To Do the Work of Men

An Operational History of the 21st Division in the Great War

Derek Clayton

Wolverhampton Military Studies Series No. 39

Helion & Company

Helion & Company Limited
Unit 8 Amherst Business Centre
Budbrooke Road
Warwick
CV34 5WE
England
Tel. 01926 499 619
Email: info@helion.co.uk
Website: www.helion.co.uk
Twitter: @helionbooks
Visit our blog at blog.helion.co.uk

Published by Helion & Company 2023
Designed and typeset by Mach 3 Solutions (www.mach3solutions.co.uk)
Cover designed by Paul Hewitt, Battlefield Design (www.battlefield-design.co.uk)

Text © Derek Clayton 2023
Images © Derek Clayton unless otherwise credited
Maps © Derek Clayton 2023

Every reasonable effort has been made to trace copyright holders and to obtain their permission for the use of copyright material. The author and publisher apologize for any errors or omissions in this work and would be grateful if notified of any corrections that should be incorporated in future reprints or editions of this book.

ISBN 9-7-81804512-33-3

British Library Cataloguing-in-Publication Data.
A catalogue record for this book is available from the British Library.

All rights reserved. No part of this publication may be reproduced, stored in a retrieval system, or transmitted, in any form, or by any means, electronic, mechanical, photocopying, recording or otherwise, without the express written consent of Helion & Company Limited.

For details of other military history titles published by Helion & Company Limited contact the above address or visit our website: http://www.helion.co.uk.

We always welcome receipt of book proposals from prospective authors.

And when the summons in our ears was shrill
Unshaken in our trust we rose, and then
Flung but a backward glance, and care-free still
Went strongly forth to do the work of men.

This is the last verse of "The Call" by W.N. Hodgson

Lieutenant William Noël Hodgson MC, of the 9th Battalion
Devonshire Regiment, was killed in action at the age of 23 on 1 July
1916, near the village of Mametz, on the Somme.
He is buried with his comrades in Devonshire Cemetery.

Contents

List of Photographs	iv
List of Maps	ix
List of Abbreviations	xi
Series Editor's Preface	xii
Foreword	xiv
Introduction: Kitchener's Armies, September 1914–September 1915	xvi

1	Loos	23
2	Somme	78
3	Arras	154
4	Third Ypres	184
5	Kaiserschlacht	207
6	Kemmel	238
7	Chemin des Dames	257
8	Somme Redux	281
9	Playing Leapfrog	304
10	The End is Nigh	323

Appendices

I	21st Division 1915-18	349
II	Divisional and Staff Commands	350
III	21st Division Brigade and Battalion Commanders	352
IV	21st Division Victoria Cross Winners	359
V	Death Sentences Passed by 21st Division Military Courts	366
VI	Map References for Original Trench Maps and How to Interpret Them	368

Bibliography	370
Index	374

List of Photographs

Lieutenant-General Sir Edward Thomas Henry Hutton.	xix
9/KOYLI Football Team. Winners of the Lady Astor Cup at Maidenhead 1914.	xxi
Major-General Sir George Townshend Forestier-Walker KCB.	xxi
The SS *St Seriol* transported the 9/KOYLI Infantry from Folkestone to Boulogne.	24
Officers of 10/Yorks, Witley Camp, 1915.	36
Second-Lieutenant Hervey Lancelot St George Swallow.	41
Second-Lieutenant Thomas Sydney Schafer.	44
Lieutenant Robert William Lee Dodds.	44
Lieutenant-Colonel Arthur de Salis Hadow.	46
Lieutenant-Colonel Hadow.	47
Major Wilfrid Harry Dent.	49
Captain Thomas Charteris.	50
Second-Lieutenant Cave Bradburne Dodds.	50
Brigadier-General Nickalls.	52
Members of *Infanterie Regiment 153*, the 'Altenburger' Regiment.	53
Obituary of Captain Duncan William Sydney Abbott.	55
Philip Vivian Rose.	56
Major John Young Storer.	57
Lieutenant-Colonel Harold Ernest Walter	58
Second-Lieutenant James Henry Rowland Hanning; Second-Lieutenant John Eric Haddon Welch; Captain James Topham; Private Joseph Goodman.	59
Pte William Thomas Thompson.	60
The Bosworth Twins. Second-Lieutenant Arthur Wright Bosworth (left) and Lieutenant Philip Charles Worthington Bosworth (right).	61
Major Lewis Charles Howard.	62
Cpl Harold John Dixon.	62
Captain W.H. Nichols.	62
The Jaques Brothers: Captain Arthur Jaques (left) and Major Joseph Hodgson Jaques, (right).	63
Lieutenant-Colonel Archibald Samuel Hamilton.	64
Second-Lieutenant Edis John William Gray.	64

List of Photographs   vii

Lieutenant-Colonel Claude Henry Campbell.	69
Sergeant C. Charlesworth.	70
Major-General Claud William Jacob. (<21stdivision1914-18.org>).	77
Major-General Sir David Graham Muschet Campbell.	79
Brigadier-General Hugo Headlam, 64 Bde. (IWM HU 123124)	82
Officers of the 9/KOYLI, Corbie, 16 April 1916.	84
Lieutenant-Colonel Colmer William Donald Lynch. (Paul Reed)	85
Captain Gordon Haswell.	86
Captain Leslie Dymoke Head.	88
Second-Lieutenant John Joseph Fritz Oldershaw.	88
Second-Lieutenant Arthur Delano Maconachie.	90
Second-Lieutenant Barry Robert Boncker.	91
Major Loudoun Shand.	97
Captain Denzil Clive Tate Twentyman.	98
Lieutenant-Colonel A. Dickson.	100
Fricourt New Military Cemetery.	101
Green Howards Memorial, Fricourt British Cemetery.	103
Captain Dennis Herbert James Ely.	107
Lieutenant-Colonel Arthur Edward Fitzgerald.	108
Officers of 9/Leics. Date unknown.	113
Lieutenant Lionel Pilkington Abbott.r)	119
Captain David Westcott Brown 6/Leics.	*122*
Lieutenant Arthur Shirley Bennett.	122
Captain Frederick Herbert Emmet.	124
Lieutenant Charles Frederick Wells Wait.	126
Captain Arthur Radclyffe Dugmore.	128
Pte Thomas Henry Garforth.	134
Sergeant G. McPherson.	135
Pte Andrew Young.	137
Second-Lieutenant G.H.Wesselhoeft.	138
Company Sergeant Major G. Potterton.	145
Second-Lieutenant W.S. Gilbart.	146
L/Cpl T. Gardner.	147
Captain Frederick William Crowther Hinings.	148
Major Wilfrid Norman Tempest.	149
Lieutenant James Humphrey Clare Schofield.	151
Second-Lieutenant F. Lillie.	153
Second-Lieutenant William Edward Crick.	165
Pte Charles Richard Renwick.	166
Captain Frederick Percy Cox.	177
Captain Audley Andrew Dowell Lee.	189

viii   To Do the Work of Men

Captain Arthur Aubrey Clarke.	191
Second-Lieutenant S.W. McClay.	198
Lieutenant Francis James Ellwood.	202
21st Division Christmas Card 1917.	205
Lieutenant John Lambert Roberts.	217
Lieutenant-Colonel Hubert Wogan Festing.	218
Captain Charles William Tone Barker.	229
Private Arthur Burkhill.	252
Private Henry Lincoln Smith.	253
Private J.H. Hutton.	265
Captain, Brevet Major, acting Lieutenant-Colonel Edward Seton Chance.	276
Brigadier-General George Gater.	281
Brigadier-General Andrew McCulloch, pictured after the War. (Peter Simkins)	282
Brigadier-General Hanway Cumming.	282
Sketch of Night Attack 23-24 August 1918.	295
Captain William Stanhope Hutchinson.	310
Lieutenant-Colonel Harry Greenwood.	337
Captain Reginald Claud Moline Gee.	341
Captain Arthur Moore Lascelles.	342

List of Maps at Centre of Volume

1. Loos 1.   i
2. Loos 1a.   ii
3. Loos 2.   iii
4. Altenberger 1.   iv
5. Altenberger 2.   v
6. Altenberger 3.   vi
7. Somme 1.   vii
8. Somme 2.   viii
9. Somme 3.   ix
10. Somme 4 Artilley Map.   x
11. Bazentin 1.   xi
12. Bazentin 2.   xii
13. Bazentin 3 (Artillery Barrage).   xiii
14. Flers-Courcelette.   xiv
15. Gueudecourt 1.   xv
16. Gueudecourt 2.   xvi
17. Gueudecourt 3.   xvii
18. Gueudecourt 4.   xviii
19. 62 Brigade Arras.   xix
20. Arras.   xx
21. Cojeul.   xxi
22. Arras 3 May 1917.   xxii
23. Arras 16 June 1917.   xxiii
24. Third Ypres 1.   xxiv
25. Broodseinde 3.10.17.   xxv
26. Broodseinde 1.   xxvi
27. Broodseinde 2a.   xxvii
28. Broodseinde 2b.   xxviii
29. Broodseinde Artillery Map.   xxix
30. 21 March 1918 1.   xxx
31. 21 March 1918 2.   xxxi
32. 21 March 1918 3.   xxxii
33. 22 March 1918.   xxxiii
34. Retreat March 1918.   xxxiv
35. Kemmel April 1918 1.   xxxv
36. Kemmel April 1918 2.   xxxvi

x To Do the Work of Men

37. Chemin des Dames 1. xxxvii
38. Chemin des Dames 2. xxxviii
39. Third Army 21-23 Aug 1918. xxxix
40. August 1918 1. xl
41. August 1918 2. xli
42. 24 August 1918. xlii
43. Luisenhof Farm 26 August 1918. xliii
44. September 1918. xliv
45. 9 & 18 September 1918. xlv
46. Third Army October 1918. xlvi
47. October 1918. xlvii
48. November 1918. xlviii

List of Abbreviations

ANZAC	Australian & New Zealand Army Corps
Bde	Brigade
BEF	British Expeditionary Force
BHQ	Battalion Headquarters
Bn	Battalion
CIGS	Chief of the Imperial General Staff
CO	Commanding Officer
Coy	Company
CSM	Company Sergeant Major
CWGC	Commonwealth War Graves Commission
DCM	Distinguished Conduct Medal
DSO	Distinguished Service Order
GHQ	General Headquarters
GOC	General Officer Commanding
GSO 1,2,3	General Staff Officer, grade 1, 2 or 3
IR	Infantry Regiment (German Army)
IWM	Imperial War Museum
MC	Military Cross
MG	Machine Gun
MGC	Machine Gun Company
MM	Military Medal
MO	Medical Officer
NCO	Non-Commissioned Officer
OR	Other Ranks
RA	Royal Artillery
RAMC	Royal Army Medical Corps
RE	Royal Engineers
RFA	Royal Field Artillery
RIR	Reserve Infantry Regiment (German Army)
RSM	Regimental Sergeant Major
TMB	Trench Mortar Battery
TNA:PRO	The National Archives: Public Records Office
VC	Victoria Cross

The Wolverhampton Military Studies Series
Series Editor's Preface

As series editor, it is my great pleasure to introduce the *Wolverhampton Military Studies Series* to you. Our intention is that in this series of books you will find military history that is new and innovative, and academically rigorous with a strong basis in fact and in analytical research, but also is the kind of military history that is for all readers, whatever their particular interests, or their level of interest in the subject. To paraphrase an old aphorism: a military history book is not less important just because it is popular, and it is not more scholarly just because it is dull. With every one of our publications we want to bring you the kind of military history that you will want to read simply because it is a good and well-written book, as well as bringing new light, new perspectives, and new factual evidence to its subject.

In devising the *Wolverhampton Military Studies Series*, we gave much thought to the series title: this is a *military* series. We take the view that history is everything except the things that have not happened yet, and even then a good book about the military aspects of the future would find its way into this series. We are not bound to any particular time period or cut-off date. Writing military history often divides quite sharply into eras, from the modern through the early modern to the mediaeval and ancient; and into regions or continents, with a division between western military history and the military history of other countries and cultures being particularly marked. Inevitably, we have had to start somewhere, and the first books of the series deal with British military topics and events of the twentieth century and later nineteenth century. But this series is open to any book that challenges received and accepted ideas about any aspect of military history, and does so in a way that encourages its readers to enjoy the discovery.

In the same way, this series is not limited to being about wars, or about grand strategy, or wider defence matters, or the sociology of armed forces as institutions, or civilian society and culture at war. None of these are specifically excluded, and in some cases they play an important part in the books that comprise our series. But there are already many books in existence, some of them of the highest scholarly standards, which cater to these particular approaches. The main theme of the *Wolverhampton Military Studies Series* is the military aspects of wars, the preparation for wars or their prevention, and their aftermath. This includes some books whose main theme is the technical details of how armed forces have worked, some books on wars and battles, and some books that re-examine the evidence about the existing stories, to show in a different light what everyone thought they already knew and understood.

As series editor, together with my fellow editorial board members, and our publisher Duncan Rogers of Helion, I have found that we have known immediately and almost by instinct the kind of books that fit within this series. They are very much the kind of well-written and challenging books that my students at the University of Wolverhampton would want to read. They are books which enhance knowledge and offer new perspectives. Also, they are books for anyone with an interest in military history and events, from expert scholars to occasional readers. One of the great benefits of the study of military history is that it includes a large and often committed section of the wider population, who want to read the best military history that they can find; our aim for this series is to provide it.

Stephen Badsey
University of Wolverhampton

Foreword

I first became truly aware, early in 1962, of the 21st Division's part in the Great War when, as a recent graduate from King's College London, I was fortunate to be appointed as an archivist and research assistant to the distinguished military commentator, Captain Basil Liddell Hart. My role, until the late summer of 1963, was to begin preparing a detailed catalogue of Basil's extensive private papers prior to their eventual transfer to King's College. This involved living and working – in some comfort I might add – for four days a week at Liddell Hart's lovely home at States House, Medmenham, near Marlow. Some evenings, when Basil stretched out on the sofa for a while after dinner, I noted that he was still occasionally bothered by the lingering effects of the gassing he had suffered at Mametz Wood on the Somme in July 1916, when he was serving as an officer in the 9th (Service) Battalion of the King's Own Yorkshire Light Infantry (KOYLI), part of the 21st Division. My curiosity about this formation was also aroused by the fact that Basil remained in touch, several decades later, with surviving fellow officers of that battalion, including Lance Spicer, who actually outlived him. It is perhaps worth observing at this point that, according to Professor Brian Bond, Basil continued to dispute Lance Spicer's right to have taken over temporary command of his company in the wake of the casualties incurred by the 9th KOYLI at Fricourt on 1 July 1916. Since that time as a hopeful young military historian, I have maintained a lifelong interest in the performance of New Army divisions which fought on the Western Front in the First World War. It was therefore a happy coincidence that – some fifteen years ago – I was asked by the University of Birmingham to supervise the MA Dissertation of Derek Clayton, whose output had already included a splendid study of the very battalion in which my former mentor had served in 1916. I am happy to add that Derek was my very first success as an MA supervisor, although most of the credit for this was undoubtedly down to him.

As Dr Clayton illustrates in this excellent and long-overdue study, the 21st Division was certainly one of the most resilient of the New Army divisions that fought on the Western Front between 1915 and the Armistice. Only weeks after arriving in France, it had experienced a serious reverse in its first major action at Loos on 26 September 1915, before being nursed back to fighting efficiency under the command of David 'Soarer' Campbell from May 1916. It had recovered sufficiently to register a highly creditable success rate in some ten attacks on the Somme that year, notwithstanding the fact that it exchanged its original 63rd Brigade for the 110th Brigade from the 37th Division on 7 July 1916. Campbell went on to become the fifth longest-serving divisional commander in the BEF.

Having seen action at Arras and Ypres in 1917, the division faced more tough challenges in the first half of 1918. It mounted an epic defence of Epéhy on the opening day of the German March offensive and then, in the next week or so, conducted a fighting retreat which saw its battalions reduced to an average combat strength of little over 200 men. It was next involved in resisting the German *Georgette* offensive on the Lys in April. Having then been sent to a comparatively quiet sector on the Aisne to rest and reorganise, it was extremely unlucky to find itself in the path of the German *Blücher* offensive, along the Chemin des Dames towards the end of May. Given the division's challenges in the spring of 1918, it is perhaps not surprising that its overall success rate in attacks during the Hundred Days, between August and November was just over 51 per cent. Even so, the division played a crucial role in certain operations, such as the recapture of Thiepval and the Ancre Heights in August. By the start of that action the division boasted three of the most outstanding brigade commanders in the entire BEF, namely George Gater (62nd Brigade), Andrew McCulloch (64th Brigade) and Hanway Cumming (110th Brigade). In this and other respects, the story of the 21st Division may be viewed as a useful yardstick of the BEF's 'learning process' in the Great War.

Derek Clayton must be commended for producing a new divisional history which is both extremely scholarly and highly readable. This volume unquestionably represents a valuable addition to the historiography of the BEF's experience on the Western Front. I am personally delighted to have been given the opportunity to be associated with the project, not least because it is the work of one of my former students!

Professor Peter Simkins
University of Wolverhampton
December 2022

Introduction
Kitchener's Armies
September 1914–September 1915

When Britain declared war on 4 August, its army, in comparison with those of Germany, France and Russia, was tiny. The first troops of the British Expeditionary Force (BEF), two Corps strong and numbering around 100,000 men, landed in France on 9 August. The bulk of the rest arrived between the12th and 17th, landing at Boulogne, Rouen and Le Havre, mostly at night. This force then moved northwards to take its place on the extreme left of the French line, first contact with the enemy occurring on 22 August near the village of Soignies.

Many were inclined to believe that the war would not be a long-drawn-out affair. In his office in London, the newly-appointed Secretary of State for War, Field-Marshal Earl Kitchener, was already convinced, however, that the conflict would be both costly and long, estimating "that the war would last at least three years and that Britain's full military strength could not be deployed until 1917".[1] Kitchener had, rather reluctantly, accepted his new post on 5 August, and immediately set about expanding the army. Parliamentary approval for the recruitment of 500,000 men was given that day, and the appeal for the first 100,000 was published in the newspapers the following morning, under the heading "Your King and Country Need You". It announced that "an addition of 100,000 men to His Majesty's Regular Army is immediately necessary in the present grave National Emergency. Lord Kitchener is confident that this appeal will be at once responded to by all who have the safety of our Empire at heart".[2] The appeal was for men aged between nineteen and thirty, five feet three inches tall and upwards, who were willing to enlist for three years, or for the duration of the war.

The result was astonishing. Recruitment into the pre-war British Army had been around the 30,000 a year mark, or an average of fewer than 100 per day. Between 4 and 8 August 1914, 8,193 men presented themselves at the recruiting stations. These figures were seen as less than encouraging, but the reality was that the number attested did not reflect the thousands who had to be turned away at the end of a day's fruitless queuing. The system in place simply could not cope. More recruiting stations were opened, more clerks and doctors drafted in, and between 9 and 15 August 45,354 men enlisted. The following week's figure was 49,982. When news of the BEF's brave stand at the Battle of Mons – and of the losses that were suffered – reached home, the week's total exceeded 63,000.

---

1   Peter Simkins, *Kitchener's Army: The Raising of the New Armies 1914-1916* (Manchester: Manchester University Press, 1988), p. 38.
2   Ibid, p.39

The 100,000 figure had been quickly surpassed. On 28 August, Kitchener's appeal for a second 100,000 appeared in the press. The upper age limit was extended to thirty-five for new recruits, forty-five for ex-soldiers and fifty for certain ex-non-commissioned officers, with the need for the last of these becoming rather pressing.

The first six divisions of the 'New Army' or 'Kitchener's Army' as it was sometimes known, officially came into being on 21 August. They were numbered 9th to 14th and became known as 'K1'. Such was the rush to enlist that the second series of divisions, 'K2', numbered 15th to 20th, was authorised on 1 September.

On 4 September, Prime Minister Asquith was able to announce that Kitchener's appeal had already produced between 200,000 and 300,000 volunteers. The Third Army, 'K3', was therefore to be raised immediately. The 21st Division was the first of this new series and came into being officially on 13 September 1914. It was destined to spend its entire period of active service on the Western Front, taking part in most of the major engagements, including the Battles of Loos, Somme, Arras and Third Ypres before involvement in the BEF's desperate defence against three massive German offensives in the Spring of 1918. It survived these – barely – to play its part in the final advance to victory through the summer and autumn, fighting its last battle only four days before the armistice. It lost more men, killed, wounded or missing, than any other New Army Division. It is perhaps no wonder then that Arthur Conan Doyle, in the final part of his six-volume history, *The British Campaign in France & Flanders,* described the 21st Division as "that hard-bitten old scrapper".[3]

The standard division in the British Army at that time was made up of three brigades, each of four battalions. With a battalion numbering around 1,000 men, simple arithmetic allows us to calculate the strength of a brigade to be 4,000 men, and a division 12,000. Once divisional artillery, a pioneer battalion and other ancillaries are added, the total would reach somewhere between 18,000 and 20,000. The division was the largest self-contained unit in the BEF that moved around as a single entity and was commanded by a Major-General. Under him would be three Brigadier-Generals, and each battalion was commanded by a Lieutenant-Colonel.[4]

In the first two 'New Armies', brigades were usually composed of four battalions from four different regiments, but in K3 it was common for two battalions or more from the same regiment to serve together in one brigade. The 21st Division, on its inception, was made up as follows:

62 Brigade:
12/Northumberland Fusiliers
13/Northumberland Fusiliers
8/East Yorkshire
10/Yorkshire

---

3   Arthur Conan Doyle, *The British Campaign in France & Flanders, Vol. VI, July –November 1918* (London: Hodder & Stoughton, 1920).
4   See Appendix III for a complete list of 21st Division battalion commanders.

xviii   To Do the Work of Men

63 Brigade:
8/Lincolnshire
8/Somerset Light Infantry
12/West Yorkshire
10/York & Lancaster

64 Brigade:
9/King's Own Yorkshire Light Infantry
10/King's Own Yorkshire Light Infantry
14/Durham Light Infantry
15/Durham Light Infantry
Pioneers: 14/Northumberland Fusiliers[5]

When a volunteer presented himself at the recruiting office, he was required to answer the eleven questions on the attestation form, (sometimes not truthfully!), undergo a medical examination, (sometimes not very thorough!) and take an oath of allegiance. He was then given the 'King's Shilling' – one day's pay for a private – and officially became a soldier. More often than not, he would then report to the local barracks and be allocated to one of the regionally-recruited regiments. There were exceptions, of course: Martin Middlebrook[6] tells of Lance-Corporal H. Fellows who joined up in Nottingham. He was an orphan, very poor and had never had a holiday or travelled far from his home town. He refused to join any of the local battalions and chose the Northumberland Fusiliers as this offered him the longest train ride. He thus became a member of the 12th battalion of that regiment.

At the local barracks, the overcrowded and confused conditions meant that allocation to individual battalions could be a rather random process: George Escritt was at Pontefract Barracks, the headquarters of the King's Own Yorkshire Light Infantry. Fed up with the food and short of money, he simply sauntered out of the barracks and walked home to Leeds with a friend, a distance of some fifteen miles:

> We had to take the chaff that we had come home for our Sunday dinner. Our mothers said we would get shot for desertion. Well, we went back by train the following Wednesday and in the field before you came to the barracks there were crowds of volunteers, so we mingled amongst them and then ambled down to the railway station.[7]

Escritt had not been missed, and by chance had joined a group of men destined for the 9/King's Own Yorkshire Light Infantry [9/KOYLI].

A major problem facing the K3 formations was a lack of accommodation in existing barracks: only 260,000 places were available and these were not enough even for the first two New Armies. Previously unused sites had to be found for K3. The 21st Division, commanded by the then sixty-five-year-old Lieutenant-General Sir E.T.H. Hutton, was to be stationed at

---

5   Over the course of the war, battalions could be moved between divisions and occasionally brigades would also be moved. Appendix I depicts how the composition of 21st Division changed.
6   Martin Middlebrook, *The First Day on the Somme, 1st July 1916* (London: Penguin Books, 1984), p.9.
7   Simkins, *Kitchener's Army*, pp.199-200.

Halton Park, between Tring and Wendover in Hertfordshire, on land owned by Lord Rothschild. Halton Park was to be a 'hutted' camp, but when the men arrived the huts had not been built and they were accommodated in tents, each one holding between fifteen and twenty men. This was initially quite "pleasant enough", but almost incessant rain from mid-October reduced the whole area to a sea of knee-deep mud. Conditions were becoming very unpleasant: "The tents had no tent-boards, we had no waterproof sheets and the blanket ration did not then allow for more than one per man. And, though the days were warm, the nights were cold".[8]

Training began almost at once, but parades had a distinctly unmilitary appearance, as the men had not yet been issued with any uniforms. The programme was unimaginative: from 06.30 to 08.00 hrs every morning, they did physical exercises. "This was much too long – half an hour would have been more than sufficient. There was not a trained gymnastic instructor amongst us, and I defy anyone who is not so trained to keep 60 men, who are longing for breakfast, healthily amused […] for an hour and a half – and that is what every officer had to do".[9] Indeed, the pool of trained officers had already been drained: in 21st Division every battalion commander had been 'dug out' from retirement and only fourteen officers in the entire division had had any prior experience in the Regular Army. The rest – over 400 of them – had been commissioned since the war began and had for the most part not undergone any officer training. Our unnamed officer continues his account, bemoaning the fact that at that point, no rifles were available:

Lieutenant-General Sir Edward Thomas Henry Hutton KCB KCMG DL FRGS (1848-1923) CO 21st Div Sept 1914–April 1915. (Australian War Memorial)

> Then, for three weeks, every day from 9 a.m. to 1 p.m. and from 2 p.m. – 5 p.m. we did Squad Drill without arms. Seven hours per day at Squad Drill without arms! If boredom could kill, we should all have died within two days. And we were absolutely forbidden to do anything else.[10]

---

8 Unpublished hand-written memoir of an unidentified 64th Bde Officer in the possession of the KOYLI Association Office, Pontefract Barracks.
9 Ibid.
10 Ibid.

xx   To Do the Work of Men

Our chronicler and a brother officer, who had both been in the Officer Training Corps at school and at Cambridge University, did show some initiative and concocted a scheme to allow some variation for the men under their command:

> We had a very fair smattering of infantry movements. We agreed that for one hour he should take half the company[11] into a remote corner of the large field, which was our parade ground, and unobserved, should carry out any small scheme that he might invent. At that time I, with the other half of the company, should 'carry on' Squad Drill, marching up and down in front of his corner, the better to obscure his movements. Also, I should be able to give timely warning of the approach of any senior officer. At the end of the hour we were to change over. This manoeuvre was successfully carried out on more than one occasion and pleased the men immensely.[12]

At the beginning of November, the men were ordered to move into huts that had been built in another part of Halton Park. It turned out, however, that the huts were still unfinished and the men immediately moved out into billets in local towns and villages, including Tring, Aylesbury, Leighton Buzzard, High Wycombe and Maidenhead. It was at about this time that, in the absence of sufficient khaki cloth to clothe the New Armies, uniforms of blue serge were issued. This was an improvement, of course, as the men's civilian clothes were beginning to wear out, and, although the blue uniforms were not greeted with universal approval by the men, parades would look more like an authentic military occasion. Training continued, and soon included simulated trench life. Trenches were dug and the men were obliged to occupy them for short periods of time in an attempt to simulate life at the front. On one occasion, A and B Companies of 9/KOYLI were occupying facing trenches, each playing the part of the other's enemy. A night exercise quickly developed into an unofficial battle between the rival companies, the men resorting to using such weapons as over-ripe tomatoes, eggs, home-made stink bombs, sticks, fists, pepper and bad language.

It was not until April 1915 that the men were able to move back into the now finished huts at Halton. The standard hutment measured sixty feet by twenty feet. Tables and benches took up the space down the centre of the hut, leaving room for thirty beds down the sides. They were constructed using a wooden frame, a corrugated iron roof and walls, lined inside with asbestos. Forty such huts could accommodate a battalion. There were also buildings for officers' and sergeants' messes, a cookhouse and a large dining room. The move back to Halton Park coincided with the resignation of Lieutenant-General Hutton.[13] He was replaced by Major-General Forestier-Walker.[14] Forestier-Walker had seen service in France since the start of the war as Chief of Staff to General Horace Smith-Dorrien (GOC II Corps) and therefore had some knowledge of the kind of war the division might be expected to fight. With his arrival, the pace of training quickened. He was a great believer in route-marching, "so we marched &

---

11   There were four companies in a battalion, each of approximately 250 men.
12   Unpublished hand-written memoir of an unidentified 64th Bde Officer held at the KOYLI Association Office, Pontefract Barracks.
13   Hutton resigned due to ill-health following a fall from his horse.
14   See Appendix II for a complete 21st Division staff list.

9/KOYLI Football Team. Winners of the Lady Astor Cup at Maidenhead 1914. The two Officers on the left of the photograph are Second-Lieutenants Buckley and Spicer. (Courtesy: Yeo Family)

marched & marched! And it was astonishing how we improved".[15]

As the new regime bedded in, the division received proper khaki uniforms. The accompanying kit, belts, pouches, pack and so on, did not however arrive until June. It was also at the end of June that the men were finally issued with rifles. The ammunition caught up two weeks later on 15 July, and a musketry course began at once. With time now of the essence, firing went on at the range at Halton continuously from 04.30 to 20.30, utilising every available hour of daylight. By the beginning of August, all the men had completed at least the basic course, and the division marched off from Halton Camp for the last time on the 9th, arriving at Witley Camp in Surrey four days later. Three days later they

Major-General Sir George Townshend Forestier-Walker KCB. (1866-1939) CO 21st Div April–November 1915.

15 Unpublished hand-written memoir of an unidentified 64th Bde Officer held at the KOYLI Association Office, Pontefract Barracks.

xxii   To Do the Work of Men

were inspected, on the march, by Lord Kitchener. Training continued, but, so intense had the training become, and so short the time left to them, that at one point, bayonet practice had to be fitted in at night, by moonlight.

Just as the first anniversary of the division's inception approached, orders were received to embark for France. Our unnamed officer continues the story:

> We were to start almost at once. We had of course guessed for the past week or two that we should not be long, but somehow or other, when the actual orders did come, to me at any rate it was a shock.

The news had been given to individual battalion commanders by Forestier-Walker and they in turn informed their subordinate officers:

> ... the Colonel made the announcement. He was brief and to the point. 'Gentlemen, you will be glad to hear that the Divisional Commander told me today that the Division has received orders to proceed overseas, it is understood to France. We shall start in about ten days. This is of course confidential.' There was dead silence for a space of about five seconds, the air was charged with electricity, then in a moment we were talking again and very soon we passed on to the closing of mess accounts and so forth. [...] We should all go to France together, but how many of us would come back?[16]

16   Ibid.

1

Loos

The 21st Division disembarked on French soil between 9 and 12 September 1915, the infantry landing at Boulogne, the rest, including transport sections and artillery, at Le Havre. Two weeks later, with absolutely no prior battlefield experience, and very little in the way of acclimatisation to the realities of the Western Front, they were thrown into action at the Battle of Loos. It is interesting to note that had the battle begun on the day originally planned, 8 September, the division would still have been in England at the time. Subsequent delays[1] condemned it to a brutal baptism of fire.

The division's performance has been a topic of controversy and argument ever since. Nick Lloyd, in his recent book, suggests that their exploits have been veiled in "myth and misunderstanding".[2] Edmonds, in his Official History, warns of the "legends [that] have grown up as regards the failure of the 21st and 24th Divisions at Loos," where they supposedly "disgraced themselves and the New Army by retiring before the enemy",[3] concluding that they were, in the end, asked to perform a "nearly impossible task".[4] The seemingly widely accepted narrative is that the two divisions advanced against the second German defensive line on the second day of the battle and were routed by enemy machine gun fire. This is far too simplistic. The true picture is much more complicated and far less damning of the divisions' performance.

The plans for a major assault in the late summer of 1915 originated from General Joffre and the French General Staff. On paper they appear attractive, if frighteningly ambitious. The Germans occupied a huge salient in north-eastern France, its farthest point of south-westerly extension being the town of Noyon, some sixty or so miles from Paris. A huge pincer attack on the southern and western flanks of this salient – the former by the French 4th, 2nd and 3rd Armies from their positions in Champagne, the latter by British and French 10th Army forces in Artois – would render it untenable. The German 1st, 2nd and 7th Armies, some 300,000 men, would be encircled and destroyed. The territorial gains would be substantial.

Field Marshal Sir John French, Commander-in-Chief of the British Expeditionary Force [BEF], was initially keen to participate. He was of the opinion that the Allies should "strike

---

1 The French needed to build more roadways prior to their attack in the Champagne region.
2 Nick Lloyd, *Loos 1915* (Stroud:Tempus, 2006). p.168.
3 J.E. Edmonds, *Military Operations France & Belgium 1915*, Vol. II (London: HMSO, 1928), p.342.
4 Ibid, p.344

The SS *St Seriol* transported the 9/KOYLI Infantry from Folkestone to Boulogne, 10 – 11 Sept 1915. (John Cowell)

as soon as possible",[5] rejecting any thoughts that they should stand on the defensive after their failed offensives of the spring. This latter course, he intimated to Lord Kitchener, could "have a disastrous effect upon the moral and offensive spirit of our troops".[6] GHQ received a draft scheme from the French Commander-in-Chief on 4 June. The BEF's part in the combined offensive would be two-fold: firstly, they would take over twenty-two miles of the French line south of Arras – this would free up the French 2nd Army to participate in the Champagne assault – and secondly launch an attack in conjunction with French 10th Army, either on its left, north of Lens, or on its right, just south of Arras. By its very nature the plan required the Allies to break through the German defensive lines – an accomplishment that had, until then, eluded them – and make substantial advances, measured in miles rather than yards, into the hinterland.[7]

On 19 June, Sir John French told General Foch (commanding the Groupe d'Armées du Nord) that he intended to attack north of Lens, with "units of First Army re-arranged to ensure that the British offensive would be delivered by the best troops".[8] The following day he asked the commander of First Army, General Sir Douglas Haig, to submit a detailed report on the feasibility of such an attack at that location.

5   Lloyd, *Loos 1915*, p.34.
6   TNA PRO 30/57/50: Kitchener Papers. French to Kitchener correspondence, 11 June 1915.
7   The strategic requirements were an advance of up to fifty miles in the north and up to seventy miles in the south. See Gordon Corrigan, *Loos 1915. The Unwanted Battle* (Stroud: Spellmount, 2006) p.7
8   Edmonds, *Military Operations 1915*, Vol. II, p.113

After personal reconnaissance of the area, Haig sent his report to GHQ on 23 June. Its five and a half pages did not make re-assuring reading. Haig had been thorough and had spoken with the commanders already in the field: GOC I Corps and COs of 1st and 2nd Divisions.

> All three officers have personally reconnoitred that area and, in addition, both divisional commanders, from having held different portions of the line with their divisions, are in a position to give from personal knowledge, detailed information regarding the ground and the enemy's defences in our front.[9]

The extensive quotation is enlightening.

The German front line in itself would be a challenge, being sited:

> ... immediately in front of the crest of the ridge, while the supporting trench is just behind it. Both trenches are wired. It is believed to be impossible to bring observed artillery fire to bear on the second line, or to cut the wire in front of it from our current position: and it is doubtful if observation stations could be got for the purpose even if we occupy the German front line trenches".[10]

Haig's assessment of the German support line is even more pessimistic:

> Any attack on the southern part of this second line[11] is enfiladed from the SPOIL BANK running south-east from FOSSE No. 5, which is itself a sort of natural fortress.
> The Germans have, nearly everywhere south of the [La Bassée] canal, the advantage of artillery observation stations and can concentrate the fire of their guns from VIOLAINES to LENS on any force which we may collect for attack in this area. The country between Loos and Fosse No. 8 [just behind the Hohenzollern Redoubt – see Map 1] is also flat and open, consequently much difficulty is likely to be experienced in supporting an attack on the German trenches, and in sending up supplies and reinforcements to the troops when the German front line of trenches has been captured. The villages in the rear of the German line are strongly defended, and the ground between them is flat and open, so that a further advance eastward would be extremely difficult.[12]

Haig predicts that an attack on the German front line in front of the town of Loos might be practicable, but that any further rapid advance would be impossible. Any attack further north was "not recommended", although he does suggest that the capture of the Hohenzollern Redoubt is "feasible".[13]

Two days later Haig submitted a supplementary report to GHQ. He had not changed his mind, affirming that "this area is not favourable for an attack".[14] He goes on to suggest that

---

9   IWM French Papers 7/2/1: Haig Report 23.6.1915.
10 Ibid.
11 The very part of the line that 21st Division were subsequently ordered to attack.
12 Ibid.
13 Ibid.
14 IWM French Papers 7/2/1: Haig Supplementary Report, 25.6.1915.

another attack at Aubers Ridge[15] would be his preferred option, in combination with an advance eastward from Givenchy, that is, north of the La Bassée Canal.

Sir John French was clearly worried by this report and his state of mind would not have been improved by the conclusions arrived at during the Allied Munitions Conference at Boulogne:

> For an offensive on the Western Front to have a reasonable chance of success, it would have to be delivered on a front of twenty-five miles by over thirty divisions and supported by 1,150 heavy guns and howitzers and the normal complement of field artillery. [...] This quantity of guns and necessary ammunition could not be produced before the spring of 1916.[16]

Not to mention the number of trained men.

The subsequent machinations and discussions between the British Commander-in-Chief and his French counterparts are beyond the scope of this work: suffice it to say that Sir John French's attempts to scale down the BEF's involvement in this grand plan were to no avail. Lord Kitchener visited French GHQ on 16 August and after long discussions, including the Russians' plight on the Eastern Front, telegraphed Sir John French on his return to London on 21 August, ordering him "to take the offensive and act vigorously".[17]

Edmonds succinctly sums up Sir John French's unenviable position:

> Under pressure from Lord Kitchener at home due to the general position of the Allies and from Generals Joffre and Foch in France, the British Commander-in-Chief was therefore compelled to undertake operations before he was ready, over ground that was most unfavourable, against the better judgement of himself and General Haig and [...] with no more than a quarter of the troops [...] considered necessary for a successful attack.[18]

The 21st Division, along with 24th and the also newly-formed Guards Divisions made up XI Corps, under the command of Lieutenant-General R.C.B. Haking. The two New Army divisions were to constitute the reserve force for the battle and would be used to exploit any success. The handling of XI Corps is one of the major controversies concerning the battle of Loos. Sir John French was favouring a "limited attack, with the reserves being employed *once* success had been achieved".[19] Indeed, Major-General Forestier-Walker had been assured by Sir William Robertson, CIGS, only days before the assault, that "under no conceivable circumstances would the 21st or 24th Division be put in unless, and until, the Germans were absolutely smashed and retiring in disorder".[20] Haig, since the submission of his reports in June, had suffered a seemingly acute attack of optimism and had adopted an "all-out plan [which] called for the reserves to be used to *ensure* this initial success".[21]

---

15 The BEF had already failed to take Aubers Ridge in a disastrous assault of 9 May 1915.
16 Edmonds, *Military Operations 1915*, Vol. II, p.117.
17 Ibid, p.129.
18 Ibid.
19 Lloyd, *Loos 1915* p.63.
20 TNA PRO CAB 45/120: Forestier-Walker to E. Edmonds, whom he addresses as 'My dear Archimedes' and then signs off as 'Hookey F-W' correspondence, 24 January 1927.
21 Lloyd, *Loos 1915*, p.63.

Sir John's failure to rein in his subordinate may be attributed to the debilitating illness he suffered during the build up to the battle: he did however rain on Haig's parade by insisting that the General Reserve be positioned well back and remain under his command until the moment he saw fit to release it to First Army. The issue dragged on into September. French intended to deploy the reserve 20,000 yards from the front line in the vicinity of the town of Lillers. This infuriated Haig, who wrote to his Commander-in-Chief demanding that the nearest units of XI Corps be placed close to Noeux les Mines, stating that "the whole plan of the First Army is based on the assumption that the troops in the General Reserve will be close at hand".[22]

Sir John finally acquiesced and agreed that the reserves would be where Haig had asked for them to be, some 5,000 – 7,000 yards from the front line on the morning of 25 September, the head of 21st Division and 24th Divisions at Noeux les Mines and Beuvry respectively. Haig's was not a total victory, however. The reserve was still to remain firmly under GHQ control until Sir John gave the order for their release.

This compromise suited neither party and the conduct of the battle was compromised by it. Haig, the scent of breakthrough in his nostrils, was able to order them forward on the 25th, but the distance of their march meant that they arrived too late to make the difference. Hindsight would seem to suggest that even a timely arrival on the battlefield would not have resulted in the wished-for decisive victory. As Major-General A.A. Montgomery, General Staff IV Corps at Loos, put it: "two people can't run one battle each on his own lines!" adding: "What a loss of life the obstinacy of the two men caused".[23]

In order to place the actions of 21st Division in context, it is necessary to outline briefly the events of the first day of the battle. At the time, the Battle of Loos was the largest fought by the British Army in its entire history. First Army attacked with six divisions of I and IV Corps in the front line (See Maps 1 and 2). The preparatory bombardment began at 07.00 on 21 September, the total number of guns available on First Army's 11,000-yard attack frontage amounting to 110 heavy guns and howitzers and 841 guns of smaller calibre.[24] This was not enough. The heavies were employed against enemy defence works, strongpoints and villages, the vital job of wire cutting being the responsibility of the field artillery. However, the allocation of one battery (four or six guns) for every 600 yards of front line was woefully inadequate, especially since ammunition was also strictly limited. Results were predictably mixed. The German wire in front of their second line was out of range of the field artillery: its destruction was therefore entrusted to the 'heavies', but at a range of 5,000 – 7,000 yards, and with very limited observation, this task was "not seriously attempted".[25]

Haig was perfectly well aware that the number of guns at his disposal and the amount of ammunition available were scarcely sufficient for a two-division attack on a 2,000 yard frontage[26], and as far back as 7 July he was considering supplementing these scarce resources with a release

---

22 TNA PRO WO 95/158: Haig to Robertson correspondence, 19 September 1915.
23 TNA PRO CAB 45/121: Montgomery to Edmonds correspondence, 11 January 1926. Another officer, in an account whose missing first two pages render it unattributable, was less kind, stating that "Our Generals […] were gentlemen with eighteen handicap minds".
24 Edmonds, *Military Operations 1915 Vol. II,* p.163.
25 Ibid, p.164.
26 Corrigan, *Loos 1915,* p. 24.

28 To Do the Work of Men

of chlorine gas.[27] On 6 September Haig briefed his corps and divisional commanders, assuring them that should sufficient gas be supplied, the proposed six-division assault was "feasible".[28]

On 26 August, Haig was told by Lt-Col Foulkes (gas expert from GHQ) that problems with the production of the chlorine gas cylinders meant that he would be unable to supply the required number by the required date".[29] It is indicative of Haig's growing obsession that gas was going to be the deciding factor in the forthcoming attack that as late as 16 September he was writing to Robertson, asking him

> "to send a special officer to London to (a) insist on gas factories working *night* and day – at present they only work 8 hours daily – and (b) make *special* arrangements to get the gas brought out and sent up to the troops. The situation was entirely a *special* one and *special* measures must be taken to ensure success.[30]

The shortfall was not made good, however, and it emerged that the planned forty-minute discharge prior to zero hour was not going to be possible.[31] A compromise solution had to be found: it was decided that the gas would be supplemented by smoke. Gas would be released for twelve minutes, followed by eight minutes of smoke, twelve more of gas and a final eight of smoke.

One vital factor in the successful use of gas was totally beyond Haig's control. The chlorine, released through rubber pipes attached to cylinders which were laboriously dug into the trench walls, would be carried over to the German positions by the wind. Unfavourable weather could therefore scupper the entire enterprise: an attack without gas, Haig proposed, would be necessarily limited to attacks by two divisions on the Hohenzollern Redoubt and the Loos salient.[32]

A breeze of six to eight miles per hour from anywhere between north-west and south-west would be perfect, and the weather forecast at 21.45 on 24 September seemed favourable. During the night, the wind direction varied between west and south-east, and at one point dropped to almost dead calm. Haig wrote:

> I went out at 5 a.m. – almost a calm. Alan Fletcher[33] lit a cigarette and the smoke drifted in puffs towards the northeast. Staff Officers of Corps were ordered to stand by in case it was necessary to counter the order to attack. At one time owing to the calm I feared the gas would simply hang about *our* trenches! However at 5:15 I said: 'Carry on.' I went to top of our lookout tower. The wind came gently from the south west and by 5:40 had increased slightly. The leaves of the poplar gently rustled. This seemed satisfactory.[34]

---

27 Gary Sheffield & John Bourne, (eds.), *Douglas Haig: War Diaries and Letters 1914-1918* (London: Weidenfeld & Nicolson, 2005) p. 130.
28 Corrigan, *Loos 1915*, p.26. In correspondence with the Official Historian, our previously unidentified officer stated, rather unkindly that "[Haig] knew as much about gas as the ignorant savage knows about a modern rifle." TNA PRO CAB 45/120.
29 Sheffield & Bourne (eds.), *Douglas Haigs*, p.138.
30 Ibid, p.149. Original emphasis.
31 It had been calculated that German gas masks were only effective for 25-30 minutes.
32 Sheffield & Bourne (eds.), *Douglas Haig*, p.149, 18 September 1915 entry. Tellingly, this entry closes with the statement: "Wind changed to the northeast in the afternoon."
33 Major A.Fletcher, 17th Lancers, Haig's aide de camp.
34 Sheffield & Bourne (eds.), *Douglas Haig:*, p.153, 25 September 1915 entry.

Nick Lloyd dismisses this account as "little more than a dramatic tale", adding that Haig's decision to go ahead was more influenced by Foulkes than Fletcher: "Just after 5 a.m. Haig asked Foulkes if his Special Brigade officers would turn on the gas if the wind was not favourable on their particular fronts. Foulkes replied that 'they won't turn the gas on if the wind is not favourable'. This seemed to reassure Haig, allowing him to order the attack secure in the knowledge that on the fronts where the conditions were completely unfavourable no gas would be released. No British troops would therefore become gassed".[35] Events were to prove Foulkes' assurance to be worthless: the gas was released at 05.50 regardless of prevailing conditions.

The men of six divisions – left to right these were 2nd, 9th, 7th, 1st, 15th and 47th (see Map 1) – climbed out of their trenches at 06.30 and advanced towards the German first line. In the south, ahead of 47th and 15th Divisions, a forty-foot high dense cloud of gas carried across the German front line trenches and then tumbled down the slope towards the village of Loos. Opposite 9th Division, "the gas produced a great effect, drifting right across the [Hohenzollern Redoubt] from south to north: most of the garrison abandoned it before the assault".[36]

On 1st Division front, however, the wind was very light, allowing the cloud to linger in No Man's Land, and further north, the 2nd Division commanders quickly ordered the release to be discontinued once they realised that the gas was simply hanging around the British trenches and beginning to drift northward *along the British front line.*

The 2nd Division assault failed, "unmitigated by any gleam of success".[37] In a little under two hours, their attack against a fully-manned German trench and uncut wire – resulting in casualties amounting to 91 officers and 2,234 other ranks killed, wounded or missing – had been completely repulsed. A second attempt planned for 09.30 was thankfully cancelled, by which time most of the survivors were back in their own front line.

The 9th (Scottish) Division, to the south, had mixed fortunes: on the left, 28 Brigade had the misfortune to advance against uncut wire and German machine guns. The attack failed. On the right, 26 Brigade was able to advance through the Hohenzollern Redoubt and by nightfall, reinforced by 27 Brigade, they held Fosse 8 and The Dump and were in touch with 7th Division to their right.

This division was able to advance the 450 yards to the German front line trench in twelve minutes and, finding the wire well cut, carried the front line and pressed on through the support line, capturing The Quarries by 09.30. Casualties had been heavy, however. Three battalions had lost their commanding officers,[38] and the 8/Devonshires, for example, lost all of their officers and 600 men, killed or wounded. The remaining troops were able to dig in and consolidate their positions facing the German second line trench system, an attack on Cité St Elie, timed for 16.00 having been cancelled.

On 1st Division right frontage, the men of 2 Brigade advanced, choking and spluttering, through their own gas clouds. The primitive 'PH' gas helmet worn by the British troops, which was to all intents and purposes a hessian sack, impregnated with chemicals that absorbed

---

35 Lloyd, *Loos 1915*, p.126. The statement by Foulkes comes from Captain Gold's correspondence with Edmonds, dated 13 December 1925. See TNA PRO CAB 45/120.
36 Edmonds, *Military Operations 1915*, Vol. II, p.179.
37 Ibid, p.251
38 Lt-Col A.G.W. Grant of 8/Devonshires, Lt-Col J.R.E. Stansfeld of 2/Gordon Highlanders and Lt-Col B.P. Lefroy of 2/Royal Warwickshires were all killed during the assault.

chlorine, with two Perspex eyepieces and a breathing tube inserted, was most uncomfortable to wear. The eyepieces quickly misted up and breathing equally quickly became laboured. Some soldiers had been caught unawares by the gas blowing back onto their jumping off positions and had been wearing the helmet rolled up on top of their heads. Others, struggling to breathe at all, would risk lifting the helmet for an unrestricted lungful of air.

As the first waves crested the Grenay Ridge they were met with withering machine gun fire. Nevertheless, the leading companies reached the German wire, only to find it intact. Attempts to cut through the obstacle were brave, but inevitably unsuccessful and small groups retired to their own trenches under intense small arms fire.

On the left, the 1 Brigade met with more success. The 8/Royal Berkshires and 1/Cameron Highlanders were able to push on past the German front line positions as far as the Lens to La Bassée road and observed German troops hurriedly withdrawing from the village of Hulluch.[39]

Realising they had been outflanked, the Germans in front of 2 Brigade surrendered and by five-thirty in the afternoon 2 Brigade troops were also digging in along the Lens-La Bassée road. An assault on the German Second Line seemed a possibility, but the division had suffered roughly seventy-five percent casualties[40] and there were substantial gaps between battalions and brigades in the newly-dug line making communication very difficult. No attack ensued.

The most successful sector of the attack on the 25 September was the most southerly, opposite the village that gave the battle its name, Loos. Perversely, the 15th Division manning the northern half of this sector probably had the most challenging objectives of any formation that day. The German front line contained two well-defended redoubts; they then had to tackle the Loos Defence Line and the village itself; 1,000 yards beyond the village was the feature that dominated that part of the battlefield, Hill 70 – believed "by the British to be well fortified and garrisoned".[41] The division's final objective, the settlement of Cité St Auguste, lay a further 1,000 yards to the east, behind the German Second Line.[42] All but the last of these objectives would be achieved, at least initially.

The 15th (Scottish) Division attacked in five columns, 46 Bde on the left, 44 Bde on the right, with 45 Bde in support. It was noticed how the volume of fire from the German front line slackened as the gas cloud rolled over it, and by 07.05, most of the line had been taken, despite machine guns in the two redoubts being able to "create[ ] large gaps in the ranks of the two leading battalions".[43] The Official History continues:

> The assaulting battalions did not delay. Their lines of companies, owing to the thick smoke, had now become intermingled, but they advanced towards the Loos Defences in good order and with determination.[44]

39   Edmonds, *Military Operations 1915 Vol. II*, p.213.
40   Ibid, p. 222 and Corrigan, *Loos 1915*, p.69.
41   Corrigan, *Loos 1915*, p.70.
42   See Map 1.
43   Edmonds, *Military Operations 1915*, Vol. II, p.194. The 9/Black Watch suffered over 150 casualties in No Man's Land.
44   Ibid, p.195.

The Loos Defence Line turned out to be thinly manned and the Scots pressed on into the village. Some Germans, surprised by the rapidity of their front-line defence's fall, fled towards Hill 70 and Cité St Laurent. Others were able to put up stubborn resistance, but bomb and bayonet won the day and by 08.00 Loos was completely in Scottish hands.

Approximately 1,500 troops, a mixture of men from numerous units, and short on officers, continued the advance. Instead of moving due east, as planned, towards Cité St Auguste, they veered to the south and up the slope towards Hill 70. The small German garrison atop the hill, on seeing this "bank holiday crowd" moving in their direction,[45] withdrew rapidly in the direction of Cité St Laurent. Lieutenant-Colonels Sandilands and Wallace (7/Cameron Highlanders and 10/Gordon Highlanders respectively) managed to halt a number of the men and began to consolidate positions just below the crest on the north-western slope of Hill 70, but some eight or nine hundred spilled over the redoubt and headed for Cité St Laurent, possibly mistaking it for their actual final objective. Lacking in cohesion, momentum and leadership, their advance faltered in the face of machine gun and other small arms fire emanating from the German Second Line defences. Pinned down on this reverse slope, with little or no cover, one or two groups attempted to rush the German positions but met with disaster. By early afternoon, survivors began to crawl back up the slope towards the hill's summit, but this general movement prompted a German counter attack which reached and successfully regained the Hill 70 redoubt.

The situation stabilised, neither side having the strength of numbers or the inclination to contest any more ground. By nightfall, units of 15th Division were holding positions facing largely south-east, stretching from Loos Crassier on the right to Chalk Pit Wood on the left. The 6/Cameron Highlanders, on this left flank, gained touch with units of 1st Division (1/Northants and 1/Gloucestershires) which had advanced at around 17.15 into positions in and around Bois Hugo.

On the extreme right of the attack frontage, 47th (London) Division was tasked with forming a defensive flank between and including the Double Crassier and Loos Crassier spoil heaps, both of which stood over one hundred feet high. At the northern end of the latter stood, clearly silhouetted against the sky, the twin winding towers known to the British as 'Tower Bridge'.

140 and 141 Bdes on the right and left respectively, followed the gas and smoke down the slope into the German front line defences, with 1/18th Londons dribbling a football in front of them, catching some of the defenders still emerging from their dug outs. By 07.30, 140 Bde troops had reached their objective – the German support trench – and were digging in between the Double Crassier and the Loos – Béthune road. Two hours later, battalions of 141 Bde, attacking to the north of the road, were able to report that they were established in the Chalk Pit, were contesting the copse to the south and had one platoon astride the Loos Crassier. A counter attack from south of the Double Crassier and stubborn resistance from German troops in trenches at the south-western tip of Chalk Pit Copse could not dent the Londoners' defences and the final prize, 'Tower Bridge', was taken by 19/London, but their commanding officer, Lt-Col H.D. Collison-Morley, was killed in the attack.

It would be fair to say that the 25 September attack was a partial success: the German front line had been breached along a substantial portion of its length and the village of Loos was in

---

45   Famously referred to thus in the relevant volume of official history, p.198.

British hands by the end of the day.[46] The cost had been high, however. The Official History puts British casualties at 470 Officers and 15,000 other ranks[47] but Nick Lloyd suggests that the total could be as high as 19,000.[48] The 6,350 fatalities mean that the average number of deaths per division is higher than were suffered on 1 July 1916 on the Somme. Senior officer casualties are staggering, with nine Lieutenant-Colonels (or acting battalion commanders) killed and a dozen more wounded. It is no wonder that none of the depleted battalions were seriously tasked with attacking the German Second Line that day. That daunting prospect belonged to 21st and 24th Divisions of XI Corps.

Haig's insistent lobbying of Sir John French on the matter of the positioning of the General Reserve seems to prove that he knew that any prospect of breaking through the German Second Line depended on the timely arrival on the battlefield – as early as possible on the 25 September – of the 21st and 24th Division troops. The failure to implement this resulted in disaster.

The 21st Division had been able to squeeze in a moderate amount of training in between their arrival in France and their arrival on the Loos battlefield: on 13 September, twenty officers of 62 Bde and a similar number from 63 Bde had spent twenty-four hours in the trenches at Nieppe and Armentières, twenty officers from 64 Bde repeating the exercise at Westoutre two days later; on the 14th, sixteen officers and thirty-two NCOs went on a four-day-course at the machine gun school at Wisques; on the 19th, 62 and 64 Bdes were able to organise Brigade Tactical Exercises during which the men practised "pushing through [a] gap forced by other troops in enemy's line and capturing strongpoints in rear".[49] On 11 September, 62 Bde constructed two 100-yard ranges among the brickfields near Hellebroucq and were able to practise sniping and machine gun firing.

Some of the officers and NCOs of 62 Bde were also able to experience the 'realities' of gas warfare for themselves on 16 September. Lt-Col Hadow, 10 Yorks, recounts the unpleasant event in his diary:

> At 2:30. parties of officers & NCOs from each battalion in the Brigade went to the brick fields for a lecture and demonstration in the use of Gas Helmets Etc. Afterwards a sample of German gas was turned on and we all walked through a trench. The smoke was so thick that men could only move slowly as everybody crowded in one after the other. Once in, all were only too keen to get out. The air we breathed through the helmet, though not poisonous, was as nasty as it could be and set me coughing. The noise of choking coughs and groans were most realistic. I was very glad when I got through the trench and had pulled my helmet off. Some of the men were rather bad, probably due to their not having put their helmets on properly. Charteris was out, he collapsed and had to go to bed when he got back. Another had to be taken to Hospital in the evening and a third was quite bad. I was all right again after a minute or two.[50]

46   See Map 2.
47   Edmonds, *Military Operations 1915*, Vol. II, p.267.
48   Lloyd, *Loos 1915*, p.156.
49   TNA PRO WO 95/2159: 64 Infantry Brigade War Diary.
50   IWM Private Papers of Colonel A. de S. Hadow. Doc. 11023.

On 21 September, Major Forster (GSO2, 21st Div) was even able to carry out aerial reconnaissance of the area around Pont-à-Vendin, some five miles or so behind the German Second Defence Line. Presumably this was on the assumption that 21st Division troops would soon be in that region. Between the 20 and 23 September they had endured a series of night marches that had seen them move from villages north-west of St Omer, covering over twenty miles on each of the first two "hot and oppressive"[51] nights before arriving near Lillers on the morning of the 23rd, where they were able to rest until the evening of the 24th.

The final march to Noeux les Mines was to prove rather testing. By moving off at 19.00 hrs, the intention was to allow the men a reasonable night's rest before the battle, and, as their final assembly positions were only between seven and eleven miles away and it was expected that they could cover that distance in three to four hours, a decent night's sleep was in the offing. Trying to move at any reasonable pace along the dark, narrow roads, carrying full equipment, including greatcoats, extra ammunition and three days' rations,[52] proved impossible. The men had to battle against motor and horse-drawn traffic coming in the opposite direction; at crossroads they were too often halted to allow other columns to cross their path; at one level crossing at Place à Bruay, units of 64 Bde were held up for over ninety minutes by an accident to a train. It was "like trying to push the Lord Mayor's procession through the streets of London without clearing the route and holding up the traffic".[53] Soon after midnight, just to add to the misery, it started to rain. The leading parties, tired and wet, arrived at their allotted bivouac areas – fields by the roadside – at around two in the morning of the 25th, the stragglers not making it until after six o'clock. Thankfully the rain had eased off by then, but sleep was to prove problematic as the final artillery bombardment, "the most intense that had yet been heard on the Western Front",[54] had begun two hours earlier. The men were to "remain in a state of readiness to move at one hour's notice".[55]

As early as 07.00 on the 25 September, when first reports began to arrive at First Army headquarters of I and IV Corps' successful breach of the German front line system, Haig sent a staff officer by motor car to Sir John French's headquarters in the chateau at Philomel, informing him that the attack was going well and asking that XI Corps be released and placed under First Army command.

At around 08.45, having received no news back regarding his earlier request, Haig sends another messenger, this time urging French to send XI Corps forward as all of his front line brigades had already been committed to the attack.

It was not until 09.30, some three hours after the attack had begun, that Sir John French finally yielded, sending the following message to XI Corps: "21st and 24th Divisions will move forward to First Army trenches as soon as situation requires and admits. On arrival there they will come under orders of First Army".[56] Haig received confirmation of this by telegram at ten

---

51 Ibid, p.273
52 The divisional commanders had been warned on 24 September that they might be cut off from their transport and "might not see their 'cookers' until the night of the 26th/27th". See Edmonds, *Military Operations 1915*, Vol. II, p.276.
53 Ibid, p.278.
54 Ibid, p.279.
55 TNA PRO WO 95/2128: 21st Div HQ War Diary.
56 Quoted in Edmonds, *Military Operations 1915*, Vol. II, p.280.

34   To Do the Work of Men

o'clock and by personal visit at around eleven-thirty. French then went to visit Haking at Noeux les Mines, the latter having received notification to march at 09.30. Haking had sent messengers to his divisions and these arrived at their destinations at around 10.30. The move onto the battlefield could finally begin.

Orders were issued to units of 21st Division at around 10.45 on the morning of the 25th to the effect that they should march eastwards to take up positions to the north and west of the village of Mazingarbe. (The 24th Division would move on a parallel course to their north). The first brigades were on the move by 11.15, but the order was delayed in reaching 64 Brigade and they did not set off until midday. The march averaged only six miles, but it was beset with the same kinds of problems the men had encountered the night before: the roads were crowded with vehicles moving in both directions, with parties of wounded men making their way to the rear and the 3rd Cavalry Division were crossing the line of march. Much has been written about the poor march discipline of the division, and although there may be some truth in the accusation, poor staff work at both GHQ and XI Corps, a lack of liaison between the two resulting in traffic congestion, and the inexperience of officers must also be taken into account. Writing to the official historian in 1926, Colonel Wethered, Brigade Major 62 Bde at the time of the battle, stated that

> the march of the 8/E.Yorks and the 10/Green Howards [10/Yorks] up to Loos was very much delayed owing to a policeman at Noeux les Mines ordering the battalions when passing a level crossing to open out with intervals between platoons. [...] This was evidently an order in force in the routine of trench warfare. It only shows how lack of attention to the minutest details may affect the timing of an attack. If the officers had been experienced, no doubt, they would have realised what had happened and disregarded the policeman.[57]

The lack of experienced officers in the division is highlighted by Wethered's later remark that "I was (I think I am accurate in stating) the only officer or man in the 62nd Brigade who had had any experience of war".[58]

The end result of all this confusion was that the final units of 21st Division were not in position until 16.00.[59] The main body of the reserves were still 5,000 – 6,000 yards from Loos village and largely ignorant of the situation ahead of them.

Even before all units of the reserve divisions were in place, XI Corps Order No.4 was sent out, timed at half past three that afternoon. In a correspondence with the official historian dated 26 January 1926, Brigadier-General C.G. Stewart, (GSO1, 24th Division at the time of the battle), accused high command of a "cult of optimism", stating that "rumours had been stated as facts", and "a rumour was accepted without apparently being confirmed, because it was optimistic".[60] This 'cult of optimism' is clearly evident in Order No. 4, which states:

---

57   TNA PRO CAB 45/121: Colonel J.H. Wethered to the official historian correspondence, 19 January 1926.
58   Ibid.
59   The 24th Division was in place shortly after 15.00 hours.
60   TNA PRO CAB 45/121: Brigadier-General C.G. Stewart to Brigadier-General Sir James Edmonds correspondence, 19 January 1926.

1. The 4th Corps has captured Hill 70 East of Loos. The 1st Corps have entered HULLUCH
2. 2. The XIth Corps (less Guards Division) will advance with a view to securing the crossings over the HAUTE DEULE Canal at LOISON-SOUS-LENS – HARNES – and PONT à VENDIN.
3. 21st Division (less one brigade detached to IV Corps)
   1st objective, the high ground around ANNAY.
   2nd objective, Canal crossings at LOISON-SOUS-LENS and HARNES.[61]

The towns of Annay and Harnes lie four and five miles respectively to the *east* of Loos, well behind the still unbroken German Second Defence Line and the town of Hulluch was still firmly in German hands. Subsequent orders would be slightly less ambitious.

The first units of 21st Division to advance to the battlefield were the four battalions of 62 Brigade (Brigadier-General E.B. Wilkinson).[62] At 10.40 on 25 September, the brigade received verbal orders to the effect that they were to be temporarily detached from 21st Division and be placed under the command of IV Corps and subsequently at the disposal of 15th Division. These orders were soon after confirmed in writing by Division Order No.7 and at 11.15 the brigade marched off to map squares L.17 and L.16.a, arriving there two and a quarter hours later. (This was near Noyelles on the Béthune – Lens road). Further orders were received at 14.30, "just as the men were about to commence their dinners",[63] requiring them to move immediately via "Quality Street"[64] to Loos. This order, hand-written on a standard message pad, and marked "PRIORITY", reflects the lack of definite intelligence getting back to divisional headquarters. It states:

> If HILL 70 beyond LOOS is still held by our troops you will support and if necessary relieve them AAA If HILL 70 has been abandoned you will retake it AAA Should you find on arrival at LOOS that the situation admits of a further advance against CITE ST AUGUSTE you will act accordingly in cooperation with the 44th & 46th Bdes now in my front line AAA The 45th Bde has orders to hold on to LOOS.[65]

Brigadier-General Wilkinson, with no knowledge of the true position or of the ground, could do no more than point out Hill 70 to his battalion commanders on the map and tell them "we do not know what has happened on Hill 70. You must go and find out".[66] He decided initially to send just two battalions, and accordingly at 15.00 hrs the 8/E.Yorks and 10/Yorks marched off via Philosophe and Fosse No.7, (that is down the main Béthune – Lens road) towards Loos. The 12 and 13/Northumberland Fusiliers followed an hour later.

---

61   TNA PRO WO 95/2128: 21st Division GHQ War Diary.
62   These were: 8/East Yorks (Lt-Col B.I. Way), 10/Yorkshire (Lt-Col A. De S. Hadow), 12/ Northumberland Fusiliers (Lt-Col H.B. Warwick) and 13/Northumberland Fusiliers (Lt-Col Lord Crofton).
63   TNA PRO WO 95/2151: 62 Infantry Brigade HQ War Diary.
64   At reference G27.a central, on the main Béthune to Lens road.
65   TNA PRO WO 95/2151: 62 Infantry Brigade HQ War Diar .
66   Edmonds, *Military Operations 1915*, Vol. II, p.296.

36 To Do the Work of Men

10TH BATTALION.
Witley Camp, August, 1915.

Back Row—Lt. P. Mathisen; Lt. W. H. Goater; Lt. R. M. Milne; 2nd-Lt. N. E. S. Gardner; 2nd-Lt. W. R. Knott; Lt. D. H. Wippell; 2nd-Lt. A. F. Jacob; 2nd-Lt. C. B. Bass; Lt. J. N. Barraclough; 2nd-Lt. V. D. K. Craddock; 2nd-Lt. J. S. Pratt; Capt. J. E. Lynch; Lt. E. D. O'Brien; Capt. S. W. Loudoun-Shand.
Middle Row—Capt. C. A. McLellan; Capt. V. Fowler; Lt. and Q.M. R. Cumming; Major W. H. Dent; Col. A. de S. Hadow; Capt. A. Hollingworth (Adjutant); Capt. T. Charteris; Capt. J. C. E. Douglas; Capt. G. A. Turner.
Sitting—2nd-Lt. F. B. Parker; 2nd-Lt. W. B. Cornaby; 2nd-Lt. P. J. Sylvester; 2nd-Lt. G. B. Hornby.

Officers of 10/Yorks, Witley Camp, 1915.

The leading battalions, marching in fours with the recently enforced hundred-yard interval between platoons, crossed the old German front line a little after 16.30 and then left the road, heading across country for the Loos Pylons, which were from here clearly silhouetted against the sky. "The direction was for Hill 70 thro' Loos and over the Slack heaps",[67] but this brought them into view of German artillery at Cité St Pierre (south of Loos village) and they came under heavy shrapnel fire. A number of casualties ensued, and their transport section, at the rear of the column and still on the main road, was "practically destroyed, the remains of the vehicles and animals completely blocking traffic".[68] Under this brutal baptism of fire, and with none of the battalions having anything other than the 1/100,000 map,[69] the line of advance became unclear and the 8/E.Yorks, followed by some men from 10/Yorks, veered to the south of Loos village and bumped into units of 1/20th Londons (47th Division) who had been holding positions just to the north of Chalk Pit Copse since the morning (See Map 2). The Yorkshiremen continued their advance, despite the best efforts of Lt-Col Hubback, commanding 1/20th London, to stop them, into and beyond the copse where they came under intense machine gun fire from German positions at its southern end. This brought the advance to an abrupt halt. The war diaries of both 8/E.Yorks and 10/Yorks fail to mention this episode: indeed, the diarist of 10/Yorks records the events of 25 and 26 September as having occurred on the 26th and 27th. The accounts of both diarists are a little unclear and at times contradictory. Both refer to their battalions' advance into and through Loos as an attack, both presumably at the time ignorant of the true location of Hill 70. The mistake was compounded by a swiftly penned, badly spelt and unsigned message from an officer of 10/Yorks, timed at 18.35 and received by 62 Bde HQ at 20.00 hours, stating:

On Hill 70. 6.35 PM.
Hold Hill 70 about 900 yards enemy's side of Loose Pilon with portions of 10 Y. 8EY & 17 Londons. Am entrenching.
    Enemy shelling Pilons and good number of machine guns & snipers are worrying us. Machine guns are said to be in wood R. of our front – about E. Unless artillery help us we shall suffer from heavy gun fire. Can our artillery engage enemy's artillery & keep down fire. Our forward position is at the outside 800 yards front of Loose Pilons.
    Have not enough men to hold position if attacked at daylight.[70]

At 17.40, Wethered, Brigade Major of 62 Bde, had sent out a message to 10/Yorks:

Push on as quick as you can to Hill 70. Report at once when you are there. AAA Have you seen anything of 8 E York R.[71]

---

67   TNA PRO WO 95/1424: 8/East Yorks War Diary.
68   Edmonds, Military Operations 1915 Vol. II, p.297.
69   Colonel Wethered, in his correspondence of 19 Jan 1926 quoted earlier, insisted that "I was the only officer in the 62nd Brigade who had a trench map!"
70   TNA PRO WO 95/2151: 62 Brigade HQ War Diary.
71   Ibid.

Ten minutes later he sent another to "Any Officer on Hill 70", which read: "62 Inf Bde urgently requires information as to the situation on Hill 70".[72]

The timings of the arrival of these messages – if indeed they did reach their destination – are not recorded. What is clear, however, is that 62 Bde Headquarters had little or no idea what was happening ahead of them. The 10/Yorks were, in fact, not on Hill 70, but astride the Loos Crassier. If we accept the officer's estimation of their distance from the 'Pilons', this would put them still almost a thousand yards short of their objective.

Thankfully, Lieutenant-Colonels B.I. Way and A. De S. Hadow (commanding 8/E.Yorks & 10/Yorks respectively) had restored some semblance of order by around half past seven. D, C and part of B Companies of the 8/E.Yorks, along with 1/19th London, dug in, extending the 20/London's line to the north over the Loos Crassier. Major Ingles, second-in-command, formed up the remainder of the men in Loos village and by eight o'clock was employing them in digging communication trenches up to the front line, though this work was hindered by machine gun and artillery fire from their right flank. Meanwhile, the 10/Yorks were gathered in positions south of Loos Crassier, to the north of Chalk Pit Copse. At 23.00 hrs, an order was sent out from 62 Bde HQ to the effect that both battalions should be withdrawn into Loos village, but Major Dent, second-in-command 10/Yorks, went back to brigade headquarters, which were by now in the village, and explained that the Germans opposite him were there in force and that he was of the opinion that the Slag Heaps should be held. Brigadier-General Wilkinson concurred and ordered 8/E.Yorks to remain in position astride the Crassier. The 10/Yorks were moved to positions to the north-east of it. The two battalions settled in for the night and awaited further instructions. (See Map 3).

Let us now turn our attention to the other two battalions of 62 Bde, the 12 and 13/Northumberland Fusiliers. As will be remembered, these units were following the two Yorkshire battalions at about one hour's distance towards Loos, and an accurate account of their actions relies largely on the respective battalion diaries: during the advance, 62 Bde had only fleeting contact with the 12th battalion and lost touch completely with the 13th until late the following evening. Orders were sent forward, but "no touch could be obtained, […] though several order-lies in addition to the Signal Section Officer were sent to find them".[73]

As the 12/Northumberland Fusiliers crested the rise on the Lens road (at about G.28.c, near the Lens Road Redoubt) they deployed left into extended order and occupied the old German front line trenches. Shortly afterwards, C Company was sent forward to occupy an outpost line. It was around quarter past seven in the evening that the men "first came under fire"[74] when the Germans sent over a number of artillery shells. Two hours later the battalion continued its move forward into Loos village, only to attract more shell fire, under which, the diarist claims, "men [were] very steady".[75] They sheltered in the church square while Captain Phillips went forward to reconnoitre the route to the Pylons. On his return, he led the men to the slag heaps where they once more came under fire, this time, and for the first time, sustaining casualties. They chose discretion over valour and withdrew a short distance back into the village.

72 Ibid.
73 TNA PRO WO 95/2151: 62 Brigade HQ War Diary.
74 TNA PRO WO 95/2155: 12/Northumberland Fusiliers War Diary.
75 Ibid.

Apparently unsure of what to do next, the CO, Lt-Col Warwick, returned to Brigade HQ and came back with orders to move to square G36 a., this putting them just outside the village to the north of the Pylons. Brigadier-General Wilkinson (CO 62 Bde) had earlier ridden to 45 Bde HQ in Loos, where he "saw a message"[76] requesting that one of his battalions be placed at the disposal of 45 Bde. 12/Northumberland Fusiliers were accordingly allocated this role and at nine o'clock, two platoons of A Company under 2nd Lts Hill and Oliver were sent forward in order to help the 45 Bde entrench on Hill 70. According to 62 Bde diary, this move was to relieve the 9/Black Watch, but the battalion diary makes no mention of this, only that (and this time in agreement with the brigade diary) the rest of A Company was sent in at a quarter to midnight to relieve the 10/Gordon Highlanders.

The other three companies spent a nervous night under sporadic shrapnel fire and were ordered to 'stand to', ready "to charge with bayonet in case of enemy appearance".[77] Their positions remained unchanged as the first streaks of dawn appeared in front of them, albeit softened by a clinging mist.

The 13/Northumberland Fusiliers, in rear of their compatriots, had, after dark, occupied the old German reserve trenches on the north side of the Lens road and began the job of reversing them. They were greeted by some shrapnel and high explosive shells, and at nine o'clock moved forward into Loos village and awaited further instructions. There, four men became casualties, victims of shrapnel fire – the battalion's first losses.[78]

Verbal orders to report to 46 Bde HQ at G.29 b. 2.4 were received at eleven o'clock.[79] The 62 Bde diary gives a different location, so it is perhaps no surprise that some confusion ensued before Lt-Col Lord Crofton bumped into Lt-Col Purvis, CO 7/Highland Light Infantry, who was representing the Brigadier-General and was able to explain the situation. He requested that one company be sent forward to "support Scottish Regiments in trench on Hill 70".[80] B Company, under Major T.V. Levinge, was accordingly dispatched. The remaining three companies lay out in the open, just to the east of the Loos-Hulluch road and awaited developments. They spent the cold hours of darkness under both persistent rain and enemy machine gun fire.[81]

Brigadier-General Nickalls, commanding 63 Brigade, had received orders on 25 September that his brigade was to march on Loos, via Philosophe and Fosse No.7 on the Loos Road "with a view to a subsequent advance to the line of the Hulluch – Loos road by night and thence continue advance against German trenches in direction of Annay".[82] The first requirement of the order was to prove practicable. The latter remained an illusory hope.

Receiving orders to move from Fosse No.7 at eight in the evening, the battalions marched down the Lens Road on the heels of 62 Brigade, but, having crossed the old British and German front lines, the 8/Lincoln and 8/Somerset battalions deployed to the north of the road, as if on parade, "with companies in column of fours at ten paces interval, that is [the] brigade occupied a

---

76   TNA PRO WO 95/2151: 62 Brigade HQ War Diary.
77   TNA PRO WO 95/2155: 12/ Northumberland Fusiliers War Diary.
78   The British soldier, at this stage of the war, did not wear a helmet. The service cap was no protection against shrapnel.
79   A guide to interpreting this style of map reference can be found in Appendix VI. This style of reference will be used extensively throughout this work.
80   TNA PRO WO 95/2155: 13/Northumberland Fusiliers War Diary.
81   See Map 3 for battalion dispositions.
82   TNA PRO WO 95/2158: 63 Brigade HQ War Diary.

40 To Do the Work of Men

frontage of about 120 paces."[83] From there, they marched across country on a compass bearing, leaving the other two battalions, (10/York & Lancs and 12/West Yorks), to turn left onto the Grenay-Benifontaine Road and skirt the northern outskirts of Loos village prior to continuing in a northerly direction as far as Point 69 (See Map 3). Three of the battalions were in place and in contact at Point 69 by eleven o'clock, but the 10/York & Lancs had been held up badly by troops from other units blocking the Loos Road, which was also being targeted by German artillery and was "in a terrible condition of mud and shell holes".[84]

Units of 24th Division to the north had, by this time, received orders to "halt and wait for daylight".[85] First Army orders to the same effect, timed at 20.17, had not reached Nickalls, however, and he pressed on. As, by 23.45, the 10/Yorks & Lancs had still not arrived at the rendezvous point, it was decided that the other three battalions would push on without them. They moved off at around half past midnight, just as the missing battalion turned up. 12/West Yorks and 8/Lincolns lead the way on a compass bearing of 112 degrees across "the great open space of rank grassland that lay between them and the Lens-La Bassée Road, three miles distant". For once, the official historian's style lapses into more relaxed, almost lyrical prose:

> At times there was fair visibility, for the enemy bombardment of Loos had turned the village into a furnace of flame, with 'Tower Bridge' silhouetted in black outline against the ruddy glow, and the sky was lightened by other burning villages, shell fire and Very lights. From time to time would come a wave of mist, when all was hidden.[86]

Given the lack of communication already in evidence, it is not surprising that 63 Brigade's eventual arrival at around three o'clock in the morning of the 26th in the vicinity of Chalk Pit Wood was unexpected. As the 63 Brigade approached the wood, they came under rifle and machine gun fire from that direction. Lt-Col Leggett, (CO 12/West Yorks), initially assumed this to be friendly fire.[87] The fire actually came from Hill 70, and luckily the two leading battalions only got as far as fixing bayonets before patrols ascertained that Chalk Pit Wood was in fact held by units of 44 and 2 Brigades,[88] who, ignorant of this mass formation's imminent appearance, had in turn almost fired on them.

By this time, another order had failed to reach Brigadier-General Nickalls: A IV Corps order concerning the projected relief of the now exhausted and much-depleted units occupying the ground that had been hard-won the previous day. Being part of XI Corps, however, Nickalls knew nothing of this plan. He met with Brigadier-General Pollard, (2 Brigade), in the Chalk Pit at the north-eastern tip of the wood and it was decided that a relief would go ahead.

63 Brigade thus took over the "line of rifle pits and the rough shelters that had been dug during the night [...] and the men, with the aid of their portable entrenching implements

---

83 Edmonds, *Military Operations 1915*, Vol. II, p.287.
84 TNA PRO WO 95/2158: 63 Brigade HQ War Diary.
85 Edmonds, Military Operations 1915 Vol. II, p.291.
86 Ibid, p.288
87 TNA PRO CAB 45/120: Leggett to Edmonds correspondence, 6 August 1926.
88 The 62 Brigade War Diary mentions only 44 Brigade. The Official History mentions only 2 Brigade. Battalion war diaries suggest that battalions of both brigades were present.

began to make them into more or less connected trenches".[89] Some sources praise the men's efforts to dig in with the far-from-effective entrenching tools, picks and shovels having been left behind on the Loos Road many hours before. Others bemoan a lack of effort in this direction, which resulted in unnecessary casualties from later artillery and small arms fire.

Praise appears in the war diaries of 8/Lincolns, 12/West Yorks, 8/Somerset LI, and Lt Alcock of the 8/Lincolns wrote to the official historian in November 1918: "By 7 a.m. on the 26th, we had a more or less connected trench with an average depth of 3'6" to 4'."[90] 63 Bde HQ diary states that "very little effort had been made […] to improve and deepen the Trenches. […] The result was that these Trenches afforded very little protection […] and many of the casualties could have been prevented if Officers and NCOs had insisted upon the Men digging themselves in properly".[91]

Second-Lieutenant Hervey Lancelot St George Swallow, 10 Yorks & Lancs, age 19, kia 25 Sept 1915. (IWM HU 118795)

In any case, Nickalls had "given his battalions to understand"[92] that their current positions were temporary and that they would shortly resume the advance.

For the time being, from north to south, the battalions of 63 Brigade were in roughly the following positions: the 10/Yorks & Lancs were in their entrenched positions on the Hulluch – Lens road, facing east, with their right flank almost at the Chalk Pit, their left at the road junction at H.19.a.5.9. "Though entrenched one had to keep down as sniping was persistent from the direction of Hill 70 or square wood." [Bois Hugo][93]

The forward units of the 12/West Yorks were to the east of the Hulluch – Lens road, aligned facing north-east, their left near the Chalk Pit, "the right of [the] battalion front line found itself digging rifle pits in the open, about twenty yards from the edge of the wood. [Bois Hugo][94] B, A and C Companies occupied this 'front line', whilst D Company were in support positions parallel to the road.

The 8/Lincolns in effect straddled Bois Hugo with one company to the north of it, facing east, the other three along its southern edge, facing south towards Chalet Wood. The 8/Somerset LI had five platoons of B and C Companies along the Hulluch – Lens road, facing east, north of

---

89 Edmonds, *Military Operations 1915,* Vol. II, p.292.
90 TNA PRO CAB 45/120.
91 TNA PRO WO 95/2158: 63 Brigade HQ War Diary.
92 Edmonds, *Military Operations 1915,* Vol. II, p.292.
93 TNA PRO WO 95/2158 10/Yorks & Lancs War Diary, Appendix I, September 1915. For this and subsequent descriptions of deployments, see Map 3.
94 TNA PRO WO 95/1432: 12/West Yorks War Diary.

Puits 14 bis[95] and another three in support in the Chalk Pit. A and D Companies had somehow become detached from the rest of the battalion during the night march and, as best as can be ascertained, had strayed south – no official word from them reached 63 Brigade HQ until 7 p.m. on 26 September, by which time they had participated in 15th Division's futile attacks on Hill 70 and had subsequently withdrawn to Vermelles.

The last brigade of 21st Division to arrive on the battle field was the 64th. As they passed Divisional HQ at Vermelles at about 20.00 hrs on the 25 September, they were able to receive instructions directly from the divisional commander: they were to follow the 63 Bde, maintaining a distance of 1,000 yards and it was raining hard as they set off. They reached the crossroads on the Lens road a mile or so south-east of Philosophe at around 9 o'clock and prepared to deploy for their final approach to the battlefield. It took three hours to issue orders, unload the machine guns, ammunition and bombs and form up the four battalions into company columns of fours, the 14 and 15/DLI in front, 9 and 10/KOYLI in the rear. The idea of following 63 Brigade was quickly abandoned as the plan was to set out across country on a compass bearing – only transport units would use the roads. The whole formation, eight columns wide, moved off into the darkness at about midnight. An officer sent ahead to liaise with 63 Brigade managed to find Brigadier-General Nickalls and returned with the news that the 63rd had moved off at 9 o'clock. "They therefore had a long start of us" asserted the 64 Brigade diarist.[96] The head of the formation reached the old British front line trenches near the Loos Road Redoubt at one in the morning. Crossing them was far from straightforward:

> Some trenches could be jumped, some had had narrow causeways filled in across them, across others we found planks. But the crossing was interminable, each trench necessitating a halt to let units file over and then reform the Brigade beyond.[97]

An hour later they were repeating the whole process at the German front line system, this time under spasmodic shell fire. Luckily, the shells landing nearest turned out to be duds. As the unwieldy formation crawled eastwards, patrols were sent forward in an attempt to make contact with 63 Brigade again. They returned without finding them.

Daylight was almost upon them as they stumbled upon a single line of German trench just to the east of the road running north from Loos village. A dilemma confronted them at this point.

> It was possible that the 63 Inf Bde had mistaken its direction and that there was nothing between us and the enemy. If this were so, it was now too late to push on to the Lens-Hulluch road as there was not enough darkness left in which to consolidate it, and the risk of moving forward on unknown ground and stumbling on the enemy without having touch with any neighbouring troops, or of being caught by him in open coverless ground at

---

95 B Coy was commanded by Captain W.H. Nichols. He was reported killed in Major Howard's account of the battle but was actually wounded and captured. He died of wounds on 15 October 1915. He was originally buried in West Munich Cemetery, but his body was exhumed in 1924 and re-buried in Niederzwehren Cemetery, Kassel, Germany. Within CWGC records, some documents list him incorrectly as a Major.

96 TNA PRO WO 95/2159: 64 Brigade HQ War Diary.

97 Ibid.

daylight in an isolated situation, was too great. On the other hand if 63 Inf Bde were ahead and had consolidated themselves on the Lens-Hulluch road as directed, we had reached just the right position in their rear from which to support them.[98]

Impeccable reasoning had removed the dilemma. The 9 and 10/KOYLI took up positions accordingly in this trench and the two Durham battalions were sent ahead to occupy another trench line discovered some short distance ahead.

Plans for the main assault on the 26 September had by this time evolved. The German Second Line would be attacked, and 21st and 24th Divisions would play the leading role. An unsupported advance would however come under severe flanking fire from both Hulluch in the north, which was still securely in German hands, and from Hill 70 in the south. Accordingly, these two locations were to be assaulted in advance of the major attack: the 1st Division would launch another attack to capture the village of Hulluch, along with Stützpunkt III and the second line trench linking the two just for good measure, and 15th Division, this time with 62 Brigade in support, would simultaneously retake the Hill 70 redoubt. The 21st Division would be required to assault the German line between Bois Hugo and Stützpunkt IV inclusive (references H.26.b.8.8 to H.20.d.3.9 – see Map 3).[99]

The first major issue to be taken into consideration here was the fact that the Germans had not been idle overnight: "in all, twenty-two additional battalions were moved into the battle area, and by daylight on the 26th, the second position was more strongly held than the first had been".[100]

Second, any preparatory or protective artillery barrage could not even begin to approach the intensity of the previous day's bombardment. It had proven impossible to get sufficient numbers of guns forward and those that were struggling to establish new positions, often in clear view of German artillery, were very short of ammunition. Neither would there be any smoke or gas. Attacking troops would inevitably encounter uncut wire entanglements in front of the German trenches.

Third, the 21st Division had already been weakened when 62 Brigade was 'loaned' to 15th Division. Subsequently, 63 Brigade had taken over the front line defences in and around the woods and as it turned out, by the time the attack was meant to go in, its units were struggling to hold back a strong German counter attack. 64 Brigade received hand-written orders at around 8 o'clock in the morning which did little to clarify their role in the coming attack: the Staff at 21st Division HQ were themselves clearly not sure of the exact situation on the battlefield. Forestier-Walker writes:

> I have sent a Staff Officer out to clear up situation and in the meanwhile you must act as you think best. AAA Try to get in touch with 63 Bde. AAA If they are helplessly astray it may be necessary for you to take their place in the first line of the attack AAA If on the other hand they are well placed to carry out attack as ordered you must consider possibility of maintaining yourself as a reserve in your present position and if necessary make any move you may think desirable.[101]

---

98   Ibid.
99   Lloyd, Loos 1915, p.163.
100 Edmonds, *Military Operations 1915*, Vol. II, p.306.
101 TNA PRO WO 95/2159: 64 Brigade HQ War Diary.

The best-case scenario, therefore, for this 'divisional' attack was for a brigade-strength assault, with a second brigade in support. At worst, it was left to the discretion of 64 Brigade commander – in ignorance of the true situation ahead of him – as to whether an attack would materialise at all.

The 26 September 1915 has been described as "a disaster for the BEF" which resulted in "an ignoble retreat".[102] The actions of the inexperienced divisions asked to perform an all but impossible task on that day have been categorised as "naïve gallantry".[103] A strictly chronological account of the day's events would produce a thoroughly tangled narrative: a blow by blow, brigade by brigade telling of the story – with a number of battalions and even companies detached from their units – would also result in an unsatisfactory muddle. A geographical framework has therefore been adopted: the attack on Hill 70 will be dealt with first, followed by events in and around the woods adjoining the Hulluch – Lens road. The attack by 64 Brigade (and other stragglers!) can then be analysed.

In the early hours of the 26th, Generals Rawlinson (IV Corps) and Haking (XI Corps) met to finalise the details of their corps' roles in the forthcoming assault. 45 and 62 Brigades would attack Hill 70 at nine o'clock, the advance being preceded by "an hour's intense bombardment by all available guns".[104] Importantly the orders contained the following instruction: "Before the bombardment of the Hill 70 Redoubt begins the infantry will be withdrawn to a safe distance".[105] Unfortunately, not all units were made aware of this prior to the eight o'clock deadline.

Second-Lieutenant Thomas Sydney Schafer, 13/NFus, age 24, kia 26 September 1915. (IWM HU 126230)

Lieutenant Robert William Lee Dodds, 13/NFus, kia 26 September 1915, age 21. (IWM HU 121332)

---

102 Lloyd, *Loos 1915* p.163.
103 Corrigan, *Loos 1915*, p.95.
104 Edmonds, *Military Operations 1915*, Vol. II, p.310.
105 Ibid, p.311.

The brigade commanders, Brigadier-Generals Wallerston (45 Bde) and Wilkinson (62 Bde), having received the orders at around five o'clock, decided that the adjustment required to conform to the proposed deployment of the troops – 45 Bde attacking to the south of the track running from Loos through the redoubt to the Hulluch – Lens road, 62 Brigade on a parallel trajectory to the north of it – would be too risky and that their formations would attack from their present positions. 45 Brigade would advance astride the track with 7/R. Scots Fusiliers on the right, 11/Argyll and Sutherland Highlanders in the centre and 13/R. Scots on the left. 62 Brigade units would advance in close support.

Attempts to get artillery batteries forward into positions north-east of Loos had floundered owing to the parlous state of the roads after the constant German shelling, and in the end the artillery barrage was supplied, at a rate of only two shells per minute per battery, by 15th Division units still in position around Maroc, Mazingarbe and Fosse No.7 – all well to the west of Loos.

Orders from brigade headquarters did not reach the assault units until after seven o'clock, and in some cases – 11/Argyll and Sutherland Highlanders, 13/R.Scots and the one forward company of 13/Northumberland Fusiliers – until after the bombardment had begun, resulting in casualties. Indeed, the orders never reached the 13/Northumberland Fusiliers, as "Signals could not find them".[106] Their CO managed to see orders meant for the Scottish regiments, but "this order was viewed too late and before the withdrawal could be ordered our shells were dropping amongst our own men, who fell back of their own accord".[107]

The early morning mist cleared quite suddenly, just as the attack was due to go in, so the German defenders on the crest of the hill had a clear view of the 45 Bde battalions who leapt to their feet and charged forward, two companies of the 8/East Yorks joining in on the right from their positions close to the Loos Crassier. This attack made it as far as the perimeter trenches of the Hill 70 redoubt, which were captured after severe hand to hand fighting. The centre of the redoubt remained in German hands, however, and attempts to push forward on either side of it were repulsed by heavy small arms cross fire and by the German artillery retaliation. The diary of 8/E.Yorks confirms that around 120 men of the battalion took part in the attack led by their commanding officer, Lieutenant-Colonel Way. Major Ingles continues the story:

> Colonel Way with the two companies entrenched on the left of our line took part in this attack but were caught by frontal fire from Hill 70 and enfilade fire from the Lens side and they suffered very heavy casualties. As Capt. Smith, commanding "C" Company, described to me afterwards in England, "His line seemed to just wither away". Capt Smith was left on the field severely wounded and Colonel Way was also severely wounded in that attack.[108]

Two hundred yards behind the 45 Bde units, the two remaining battalions of 62 Bde that had correctly interpreted their orders, the 10/Yorks (Lt-Col A. de S. Hadow), and 12/

---

106 TNA PRO CAB 45/121. Colonel J.R.Wethered (Bde Major 62 Bde) to Edmonds correspondence, 19 January 1926.
107 TNA PRO WO 95/2155 War Diary 13/Northumberland Fusiliers.
108 TNA PRO CAB 45/120. Major R.J. Ingles to Edmonds, 6 March 1926. According to the 8/E.Yorks War Diary (TNA PRO WO 95/1424), Colonel Way was wounded on or near the slag heap after the battalion withdrawal.

Northumberland Fusiliers (Lt-Col H.B. Warwick), advanced up the slope into a hail of machine gun fire.[109] They were met by some of the Scots retiring from the crest, but pushed on, carrying some of the Scots with them, back over the crest on either side of the redoubt. It was here that the attack began to falter: the diarist of 12/Northumberland Fusiliers wrote:

> After enemy's first line trench the attack appears to have come under machine gun [fire]. Attack held up and many casualties. Troops on our left began to go back. CO went forward to encourage men but further progress impossible. CO slightly hit in ear and casualties in officers heavy. The crest of the hill was held for some time but MG very severe and troops obliged to fall back to front line trench. Enemy attempted to follow over crest but were easily repulsed. 'A' Coy report having taken enemy's first line trench and bayoneted several Germans but were afterwards very heavily fired on by MG's while in pursuit of enemy. Obliged to retire to crest and afterwards to front line trench.[110]

Lieutenant-Colonel Arthur de Salis Hadow, commanding 10/Yorks. kia 26 Sept 1915. Age 57. (Harrow School)

The 10/Yorks, on their right, were likewise pinned down by machine gun fire, seemingly just short of the German front line defences. Gallant, but ultimately unsuccessful attempts were made to get the men forward. Lt-Col Hadow stood up, shouted "Charge!" and rushed forward, only to be cut down immediately and killed.

This was Hadow's first action. He wrote a series of letters to his wife, Maud, beginning the day after embarkation for France:

---

109 It appears the 13/Northumberland Fusiliers sent two platoons forward from their positions on the Loos – Hulluch road. Their War Diary states that the attack "swayed to and fro" but provides no other details. The memoir of Private W. Walker does not help much, other than to establish that they did advance, but were immediately cut to pieces by severe machine gun and artillery fire. It is possible, from his account, to conclude that the advance never made it up the slopes of Hill 70, but could perhaps have veered to the left, coming up against German troops in the vicinity of Chalet Wood. 62 Bde diary confirms that the battalion took part in attacks here in conjunction with 63 and 64 bde troops later in the day. As a result, casualties for the day were severe: 17 Officers and 379 Other Ranks. Just over one hundred of these were fatalities.

110 TNA PRO WO 95/2155: 12/Northumberland Fusiliers War Diary.

Lieutenant-Colonel Hadow. CO 10/Yorks is buried in St Patrick's Cem., Loos. The headstone erroneously records his date of death as 27 September 1915. (Author)

48   To Do the Work of Men

Yesterday was a real hateful day and it was very, very horrid having to say goodbye to you all. I felt terribly near breaking down, you and the children have been so sweet to me lately, it makes the parting worse. God grant we shall meet again, it's something to look forward to.

He managed to write every day, up to and including the morning of the ill-fated attack on Hill 70. His letters are perhaps typical of the era: he regrets leaving his family behind, hopes that he will be able to do his duty, and is accepting of his possible fate.

20 September
Though what I'm telling you will make you feel anxious, but I'm certain you will be brave, as you were about Gerry.[111] I hope with God's will, I may come through all right, but should I not, both you and I will have done our duty to our country.

24 September
I know full well I shall be in God's hands. I trust I may do my duty as I ought to do, and if it is fated I am to die, I feel I shall have fallen doing the right thing and that I shall be allowed to join Gerry in heaven. I think it right to look things squarely in the face, though naturally I hope I may come safely through and that we shall all spend a good many happy years together. I was so glad I got the little photo case this morning, I shall carry it with me always.

26 September
My darling Maud,
    I wonder if I shall ever finish this or whether this morning is my last on earth. […] We are just off. Goodbye, with love,
    Arthur."[112]

On seeing his commanding officer killed, Major W. Dent also stood up in order to initiate an advance but met the same fate. It is difficult to understand what followed. Bravery is to be commended, but here naivety overbore pragmatism: three more officers, Major R. Noyes, Captain T. Charteris and Captain J. Lynch all made similar unsuccessful, and ultimately fatal, attempts to lead the battalion forward.[113]

---

111 Colonel Hadow's son, Second Lieutenant Gerald Francis Hadow, 2nd Yorkshire Regiment, was killed in action at Givenchy on 15 June 1915. He had survived the initial assault, but was killed by shell fire as he made his way back to report to Headquarters. He had earlier survived Neuve Chapelle and Festubert. He was twenty years old.
112 IWM Hadow Papers.
113 Hadow, an Old Harrovian, (as were his seven brothers), retired from the army as a Brevet Colonel in September 1909. He was appointed commanding officer of 10/Yorks on 21 September 1914. He is buried in St Patrick's Cemetery, Loos, Grave reference III G 8. Major Dent was an Old Etonian. He is buried in Cabaret Rouge British Cemetery, grave XVIII E 1. Noyes, Charteris and Lynch are all commemorated on the Loos Memorial at Dud Corner Cemetery. The Commonwealth War Graves Commission incorrectly records Lynch's date of death as 25 September, and that of Hadow as the 27th.

Major Wilfrid Harry Dent, 10/Yorks kia 26 Sept 1915, age 48. Cabaret Rouge Br Cem XVIII.E.1. (Author)

The assault on Hill 70 had, effectively, failed. Troops from both brigades were inextricably mixed up, some parties clinging on to the flanking shoulders of the redoubt, others hanging on to fire-swept positions just down the slope in the old German first defence line. At around eleven o'clock, renewed and heavy German artillery fire from positions near Lens and Cité St Auguste, including some gas shells, proved to be the final straw for some of the men, who, ignoring the entreaties of their officers, began to withdraw down the casualty-strewn slope towards the relative shelter of Loos village. A more general withdrawal by 45 Brigade troops at around 4 o'clock in the afternoon, proved to be, according to the 12/Northumberland Fusiliers diarist, the prompt for Colonels Way and Warwick to decide to give the order for their men to retire. Later reports of men coming in from Hill 70 after dark confirm that the order failed to reach everyone, but the majority of those involved in the attack streamed back towards, and in some cases, through Loos: the survivors of the 10/Yorks, with the exception of two officers and their attached party who rallied and took up defensive positions on the Loos Crassier, were bivouacked near Philosophe by midnight; a number of 12/Northumberland Fusiliers were collected under the command of Major Graham-Pole at Noyelles-les-Vermelles by around ten o'clock. The rest of the battalion, under Captain Edlmann, (A Coy), remained in defensive positions in Loos village until relieved by the Guards at 04.30 the following morning. Lt-Col Warwick, ushering his men back across the slag heaps, had suffered a bullet wound between the shoulder blades and had been "placed in a dugout"[114] until he could be safely evacuated.

The 8/E.Yorks, back in their original positions on the Crassier, reported that an enemy attack developed at around five o'clock, the Germans advancing "in extended order". Major Ingles continues the story:

Captain Thomas Charteris, "A" Coy 10/Yorks, kia 26 September 1915. (*De Ruvigny's Roll of Honour*, Vol. 2)

Second-Lieutenant Cave Bradburne Dodds, 12/NFus, kia 25 September 1915. (*The War Record of Old Dunelmians 1914-1919*)

114 IWM Hadow Papers.

> I could see them with my glasses slowly advancing at a walk, kneeling to fire and then advancing again. Their rifle fire was accurate, the bullets skimming close over our parapet.[115]

A rather untidy withdrawal to trenches on the other side of the Crassier was then instigated by an already wounded Lieutenant-Colonel Way, but Ingles managed to restore some vestiges of order as the German attack petered out. He found some officers of 20/London Regt and the two 10/Yorks officers, whose men were holding that stretch of trench line, and was told that his men could best be employed in improving the state of the communication trenches. They were soon put to work accordingly, and at around daybreak on the 27th, Ingles was considering re-occupying their original positions when

> a large party of the 3rd Dragoon Guards arrived as reinforcements. I had a consultation with the officer commanding, who agreed to take his men up and occupy the trenches we had vacated, and this was done. By daybreak I could see my officers and men were beginning to feel the strain: we had had no rest since the morning of the 25th and practically nothing to eat or drink. However, we spent the morning doing trench work. [...] About midday the senior officer of the 20/London Regiment, in the front trenches, showed me a written despatch from Headquarters directing any details of the 21st Division that happened to be still in the line to withdraw and report to the one hundred and something Brigade Headquarters (I cannot now remember the exact No. of the Brigade or map reference of its place) behind Loos. Acting on this order I gave instructions to my officers and those of the 10/Yorks to collect their men and prepare to move back.[116]

The five officers and 200 men of the 8/E.Yorks and two officers and eighty men of 10/Yorks moved back along an old, deep, German communication trench to the required Brigade Headquarters, where they were given something to eat and drink and then told to make their way back to 'Quality Street'.

Their attacks on Hill 70 and their defence of Loos village had cost the units of 62 Brigade dearly: the Official History details their casualties as follows:

	Officers	Other Ranks
12/Northumberland Fusiliers	22	459
13/Northumberland Fusiliers	17	379
8/East Yorks	21	299
10/Yorks	13	286
Total	**73**	**1,423**

Brigadier-General Nickalls had established 63 Brigade's headquarters in the Chalk Pit adjacent to the Hulluch-Lens road. As he surveyed the still-mist-covered battlefield in front of him, just as the sun began to rise at about seven o'clock, he made the decision to push his men forward at the earliest opportunity in an attack on the German second position. He gathered his battalion

---

115 TNA PRO CAB 45/120: Major R.J. Ingles to Edmonds correspondence, 6 March 1926.
116 Ibid.

commanders together and was issuing orders for an attack at eight o'clock when a "staff officer of 21st Division arrived and told him that a general attack had been ordered for 11 a.m."[117] Nickalls decided to wait. Norman Tom Nickalls was fifty-one years old. He had been educated at Eton and was commissioned in the 17th Lancers in August 1886 and served in the Boer War. By the outbreak of the Great War he was a colonel commanding the York Brigade of Mounted Infantry. He took over as commanding officer of 63 Brigade on 31 August 1915. By the appointed time of the general attack on 26 September, Nickalls was dead and his brigade was in no position to join in any advance, fighting desperately as they were to hold back a strong German counter attack.

It would seem in any case that the orders for the attack were at best vague, and at worst devoid of necessary details, such as information on the German defences, the direction of the attack or clearly delineated objectives. The 8/Lincolns, dug in astride Bois Hugo, received

Brigadier-General Nickalls, kia 26 Sept 1915. (IWM HU 118390)

their orders for the forthcoming attack at around eight o'clock: Major J.Y. Storer, second in command, passed the word along the line of trenches, telling Second-Lieutenant Alcock "that we were to attack at 11 a.m. He could give me no information beyond that fact that we were to attack the enemy trenches 'over there', [shades of Captain Nolan!] i.e. somewhere to the E., but he appeared to have no idea of their distance from our position". [118]

Battalion war diaries report that the 63 Bde positions began to come under artillery and sniper fire at around dawn, and by nine-thirty reports were reaching Brigade HQ that "the situation was distinctly unfavourable".[119]

The German infantry advancing towards the British positions were from *153rd Infantry Regiment*, [IR153], the *"Altenburger Regiment"*, part of *8th Division*. On 25 September this division was in reserve positions near Douai, and orders were given to commence their move to the front that morning. IR153 marched to the railway station at Pont de la Deule and entrained for Harnes, some three miles east-north-east of Lens. From there they continued on foot to Loison, arriving just as it began to get dark. There, officers were briefed on the current position by Oberstleutnant Pohl,[120] the brigade adjutant: the 'English' had broken through to the north of Lens and had taken Hill 70; it was likely that they would threaten the German Second Line.

---

117 Edmonds, *Military Operations 1915*, Vol. II, p.292.
118 TNA CAB 45/120: Alcock to Edmonds correspondence, 29 November 1918.
119 TNA PRO WO 95/2158: 63 Brigade HQ War Diary.
120 *Oberstleutnant* is the German Army equivalent of Lieutenant-Colonel.

Members of *Infanterie Regiment 153*, the 'Altenburger' Regiment.

54 To Do the Work of Men

Even if this second phase did not materialise, their continued occupation of Hill 70 – with the clear observation to the east that the position offered – would be "disastrous".[121]

IR153 was ordered to retake Hill 70 and the woods to the north of it, before occupying a line along the Hulluch-Lens road. Battalion commanders were given more detailed verbal orders at around seven o'clock that evening: *1st Battalion* would attack the woods, advancing in a westerly direction from positions north of St Auguste; *2nd Battalion* would attack Hill 70 and Chalet Wood from the south. The battalion would subsequently advance to the Hulluch-Lens road, gaining touch, it was hoped, with *1st Battalion* at or near Puits 14 bis. The *3rd Battalion* was to remain in support on the north-western edges of St Auguste.[122]

The march forward to their jumping off positions began almost immediately. It was pitch black and was raining heavily. To make matters worse, the area around St Auguste was being shelled sporadically by the British artillery. The messages sent back to Regimental HQ informing them of the *1st and 2nd Battalions'* arrival at their assembly positions both arrived together, by chance, at 21.40. Orders were almost immediately sent back to the two battalions: "11 Uhr antreten!"[123] ("Advance at 11 o'clock!").

Forward units of *1st Battalion*, under Hauptmann Freiherr von Stein, went forward "in the dark into the unknown",[124] initially unopposed, and were able to occupy the north-eastern section of Bois Hugo. Coming across the track that runs parallel to the Hulluch-Lens road, some 600 yards to the east of it, Stein's men mistook it for the road and halted there, reporting their position – mistakenly – to HQ at one o'clock in the morning. At this point, their presence was noticed by the British and they were fired upon from directly ahead and both flanks, making any further mass advance impossible without additional support. Casualties had begun to mount, but some troops were able to infiltrate the British positions in Bois Hugo: the 8/Lincolns had troops to the north and south of the wood, but none actually in it. Two outposts made up of Cameron Highlanders and Northants that had been overlooked in the earlier relief, were overrun and small numbers of "Germans penetrated to the western portions of Bois Hugo".[125] These began to cause trouble as soon as the morning mist lifted, being able to fire into the flanks and rear of the Lincolns.

Rittmeister[126] von Viereck had led the *2nd Battalion* from their jumping off positions north of Lens up the southern slopes of Hill 70, encountering first a lightly held German defensive line made up of men from the *106th* and *178th Regiments*. Crossing this position they came under machine gun fire from their left and began to incur very heavy casualties. The right flank made better progress and was able to infiltrate the north-eastern sector of Chalet Wood but began to suffer casualties as they were fired upon from their right. Touch with *1st Battalion* had not been made, and it is possible that this, and some less than accurate map-reading, had led to the two German battalions firing on each other. *1st Battalion* had mistaken the track for the road, and *2nd Battalion* had mistaken Chalet Wood for Bois Hugo. Both assumed that they were firing at

---

121 Ernst Schmidt-Osswald, *Das Altenburger Regiment (8. Thüringisches Infanterie-Regiment Nr. 153) im Weltkriege* (Oldenburg: Stalling, 1927) p.181.
122 See Map 4. Chalk Pit Wood, Bois Hugo and Chalet Wood were known to the Germans as *Rebhuhnwäldchen, Steinwald* and *Buschwald* respectively.
123 Osswald, *Das Altenburger Regiment*, p.183.
124 Ibid, p.183.
125 Edmonds, *Military Operations 1915*, Vol. II, p.318.
126 Cavalry rank equivalent to a captain of infantry.

British troops during the night.[127] When orders went out the following morning to continue the advance to the Hulluch-Lens road, only the *1st Battalion* was able to comply: the *2nd Battalion* had suffered such severe losses that they could do no more than follow up the *1st Battalion's* attack. Indeed, the *2nd Battalion's* left flank company, which had marched from Harnes with 147 rifles, could, by the morning of the 26th, muster no more than fourteen (For positions in the early morning of 26 September, see Map 5).

The *1st Battalion* was ready to launch this attack, when it came under heavy British artillery fire as the preparations for 15th Division's nine o'clock assault on Hill 70 began. The Germans decided to await developments. Orders received subsequently included an advance on Loos itself.

Once the 15th Division assault had been repulsed, thoughts of a further German advance could resurface. The first reports in British unit war diaries of this renewed assault put it somewhere between nine and half past nine in the morning. The Germans were pushing forward in some force, IR153 having finally received reinforcements from *106th Regt,* and the 8/Lincolns were beginning to lose heavily. In response to the developing situation, Brigadier-General Nickalls, all thoughts of an attack dispelled, tried to reorganise his troops so as to prevent being outflanked on the right by Germans emerging from Bois Hugo: he ordered the two companies of 8/Somerset LI near the Chalk Pit to line its southern edge, facing the wood, and sent a message to the 10/ York & Lancs asking that two companies be detached and sent to line the southern edge of Chalk Pit Wood. This "verbal order"[128] was misunderstood and in the end three companies advanced, believing they were part of an attack, through the wood and into the open ground beyond it. Here, "a very heavy machine gun fire from concealed positions drove us back".[129] 'C' Company had lost particularly heavily during the advance, losing all their officers, including the commander, Captain D.W.S. Abbott[130], who "was shot and died shortly after while being carried back".[131]

ABBOTT, DUNCAN WILLIAM SYDNEY ELPHINSTONE, Capt. 10th (Service) Battn. The York and Lancaster Regt., 3rd *s.* of the late Major Duncan Dunbar Abbott, of Rockenham, co. Cork; *b.* Oldwood, Rochestown, co. Cork, 23 July, 1879 ; educ. Rosscarbery College, co. Cork : gazetted Lieut. 5th (Militia) Battn. The Royal Munster Fusiliers in 1897, and served in the South African War of 1900–1902 (Medal). Shortly after the outbreak of war in 1914 he was gazetted temp. Capt. 17 Oct. 1914 ; went to France with his regiment 10 Sept. 1915, and was killed in action 26 Sept. following, while leading his company at the Battle of Loos. Buried at Loos. His Commanding Officer wrote : " He died leading his men bravely and wonderfully, and all the men and his brother officers feel his loss very keenly." The Adjutant : "I last saw my dear chum in a trench where he had been carried. . . . We have indeed lost a brave leader." The men of his company wrote that they felt that with him at their head they could do anything, and would have followed him anywhere. He *m.* at St. Mary's Church, Finchley, London, N., 6 Feb. 1915, Florence (Church End, Finchley), only dau. of the late Henry Cooper.

Obituary of Captain Duncan William Sydney Abbott, 10 Y&L, kia 26 Sept 1915. (*De Ruvigny's Roll of Honour,* Vol. 2)

127 Osswald, *Das Altenburger Regiment,* p.186.
128 TNA PRO WO 95/2158: 10/York & Lancasters War Diary.
129 Ibid.
130 Duncan William Sydney Abbott has no known grave and is commemorated on the Loos Memorial to the Missing at Dud Corner Cemetery.
131 TNA PRO WO 95/2158: 10/York & Lancs War Diary.

The three companies fell back as far as the Loos–Hulluch road before officers were able to rally them, along with "a number of the Scotch Brigade".[132] Even here, they were under enfilade machine gun fire from German positions near Bénifontaine and it became clear that the position was untenable: "A Lt-Colonel of the Scotch Brigade considered that this line should move back into the Southernmost German trenches. On this retirement as no reports were received we had no means of communicating with troops on the left, the Colonel made the above decision under very heavy machine gun fire. This movement was taking place when Captain Foster, Div Staff, suggested a rally on a line parallel to a track running NE. I[133] took charge of this which consisted of cover from this line. Other lines were formed in rear."

It was at about this time that Brigadier-General Nickalls sent a message back to Brigadier-General Gloster, commanding 64 Brigade, asking that a battalion be sent forward to reinforce his right flank. The 14/DLI were accordingly sent forward, but events had developed further before they reached Bois Hugo.

Three reserve platoons of 8/Somerset LI had been ordered forward under Major Howard to reinforce the south-eastern face of Chalk Pit Wood and they were able to find "good natural cover and an old deserted shallow trench. A continuous heavy rifle fire was then opened upon us but I [Major Howard] only had about three casualties as my men were well under cover."[134] It was around 09.20 when Captain Rose, Staff Captain, became aware of the perilous state of the brigade's left flank, the Yorks & Lancs having largely vacated their trenches in square H.19.c (See Map 3). Howard was asked to send a messenger to the York & Lancs, who were still, at this point, forward of Chalk Pit Wood, asking that a company be sent back to the abandoned position. Finding no volunteers to take the message, Howard went himself and managed to get about a hundred officer-less men back into the original trenches, along with an extra platoon of 8/Somersets under Lieutenant Marsh.

Philip Vivian Rose, Staff Officer, 63 Bde, (7/Ox & Bucks LI) wounded 26 Sept 1915. Died of wounds 17 April 1917. Buried in St Margaret Churchyard, Tylers Green, Bucks. (*Harrow Memorials of the Great War* Vol. 5)

132 Ibid.
133 Major Raven.
134 TNA PRO WO 95/2158: 8/Somerset Light Infantry War Diary.

These men, along with the still entrenched 12/W.Yorks, came under artillery fire at about this time: it ceased at ten o'clock and a party of Germans were seen advancing in line from positions near *Stützpunkt IV* across the open ground to the north of Bois Hugo. Shelling by British guns deployed near Vermelles and small arms fire from the 12/W.Yorks and the mixed formation now on their left stemmed the tide for a while: "The firing grew heavier. The Scottish regiment retired for some reason from Puits 14 bis[135]. Two of the battalion machine guns, in position on the left flank of C Company, found a target in a body of Germans who came out in the open in front of them, and only about a dozen of these escaped by bolting into the wood. One of the guns jammed. Captain Branch continued working the other".[136]

Astride Bois Hugo, the units of 8/Lincolns were under serious pressure. Second-Lieutenant Alcock stated that the battalion was taken by surprise: "the enemy suddenly attacked in considerable force and, as far as we in support were concerned, utterly unexpectedly".[137] Having earlier infiltrated the wood, the Germans were able to attack some of the Lincolns' trenches in the flank and, forcing a gap, drove them back through the wood, inflicting heavy casualties. Lieutenant-Colonel Walter found Alcock and "shouted to me to get up and to the left and rally them and I therefore left my position in the centre, ran up to the left, and got as many men as possible back into the trench and then jumped in myself".[138] Six officers, including two company commanders had by this time become casualties and the right flank began to fall back in some disorder: "within a few seconds there was a perfect stream of them running back in considerable confusion".[139] Colonel Walter was able to rally some of his men and attempted to regain the lost trenches, but as he led the charge he fell mortally wounded.[140]

Very soon afterwards, Major J.Y. Storer, second in command, was also killed, though conflicting stories have him blown up by a shell or shot through the head.[141] Losing so many officers was a severe blow to the battalion, and

Major John Young Storer, 8/Lincs. Kia 26 Sept 1915. (IWM 118664)

---

135 As per above, this would be in conjunction with 10/ York & Lancs.
136 TNA PRO WO 95/1432: 12/West Yorks War Diary.
137 IWM Private papers of Lieutenant J H Alcock. Doc. 5523.
138 Ibid.
139 TNA CAB 45/120: Alcock to Edmonds correspondence, 29 November 1918.
140 Lieutenant-Colonel Harold Ernest Walter was captured by the Germans on the evening of 26 September and taken to a hospital in Douai. He died of his wounds three days later and was buried in Douai Communal Cemetery, Grave D 2.
141 See Nigel Atter, *In the Shadow of Bois Hugo: The 8th Lincolns at the Battle of Loos* (Solihull: Helion & Company, 2017) p.51. John Young Storer has no known grave and is commemorated on the Loos Memorial .to the Missing.

Lieutenant-Colonel Harold Ernest Walter, CO 8/Lincs. Died of Wounds 29 Sept 1915. Douai Comm Cem D.2. (Author)

Top left: Second-Lieutenant James Henry Rowland Hanning, 8/Lincs, age 18, kia 26 Sept 1915. (IWM HU 122836)
Top right: Second-Lieutenant John Eric Haddon Welch, 8/Lincs, age 19, kia 26 September 1915. (IWM) HU 127247
Above left: Captain James Topham, Adjutant, 8/Lincs. Kia 26 Sept 1915. Loos Memorial. (IWM HU 119134)
Above right: 10449 Private Joseph Goodman, 'A' Coy, 8/Lincs, kia 26 Sept 1915. (IWM HU 115183)

despite Captain McNaught-Davis leading three bayonet charges against the advancing Germans,[142] most of the Lincolns were forced to abandon their trenches and "retired across the road towards the Chalk Pit where I believe they joined the supporting coys of the S.L.I. & Y & L."[143] The remnants of the battalion, under Lt Alcock and Lt Hall, hung on, to the north of the wood, (McNaught-Davis was by this time lying with a serious head wound in one of the abandoned trenches[144]), completely isolated.

Alcock carried on with the remainder of the story:

Pte William Thomas Thompson 8/Lincs, kia 26 September 1915. (IWM HU 96737)

> We hung on to the trench in the hope that units behind us, when they attacked, would be able to carry us forward with them. What happened I do not quite know, but the attack from behind, (if it ever took place at all), never reached our position, and owing to the contours of the ground I was unable to see what was happening there. [...] We were practically surrounded by 11:45 a.m. and during the day the position grew gradually worse, until finally it was merely a question as to whether the survivors could maintain their position till dark [which] should allow us to retire across the open ground to the N.W. We suffered severely from enemy shell fire, and also from the rifles and machine guns in the BOIS HUGO on our right flank. We also had a good number of casualties from British shrapnel which was bursting short. By about 5:30 p.m. we had very little ammunition left, and the enemy were bombing their way up the trenches from the wood. Our men could make no effective reply (we had no bombs at all). Lt. Hall, senior officer in the trench, who was on my right and thus nearer to the wood, decided that the only thing to do was surrender. Personally I was not consulted – I had been knocked down by a shell about 5 p.m. and Lt. Hall had been told that I was killed. I was forced to conform as I had only four unwounded men left, all of whom had very few rounds of ammunition, and the enemy were by now all around us.[145]

Both Alcock and Hall were taken prisoner. Both survived captivity and were repatriated in 1918. All of the officers that had gone into action with the 8/Lincolns became casualties.[146]

---

142 Ibid. p.51.
143 TNA CAB 45/120: Alcock to Edmonds correspondence, 29 November 1918.
144 McNaught-Davis was taken prisoner. Recovering from his wounds, he was repatriated in October 1918.
145 TNA CAB 45/120: Alcock to Edmonds correspondence, 29 November 1918.
146 Two of the 8/Lincolns officers killed on 26 September were twin brothers: Second Lieutenant Arthur Wright Bosworth and Lieutenant Philip Charles Worthington Bosworth, born 9 June 1885 into a

The Bosworth Twins. Second-Lieutenant Arthur Wright Bosworth (left) and Lieutenant Philip Charles Worthington Bosworth (right), both 8/Lincs, both killed in action 26 Sept 1915. (*De Ruvigny's Roll of Honour*)

Meanwhile, the 8/Somerset LI were coming under increasing pressure too. Major Howard and his men near the Chalk Pit were under enemy artillery fire, but luckily most of the shells were landing in the pit itself and doing little damage. Rifle fire, however, was "deadly"[147] and within the space of a few minutes, Lieutenant Hopkins and Second-Lieutenant Basker[148] were killed and Lieutenant Fitzmaurice wounded. Ten volunteers who had earlier been sent back to bring ammunition arrived back at around eleven o'clock with 2,000 rounds, this being all they could find, and the Somersets were able to "blaze away at the Germans who were coming into full view all the time now. […] Things began to get warm now and we all took rifles and shot carefully along the wood wherever the enemy debouched, at ranges varying from 400 to 800

---

wealthy family in Cadeby, Leicestershire. Both brothers had worked in banking before the war. Philip was an able sportsman and a first class shot. He was an excellent cricketer and played hockey for Leicestershire and Derbyshire. When war was declared, both brothers were abroad, Philip exploring the arctic regions of Canada with his elder brother, Dr T.O. Bosworth, and Arthur was living in Valparaiso, Chile. Both returned to England to enlist and are commemorated on the Loos Memorial to the Missing.

147 TNA PRO WO 95/2158: 8/Somerset Light Infantry War Diary.
148 Second-Lieutenants Lewis Hopkins and Reginald Hugh Basker are commemorated on the Loos Memorial.

62   To Do the Work of Men

15218 Cpl Harold John Dixon, 8/SomLI. Kia 26 September 1915 age 21. (IWM HU 121308)

Major Lewis Charles Howard 8/SomLI. He was later promoted Lieutenant-Colonel and commanded 8/Som LI from 11 October 1915 until he was killed in action, age 34, on 23 December 1915 whilst leading a patrol in No Man's Land. He is buried in Cité Bonjean Mil Cem, Armentières. Grave Ref. IX.D.71. (The Sphere 29 Jan 1916)

yards. Ammunition ran low so we stripped the dead of theirs and got enough to keep going".[149] The Somersets had managed to keep the Germans pinned down and by 12.30 they were relieved to see reinforcements arrive in the form of the 8/Buffs[150] who brought along with them a very much-needed machine gun.

It was somewhat earlier than this, however, that 63 Brigade's defences began to crumble:

Captain W.H. Nichols 8/SomLI, died as Prisoner of War, 15 October 1915, and is buried in Niederzwehren Cemetery, Kassel, Germany, grave ref. II.A.17. (*Tonbridge School and the Great War of 1914-1918*)

149 Ibid.
150 Part of 24th Division.

this was possibly initiated, perversely, by the arrival of the 14/DLI on the battlefield. The sight of troops appearing to their right rear – and being mistaken for Germans – may have caused some consternation amongst the men of 12/W.Yorks, whose commanding officer, Lieutenant-Colonel Leggett, had earlier been wounded by a shell on his way to a conference with Brigadier-General Nickalls: "A sudden order to retire, which cannot quite be accounted for, began on our right & passed along the line to the left. The men began retiring"[151] A number of 12/W.Yorks officers were killed as they tried to rally their men, including Major J.H. Jacques, who had taken command of the battalion after Leggett's incapacitation, his brother Captain A. Jacques[152] and the adjutant Captain A.H.A.Vann. The aforementioned Captain Branch kept his machine gun in action, firing from a shell hole at the Germans emerging from the woods until he ran out of ammunition. He was subsequently wounded.

The Jaques Brothers: Captain Arthur Jaques (left) and Major Joseph Hodgson Jaques, (right) both 12/WYorks, both killed in action on 26 September 1915, aged 27 and 28 respectively. Both are commemorated on the Loos Memorial. (IWM HU 116322 & HU 116323)

---

151 TNA PRO WO 95/1432: 12/West Yorks War Diary.
152 Joseph Hodgson Jacques was born in Shanghai, China in 1887. His brother Arthur was born in 1888 and went to Cambridge University in 1908, just as his elder brother was travelling to New York on RMS *Lusitania*. By 1914 they were both married, living in Hampshire, men of 'private means'. The sums of money left in their wills amounted to over £92,000. Both are commemorated on the Loos Memorial to the Missing.

Unfortunately, the infection spread and most of the 63 Bde men to the north of the woods joined in this retirement, including those men of 10/York & Lancs still lying out near the wood, and some of the Lincolns who had been forced out of their positions to the south of Bois Hugo. "Efforts by other officers to rally the men along the Lens road and in the Chalk Pit, under a continuous rifle and machine gun fire from Bois Hugo, were of no avail".[153] Brigadier-General Nickalls ran forward from his headquarters in an attempt to rectify the situation, but he was killed almost immediately.[154] To add to the confusion, the advancing 14/DLI initially mistook the retreating Yorkshire battalion for Germans and opened fire. The mistake was soon realised, but a small number of the 14/DLI men were caught up in the retreat. The rest, as they continued towards Bois Hugo, came under withering machine gun fire from the edges of the wood which enfiladed their lines as they naturally veered away from the source of danger. As they crossed the open fields and approached the slopes of Hill 70, seventeen 14/DLI officers became casualties, including the commanding officer, Lieutenant-Colonel A.S. Hamilton, who was wounded. All four company commanders were lost, along with the machine gun officer and 220 men. Not surprisingly, the men were driven back.[155]

Coincidentally, it was about this time that some IV Corps troops began to retire also from the upper slopes of Hill 70 – they were later to claim that they had been shelled by the British artillery and attacked in the rear by the British 9:00 a.m. assault on the hill. Subsequently, further shelling by their own guns had been the last straw.

Three battalions of 64 Bde were still in position to the north of Loos. In accordance with the original orders for the general attack at 11 o'clock, and regardless of the changing situation in front of them,

Lieutenant-Colonel Archibald Samuel Hamilton, age 50, commanding 14/DLI. Died of Wounds 13 October 1915. Buried in Hendon Cemetery, Grave Ref. B.9.21421.(*The Sphere*, 13 Nov 1915)

Second-Lieutenant Edis John William Gray, 14/DLI, Age 19. Kia 26 Sept 1915. (IWM HU 115351)

---

153 Edmonds, *Military Operations 1915*, Vol. II, p.320.
154 Nickalls' body was never recovered and he is commemorated on the Loos Memorial to the Missing.
155 Lieutenant-Colonel Archibald Samuel Hamilton, OC 14/DLI, age 50, died of his wounds on 13 October 1915 and is buried in Hendon Cemetery, London.

the men of 15/DLI went forward. Just prior to this advance, Major Johnson had observed the general retreat from the woods, "amazed to see a few men leisurely emerge and walk towards our left flank. At first we took them for Germans in Khaki, but only for a moment. Soon they were followed by others, and yet more disorganised bodies"[156] Some retreated through the Durhams' positions, some reformed and advanced again, some were caught up in the new attack. Lieutenant-Colonel Logan, commanding the 15/DLI, jumped to the front of the Durhams' shallow entrenched positions and shouted the order to advance. They were under artillery fire as soon as they emerged: "a high explosive shell burst near the right company, throwing up a black cloud, the characteristic mark of what was nicknamed a 'coal box'."[157] Continuing his narrative, Johnson observed:

> Approaching the first road I ordered a 'double' to cross the road quickly, thinking that perhaps the Germans might range on it. [...] We came under shrapnel fire, mixed with high explosive shells, and I continued to lead the advance across the flat ground by short rushes, lying down after each, and endeavouring to keep the line straight. In this manner we reached the second road which crossed our front. Now we met with heavy rifle fire, and the noise of firing increased but still no objective upon which to fire was visible. The hill to be taken was yet a long way off.[158]

This final statement is important: Johnson, writing shortly after the event, was clearly of the opinion that the battalion's objective had been Hill 70. The 11 a.m. attack should have been directed against the German Second Line to the north of Bois Hugo, "to the northward of the German 'keep' in H.20.d".[159] The 24th Division attack went in more or less due east, as required, but each advance by units of 21st Division veered to the right in the direction of Hill 70.

Johnson goes on:

> After a short halt I again led the advance. We had many casualties, and there was more hesitation to follow on. For the first time I became aware of two more woods on our left flank, from which direction with each advance the firing very greatly increased: we were enfiladed by rifle and machine guns. This was entirely unexpected, and a little disconcerting. Examining the position through glasses I believed I could locate machine guns in an upper storey of a house on the edge of the middle wood, and finding A and B Companies somewhat ahead I formed line half left, to face the woods with the objective of assisting the advance of those who followed. The din was extraordinary, and I found it impossible by shouting my loudest to make my voice carry as far as the third man from me.[160]

Johnson's company fired their first shots of the war in the direction of the house in Bois Hugo, but at long range the effects would have been negligible.

---

156 TNA PRO CAB 45/120: Major R.B. Johnson to Edmonds correspondence. This account also appears in TNA WO 95/2161: 15/Durham Light Infantry War Diary.
157 TNA PRO CAB 45/120: Major R.B. Johnson to Edmonds correspondence.
158 Ibid.
159 TNA PRO WO 95/2161: 64 Brigade HQ War Diary.
160 TNA PRO CAB 45/120. Major R.B. Johnson to Edmonds correspondence.

66   To Do the Work of Men

In one way and another the line got thinner, and few came up. We were on the lower slope of Hill 70, a bare stretch of open country covered with long rank grass. No rifle fire appeared to come from that direction, and I thought the Germans were reserving it for the time we should be nearer. Well directed shells, however, came over the hill in plenty.[161]

By 11.45, Lieutenant-Colonel Logan was dead,[162] and the forward lines of the battalion, led by the adjutant, Captain Babbage, were within 200 yards "of the objective".[163] It was at this point that some of the wayward elements of 8/Somerset LI appear on the scene once more. Lieutenant-Colonel Denny, along with a lieutenant, a corporal and a handful of men stumbled upon Johnson's position. Johnson had by this time been wounded and was finding it difficult to move about, hampered by his kit and the loss of blood. Babbage, with only fifty or so[164] unwounded men with him by this stage, decided to withdraw and ordered a retirement that was carried out "coolly and orderly".[165]

Johnson, Denny and Lieutenant Barker of 'A' Company, 15/DLI, found themselves out on a limb. Retracing their steps across the face of the woods did not seem an attractive prospect, but they noticed what appeared to be the roof of a dugout some 150 yards behind them in the direction of Loos village. They set off to crawl towards it. Just as they reached it, a shrapnel shell burst almost directly overhead; "I felt as if I had been hit with a hammer on the head, and found that a bullet had struck my cap just below the badge without penetrating".[166] Barker sprinted back further towards the village and soon returned to report that a British-held trench was some 120 yards away. Denny and his subaltern sprinted to it, but Johnson, weak with loss of blood, doubted his ability to reach it. He removed his pack, rid himself of all extraneous impedimenta, and gave his revolver to Barker. The two set off, Barker almost carrying his comrade, and they fell into the trench which was held by a company of Gordon Highlanders. Johnson eventually made his way back through the village and found a dressing station back in 'Quality Street'. Barker left him there and rejoined the remnants of his battalion.

The withdrawal of the Durham battalions was observed from 64 Brigade HQ. It coincided with the withdrawal of the 24th Division units that had gone up against the heavily-wired German Second Line and had been beaten back. The time was 12:30 p.m. The Durhams were eventually rallied in rear of their original jumping off trenches. Almost 30 officers and over 600 other ranks had become casualties. The official history sums up the situation succinctly: "Thus it seemed that the fighting power of the 63rd and 64th Brigades, that is of the 21st Division – for the 62nd Brigade was detached with the 15th Division – was already broken".[167]

The three woods north of Hill 70 were by this time firmly in German hands: the regimental history describes the final stages of their capture in an exaggerated and heroic fashion. At around

---

161 Ibid.
162 Lieutenant-Colonel Edward Townshend Logan DSO, Cheshire Regiment, OC 15/DLI, age 49, is commemorated on the Loos Memorial to the Missing. He had served in the Boer War and had been Mentioned in Despatches twice.
163 TNA PRO WO 95/2161: 15/Durham Light Infantry War Diary. It bears repeating that Hill 70 was not their objective.
164 Ibid.
165 Ibid.
166 Ibid.
167 Edmonds, *Military Operations 1915*, Vol. II, p.321.

midday, during a lull in the British artillery action, "a line of field-grey advanced, followed by more waves, and stormed through the woods as far as the track, their thundering cheers audible above the 'tack-tack' of the enemy machine guns". Puits 14 bis was overrun and "a large number of unwounded Englishmen were taken prisoner".[168]

It was a costly gain. The 63 Brigade had exacted a heavy toll on the attacking Germans. The IR153 had left Loison 2,000 strong. Their assault on the woods had cost the two leading battalions over 700 men. All thoughts of retaking Loos village were dashed: the survivors were ordered to dig in where they were, ready to defend their positions.

"The Brigadier and I took stock." Thus wrote Lieutenant-Colonel K. Henderson, Brigade-Major of 64 Brigade at the time, in his memoirs.[169] He was at brigade headquarters, a little way south of Point 69 (see Map 3), in conversation with Brigadier-General Gloster at around 12.30 on 26 September. All around their headquarters, officers and NCOs were desperately trying to rally the men streaming back from Hill 70 and the woods. They came to the conclusion that 62 and 63 Brigades were broken up and scattered to such an extent that it would be some time before they were once more capable of cohesive action. From what they could see, and from reports coming back with some of the stragglers, Hill 70 appeared lost, and Puits 14 bis and Chalk Pit Wood "obviously were. I urged that with two remaining intact battalions [9 & 10/ KOYLI] it was hopeless to expect success where so many had failed, and that the moment for local uncoordinated effort had passed".[170]

The 9 and 10/KOYLI had arrived in their current positions on the Loos – Haisnes road at dawn and had not moved since, sitting tight under intermittent shell fire. Brigadier-General Gloster was faced with a dilemma. His original orders were to attack, and no messages had arrived at headquarters from higher command to alter the situation. He had, however, watched two of his four battalions cut to pieces on the slopes of Hill 70 and in front of Bois Hugo and his fear was that his two remaining units might have to withstand a German counter attack. If any further offensive action was to have any chance of success, higher authority would need to be appraised of the situation[171] and advised that proper artillery support would be needed. Gloster seemed to be heeding Henderson's counsel that caution was the smart card to play, particularly when the latter "pointed out that at any moment the Germans might try and follow up their success and advance on us, in which case all depended on the intact battalions",[172] and had all but made up his mind to adopt the defensive option. Everything was about to go wrong.

> [U]p came Campbell, GSO III of our division,[173] very hot and excited, and fresh from frantic efforts assisting to rally retiring troops in our rear. He urged General Gloster to resume the advance at once at all costs. I [Henderson] argued the point. He turned his shoulder on me and said he was sure the divisional commander would insist on attacking

---

168 Osswald, *Das Altenburger Regiment*, p.188. For final positions on 26 September, see Map 6.
169 IWM The Private Papers of Lieutenant-Colonel K. Henderson DSO. Doc. 10942.
170 Ibid.
171 According to Captain Pattison of the 8/Lincolns, Major-General Forestier-Walker had, by this time, no idea exactly where 63 Brigade was. See TNA PRO CAB 45/121.
172 IWM Lieutenant-Colonel K. Henderson DSO Papers, Doc. 10942.
173 Major Claude Henry Campbell DSO.

68 To Do the Work of Men

again, and I gathered he had been shouting to every officer and man he met to turn and advance again.[174]

Gloster was wavering, now afraid that he might be blamed if he did nothing and suggesting that he could avoid any censure from high command if he at least tried to do something. He caved in, but still preferred to err on the side of caution. This stance was soon to be overtaken by events and it is clear that Henderson puts the blame for this squarely on Campbell's shoulders:

> We gathered from Campbell that he had arranged for the 63 Bde to attack and reoccupy its original position, and that we must go for Hill 70 again. But there was no clear assignment of objectives, no arrangement for artillery cooperation, no time named. His own idea was to get the whole crowd turned and blindly barging forward once more, and as I will now show, he must have already given orders which nullified any small local efforts towards cohesion it was possible for us to make on our own.
>
> I hurriedly sent for Lynch and Pollock, commanding respectively the 9th and 10th KOYLI. Logan commanding 15 DLI had been killed and Hamilton commanding 14 DLI severely wounded (later died) but I did not then know this and had no idea where the bn HQs of the two Durham battalions now were.
>
> But our idea was briefly to attack with the two Yorkshire battalions, and trust to having reformed the two Durham battalions soon enough thereafter to make of them a Bde reserve.
>
> Conscious of the poor chances of success we had also decided to give strict orders that if progress should be impossible beyond any given point, the line was to dig in and hold tight there, and not to come back again.
>
> We were in the act of explaining the project to Lynch and Pollock when suddenly, over our trench from behind us and also all along the line to the left of us, as of one accord every man rose up and surged forward. This included the 9th KOYLI. We asked Lynch who had given them orders to move, and he said he didn't know; he certainly had not. In a few moments the advance was swelled by large numbers of the previously repulsed troops, 63 Bde, Durham and 4th Corps troops, who had apparently been reformed behind us. Who sent them all forward, and with what orders they went, it is doubtful if anyone will ever know for certain. My own conviction is that this was the result of poor Campbell's interference and wild incitements. He was killed some six months later.[175]

Three companies of 9/KOYLI had responded to the call to advance, but they had no idea where they were going or what they were to do when they got there. Lieutenant-Colonel Pollock was swiftly despatched to use the 10/KOYLI as a second or support line and render

---

174 IWM Lieutenant-Colonel K. Henderson DSO Papers, Doc. 10942.

175 Ibid. Lt-Colonel Campbell was killed in action on 14 March 1916, near Arras. He was born in 1878, the second son of the late Henry Alexander Campbell of Lynford Hall, Norfolk. He passed through Sandhurst and was commissioned into the Queen's Own Cameron Highlanders in 1899. He attained the rank of Major by 1915 and subsequently commanded the battalion in France, having accompanied it to the Western Front in September 1914 as its adjutant. He was mentioned in dispatches and awarded the DSO. He served on the staff of 21st Division from July to November 1915 and was then appointed to command 12/West Yorkshire Regiment. At the time of his death he was OC 4/Seaforth Highlanders.

any assistance that they could. Lieutenant-Colonel Lynch was by now running after his battalion with orders that the advance should under no circumstances go beyond the Loos – Hulluch road. These orders never reached the 9/KOYLI: only two companies of 10/KOYLI received them and acted upon them. Urged on by their company commanders, the Yorkshiremen surged across the road and, assuming that the greatcoat-clad men visible near the crest of Hill 70 were their enemy – they were in fact the remnants of British units that had attacked the hill at nine o'clock – veered to the south and advanced towards the slope.

The German machine gunners in Bois Hugo and Chalet Wood, once again escaping a frontal assault, poured withering fire into the flanks of the KOYLIs. They were joined in this endeavour by German troops in the Hill 70 redoubt, so the unfortunate KOYLIs were therefore taking fire from both front and left with little or no chance of reply. It is no surprise that the advance stalled.

Lieutenant-Colonel Claude Henry Campbell, GSO 3, 21st Div. (Author)

> Lynch and a few small bodies [of men] near him whom he was able to influence, stopped at the bottom of the valley and started to dig in. But they were too few, and he soon realised that if he stayed out he might at any moment be overrun and captured if the Germans counter attacked.[176]

Lynch's men and most of those involved in the attack began to make their way back as best they could across the *Leichenfeld* or "field of corpses"[177] to their original trenches. Others had advanced a little further and withdrew through Loos village, as illustrated by the account of Lieutenant Harold Yeo of 9/KOYLI:

> Anyway we went ahead in a sort of line with everyone just where they happened to be when the forward impulse came. I was nowhere near my platoon, nor was anyone else, but one merely had to get up each time and call out to come on, irrespective of who they belonged to. Eventually, after several rushes I found myself with a following of men of an altogether different Division and about half a dozen of our own. A machine gun (or rather several ditto) was making progress rather difficult and I was just lying down thinking of how to shut them up when the CO of my new hearties sent orders to retire. Thinking he must be mistaken or have developed chilly feet I told such as I could make here to stay with me. There was a devilish row going on, and I found that my crew had diminished from forty

---

176 Ibid.
177 Named thus by the Germans in their accounts of the engagement.

19749 Sergeant C. Charlesworth, 10/KOYLI, kia 25 Sept 1916. (Author)

to six, among whom I found Morris,[178] who was as surprised to see me as I to see him. A sniper neatly bagged one of the party at once, and we decided that we could hardly carry on to much effect as we were, so we decided to stay and await eventualities. After two hours (during which time we passed round pills to the wounded and shot at whatever might hold Germans in front in turns) it seemed as though our winter would be spent in making sausages on a black bread diet if we didn't get a move on. Therefore we trotted back and on the way called in a small house in Loos, and there found about twenty wounded all over the place, and a French woman giving them coffee and hot milk. We patched up that lot and distributed such cigarettes and grub as we had as we had to push off and find the battalion, which had meanwhile been withdrawn. As it was just getting dark we found the main body and we all eventually occupied a line of trench running in front of the one we had been in the night before.[179]

The majority of the men had regained their original positions long before Yeo and his group returned, having been rallied there by the remaining KOYLI company and the 64 Brigade staff. The question of what to do next still remained and the position was now more precarious than it had been two hours earlier. Henderson, having witnessed the retreat, went back to 64 Brigade HQ, arriving at precisely the same moment as Major-General Forestier-Walker appeared from the opposite direction:

We both jumped down into the trench, and there I found [...] Campbell as well, and also the Brigade Major RA. We all cowered down in the trench, and while continuously sprayed with dust and gravel and once nearly buried by falling earth, all from the shelling, we explained the situation. He then started dictating to Campbell a very long message to the Corps Commander. In this he described the situation and intimated that he had approved, in view of our small numbers and our isolated position, of our withdrawing under cover of darkness to the old German Front System, where he asked that reinforcements should meet us.[180]

Luckily, two copies were despatched: the Brigade Major RA, entrusted with one of them, was killed on his way back to Headquarters. The message, timed at 14.45, gives the position of the remnants of 64 Brigade as "trenches roughly from the figure 9 in square G.29 to an unknown distance northwards. 63 Brigade position cannot be definitely ascertained. [...] [T]he men appear to be considerably shaken and demoralised".[181]

A reply was received just before dusk "to say we were to hold our ground at all costs because the Corps Commander feared that if we moved back we would lose Loos".[182] So the men of 64 Brigade remained where they were for several more hours, once more under shell fire and sustaining more casualties.

---

178 Second-Lieutenant F.G. Morris, 9/KOYLI.
179 IWM Colonel H.E. Yeo MBE MC Papers, Doc. 3132, Correspondence to father, 7 November 1915.
180 IWM Lieutenant-Colonel K. Henderson DSO Papers, Doc. 10942. The message, in Campbell's handwriting, is in 21st Division General Staff HQ War Diary.
181 TNA PRO WO 95/2128: 21st Division General Staff HQ War Diary.
182 IWM Lieutenant-Colonel K. Henderson DSO Papers, Doc. 10942.

72 To Do the Work of Men

Relief was on its way. The Guards Division was moving forward from their positions near Noeux les Mines, and 64 Brigade received news to this effect at around eight o'clock that evening. The Guards' march was, however, beset by the same problems encountered by 21st and 24th Divisions twenty-four hours earlier. They did not reach the old German front line until midnight and it was almost four o'clock on the morning of the 27th by the time they had taken over the 64 Brigade positions:

we withdrew to bivouac between NOYELLES LES VERMELLES and SAILLY LA BOURSE which was reached about 6 a.m. halted for rest of day and night 27th/28th. Rainy.[183]

The column that had been formed for the march back had been less than 300 strong. Just prior to this, Henderson witnessed a "horrible sight":

The Guards had captured two German prisoners whom they had found in the old German line telephoning to their friends from our rear by a line that had managed to escape being cut. These two unfortunate men were there and then stood up and shot in cold blood. […] The prisoners were in no sense of the word spies. They were wearing their own uniform and had obviously merely been isolated when our attack the day before overran their position. But finding that telephone communication with their own people remaining intact, they very naturally and pluckily took advantage of the fact and no doubt gave their friends valuable information during the 24 hours they remained undiscovered.[184]

The 21st Division's involvement in the Loos offensive was over. The town of Loos was still in British hands, and the line extended northwards through the 64 Bde's final positions. The battle dragged on into the middle of October, but no further substantial gains were made. The German Second Line remained unbroken.

It is difficult to be accurate where 63 and 64 Brigade casualties are concerned. The War Diary returns are inevitably inaccurate, as the missing were subsequently either confirmed as killed or captured, or they returned as stragglers some hours or even days later. Some of those reported wounded had in fact been killed, or vice versa. The 21st Division Diary lists them as follows:

	Officers			Other Ranks
	K	W	M	Aggregate
63 Brigade	21	40	8	1,333
64 Brigade	3	32	0	1,022

Overall casualties for 21st Division are probably most accurately reflected in the Official History, which gives the figures as follows:

---

183 TNA PRO WO 95/2159: 64 Brigade HQ War Diary.
184 IWM Lieutenant-Colonel K. Henderson DSO Papers, Doc. 10942.

	Officers			Other Ranks		
	K	W	M	K	W	M
	33	128	37	219	2,271	1,363
Total:		198			3,853	
Overall Total:						4,051[185]

Officer casualties must be regarded as high. If one assumes that a battalion went into action with 24 officers and accepts a corrected figure for casualties (counting only those from the twelve attacking infantry battalions), the rate is a disturbing 60 percent. Particularly badly hit were the 8/Lincolns, who lost nineteen officers. The 14/DLI lost its commanding officer, all four company commanders, the adjutant and ten other officers. The 12/West Yorks lost twenty. Not only were the men thrown into battle with no combat experience, they were also quickly deprived of leadership and the stability that this lends.

Overall fatalities for the twelve infantry battalions can be gleaned from the Commonwealth War Graves Commission.[186]

	Officers	Other Ranks
62 Brigade	25	402
63 Brigade	29	392
64 Brigade	11	224
Total	**65**	**1,018**
Overall Total		**1,083**

The use, or misuse, of the reserve divisions at Loos has been a subject of debate ever since the events of 26 September 1915 and the repercussions were very soon felt at the highest level of command. The details of the immediate aftermath do not lie within the remit of this narrative, but the end result was the resignation of Sir John French as Commander-in-Chief on 17 December 1915 and his replacement by Sir Douglas Haig.

The reputation of 21st Division does, however, merit a review. This chapter has shown quite clearly that the accepted version of events, 21st Division and 24th Division advancing against the German Second Line and being routed by enemy machine gun fire, is a simplistic and dismissive travesty of the truth. When Sir James Edmonds was compiling his Official History in the 1920s, a number of officers who had taken part in the battle were keen to enter into correspondence with him and offer their version and their opinions.

One or two had reputations to defend: Haking, commander of XI Corps in 1915, was quick off the mark and on 27 October, just over a month since the engagement, he wrote defending

---

185 The 24th Division casualties amount to 187 officers and 3,991 other ranks or a total of 4,078.
186 This is not without problems: unaccountably, the CWGC wrongly gives 27 September 1915 as the date of death for many men who were clearly only in action on the 26th. The figures quoted also include those who died of wounds in the days following the engagement.

the detachment of 62 Bde from 21st Division so that they could attack Hill 70; he denied that British troops had suffered under 'friendly' artillery fire; he writes disparagingly at length of unwounded men retreating, having discarded their rifles so as to better help a wounded colleague.[187] Nothing, it seemed, was his fault.

Forestier-Walker, GOC 21st Division, wrote to the official historian on 24 January 1927, declaring that his Division's march discipline was "extraordinarily good".[188] It was not. He also assured Edmonds that 21st Division was an "exceptionally well-trained one. [...] I doubt if a better one ever crossed the channel".[189] Eleven months later, he wrote to Edmonds again, claiming that his memory of 1915 was rather "foggy". He also stated that by April 1915, the division was "very little advanced in the matter of Company or Battalion training, and until the middle of June, or perhaps rather later, nothing could be attempted in the way of Dvnl or Bde training except a weekly route march". Thereafter, a few Divisional and Brigade training schemes were organised, but "training was not continuous" as other things, such as musketry, got in the way. He concludes that there was "inadequate time [...] for complete training".[190] Forestier-Walker was right to point out that one of the division's weaknesses was "a paucity of regular officers. [...] No battalion had more than one regular officer other than the CO, who was in all cases a 'dug out'".[191]

Other officers, with perhaps no real axes to grind, offer opinions that, although never totally devoid of 'unit solidarity and pride', largely plough a similar furrow.

Major Buckley, Staff Captain, 64 Brigade, believed that

> the real reason for the failure of 21 Div is to be attributed to their appalling ignorance of the situation. [...] Neither battalion commanders nor company officers had a map of the ground, in fact I believe the only officer of 64 Bde who saw a detailed map of the area was the Brigade Major. Speaking from memory even he was only allowed to look at one when he was at Div HQ on the afternoon of 25th September.[192]

He also defended the two KOYLI battalions who were sent forward in error:

> "Mention should be made of the fact that quite a large number of both battalions did not retire but remained in position until after dark, well beyond the Loos – Hulluch road".[193]

Lieutenant-Colonel Leggett, CO of 12/W.Yorks, points a finger in the direction of higher command, asserting that "we COs never during the whole period before or during the battle, ever received a coherent order. [...] We were left apparently on our own without any knowledge of the course of events. [...] The officers were splendid and brave, if ignorant, and the men after all they had to endure, 'sans rapproche'."[194]

187 TNA PRO CAB 45/120
188 Ibid.
189 Ibid.
190 TNA PRO CAB 45/121: Handwritten correspondence to Edmonds, 10 December 1927.
191 TNA PRO CAB 45/120: Forrestier-Walker to Edmonds correspondence, 24 January 1927.
192 TNA PRO CAB 45/120: Buckley to Edmonds correspondence, 1 January 1927.
193 Ibid.
194 Ibid. Leggett to Edmonds correspondence, 6 August 1926.

Colonel Stewart, GSO I, 24th Division, dismisses the idea of a rout:

> Between 3 p.m. and 6 or 7 p.m. on 26th I rode up and back along the line of the 21st and 24th Divisions while they were coming back under fairly heavy shell fire, and I saw no case of panic or fear. Men had their arms and had no officers or NCOs. They were tired out, hungry and thirsty, and though suffering a fair number of casualties as they walked back, never hustled and obeyed my orders at the time to reoccupy the trenches. [...] I saw plenty of attacks later – very many. I never saw one worse prepared than this, bar one, at Fromelles.[195]

Lieutenant-General R.D. Wigham, GHQ, offers a view from the higher echelons of the command structure. He accepts that GHQ was at fault for not having the reserves in position in time to support the initial attack, but adds that

> the subsequent difficulties which beset them were due to faults in the exercise of Command and Staff work by XI. Corps H.Q. It is no excuse to put them all down to inexperienced troops; the Corps H.Q. was out of touch with its divisions and that was the beginning and end of it.[196]

Modern historians have moved beyond the myth. Gordon Corrigan summed up the performance of the reserves as follows:

> The inescapable fact is, however, that the use of the New Army divisions was a disaster. The men were excellent material – physically and educationally superior to most regular soldiers – and they showed quite remarkable bravery, but through no fault of their own they simply did not have the experience and training to see them through when command and communications broke down and when their leaders were incapacitated.[197]

Nick Lloyd emphasises the difficulty of the task assigned to the reserve divisions, opining that "even had both divisions been hardened veterans with good support, the results would not have been much different to what actually occurred".[198]

The original role assigned to the 21st Division was to attack and break through the German Second Line to the north of Bois Hugo. That it failed to do so is down to a number of factors. Its arduous march onto the battlefield, coupled with shortages of food, water and sleep, meant battalions arrived too late to be of practical use. By the time they did arrive, 62 Brigade had already been attached to 15th Division and were destined to support an abortive attempt to capture Hill 70, a mission nevertheless deemed critical to the success of the main follow up attack. The 63 Brigade, having taken over trenches in and around the woods to the north of Hill 70, was in no position to attack anything, as they were fighting desperately to defend themselves against strong German counter attacks. So, well before the appointed time for the attack, 21st

---

195 TNA PRO CAB 45/121. Stuart to Edmonds correspondence, 3 August 1925.
196 Ibid. Wigham to Edmonds correspondence, 9 July 1926.
197 Corrigan, *Loos 1915,* pp. 137-138.
198 Lloyd, *Loos 1915,* p.217.

Division was already down to one-third strength. 14 and 15/DLI were then in turn despatched from 64 Brigade to reinforce their embattled colleagues, manoeuvres that ended badly due once more to a lack of realistic command decisions. Parts of the two remaining Yorkshire battalions were then sent forward in error, only to commit the same directional mistake as the Durhams, resulting in more losses for no gain.

The original order for the 11 a.m. attack came from a commander with absolutely no idea of the actual situation on the battlefield. Subsequent modifications were made from a similar position, but communication problems meant that the forward units were left to improvise, but, fatally, from a position of ignorance of the bigger picture. In short, command and control fell apart with inevitable consequences.

That the men withdrew cannot be disputed, but 'green' troops in their first battle, inadequately trained, with absolutely no experience of war, devoid of leadership resulting from the high casualty rate amongst their officers, and facing determined and deadly opposition, cannot be blamed for such actions.

Attacks did indeed fail, but it has to be noted that the men of 63 Brigade performed heroically and effectively in their defence of the woods. They were eventually forced out, of course, but not before they had meted out such severe punishment to their opponents that any possibility of the Germans recapturing the village of Loos was negated.

The final word must go to the men themselves: in the Official History, as the "sheep without a shepherd" were reorganised in their final defensive positions as night fell on the 26 September, General Haking spoke to some of them. They gave similar replies to his questions: "We did not understand what it was like; we will do all right next time".[199] The next time would be the first day of the Battle of the Somme.

The 21st Division spent the winter of 1915-1916 initially holding trenches in Ploegsteert Wood in southern Belgium. Mid-November saw them move a little way to the south to a sector adjacent to the northern French town of Armentières. Conditions there were generally poor, and during their turns in the front line trenches a lot of their time was spent trying to cope with the flooding caused by the extremely wet weather. The men became accustomed to the normal routine of trench life: the occasional raid on enemy positions, German artillery retaliation, sniping, mending the wire, trenches knee-deep in water for days on end. Shelled while in the front line and used as pack mules in working parties while out of it, the men simply learnt to put up with the conditions. Harold Yeo, 9/KOYLI, summed up conditions succinctly in a letter home written on 17 November 1915: "Life goes on in the ordinary (!) way. The trenches here are very muddy and it's difficult to get along in places [...] one almost has to swim".[200]

During this period, after its experiences at the Battle of Loos, it was deemed that the 21st Division might need some 'stiffening up'. Accordingly, in November, one battalion from each brigade was replaced by a 'more experienced' unit: in 62 Bde, the 8/EYorks was replaced by 1/Lincolns; in 63 Bde, the departure of 12/West Yorks saw the arrival of 4/Middlesex; and in 64 Bde the 14/DLI swapped places in 6th Division with the 1/East Yorks. The division also bid farewell to Major-General Forestier-Walker, who was replaced in November 1915 by Major-General Sir C.W. Jacob, the latter only remaining in post until May the following year.

---

199 Edmonds, *Military Operations 1915*, Vol. II, p.335.
200 IWM Colonel H.E.Yeo MBE, MC Papers, Doc. 3132.

It was as their time in Flanders was drawing to a close in March 1916 that 64 Bde was chosen to 'meet' and be inspected by Sir Douglas Haig, by then the Commander-in-Chief of the BEF. On the 25th, the men were drawn up along the Bailleul to Ousterteen road and it fell to Lieutenant Spicer, 9/KOYLI, in the absence of his company commander, to greet the General:

> We were lined up at the side of the road, and as he came along, each company had to present arms – then slope them – and then the Company Commander had to fall out and be introduced to the C-in-C and walk alongside him down the length of his company while he asked the usual inane questions. […] You trot up to him, salute him, then shake hands. His first remark to me was: 'Well, this is a great responsibility on your young shoulders, isn't it?' I feel the correct reply would have been either;
>
> 1) What about yourself?, or
>
> 2) You can talk!. As it was I merely murmured 'Yes, Sir' and let him carry on.[201]

Major-General Claud William Jacob (1863–1948) GOC 21st Division from November 1915 to May 1916. (<21stdivision1914-18.org>)

Seven days later, 21st Division, having travelled by train to Longeau, just to the south-west of Amiens, marched into La Neuville, a pretty little village situated close to where the River Ancre joins the meandering River Somme. Second-Lieutenant Ellenberger, C Company, 9/KOYLI, describes the billeting arrangements:

> It was one of the best billets we ever had: Madame was very nice and hospitable. Indeed, we were to find all the inhabitants down here were kindly disposed to us. We soon found she baked excellent bread and had some home-brewed beer, which was better than most French beer. To celebrate our arrival in this new part of the world we bought two barrels from her and had a beer parade – the most popular parade the company ever attended!.[202]

Of course, this new idyll was destined to be short-lived. Working parties of up to 600 men were soon the order of the day as tons of essential materiel for the coming offensive arrived by lorry or train and had to be man-handled the last few miles to the trenches. The men were feeling confident that they were not going to be left out of the Big Push for 1916.

---

201 Lancelot Dykes Spicer, *Letters from France 1915-1918* (London: Robert York, 1979), p.41.
202 IWM Brigadier G.F. Ellenberger MC Papers, Doc. 4227.

2

Somme

Part I

The Battle of the Somme, or at least the events of its first day, 1 July 1916, has come to represent, in British folk memory, "all that was wasteful, incompetent and futile about the fighting on the Western Front".[1] Thankfully, recent scholarship has attempted to provide a more balanced interpretation of events to the already huge historiography of the 141-day campaign. This work does not aim to cover the wider picture in any great detail: for those who desire such an overview, the list of works is extensive.[2] This chapter will focus on the involvement of 21st Division, which took part in attacks twice in July, including the first day of the battle and again in September before its transfer out of the area in October.

On 22 May 1916, a significant event had taken place: Major-General David Graham Muschet Campbell had taken over command of 21st Division. 'Soarer' Campbell had earned his nickname by riding a horse of that name to victory in the 1896 Grand National, Irish National Hunt Cup and Grand Military Steeplechase. He was a cavalryman who had led his men in a charge near Mons in 1914, where he became probably one of the last men in military history to be wounded by a lance. By 1918 he was personally making aeroplane reconnaissance flights as observer, often requesting his pilot to attack targets of opportunity. He adopted the code name "Barbara", and often the hurried message sent down the chain of command of 'Barbara

---

1   Gary Sheffield, *The Somme* (London: Cassell, 2003), p. xii.

2   This list does not claim to be exhaustive. To it could be added the series of 'Pals' histories published by Pen & Sword and innumerable unit and formation histories: J.E. Edmonds, *Military Operations France & Belgium 1916*, Vol. I (London, Macmillan, 1932). W. Miles, *Military Operations France & Belgium 1916*, Vol. II (London: Macmillan, 1938); Martin Middlebrook, *The First Day on the Somme, 1st July 1916* (London: Allen Lane, 1971); Robin Prior & Trevor Wilson, *The Somme* (London: Yale University Press, 2005); Robin Prior & Trevor Wilson, *Command on the Western Front* (Oxford: Blackwell, 1992); Peter Hart, *The Somme* (London: Weidenfeld & Nicolson, 2005); Peter Simkins, *From the Somme to Victory. The British Army's Experience on the Western Front 1916-1918* (Barnsley: Pen & Sword, 2014); William Philpott, *Bloody Victory* (London: Little Brown, 2009); Peter H. Liddle, *The 1916 Battle of the Somme: A Reappraisal* (London: Leo Cooper, 1992); Lyn Macdonald, *Somme* (London: Papermac, 1983). Chris McCarthy, *The Somme: The Day-by-Day Account* (London: Arms & Armour Press, 1993); Malcolm Brown, *The Imperial War Museum Book of the Somme* (London: Sidgwick & Jackson, 1996); Gary Sheffield, *The Somme*, (London: Cassell, 2003); Andrew Rawson, *The Somme Campaign* (Barnsley: Pen & Sword, 2014).

on the loose' warned subordinates to expect an otherwise unannounced visit. He was an excellent divisional commander who did not suffer fools gladly and was quite prepared to protest to his seniors when he perceived his orders to be unreasonable. But he was equally prepared to listen and was tactically astute. By the end of the war he was the fifth longest serving divisional commander in the BEF.[3]

On 30 December 1915, the day after a conference at Chantilly, the newly-appointed Commander-in-Chief of the British Expeditionary Force, Sir Douglas Haig, received a letter from his French counterpart, General Joffre, proposing a large-scale combined Franco-British offensive on a sixty-mile front straddling the River Somme, this to take place the following spring or summer. This was part of a wider Allied strategy for 1916 which would also include offensives by the Russian and Italian armies. Haig did not want to attack on the Somme, however, preferring to launch an offensive further north in the Ypres area. Joffre at first acquiesced, allowing this plan to go ahead, providing the British would also take part in a subsidiary battle on the Somme sometime in the spring. Various factors combined to frustrate Haig's idea, including the inability of the Russians to launch any meaningful attack before the summer, and it was agreed on 14 February that the main effort would be on the Somme after all.

Major-General Sir David Graham Muschet Campbell GCB, commanded 21st Division from May 1916 until the end of the war. (21stdivision1914-19.org)

The plan as originally envisaged did not come to fruition: the scheme was pre-empted by the German attack on French positions near the town of Verdun on 21 February. This battle, which lasted for nine months, grew into an attritional struggle on a scale not yet seen during the war, involving eventually seventy-eight French Divisions and costing them around 315,000 casualties. The desperate defence of Verdun, from which was born the maxim *Ils ne passeront pas*,[4] meant that the French Army was bleeding to death: Joffre implored Haig to support their efforts

---

3 Brigadier-General Hanway Cumming, who commanded 110 Bde from February 1918, described Campbell thus: "Very quick and alert, with an inexhaustible supply of energy, a great sense of humour and a fund of common sense, he was the perfection of a Divisional Commander. He was very popular with all ranks, and rightly so, as he never spared himself in looking after their comfort and efficiency in every way. Added to which he was a fine soldier, with sound and original ideas on training, and possessed a strong will of his own without being in any way obstinate". Hanway R. Cumming, *A Brigadier in France* (London: Jonathan Cape, 1922), p.95.

4 'They shall not pass'.

80 To Do the Work of Men

by attacking as soon as possible on the Somme, fearing that British inaction could result in the Allies losing the war that year. It also became clear, as time went on, that the level of French involvement on the Somme would have to be reduced. That is not to say, however, that the French contribution was, in the end, insignificant: on 1 July, five French divisions, to the right of the British frontage, attacked astride the Somme.[5] Nevertheless, the battle of the Somme would be very different to the one originally envisaged. Haig promised that the newly-formed Fourth Army, commanded by General Sir Henry Rawlinson, would be ready by 20 June, but he was careful to add that he would have preferred to wait until at least mid-August in order to allow more troops to be assembled. On hearing this date, Joffre "at once got very excited and shouted that 'The French Army would cease to exist, if we did nothing till then!'"[6] Joffre eventually reassured Haig that "the British would not be called on for their effort until about the 1 July".[7] It was an uneasy compromise: Haig, on one level, was not confident that the New Armies were ready for the task allotted to them, confiding to his diary on 29 March: "I have not got an Army in France really, but a collection of divisions untrained for the field".[8] As prior to the Battle of Loos, however, Haig's optimism was to get the better of him. The wrangling between Haig and Rawlinson that ensued regarding the detailed planning of the battle is beyond the scope of this narrative,[9] but in essence Rawlinson favoured a "slow, methodical advance, assaulting and capturing one German defensive position at a time before moving up the guns to attack the next".[10] Haig's ideas developed to include the possibility of a complete breakthrough including cavalry exploitation, but also allowed for the development of an attritional struggle instead. A continuation of Fourth Army Operation Order No.2, issued on 14 June 1916 begins:

> During the first two phases of the operation, [...] there may arrive a moment when the enemy's resistance may break down, in which case our advance will be pressed eastwards far enough to enable our cavalry to push through into the open country beyond the enemy's prepared line of defence. Our object will then be to turn northwards, taking the enemy's lines in flank and reverse, the bulk of the cavalry co-operating on the outer flank of this operation while suitable detachments will be detailed to cover the movement from any offensive of the enemy from the east. [...] During which phase of the operation the enemy's resistance is likely to break down it is impossible to foretell, but the Army Commander wishes to be prepared for the most favourable situation to ourselves, while at the same time running no risk of a less favourable situation finding us unprepared.[11]

The breakthrough would never materialise, of course, but as long as this attractive trump card remained on the table, the final plan could be nothing other than an impossible compromise:

---

5   The British attacked with thirteen divisions in the front line. This figure includes the two divisions of Third Army(General Sir Edmund Allenby) involved in the subsidiary attack at Gommecourt.
6   Gary Sheffield & John Bourne (eds.), *Douglas Haig*, p.188 (Diary entry for 26 May 1916).
7   Edmonds, *Military Operations France and Belgium 1916*, Vol. I, p.44.
8   Sheffield & Bourne (eds.), *Douglas Haig War Diaries*, p.183. Approximately 60 per cent of the men assembled for the attack belonged to New Army divisions.
9   See Philpott, *Bloody Victory*, pp.88-130 for an in-depth analysis. See also Peter Hart, *The Somme*, pp.64-71.
10   Ibid, p.107.
11   TNA PRO WO158/234: Fourth Army War Diary.

"The British plan was a product of two minds, certainly with different conceptions of the nature of industrial battle, often competing over details, one thinking strategically, the other tactically".[12]

The 'two minds' were even at odds concerning the nature of the preparatory artillery bombardment: Haig wanted a short, intense bombardment; Rawlinson envisaged a four to five-day pummelling of German positions. In the end, there were just not enough guns available to Fourth Army for a 'hurricane' bombardment and Rawlinson's five-day plan was adopted. Haig still insisted, however, that north of the main Albert – Bapaume road first day objectives should include part of the German Second Line where it lay nearest to the Front Line. The resultant thinning out of the British artillery effort would cost the assaulting battalions dearly. Of course, the overall strategy was of little, if any, interest to the men of the front line divisions assembled in the jumping off trenches on the morning of 1 July: the limits of their concerns were necessarily constrained to include only what lay directly in front of them; the German trenches to be assaulted, the state of the German wire, the objectives to be gained and consolidated.

The German front line on the Somme roughly formed the shape of a capital "L", with the heavily fortified village of Fricourt nestled in the apex of the resultant salient.[13] The main attack was to take place between the village of Serre in the north and Montauban in the south. Fricourt was not to be assaulted frontally, however: pincer movements to its north and east would render the heavily defended position untenable. The northern outflanking manoeuvre would be undertaken by 21st Division, that to the east being entrusted to 7th Division. Troops would 'join hands' at a pre-determined point to the village's north-east and their day's work would be all but done. The men of the German *111th Reserve Regiment* manning the trenches and sheltering in the deep dugouts in and around Fricourt were determined to thwart such ambitions. For almost two years, the German military engineers had been active: their line had been positioned most carefully:

> Here giving up a stretch of low-lying ground, there withdrawing from a steep river valley, they had backed off to build a line that hugged the high spurs and contours of the chalky downland, so that every slope, every natural ravine, each natural declivity, every wood and hilltop could be turned to maximum advantage for observation, for concealment, for defence. [...] By the summer of 1916, every hilltop was a redoubt, every wood an arsenal, every farm a stronghold, every village a fortress.[14]

On the left flank of 21st Division's frontage was 64 Brigade (Brigadier-General H. R. Headlam). Next, on their right, came 63 Brigade (Brigadier-General E.R. Hill). 62 Brigade (Brigadier-General G.C. Rawling) was in reserve. Facing Fricourt itself were two battalions of 50 Brigade ((Brigadier-General W.J.T. Glasgow), on loan from 17th Division. Its left-hand battalion, the 10/West Yorks, was to form a defensive flank to the north of the village, facing south-east. The 7/Yorkshire on their right, were to advance through Fricourt, but not until it was deemed feasible to launch 'Phase Two' of the attack, which in the end was judged to be at 14.30 hours that afternoon (See Map 8).

---

12 Philpott, *Bloody Victory*, p.127.
13 See Map 7.
14 Macdonald, *Somme*, pp. 10-11.

The 64 and 63 brigades were to attack across the Fricourt Spur: the convex nature of the ground, rising for 500 yards in front of their jumping off positions, meant that the German front line was initially just out of sight. Once over the crest, with Fricourt village now visible a mile away to the south-east, the ground fell away gradually for a further 5-600 yards, containing a labyrinth of German support and communication trenches, until it reached a sunken road heading due north from the village. The first objective, Crucifix Trench, lay a further 2-300 yards to the east. The advance to the second objective, including gaining touch with the 7th Division advancing northwards from Mametz, would see them skirt to the north of Fricourt Farm before reaching Bottom Wood, another 1,000 yards to the east. In retrospect it can be seen that the objectives for 1 July were over-ambitious.

Brigadier-General Hugo Headlam, 64 Bde. (IWM HU 123124)

The key to any successful assault of a well-prepared trench system was the quality and intensity of the artillery bombardment that would precede it. The properly developed artillery 'creeping barrage' lay, as yet, some way off in the future, however, but the 21st Division was able to advance behind a basic version which involved the guns 'lifting' from one line of targets to the next at specific intervals: the heavier guns would indeed 'lift' directly onto the next designated line, but the 18 pounders "in lifting their fire […] will search back to the next barrage, in order that the whole ground may be covered by fire immediately before our infantry advance over it"[15] (See Map 10).

In his Operation Orders, Lieutenant-Colonel King, commanding 10/KOYLI, assured his men that "the enemy wire will be cut and trenches destroyed up to and beyond the second objective", and that they should follow "the line of the burst of shells as closely as possible", adding reassuringly, that "Shrapnell [sic] always bursts forwards".[16]

Such optimism was misplaced: although the German front line trench system on the Fricourt Spur was very badly damaged by the bombardment, there were a number of problems with the artillery barrage. The first was the density of the barrage – spread over the extensive depth of the German defensive system of trenches, it was too weak to have the desired effect; the German defenders, though far from comfortable in their deep dugouts, were relatively safe against all but direct strikes from the heaviest shells and were thus able to man their trenches once the barrage had lifted beyond them; although the 21st Division artillery fired over 32,000 shells on 1 July

---

15 TNA PRO WO 95/2136: 21st Division Commander Royal Artillery [CRA] War Diary, 'Instructions for the Offensive No.3' 15 June 1916.
16 TNA PRO WO 95/2162: 10/KOYLI .War Diary

(a mixture of high explosive and shrapnel from the 18 pounders and 4.5" Howitzers), a significant number did not explode.[17] Lastly, the speed at which the lifting barrage advanced made it almost impossible for the infantry to keep up: it would lift from the German front line trenches at Zero – a costly error in itself – and from the sunken road at Zero plus seventeen minutes. It would move beyond the first objective line at Zero plus forty-five.[18]

Nevertheless, ignorant of what was to come, some of the men in the front line trenches were impressed by the preparatory bombardment, particularly as it intensified in the final minutes before zero: Lieutenant B. L. Gordon of 9/KOYLI later wrote that it was "more violent than anything I have ever heard, its intensity was terrific".[19]

The 64 Brigade had been in the Somme area since the end of March 1916: they had done a number of stints in the line opposite Fricourt and had been able to take part in 'practice attacks' on 17 and 21 May over ground selected specifically for its similarity to that over which they were to do it for real six weeks later. Enemy 'positions' marked out with flags and tapes were taken within a couple of hours and consolidated. No casualties were reported.

It was now the real thing. They marched into the front line in the early hours of 28 June and settled in, ready for the off on the 29th, 10/KOYLI on the left Brigade frontage, 9/KOYLI on the right, with 1/East Yorks and 15/DLI in support respectively. That afternoon, a message arrived stating that the attack was postponed for forty-eight hours. Poor weather conditions had hampered artillery-spotting and observation – only one day out of five since the beginning of the bombardment on the 24th had been fine. Low cloud, mist and rain had led Rawlinson to decide that the attack would now go in on 1 July. All the men could do now was wait.

That evening, the officers of 9/KOYLI received a summons to meet at Battalion HQ. When they got there, a glass was put in their hands: there was to be a final drink together before the attack. An already nervous atmosphere became markedly more strained when the commanding officer, Lieutenant-Colonel Lynch, entered the room.

Over the nine months since Loos, Lynch had contrived to make himself very unpopular with the men and the officers – particularly the latter. In March, C Company had been pumping out flooded trenches near Armentières for four days and nights. Just prior to their relief, a sharp downpour had put paid to all their efforts. Lynch was furious and ordered them back into the front line to pump out the positions for another eight hours for the incoming battalion. C Company very nearly refused to go, but their officers, who were themselves indignant at the orders, persuaded them not to disobey. A month later, Lynch took another decision that did nothing to improve his relationship with the other officers. He promoted Captain Stephenson to Temporary Second-in-Command of the Battalion. Stephenson was a personal friend of the CO and this move catapulted him from mere second-in-command in his company, thus passing over all the existing company commanders. Captain G.E. Griffin, commanding C Company, Stephenson's company, had a row with Lynch and soon after, he and two other officers, including Lieutenant L.D. Spicer, put their names down for a transfer to the Balloon Section. Lynch was apoplectic. Spicer continues the story:

---

17 Research has suggested that the figure might be as high as 30 per cent.
18 See Map 10. Standard creeping barrages later in the war would tend to advance at a rate of 100 yards every four minutes.
19 *The Bugle* [journal of the KOYLI] *Vol. 24. No.6,* article by B.L. Gordon, p.24.

84 To Do the Work of Men

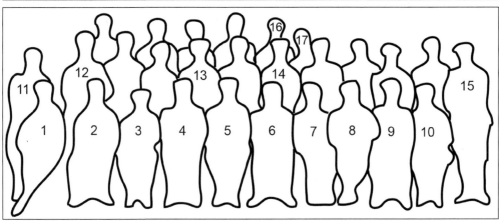

Officers of the 9/KOYLI, Corbie, 16 April 1916. (Courtesy: Paul Reed)

Key:
1. Capt. Revd A. Bouchier (Chaplain), 2. Capt. G. Haswell (B Coy), 3. Capt. L.D. Head (A Coy), 4. Major H. Greenwood, 5. Lt-Col. C.W.D. Lynch, 6. Lt A.G. Spark, 7. Capt. W. Walker (C Coy), 8. Capt. G.E. Griffin (D Coy), 9. Lt-QM. W.K. Pethed, 10. Capt. A. Stephenson, 11. Lt H.A. Telfer, 12. 2/Lt E.R. Nott, 13. Lt. J. Buckley, 14. Lt L.D. Spicer, 15. Lt A Malseed RAMC, 16. 2/Lt C.W. Ellis, 17. 2/Lt J.J.F. Oldershaw

Lynch summoned in all the officers. [...] He first of all started fairly reasonably by justifying himself in promoting Stephenson. [...] He then praised Griffin's work and generally soft-soaped him, and said it was no slur on him that he was being passed over. Having said all this he then asked Griffin to leave the room, the ostensible reason being that he wished to tell us that he had not promoted Griffin because of his 'not being a gentleman'. As a matter of fact, from this moment onwards he became purely insulting – so insulting that it was quite unbelievable, and his insults were all directed at me! He told us that he was now addressing the officers of D Company (my company). He then stated the facts as to our applying for this balloon job and said that in the first place it showed that we were insubordinate, and secondly it showed cowardice. The latter charge he dwelt on for some time.[20]

Lynch blocked the transfer requests but took no further action.

Lynch's entry to the drinks party on the eve of battle prompted the adjutant to ask Captain Gordon Haswell, the senior captain present, quietly to propose a toast to the CO. "I'm damned if I will", replied Haswell, adding "I don't wish him good health and I am not prepared to be insincere on this occasion". The adjutant insisted, however, and after a few seconds of restrained argument, Haswell reluctantly stepped forward and raised his glass, saying: "Gentlemen, I give you the toast of the King's Own Light Infantry, and in particular the 9th Battalion of that

20 Lancelot Dykes Spicer, *Letters from France 1915-1918* (London: Robert York, 1979), p.47.

Lieutenant-Colonel Colmer William Donald Lynch, CO 9/KOYLI, kia 1 July 1916, age 35. (Paul Reed)

Regiment" During a slight pause here he recalled a phrase which occurred repeatedly in the written orders for the attack: "Gentlemen, when the barrage lifts". His brother officers emptied their glasses in silence. An unpleasant scene had been side-stepped.[21]

Unpopular amongst his fellow officers Lynch may have been, but his detailed instructions regarding the method of attack for the morning of 1 July, all twelve pages of them, portray a meticulous and careful planner. The commonly held perception that all battalions instructed their men to walk slowly towards the enemy trenches on that fateful morning is here demonstrated quite clearly to be nonsense. Divisional orders dating back to the middle of May 1916 made sure that officers of 21st Division knew to move their first waves forward as close to the lifting artillery barrage as possible. This is clearly illustrated by the following paragraph:

> During the advance, it is necessary to have the leading lines close up to the Artillery barrage, so that positions may be occupied the moment the barrage lifts.
>
> To ensure this, in the first instance, the leading two lines must leave their trenches before the bombardment ceases and advance as far as possible towards the German lines.[22]

Lynch's instructions also advise as to just how quickly his men should advance:

Captain Gordon Haswell, "B" Coy, 9/KOYLI. kia 1 July 1916. Age 24. (Harrow County School)

> The advance will be made in quick time and no faster. If it is necessary to charge a body of the enemy who are in the line of advance, or an occupied trench, the advance must be

---

21 The toast was not forgotten. It appeared subsequently in the In Memoriam column of *The Times* every 1 July well into the1960s. Both Lynch and Haswell were killed on 1 July 1916. They lie close together in Norfolk Cemetery, Bécourt, France.
22 TNA PRO WO 95/2130: 21st Division HQ War Diary.

Getting his men as close to the German lines prior to Zero was also helped by the construction of a "Russian Sap" dug by the Engineers across the re-entrant in the front line in front of the 9/KOYLI positions (See Map 9). This, to all intents and purposes, was a trench with a thin layer of soil left in place as a roof, thus disguising it from enemy observation. It was to be opened up the night before the attack and reduced the distance to be covered in the open from 300 to 180 yards. To reduce this distance even more, the first waves were to leave this sap five minutes before Zero "and creep as near to the enemy front trench as our barrage will permit".[24] On 30 June, the news of the efficacy of the artillery bombardment was also encouraging: "Brigadiers concerned reported that they were satisfied that the enemy's wire had been sufficiently destroyed".[25] No matter how detailed and thorough the planning, however, and no matter how well the men understand their tasks, the enemy always has other ideas.

The morning of 1 July dawned dry, bright, warm and sunny. The last units of 21st Division, the 1/E. Yorks and 15/DLI, had reached their jumping off positions at three o'clock that morning. They should have in position earlier, but one of the communication trenches, Pioneer Avenue, was blocked by a working party from the 14/Northumberland Fusiliers, many of whom, including the officer in command, were reported to be drunk.[26]

The artillery barrage had increased in intensity at 06.25 and at 07.22 a hurricane 3-inch Stokes Mortar bombardment was added to the mix. At 07.25 the heavy artillery lifted off the enemy front line and three minutes later 178 Tunnelling Company of the Royal Engineers exploded three comparatively small mines in No Man's Land near the German Tambour. These detonations were meant to distract the German defenders and the resulting crater lips would shield the right flank of the 10/W.Yorks as they created a defensive flank across No Man's Land and to the north of Fricourt to protect the assault across the spur. Smoke was also released across this sector of the front, by both hand-thrown bombs and 4" Stokes Mortars.

On the extreme left of 64 Brigade frontage the men of 10/KOYLI (Lieutenant-Colonel H.J. King) left their trenches and crawled out into No Man's Land at 07.25, the first two platoons of A Company on the left and those of B Company on the right. As they inched forward, they could not have helped but notice, over their left shoulders just to the south of the village of La Boisselle, the detonation at 07.28 of 60,000 pounds of ammonal which formed the brutally contested Lochnagar Crater on 34th Division front. Behind the leading wave, D and C Companies, left and right respectively, were designated as "clearing parties" who, with bombing squads attached, would follow closely on the heels of the assaulting companies, clear the German dug-outs and form blocks in captured trenches on their left flank. To aid the swift capture of dug outs, the men were carrying "two Vermoral (sic) Sprayers per platoon" and "all available electric torches".[27] Those men of the supporting companies not designated as clearing

---

23 TNA PRO WO 95/2162: 9/KOYLI War Diary.
24 Ibid.
25 TNA PRO WO 95/2130: 'Operations Carried out by 21st Division', 21st Division HQ War Diary.
26 TNA PRO WO 95/2159: 64 Brigade War Diary.
27 TNA PRO WO 95/2162: 10/KOYLI War Diary. Vermorel Sprayers were employed to neutralise dugouts that had been contaminated with chlorine gas. The need to form a defensive flank on the left

parties were to carry forward the following: each man would have a pick or shovel and between them they would transport twenty boxes of small arms ammunition and forty buckets of Mills Grenades. A detailed account of the actions of 10/KOYLI cannot be given, unfortunately: the battalion war diary, unhelpfully, devotes only four lines to this momentous day's events and R.C. Bond's *The King's Own Yorkshire Light Infantry in the Great War*[28] offers little in addition. Their story must be gleaned from the accounts of the other battalions in the brigade. It appears that their commanding officer, Lieutenant-Colonel King, was wounded in the chest by two bullets from a German machine gun just after he crossed the German front line.[29]

On 10/KOYLI's right, the men of 9/KOYLI were also crawling into No Man's Land from the Russian Sap, A Company (Captain L.D. Head) and C Company (Captain W. Walker) in the lead. The leading platoons, under Second-Lieutenants N.L. Alexander and J.J.F. Oldershaw had gone no more than twenty-five yards when they "were greeted by a hail of Machine Gun and Rifle fire; the enemy, in spite of our barrage, brought his machine guns out of his dug-outs and, placing them on the top of his parapet, opened rapid fire".[30]

Some of this machine gun fire was coming from the German trenches on the higher

Captain Leslie Dymoke Head, "A" Coy, 9/KOYLI, kia 1 July 1916, age 28. (Lloyd's Men War Memorial)

Second-Lieutenant John Joseph Fritz Oldershaw, 9/KOYLI, kia 1 July 1916, age 23. (england1418.wordpress.com)

was born from the mistaken belief that 34th Division were not to attack at the same time as 21st Division. The failure of the former to advance as quickly as was envisaged quickly rendered this tactic necessary, however.

28 R.C. Bond, *The King's Own Yorkshire Light Infantry in the Great War* (Bradford: Percy Lund, Humphries & Co Ltd., 1929).
29 TNA PRO CAB 45/135: Major Laskie to official historian correspondence, 30 June 1930. Laskie recovered after several months in hospital and returned to France to command a different battalion.
30 TNA PRO WO 95/2162: 9/KOYLI War Diary.

ground near La Boisselle, their position allowing the gunners to enfilade these exposed troops from the left. The German response also included a shrapnel barrage, but this mainly caught the supporting companies. Lieutenant Gordon, B Company, led his men from the original front line trenches into this barrage at 07.29:

> The advance was by crawling and by rushes from shell-hole to shell-hole. The noise was deafening and the German machine-gun fire was terrible. Just before reaching the Russian sap I was struck on the chin by a bit of shrapnel. When I reached the sap I lay down and looked into it. I saw Colonel Lynch, who said: "Hullo, Gordon, are you hit?" I put my hand to my chin and found it was covered with blood. The Colonel then began to get out of the sap. He was killed by a shell almost immediately afterwards.[31]

Ahead of Gordon, with C Company, Second-Lieutenant G.F. Ellenberger reported that his men, as they got closer to the German front trench, in addition to the machine gun fire, were greeted by a hail of stick grenades. His company commander, Walker, was already dead, killed by machine gun fire. Gordon, coming up from behind and closing in on the leading platoons, passed close enough to the body to recognise him. He continues his story:

> By this time our waves were jumbled together and, owing to the smoke, it was difficult to keep direction [and] after a few more minutes, which seemed ages, I reached the German front trenches. Several 'B' Company men joined me, and I sat in a shell hole while one of them bandaged my chin.[32]

On reaching the front line, Ellenberger saw that it had been "frightfully ploughed up"[33] by the British artillery bombardment. Gordon further observed:

> Although our bombardment had failed to knock out the enemy machine guns, its effect on their trenches had been great. For the most part they were entirely knocked in, one long succession of shell-holes, brown craters mainly, for the soil is thick. Now and then one came to an enormous white crater, caused, I believe, by our trench mortars. These were 15 or 20 feet deep and as many yards across.[34]

The KOYLIs , "in spite of heavy losses carried the front line with little delay".[35] The losses had, indeed, been heavy. The battalion suffered the majority of its day's casualties in crossing No Man's Land. Of the twenty-four officers who had led their men forward, only five succeeded in crossing the German front line trench. They were Lieutenant Gordon, and Second-Lieutenants

---

31 *Bugle,* Vol. 24, No. 6, p.30. Major Laskie (10/KOYLI) added that Lynch had been hit in the shoulder by machine gun bullets before a shell splinter hit him in the head, killing him. This must have been hearsay, as Major Laskie was well back behind the lines with the Transport before being ordered forward at 4 p.m. on 1 July. See TNA CAB 45/135: Major Laskie correspondence with official historian, 30 June 1930.
32 *Bugle,* Vol. 24, No. 6, p.30.
33 IWM Private Papers of Brigadier G.F. Ellenberger MC, Doc. 4227.
34 *Bugle,* Vol. 24, No. 6, p.30.
35 TNA PRO WO 95/2162: 9/KOYLI War Diary.

Ellenberger, A.E. Day, R.F. Frazer and G.H. Featherstone, the Signalling Officer. A Company had already lost all its officers and Ellenberger was the only C Company officer left. Eighteen-year-old Second-Lieutenant Frank Golding, who had joined the battalion only twelve days before, lay dead in No Man's Land.[36] Also killed during the first stage of the attack, seemingly by the same shell, were brothers 19877 Lance Corporal Samuel Cooper and 19878 Private Lawrence Cooper. They had both worked as miners at Kiveton Park Colliery near Sheffield and enlisted together on 11 November 1914. Aged 23 and 20 respectively, they are commemorated on the Thiepval Memorial.[37]

Behind the two KOYLI battalions, the two battalions in support, the 1/E.Yorks (Lieutenant-Colonel M.B. Stow) on the left and 15/DLI (Lieutenant-Colonel A.E. Fitzgerald) on the right, moved forward at 07.30.

Second-Lieutenant Arthur Delano Maconachie, "C" Coy, 9/KOYLI, kia 1 July 1916, age 22. (*Northern Assurance War Records*)

The 1/E.Yorks advanced in column of platoons, B and D Companies (Captains Huntriss and Besant) in the lead, followed by Battalion Headquarters troops, with A and C Companies (Captains Hawkesworth and Anderson) bringing up the rear. They followed 10/KOYLI across the Fricourt Spur and onwards down the slope to the Sunken Road.

The diarist of 15/DLI tells their particular story in a more heroic style: under a clear blue sky in which "our aeroplanes were scudding about", the men

> clambered up the assaulting ladders and with magnificent dash made straight for the German line. […] Many officers and men were wounded soon after mounting the parapet. But there was no hesitation. All were eager to get across and meet the enemy at close quarters. Among the officers who were wounded quite early were Capt. F.P. Stamper and 2nd Lieut. C.S. Haynes – the former in the leg, the latter slightly wounded in the arm. The latter gallantly continued and subsequently met his death at the head of his men. What opposition that survived was quickly overcome by grenade and bayonet and the prisoners who came up from their deep dug-outs were sent to the rear to QUEEN'S REDOUBT under charge of slightly wounded cases.[38]

---

36   Second-Lieutenant Frank Alfred Golding is buried in Gordon Dump Cemetery, Grave Reference II N 4.
37   Pam Linge & Ken Linge, *Missing But Not Forgotten* (Barnsley: Pen & Sword, 2015), p. 193.
38   TNA PRO WO 95/2161: 15/DLI War Diary. Second-Lieutenant Clifford Skemp Haynes was 25 years old and is commemorated on the Thiepval Memorial.

Despite claims of rapid advances, the support battalions soon caught up, and to some extent became mixed up, with the leading units. Casualties were also high amongst the supporting battalions: the 1/E.Yorks, advancing behind 10/KOYLI, encountered heavy machine gun fire.

The German front line trench had been "badly damaged", but "there were still a few machine guns untouched and these took a heavy toll of the battalion".[39] The battalion diary is unclear, but it is likely that the commanding officer, Lieutenant-Colonel Stow, was wounded at about this time. He was taken back to Heilly Casualty Clearing Station but died of wounds later that day.[40] Captain Willis, the Adjutant, took command.

It would seem that the dug outs in the German front line system had been effectively dealt with, as "once the main network of trenches was passed, we suffered no damage from hostile rifle or M.G. fire from our immediate rear".[41] The 9/KOYLI diarist continues the story:

Second-Lieutenant Barry Robert Boncker 1/EYorks, age 19, kia 1 July 1916. (Croydon Roll of Honour)

> the whole Brigade was united, irrespective of battalions, and driving the enemy rapidly out of his support trenches. From here to the SUNKEN ROAD the attack became a running fight or series of small fights: much work was done with bomb and bayonet, and some prisoners were taken.[42]

Lieutenant Gordon's party had begun to stray too far to the south in all the smoke and confusion, so he and his now mixed group, including a number of men from 8/Somerset LI and a private from the Durhams, did their best to veer left as they fought their way down the slope:

> While we were moving to our left we suddenly came upon about a dozen Germans, about ten or twelve yards off. They fired at us with rifles. I whipped out my revolver and fired several rounds, and some of my men also fired. One of the Germans dropped and suddenly

---

39 TNA PRO WO 95/2161: 1/East Yorks War Diary.
40 Lieutenant-Colonel Montague Bruce Stow, age 32, is buried in Daours Communal Cemetery Extension, grave reference II.A.7. His date of death is recorded as 2 July 1916.
41 TNA PRO WO 95/2159: 64 Brigade HQ War Diary. Note, however, the experience of 10/Yorks later in the chapter.
42 TNA PRO WO 95/2162: 9/KOYLI War Diary.

my 'Faithful Durham' rushed forward shouting: "Come on, boys, the b--------s are on the run." The enemy would not face the bayonet. We captured the wounded man and one other, who threw down his rifle and held up his hands. The rest fled.[43]

Second-Lieutenant Ellenberger gave his own personal account in a letter home written six days after the attack. He also highlights the Germans' dislike of hand to hand fighting:

> The whole thing was so very fast and it was such hot work that you hadn't time to sit and think over the horrors, but just went on and on, pursued by a decided but unexpressed feeling that you would sooner be anywhere but there. The Hun ran, and we took a lot of prisoners; he has a very unsporting idea about fighting, has the Hun. He'll poop away his machine gun at you, and he'll snipe at you, and he'll throw bombs at you, but as soon as you get to close quarters, with the bayonet, he puts up his hands. [...] I saw a lot of Huns, and a lot of Hun rifles, and it's an absolute fact that none of them had a fixed bayonet – when it came to bayonet work they put up their hands; the bayonets we found afterwards down in their dugouts.[44]

Ellenberger and Gordon met up somehow on the reverse slope and they pressed on together, rushing the last two hundred yards over open country under enemy shell fire, and made it safely across Lozenge Trench to the Sunken Road, arriving just after eight o'clock. The situation was one of confusion and disorganisation. The Sunken Road, with ten-foot-high grass banks on both sides, seemed the ideal spot in which to pause and attempt to establish some sort of order. Lieutenant Gordon continues:

> Just in front of the Sunken Road, which is about 1,100 yards in front of the original British fire trench, was a German subsidiary line of trenches. [This would be Lozenge Trench – see Map 9] Here I found many of our own men and others from different battalions in our brigade, but no senior officers except Colonel Fitzgerald of the Durhams. After a short time I realised what had happened, took command of my battalion and reported myself to Colonel Fitzgerald.
>
> About 3 or 400 yards in front of the Sunken Road there is a trench called Crucifix Trench by the British, because just above it there is a crucifix standing between three tall trees.[45] This trench was the ultimate objective of our battalion. I asked Colonel Fitzgerald if I should lead my men to it, but he instructed me not to do so at that time, as owing to the rapid advance of our brigade, both our flanks were exposed. Indeed the Sunken Road itself was being continuously enfiladed by enemy machine guns firing from the direction of Fricourt on our right and from Birch Tree Wood on our left. I instructed my men to dig themselves in on the line of the Sunken Road, which they began to do, gradually improving the cover against the machine gun fire, but not before we had sustained further losses.[46]

---

43 *Bugle*, Vol. 24, No. 6, p.30.
44 Private Papers of Brigadier G.F. Ellenberger MC, IWM. Doc. 4227,7 July 1916 correspondence.
45 There is still a crucifix at this location, but nothing to indicate that it is the original.
46 *Bugle*, Vol. 24, No. 6, p.31.

We can now move our focus to the south and examine the first phases of 63 Brigade's attack. This brigade lined up with 8/Somerset LI (Lieutenant-Colonel J.W. Scott) on the left, with 8/Lincolns (Lieutenant-Colonel R.H. Johnston) behind them in support. On the right brigade frontage was 4/Middlesex (Lieutenant-Colonel H.P.F. Bicknell) with 10/Yorks & Lancs (Lieutenant-Colonel J.H. Ridgway) behind them. The 10/Yorks, (Lieutenant-Colonel W.B. Eddowes), despite being located in Queen's Redoubt, 62 Brigade being designated as Divisional Reserve), would send one company forward behind 4/Middlesex "for the purpose of clearing hostile trenches".[47]

The 63 Bde's first objective was a line from Fricourt Farm to Crucifix Trench and they were expected to send advance parties as far forward as Railway Copse. The second and final objective would be along the edge of Bottom Wood, but as neither of these objectives was reached, they are included here purely for academic interest.

The men of the leading companies of 8/Somerset LI, C Company on the left and B Company on the right, crawled out into No Man's Land at 07.25. A Company would be directly behind them in support and D Company would bring up the rear in artillery formation, carrying ammunition, grenades, picks and shovels. They stood up at Zero and "advanced in quick time",[48] only to be met by very heavy machine gun fire. The attack faltered as around half of the men in the leading platoons became casualties, and by the time the German front line was reached, all the officers in the battalion except Lieutenants Hall, Kellett and Ackerman had been either killed or wounded,[49] and "...although Officers and men were being hit and falling everywhere, the advance went steadily on, and was reported [...] by a Brigade Major who witnessed it to have been magnificent".[50] One particular German machine gun in the front line proved particularly stubborn, but a grenade attack eventually silenced it. "The only enemy found alive in his front line were a few machine gunners, who were immediately killed".[51]

The Germans had opened an artillery barrage on No Man's Land almost as soon as the assault had begun, and the supporting companies were forced to advance through it, suffering heavy casualties in the process, but Arrow Lane was soon overrun and the advance continued along it over the crest and down the reverse slope into an area described by the battalion diarist as "a mass of craters".[52] The advance was supported by one Stokes Mortar gun and a Lewis Gun team, until the former was knocked out by enemy fire, and a party under Second-Lieutenant Kellett was able to work its way from crater to crater until it entered the relatively undamaged Lozenge Alley. Enemy shrapnel fire was making any further advance perilous, so it was decided to consolidate the positions they had gained thus far: this meant making firesteps in what was only a communication trench and being ready to face any counter attack from the direction of Fricourt village. Second-Lieutenant Hall and his men joined Kellett's party: this made a total of about one hundred men. Lieutenant Ackerman and his party of about thirty men, it would seem, made it no further than Brandy Trench: they were found there the following morning when rations were brought forward.

47 TNA PRO WO 95/2130:. Orders issued 17 June 1916, 21st Division HQ War Diary
48 TNA PRO WO 95/2158: 8/Somerset LI War Diary.
49 Initial estimates show eighteen officer casualties, including nine fatalities. Commonwealth War Graves Commission records show this figure to be correct.
50 TNA PRO WO 95/2158: 8/Somerset LI War Diary.
51 Ibid.
52 Ibid.

94   To Do the Work of Men

The support battalions were under orders not to advance until 08.30: this would allow them to pass through the leading battalions and onto the second objective in time to follow the artillery barrage. The difficulties encountered by the leading battalions meant that this order was cancelled and word was sent at 08.20 to the effect that 8/Lincolns and 10/Yorks & Lancs were not to move until ordered to do so.

Lieutenant-Colonel Johnston of 8/Lincolns received the order, but D Company had already advanced behind the Somersets and was helping to clear out the German front line trench system. A and B Companies also advanced before word could be got to them. Johnston quickly telephoned Brigade Headquarters for instructions. With A, B and D Companies already across No Man's Land and beyond recall, Johnston was told to take C Company and join in the advance. He reached the junction of Arrow Lane and Lozenge Alley (see Map 9) before being able to exert any influence on what was happening. He sent one party down Dart Lane to the right with one bombing squad, and another along Brandy Trench with orders to move subsequently to the Sunken Road. Others of his battalion were moving along Lozenge Alley. Johnston continues the story:

> I advanced [up Lozenge Alley] trying to find out the situation on the right. I could not see any advance here. It was therefore necessary to watch our Right Flank. I pushed up men to Lozenge Wood and along Sunken Road, getting touch with 64th Brigade. […] Those advancing up Lozenge Alley meeting (sic) Germans coming from FRICOURT Farm. The Germans made 2 bombing attacks up LONELY TRENCH, both of which were repulsed. Though at one time the Germans got a few men into LOZENGE ALLEY here. They used Rifle Grenades as well as bombs and so could out distance our bombers until we got up Rifle Grenades. The Germans left at least 20 dead in LONELY TRENCH close up to LOZENGE ALLEY and some in LOZENGE ALLEY.[53]

Johnston had put Second-Lieutenant Preston in charge of the block at the junction of Lonely Trench and Lozenge Alley at around ten in the morning and had himself fired off all of their rifle grenades to repel the first German attack. He is in no doubt as to the importance of this action:

> From a plan of the trenches it is clear that if these bombing attacks had been successful, and the Germans had got a foothold in Lozenge Alley at this point (they actually did get a few men in for a few minutes) they would have taken our troops in Sunken Road to the North of Lozenge Alley in flank as well as in rear, and turned them out. 2/Lt Preston & his party prevented this.[54]

Johnston was then ordered by Division at around 16.35 to hold the trenches they were in. He was able to get four Stokes Mortars in place, but a British artillery barrage prevented any further counter attacks coming their way. It would appear that a number of the men previously ordered forward to the Sunken Road made it, and some even advanced as far forward as Crucifix Trench

---

53   TNA PRO WO 95/2158: Appendix X, 8/Lincoln War Diary.
54   TNA PRO CAB 45/135: Lt. Col. R.H. Johnston correspondence with official historian, 15 February 1930.

but were forced to retire when they ran out of grenades.[55] The 8/Lincolns suffered five officers killed, with a further eight wounded. Other ranks casualties amounted to 254, thirty of them fatalities.[56]

On the right brigade frontage, the 4/Middlesex had suffered a number of casualties in the hour prior to Zero amongst the two companies occupying the front-line trenches: a German retaliatory barrage had proven to be disconcertingly accurate, if not particularly heavy. As per orders, the two leading companies (A and B) had begun their move forward into No Man's Land from the jumping off positions at 07.25. They were met with machine gun fire of such intensity, particularly from their right flank, that they were forced to return to their trenches. The losses, even at this early stage, were deemed severe enough to merit a change to the attack formation: A and B Companies were now to advance in one line rather than two. They moved out into No Man's Land for a second time one minute before Zero and this time "went across without hesitation".[57] C Company followed 100 yards behind them, with D Company a similar distance further back.

By the time the two leading companies had managed to cross the German front line, the six enemy machine guns, two of which were in the open between Empress Trench and Empress Support, with the other four firing from the right flank near the Tambour, had taken a decisive toll on the Middlesex units: all the officers and a number of the NCOs in A and B Companies had been hit. Most of the now leaderless remnants, it seems, pushed on in small groups towards the Sunken Road. Those who made it that far attached themselves to units of 8/Lincolns and remained with them until the morning of 3 July when the survivors were brought back to Battalion HQ by Sergeant Millwood. Their claim to have reached the Sunken Road can be verified by the fact that the 9/KOYLIs, on their arrival at that point, sent a certain 19970 Private J. Kearford of B Company down the road towards Fricourt to make contact with their neighbouring unit: he reported back that he had met members of 4/Middlesex.[58]

C and D Companies of 4/Middlesex, along with Battalion HQ personnel who had advanced with the rear line of the second wave, had also suffered heavy casualties as they crossed No Man's Land through the enfilade machine gun fire. They were able to establish themselves in Empress Trench (see Map 9) but had already been reduced to a strength of four Officers, around 100 Other Ranks and two Lewis Guns.

The 50 Brigade assault on the right, designed to form a defensive flank along the northern edge of Fricourt, had failed.[59] This meant that the battalion's right flank was open and the Germans were able to bring machine guns and bombing parties up from Fricourt to threaten the Middlesex position. They were observed as they advanced across the open in places, and Lieutenant-Colonel Bicknell decided that his only course of action was to "hang on to Empress Trench and consolidate it".[60] A message to that effect was sent back to Brigade HQ at 08.15.

---

55 TNA PRO WO 95/2158: 'Account of Operations July 1st – 4th 1916', 63 Brigade War Diary.
56 These figures are for 1-3 July, as recorded in 63 Brigade HQ Diary. (WO 95/2158). Fatalities for 1 July can be ascertained from Commonwealth War Graves Commission records: 2 Officers (Second-Lieutenants W. Swift and J.H. Cragg) and 14 Other Ranks.
57 TNA PRO WO 95/2158: 'Account of Operations, July 1st -4th 1916, 63 Brigade War Diary.
58 TNA PRO WO 95/2162: 9/KOYLI War Diary.
59 This attack is dealt with in more detail later in this chapter.
60 TNA PRO WO 95/2158: 'Account of Operations, July 1st-4th 1916, 63 Brigade War Diary.

96　To Do the Work of Men

The consolidation – the 'reversing' of the trench and the creation of a firestep – was far from complete, but they were able to create blocks in the trenches on their right flank which helped them to repulse three attempts by the Germans to bomb their way up them.

By default, the 4/Middlesex (and 8/Somerset LI) had become the flank guard of the division. Their short advance had cost them well over 50 percent of their number: the 63 Bde War Diary puts their casualties for July at twenty Officers, of which fifteen were killed, and 521 Other Ranks: 114 killed, 314 wounded and 93 missing. Fatalities for 1 July can be confirmed at 13 Officers and 79 Other Ranks.[61]

The 62 Brigade was in divisional reserve: on 1 July they were to act as carrying parties for the assault units. B Company of 10/Yorks, however, was the exception. They were given the task of following the 4/Middlesex and mopping up their first objective. Accordingly, this company was moved up from Queen's Redoubt to the front line just before zero. They watched as the Middlesex men forced their way across the German front line and prepared to follow them. As they climbed out of their trench, however, it became clear that one of the machine guns in the German front line was still in action and was cutting down the men as they appeared above ground. The commanding officer, Major Stewart Walker Loudoun-Shand, leapt up onto the parapet and started to help his men forward.

> [He] won his Victoria Cross for superb courage in leading his men in the teeth of a murderous machine gun fire, from a gun that had been brought into action after the first wave had passed it. Unfortunately he was not destined to live to enjoy his distinction, as, after being hit three times, he was mortally wounded. Even then he continued to cheer on his men, and he died just as they silenced the gun and the Huns who were causing the trouble.[62]

Their subsequent actions are lost in the 'fog of war': they advanced to clear out the German front line trench system, but any further details are missing from all the unit and formation diaries of the time. Wylly asserts that the company started the day five officers and 117 other ranks strong and ended with only one officer and twenty-seven men.[63]

At about 09.15, the men of 10/Yorks and Lancs arrived on the scene and passed through the 4/Middlesex positions. They were able, in the face of sustained machine gun fire, to drive the enemy from the support line and to make it forward "some distance in advance of Dart Lane".[64] In spite of machine gun fire from Fricourt Wood, parties of bombers were able to get as far as Lonely Trench where they destroyed three enemy trench barricades and repulsed attacks from three large groups of Germans advancing from Fricourt. They then erected their own block at the junction with Lozenge Alley. At around the same time, a number of D Company men were sent back to Arrow Lane with one gun from the Machine Gun Corps in order to prevent any German infiltration behind their right flank.

61　Commonwealth War Graves Commission records also show a further 82 fatalities, three of them officers, on 2 July 1916.

62　H.C. Wylly, *The Green Howards in the Great War* (Uckfield: Naval & Military Press reprint of 1926 edition), pp.334-335. For the full VC citation and a brief biography, see Appendix D.

63　Ibid, p.335. There is no further mention of B Company until their "remnants" are found occupying part of Lozenge Alley later in the day.

64　TNA PRO WO 95/2158: 'Operations July 1st 1916 – July 4th 1916', 10/Yorks & Lancs War Diary.

Major Loudoun Shand VC 10/Yorks, kia 1 July 1916, age 36. Norfolk Cem. I.C.77. (Author)

The battalions of 63 Bde were rather mixed up: orders came down from Division at around 16.35 requiring the flank positions to be maintained but also battalions to reorganise. All the men of 10/Yorks & Lancs that could be gathered made their way back to Dart Lane and commenced consolidation. Lieutenant-Colonel Ridgway placed bombers at the junctions of Dart Lane, Empress Support and Lonely Lane and some men in Arrow Lane. They held these positions for the rest of the day and the night of 1- 2 July. Casualties were significant: 63 Bde Diary records 10/Yorks & Lancs as losing 13 Officers and 307 Other Ranks during the month of July 1916. Fatalities for 1 July can be confirmed at five Officers and twelve Other Ranks.

The situation therefore settled down as follows: 4/Middlesex was in Empress Trench, Empress Support and Ball Lane. Forty-three of their number remained in the Sunken Road. A mixed force of 8/Lincolns and 8/Somerset LI stretched from the western edges of Lozenge Wood, across the Sunken Road and along Lozenge Alley. It is possible that some isolated groups of men of 10/Yorks & Lancs remained in position to the south of this trench, facing Lonely Lane, and that some made it some distance down Lonely Trench towards Fricourt.

Captain Denzil Clive Tate Twentyman 10/Y&L, kia 1 July 1916, age 26. (*Yorkshire Rugby Union Roll of Honour*)

The focus of the narrative must now shift southwards again and the exploits of 50 Brigade. The 10/West Yorks (Lieutenant-Colonel A. Dickson) were on the left brigade frontage, their task being, as mentioned earlier, to advance and form a defensive flank across the northern outskirts of Fricourt. 7/Yorks (Lieutenant-Colonel R. D'A Fife), on the right, were to attack the village as part of Phase Two of the assault, but not until it was deemed appropriate to do so. The plan was to go very badly wrong.

If all had indeed gone as planned, 10/West Yorks would have advanced across four German trench lines and captured positions at Red Cottage and Lonely Copse. (See Map 9). The right flank of 63 Bde troops attacking across the Fricourt Spur would thus have been protected.

The men lined up in four waves, one company making up each one. The explosion of the Tambour Mines at 07.28 served to distract and disorientate the Germans long enough for the first two waves, who left their trenches at precisely 07.30, to get across No Man's Land and into König Trench, the German front line, relatively unscathed. Among this group was Lieutenant Philip Howe, whose story is told in some detail (though spread over many pages) in Martin

Middlebrook's *The First Day on the Somme*.[65] His orders were to take his platoon and make for Lonely Trench, his objective. Crossing No Man's Land he "could hear bullets whistling all around him but, heeding his instructions, he kept going and did not bother about those behind him. As he reached the German wire he could see that it was well cut and in the German front line trench he could see only one of the enemy".[66] One of Howe's platoon shot the German and the advance continued. Within half an hour, he and his men, the remnants of two platoons numbering around twenty, made it into Lonely Trench, which they found was deserted. "Of the rest of the battalion there was not a sign".[67]

By midday, Howe's little group were in dire straits. Howe had been wounded by a bullet through the palm of his right hand. They were short of ammunition, many of the men were wounded, and, with no sign of reinforcement from the rear, it was agreed that they would surrender once their ammunition was gone. Luckily, it was soldiers from 10/Yorks & Lancs who reached them first, and they were able to make their way back to the British lines along Lozenge Alley.[68] His story is corroborated by the 50 Brigade diarist who tells of "a junction [...] effected with the 21st Division on the left in Lonely Support trench but only by a detachment".[69]

By the time the third and fourth waves of the 10/West Yorks climbed out of their trenches, the Germans opposite the Tambour had had time to get their machine guns in place. The artillery screen across the Tambour position was "not intense enough to keep the enemy down in his shelters",[70] and, not being attacked frontally themselves, they were free to enfilade the Yorkshiremen crossing the open space to the north. They were annihilated. The commanding officer, Lieutenant-Colonel A. Dickson,[71] his Second-in-Command, Major J. Knott,[72] along with the Adjutant, Lieutenant J.W. Shann, were all killed very early in the attack: a few men made it into König Trench, but they were under enfilade fire from Fricourt and could move neither forward nor back. By two in the afternoon, German bombing parties were moving up König Trench from the south.

The 10/West Yorks suffered more casualties than any other battalion on 1 July 1916. The Official History puts the toll at 22 Officers and 688 Other Ranks.[73] One hundred and thirty-five of them now lie in Fricourt New Military Cemetery, located to the north west of the village, in what was No Man's Land.

The 7/Yorkshires, as noted above, were positioned directly opposite Fricourt village and were not scheduled to take part in the assault until higher command deemed it appropriate. At Battalion Headquarters, situated in a dug out at Fricourt railway station (see Map 9),

---

65   See pages 129-130, 144-145, 173, 202, 205-207, 241, 243, 268, 296, 298, 302, 303, 304, 311, 316.

66   Middlebrook, *First Day on the Somme*, pp.129-130.

67   Ibid, p.145.

68   For his exploits on 1 July, Howe was awarded the Military Cross. London Gazette 29724, 25 August 1916.

69   TNA PRO WO 95/1998: 50 Brigade HQ War Diary.

70   Ibid.

71   Lieutenant-Colonel A. Dickson, age 41, South Lancs Regt (attached 10/WYorks) is buried in Fricourt New Military Cemetery, grave reference C.12.

72   Major James Leadbitter Knott DSO is buried in Ypres Reservoir Cemetery next to his younger brother, Captain Henry Basil Knott, 9/Northumberland Fusiliers, who was killed on 7 September 1915.

73   JEdmonds, *Military Operations France & Belgium 1916*, Vol. I, p.357.

Lieutenant-Colonel A. Dickson, commanding 10/WYorks, kia 1 July 1916, age 41. (Author)

Fricourt New Military Cemetery. (Author)

Lieutenant-Colonel R. D'A. Fife awaited developments: Battalion Order No. 53 stated that "[the] 2nd stage of the attack […] will clear Fricourt village and Fricourt Wood in conjunction with 22nd Infty Brigade of the 7th Division. A 2nd Zero Hour for this assault will be ordered".[74] Fife was worried. His diary details his thoughts:

> It appeared to me that the key to the village of Fricourt was a salient, known as Wing Corner, opposite to the extreme right of our line. I knew that this salient held machine guns which could enfilade almost the whole of the front which had been allotted to our assault, and in front of our left centre was another salient, known as Wicket Corner, which could also bring enfilade machine gun fire to bear on our left as it advanced. Wing Corner was the nearest point to our line, and I formed the opinion that it was of the utmost importance to capture it first in order to silence the enemy machine guns. The method of the assault as ordered by the Higher Command was that, on leaving the trenches, the successive waves were to throw themselves flat on the ground and crawl forward behind the artillery creeping barrage until it lifted beyond the enemy's front trench, when the remainder of the intervening ground was to be crossed as fast as possible. […] We had of course practised crawling, and as far as I recollect had found that fifteen yards a minute for men in battle kit was fairly good going".[75]

---

74 TNA PRO WO 95/2004: Operation Order No. 53, 7/Yorks War Diary.
75 Quoted in Wylly, *The Green Howards in the Great War*, pp.219-220.

102   To Do the Work of Men

His fears of enfilade machine gun fire were to be proved right.

The 7/Yorks had moved forward into their front-line positions late on the evening of 27 June and had remained there under intermittent rain and enemy shell fire for the duration of the forty-eight-hour postponement of the attack. D Company, (Captain H.L. Bartram) the battalion reserve, was in Bonte Redoubt, approximately 1,000 yards behind the front line. B Company (Captain L.G. Hare) was in the support trenches, leaving C Company (Captain R.W.S. Croft) to man the front-line trench on the left, and A Company (Major R.E.D. Kent) similarly placed on the right. As the main assault went in on their left at 07.30, dense smoke hid the scene from the 7/Yorks men. It was only the rattle of enemy machine guns that told them that the 10/West Yorks were in action.

At around 09.00, Lieutenant-Colonel Fife received a disconcerting telephone message from B Company: for some inexplicable reason, Major Kent had led A Company in an assault on the enemy positions at 08.20.[76] The battalion war diary succinctly chronicles their fate:

> As soon as they began to climb over our parapet, terrific machine gun fire was opened up by the enemy and the company was almost at once wiped out.[77]

What remained of A Company huddled in shell holes in No Man's Land, able to move neither forward nor back amidst continued machine gun and rifle fire. Major Kent and Lieutenants David and Tenney were wounded. All they could do was wait until the second attack passed over them. All Fife could do was bring D Company up into A Company's previous front line positions and await the order to attack. The said order from Division arrived at one o'clock: an artillery barrage would begin at 14.00 and the men would attack half an hour later.

The promised barrage was, according to the 7/Yorks diarist, "feeble".[78] The efficacy of the bombardment was hampered by the knowledge that A Company survivors were still lying out in No Man's Land and subsequently the German trenches suffered very little damage, the wire remaining largely intact.

Nevertheless, D, B, and C Companies went over the top at the appointed time and "were literally mown down and were finally brought to a standstill about half way across to the enemy's trenches".[79] Some of the handful of survivors found a little protection in a ditch, but it had only taken around three minutes for the battalion to suffer over three hundred casualties, including thirteen of their officers. From where Lieutenant-Colonel Fife was, he could not see what was happening to his men, but from what he could hear "it was evident that the assault was under enfilade fire from both flanks and that it would be a miracle if it succeeded against such a storm of bullets".[80] His earlier fears had materialised.

---

76   The actual timing of the assault is uncertain: Wylly, quoting Fife's diary and 50 Brigade War Diary, gives the time as 08.20. The battalion war diary and the official history record the assault as going in at 07.45. Kent was later promoted Lieutenant-Colonel and was killed leading the 4/Yorks on 27 May 1918 near Craonnelle on the Chemin des Dames.. He is commemorated on the Soissons Memorial.
77   TNA PRO WO 95/2004: 7/Yorks War Diary.
78   Ibid.
79   Ibid.
80   Wylly, *The Green Howards in the Great War*, p.221.

Green Howards Memorial, Fricourt British Cemetery. (Author)

104   To Do the Work of Men

It was initially proposed that a second attempt be made to assault the German trenches, but Fife, with the agreement of the brigadier, decided that enough lives had been wasted already.

The battalion was relieved by 6/Dorsets that evening, by which time many gallant deeds by the survivors to bring in their wounded had been witnessed, Captain Harper, the Medical Officer, and Reverend Potter being worthy of special mention.[81] Casualties had indeed been heavy. A Company's inexplicable blunder had left only thirty-two unwounded from the 140 who had gone over the top. B Company lost seventy out of 160, C Company ninety-seven out of 177. D Company's losses numbered sixty-one out of 130.

In all, five Officers were killed, and ten wounded. Other Ranks casualties totalled 336. Ninety-three of their dead lay near their battalion memorial in Fricourt British Cemetery.

At this point in the narrative we must return to those men who had made it across the Fricourt Spur and had fought their way into the Sunken Road to the north of the village. A thoroughly mixed force comprising all four battalions of 64 Bde were doing their best to consolidate the positions in the Sunken Road. Lieutenant Gordon, the most senior officer remaining of 9/KOYLI, had come across a large German dug out, which had been a battalion headquarters, in the forward bank of the road. It was about twenty-five feet deep and consisted of several rooms. Gordon found some cigarettes and, more importantly, a substantial store of sparkling mineral water, which he immediately began to distribute to the men who were extremely thirsty: the day had turned out very hot and sunny.

The Sunken Road was, of course, not the ultimate day's objective, so the question now arose: what to do next? The senior officer present, Lieutenant-Colonel Fitzgerald of 15/DLI, along with the small number of officers from the other battalions still able to continue at duty, were doing their best to reorganise their men and find some protection against the enfilade machine gun fire that was coming from German positions on the left in Birch Tree Wood and the right in Fricourt village.

What no-one in the Sunken Road knew at that time, was that a mixed force of KOYLIs, Durhams and East Yorks under Second-Lieutenant A.E. Day, 9/KOYLI, was already two hundred yards in front in Crucifix Trench. Day, already wounded in the leg by shrapnel while crossing No Man's Land, had clearly reached the Sunken Road before anyone else and had pressed on immediately to find Crucifix Trench unoccupied. Crucifix Trench, being a subsidiary line, was not very deep, had no dug outs and had in any case been badly knocked about by the British artillery barrage. The position was a precarious one.

News back at 64 Bde headquarters was somewhere between sparse and non-existent. At around 07.50, Brigadier-General Hugo Headlam sent Captain Harold Yeo – now a staff officer – forward to find out what he could about the situation ahead. Half an hour later, he had still not returned, so Headlam decided to move his headquarters forward and set off, accompanied by his Brigade Major, Major Graham Bromhead Bosanquet, and followed by the brigade signallers who were doing their best to lay a telephone line. As his party crested the Fricourt Spur – he was moving across the open, not along trenches – he became aware that "there were no British troops on [his] left".[82] He continues:

---

81   Ibid, p.222.
82   TNA PRO CAB 45/134. Hugo Headlam correspondence to the official historian, 3 March 1930.

Consequently I was nervous about my left flank & seeing some parties of my men in groups in a communication trench (I think it was called Patch Alley) leading to sunken road, I tried to organise them & ordered them to face north & guard left flank.[83]

Headlam had noticed a party of about 100 men from what he assumed to be 34th Division retiring from the vicinity of Round Wood and feared that a German counter attack was either in progress or imminent.[84] At the eastern end of Patch Alley he came across some men of 34th Division and ordered them also to form a defensive flank facing north.[85] He arrived at the Sunken Road with Major Bosanquet and his artillery liaison subaltern to find the consolidation in progress.[86] Still worried by the situation on his brigade's left flank, Headlam despatched Captain Bevan of the Machine Gun Company with orders to get some of his guns into Round Wood. He then, with Bosanquet, rounded up a small party and advanced in the open towards the northern end of Crucifix Trench, "with the idea of passing over it and getting Birch Tree Wood while it was still possible to do so".[87] It was an ill-fated move: "a German machine gun suddenly popped up and loosed off a belt which did in most of the party".[88] Headlam was forced to beat a hasty retreat back to the Sunken Road. Here, he found Lieutenant-Colonel Fitzgerald in the large German dugout, who informed him that he had sent Lewis Gunners to the northern edge of Lozenge Wood to secure their right flank. Headlam's mind was still focussed on the brigade's left flank, however, and he sent Captain Willis of 1/East Yorks "to see to the consolidation of Round Tree (sic) Wood and the left flank generally".[89]

By this time there was no sign of the signallers who had gone forward from headquarters with their telephone line, so Headlam sent a runner back to Brigade HQ with a written situation report for transmission from there by telephone to Major-General Campbell. At around ten o'clock, having received neither reply nor new orders, and leaving Lieutenant-Colonel Fitzgerald in charge, Headlam set off back to his brigade headquarters in the old British front line. He arrived there about half an hour later and was able to speak to Campbell on the telephone. His original message had not yet arrived – it reached Brigade HQ around half an hour after he did. In response to Headlam's report, Campbell said that he would send forward units of 62 Bde to form proper defensive flanks.

---

83 Ibid.
84 TNA PRO WO 95/2159: 64 Brigade HQ War Diary.
85 He mistook them for Tyneside Scottish. They were more likely to have been 15 or 16/Royal Scots.
86 In his letter to the official historian, Headlam states that at this point Lieutenant Day returned from Crucifix Trench to report to him that it was in British hands. This would seem to be a lapse in memory after fourteen years: in his own account in the 64 Bde War Diary written on 6 July 1916 he makes no mention of this meeting and the 9/KOYLI war diary reports that Day sent word back to Lieutenant Gordon from Crucifix Trench regarding his situation at around midday. By that time, Headlam had returned to Brigade headquarters.
87 TNA PRO WO 95/2159: 64 Brigade HQ War Diary.
88 TNA PRO CAB 45/134. Hugo Headlam correspondence to official historian, 3 March 1930. Major Graham Bromhead Bosanquet MC was killed in this attack. He is buried in Gordon Dump Cemetery, grave reference IV.H.10.
89 TNA PRO WO 95/2159: 64 Brigade HQ War Diary. In his correspondence with the official historian in 1930, Headlam suggests that Willis ought to be mentioned in the official narrative. He is not.

Even then, confusion ensued. The original order placing one battalion at Headlam's disposal for use on his left flank, confirmed by wire at 11.30, was an hour later altered by a further wire which stated that 34th Division was now advancing through Peake Wood and that the reserves should be used on the right flank. Eventually, two battalions were sent forward, the 1/Lincolns to occupy a position in the Sausage Support system, and the remainder of 10/Yorks to the aforementioned right flank position. In the end, due to 1/Lincolns blocking Aberdeen Avenue, a communication trench in the British front line system, for some inordinate amount of time, the Yorkshire unit was not able to reach their intended positions until around half past six in the evening.

In the meantime, the men in Sunken Road were now aware that Lieutenant Day's party in Crucifix Trench was in dire need of reinforcement. Orders came from Brigade at 13.30 to attack from the Sunken Road and take Crucifix Trench and an artillery barrage was promised. The order arrived too late for the barrage to be of any use, if indeed any proper barrage occurred: some accounts do not mention any artillery support. Nevertheless, the men advanced at the double in three waves across the two hundred yards or so of open ground under the three remaining 9/KOYLI officers, Lieutenant Gordon and Second-Lieutenants Ellenberger and Frazer, and made it to their objective. Gordon managed to establish something of a headquarters near the crucifix and sent out bombing squad and machine guns to cover both flanks. By this time, Second-Lieutenant Day's leg wound was threatening to incapacitate him totally if he did not receive medical attention, but he refused to go back until directly ordered to do so by Gordon. Frazer had also received a head wound and was forced to go back for treatment.

The 15/DLI had also received orders to continue their advance, this time towards Shelter Wood, with the ultimate aim of reaching Quadrangle Trench. The attack failed to reach either objective. The 15/DLI diarist recounts events:

> Parties accordingly pressed on in this direction and two parties in particular deserve special mention – one under 2nd Lieut F.J. Cartman and one under 2nd Lieut A.S. Morley who both reached positions between 30 and 40 yards from the edge of the wood. The smallness of their numbers made it impossible for them to proceed further so they took up a precarious position in shell-craters and proceeded to snipe any of the enemy who showed themselves. One incident in connection with this is worthy of note – Capt D.J. Ely though wounded slightly in the foot pressed on with his men towards Shelter Wood. He showed a magnificent example to his men and until his death by a sniper's bullet he was full of enthusiasm and courage. That sniper's time was short. One of our men – Pt J.Jolley saw him. They saw each other and fired. The German's bullet grazed Jolley's nose. Jolley's bullet struck fair and square in the head. A second bullet in the same place completed the work of NEMESIS.[90]

Captain Ely's role in the assault is described in more detail in a short book commemorating his life:

> 'Ely was splendid', said the colonel that night, as he lay severely wounded in a dug-out captured from the Germans. 'He was out on the top, running about getting his men along,

---

90   TNA PRO WO 95/2161: 15/DLI War Diary. Curiously, the last sentence is crossed out in the original document but remains legible.

and treating the shells as so much dirt.' The company, in strength little more than a platoon, was thinned out by machine gun fire from the beginning, and the task set them proved to be too hard, the enemy being strongly posted and commanding all the approaches. They had advanced up the slope to within fifty yards of the wood when their captain was shot through the head by a sniper, and fell into a shell-hole, where he died almost immediately in the presence of one of his subalterns who had followed him. The Germans tried to reach them in the hole but were held off by gun-fire; and after lying there for many hours the lieutenant escaped with one man under cover of darkness. 'It was a splendid charge,' writes a lance-corporal, 'and I assure you that no-one could die a more noble death than Captain Ely'.[91]

Captain Dennis Herbert James Ely, 15/DLI kia 1 July 1916.

At around five in the afternoon, it was reported to 15/DLI's commanding officer, Lieutenant-Colonel Fitzgerald, in the deep German dug out in the Sunken Road, that the Germans had been seen massing on the left flank between Shelter Wood and Round Wood, presumably with the intention of counter attacking. The 15/DLI diarist again continues the story:

> The C.O. hurried out to supervise arrangements to meet them. Machine guns and bombers were moved up to the left. A party of about 300 Germans actually did appear on the left but were mowed (sic) down by our Lewis Gunners. It was while supervising these arrangements that the C.O. was wounded – a M.G. bullet striking him full in the leg about half way between the knee and the thigh. [?] It was roughly dressed there and then and he was carried back to his headquarters in Sunken Road – a place of only tolerable safety. He refused to be carried downstairs as this would mean moving a badly wounded man from the only stretcher on (sic) the place. He stayed here – tended by his servant – until it was possible to remove him – nearly 14 hours later.[92]

---

91 Anon., *Dennis Ely: Captain, Durham Light Infantry* (Oxford: Frederick Hall, 1916). The author of the work is unclear, and it has to be said that the account would appear to be (typical for the period) rather over-romanticised. Although it is mentioned in the book that Ely was buried in Fricourt the day after the attack, his grave must have been subsequently lost, as he is commemorated on the Thiepval Memorial.

92 TNA PRO WO 95/2161: 15/DLI War Diary. Lieutenant-Colonel Fitzgerald was evacuated to England but died in hospital in London. He is buried in Twyford (The Assumption) Churchyard in Buckinghamshire. Commonwealth War Graves Commission records give his date of death as 11 July 1916. On his headstone, it is given as 13 July 1916, as stated on the CWGC Grave Registration Form.

The situation had begun to settle down on 21st Division front and word was sent out that 62 Bde units were to relieve the men currently in the front-line positions. With officer casualties having been so severe, battalions had ordered forward officers who had been left out of the initial assault. At around 16.15, Lieutenants L.D.Spicer and B.H.L. Hart,[93] and Second-Lieutenants W.F. Keay, H.F. Kingston and W.W. Shepherd of 9/KOYLI started their trek up to the front line. It was to take them until 19.00 to reach their destination in the Sunken Road. There, Spicer was directed to the old German dug out by CSM Warren, whom he stumbled across digging himself into the bank:

Lieutenant-Colonel Arthur Edward Fitzgerald, age 44, commanding 15/DLI. Died of Wounds 11 July 1916. (*Harrow Memorials of the Great War*)

> This was approached by a covered entrance, which had been converted into a temporary dressing station. It was very difficult to get in without treading on the wounded [...] standing on top of the stairs, I called down to Gordon. A long white figure rose from down the steps, and uttered in fervent tones: 'Is that you, Spicer, is that you? Thank God, thank God.'[94]

Captain Santar of 10/KOYLI had relieved Gordon in Crucifix Trench during the afternoon and the latter had been able to make his way back to the dugout. Santar was also later wounded in the chest and forced to go back. With Ellenberger also coming back to the Sunken road to receive orders, this left RSM Crossland in charge of the men in Crucifix Trench until Lieutenant Hart was sent forward to impart the welcome news of the relief. Gordon, in the meantime, had made his way back to the Regimental Aid Post, a long, exhausting and eerie walk back across the battlefield. The doctor cleaned up his wound and gave him an enormous whisky and soda, telling him to get some sleep. Gordon was content to do as he was told and found a space on the floor. Major Johnson, now in command of 15/DLI, was also happy to see reserve officers of his battalion arrive to bolster both numbers and morale. He was able to lead his men out of the trenches at around midnight.

---

93 Basil Liddell Hart, the celebrated military historian.
94 Spicer, *Letters from France 1915-1918*, pp. 61-62.

Captain Willis had been in charge of 1/E.Yorks operations since early in the morning when Lieutenant-Colonel Stow had received his fatal wound. Major Saunders, along with Lieutenant Marshall and Second-Lieutenants Eames, Benson, and Stockham arrived at 19.30 to ready the survivors for relief. Delays meant, however, that the relief was not completed until 06.30 the following morning.

The 10/KOYLI diarist, with customary brevity, merely states that the battalion, now under the command of Major F.B. Laskie, was relieved by 1/Lincolns and moved to Sausage Support Trench.

The 21st Division Headquarters Diary sums up the positions of its units at 10 p.m. on 1 July as follows:

> 50 Bde: the 7/Yorks and 10/West Yorks had been relieved and moved back into reserve positions. The 6/Dorsets and 7/East Yorks had been moved forward and were holding the original front line trenches.
>
> 63 Bde: 4/Middlesex were largely in Empress and Empress Support Trenches.
>
> 10/Yorks & Lancs and 8/Lincolns were in Lonely Lane, Lonely Trench and Lozenge Alley.
>
> 8/Somerset LI were in Lozenge Wood.
>
> 62 Bde: 10/Yorks and 1/Lincolns were, right and left respectively, in Lozenge Wood, and thence strung out along Crucifix Trench as far as Round Wood, where they had established touch with 34th Division.
>
> 12/Northumberland Fusiliers were moving forward into the Sunken Road, while their sister battalion was on its way up to Brandy Trench.
>
> 64 Bde: the 9 & 10/KOYLI were moving back into South Sausage Trench and South Sausage Support.
>
> 15/DLI and 1/East Yorks were moving back to positions in the original British Front Line.
>
> The movements of 62 and 64 Bdes were not complete until 06.00 on 2 July.[95]

The 2 July was a day largely occupied by consolidation and adjustments in battalions' positions so as to prepare for further action on the 3rd. The 64 Bde had a mostly quiet and uneventful time. The 1/E. Yorks, however, were notified around midday that some of the trenches to their left, in and around Sausage Redoubt, were still occupied by a force of German troops whose presence was "endangering our communications", and were required to send a patrol to "clear up the situation".[96] A bombing party was accordingly dispatched under Second-Lieutenant Eames to reconnoitre the position, but in encountering a larger than anticipated number of Germans, Eames was killed.[97] The Germans were eventually subdued by men of the East Lancashire Regiment and a defensive flank was subsequently established by C and D Companies of the East Yorks under Captain Hawkesworth.

---

95   TNA PRO WO 95/2130 War Diary 21st Division, 'Operations carried out by 21st Division, July 1st – July 3rd 1916.'

96   TNA PRO WO 95/2161 War Diary 1/East Yorks.

97   Second-Lieutenant Arthur Horwood Eames is commemorated on the Thiepval Memorial. His date of death is recorded erroneously as 1 July 1916.

110   To Do the Work of Men

63 Bde units were also able to consolidate and reinforce their positions: 4/Middlesex's Lewis Gunners were able to harry any German soldier in Fricourt brave or foolhardy enough to break cover but remained in previously gained positions. A sad postscript to their involvement at Fricourt occurred early in the morning of 3 July as a grave was being dug for their officer casualties, whose bodies had been recovered during the hours of darkness: a single German shell landed in a trench killing Second-Lieutenant Barnett, Sergeants Millwood and Prosser, and killing or wounding around thirty Other Ranks.[98] This, and a move to Lozenge Alley at around noon, meant that the burials were unable to take place.

8/Somerset LI and 10/Yorks & Lancs were moved into positions during the day so as to be ready to support an attack planned for the following morning. An 8/Lincs patrol found Red Cottage and Fricourt Farm to be empty.

The battalions of 62 Bde in reserve, 1/Lincolns, three companies of 10/Yorks and the 12 & 13/Northumberland Fusiliers had been originally detailed as carrying parties for the attacking battalions of the division. As 3 July dawned, they were soon to become the main players in the continuing efforts to encircle and capture Fricourt. Original orders for the attack had been sent on the evening of 2 July, but these were very quickly countermanded and at 05.30 on the 3rd, orders to attack Birch Tree Wood and Shelter Wood were received. Zero Hour would be 09.00.

The battalions were arranged as follows: 1/Lincolns, who were to spearhead the assault, were in Crucifix Trench between Round Wood and its junction with Patch Alley. To their right, extending as far as Lozenge Wood, were men of 10/Yorks. The 12/NFus were in the Sunken Lane, with the 13/NFus back in Sausage Support Trench. The objective was a trench running along the northern edge of the woods, as far as the light railway line (See Map 9).

An intense artillery bombardment of the two woods began at 08.40, five Stokes Mortars positioned in Crucifix trench joining in at 08.58. Fire support was also given by 10/Yorks and 62 Machine Gun Company, and at exactly 09.00, with A and B Companies in the front wave, left and right respectively, "[the] leading platoons [of 1/Lincs] left the trench to rush the enemy".[99] As they crested a low ridge in front of the woods, they came under heavy machine gun fire, A Company suffering particularly badly. C Company was immediately rushed forward to maintain the attack's momentum, but B Company "were more fortunate and reached the objective without serious loss".[100] D Company moved up to support them and consolidation of the newly-won position began. A Company had managed to reach the edge of the trees, but the Commanding Officer, Lieutenant-Colonel Grant, had been seriously wounded in the head. To add to their troubles, their left flank was quickly found to be under threat from a German counter attack. Bombers managed to hold the Germans back until a company of 12/N Fus was sent forward at about 09.15: the enemy bombing party at this point seemed to lose heart and were soon taken prisoner. The Lincolns were now able to get through the wood but discovered that they were suddenly threatened from the rear by troops emerging from dug outs that had been bypassed in the rush to get forward. "Bombing parties were sent [back] to deal with these and the enemy, who put up a stubborn

98   Second-Lieutenant Phillip Barnett and Sergeants Millwood and Prosser are buried in Gordon Dump Cemetery. The Sergeants' dates of death are both incorrectly recorded as 1 July 1916.
99   TNA PRO WO 95/2154: 1/Lincolns War Diary.
100 Ibid.

resistance, suffered heavily".[101] The woods were clear by 14.30 – but only after two squads of bombers from 13/N Fus had been thrown in to clear the north-west corner of Shelter Wood – and at this point "the enemy surrendered in large numbers, 600 giving themselves up in Shelter Wood".[102] The position was now secure in the centre and on the left. The right flank had been protected only by a machine gun barrage, but 10/Yorks were able to move forward and occupy 250 yards of trench stretching south-eastwards from the eastern corner of Shelter Wood. Here, they were able to gain touch at around 18.30 with troops of 7th Division. Troops of 51 Bde had been able to capture Railway Alley at 11.30 and one company of 7/Border Regt entered the western part of Bottom Wood. As they pressed on to capture the rest of the wood, they encountered 21/Manchester (7th Division) who had occupied the eastern end, having met no opposition. The encirclement of Fricourt was complete.

The 1/Lincolns were relieved by 12/N Fus and withdrew to the Sunken Road. The war diary was able to claim 700 prisoners, including a battalion commander, but also had to count the cost of the day's action. It recorded three Officers and 34 Other Ranks killed, six officers and 191 Other Ranks wounded, with nine missing. Fatalities can be confirmed at 68.[103] The 21st Division had played its part. By the morning of 4 July, its units had been relieved and were busy entraining at Dernancourt, just to the south-west of Albert, bound for Ailly-sur-Somme.

The first day of the Somme is rightly remembered for the huge losses suffered by the British Army. It is also often forgotten that, in spite of the losses, a number of the attacks met with a certain degree of success. The 21st Division's involvement belongs in the latter category. The village of Fricourt was surrounded, as planned,[104] and subsequently occupied without a fight. On the right wing of the assault, the 7th, 18th and 30th Divisions captured their initial objectives, including the villages of Mametz and Montauban; to their right, the French Army made substantial gains. To the north of the Fricourt Spur, however, the picture is bleak.

An accurate figure for 21st Division manpower losses between 1 and 3 July is impossible to calculate. Fatalities for these days can be ascertained through the record of Commonwealth War Graves Commission burials, but later losses resulting from soldiers who died of wounds or from those on the 'missing' list who were later confirmed as dead, can only blur the figures. Any attempt to produce an 'exact' figure immediately invites challenge – the author therefore makes no such claim – and the figures below must be regarded as estimates. Estimates can still illustrate the scale of the cost of the enterprise.

The following table is based on figures given in the 21st Division A & Q diary[105] and by the 50 Bde war diarist:

---

101 Ibid.
102 TNA PRO WO 95/2151: 62 Brigade HQ War Diary.
103 Commonwealth War Graves Commission records.
104 Even if it did take longer than was anticipated.
105 TNA PRO WO 95/2135: 'Appendix A, Battle Casualties from midnight June 30th to midnight 3rd July 1916', 21st Division HQ War Diary.

112   To Do the Work of Men

	Killed		Wounded		Missing		Total	
	Off	OR	Off	OR	Off	OR	Off	OR
62 Bde[106]	8	126	41	639	–	146	49	911
63 Bde	34	224	29	929	3	330	66	1,483
64 Bde	38	200	53	1,056	7	597	98	1,853
Pioneers[107]	–	4	2	89	1	12	3	105
Div. Art.	1	1	3	15	–	–	4	16
Div. Eng.	1	3	1	48	–	8	2	59
Field Amb.	–	1	1	11	–	1	1	13
Div. Total	**82**	**559**	**130**	**2,787**	**11**	**1,094**	**223**	**4,440**
50 Bde[108]	16	337	21	626	2	187	39	1,150
Total	**98**	**896**	**151**	**3,413**	**13**	**1,281**	**262**	**5,590**
Overall Total:								**5,852**[109]

Accepting that the 50 Bde totals are probably slightly high, (this possibly negated by 62 Bde's limited involvement on 1 July), assuming that a battalion would go into action with around 25 Officers and 750 Other Ranks, and removing Artillery, Engineering and Field Ambulance figures, percentage casualty rates for infantry going into the attack can be roughly estimated at a frightening 80 percent for officers and 60 percent for other ranks. The cost had indeed been high.

Part II

By 11 July, the units of 21st Division, after a brief respite away from the Somme area, were back: 62 Bde was billeted in the village of Méaulte, just south of the town of Albert and 64 Bde was some two miles further to the south-west in Ville-sur-Ancre. Also billeted in Méaulte was 110 Bde, made up of the 6th, 7th, 8th and 9th battalions of the Leicestershire Regiment. It had been decided that 63 Bde, after its mauling on 1 July, should be taken out of the line and rested for some considerable time: on 7 July, the 110 Bde took its place in 21st Division, a move that was to prove permanent.[110]

Recruitment for the Kitchener battalions of the Leicestershire Regiment had begun in September 1914. Originally, the 6th Battalion was destined for 9th Division, the 7th earmarked for 15th Division, and the 8th and 9th were to become part of 23rd Division. On 12 April 1915, it was decided, however, that the 16th (Irish) Division, part of the Second New Army, should

---

106 Brigade totals include headquarters, trench mortar battery and machine gun Company figures.
107 14/Northumberland Fusiliers.
108 Includes 10/West Yorks and 7/Yorks only.
109 TNA PRO WO 95/1998: 50 Brigade War Diary. These figures include casualties sustained between 1 July and 11 July 1916.
110 In effect, 63 Bde and 110 Bde swapped places, with 63 Bde becoming part of 37th Division. Curiously, the 63 Bde had suffered fewer casualties than 64 Bde, but the former was nevertheless chosen for replacement.

Officers of 9/Leics. Date unknown, but probably early 1915. (War Illustrated Vol. 8)

be replaced. The 44th Division was chosen, renumbered 37th, and its Infantry Brigades became the 110th, 111th and 112th. The four Leicestershire battalions were gathered together in 110 Bde and joined the rest of the division at Perham Down Camp on Salisbury Plain at the end of the month.[111]

Training ensued, and the men guessed that an inspection by King George V on 25 June surely meant that embarkation for a foreign theatre of war could not be far away. Rumour favoured the Middle East, or perhaps Gallipoli, but they were destined for the Western Front.

The Leicesters disembarked from their troop ships in Boulogne during the night of 29 – 30 July 1915 and by mid-August were in Belgium, half-battalions being introduced in turn to trench routine in the front line near Kemmel. Seven days of gradual induction was followed by a move to the village of Mondicourt, just south of Arras. After another week's training, which sadly included an accident during a grenade-throwing exercise that resulted in the deaths of one Officer and eight Other Ranks, they took over French-held trenches facing Monchy-au-Bois. They spent several months in this sector, just to the north of Gommecourt, and battalions rotated in and out of the front-line positions, spending their 'rest' periods in the village of

---

111 For a detailed account of 110 Bde's activities prior to their joining 21st Division, see Matthew Richardson, *The Tigers, 6th, 7th, 8th & 9th (Service) Battalions of the Leicestershire Regiment* (Barnsley: Pen & Sword, 2000), pp. 45-116.

Berles-au-Bois. A very wet November and freezing weather in January meant that they had to endure very trying conditions and were no doubt very relieved to move back to Doullens in April, where they spent six weeks resting, cleaning up and training.

They were back in the trenches by the end of May 1916, occupying the line near Bailleulment, a short distance to the north of their previous positions. They were destined to miss the 1 July attack: the 7/Leicesters mounted a trench raid in the early hours of 29 June, four officers and seventy men attempting to divert German attention from preparations further to the south,[112] and on the day of the main attack 110 Bde was designated as reserve unit for 46th Division and was in the end not involved.

Orders for the transfer to 21st Division were received at 16.30 hours on 5 July and after breakfast on the 6th, the men were tasked with sewing the yellow insignia of their new parent division onto their tunics before setting out on the four-day march to Ailly-sur-Somme where they entrained for Méricourt. A final short march saw them arrive in Méaulte on the 11th. By the evening the brigade was in positions in the vicinity of Bottom Wood. They remained there, under intermittent German shell fire, for two days: the 9/Leicesters' War Diary records the deaths of Major A.W.L Trotter and Second-Lieutenant A.B. Taylor on 12 July,[113] along with the wounding of Second-Lieutenant H.F. King. Total casualties for the period 11 – 13 July are reported as three Officers and fifty Other Ranks. On 13 July, the Leicesters were back in Fricourt drawing rations and equipment in preparation for their role in the coming attack, their first major engagement.

Sir Douglas Haig met with Generals Joffre and Foch at three o'clock in the afternoon of 3 July to "discuss future arrangements".[114] Joffre was keen that the British make another attempt to capture the Thiepval heights, but Haig favoured developing the relative success of the right wing of the attack and pressing on towards the German Second Position between the villages of Bazentin-le-Petit and Longueval. Joffre initially flew into a rage and "ordered"[115] Haig to attack at Thiepval. Haig's diary entry continues, perhaps rather unkindly: "I waited calmly till he had finished. […] The truth is the poor man cannot argue, nor can he easily read a map".[116] Haig then reminded Joffre that he, Haig, was responsible for the actions of the BEF and pointed out calmly that the current situation favoured the Bazentin Ridge operation. Joffre eventually backed down.

On 8 July, Rawlinson, commanding Fourth Army, issued the preparatory orders for such an attack by four divisions, to be launched on the morning of the 10th. The timing was overly optimistic, however, as before this assault could go in, Fourth Army would need to edge its front line closer to the German Second Position, and this still required the capture of the village of Contalmaison, Mametz Wood and Trônes Wood. An initial assault on Contalmaison on 7 July

---

112 The raid cost the 7/Leicesters one officer and two men killed. Twenty-eight men were wounded.

113 Major Alexander William Lewis Trotter, age 46, is buried in Dantzig Alley British Cemetery, Grave III H 8. Second-Lieutenant Arnold Bradley Taylor, age 22, is commemorated on the Thiepval Memorial. Two of his brothers, John William and Gerard Bardsley Taylor were also killed during the war. It appears that Second-Lieutenant Henry Frederick King died on 7 May 1917, aged 25.

114 Sheffield & Bourne (eds.), *Douglas Haig War Diaries*, p.198, Monday 3 July 1916 entry.

115 Ibid, p.198.

116 Ibid, p.198.

had failed, and it was not until the 10th that it fell to 23rd Division. 38th (Welsh) Division only completed the capture of Mametz Wood on 12 July after a costly struggle.

By then the plan had changed: Rawlinson and Congreve[117] proposed a simultaneous attack by XV and XIII Corps. The troops would assemble under the cover of darkness and attack at dawn. A five-minute 'hurricane' artillery bombardment would, it was hoped, lend the attacking troops the element of surprise. Haig was sceptical. His diary entry of 11 July sums up his thoughts:

> I am not quite satisfied with Rawlinson's plan of attack against Bazentin le Grand – Longueval. His proposal to attack at dawn over an open plateau, for 1000 yards distance, after forming up two divisions in mass in the dark, and this with a force of two divisions, appears to me a manoeuvre which one cannot do successfully against flags in time of peace![118]

He had suggested instead a more complicated plan: XV Corps would attack two hours before dark on 12 July, capture the two Bazentin villages and their eponymous woods, wheel to the right and continue their advance eastwards towards Longueval, whereupon XIII Corps would commence their advance from the south at daybreak on the morning of the 13th.

The dilemma was unresolved as the initial artillery bombardment began on the morning of 11 July and at a Fourth Army conference that afternoon, both Corps commanders, Congreve and Horne,[119] and all the divisional commanders expressed their preference for Rawlinson's plan. Preparations duly went ahead "in the general hope that the sanction of GHQ would yet be obtained".[120]

Haig was finally persuaded. Four divisions, 21st and 7th (XV Corps) on the left, and 3rd and 9th (XIII Corps) on the right, would assault the Bazentin Ridge at 03.25 on 14 July. 18th Division, on the extreme right, would complete the capture of Trônes Wood.[121] Hopes of French collaboration on the right wing were, however, dashed: the French commanders "were convinced that the dawn assault of Fourth Army stood no chance of success"[122] It had been assumed that the French XX Corps would attack south of Guillemont, but in the end the decision was taken that it should remain on the defensive.

It was a modest plan, initially, even if it did include the 2nd Indian Cavalry being on hand to gallop forward and seize High Wood should the opportunity arise after Longueval's capture. Rawlinson's ambitions quickly grew, however, as Z-Day approached: the Indian Cavalry, having taken High Wood, were then expected to push patrols out to the villages of Flers and Le Sars, some two to three miles beyond the wood. 1st Cavalry Division would then push on to Morval and Les Boeufs and would hold those positions until XV Corps arrived to relieve them. For once it was Haig who experienced doubts about the feasibility of the cavalry exploitation, even as Rawlinson's ambitions extended to the possibility of adding Pozières, Courcelette, Martinpuich and Guillemont to the list of distant objectives.

---

117 Lieutenant-General Sir Walter Norris Congreve, GOC XIII Corps 1915-17.
118 Sheffield & Bourne, *Douglas Haig War Diaries*, p.202. Entry for 11 July 1916.
119 Lieutenant-General Henry Sinclair Horne, GOC XV Corps January – September 1916.
120 Miles, *Military Operations France & Belgium 1916 Vol.II*. p.65.
121 See Map 11.
122 Miles, *Military Operations France & Belgium 1916*, Vol. II. p.67.

116   To Do the Work of Men

The exploitation phases of the attack would of course prove illusory, but its initial phase, the capture of the ridge, has been trumpeted as a crushing victory, even if Gary Sheffield sums up the day's action as "tantalizingly incomplete".[123] Its success is often attributed, at least partly, to the efficacy of the artillery bombardment. On a narrow two-corps frontage, Rawlinson had at his disposal two-thirds of the guns used in the whole 1 July attack:

> On 1 July, the British had shelled 22,000 yards of front and 300,000 yards of trench behind the front line. A fortnight later, the comparative figures were 6,000 and 12,000 yards. […] Every yard of German trench was subjected to 660 pounds of shell.[124]

This provided an intensity of fire five times greater than that achieved on 1 July.[125]

The intensity of the bombardment, the achievement of surprise, and "sensible"[126] infantry tactics all proved crucial to the successful capture of the Bazentin Ridge. The orders issued for the attack by 21st Division HQ on 11 July are, particularly in comparison to those distributed a fortnight earlier, remarkably concise. The objectives are strictly limited: the first is the capture of the first two lines of German trenches (Flatiron and Forest trenches – see Map 12). Second is the capture of Bazentin-le-Petit Wood and the village itself. There is no mention of wider exploitation. A slight amendment to the first objective issued on 13 July also includes an encouraging report on the state of the German defences:

> Identifications obtained from prisoners shows [sic] conclusively that the enemy appears to be very disorganised. […]
> Many of the prisoners have owned to the fact that they have been hurried up to the front line and have had little or no idea of where they were going to and what they were to do.
> There seems little doubt that the German heavy guns have been withdrawn to positions further in the rear, but we must expect to meet a considerable number of machine guns, though it is hardly probable that the emplacements will be so strong as those which we have met with in the front line system. […]
> Our heavy and field artillery have been very successful with their fire on the German 2nd Line during the last two days. We may, therefore, confidently assume that the enemy are not in the same fighting form as they were on the 26th June and will probably not fight so well as they did on the 1st July.[127]

It was to be the newcomers to the division that would lead the assault. They would line up along the northern edge of Mametz Wood on the night of 13/14th July, D Company of 8/Leicesters on the left, 7/Leicesters in the centre and 6/Leicesters extending their line beyond the wood on the right flank (See Map 12). The rest of 8/Leicesters and 9/Leicesters were in support, ready to consolidate captured positions. The 1/East Yorks (64 Bde) were originally placed at 110 Bde's disposal in order to protect their left flank, but this order was cancelled at the last minute, the

---

123 Sheffield, *The Somme*, p.83.
124 Ibid, p.83.
125 Prior & Wilson, *Command on the Western Front*, pp.191-192.
126 Sheffield, *The Somme*, p.83.
127 TNA PRO WO 95/2130 'Amendment to Order 00.59, 13 July 1916, 21st Division HQ War Diary.

job of flank guard reverting to the 8/Leics. 62 Bde would be in support in Mametz Wood and 64 Bde in reserve near Bottom Wood. It fell to D Coy, 9/Leics, to form carrying parties on the day before the scheduled attack in order to establish forward dumps of large numbers of Mills bombs:

> "Our task – a dangerous one – for the day was to carry at least 80,000 Mills Bombs from Rose Dump and establish two new dumps as nearly as possible in the rear of the front firing line. Needless to say, the Huns were shelling all the approaches to stop the passage of all supplies as far as possible. Luckily, the old German light railway was still intact, but farther onwards it was so knocked about by shell-fire that it was rendered useless. This part of the journey was fairly safe, as the railway ran up a valley, so we experienced little difficulty in carrying the bombs from one point to another. At the second point we unloaded the trucks, unpacked the bombs, detonated them and placed them in bucket-satchels which were closed by strings, like a sponge-bag. When this had been done, we got to work in parties of 50 each, under an officer, and carried the bombs in these bags. Each man had two bags. As soon as the bombs were deposited, other parties of 50 were ready to carry them forward up the centre track in Mametz Wood. At the corner of the wood we came across a well-constructed German Artillery Observation Post – a tree, with ladders leading up to wooden platforms in three tiers – a good piece of work and construction, but now no longer belonging to the invaders of the fair land of Sunny France! [...] We spent the whole day carrying these bombs and establishing these dumps. We had no lunch, but we worked on, for the success of our attack of the morrow depended upon it".[128]

The assembly, though complete by 02.55 on the 14th, was not without difficulties: the 7th and 8th battalions came under heavy artillery fire as they advanced along the light railway that ran south to north through the wood, the former losing its commanding officer, Lieutenant-Colonel W. Drysdale on the way. The battalion war diary recounts the episode only briefly: "A number of casualties were suffered during this operation, one platoon of C Coy losing almost half its number. The men behaved admirably under trying conditions".[129] The battalion adjutant, Captain A.A. Aldworth, took over command. The 8th Battalion also came under fire: C Company's Lewis Gun team was knocked out on the way up to the assembly positions, but the first wave was in position 30 yards beyond the northern edge of the wood by 02.15, only to come under hostile artillery fire thereafter. By zero hour, D Company had moved forward some 200 yards further forward. With their "raiders and bombers"[130] out ahead, some distance ahead of the first wave, they were ready to race for the German parapet as soon as the whistles blew. C Company was positioned at the edge of the wood and B and A Companies were, respectively, in support behind 7/Leics and 6/Leics.

The assault would be made in four waves: 'A' wave would consist of twelve platoons of 6/Leics, and twelve platoons of 7/Leics, these in three lines of columns of platoons at thirty yards

---

128 Leicester Record Office DE8145/38. Lieutenant A C N March Phillips De Lisle, 'The Story of a Leicestershire Company in the Great Push' by 'One who was there'. An account of the actions of 'D' Company, 9th Battalion on the Somme, July 1916.
129 TNA PRO WO 95/2164: 7/Leics War Diary.
130 TNA PRO WO 95/2165: 8/Leics War Diary.

118   To Do the Work of Men

distance. 'B' wave, four platoons of each battalion, were to follow as soon as the first wave had gained the German front line, Flatiron Trench. 'C' Wave, made up of four platoons of the 8/Leics, would advance at Zero plus 60 minutes with 'D' wave carrying supplies close on their heels with orders to occupy Forest Trench. The first wave of the 8/Leics would secure the flank by occupying Villa and Aston Trenches, along with Left Alley (See Map 12).

By 03.15, the men of the first wave were in positions along tapes laid out earlier by 64 Bde. No reaction at this point by the German defenders gave them hope that the element of surprise was still theirs. The advance was to be uphill, across open ground, but by edging out one hundred yards or so beyond the northern edge of Mametz Wood, the Leicesters were hoping to win the race for the parapet. Dawn was just beginning to break as an avalanche of shells fell on the German Front Line trench at 03.20, "the whole sky behind the waiting infantry […] seem[ing] to open with a great roar of flame. For five minutes the ground in front was alive with bursting shell, whilst the machine guns, firing on lines laid out just before dark on the previous evening, pumped streams of bullets to clear the way".[131]

At 03.25, the first waves of the three battalions surged forwards. On the left, D Coy of 8/Leics immediately came under heavy machine gun fire from the German front line. Captain Ward, the company commander, was hit before he had gone many yards: indeed, "not a single officer of this Coy reach[ed] Villa Trench. The Coy was led by its NCOs".[132] Once the Leicesters had forced their way into Villa Trench, opposition crumbled and their Lewis Guns were able to wreak havoc amongst the retreating Germans. Dug outs were bombed and the men then pushed forward into Aston Trench, repeating the process before bombing their way westwards towards the left flank along both trench lines and forming blocks.

In the centre, the men of 7/Leics knew that the success of the attack – not to mention their survival – depended on the speed of their advance, aware of the need to "rush the first line before the enemy could man it".[133] The two flank companies fared best: D Company, on the left, encountered some machine gun fire, but was able to rush the German front line trench quite promptly, as were the men of A Company on the right. In the centre, German machine guns proved to be much more stubborn and much more effective and pinned down the men of B and C Companies for twenty minutes or so. It was not until bombers from the two flanking companies were able to work their way inwards and capture the machine gun positions that their comrades were able to complete their advance. By this time, the second and third waves came on and "swept the remainder of the first line with them and made for the second line, (Forest Trench)".[134] The war diarist continues the story:

> The first line trench at first made some resistance but many were caught in their dug outs, & the rest, seeing that they could not stop our rush, retreated into the Wood & made no resistance in the FOREST trench. By 4 a.m. our whole line was in occupation of FOREST trench and the work of consolidation was begun.[135]

---

131 Miles, *Military Operations France & Belgium 1916*, Vol.II. p.78.
132 TNA PRO WO 95/2165: 8/Leics War Diary.
133 TNA PRO WO 95/2164: 7/Leics War Diary.
134 Ibid.
135 Ibid.

Lieutenant Lionel Pilkington Abbott, 7/Leics, kia 14 July 1916, age 28. (Author)

120   To Do the Work of Men

The first objective had thus been gained, but the cost had been heavy: all the officers in D Company had become casualties and B and C Companies were down to one remaining officer each, respectively Second-Lieutenant Evans and Second-Lieutenant Reed. Captain A.A. Clarke was now commanding the battalion.

There was no time to rest on any laurels, however. CSM Geary was sent back to Flatiron Trench with a small party of men to ensure that it had been properly cleared of the enemy and "found a number […] who had been passed over in the rush".[136] In the meantime, D Coy had pushed forward on the left, but after running into the tail end of their own creeping barrage,[137] turned to the flank and established touch with the 8th battalion. Captain Clarke, leaving Evans in charge of the Forest Trench position, was ready to take his party of men forward at 04.25 to capture the next objective – the northern edge of Bazentin-le-Petit Wood.

On the right of the brigade frontage, the two companies on the left of the two leading waves of 6/Leics made it across No Man's Land with relatively little trouble. Those on the right suffered a good many casualties from German machine gun fire coming from Bazentin-le-Grand Wood on the right flank, as this area had not yet been cleared by 7th Division. On reaching the German front line, the 6/Leics found it "very much knocked about"[138] and were able to take a couple of dozen prisoners. Within five minutes, the third and fourth waves had swept through and, having charged two German machine gun posts situated in the south-east corner of the wood, killing the gunners and capturing the guns, had entered the German second line. "There were not a large number of Germans in second line when it was entered".[139] At around 04.00, leaving small parties in the German first line to deal with any enemy still in the dug outs, the men of the first and second waves went forward to join their compatriots in Forest Trench. Twenty minutes later, with three platoons remaining behind, the rest of the battalion went forward through the wood to the "One Hour Line" reaching it only after having once again come under enfilade fire from Bazentin-le-Grand Wood. Revenge was soon theirs, however: as 7th Division advanced, those Germans in Bazentin-le-Grand Wood began to retire across the open ground towards the village, only to suffer heavy casualties from the 6/Leics Lewis Gun teams. Particularly hard hit were those who mistakenly headed for Bazentin-le-Petit Wood, not realising at first that it was in British hands.

The barrage lifted from the "One Hour Line" and the men of 110 Bde were ready to continue the advance: their positions at this point were roughly as follows:

> 6th Bn Leic Regt on right and 7th Bn Leic Regt on the left in FOREST and FLATIRON trenches – D Coy 8th Bn Leic Regt in LEFT ALLEY, with blocks in ASTON and VILLA trenches – one company 8th Bn in support of D Coy in N. of MAMETZ Wood, immediately west of tramway. Two companies 8th Bn supporting the 6th and 7th Bns were lying in open ground East of MAMETZ Wood and in northern edge of MAMETZ Wood respectively. 9th Bn Leic Regt and 1st Bn E. Yorks in Reserve at SE end of MAMETZ

---

136   Ibid.
137   The barrage would still have been on the "One Hour Line" at this point. See Map 13.
138   TNA PRO WO 95/2164: 'Narrative of Action of 6th Leicestershire Regiment from 3 a.m. 14.7.16 to 8 a.m. 17.7.16', 6/Leics War Diary.
139   Ibid.

Wood. [...] About 4 a.m. touch was gained with the 1st Division at the SW corner of BAZENTIN-le-PETIT Wood.[140]

All three front line battalions were trying to push further forward through Bazentin-le-Petit Wood toward the "Two Hour Line" (see Map 13): on the left, C Coy and the first waves of A and B Coys of 8/Leics traversed the 450 yards of No Man's Land and entered the wood. C Coy moved up the western edge of the trees as far as Forest Trench and then conformed, as best they could, to the movement of 7/Leics on their right, bombing enemy dug outs in the wood as they went. The Battalion War Diary reports casualties "Due to enemy machine guns situated in the middle of the wood on platforms up large trees".[141]

A and B Coys advanced in support of the 7 & 6/Leics, moving eventually to the northern edge of Bazentin-le-Petit Wood, the German garrison retreating before them into the village. At about 05.00, the Battalion CO and Adjutant came up and established Battalion HQ in the south-west corner of the wood. It was about this time that the Germans counter-attacked along Aston and Villa trenches, launching bombs and rifle grenades as they advanced. This particular assault was halted and then driven back by bombing parties organised by Second-Lieutenant Alexander of C Coy, along with the CO himself, Lieutenant-Colonel Mignon. Both of these officers were killed.[142] The Germans contented themselves thereafter with launching rifle grenades at the British positions, this carrying on until around 14.30.[143]

The 7/Leics in the centre pushed onward with D Coy advancing a little too eagerly and being caught by the tail of the British artillery barrage. Being forced to retire temporarily, these men then turned towards the flank and established touch with the 8/Leics on their left. The rest of the battalion, under Captain Clarke, moved forward and encountered almost no resistance on their right flank. Those on the left came under machine gun and rifle fire from a nearby observation post and both Captain Clarke and Lieutenant Wakeford were hit. Captain Arthur Aubrey Clarke was later awarded the Military Cross for his part in this attack.[144] Now with no officers left in this assault, it fell to Sergeant Walker of A Coy and Lance-Sergeant Sherlock of C Coy to rally the men and lead them on to their objective. One party of 7/Leics, under Lance-Corporal Bush, in trying to outflank a German machine gun post, got lost in the trees and ended up bumping into a group of 6/Leics. Bush immediately "placed himself [and his men] under orders of an officer of that battalion".[145]

Sergeant Walker's men were determined to reach the northern edge of the wood and managed to rush a party of Germans in their trench. The Germans did not put up a fight and made to retreat towards the village. Caught between the advancing Leicesters and the British artillery barrage, however, and with nowhere to go, they gave themselves up. By 06.45, the 7/Leics were in position along most of the northern edge of Bazentin-le-Petit Wood and being reinforced by the

---

140 TNA PRO WO 95/2163: 110Brigade HQ War Diary.
141 TNA PRO WO 95/2165: 8/Leics War Diary. No other source mentions this phenomenon.
142 Both Lieutenant-Colonel Jepson George Mignon, age 46, and Lieutenant John Alexander, age 24, are commemorated on the Thiepval Memorial. The Commonwealth War Graves Commission records their deaths incorrectly as 15 July 1916.
143 TNA PRO WO 95/2165: 8/Leics War Diary.
144 Clarke was killed in action at Hooge on 1 October 1917. He is buried in Hooge Crater Cemetery, grave X.L.17.
145 TNA PRO WO 95/2164: 7/Leics War Diary.

rear waves of 8/Leics. Half an hour later, Captain Gwyther, now in command of the battalion, sent a party under Second-Lieutenant Evans to reconnoitre the north-western corner of the wood. He encountered an enemy strongpoint and took up positions facing it. The battalion war diary tactfully reports: "Possession of NW corner doubtful".[146]

It was once more time to take stock. The men were able to pause and rest for a short while but came under increasingly intensive German artillery fire as the time approached midday.

In the meantime, parties of 9/Leics had moved forward in support of their sister battalions: at around 08.15, Lieutenant-Colonel Haig, along with D Coy and half of C Coy, set off across No Man's Land into Bazentin-le-Petit Wood with orders to take over the western and north-western edges:

> We moved off in artillery formation. [...] The ground we stood on was literally ploughed up, and deep shell holes were sunk about everywhere, comparable only to a thousand miniature volcanic craters. We traversed the old Bosche front line. Here we saw a heap of dead resting in every possible grotesque position on or near the flattened-out trench, quite beyond recognition; a heap of discarded rifles, all twisted and torn by shell fire and by the violence of the fighting; a heap of battered dug-outs, in all forms of disrepair; and, finally, a most vivid picture of war was now visible – a machine-gun still pointing towards our lines with the Hun gunner still grasping, in the rigors (sic) of death, the traversing-handle of the gun.[147]

Captain David Westcott Brown 6/Leics, kia 14 July 1916, age 23, Thiepval Mem, BA Balliol, Oxford "One of the War Poets". (*Balliol College War Memorial Books*)

Lieutenant Arthur Shirley Bennett, 9/Leics, kia 14 July 1916. (*Rugby Roll of Honour*)

146 Ibid.
147 Leicester Record Office. DE8145/38. Lieutenant A.C.N.M.P. de Lisle. "The Story of a Leicestershire Company in the Great Push" by one who was there. An account of the action of D Company (9th Bn) on the Somme.

D Coy, under Lieutenant Nolan then drew the short straw and was directed to clear the remaining Germans out of the north-west corner. This failed attack cost Nolan his life.[148] Lieutenants de Lisle and Smith were wounded. Lieutenant de Lisle survived to write an account of the attack:

So as one man we are up and off, not knowing how far the enemy is ahead, but knowing that he is somewhere within the next hundred yards of wood right in front of us. We could only double about ten yards, for the wood was blocked by shell-split fallen trees; and other undergrowth is so thick that soon even walking is impossible: crawling is the only means of progress possible. Then the whole line halts and replies to the murderous hail of bullets still coming from unseen rifles. Once more we crawl forward, but only for a few dozen yards. For we come to an evacuated trench which we man and wait for the next burst of murderous rapid fire. We do not wait long. At first small in volume, it increases till the whole wood resounds with the deadly echo. Again our men are silently crawling forward until another shallow line of trench is encountered, and rapid fire is again opened in increased volume. We had now gone about a hundred yards from the road, so there was but another hundred yards for us to get the Huns out of the wood.[...] Then we yell out 'For God's sake stop this useless firing and go forward with bayonet and bombs.' [...] I get up to urge the men to stop firing; but almost as soon as I do so, I receive a bullet in my neck at close range. It penetrated deep and the blood gushed out. I fell downwards into a shell hole. One of the men quickly applied my first field dressings as tightly as possible to try and stop the bleeding, for it was bleeding fast. In fact, I thought my number was up, as it bled so hard.[149]

It was not until very late in the afternoon that the Germans were finally forced out of that sector of the wood, and this only after an attack led by the Brigadier, the Colonel and men from the Headquarters Staff: Quarter Master Sergeant D.A. Bacon described it in lurid detail in his personal memoir:

Accordingly, every available unwounded Officer and man [...] was ordered forward to the attack. [...] Our artillery opened with a heavy barrage on the enemy's position which was immediately answered by the enemy who fired promiscuously (sic) with Machine Guns and Trench Mortars from three directions; the din thus created was awful, bullets whistled and cracked at all elevations and angles, and one had literally to crawl or lie on the ground in shell holes to avoid them. Our positions were some 20 yards from the enemy and ran down the light railway for about 40 yards and then west through the wood. At a given signal rapid rifle fire was directed on the enemy for two minutes and then a charge was ordered; every man who got up was knocked down, wounded or killed immediately. Some minutes later this was repeated with the same result; it was Hellish – the men dropped like stricken sheep. The enemy were not in large force, but were concealed behind the brushwood and a bank, and well supplied with Machine Guns which they used to devastating effect. Finding that it was impossible to take the position by frontal attack, it was decided that stealth

148 Lieutenant William Henry Nolan is commemorated on the Thiepval Memorial.
149 Leicester Record Office. DE8145/38. Lieutenant A.C.N.M.P. de Lisle, 'The Story of a Leicestershire Company in the Great Push by one who was there' – an account of the action of D Company (9th Bn) on the Somme.

would have to be employed. To this end certain of the men were ordered to crawl within a few yards of the enemy and then rush him; this succeeded were (sic) bolder methods failed, but our casualties were exceedingly heavy. After hand to hand fighting for some thirty minutes and suffering severe loss, the position was captured together with many Machine Guns, while such of the Bosche as were able, retired to a trench some fifty yards in front of the Wood.[150]

Another ill-fated attack, this time led by Captain Emmet with forty of his men attempted to charge the German trench fifty yards to the north of the wood, but they were cut down by machine gun fire. Emmet and thirty-six of his men were killed.[151] Another later attempt to complete Emmet's mission also met with failure and at around 19.00 it was finally decided to consolidate the positions already held.

Captain Frederick Herbert Emmet, 9/Leics. Age 26, kia 14 July 1916.(*The Sphere*, 28 Oct 1916)

Our attention now moves to the right wing of the attack. The right-hand company of 6/Leics had been preoccupied with groups of Germans retreating from Bazentin-le-Grand Wood in face of 7th Division's advance and had remained in a defensive flank position along the eastern edge of the Bazentin-le-Petit Wood. Only at 05.20 did the battalion move forward to the "Two Hour Line", remaining there until 06.00 when they were reinforced by "several platoons"[152] of 9/Leics. Five minutes later they advanced towards Bazentin-le-Petit village. They should have had 7th Division on their right at this point, but these were still behind schedule and the 6/Leics assaulted the village alone. The battalion diarist makes little fuss of this excursion: "The whole village was assaulted and taken, and 3 Officers and some 200 prisoners".[153] Forty minutes later, the Royal Irish Rifles of 7th Division arrived in the village and the eastern sector (to the east of the Martinpuich road) was handed over to them.

At 08.30, a German counter attack pushed the Irish back as far as the cemetery and a nervous 6/Leics reformed their defensive flank. By 09.15 the situation had been restored by 7th Division reinforcements, however, and 6/Leics were able to consolidate their positions to the north of

---

150 Leicester Record Office. 22D63/146. D.A. Bacon MM, '110th Leicestershire Brigade, 21st Div. A Personal Account'.
151 Captain Frederic Herbert Emmet, age 26, is commemorated on the Thiepval Memorial.
152 TNA PRO WO 95/2164: "Narrative of Action of 6th Leicestershire Regiment from 3 a.m. 14.7.16 to 8 a.m. 17.7.16", 6/LeicsWar Diary.
153 Ibid.

the village once and for all. From here they were able to repel another German counter attack at around 15.00 with rifle and Lewis Gun fire.

By this time, the only objective still in German hands was the road running from the most northerly point of Bazentin-le-Petit Wood (S.8.a.1.3) to the northern tip of the village itself (S.8.a.8.6). Orders were received at 19.30 to capture this stretch, but persistently heavy machine gun fire from the left brigade flank persuaded commanders to cancel this attack. Other than two companies of 1/E.Yorks coming up into Bazentin-le-Petit Wood as support – and suffering casualties under both British and German artillery barrages – the day's work was done.

Both Bazentin woods were seized, along with the village which gave them their names, but any ideas of expansive exploitation had to be quickly forgotten. It is well documented that the Deccan Horse and 7th Dragoon Guards advanced against High Wood that evening,[154] but their gains could not be consolidated and the cavalry were eventually forced to withdraw. On the broader front, 6,000 yards of the German Second Position had been captured, including Contalmaison Villa, the Bazentins, most of Longueval and Trônes Wood. The formation of this new salient had cost the British somewhere around 9,000 casualties.

The final positions of 110 Bde troops are neatly described in tabular form in the Brigade War Diary. The diarist entitles it "Dispositions of Brigade at 11 a.m.", but it serves equally well for later in the day:

No. of Platoons of…	6/Leics	7/Leics	8/Leics	9/Leics	1/E.Yorks
Village of Bazentin-le-Petit, E. Portion of wood, N.edge.	16	4	2	5	
W. portion of Bazentin-le-Petit Wood, N. edge.		8	3		4
Operating near NW corner of Bazentin-le-Petit Wood		4		4	4
Western edge of Bazentin-le-Petit Wood			8		
Forest Trench			3	2	
Flatiron Trench				3	
Mametz Wood (various parts)					8
Carrying				2	

The action dragged on through the next two days. On the 15th July, 64 Bde were ordered to take up positions to the south of Mametz Wood and be ready to support an attack by 33rd Division, should the necessity arise. It didn't, but 10/KOYLI was required to go forward into Bazentin-le-Petit village, where General Hessey's (110 Bde) position was deemed less than stable. They arrived, with four machine guns, just before eleven in the morning, but found the village crammed with troops of 7th and 33rd Divisions. The Germans were shelling the village and casualties began to mount. The CO, Lieutenant-Colonel Bridge, decided that a withdrawal to positions south of the village would be advisable. Brigadier-General Headlam (CO 64 Bde) arrived at about that time and confirmed the withdrawal to trenches about a mile to the south.

---

154 See Miles, *Military Operations France & Belgium 1916*, Vol. II. pp. 84-87.

It became clear that a number of Germans were still ensconced in the strongpoint to the north of Bazentin-le-Petit Wood. Accordingly, at around nine o'clock in the evening, a party of 9/Leics was given the dubious honour of attacking it once more. The 110 Bde diary describes the subsequent failure of the attack in a matter-of-fact tone, stating that the entire party was either killed or wounded as they rushed the strongpoint. The 9/Leics diarist tells a slightly different story, but with a similar outcome:

> 2/Lt Sargeant and 20 men went to dig themselves in at NW edge of wood. They arrived at position but were isolated with a barrage of Rifle Grenades behind them and are believed to have been all killed or wounded.[155]

Orders arrived at 110 Bde HQ at around 23.00 on the 15th to the effect that the road running from the northern tip of Bazentin-le-Petit Wood to the northern end of Bazentin-le-Petit village (S.8.a.15.45 – S.8.a.8.7, see Map 12) was to be assaulted by 62 Bde, with one company of 1/E.Yorks in support. The attack, led by one company of 10/Yorks under Captain Crone and Captain Coater, went in at 02.15 on the 16th, with a bombing squad from 1/Lincs, and two hours later the brigade received a report that the "road had been seized and handed over to the 1st East Yorks R".[156] The Yorkshiremen's attempts to consolidate the position proved problematic: the one officer and fifty men came under enfilade fire from their left and were eventually reinforced by one platoon of the 9/Leics.

At approximately 14.00, it was decided that 110 Bde was to be relieved by 64 Bde. Accordingly, 10/KOYLI and 15/DLI were sent forward, the former allocated the north-eastern portion of Bazentin-le-Petit Wood, the latter to the western and north-western edges. Not surprisingly, there was a great deal of confusion as mixed up units tried to organise an orderly withdrawal, and the relief was not complete until 06.00 on the 17th.

Lieutenant Charles Frederick Wells Wait, 10/KOYLI, kia 15 June 1916, age 21. (england1418.wordpress.com)

---

155 TNA PRO WO 95/2165: 9/Leics War Diary. The following day, the 16th, a platoon under Second-Lieutenant Lee was dispatched to search for Sargeant's party but found no trace. Second-Lieutenant Arthur Percival Sargeant, age 20, is buried in Flatiron Copse Cemetery, grave XI.B.3. The Commonwealth War Graves Commission give his date of death incorrectly as 14 July 1916. This strongpoint was eventually taken at around 10.00 on the morning of 17 July, when reconnaissance revealed that the Germans had evacuated the position, allowing 15/DLI to occupy it unopposed.

156 TNA PRO WO 95/2151: 62 Brigade HQ War Diary.

As part of the relief, C Coy of 9/KOYLI was sent up on the evening of the 16th to occupy the old German front line trench system. In command was Lieutenant Basil Liddell-Hart. He recounts the events in his memoirs:

> The enemy's harassing fire was all the more unpleasant here because the shells often hit branches of trees and exploded with a shower of descending splinters. On the way I got a puncture in my right hand, but after having it bandaged had carried on, as only one other officer was left, and he was too inexperienced to take over. When two companies of another battalion eventually came up to relieve us, [on the 17th], my company was withdrawn and moved back to rejoin our own battalion. As we were passing through Mametz Wood in the dark we heard a lot of shells hitting the ground around us, but only with a faint 'plop' which suggested they had failed to explode. In a few moments there was a pervasive smell of gas. It was the first intimation that the Germans has started to use a lethal gas-shell filled with a new kind of gas, phosgene, more deadly although less painful than the chlorine gas first used in the war the year before. [...] I was coughing violently but stayed on the spot to warn and direct the platoons that were following, and then hurried on to catch the leading platoon at the rallying point and lead them all back to the battalion bivouac.[157]

Hart went to the nearest field ambulance to have the wound to his hand properly assessed and dressed. The doctor, noticing his breathing difficulties, examined his chest and sent him immediately to the Casualty Clearing Station at Corbie. He was soon back in King Edward VII's Hospital in London. His convalescence dragged on into 1917 and he never rejoined his old battalion.

By the evening of 17 July, 110 Bde units were on their way back to billets in the village of Ribemont, and 64 Bde was about to be relieved by 1/Middlesex and 1/4th Suffolk of 98 Bde, 33rd Division. The last units reached Méaulte at around 08.00 on the 18th.

On 16 July, Captain Harold Yeo and the rest of the 64 Brigade Staff had established their headquarters in a French chateau that had been, up to a few days ago, a German HQ. Yeo marvels at the excavations under the building:

> The Huns dig the most enormous dugouts for themselves; this one is three storeys down, two below the original cellar, and must be at least 30 feet down.

In the same letter to his mother, Yeo tells of an encounter with a German prisoner:

> I had quite an interesting talk with a young Hun officer, who had only been up in the line forty days, having been in Berlin before, passing his commission exam. There the talk was that the war was to end on August 17th. I asked him who said so and he pointed upwards, but whether he meant the Almighty or the Kaiser, I couldn't make out. I asked him who was to win by that date and he was rather bashful to say.[158]

---

157 Liddell Hart B.H. *Memoirs* (Cassell, 1965) pp. 25-26.
158 IWM Colonel H.E. Yeo MC Papers, Doc. 3132, correspondence to mother, 16 July 1916.

Captain Arthur Radclyffe Dugmore, 10/KOYLI. Author of *When the Somme Ran Red: The Experiences of an Officer of the King's Own Yorkshire Light Infantry During the First World War* (Barnsley: Pen & Sword reprint of 1918 edition) Dugmore was 44 years old when the war began, but nevertheless acquired a commission in the 10/KOYLI. He was gassed, probably in mid-July 1916, and was declared unfit for further duty. He wrote his memoir in 1917 and went on to be a celebrated naturalist, photographer, author and artist. By the time he published *Two Boys in Beaverland* (1920), he was Major A. Radclyffe Dugmore. He died in 1955. (IWM HU 118166)

The 14 July night assault is often written in histories as a crushing success; as an example of lessons learnt from the events of 1 July; as a blueprint for future assaults, the innovative artillery bombardment in particular being held up as a major step forward in the 'learning process'. Often omitted, however, are two obvious negatives: the failure of the exploitation phase, in particular the failure to capture and hold High Wood and Delville Wood which would prove very costly to those men who had to finish the job; the capture of the Bazentins and their eponymous woods had been very costly. Casualty figures were very high, particularly amongst officers. The diarist of 7/Leics provides a depressingly lengthy list of officer casualties, concluding initially that overall losses for the battalion came to 18 Officers and 535 Other Ranks. The 110 Bde diary gives figures for the period 12 to 17 July 1916:

	Killed		Wounded		Missing		Totals	
	Off.	OR	Off.	OR	Off.	OR	Off.	OR
6/Leics	5	55	20	362	2	76	27	493
7/Leics	14	72	6	309	–	147	20	528
8/Leics	3	57	13	278	1	95	17	430
9/Leics	8	47	9	294	1	52	18	393
110 MGC	–	4	5	16	–	4	5	24
110 TMBty	1	1	2	7	–	–	3	8
Attached, 14 – 16 July					Total		90	1,876
1/EastYorks	–	36	6	186	–	126	6	348

Calculations to show percentage casualties are problematic: the total number of men going into action is impossible to know. If one accepts an estimate of 27 officers and 750 men per battalion, the arithmetic throws up figures for the four assaulting infantry battalions as follows: Officers: 76 percent. Other Ranks: 61 percent. These figures could well be too low, but are nevertheless shocking. Matthew Richardson, in his book *The Tigers*, describes them as "truly appalling".[159] The relative success of an attack should always be assessed against the human cost.

By the close of July, 21st Division had been moved north into the Third Army sector. They would occupy trench lines near Arras until being returned to the Somme area on 13 September, in time to take part in the Battle of Flers-Courcelette.

Part III

The Battle of Flers–Courcelette, which opened on 15 September 1916, is today remembered for the debut of the tank. It was another attempt to force a breakthrough and reintroduce mobile operations beyond the trench lines that constituted, on this occasion, the German Third Position. The attack would involve five British corps of Fourth Army. The twenty-one divisions in the front line would punch through the German lines, thus allowing the Cavalry Corps to leapfrog and capture the town of Bapaume.

Writing to "C.G.S." on 29 August, Sir Douglas Haig, in a memorandum entitled "Notes on Sept. Offensive", was of the opinion that "a stage in the Battle is approaching when it will be possible to reap decisive results. […] Our general objective is the same as hither to – destruction of Enemy's field force, […] namely to break the enemy's front, advance on Bapaume at the same time widening the gap." The British would then "Pass through the gap and roll up the Enemy's lines of defence North Westwards towards Miraumont by operating against their front, flank, and (with a force of all arms) rear".[160]

Fourth Army GOC General Rawlinson, typically, had favoured a rather more measured, step by step approach, but the plan in the end reflected the Commander-in-Chief's usual optimistic stance. And as usual, the reality rendered the disagreement irrelevant – no breakthrough ensued.

On the left of the assault frontage,[161] the 3rd and 2nd Canadian Divisions, marking their first appearance on the Somme, attacked either side of the Albert – Bapaume Road and succeeded in capturing the village of Courcelette. To their right, Martinpuich fell to the 15th (Scottish) Division as their neighbours, the 50th Division, pushed on between the town and High Wood. The latter was the first objective of 47th Division, and Lieutenant-General Pulteney (III Corps) had decided that the front lines there were too close to risk an artillery bombardment and used tanks as a risky substitute. Against Tank Corps advice, he insisted that their machines enter the wood, which was by then reduced to a chaotic mixture of shell holes and tree stumps. Only one tank (D-13) made it into the wood, and the decisive factors in the wood's capture were a combination of hurricane trench mortar fire, the outflanking of the wood by neighbouring units

---

159 Richardson, *The Tigers*, p.129.
160 TNA PRO WO158/235: 'Notes on Sept Offensive', Sir Douglas Haig to CGS, (Sir William Robertson), 29 August 1916, Fourth Army War Diary.
161 See Map 14.

130   To Do the Work of Men

and the undaunted courage of the London Territorials. Their significant losses meant, however, that they were unable to push on any further than the wood's northern boundary, this leaving the New Zealanders on their right in a salient that extended beyond the village of Flers.

The assault on this village has become the most celebrated action of the day, with units of Major-General Lawford's 41st Division – which had only been in France for four months – reportedly marching up the main street, accompanied by Lieutenant Hastie's tank, D-17. They eventually reached and consolidated positions to the north and east of the village.[162]

To the right, the 14th Division was able to match the advance of 41st Division, whilst to their right, the Guards, with little or no help from the tanks allocated to them, made it halfway to their day's objective, the village of Lesboeufs. When the advance faltered under heavy enemy machine gun fire, Lieutenant-Colonel Campbell of 3rd Coldstream Guards managed to rally the men and led them onto their next objective, winning himself a Victoria Cross in the process.

On the far right flank of the attack, the 6th and 56th Divisions advanced against machine gun posts in the Quadrilateral redoubt that had not been suppressed by the artillery barrage and against uncut wire. They suffered heavy casualties and made only limited progress.

The 21st Division took no part in the fighting of 15 September 1916, spending the day some distance back in reserve in positions in and around Fricourt. That afternoon, 64 Bde was moved forward to Pommiers Redoubt and at 21.30 orders came in from XV Corps HQ requiring that one brigade of 21st Division be placed at the disposal of 41st Division to carry out an attack the following morning. The 41st Division, exhausted by their efforts on the 15th, needed fresh blood. That honour fell to 64 Bde. Divisional orders, issued at 23.45, stated, optimistically:

> The attack will be continued to-morrow on the GIRD LINE and GIRD SUPPORT LINE west of GUEUDECOURT between N.26.c.3.5 and N.19.d.9.4 to enable the cavalry to push through.
> The 64th Inf Bde has been placed under the command of the G.O.C. 41st Division to carry out the attack.
> The 14th Division will attack GUEUDECOURT and the N.Z. Division will form a defensive flank facing N.W.[163]

At about half past ten in the evening of the 15th, a motor car arrived at 64 Bde HQ and took Brigadier-General Headlam to 41st Division headquarters, where he was briefed on the forthcoming attack. He was back in his own headquarters by 01.00 and held a hastily convened conference of his battalion commanders in order to explain the situation – and the expectations – to them. The conference was evidently quite short, as by 01.30 Headlam was on his way forward once more, this time to meet with Brigadier-General Clemson (124 Bde) in York Trench, having left his Brigade-Major to "bring along the Brigade".[164] The men of 64 Bde finally moved off at around 02.10, "having six miles to cover in rain and darkness, over trenches, shell craters and other obstacles".[165]

---

162 For the real story, see Trevor Pidgeon, *The Tanks at Flers* (Cobham: Fairmile Books, 1995) pp. 163-179.
163 TNA PRO WO 95/2159/3: 64 Bde HQ War Diary. Note that the cavalry advance was still anticipated.
164 TNA PRO WO 95/2159: Report by Brigadier-General Headlam, 19 Sept 1916, 64 Bde HQ War Diary.
165 Miles, *Military Operations France & Belgium 1916*, Vol. II, p.346, fn 1.

General Rawlinson, commanding Fourth Army, had realised that the 15 September attack had lost impetus by the middle of that afternoon and knew that he would have to call on his reserve formations if any further progress was to be made. He, therefore, after a meeting with Sir Douglas Haig, issued orders that, with one or two exceptions where the line gained had to be "tidied up", no more advances would be attempted that day. Artillery would be brought up in readiness for a renewed effort on the morrow.

Orders for XV Corps, issued at 20.25, required only that the previous day's objectives, the Gird Trenches and the village of Gueudecourt, be captured. As previously mentioned, 14th Div, on the right of the Corps frontage, was to take the village, and 41st Div would be responsible for the capture of the two trench lines to the west of it (See Map 15). At 20.30, Major-General Lawford telephoned Corps HQ to report that he only had one battalion in the 41st Division that was in any fit state to prosecute an attack. Lieutenant-General Horne (XV Corps) therefore placed 64 Bde at his disposal.

The plans for 64 Bde's attack were relatively straight forward: one battalion was to be in place in Flea Trench (square N.31.b, see Map 15) by 06.00 hrs on the 16th, with a second in close support. The third battalion would be in Flers Trench, ready to send troops forward if requested, and the fourth was to be in reserve in Switch Trench. An artillery bombardment meant to cut the German wire would begin as soon as it was light enough for observation. At 09.15, a line of barrage would form 200 yards ahead of Flea Trench which would begin to creep forward at 09.25 (Zero Hour) at a rate of 30 yards per minute, the leading infantry close behind. Five tanks would assemble initially on the line of Flea Trench and then advance with the infantry. Later orders reduced this number to three.

More detailed orders issued at 05.10 on the 16th revealed that the leading assault battalions would be the 9/KOYLI, on the left, and 15/DLI on the right. 1/EYorks were to be the support battalion and 10/KOYLI would be back in reserve. As soon as the assaulting battalions moved forward, 1/EYorks would also advance and take up positions in Flea Trench. In turn, 10/KOYLI would subsequently occupy Flers Trench.

The advance of 64 Bde from Pommiers Redoubt to the jumping off positions was a difficult one, and the men arrived late on the battlefield:

> It is exactly five miles from POMMIERS to the FLERS Trench. The Brigade started at 2:10 a.m. It could hardly have started before this. Considering that it was raining, that it was hung up for half-an-hour in MONTAUBAN, and that the ground was slippery, it was good work for the leading Battalion to reach FLERS Trench by 5:45 a.m.[166]

At this point, there was some confusion as to where the 41st Division troops manning the front line actually were: an RE Officer of 124 Bde informed Headlam that they had been withdrawn from Flea Trench and were some 800 yards or so further back, to the east of Flers in squares N31.c & d. Headlam continues his report:

---

166 TNA PRO WO 95/2159/3: . After Action Report written by Brigadier-General Headlam on 19 September 1916, 64 Brigade War Diary.

132   To Do the Work of Men

This situation made my idea of forming up as I had intended impracticable, and orders were altered accordingly. Captain YEO, my Bombing Officer, was with me, and I sent him to meet the Battalion as they passed, explain the new situation to the C.O.'s, and arrange for 9th K.O.Y.L.I. and 15th Durh. L.I. to endeavour to form up just S. of the line, as it was supposed to be held, the other two battalions to be placed as originally ordered. Captain YEO was to assist Battalions to form up.[167]

As it turned out, the RE officer was wrong, and Yeo found 41st Division troops in Flea Trench, but the confusion had caused further delay and when Headlam returned from establishing his headquarters in Longueval, it was 06.15, broad daylight and the two forward battalions had only just managed to form up as best they could, not in Flea Trench as planned, but with 9/KOYLI in the sunken Flers to Ginchy Road – in the vicinity of Flers Avenue – and 15/DLI in shell holes behind Flers Trench.

Headlam went around and spoke to all four battalion commanders. It had become necessary to improvise: the forward troops were 1,400 yards behind the line on which the artillery barrage was going to start, and somehow 15/DLI were behind 1/EYorks. The assaulting battalions were therefore ordered to begin their advance twenty-five minutes before the commencement of the barrage, with 9/KOYLI shifting to the left in order to allow the 15/DLI to come up on their right. The CO of 1 EYorks was told to follow about 200 yards behind and that "if he saw any hesitation or difficulties or was asked for support, he was to send forward one or more companies at once without reference to me. [Headlam][168]

Headlam then decided it was wiser to have his HQ in Switch Trench, Longueval being too far back to have any control over matters. There, he asked a Heavy Artillery Forward Observation Officer to try to get a message back to Corps Heavy Artillery, asking that the barrage begin earlier, in order to help his advance. If the message did get through, it was not acted upon.

It was therefore at around 08.45 that the 64 Bde men began their advance from Flers Avenue, in the open, in daylight, in full view of the German positions in the Gird trenches, and with no artillery barrage to help them. Indeed, within ten minutes, they were greeted by a German barrage. Luckily, it was not very accurate and fell mostly behind the advancing troops. The war diary of 15/DLI offers the most detailed account of this stage of the attack. They advanced with A and B Companies in the front line, C and D Companies 300 yards behind:

> 1st Stage: At 8:45 a.m. "C" and "D" Coys with Battalion Headquarters Detachment, commenced the advance in order to bring them closer to the two leading Coys. "A" and "B" commenced their advance as "C" and "D" closed upon them. A heavy barrage was put up by the enemy causing only moderate casualties as part of their shell fire fell behind our advancing lines.
>
> 2nd Stage: At about 9 a.m. all four Coys had reached a roadway at right angles to the line of advance, which ran through a deep cutting.[169] Here Companies were reformed and passed on towards enemy's position in the order in which they started. All ranks pressed bravely on through shell, rifle and machine gun fire. Casualties became heavier as they

167 Ibid.
168 Ibid.
169 This road must be 'Bulls Road'. See Map 15.

progressed and gradually, though a few still moved forward, the attack fizzled out and by 10 a.m. all in the attacking lines were sheltering in shell holes from which no movement was possible owing to machine guns and accurate sniping.[170]

The Durhams had managed to advance to within 150 yards of the German First Line (Gird Trench), but they would get no further.

The 9/KOYLI on the Durham's left flank also advanced across the valley floor and began to toil uphill towards the enemy trenches. They had approximately twice the distance to cover to get to Gird Trench and met with the same fate as their compatriots.

They began their advance behind one of the tanks, D9. It was a sorry tale of inadequate communication between tank and infantry. Owing to the late arrival of the 64 Bde troops, Second-Lieutenant Victor Huffam, commanding "Dolly", a female tank,[171] assumed that the infantry attack had been cancelled. His CO, Major Frank Summers, decided, however, that the tank attack would proceed as planned, and D9 accordingly set off towards Gird Trench along Grass Lane (See Map 16). Tank D14, also 'female', commanded by Second-Lieutenant G.F. Court, in front of 15/DLI, though ignorant of their presence, moved directly towards Gueudecourt village. The third tank, on the left flank of the attack, was D11, "Die Hard", another 'female' commanded by Second-Lieutenant Herbert Pearsall. This tank was knocked out just to the north of Flers and would not have been visible to the 64 Bde troops.[172]

D14 made it almost as far as Gird Trench but was forced to stop with mechanical problems. While stationary, it was hit by German shell fire and exploded, killing all of its crew.

D9, meanwhile, although already hit, its prismatic mirrors and periscopes shattered, lumbered on up Grass Lane. The two right-hand machine gunners were able to pour some devastating fire into German troops who had taken up advanced positions in shell holes, but it was soon after hit by one large shell that disabled it completely. Two of the crew were already dead, the left-hand gunners having been killed by armour piercing bullets, but Huffam, who was briefly knocked unconscious by the impact of the shell, managed to drag a badly-wounded crew member out of the tank. The other surviving four men, also wounded, managed to scramble out of the burning hulk and all were able, eventually, to make their way from shell hole to shell hole close enough to the British lines that the men there were able to come out and rescue them.[173]

The War Diary of the 9/KOYLI describes this day's actions in the briefest of terms, but Lieutenant G.F. Ellenberger gave an account of the events in a letter home to his family on 23 September:

> ... we had about a thousand yards to go before reaching the German trench under heavy fire, especially MGs all the way; however we started off and pushed on though nobody knew exactly

---

170 TNA PRO WO 95/2161: 15/DLI War Diary.
171 D9, 'Dolly', was a 'female' tank. These were armed with machine guns in the side sponsons; 'Male' tanks had six-pounder guns.
172 It is a strange coincidence that Pearsall was a pupil at the school where the author taught, (King Edward VI Five Ways, Birmingham) and taught at the school where the author was a pupil, (Batley Grammar School, Yorkshire). All the crew of D11 survived the action, though two were wounded.
173 For a detailed account of the tank action on 16 September, see Trevor Pidgeon, *The Tanks at Flers*, pp. 180-185.

17815 Pte Thomas Henry Garforth, 1/EYorks, age 19, 16 Sept 1916. AIF Burial Ground I.C.27. (Author)

45566 Sergeant G. McPherson, 15/DLI, kia 16 Sept 1916. AIF Burial Ground I.L.2 (Author)

136 To Do the Work of Men

where we had to go, and we seemed to have no supports, and in fact it was very badly organised altogether, and by the time some of us had got within 100 yards of the Hun trench, the attack had collapsed – there was no more control – I don't mean that we ran away. For [we] certainly didn't, but we were scattered about in shell holes and could do nothing except wait for support which never came. Nobody behind knew what had happened to us, nor apparently made any efforts to find out. We had a 'Caterpillar' ('tanks' as the papers call them) in front of us, but when it reached the German trenches it just sat there, ceased fire, belched forth columns of black smoke and burst into flames.[174] You only had to show the slightest signs of movement to get a bullet over: that was how I first got pipped. I looked up and saw a Bosche in their trench wearing one of our steel helmets. I bent down to tell this to the fellow with me and just as I was bringing my head down, 'ping' went my steel helmet and fell off and I felt a nasty knock at the side of my head and blood poured forth in torrents. It was a very lucky shot for me: made a hole clear through the brim of my helmet and the top of my left ear and grazed my head.

Later in the morning I tried to get back to let people behind know what was happening but it was no good. I got a bullet through my haversack, knocking a piece of tin into my back, and shortly afterwards a bullet in the top of my left leg, it went in at the side of my leg and on its way out hit some ammunition in my trouser pocket, bent it all about and made a fairly big hole, about one inch by one-and-a-half inches in my leg. I then had to lie in a very shallow scoop in the ground, not a proper shell hole, for about eight hours until it was dark. There was another fellow there and we found we were lying each one's head by the other one's feet, but we couldn't move about and had to lie in almost the same position the whole time. A third man was just getting into the same hole when he got a bullet through the brain and so kept us company as a corpse for the rest of the day. In the afternoon we were shelled by the Bosche, and later equally heavily by our own artillery: it was a marvel I wasn't hit: the man with me was killed about six o'clock.[175]

Ellenberger was able crawl back to the British lines after dark and was soon on his way back to England, via No.36 Casualty Clearing Station at Heilly and No.8 General Hospital at Rouen. His basic story would have been repeated all along the line, as men were pinned down by the enemy gun fire.

There was much dispute about just how far forward the attacking troops were able to get: neither made it to Gird Trench, but some German outpost positions must have been overrun by 9/KOYLI, as the 1/E.Yorks War Diary tells of two groups of prisoners being sent back and this story is backed up by Headlam's after-action report:

On the left some parties of 9th K.O.Y.L.I. got into what were apparently advanced German trenches in front of their main line. Here some Germans were killed, and two parties of prisoners taken. One of these parties (12 men) was sent back via FLERS and a German big shell dropped among them and appears to have knocked out the whole lot and their escort – the second party of 19 was successfully brought back.[176]

174 This is likely tank D14.
175 IWM Brigadier G.F. Ellenberger Papers, Doc. 4227.
176 TNA PRO WO 95/2159/3: After Action Report written by Brigadier-General Headlam on 19 September 1916, 64 Brigade HQ War Diary.

35011 Pte Andrew Young, 10/KOYLI, kia 16 Sept 1916, age 20. Guards' Cem, Lesboeufs, IV.N.10. (Author)

Second-Lieutenant G.H.Wesselhoeft, 15/DLI, kia 16 Sept 1916, age 19, AIF Burial Ground, III.J.6 (Author)

Headlam had noted from his HQ that the attack had faltered and sent Captain Yeo forward to see what had happened. Yeo returned with a message from 15/DLI at about 09.35, to the effect that the attack required further impetus. Orders were duly dispatched to 1/E.Yorks to sent men forward, but 1/E.Yorks had already done so. B Company had gone forward at about 10.00 hrs to reinforce the left flank of 9/KOYLI, but had lost three officers, including the company commander, on the way up. They made contact with some KOYLI positions, but no further advance was possible. Attempts by 15/DLI to arrange an attack in conjunction with the remaining companies of 1/E.Yorks were twice postponed, and a message eventually arrived from brigade stating that arrangements were in hand for a resumption of the attack at 18.15-18.45.

Headlam had received orders from 41st Division at 17.25: 64 Bde was to attack again at 18.30. Messages were duly dispatched, but 15/DLI did not receive notification of the attack until twenty minutes before the proposed zero hour and the CO replied that it was too late for arrangements to be made and took the unilateral decision to cancel. By this time the 10/KOYLI had moved up to support this new effort but were sent back by Lieutenant-Colonel Pedley (15/DLI). Unfortunately, the cancellation came too late to stop the artillery barrage and, as noted earlier by Lieutenant Ellenberger, some of the British troops still out sheltering in shell holes became casualties as a result of this 'friendly' fire. This barrage also caught some of the men of A Company of 1/E.Yorks, who had been sent up to reinforce the evening attack.

At dusk, as survivors began to make their way back across No Man's Land to their own lines, the units of 64 Bde were positioned as follows:

> Notwithstanding the men still 'out', 9/KOYLI and 15/DLI were withdrawn to Bulls Road. The 1/E.Yorks were manning Flea Trench, with one company just to the rear in support, and 10/KOYLI were in Flers Trench.
> The attacks on either side of 64 Bde also failed. The cavalry was not deployed.

64 Bde casualties in the attack had been quite heavy. The respective battalion war diaries reported them thus:

> The two assaulting battalions came off worst, of course: 9/KOYLI lost thirteen officers, seven killed and six wounded. Other Ranks casualties amounted to forty-three killed, 180 wounded and 153 missing.

15/DLI had six officers killed, ten wounded and three missing. Other Ranks casualties were recorded as thirty-six killed, 209 wounded and 174 missing. The battalions in support did not emerge unscathed by any means: 1/E.Yorks had six officers wounded. Eighteen Other Ranks were killed, with 117 wounded and forty missing.The 10/KOYLI recorded three Officers wounded, eight Other Ranks killed, with eighty-nine wounded and eighteen missing.

140 To Do the Work of Men

The War Diary of 64 Bde presents the casualty figures in the following table:
Casualties of 64 Bde 16-17 September 1916

		KIA	Wounded	Missing
1/E.Yorks	Officers	–	6	–
	Other Ranks	18	106	59
9/KOYLI	Officers	4	6	3
	Other Ranks	43	180	150
10/KOYLI	Officers	–	6	–
	Other Ranks	23	117	39
15/DLI	Officers	5	8	4
	Other Ranks	33	228	170
64/MGC	Officers	–	1	–
	Other Ranks	1	6	2
64 Bde HQ	Officers	–	1	–
Totals:	**Officers**	**9**	**28**	**7**
	Other Ranks	**118**	**637**	**420**
Overall Total:				**1,219**[177]

The brigade was finally relieved by units of 165 Bde during the night of 16/17 September, the last troops reaching Pommiers Redoubt at around 07.00.

The attack had been a failure and high command wanted to know why. Brigadier-General Headlam submitted his report on 19 September. Major-General Campbell appended his comments on the 22nd, and word came back from Corps four days later.

Headlam offered a number of reasons for the failure. He notes the "very short notice"[178] given to 64 Bde of their involvement in the assault, which meant that no reconnaissance was possible, and concludes that "An attack over ground which has never been even looked at before can seldom be successful".[179] He goes on to mention the confusion caused by misinformation received over the positions of 41st Division troops in the trenches to the north of Flers village and the subsequent delay in 64 Bde troops' arrival on the battlefield. The men were therefore forced to advance well behind a barrage that could not, at that late stage, be altered. He then insists that protocol regarding preparation for the attack had been breached, stating that:

> The circulars founded on lessons of the war invariably point to the absolute necessity of every Officer and man thoroughly knowing where he is to go and what he is to do. In this attack, it was absolutely impossible for this to be done. CO's had no chance of holding thorough conferences with their Officers.[180]

---

177 TNA PRO WO 95/2159: 64 Bde HQ War Diary.
178 TNA PRO WO 95/2159/3: Report written by Brigadier-General Headlam, B.M. 111, 19 September 1916, 64 Brigade War Diary.
179 Ibid.
180 Ibid.

It is understandable that Headlam would defend his own men, as well as trying to deflect any direct blame from himself. He sums up his thoughts:

> […] the Brigade was called on to make an advance of over 2,000 yards, over open country, which had never been seen before, full (sic) exposed to view, and with at least 25 mins. of the advance being unassisted by barrage fire. It was met by gun fire and Machine Gun fire.
>
> However demoralised the Germans may be in front of us, I submit that the task was one which was beyond the power of the very best troops. As a matter of fact, elements of the Brigade reached within 100 yards of the German wire, and others captured Germans in advanced trenches.
>
> From what I saw myself, and from the evidence of witnesses, I consider that the conduct of Officers and men was excellent. I deeply regret the failure of the attack, and the losses incurred.[181]

Major-General Campbell agrees with much of what Headlam had to say, adding that the brigade's casualties between 1 and 18 July meant that the units were "largely composed of young Officers and men who have had little or no experience of fighting. Since being withdrawn on July 18th, this Brigade has only had 6 days out of the line for training. These circumstances rendered their task an extremely difficult one".[182]

He then goes on to attempt to deflect blame onto 41st Division: he attests that "with the exception of a Major attached to the 41st Divisional Staff, who came to 64th Brigade H.Q. for a few minutes early on the morning of the 17th, [i.e. after the attack] no Staff Officer came near General Headlam all the time or assisted him in any way. Moreover, no attempt was made by the 41st Divl. Signals to connect the 64th Brigade H.Q. with the Division".[183] A major part of his report is an indignant response to "remarks made" by Major Otter, the CO of 11/Royal West Surrey, who had been put in charge of the 41st Division troops in the trenches to the north of Flers, and thereby responsible for the defence of the village.

Campbell took offence at a comment allegedly made by Otter to the effect that the 64 Bde troops "never attacked". He defended his two battalion commanders, Heathcote (9/KOYLI) and Pedley (15/DLI), stating that the former is "a first class officer" and that the latter has "nearly 31 years of service",[184] and spoke to Major-General Lawford (41st Div) on the matter:

> I have already brought privately to General Lawford's notice some most insulting remarks made in public about this Division by Major Otter.
>
> I took the matter up privately in order to avoid, as far as possible, creating bad feeling between units, and it is only after Major Otter's official report that I mention this matter now.[185]

---

181 Ibid.
182 TNA PRO WO 95/2159: Report written by Major-General Campbell, G.790, 22 September 1916, 64 Brigade War Diary.
183 Ibid.
184 Ibid.
185 Ibid. The only report found by the author that was written by the then Lt-Col R. Otter was in the War 11/Royal West Surreys war diary. See TNA PRO WO 95/2638/5, 19 September 1916. It stated:

142   To Do the Work of Men

He counters Otter's remarks by reiterating the fact that the attacking troops "got close up to the German wire" and that "prisoners were taken".[186] He concludes by taking a general swipe at 41st Division and the fact that they even needed to call up 64 Bde:

> In conclusion, I would point out with reference to the last paragraph of general Lawford's letter, that I understood from him that the reason the 64th Brigade was required to attack the next day was that his Division was so disorganised that he was unable to carry out the attack with his own Division, although it had the night in which to re-organise.
> The 41st Division was a fresh Division which had only been engaged for one day. Perhaps there are facts of which I am not aware.[187]

It was one week later, on 26 September, that XV Corps' remarks on Headlam's report were released. The report emphasises the necessity of attacking on the 16 September, given the state of demoralization amongst the German defenders, adding that this "greatly reduced the difficulties to be faced" and particularly that if the attack could be pressed home before the Germans could bring up reinforcements, it "held out every hope of achieving the principal object of the operations, viz:- the launching of the cavalry".[188]

It goes on to acknowledge the short time given to 64 Bde to prepare for the attack and the disarray in which 41st Division found itself on the morning of 16 September as contributory – and mitigating – factors in the failure of the assault, although it admonishes Headlam for not issuing his warning orders earlier.

Headlam is also criticised for ordering 1/E.Yorks to follow only 200 yards in the rear of the assaulting battalions: "This was much too close. The battalion could not be kept in hand. If the slightest check occurred, it was bound to become mixed up with the assaulting battalions as indeed happened".[189] This, coupled with the presence of 124 Bde troops north of Flers, resulted in "much crowding, and consequent disorder and loss".[190]

The conclusions are fairly even-handed, with blame shared between 41st and 21st Divisions: 64 Bde arrived on the battlefield too late, its assaulting battalions did not attempt to dig in and hold the ground it did make, but the failure of 41st Division to withdraw its unneeded units

---

'At 9:30 a.m. 64 Bde attempted an attack which failed with heavy casualties after which the line was heavily barraged. […] In the afternoon further units of the 64 Bde appeared for a further attack. During our preparatory barrage enemy were reported advancing and battalions stood to. The attack did not develop. The units ready for the attack on the German lines did not leave our trenches and thereby caused great overcrowding and delayed work in progress'. It is possible that Otter's remarks in the last paragraph refer to the later, second attack which in the end did not take place anyway. It is possible that Campbell took this remark as meaning the initial assault. It is also possible that Campbell refers to comments made verbally by Otter to fellow officers and therefore not included in the report. The matter remains unresolved at the time of writing.

186 TNA PRO WO 95/2159: Report written by Major-General Campbell, G.790, 22 September 1916, 64 Brigade War Diary.
187 Ibid.
188 TNA PRO WO 95/2159/3: XV Corps Report, 42/2 G.X., 26 September 1916, 64 Brigade War Diary.
189 Ibid.
190 Ibid.

from their positions north of Flers exacerbated an already difficult situation, and "crowding and congestion of troops was serious and led to loss".[191]

Recriminations aside, the Gird trench system and the village of Gueudecourt were still in German hands. It would be 21st Division's responsibility to rectify that situation. To make matters slightly more difficult, German troops had managed to infiltrate about 100 yards of Gas Alley and would therefore be able to enfilade any repeat attempt at taking Gird Trench. These positions would have to be cleared out first. A first attempt on 18 September, following up a bombardment by Heavy Artillery on the area around Point 91 (reference N.33.c.0.1, see Map 17) by bombers of 13/N.Fus was beaten back by enemy machine gun fire. Two days later, a second attempt proved more successful. This time, with support from Stokes Mortars, fifty yards or so of Gas Alley was captured, and a counter attack repulsed by field gun and Lewis Gun fire. Further infiltration northwards up the trench was possible during the night, but Point 91 remained in German hands.[192] It would be up to the 1/Lincs and 4/Grenadier Guards to complete the job on the day of the main attack.[193]

The attack would be a joint venture by 110 Bde on the left of the attack frontage and 64 Bde – with 1/Lincs temporarily attached from 62 Bde – on the right. Zero Hour would be at 12.35, much later than had been the norm in previous offensives. This was so as to give the Germans fewer daylight hours in which to organise any counter attack. From left to right, the assault battalions were 8/Leics, 9/Leics, 1/EYorks and 10/KOYLI. Three objectives were clearly defined in brigade orders: the first for both brigades was the Gird trench system. 110 Bde would then advance into the village of Gueudecourt, stopping at the main road that bisected it from north-west to south-east, 64 Bde reaching the track some 600 yards beyond Gird Support. The final objective required 110 Bde to capture the rest of Gueudecourt village, 64 Bde reaching the main Gueudecourt to Lesboeufs Road (See Map 17).

An artillery bombardment would commence on 24 September, concentrating initially on the wire in front of the Gird trench system. A creeping barrage was to accompany the infantry advance. On the nights of 23/24 and 24/25 September, patrols sent out by 64 and 110 Bdes were able to report that the wire "in front of GIRD TRENCH had been successfully destroyed".[194] The men of 64 Bde advancing on the 25th were to find out to their cost that these reports were wildly optimistic. The wire in that sector was largely intact.

The 8 and 9/Leics were in their jumping off trenches by 02.00 on 25 September. 1/EYorks and 10/KOYLI on their right were similarly placed by 07.00. These 'trenches', rather unimaginatively

---

191 Ibid.

192 TNA PRO WO 95/2131: 'Report on the Operations of 21st Division 15th September to 1st October 1916' 21st Division HQ War Diary.

193 The War Diary of 13/Northumberland Fusiliers states: "22/9/16: The enemy having evacuated Point 91 a company and one squad of bombers of 4th Bn Grenadier Guards on our RIGHT took possession of it supported by one squad of our company bombers". TNA PRO WO 95/2155. The diary of the 4/Grenadier Guards makes no mention of this action nor indeed of any subsequent loss of the position and the 1/Lincs account clearly tells of a joint attack on Point 91 in conjunction with the 4/Grenadier Guards on 25 September. For both accounts to be true, one must assume that the Germans retook Point 91 at some juncture between 22 and 25 September. At the time of writing, this discrepancy remains unresolved.

194 TNA PRO WO 95/2131:'Report on the Operations of 21st Division 15th September to 1st October 1916', 21st Division HQ War Diary.

144   To Do the Work of Men

christened "New Trench", had been hastily dug by the divisional pioneers and did not impress the men of the Leicester battalions who found them much too shallow. (The War Diary of 9/Leics claims that New Trench was only one foot deep.[195]) They spent the pre-dawn hours doing their best to deepen them. All the men could then usefully do until Zero Hour was to keep out of sight so as not to advertise the fact to the Germans that their trenches were heavily-populated and to check and re-check their equipment. Each man would carry 170 rounds of small arms ammunition, two sandbags and one or two Mill's Grenades. Each battalion would also be equipped with around 150 shovels. In order to suppress enemy machine gun fire, the East Yorks and the KOYLIs would each send one Lewis Gun forward with the first wave of the attack.

At exactly 12.35, just as the artillery put down the protective barrage some 200 yards in front of the jumping off positions, officers' whistles blew and the first waves clambered out of their trenches and set off across the shell-cratered fields, up the slope towards the ridge that hid Gueudecourt village from sight.

Patrols sent out between 01.00 and 03.00 that morning by C and D Companies of 9/Leics were able to report that the enemy wire was "completely smashed" and that Goat Trench was "lightly held".[196] Just before Zero Hour, the first waves – C and D Companies – formed up in front of New Trench before advancing in extended order, with A and B Companies behind them in artillery formation. As soon as the men appeared, the Germans put down a very heavy artillery barrage, but the Leicesters occupied Goat Trench "without serious opposition"[197] within the first ten minutes. Gird Trench was to prove more problematic. The first two waves of D Coy pushed on from Goat Trench but were subject to intense enfilade machine gun fire from their right, and although a number of men made it as far as Gird Trench, all D Coy officers had become casualties: Second-Lieutenants Peter and Gilbart were killed, as was CSM Potterton. C Coy, on the right battalion frontage, fared even worse: only remnants of the first wave made it as far as Gird Trench, but they were "all killed or wounded",[198] including Second-Lieutenant Rennie, who was killed in Gird Trench itself. Captain Webb, advancing with the third and fourth waves of C Coy, soon realised that the sensible course of action was to wheel his men to the right and form a defensive flank along the sunken road, Watling Street. By 13.00, his CSM, Rhodes, had been killed and Webb himself wounded. Meanwhile, at around 14.00, A Coy's advance was also halted by the machine gun fire coming from the right, its commander, Captain Allberry being killed almost as soon as the advance began.[199]

On the left brigade frontage, the attack of the 8/Leics was also able to push past Goat Trench but came under severe enemy fire as they approached Gird Trench. Small parties fought their way into this line, and the Leicester men – seemingly remnants of both 8th and 9th battalions -were able to capture about eighty yards of the trench straddling Pilgrim's Way (see Map 17) and established a block facing south-east. A bombing duel then developed between the two

195 TNA PRO WO 95/2165: 9/Leics War Diary.
196 Ibid. This trench was not on earlier British trench maps. Presumably it had been created since 16 September by joining up the 'advanced positions' in front of Gird Trench.
197 TNA PRO WO 95/2163: 110 Brigade HQ War Diary.
198 TNA PRO WO 95/2165: 9/Leics War Diary.
199 Captain (?) Alfred Edwin Peter, Second-Lieutenant Cyril Thomas Rennie and Captain Cecil Charles Allberry are commemorated on the Thiepval Memorial. Second-Lieutenant W.S.Gilbart is buried in Heilly Station Cemetery, Grave IV. G. 32. 12696 CSM G. Potterton is buried in A.I.F. Cemetery, Grave II. J. 30 and 14796 CSM Walter Henry Rhodes is commemorated on the Thiepval Memorial.

12696 Company Sergeant Major G. Potterton, 9/Leics, kia 25 Sept 1916. AIF Burial Ground II.J.30. (Author)

Second-Lieutenant W.S. Gilbart, 9/Leics, kia 26 September 1916, age 22, Heilly Station Cemetery, IV.G.32. (Author)

12977 L/Cpl T. Gardner, 8/Leics, kia 25 Sept 1916. Guards Cem Lesboeufs, V.I.1. (Author)

sides sharing Gird Trench, the Germans at one point leaving the trench in an attempt to advance above ground. This brave move was thwarted by Lewis gun fire from Sergeant Read and Private Briggs of 8/Leics, who were in a shell hole between Goat and Gird Trench.[200]

The 8/Leics war diarist is, after the capture of this stretch of Gird Trench, at odds with most other accounts of the day's events. The men of this battalion got no further than Gird Trench that day.[201]

Lieutenant-Colonel Haig, commanding 9/Leics, and Lieutenant Tooth, made their way forward along Pilgrim's Way, following the fourth wave of the attack, as far as Gird Trench, where they found around forty 8/Leicesters men without an officer. Haig set about re-organising the men and decided to remain with them until reinforcements arrived. The Lieutenant-Colonel had been wounded in the hand during the advance but remained at his post until relieved on the 26th.

Meanwhile, a party of 8/Leics under Sergeants Chesterton and Read tried to bomb their way eastwards along Goat Trench in an attempt to reach Gird Trench and thereby outflank the German defenders therein. It was a gallant attempt, but one

Captain Frederick William Crowther Hinings, 1/EYorks. Kia 25 Sept 1916. Thiepval Mem. Played rugby union for Headingley R.F.C. (*Yorkshire Rugby Union Roll of Honour*)

---

200 See Richardson *The Tigers*, p.155.
201 The diary, written by the Adjutant, Lieutenant J.W. Dixie-Smith, at this point seems to be at worst a work of fiction, and at best one of wishful thinking, stating "They pressed on to the second objective which was the village of Gueudecourt. By the time they reached the village, their ranks were sadly thinned by the tremendous artillery barrage the enemy put up, and by machine guns, which wrought terrible havoc. Nevertheless with dauntless gallantry they pressed on, reaching the village and engaging the enemy in hand to hand fighting, which took place all the night. In the morning the 7th Bn relieved the 8th Bn in the village and the enemy were finally driven out". TNA PRO WO 95/2165 : 8/Leics War Diary. The dating of the diary entry (24-31[sic] Sept) shows that the account was not written until 30 September at the earliest. The only reference to any British soldiers possibly reaching Gueudecourt on 25 Sept appears in the Official History, which states: 'Some men of the 8/Leicesters are said to have pushed on into Gueudecourt; if this be true they were not seen again". See Miles, *Military Operations France & Belgium 1916*, Vol. II, p.379. The 7/Leics war diarist makes no reference to "relieving" the 8/Leics in Gueudecourt. This battalion did not enter the village until the night of 26/27 Sept, Gueudecourt having been occupied without opposition by 6/Leics on the evening of the 26th.

which failed: Chesterton and his men were forced to improvise a block when German opposition stiffened and they resolved to hold on where they were.

The 6/Leics, from their support positions in Gap and Switch Trenches, had been ordered forward at 16.25 to help the advanced battalions consolidate their somewhat precarious situation in Gird Trench. Four platoons, two from C Coy and two from D Coy, went forward and reached these forward positions, but were met by the same intense machine gun fire from the right flank that had so badly disrupted the initial attack. Major H.H. Emmerson, commanding C Coy, was killed,[202] and Captain Quayle, commanding D Coy, was wounded. The rest of the battalion took up positions in Bulls Road Trench.

As the day's fighting slackened off, the men of 110 Bde set about consolidating the positions they had gained that day: the 300 or so shovels that had been carried forward now proved their

Major Wilfrid Norman Tempest, 9/KOYLI, kia 25 September 1916, age 27. (*Stonyhurst War Record 1914-1919*)

worth. Although some Germans were seen during the night working around to the west of Pilgrim's Way, no counter attack was forthcoming.

The assault had been effectively disrupted by heavy enfilade fire from the right flank. The reason why the Germans were able to put down this fire was the failure of the 64 Bde attack to capture the stretch of Gird Trench between Watling Street and Point 91 (See Map 17).

The story of this failure can be briefly told.

The 1/E.Yorks, on the left of 64 Bde frontage attacked with C & A Coys in the first wave, B & D Coys one hundred yards behind. They immediately came under heavy shell and machine gun fire, but, pressing on, they "found the German barbed wire [illegible] untouched by our artillery fire".[203] The second wave soon ran into the survivors of the first and the men took shelter in shell holes "where possible close up to the German wire & remained there opening fire on the enemy wherever they showed themselves over the parapet of GIRD TRENCH".[204] The 1/E. Yorks got no further that day, the men remaining where they were, out in the open, for the rest of the day.

On their right, the 10/KOYLI met with a similar fate: at 13.50, a message was received at 64 Bde HQ to the effect that the first objective, Gird trench, had been taken. This proved to

---

202 Major Henty Hetherington Emmerson is commemorated on the Thiepval Memorial.
203 TNA PRO WO 95/2161: 1/E.Yorks War Diary.
204 Ibid.

be incorrect; the men were held up short of the uncut German wire in front of this trench. A telephone call from 21st Divisional HQ timed at 16.20 reported that a contact aeroplane had reported Gird Trench to be still full of Germans. Major Milward, attached to Brigade HQ from 10/KOYLI, was sent forward to find out just what was happening. His subsequent written account reflects the confused nature of the 1916 battlefield: it was a half hour walk to the advanced brigade HQ in Sunken Road, (Watling Street), where he found Lieutenant-Colonel Bridge under the mistaken impression that his men had advanced to the third objective. "All his runners with messages had been shot, and he was cut off".[205] Milward found the original front line full of dead and wounded, "and full of a mixture of men – men of the two supporting battalions who had reached it after passing through the enemy's barrage – the 9th K.O.Y.L.I. and 1st Lincolns. They had lost heavily, had few officers left, and no organisation – no sentries – all mixed up. They did not realise they had the enemy in front of them. I got them organised and sorted out, and sentries posted, and returned to Battn Headquarters".[206] He was on his way back to report to Brigadier-General Headlam when a message finally made it back from the front line, confirming that the men had never entered the German front line. They too, like the 110 Bde troops on their left, were sheltering in shell holes and waiting for darkness.

The 1/Lincs had advanced as required at 12.35, expecting to leapfrog the leading battalions and advance onto the third objective. A and C Coys, commanded respectively by Captains J. Edes and J.E.N.P. Denning, made it through the enemy artillery barrage and the machine gun fire emanating from their right as far as the original British front line. Here, they were surprised to find it still occupied by the first line battalions, some survivors of which had made it back to their jumping off positions. Denning had been wounded by this stage, and remained in the trench to reorganise his men, but Edes decided to go on, and, encountering an officer of the 4th Grenadier Guards, went to the assistance of the guardsmen who were trying to take Point 91.

> This manoeuvre was carried out with the Company's left flank 'in the air'. The men bayoneted and bombed their way up GAS ALLEY until thinned in numbers by heavy casualties. It was then decided to consolidate in front of the strong point. While this was being done our left got in touch with a party of the 9th K.O.Y.L.I who had advanced and succeeded in occupying a line of shell holes which they had connected together.[207]

B and D Coys of 1/Lincs undertook an advance of around 1,500 yards through the enemy barrage in order to support their comrades, but, having suffered heavy casualties, and making it only as far as the original front line, were subsequently ordered to withdraw to Bulls Road. A Coy remained where it was until finally being able to withdraw at midnight.

Gueudecourt was still in German hands, as was most of the Gird trench system. Orders were issued at around 19.30 that 64 & 110 Bdes were to renew their attack during the night but following a discussion between the Corps and Divisional Commanders, (Lieutenant-General Horne and Major-General Campbell), it was decided that the Gird trench system

---

205 TNA PRO WO 95/2162: Report written by Major C.A. Milward, 10/KOYLI War Diary.
206 Ibid.
207 TNA PRO WO 95/2154: 1/Lincs War Diary. It is likely that it was 10/KOYLI with whom they formed this advanced position. The 9/KOYLI war diarist asserts that they advanced no further that day than the original British front line.

be secured before any further attack on Gueudecourt was attempted and that a tank would be used for this purpose – but not until the morning. In the meantime, 15/DLI took over the 64 Bde front line, the other three battalions being withdrawn. The battalions of 110 Bde remained largely in the positions they had gained during the day.

On the morning of 26 September, Second-Lieutenant C.E. Storey, commander of tank D4, received orders to proceed from Flers and lead an attack on Gird Trench.[208] He would be supported by the bombers of 7/Leics, with C & D Coys of the same battalion in support. Captain H.W.H. Tyler and Second-Lieutenant H.J.Walsh would command the detachment of Leicesters.

The tank, a 'female' version, moved off from Flers village at about 06.30 and rumbled northwards up Pilgrim's Way. It arrived at the junction with Gird Trench at 07.15 and turned south eastwards along its length. The Germans, both surprised and bewildered by the arrival of the tank, put up little resistance as the machine, spitting fire from its six machine guns, made inexorable progress, followed closely by the 7/Leics bombers. Those Germans not wounded or killed by the enfilade were either quick to surrender or took refuge in dugouts. These were effectively dealt with as the bombers threw a mixture of Mills, smoke and phosphorous bombs down the stairways. As the tank progressed, C and D Coys' Lewis Gunners were quick to deal with any Germans who attempted to escape across the open. Men from 15/DLI also advanced and occupied Gird Trench in the wake of the tank. By 07.45, the trench had been cleared as far as Watling Street. The 7/Leics war diarist continued the story:

Lieutenant James Humphrey Clare Schofield 15/DLI, kia 26 Sept 1916, age 28. (*British Roll of Honour*, Vol. 2)

> Here a break in the trench caused by the SUNKEN Road caused a temporary check, but 2/Lt Walsh pushed his men across the gap in sections & continued the advance without loss. Our men entirely out-threw the German bombers & when 200 yards beyond Watling St

---

208 This was the second tank under Storey's command to be designated "D4". The first had been supposed to take part in the attack on Flers village on 15 September 1916, but it had become ditched in Delville Wood on its way up to the front line.

the tank left the trench and proceeded towards the village, the bombers were able to carry on without a check.[209]

The remains of the German garrison were being herded towards the positions in the vicinity of Point 91 now held by the Grenadier Guards. Some were cut down by Lewis Guns, others surrendered. By 09.45, it was all over: the Leicesters had linked up with the Guards and the tank had run out of petrol before reaching Gueudecourt village.[210] German prisoners amounted to 8 Officers and 362 Other Ranks. British casualties totalled five men wounded.

The 4/Grenadier Guards diarist reported seeing "several hundred" Germans retiring across open ground at midday between Gueudecourt and Transloy "in great disorder, apparently leaving their rifles behind them".[211] This coincided with a two-pronged advance by the cavalry. A troop of the South Irish Horse, by this time on foot, had reached the north-west corner of Gueudecourt, and a squadron of the 19th Lancers (Sialkot Cavalry Bde) had trotted up Watling Street and on as far the outskirts of the village. There they tied up their horses and continued on foot. They were met with machine gun fire and promptly withdrew. The South Irish Horse also withdrew at about 18.00 hours. It was left to the men of 6/Leics to make the final advance to occupy Gueudecourt, which they did without opposition at about 17.30 on the evening of 26 September. They were able to establish a line through the orchards in the northern and eastern outskirts of the village and continued to consolidate, gaining touch with 10/Yorks of 62 Bde who had advanced to the third objective on their right and had relieved 64 Bde. It was not until the following morning that they were able to link up with 55th Division troops on the left (See Map 18).

By this time, the 7/Leics had relieved the 8 & 9/Leics in Gird and Bull Road trenches, the latter battalions being temporarily reorganised into a composite battalion owing to a shortage of officers. On 29 September, the 7/Leics moved forward to relieve the 6/Leics in Gueudecourt, but not before their commanding officer, Lieutenant-Colonel Drysdale, had been killed by sniper fire as he reconnoitred their new positions in the village.[212]

By 1 October, all units of 21st Division had been moved back into the area between Delville Wood and Bernafay Wood, and the following day entrained "for the back area".[213] The division's involvement in the 1916 Battle of the Somme was over, but the final episode had been costly. Casualties for the period 25 September to 1 October can be estimated at:

209 TNA PRO WO 95/2164L: 7/Leics War Diary.
210 Tank D4 had become ditched and Storey was wounded. He and his crew, four of whom had also suffered wounds from splinters, withdrew, taking the machine guns with them. A later attempt to unditch the tank was unsuccessful, resulting in the tracks breaking. See TNA PRO WO 95/110: 4 Bde Tank Corps War Diary.
211 TNA PRO WO 95/1223: 4/Grenadier Guards War Diary.
212 Lieutenant-Colonel William Drysdale DSO, age 39, Royal Scots, (OC 7/Leics) is buried in Caterpillar Valley Cemetery, grave reference VI.E.11.
213 TNA PRO WO 95/2131: 21st Division HQ War Diary.

64 Bde:

	Killed		Wounded		Missing	
	Off	OR	Off	OR	Off	OR
1/EYorks	6	40	8	152	–	59
9/KOYLI	1	6	5	65	–	29
10/KOYLI	7	51	7	162	1	110
15/DLI	–	7	3	39	1	9
1/Lincs (Att)	4	21	6	132	–	28
Totals	18	125	29	550	2	235
Grand Total:						959

110 Bde: Battalion casualty returns are either incomplete or non-existent. Therefore, Brigade diary figures must be accepted as follows:

	Killed		Wounded		Missing	
	Off	OR	Off	OR	Off	OR
	12	168	41	812	1	106
Grand Total:					1,140	

This provides an overall casualty figure of almost 2,100.

The 21st Division spent the winter of 1916-17 in and out of trenches in front of Noeux-les-Mines and Béthune. Their next major engagement would be on the first day of the Battle of Arras, on 9 April 1917.

Second-Lieutenant F. Lillie, 9/KOYLI, killed in a training accident 18 December 1916. He was due to go home on leave for Christmas. (*Yorkshire Rugby Union Roll of Honour*)

3

Arras

The relevant volume of Official History[1] views the first day of the Battle of Arras, 9 April 1917, as "one of the great days of the War". Cyril Falls, its author, continues in effusive tone: "It witnessed the most formidable and at the same time most successful British offensive hitherto launched".[2] He compares the scale of the offensive to that of the first day on the Somme, and attributes the greater initial gains at least partly to the much improved, much more powerful and numerically far larger artillery component of the attack. The BEF had also revised its artillery priorities over the winter of 1916-17: counter-battery techniques – including flash-spotting and sound-ranging – had been improved and the neutralisation of enemy batteries became an integral part of any artillery fire plan; the creeping barrage had also developed – depth was increased as several lines of 18 pounder shells were incorporated and 4.5 inch howitzers were added to the advancing curtain of fire ahead of the 18 pounders. The heavier guns – 6-inch, 8-inch and 9.2-inch howitzers – that hammered away at the German defences were also equipped at this time with the new 106 fuses.[3] Shell production had increased from 45 million in 1916 to 76 million in 1917 and better quality control ensured less 'duds' reached the German lines. Emphasis was also shifted so that initial bombardments would concentrate on the German front line defences rather than being dissipated across numerous support and reserve trench lines.[4]

All this said, the Arras offensive was, however, merely a diversionary attack meant to support a decisive French assault against the German lines in the Champagne region. Planning began some five months earlier in November 1916, when allied Commanders-in-Chief met at

---

1   C. Falls, *Military Operations France and Belgium 1917*, Vol. I (London: HMSO 1940), *passim*.
2   Ibid, p.201. Such an accolade may not be as impressive as it sounds: previous British offensives on the Western Front had not been overwhelmingly successful.
3   The 106 fuse was a great improvement on earlier versions as its far more sensitive setting meant that a shell would explode immediately on contact with the ground or with barbed-wire, resulting in greater destructive power and reduced cratering. By April 1917, 150,000 of these fuses had been issued to the artillery in France, but only to 6-inch, 8-inch and 9.2-inch batteries, and this figure made up only 50% of their total allocation. The authority for 106 fuses to be supplied to 18-pounder batteries was not granted until 20 May 1917. Some 18-pounder batteries did not receive 106 fuses until early 1918. See A.J. Nannini to Sir Noel Birch correspondence, 22 November 1937. See TNA PRO CAB 45/116.
4   For further details, see Paul Strong & Sanders Marble, *Artillery in the Great War* (Barnsley: Pen & Sword, 2011), pp. 122-129.

Chantilly for the purpose of long-term planning for the following spring. Initial plans envisaged combined, if not simultaneous, attacks by British and French forces: the British Fourth and Fifth Armies would resume the Somme offensive, Third Army under Allenby would launch an assault from the north of Arras in a south-easterly direction and further north, First Army would form a defensive flank in order to protect Allenby's left and rear. A limited French attack south of the River Somme would complete the picture. All this would distract the German forces prior to the Champagne offensive.

A number of factors would subsequently derail this plan. Firstly, the French dismissed their commander in chief, Joffre, and replaced him with General Robert Nivelle. Once in command, Nivelle proposed a much more spectacular role for the French in the 1917 offensives: his plan promised a rapid breakthrough, using twenty-seven divisions, and decisive exploitation thereafter.[5] Collecting so much manpower – three full Armies – in one area would require the British to take over part of the line occupied at that time by the French: an extra twenty miles were added to the British right flank, a move that was eventually agreed upon and finally completed on 26 February. Haig, for his part, had no objections to the French taking the major role that spring. He had been wanting to implement his own pet scheme – an attack along the Belgian coast from Ypres – for some time and saw the summer of 1917 as the perfect time to do it. A limited-duration subsidiary attack by the British therefore suited him and would allow him to deploy enough troops northwards in time for his own major offensive.

Second, at a conference in Calais on 26 February 1917, Nivelle, with, it must be said, the connivance of the British Prime Minister, David Lloyd George, threw a metaphorical spanner of huge proportions into the Allied works: the proposal was that the British forces would be placed effectively under Nivelle's command for all matters concerning the conduct of operations, including plans for offensives and troop deployments. Haig and Robertson, aghast at the suggestion, protested vehemently, the latter threatening resignation, and were able, eventually, to scale back the proposal so that Haig would only be under Nivelle's command for the duration of the planned offensive and he would "have the right of appeal to his own government and liberty as to the means he employed and the methods of utilizing his troops in the sector allotted to him".[6] The uneasy compromise rumbled on.

Third, the Germans had plans of their own. They had been constructing a new defensive position well behind the existing front line since September 1916. The 'Siegfried Stellung', known to the Allies as the 'Hindenburg Line', ran from Neuville St Vaast, close to Vimy, skirted Arras to the north-east and continued south to Soissons. It would shorten the overall German line by twenty-five miles, thus requiring approximately fourteen fewer divisions to man it. It was a system like no other on the Western Front, based on the principle of defence in depth, but with a remarkably strong front edge: it comprised

> a system of strongpoints and wide – sometimes hundreds of yards wide – belts of wire, covered by an interlocking field of machine guns and artillery fire, trenches and strong points equipped with deep dugouts: to all this were added well-constructed observation

---

5   The details of this plan need not encumber this narrative, as its subsequent failure renders them redundant.

6   Falls, *Military Operations France and Belgium 1917*, Vol. I, p.57.

156   To Do the Work of Men

posts on higher ground, deeply dug communications and telephone lines, and adequate supplies of food, water and ammunition.[7]

Secret orders for 'Operation Alberich', named after the malicious dwarf of the *Nibelungenlied*, the code name for the German withdrawal to the Hindenburg Line, were issued on 4 February 1917. By 19 March, some thirty-five divisions had effectively melted away from their trenches facing the British and were safely ensconced in their new positions. The British 'pursuit', once the reality of the situation had dawned, was, perhaps understandably, less than vigorous. The Germans, in their retreat, had left villages destroyed, water supplies poisoned, bridges and crossroads blown up and countless booby traps for the unwary Tommy. The British advanced across a wilderness.

All of the above meant drastic modifications to the British plan of attack. The recommencement of the Somme offensive was made redundant by the German withdrawals: the Bapaume salient, one of the original objectives, no longer existed. The main role in the forthcoming assault would now fall to Third Army, to the north, which would attack due east from Arras. First Army, on their left, would seize Vimy Ridge, thus securing the attack's left flank. On the southern sector of the attack frontage, the Hindenburg Line was effectively the German's front line of defence, and it was here that 21st Division, as part of VII Corps (Lieutenant-General Sir T. D'O. Snow) were to take their place in the line.

The line occupied by 21st Division at the beginning of April was, however, deemed in need of adjustment: the jumping off positions would need to be nearer the Hindenburg Line and this meant that a small-scale attack was needed to push the current line forward by a thousand yards or so between the villages of Hénin sur Cojeul and Croisilles. Both villages were still in German hands, however. They too would have to be captured before the main assault could go in. The task of pushing the line forward fell to units of 62 Bde, whilst the capture of the villages was the responsibility of neighbouring divisions: 30th Division on the left would take Hénin sur Cojeul and 7th Division would assault Croisilles. This preliminary attack would take place early on the morning of 2 April.

The 62 Bde had been in the line since the night of 27/28 March and had pushed patrols forward, probing the German outpost positions, establishing advanced posts and provoking several skirmishes. In one such, on the morning of 29 March, a patrol under Sergeant Martin of 12/Northumberland Fusiliers attacked and took the small cemetery south of Hénin, killing three men from *207 R.I.R.*[8] The following night, a number of Germans attempted to recover the bodies of their comrades. This resulted in another fight for Martin's men who chased the Germans back into Hénin, killing a further two and capturing two more. Lieutenant Noble was wounded during this encounter. Further south, the 1/Lincolns pushed forward towards the Hénin – Croisilles road and captured an enemy machine gun along with one of its crew.

Orders were finally issued for the 2 April attack: 62 Bde would advance with three battalions in the front line, 12 NFus (Major Edlman) on the left, 1/Lincs (Lieutenant-Colonel Evans) in the centre and 13 NFus (Lieutenant-Colonel Dix) on the right. The 10/Yorks (Lieutenant-Colonel Matthias) would be in support (See Map 19). Zero Hour was set at 05.15. By 03.30

---

7   Robin Neillands, *The Great War Generals on the Western Front 1914-18* (London: Robinson Publishing, 1999), p. 322.
8   *The 207th Reserve Infantry Regiment*

men of the front-line companies had crawled out unobserved to within 200 yards of the first objective.

The 12 NFus lined up with D and B Companies in front, left and right, with A Company in support and C Company in reserve. The artillery bombardment came down on time at 05.15 and "on account of the extreme accuracy of the covering fire […] the assaulting troops were able to follow the barrage within 50 yards".[9] The barrage lifted at 05.25 and the men surged forward. The only real resistance encountered was on the left from a strongpoint at T.3.c.8.8 where, after a "brisk encounter",[10] the German machine gun was overrun. Both objective lines were gained in quick time and with few casualties. Nine prisoners from *99th R.I.R.* were captured and the 12/NFus diarist estimates forty Germans killed. As consolidation was begun, and strongpoints put in place along the left flank, Lewis Gun teams were sent out to establish posts some 150 yards ahead of the captured position. The retaliatory artillery barrage was poor and fell mainly behind the advancing troops, but some casualties were suffered from rifle fire emanating from Hénin village, which was not captured until the afternoon when 12/NFus were able to establish contact with 2/Yorkshire Regt.

In the centre, 1/Lincolns had already gained a foothold along the first objective by the morning of 31 March. Attempts to dislodge them were less than energetic and relatively easily repulsed. On the morning of 2 April, the Lincolns were able to push patrols forward into the second objective, again with relative ease, while a Lewis Gun team sent out into square T.10.b was able to wreak havoc among Germans retreating northwards along the sunken road from Croisilles village.

On the right, 13/NFus stormed the first objective, D and B Companies arriving at, and capturing, the position within one minute of the artillery barrage lifting. D Company remained on this line and B Company crawled out as far as possible behind the new standing barrage. Ten minutes later, the barrage lifted once more and the second objective was in British hands thirty seconds later. The after-action report, written by Lieutenant-Colonel Dix, was fulsome in its praise of 21st Divisional Artillery:

> "The barrage and timing were perfect and we suffered no casualties from our own barrage. […] The 21st Divisional Artillery covered my advance and formed the barrage which as has already been mentioned was perfect. 2nd Lt Bracecamp RFA was liason (sic) Officer and every praise is due to him for his unstinted energy in the performance of his duties".[11]

Casualties had been minimal: four officers were wounded, including Captain Haines who had led the assault, and ten Other Ranks were killed, with a further 49 wounded. Two enemy machine guns had been captured.

On the right, 2/Queen's (7th Division) were attacking the village of Croisilles: some progress was made on its eastern side, but the initial assault on the village itself failed. A second attempt proved more successful, but Croisilles was not cleared of the enemy until dusk. This delay allowed the German units in dug outs to the west of the village to launch a counter attack at 06.30 up the two sunken roads in T.17. They were able initially to fire into the rear of the

---

9   TNA PRO WO 95/2152: 62 Bde HQ War Diary.
10   TNA PRO WO 95/2155: 12/Northumberland Fusiliers War Diary.
11   TNA PRO WO 95/2155: 13/Northumberland Fusiliers War Diary.

158   To Do the Work of Men

newly-won positions, but A Company of 13/NFus, moving up in support, managed to get Lewis Guns and machine guns into a flanking position quickly enough to halt the Germans' advance. Lieutenant Armstrong personally accounted for nine of the enemy with shots from his revolver. The battalion bombers then drove the Germans back into their dug outs, wherein they sheltered for the rest of the day under constant fire from 62 Trench Mortar Battery.

By noon on 2 April, consolidation of the newly-gained positions was proceeding rapidly, all of the objectives having been gained except for a stubborn German strongpoint still holding out at the crossroads in T.17.d. Six attempts were made to dislodge the defenders, but the target was only gained once the enemy slipped away under the cloak of darkness that night. The 13/NFus were relieved just after dusk by 10/Yorks and a strong patrol under Lieutenant Storey was sent into Croisilles around midnight. A search of the German dug outs found them evacuated and the party was able to gain touch with 7th Division troops at around 02.00 on the 3 April. The weather throughout these operations had been awful. Snow, sleet and bitterly cold winds during the day were followed by frost during the night. Casualties for 62 Bde were estimated as follows:

	Killed	Wounded	Missing
Officers	1[12]	8	–
Other Ranks	37	114	2

Seventy of the enemy were recorded as killed, and twenty-nine were taken prisoner, including two officers. The jumping off positions for the 9 April attack were now established

A detailed account of the action along the entire front on 9 April is not necessary here, but a brief synopsis will provide context for the 21st Division attack. General Allenby had originally proposed a two-day bombardment prior to the assault in order to obtain at least some element of surprise. He was overruled: a four-day bombardment, preceded by three weeks of wire-cutting, would be provided by over 2,800 guns, over a thousand of them 'heavy', comprising one gun for every nine yards of front.

The assault was delivered by the Canadian Corps of First Army on the extreme left, and by XVII, VI and VII Corps of Third Army, listed north to south (See Map 20). The Canadians would assault Vimy Ridge and thereby secure Third Army's left flank. Ferguson's XVII Corps would attack to the north of Arras, with 51st, 34th and 9th Divisions in the front line and VI Corps (Haldane), from a quite narrow front, would send 15th, 12th and 3rd Divisions forward from directly east and south-east of the city. VII Corps, on the right, had 14th, 56th, 30th and 21st Divisions in the line.

Objective lines were designated 'Black', 'Red', 'Blue', 'Brown' and finally 'Green'.[13] The British front line on the right flank of the attack turned to the south-east. This meant that the first targeted line in front of most of VII Corps was the Brown Line. Zero Hour for the main assault was 05.30, but the planned capture of the Brown Line was not scheduled until Zero plus eight hours, that is 13.30, followed by a further two-hour delay before advancing to the Green Line.

---

12   This was Second-Lieutenant T.W. Ewens of 13/NFus. The brigade diary gives his date of death as 2 April, but the 13/NFus Battalion War Diary notes his death on 30 March. This latter date is confirmed by the Commonwealth War Graves Commission. He is buried in Douchy-les-Ayette British Cemetery, grave IV.H.19.

13   These objectives are marked in appropriate colours on Map 20.

Lieutenant-General Snow was therefore forced to stagger the times that his divisions would move off into the attack, the 14th going in first. This meant that the designated units of 21st Division would not be required to advance until around four o'clock in the afternoon and only then if the attack of 30th Division on their left had been successful.

The 64 Bde, on the left of 21st Division's frontage, would prosecute the attack. 110 Bde, on the right, would form a defensive flank facing east in order to discourage any German counter attack from that direction.

The first line of the 64 Bde orders for the attack indicates the level of ambition present among the higher echelons of command, stating that "The Third Army is to break through the enemy's defences and advance on CAMBRAI".[14] Thereafter it returns to more realistic objectives: VII Corps' job was to gain the high ground to the south-east of the Cojeul River. 89 Bde, of 30th Division, on 21st Division's left, had orders to attack along the Cojeul River valley and were expected to "secure" the village of St Martin sur Cojeul (see Map 21) "prior to the general attack taking place".[15] Thereafter, the German first and second line trenches in the Hindenburg Line would fall by Zero plus 10 hours and 57 minutes (approximately 16.27) and three quarters of an hour later the brigade would launch an assault on the village of Héninel, its final objective for the day, behind a renewed creeping artillery barrage. Jumping off times were to be so arranged that the troops of 30th and 21st Divisions would reach the Hindenburg Line at the same time.

The density of the artillery barrage for the Arras offensive was far greater than any previous assault on this scale along most of the frontage. On the right flank, however, difficulties in moving guns into position – VII Corps did not "close up"[16] to the Hindenburg Line positions until 2 April – meant that the plans to use trench mortars and 18 pdrs to supplement the heavier guns in their task of cutting the German wire could not be fully implemented. The best that could be hoped for in the end was for "lanes 100 feet wide"[17] to be cleared through the double line of barbed wire entanglements in front of the German trenches. To monitor developments, "careful reconnaissance [was to] be made each night to observe and report on the effect of the Artillery wire-cutting operations. Reports [were to] be forwarded to Div. H.Q. as soon as possible, being repeated to Colonel Lyon, 46th H.A. [Heavy Artillery] Group at Boiry St Martin".[18] Divisional orders went on to state that

> 64th Inf. Bde. will not attack the enemy's position where it is found that the gaps in the wire are not passable. If no gaps exist, a report (repeated to G.O.C. Right Brigade, 30th Division) will be made at once to Div. H.Q. so that the attack can be postponed, and arrangements made for cutting the wire properly.[19]

It is interesting to note that this caveat does not appear in 64 Bde orders issued on 8 April: presumably it had been ascertained by that point that the wire cutting had been successful, at

---

14   TNA PRO WO 95/2159. "64th. Inf. Bde. O.C. 115" issued 8.4.1917, 64th Bde War Diary.
15   TNA PRO WO 95/2132: Appendix E, 'Plan of Attack of Right Brigade, 30th Division', April 1917, 21st Div HQ War Diary.
16   Falls, *Military Operations France and Belgium 1917*, Vol. I, p.183.
17   TNA PRO WO 95/2132: 'O.C. No. 97, Instructions for Attack', 21st Div HQ War Diary.
18   Ibid.
19   Ibid.

160   To Do the Work of Men

least to some extent. Any battalion coming up against uncut wire was to search to its left and right and then follow in the steps of any neighbouring battalion lucky enough to find a gap before "then inclin[ing] to its own objective".[20] Should the worst-case scenario result, a fall- back position was available:

> If it is seen that the leading waves are unable to force their way through the gaps in the wire the support companies will form a line on which battalions will reform and dig-in. This line is to run approximately through T.5.c. – T.4.b. – T.4.a. – N.34. c & a.[21]

The 64 Bde would line up with 9/KOYLI on the left, 15/DLI in the centre and 1/E.Yorks on the right. 10/KOYLI would be in support.

The artillery bombardment proper began at 06.30 on 4 April, but it was decided at a meeting between Douglas Haig and Robert Nivelle the following day that the attack would have to be delayed by twenty-four hours: the French were not ready and the weather was awful, with snow storms hindering artillery observers. The troops would now attack on Easter Monday, 9 April 1917. The extra day proved valuable to the artillery: 8 April was a sunny day and improved observation allowed "a great deal to be accomplished that day. It was felt that the artillery preparation had done all that could be expected of it".[22]

The weather took a turn for the worse overnight, however, and as fifteen divisions huddled in their jumping off trenches on that Easter Monday, it was bitterly cold, with a strong westerly blowing. The ground was very wet and it was beginning to snow again.

The events of the day, so far as the main attack is concerned, can be quickly summarised, moving north to south. (See Map 20). On the left, or northern flank, the Canadian Corps stormed up the slopes of Vimy Ridge. Only on the extreme left did the German defenders hold out for any length of time. The German positions on the crest were overrun, but the cost had been high, the Canadians suffering over 10,000 casualties, 3,598 of them killed.

51st Division, on the left of Allenby's Third Army, ended the day slightly short of their final objectives, but 34th Division on their right managed to gain a toe-hold just short of the Green Line. The 9th Division's attack was a complete success and with 4th Division leapfrogging to reach the village of Fampoux, this section of the front saw the day's furthest advance – three and a half miles.

The 12th and 15th divisions, attacking directly east from Arras itself, had had the good fortune of being able to spend the five days prior to the assault safe and dry in the extensive system of tunnels under the town. They quickly seized the town of Blangy before fighting their way across Railway Triangle and securing Battery Valley. 12th Division's advance with its right on the arrow-straight Arras-Cambrai road was eventually held up on the Wancourt-Feuchy line. 3rd Division was able to capture the town of Tilloy, but the attempt to push 37th Division through and on to Monchy-le-Preux came too late in the day and the advance petered out in the gathering gloom of evening.

---

20   TNA PRO WO 95/2159: '64 Bde. O.C. No. 115, issued 8.4.1917', 64th Brigade War Diary.
21   Ibid. This line approximates to the track that runs south-east from St Martin sur Cojeul across the line of advance. See Map 21.
22   Falls, *Military Operations France and Belgium 1917*, Vol. I, p.185.

The VII Corps divisions, as previously mentioned, had staggered start times: the 14th would start at 07.30, the 56th at 07.45, and 30th Division would send one brigade in at 12.55, the other two only following at 16.15 in order to coincide with the 21st Division's assault.

The 14th Division had the Blue Line in its possession by 08.45, but the attack could not proceed much further. Part of the Hindenburg Line was occupied, but any further advances were denied by heavy German machine gun fire. By midday, an uneasy stalemate had been reached.

56th Division faced the town of Neuville-Vitasse, behind which ran the Hindenburg Line, here a triple trench system. Neuville-Vitasse did fall, but determined resistance by the German defenders meant that the Blue Line was not reached here until four o'clock in the afternoon. The attack on the Hindenburg system went in long after schedule, and initial advances were promising, but by the end of the day only the first line was still in British hands.

The advance of the left-hand brigade of 30th Division, 21 Bde, was timed so that the first wave would reach the Hindenburg Line at 12.55, but the delays to the north meant that they were met by heavy enfilade machine gun fire and an enemy artillery barrage. By the time they reached the enemy wire, the momentum of the attack had gone, and survivors fell back to the Neuville – St Martin road and began to dig in.

The right-hand brigade of 30th Division, 89 Bde, (Brigadier-General the Hon. F.C. Stanley) was to go forward simultaneously with 64 Bde (See Map 21). 20/King's Liverpool were on the left, with their sister battalion, the 19th, on the right. Their initial target was the Hindenburg Line, but 19/King's were then to go on and capture Héninel. As a preliminary objective, the 2/Bedfordshires had occupied St Martin sur Cojeul at 01.30 that morning and were to follow on later in support of the Liverpool battalions. The latter were able to begin their advance unmolested and reached St Martin soon after 15.30. From here on, things went badly wrong. The wire in front of the Hindenburg complex was found to be virtually intact and the attackers, brought to a halt by both wire and intense machine gun fire, attempted to dig in where they were. The two battalions had suffered around 400 casualties between them. Brigadier-General Stanley, assessing the situation, realised that any resumption of the attack could only succeed after a new artillery bombardment. With his men too far forward for this to be carried out safely, he ordered them to withdraw under the cover of darkness to positions in the northern outskirts of St Martin.

With the wire largely uncut and 30th Division's attack having failed, Brigadier-General Hugo Headlam, 64 Bde, must surely have been expecting his attack to be postponed – as per original orders. The fourth paragraph of his subsequent after-action report clearly outlines his thoughts on the matter:

> In the general plan of the battle a promise was given that the Brigade would not be called upon to advance until the troops on the left had seized and consolidated the NEPAL trench north of the Cojeul River and were ready to advance thence on HENINEL and WANCOURT simultaneously with the advance of the Brigade. It is unnecessary to point out here that this arrangement was vital to the success of my attack, since the defenders of such a position as I was called upon to attack could scarcely be expected to be dislodged unless they felt that by staying in their positions they would be captured by the advance of the troops on their flank and towards their line of retreat.[23]

23   TNA PRO WO 95/2159: 64 Bde War Diary.

162   To Do the Work of Men

Hindsight notwithstanding, he makes a valid point. He continues in rather vague terms: "Circumstances arose which made it necessary to make my attack in conformity with the advance of 30th Division on my left".[24] Headlam's original plan had been to attack only on the southern portion of his division's sector using two battalions in the front line. Major-General Campbell could not allow this, as there would have been a "considerable gap"[25] along the Cojeul River valley between 64 Bde and 89 Bde: Headlam was told to attack along the whole of his front and accordingly altered his thinking and put three battalions in the front line. For three nights prior to the attack, 2,400 yards of assembly trenches were dug on both sides of the road running south-east from St Martin sur Cojeul. A number of dumps were created, these containing in total around 2,000 [Mills] bombs, 500 gallons of water, 800 rifle grenades and 500 Stokes bombs. The road itself was sunken along the 9/KOYLI section of the line, the banks either side varying from six to ten feet high. It climbs gently from the river valley before levelling out on the 15/DLI sector. In front, across the gently undulating and open grassland, the enemy wire – just over 1,000 yards away – would be clearly visible, the last few dozen yards of the approach being uphill. The undulations created some areas of 'dead ground' where the advancing troops would be safe from direct defensive machine gun fire. Headlam's report gives us some idea of the task facing his men when he describes the fortifications of the Hindenburg Line, and underlines the difficulties of wire cutting by the artillery:

> The line to be attacked was one of very great strength. It was a carefully selected position upon which an immense amount of labour had been expended. Aeroplane photos showed plainly the depth and thickness of the wire which was in two belts in front of first line and in three belts in most parts in front of second line, moreover, owing to short time available and lack of artillery ammunition only about 9 gaps had been cut in wire on the whole front.
>
> Concrete M.G. emplacements, absolutely safe dugouts, and numerous protected snipers posts added to the power of defence of a position which prisoners frankly confessed was considered impregnable".[26]

The Hindenburg Line defences were indeed formidable, and the paucity of gaps created in the wire meant that it was down to the luck of the draw as to whether a column of men in the first wave stumbled upon one or were faced by impenetrable entanglements. A report in 21st Division's 'Daily Summary of Operations' for 5 April gave little in the way of optimism in this matter: "Wire from T4.b.8.6 to N34.c.9.6 [directly in front of the 15/DLI] examined and found very thick. Seven rows iron screw pickets about 2 feet apart and wire about 5 feet high so thickly entangled as to resemble a thorn fence".[27]

---

24   Ibid.
25   Ibid.
26   Ibid. A word of caution to the reader: Brigadier-General Hugo Headlam's reports and correspondence with the Official Historian – which is quite extensive – always tend to put himself and his brigade in a favourable light. An inclination to self-criticism or self-deprecation is not one of his obvious traits.
27   TNA PRO WO 95/2132: 21st Div HQ War Diary.

Patrols had been sent forward to assess the situation. 10/KOYLI had been in the line along the road running south-east from Hénin sur Cojeul since the night of 3/4 April, and on the afternoon of 7 April a patrol "worthy of note" went out.[28]

> CSM Gill and Cpl Hammond of A Coy went out covered by a Lewis Gun. In broad daylight while our artillery was shelling the German wire & line [...] they walked 1500 yds up to the German wire. They walked along the German wire and made a careful inspection of it. They got back safely bringing with them very valuable information about the gaps which had been cut by our artillery. For this & other good service CSM Gill was awarded the DCM & Cpl Hammond the Military Medal. 2nd Lt Hobbs (killed on the night of the 10th)[29] was in charge of the Lewis Gun.[30]

Arrangements for the creeping barrage behind which the infantry would advance were as follows: at Zero minus twenty-two minutes, an eighteen-pounder barrage would be put down on a line south-west of the German wire (marked A ------- A -------- A on Map 21). At twelve minutes before Zero, the barrage would begin to creep towards the wire. Four minutes later it would reach the enemy's front trench. At Zero minus one the barrage would leave the front trench and creep forward once again, forming a standing barrage 200 yards beyond it, remaining there for a further half hour. It would then advance once more at a rate of fifty yards per minute, passing over the German second line and forming another standing barrage on the far side of it.

With the barrage lifting off the German front line at Zero minus one, and with 1,000 yards to cover, it was necessary for the men of 64 Bde to leave their trenches well before zero in order to arrive at the wire tight on the heels of their artillery support, and, equally importantly, at the same time as the men of 89 Bde on their left.[31]

The other battalions of 64 Bde came into the line on the night of 8 / 9 April. The 15/DLI had been helping to dig the assembly trenches on the 6th and 7th and lost one officer whilst out on patrol.[32] The 9/KOYLI and 1/E.Yorks, whilst also called upon to dig, were able to practise the forthcoming attack on the 6th over ground near Adinfer. All were in place around midnight.

---

28 TNA PRO WO 95/2162: 10/KOYLI War Diary.
29 Second-Lieutenant Arnold William Hobbs, age 23, lies in Hénin Communal Cemetery Extension, grave I.A.5. He had previously served with the 18th (University and Public Schools) Battalion, Royal Fusiliers and had been awarded the Military Medal. The Commonwealth War Graves' Commission gives his date of death as 9 April 1917. The inscription on his headstone reads: 'Arnold Dear We Know That Your Spirit Has Continued Life. Au Revoir'.
30 Ibid. It is interesting to note that the patrol went forward in broad daylight yet was able to inspect the German wire unmolested. How this was possible is hinted at in a letter to the Official Historian on 21 June 1937 from Lt-Col G.H. Addison, 21st Div CRE (from 16 Jan 1917 to 19 July 1918), in which he claimed that the thickness of the wire in front of the German front trench was a hindrance to the defenders: "Owing to the undulating ground there were many places where, though the inner edge was under fire from the trenches, the outer was not, and the thickness of the wire combined with the usual smoke and fog of an attack gave such good cover that parties of men could come right up to the wire". See TNA PRO CAB45/116.
31 As we have already seen, however, the men of 89 Bde would not reach the German front line trenches.
32 Lieutenant Victor Albert Villiers Zacharias-Jessel, age 21, is commemorated on the Arras Memorial.

164   To Do the Work of Men

The men of the DLI and E.Yorks were content to wait in their trench lines, but after Brigadier-General Headlam had inspected the new positions, 9/KOYLI were instructed to form up in the sunken road just behind their front trench. This move caused the diarist of 15/DLI to complain that it made liaison between his left companies and the right companies of the KOYLIs rather problematic, as "these companies were not in the same trenches".[33]

After a long, wet – the men's greatcoats had been stored neatly some distance back from the front line – and no doubt frustrating wait throughout most of 9 April, the men of 64 Bde finally climbed out of their trenches at 15.52, Zero minus twenty-three minutes, and formed up, ready to move forward. The advance was to be made in half-platoon columns, 25-35 yards apart, with the second wave similarly deployed 200 yards behind. Each man carried, in addition to his rifle, bayonet, haversack and groundsheet, 120 rounds in one bandolier and a grenade in each breast pocket. With entrenching tool, full water bottle, two days' rations and three empty sandbags, not to mention shovels, pickaxes, flares and wire-cutters, a slightly-built man might end up carrying half his own weight in equipment into battle.

The twelve officers and 550 men of 9/KOYLI set off, A and C Companies, left and right, in the first wave, B and D Companies similarly placed, making up the second. The leading wave was to capture and consolidate the front line German trench, allowing the second wave to leapfrog them and do likewise to the second line position. If all went to plan, this section of the Hindenburg Line would be in British hands within the hour.

To begin with, there was very little in the way of a reply from the German garrison: a retaliatory artillery bombardment began quite promptly, but this was rather weak and ineffective; some German outposts had been reported to be situated between the wire and the first trench, and one or two possibly in front of the wire – as already mentioned, the men in the front line trench had very limited visibility owing to the thickness of the wire – so during the night 8/9 April, Headlam had sent forward two of his Vickers Machine Guns to take up a position at T4.b.2.7 (See Map 21). This was in the sunken section of the St Martin to Fontaine road that ran north-west to south-east across the line of advance and was about 300 yards from the German wire. Their job was, once the attack began, to traverse their guns along the German positions to encourage the defenders to keep their heads down, a task in which they were very effective. The orders given to the machine gun teams by the Brigadier reflected the ambiguous nature of 64 Bde's situation:

1. I cannot tell you if we will attack or not: it all depends on how things go on our left.
2. I cannot communicate with you at all.
3. The only way you will know if we are advancing is if you see & hear a barrage come down on the wire in front of you.
4. If the barrage comes down you are to get your guns into action at once on to the wire in front & traverse as far to left and right as you possibly can.
5. When the leading troops reach you, pack up, follow them and use your guns to help in consolidation of captured position.[34]

---

33   TNA PRO WO 95/2161: 15/DLI War Diary.
34   TNA PRO CAB45/116. Brigadier-General Headlam to Official Historian correspondence, 9 June, (no year given, but likely 1937). Later in the letter, in typical fashion, Headlam asserts that this use of his machine guns was 'the best example of "forward M.G.s" in the war!'

The KOYLIs suffered very few casualties until they came within 150 yards from the German wire. By this time, the creeping barrage had moved beyond the German front line, allowing their riflemen and machine gunners to direct intense fire onto the approaching khaki columns. Arriving at the wire, some troops were able to pass quite easily through the gaps, whereas others were held up for some time as they came up against uncut sections. Detachments of Stokes Mortars had gone forward with the second wave, and these immediately went into action in an attempt to cut more of the wire. One mortar was able to fire on a concrete strongpoint and put it out of action, but in attempting to observe the effects of his fire, the gallant officer directing this work was mortally wounded.[35]

The KOYLIs of A and D Companies made their way through the first belt of wire, but were held up by the still intact second belt. Individuals tried to use their wire cutters, but the task was impossible and the German rifle and machine gun fire began to inflict severe casualties. In effect, the KOYLIs were stuck out in the open between two belts of barbed wire. It is not surprising that the impetus of the attack was lost and the men sought what little cover was available, lying either in shell holes or behind any fold in the ground that they could find. B and D Companies, in the second wave, with both commanders having already become casualties, "pushed forward under the impression that the leading wave had established a footing in the German front line trench",[36] only to meet a similar fate to that of the leading companies.

On the KOYLI's right, the two leading companies of 15/DLI, (C & D Companies, commanded respectively by Lieutenant Sanders and Captain Thorpe), following very close to the advancing creeping barrage, were able to pass through a wide gap in the German wire and had soon secured their first objective – the German front line trench. A and B Companies (Lieutenant Hall and Captain Cartman) had halted at the sunken road until red flares could be seen burning ahead of them, this being the pre-arranged signal that the first trench had been

Second-Lieutenant William Edward Crick, 9/KOYLI. kia 9 April 1917, age 20. (*Mill Hill School Book of Remembrance*)

---

35 This was Acting Captain Daniel Piza, attached 64th Trench Mortar Battery, (formerly East Yorkshire Regiment). His body was never recovered and he is commemorated on the Arras Memorial.
36 TNA PRO WO 95/2162: 9/KOYLI War Diary.

captured. As these latter units approached the trench, they came under a heavy barrage and cohesion was briefly lost. The trench itself was very wide and proved difficult to cross, and with the companies somewhat mixed up, it was decided to re-organise the men before leapfrogging onto the second objective.

Captain Cartman had received a report to the effect that the KOYLIs were held up short of their first objective and that the 1/E.Yorks on the right were not attempting to reach the German second line. A patrol under Second-Lieutenant Williams was sent forward to examine the wire belts between the two German trench lines. Williams was one of the very few men of this patrol to make it back to the Durhams' position and was able to report it "very strong and quite uncut by our artillery – also that it was under enfilade machine gun fire from the left".[37] A decision had to be made: Cartman's assessment was that a further advance was impossible without artillery support and he sent a message to that effect back to Brigade HQ.

53172 Pte Charles Richard Renwick, 15/DLI. Kia 9 April 1917, age 19. (*Lloyd's Men War Memorial*)

On the right of the Brigade front, C and A Companies of 1/E.Yorks went forward. C Company, on the left, was in the German front line trench by 16.15. A Company, on the right, having been held up by the wire, caught up a few minutes later. Some of the men, unsure of their location, pushed on immediately toward the German second line and became casualties under the British barrage. They were forced to lay out in the open until darkness allowed them to make their way back to the German front line. After a consultation with Captain Cartman of 15/DLI, the 1/E.Yorks officers agreed that the uncut wire in front of their second objective precluded any further advance and consolidation of the captured line began. A Company created a block in the trench on their right flank and were to spend the night in a bombing fight with the Germans beyond it.

The narrative now returns to the 15/DLI in the centre of the brigade attack. As the work of consolidating the newly-won position began, Lieutenant Saunders (D Coy) attempted to gain touch with troops of the 9/KOYLI on the left. Unable to do so, he organised a bombing party and they began working their way northwards along the German front line into the 9/KOYLI sector. They had advanced almost 300 yards and Saunders was able to locate the German machine gun that had the Yorkshiremen pinned down. Unfortunately, Saunder's party

---

37 TNA PRO WO 95/2161: 15/DLI War Diary.

was running short of grenades and was forced to withdraw. The lieutenant reported that had he had sufficient grenades, he would have been able to silence the machine gun.

Perhaps encouraged by this bombing party's retreat, the Germans organised a bombing party of their own and made substantial inroads into the DLI-held section of the trench, forcing a large number of A and D Company men from the section they had captured. Major Falvey-Beyts, commanding 15/DLI, ordered Captain Thorpe (C Coy) to gather a small force together and form a strongpoint to deter any further incursions. The situation became less dynamic at this point, and as things settled down, Thorpe and his men began digging a communication trench from his strongpoint back to the sunken lane in square T.4.a.

It was at about 17.25 that Lieutenant-Colonel Daniell, commanding 9/KOYLI, sent Second-Lieutenant R.H. Box forward from Battalion HQ to find out what the situation was concerning the battalion. Box returned and reported, but Daniell, anxious to see for himself and actually instructed to do so by Headlam, went forward himself at 18.00 hours. He found it much as Second-Lieutenant Box had said: "the Battn. were established in shell holes, mostly inside the wire, and saw that it was useless to try and reorganise them until dark, as the German snipers were very active, both on our own front and from the other side of the valley on our left".[38] His intention, as he made clear to Brigade HQ, was to reorganise the battalion, as soon as daylight on the 10th would permit, in order to cover the high ground across the valley, "from which the enemy had not been dislodged",[39] with Lewis Gun and rifle fire. Whilst in the front line, just after dusk he noticed reinforcements advancing to occupy the road in front of the German positions. These were men of B and D Companies, 10/KOYLI, under Captain Holdstock, who had received orders at 19.10 to send two companies forward to support their sister battalion. A and C Companies, (Captain Marsh), set out at 19.30 to reinforce the 15/DLI and 1/E.Yorks who were "holding about 1,000 yards [of the Hindenburg Line] from T.5.a.3.4 to N.34.d.5.5".[40]

Lieutenant-Colonel Daniell, clearly still worried by the perilous positions held by his men, made the decision just before eight o'clock not to wait until the morning, but to withdraw his men immediately and get them to form up to the left of 10/KOYLI and dig in along the St Martin – Fontaine road. Under the supervision of Second-Lieutenant Box, as many wounded men as possible were collected from amongst the wire entanglements and shell holes between the two banks of German wire and brought safely back to the new positions. There was some urgency to his mission, as it was understood that the area was to be subject to an artillery bombardment the following morning. Rations arrived at around 23.30: tea, cold meat, biscuits and rum did much to enliven the men's spirits. Even so, Lieutenant Ibbotson, sent forward from Brigade HQ, reported back to Headlam that the men of 9/KOYLI were in an exposed position and "too tired to dig effectively".[41] Accordingly, at 04.47 on the 10 April, orders were sent to the effect that 9/KOYLI would withdraw to positions behind the sunken road from which 10/KOYLI had originally advanced (See Map 21). Twelve Officers and 550 Other Ranks had taken part in the attack: seven Officers and 176 Other Ranks were reported as casualties.

Headlam had, in the meantime, sent specific orders to Lieutenant-Colonel Postlethwaite, commanding 10/KOYLI. B and D Companies were to dig in along a "line just our side of the

---

38   TNA PRO WO 95/2162: 9/KOYLI War Diary.
39   Ibid.
40   TNA PRO WO 95/2162: 10/KOYLI War Diary.
41   TNA PRO WO 95/2159: 64 Bde War Diary.

168 To Do the Work of Men

Hindenburg Line wire – (the wire would thus protect our new trench)".[42] A number of lanes would then have to be cut through the wire "to enable a counter attack to be made easily".[43] Headlam was sure that the Germans would counter-attack the next day and attempt to eject the 64 Bde men from their hard-won section of trench. Postlethwaite was told to rush these men forward "on his own initiative"[44] as soon as any such attack began. C Company was in the old German front line to the left of 15/DLI, effectively forming the left flank of the brigade frontage, and A Company was in the same line between 15/DLI and 1/E.Yorks.

The Germans' first attempt to recapture their front line began at around 08.00 on the morning of the 10th.[45] A strong bombing party attacked the trench block on the left flank held by the men of 10/KOYLI: luckily, the recently-dug communication trench allowed supplies of bombs to be brought up, and after an exchange lasting an hour and a half, during which time over 300 bombs had been thrown – including some German ones found lying in the trench – the Germans were repelled. 30144 Private Horace Waller of C Company, 10/KOYLI, "distinguished himself on this occasion",[46] continuing to throw bombs for over an hour after five of his comrades had been killed.

The re-supply mission continued throughout the day as the 64 Bde men steeled themselves for the inevitable: a massive German counter attack was launched at 19.00 hrs. On the left, Pte Waller and his comrades were once more engaged in a vicious exchange of bombs. This time, "all the garrison became casualties, except Pte Waller, who, although wounded later, continued to throw bombs for another half an hour until he was killed". Waller was awarded the Victoria Cross.[47]

Simultaneously, a well-organised attack was driven in against the right flank of the 1/E. Yorks positions. The Germans pushed in from the flank along the old front line, in the open along both sides of the trench and also advanced from their own second line, supported by rifle grenade and trench mortar fire. The East Yorks men were unable to hold on and the right flank began to withdraw, only for the rest of the line, including the 15/DLI and the 10/KOYLI, to conform and take up positions in the new support trench. A gallant attempt had been made by Second-Lieutenant B. Cookson of 1/E.Yorks to rescue the situation, but this had come to nought: he rallied about fifteen of his men and led a bayonet charge back towards the advancing Germans, only to quickly fall, mortally wounded.[48]

Lieutenant-Colonel Postlethwaite of 10/KOYLI does not come out of this engagement well. In a letter to the Official Historian, written 23 July 1937, Lieutenant-Colonel R. Waithman, commanding 1/E.Yorks, bemoans the inaction of Postlethwaite's men:

42 TNA PRO CAB45.116: Headlam to Official Historian correspondence.
43 Ibid.
44 Ibid. The order was repeated at noon on 10 April.
45 The exact timing of this attack is uncertain. The 10/KOYLI war diarist puts it at 08.00. The 15/DLI war diarist has it starting at 05.00, and the diary of 64 Bde simply states that the attack took place in the early morning. The Official History offers no time at all.
46 TNA PRO WO 95/2162: 10/KOYLI War Diary.
47 Philip L.Wheeler, Stuart M. Archer, Peter Wrigley & Ian B. Fallows, *Batley Lads. The Story of the Men on the Roll of Honour at Batley Grammar School who died in the Great War.* (Privately published, n.d.), p.150. Quotation taken from the Citation for Pte Waller's VC. For the full VC Citation and a brief biography, see Appendix IV.
48 Second-Lieutenant B. Cookson, age 22, is buried in Wancourt British Cemetery, grave reference VIII A 6.

Their chief object, as I understood it, was to prevent (by counter-attack) the German troops from issuing out of their own trench and getting round my flank so as to attack my Bn from the rear. The inaction of 10/KOYLI allowed the Germans to do exactly this. We could have coped with their attacks in front and flank, but when they got round and in rear of my right flank, it was a different story and we were compelled to withdraw some 200 yards.[49]

Why did Postlethwaite not attack? The diary of the 10/KOYLI has little to say on the matter, save that as soon as the E.Yorks began their withdrawal, "the artillery [British] opened and shells were falling on our front line". A telephone message was sent to the artillery to ask them to lift "so that a counter attack could be made".[50]

At about the same time, Major Falvey-Beyts, commanding 15/DLI, instructed Captain Thorpe of C Company to organise a counter-attack to regain at least a portion of the positions they had just vacated. The half-hour delay caused by Postlethwaite's cautionary stance was crucial, however. Headlam was about to order 10/KOYLI forward, but the Germans had managed to get machine guns into position in their old front line and Major-General Campbell, apprised of the situation,[51] quickly ordered Postlethwaite to stay put. Luckily, word was also sent to Thorpe in time to halt his preparations. Headlam's after-action report concedes that the delayed counter-attack "would not have succeeded",[52] but his correspondence with the official historian twenty years later is rather less conciliatory: "I have no doubt whatever that if Lt-Col Postlethwaite had acted on my orders & rushed forward we should have defeated the counter [attack] and held line". The Official History smooths over the issue, concluding that Campbell "was acting on the principle that, though a counter-attack carried out within a few minutes while the victorious enemy is still in confusion may well be successful, in default of that it is advisable to wait and mount one deliberately. He now preferred to entrust the operation to the fresh 62nd Brigade, which was already under orders to relieve the 64th".[53]

This relief took place during the night of 10/11 April and by 02.00 on the 10th, 64th Brigade HQ was established in the village of Boiry St Rictrude.

The 'front line' positions were now occupied by 1/Lincs, on the right, with 10/Yorks on the left. The two Northumberland battalions took up positions slightly to the rear, ready to support if necessary. Orders for the attack on the following morning were received at Brigade HQ from Division at 19.30: the assault would go in at daybreak and would occupy the enemy's front line trench from T.5.a.4.2 to N.34.a. Details reached the 1/Lincs at 03.30 on the 11th: zero hour was 06.00, and a second objective was included. This was, predictably, part of the German

---

49 TNA PRO CAB45/116: Lieutenant-Colonel R. Waithman to the Official Historian correspondence, 23 July 1937.

50 TNA PRO WO 95/2162: 10/KOYLI War Diary.

51 Telephone communication between the front line, Brigade HQ and Divisional HQ was maintained throughout. See after-action report by Major Falvey-Beyts, War Diary 15/DLI. TNA PRO WO 95/2161.

52 TNA PRO WO 95/2159: 64 Bde HQ War Diary.

53 Falls, *Military Operations France and Belgium 1917*, Vol. I, p.247. Lieutenant-Colonel Postlethwaite continued in command of 10/KOYLI, but on 6 May, Major Brewis took over as Postlethwaite "needed a rest". On 24 July, Postlethwaite was "admitted to hospital" and on 22 August Major Festing of 15/DLI arrived and "took command of the battalion". TNA PRO WO 95/2162: 10/KOYLI War Diary.

170   To Do the Work of Men

Second Line, but it was only to be occupied "if found by Patrols not to be held, or, only lightly held. It was not to be regularly attacked".[54]

The supporting artillery barrage began at 05.35 and at Zero minus 12, the leading platoons began their advance and were able to follow the barrage right up to the German wire. They went forward "in excellent order and with great steadiness",[55] but then met with both intense machine gun fire "along the wire and to the front through existing gaps"[56] and largely intact wire entanglements. On the 10/Yorks frontage, only one "entirely cut lane and a second one partially cut"[57] were found. The 1/Lincs were only slightly luckier, in that they identified three lanes cut through the enemy wire. With only four gaps on a frontage of 1,200 yards, most troops inevitably came up against uncut wire.

> "All cuttings were completely dominated by the enemy's machine guns, which were fired from concrete emplacements in the front line. Enemy's snipers were active on the flanks and in the narrow trenches situated in the midst of the densest portions of the wire. Great but useless gallantry was shown by both leading battalions".[58]

The 10/Yorks failed to penetrate the wire, the first row of which they estimated to be thirty-five feet wide. They clung on to their precarious positions until dusk, at which point they were ordered to withdraw to their original jumping off trench in order to allow the heavy artillery to bombard the wire one more time. The failed attack had proven costly: two Officers were killed and three wounded, and the war diary estimates their Other Ranks casualties at 120.[59] The battalion was relieved during the night by 13/NFus.

The 1/Lincs met with a similar fate. Gallant attempts to get through – and sometimes under – the wire eventually came to nought. The war diary records one officer killed and six wounded, but tellingly emphasises the number of NCO casualties, (13 killed, 27 wounded and 2 missing), which "speaks for the determination with which they led their sections forward to a task believed to have been impracticable".[60] One NCO merits special mention in the battalion account:

> Sergt Walker with his Lewis Gun detachment specially distinguished himself in his efforts to overcome the enemy machine gun fire, firing the gun continuously himself from 6:30 a.m. to 12:30 p.m. and returning alone 7 times across the open for ammunition. He was finally killed about 12:30 p.m.[61]

---

54   TNA PRO WO 95/2154: 1/Lincs War Diary.
55   TNA PRO WO 95/2152: 62 Bde War Diary.
56   TNA PRO WO 95/2154: 1/Lincs War Diary.
57   TNA PRO WO 95/2152: 62 Bde War Diary.
58   Ibid.
59   The two officers killed were Lieutenant John Selbey Pratt, age 19, who is buried in Wancourt British Cemetery, grave reference VII D 33, and Second-Lieutenant Maurice Kemp-Welch, age 36, who is commemorated on the Arras Memorial.
60   TNA PRO WO 95/2154: 1/Lincs War Diary.
61   Ibid. 9675 Lance-Sergeant Arthur Walker was Mentioned in Despatches and is buried in Cojeul British Cemetery, grave A 73. (On the original Graves Registration Report Form his regimental number is recorded as 7675.) The officer fatality is likely Second-Lieutenant Harold James Marlin, OC "B" Coy, age 32, who is buried in Henin Communal Cemetery Extension, grave I D 1. (On the

Over 100 rifle grenades were fired by a party under Second-Lieutenant Hine in an attempt to silence one particular enemy machine gun, but their efforts were in vain: the narrow slit in the concrete emplacement was only inches above ground level and it proved to be an impossible target. A report sent back by Hine was misinterpreted by Brigade HQ as meaning that the first objective had been won, and Major Wales, sent forward to supervise its consolidation, was badly wounded on his way back, having ascertained the true position. Just as with 10/Yorks, the forward positions were evacuated to allow a further bombardment of the wire. The 12/NFus came up to relieve them, completing the task by 21.30 that evening. The diarist feels obliged to mention one more member of the battalion:

> Prior to relief all wounded had been brought in, it was snowing hard and there was to be a fresh attack the next day. Much good work was performed by Capt. G. Jacobs, the Battalion M.O. [Medical Officer], who has on several occasions been recommended for gallantry but so far without recognition. His devotion to duty and cheerful bearing in the face of heavy fire were and always have been an example to all.[62]

It was still imperative that the Hindenburg positions be taken as soon as possible. At five o'clock the next morning, an artillery barrage was due to begin that would presage one more effort to oust the defenders, this time by the two Northumberland battalions.

By the morning of the 12th, however, the situation had changed: 62 Bde HQ had received messages the previous evening to the effect that 21 Bde troops on the left had penetrated the Hindenburg Line and were bombing southwards down the line towards the Cojeul River. A patrol sent out by 13/NFus under Captain Graham could find no evidence of this and his party was withdrawn at 04.30. The 05.00 artillery barrage began as planned, but 21st Division was able to report, at 06.00, that 169 Bde, which had relieved 21 Brigade, were continuing the advance down the Hindenburg Line and should be entering the trenches opposite 62 Bde positions at any moment. Further patrols were sent out but were only able to report that they had been fired upon from the German lines.

By 10.30, however, as the artillery bombardment ceased, enemy troops were seen retiring across the open ground behind their lines: this time patrols found the German front line trench empty and this was quickly occupied, with men from 13/NFus entering the support line – likewise evacuated – by 11.30. On their right, the 12/NFus CO, Captain Lockie, also ordered his men forward, and both German trench lines were occupied by 14.00, the Fusilier's right flank being approximately at T.6.a.10.76 (See Map 21). B Company formed a defensive flank along a communication trench and battalion HQ was moved forward into one of the vacated concrete machine gun emplacements. The extent and quality of the dugouts that were discovered came as a surprise to their new tenants:

> A very fine system of dugouts were found in the Support Line, being connected up through the whole length of the line by a tunnel 8ft high & 6ft wide, the top, sides and bottom well-made and completely boarded with 3" thick planks, sleeping berths and small recesses

---

original Graves Registration Report Form he is recorded as H.J. Martin, date of death 11.4.1917. On his headstone, he is correctly identified as H.J. Marlin, but his date of death is given as 12.4.1917.)

62   Ibid.

and rooms led off the tunnel; a good deal of Booty was found, the enemy having evacuated in a great hurry. Boxes of grenades, ammunition & Very Lights & also 4 small Trench Mortars were seized, numbers of blankets, clothing, Iron rations, lamps, tools, etc. There was an entrance to the tunnel down a shaft – well boarded and made – every 50 yards from the trench, 50 ft down & steps well made, each entrance was numbered with a tin plate.[63]

In these dugouts were discovered a number of prisoners from 64 Bde: they had apparently been well-treated before being left behind by the retreating Germans. A wounded NCO of 10/KOYLI informed Lieutenant-Colonel Dix, (CO 13/NFus) that the Germans had stood to at about 03.30 that morning, had given their wounded prisoners coffee, and had begun their evacuation at 08.30.

The right flank of 12/NFus butted up against strongly held German positions in both trenches of the Hindenburg Line. Lieutenant-General Snow ordered the 21st Division to continue its advance on the 13 April: the proposed attack involved a "bombing operation down the Hindenburg Line and [...] an advance across the open on either side of it".[64] To the north of the line, units of 56th Division would advance in an easterly direction, and to the south, two companies of the 6/Leics would do likewise. It was down to the 12/NFus to execute the bombing operation: A Coy and two platoons of B Coy would continue the advance down the support line; D Coy along with the remaining two platoons of B Coy were to do the same along the enemy front line. C Coy would advance in the open just to the north of the support line. Two tanks were to support the infantry advance. Unfortunately, one of them broke down before it had moved at all, and the other suffered the same fate soon after zero. This second tank later managed to get as far as square T.5.b, fired 400 rounds, promptly retired "and was no more seen".[65]

None of the attempts to advance over open ground made any real headway: C Coy barely got away from its jumping off positions before being pinned down by machine gun fire from the sunken road in N.35.d and from a hedge on N.36.a. The diary of the 6/Leics barely mentions the event at all, stating that "The attack held up after a very small advance".[66] The bombers managed to work their way some distance along the two trench lines, but resistance was stubborn and by 18.00 hours they had, according to the battalion war diary, come to a halt in positions in square T.5.b. This is not clear, however: the diary claims an advance of 1,000 yards, and the 62 Bde diary states that the bombers pushed on as far as square T.6.d before being held up by a machine gun in a concrete emplacement. The distance claimed and the map reference would then tally, leaving only the 12/NFus diarist's map reading in question. In any case, with the men exhausted after struggling through deep, sticky liquid mud in the trenches, any further attempts to continue the advance were suspended. By the early hours of 14 April, the Northumberland Fusiliers and the Lincolns had been relieved by men from 19 Bde and twenty-four hours later the remaining 62 Bde units were withdrawn. By nightfall on the 15th, they were in billets in Bellacourt, Grosville, Beaumetz and Bretencourt, their involvement in the initial stage of the Battle of Arras finally over. 62 Bde casualties for the period 10 – 14 April amounted to 3 Officers killed, with 10 wounded, 61 Other Ranks killed, with 226 wounded and 55 missing.

---

63   TNA PRO WO 95/2155: 13/Northumberland Fusiliers War Diary.
64   Falls, *Military Operations France and Belgium 1917*, Vol. I, p.285.
65   TNA PRO WO 95/2152: 62 Bde HQ War Diary.
66   TNA PRO WO 95/2164: 6/Leics War Diary.

The 21st Division was out of the line for the next fortnight, having been moved back to "rest areas".[67] Casualties for the entire operation so far, 9–15 April, were reported as follows:

	Killed	Wounded	Missing	Total
62 Bde				
Officers	3	11	–	14
Other Ranks	61	228	55	344
64 Bde				
Officers	12	26	1	39
Other Ranks	120	450	225	795
110 Bde				
Officers	3	9	–	12
Other Ranks	35	138	10	183
14/NFus (Pioneers)				
Other Ranks	–	5	1	6
Total				
Officers	18	46	1	65
Other Ranks	216	821	291	1,328
Overall Total				**1,393**

Other than Private Waller VC, one more "Other Rank" casualty merited special mention in the newspapers back in Yorkshire. Corporal Sydney James, of 9/KOYLI, was the subject of a short article in the *Huddersfield Examiner* of 27 April:

> News is at hand that Corporal Sydney James, KOYLI, who played centre half-back for Huddersfield Town before joining the forces last year, was killed in action in France on April 9th. James, who hails from Sheffield, played for the Tinsley Church and Bird-in-Hand Clubs in that town previous to coming to Huddersfield Town, who secured him as a centre-forward. A stylish and clever player, he had scarcely the physique necessary to achieve a big result in that position, and later he was moved to centre-half, an experiment which was attended with great success. His work was consistently good, and when called up he promised to be one of the finest centre half-backs in the Second Division of the English League. The news of his death was received yesterday by his mother, who lives at Tinsley, and many players and lovers of football will read the announcement with regret".[68]

The 64 Bde was not allowed to "rest" for long. The struggle for the Hindenburg Line position was continuing, and on 23 April, orders attached the brigade temporarily to 50th Division. The following day, 64 Bde was moved again, this time to join 33rd Division: 9/KOYLI were then given the unenviable task of attempting yet another bombing attack down the Hindenburg Line, scheduled for 28 April. On the afternoon of the 25th, they joined 19 Bde in the Hindenburg

67   TNA PRO WO 95/2132: 21st Division General Staff War Diary.
68   35274 Lance-Corporal Sydney James, age 26, is buried alongside many of his comrades in Cojeul British Cemetery, grave D9.

front and support lines where they relieved the 1/Cameronians, only to attract immediate attention from German artillery which shelled the front line section. A Company suffered a few casualties, including Lieutenant A.E. Day and Second-Lieutenant S.G. Richards wounded. Five other ranks were killed.

The 9/KOYLI were approximately one and a half miles to the south-east of the section of the Hindenburg Line they had previously attacked and opposing sides here held adjacent sections of the same trenches. Zero hour was 03.00 on 28 April: whilst the main attack made its way down the two trench lines, another party would advance across the open ground on the left, that is, to the north-east of the German support line.

The advance began on time, with the supporting artillery barrage scheduled to start five minutes later. On the right of the attack front, however, four shells fell short, landing right in the middle of the attacking party. Unsurprisingly, this disorganised and delayed them considerably. They gathered themselves together once more and managed to advance a further 200 yards before encountering a German block. Their efforts to take this block failed and it was decided to construct one of their own in front of it. The men advancing on the left, down the support line, experienced similar problems, coming across a twelve-foot-high block approximately 250 yards short of their objective. A bombing fight ensued which lasted for several hours, but in the end, the block remained intact. On the extreme left, those men attempting to attack across the open ground were unable to advance in face of heavy machine gun fire and were forced to go to ground.

The attack had stalled, had gained only about fifty yards of trench and had cost the battalion some fifty casualties, including Second-Lieutenants Teaz and Brierley wounded. Seven Other Ranks had been killed. At 19.45, the 9/KOYLI were relieved by 1/EYorks, who placed two companies in each trench, one holding the block, the other a short distance behind in support.

At 07.30 on the following morning, the Germans launched a counter attack against B Company in the support line, pushing them back and beginning a sequence that saw the block change hands several times during the day. A scheduled bombardment by British heavy artillery that evening meant that the 1/EYorks men were obliged to pull back some 200 yards in order to avoid casualties from 'friendly fire'. This meant that all the ground gained the previous day was lost. Defending those gains had cost the 1/EYorks three Officers wounded, seven Other Ranks killed, with one missing and forty-five wounded.

The situation settled into a stalemate as both sides consolidated the positions they held and refrained from antagonising each other into action. A series of reliefs saw the 1/EYorks and 15/DLI swap places a number of times in the following few days before rejoining the rest of 21st Division in billets away from front line duties. The 21st Division would play its part in the Battle of Arras on two more occasions.

The main French attack had gone in on the Chemin des Dames ridge on 16 April: although some ground had been captured, this "modest success" had "fallen catastrophically short of [Nivelle's] grandiose goals". [69] Hints from Paris and London that Nivelle was about to be replaced by Pétain gave Sir Douglas Haig pause for thought. Haig knew that once Pétain was in charge, the French Army would be likely to adopt a more defensive strategy and this would render pointless any continued efforts by the British to push on to Cambrai. Instead, he made his mind up to push " 'steadily forward to a good defensive line' by the middle of May and then

---

69   Gary Sheffield, *The Chief: Douglas Haig and the British Army* (London: Aurum Press, 2011), p. 218.

'consolidate it' and wait on events before deciding on future operations".[70] With this in mind, and with French attacks already planned for 4 and 5 May, the British would launch another general offensive on 3 May: First, Third and Fifth Armies were to "advance to a given line which [Haig] believed would be equally well suited 'for a renewed offensive or for defence'".[71]

The 3 May attacks proved to be litany of failure, the "only bright feature of a terrible day"[72] being the capture of the village of Fresnoy by the Canadians at the northern end of the sixteen-mile front. The planning was flawed, and the eventual zero hour of 03.45 was an uneasy compromise: Allenby (Third Army) had wanted to attack in the light, but the Australians on the right flank (part of Gough's Fifth Army) were pushing for a night attack. Haig insisted that all units should begin their advance at the same time and imposed this hasty compromise. The attack would begin in the dark after all. Planners had only two days in which to finalise the orders and this led to some units not receiving theirs "until one hour before zero. It was a recipe for disaster".[73] Indeed, the official historian concludes that 3 May was the "blackest of the war".[74]

The 21st Division was called upon to attack in the southern sector of the front (See Map 22). The 110 Bde was to advance in a south-easterly direction *behind and paralleling* the Hindenburg positions and capture the town of Fontaine-lez-Croisilles before possibly being required to push on to positions which effectively formed a flank to the advance of 62nd Division, whose job it was to capture the town of Bullecourt and then push on in a north-easterly direction, that is, at ninety degrees to the 110 Bde attack. Meanwhile, a heavy artillery barrage would fall on the area between the two divisions until they were in a position to gain touch with each other, and 64 Bde, from positions well in advance of 110 Bde's right flank, was given the unenviable task of once more bombing its way down the section of the Hindenburg Line still occupied by the German forces. Tanks would be available to support these attacks. One was allocated to 64 Bde, two to 110 Bde, and one would remain in reserve.

This latter objective was entrusted to 15/DLI. Just behind them, in support would be 10/KOYLI. The 15/DLI relieved 1/EYorks in square T.6.d on the evening of 2 May, orders for the attack not arriving until 22.00 hrs.

The story of this attack can be relatively quickly told. The attack went in at 03.47 and immediately ran into a German retaliatory artillery bombardment. The promised tank was as yet nowhere to be seen: it was inching its way forward in the dark, clinging to the edge of the Hindenburg support line trench in order to keep direction. The men ran almost immediately into a substantial trench block, and in trying to circumvent it by advancing across the open found that the trench beyond it was full of wire. The first 15/DLI bombing squads were stopped in their tracks by enemy sniper and machine gun fire, and any attempts to climb over the block only resulted in more casualties. A message sent back to Brigade at 04.28 reported their inability to get any further forward.

---

70 Ibid. pp.219-220. Within this reference, Sheffield is citing an article by David French entitled 'Who Knew What and When? The French Army Mutinies and the British Decision to Launch the Third Battle of Ypres' in Lawrence Freedman et al, *War, Strategy and International Politics* (Oxford: Clarendon Press, 1992).

71 Jonathan Nicholls, *Cheerful Sacrifice: The Battle of Arras 1917* (London: Leo Cooper, 1993), p. 195. Nicholls cites TNA PRO WP158/23.

72 Ibid, p. 201.

73 Ibid. p. 196.

74 Falls, *Military Operations France and Belgium 1917*, Vol. I , p.450.

176 To Do the Work of Men

Just after five o'clock, the tank arrived. It had reached the road at U.1.c.2.6[75] and began firing down the Hindenburg Support Line trench, only to be greeted by a hail of German trench mortar rounds. At 05.48, Captain Thorpe, (15/DLI), commanding the left attacking company, made another attempt at getting over the first German block, taking eight of his men with him. No sooner had they appeared above ground, when a German shell took out seven of the party. Thorpe and his one remaining unwounded man were forced to retire and Thorpe was able to report that the tank had been crippled and could not advance any further. It had not reached the first trench block. Stranded in the open, it attracted a great deal of enemy artillery fire, much of which fell amongst the 15/DLI men. The choice was stark: remain where they were and continue to take casualties or advance once more. Lieutenant-Colonel Falvey-Beyts decided that the latter course was preferable and led his men across the open between the two trench lines. They soon came up against a strongly-wired and equally strongly-defended communication trench and this assault also ground to a halt.

It was the subsequent arrival of Second-Lieutenant Cundall and the A Coy bombers of 10/ KOYLI at around 06.45 that re-energised the advance and some of the men were able to push on about 200 yards along the trench. Unfortunately, Cundall was killed whilst leading his party and momentum was lost.[76] The war diary of 15/DLI claims that fourteen separate attempts were made to advance beyond the first German block that day, but they were all to no avail. They were eventually relieved by 1/EYorks that evening, having lost eight officers and 106 Other Ranks[77], but having gained little or no ground.

Three days later, on 6 May, the 15/DLI were back in the front line trenches, "holding the line".[78] An event that took place that day is remarkable in that it merited no mention in the battalion war diary, neither then, nor subsequently. A wounded man was spotted lying out in No Man's Land some forty yards from the German wire. Private Michael Heaviside volunteered to take some food and water out to him. He managed to reach him despite heavy enemy fire and soon realised that the man had been out there since the failed 3 May attack. Heaviside succeeded in getting the man safely back to the British line and was subsequently awarded the Victoria Cross for his actions.[79]

By 03.15 on the morning of 3 May 1917, 110 Bde troops were in position in the front line (designated the Brown Line) ready to launch their attack on the village of Fontaine-lez-Croisilles. The 8/Leics occupied 800 yards of the brigade frontage on the right, with three companies in the front line and one in support. To their left, along a shorter frontage of 500 yards, and deployed in depth with only one company in front, were 9/Leics. Each battalion had one tank allocated to it, along with one section of machine guns and two Stokes mortars. The brigade's first objective, the Blue Line (see Map 22) was about 1,500 yards from the Brown Line and more or less followed the course of the Sensée River which ran just to the north of

---

75 This is where York Trench meets the Hindenburg Support Line and is barely in advance of the original jumping off line. See Map 22.

76 Second-Lieutenant John Earnest Cundall, age 36, is buried in Henin Communal Cemetery Extension, grave II.B.2.

77 There was one officer fatality. Second-Lieutenant Christopher Nevile Baildon, age 24, is commemorated on the Arras Memorial.

78 This phrase constitutes the entire entry for TNA PRO WO 95/2161:15/DLI War Diary.

79 See Appendix IV or the full VC Citation and brief biography.

the village of Fontaine-lez-Croisilles. Reaching the second objective, the Yellow Line, required the capture of the village itself. At Zero plus three and a half hours, the heavy artillery barrage would cease and "[t]he area enclosed in these Barrages as far South East as the Army Boundary will then be mopped up by 110th Inf. Bde".[80] On the left was 54 Bde, 18th Division. The 7/Bedfordshires were to capture, and then push on beyond Chérisy.

Artillery arrangements were as follows: before Zero, Fontaine Wood was to be bombarded using incendiary shells.[81] A standing barrage just ahead of the Brown Line would come down at Zero, and at Zero plus two minutes, it would begin to creep forwards at a rate of 100 yards every two minutes until it reached River Road, at which point (Zero plus twenty-four minutes) it would slow to a rate of 100 yards every six minutes before halting 200 yards south of the Sensée River. This standing barrage would remain in place until Zero plus two hours, whereupon it would recommence its forward movement at the previous rate before forming a final standing barrage 200 yards south-east of the Yellow Line. The barrage would cease completely at Zero plus three hours. 110 Bde orders reinforced this rate of forward movement, stating that "Bns will advance in accordance with barrages […] and leading waves will advance as close as possible to the creepers".[82]

The two Leicester battalions' leading waves were already lined up approximately fifty yards ahead of the Brown Line at Zero and were greeted by an immediate German defensive barrage. Unsurprisingly the men were "unnerved and the start of the battle was a hurried and disorganised affair as they struggled to get clear of the German shell fire".[83] At Zero plus two, (03.47), they began their advance.

Both battalions veered slightly to the right, pushed across by the 7/Bedfords who themselves had lost direction and encroached into 110 Bde territory.

On the left, 9/Leics suffered heavy casualties from the shell fire as they struggled forward, with Captain F.P Cox being killed almost immediately.[84] It was noticed at this point that "their" tank was advancing alongside Wood Trench, but it was forced to withdraw after coming under heavy enemy machine gun fire. It played no further role in the assault.[85] By 04.15 the attack had faltered and the men were held up just short of Fontaine Trench. A further five officers had been wounded by this point.

Captain Frederick Percy Cox, 9/Leics. Kia 3 May 1917, age 37. (*The Sphere*, 11 Aug 1917)

80 TNA PRO WO 95/2132: 21st Division GHQ War Diary.
81 Ibid. Rather quaintly, the orders add: "weather permitting".
82 TNA PRO WO 95/2163: 'Operation Order No. 62', 2 May 1917, 110 Bde War Diary.
83 Richardson, *The Tigers*, p.179.
84 Captain Frederick Percy Cox, age 37, is commemorated on the Arras Memorial.
85 The tank allocated to 8/Leics broke down and played no part in the attack.

On the right, 8/Leics had lined up with C Coy (Major T.L.Warner) on the left, B Coy (Captain A.G. Astle) in the centre and A Coy (Lieutenant F.R. Oliver) on the right. D Coy (Second-Lieutenant J.W. Corbett) was drawn up in two lines, sixty yards to the rear. The diarist was at pains to point out the inadvisability of attacking in the dark:

> The morning was very dark – sunrise was not until 5:23 a.m. (summer time), the dust and smoke from our own barrage and that of the enemy which opened almost immediately, making it impossible to see more than a few yards ahead.[86]

It was not long before C Coy was held up by heavy machine gun fire and found themselves sheltering in positions along the sunken road, known as Rotten Row, which led into Fontaine village. The other three companies, as reported to Brigade HQ at around 04.40, were also held up "on a line 300 yds N.E. of RIVER ROAD by machine gun fire, especially from the direction of CHERRY WOOD and HINDENBURG FRONT LINE, about the point where RIVER ROAD crosses it".[87] This was confirmed by a report – clearly arriving out of sequence at HQ – that the 8/Leics had taken York Trench and had advanced a short distance beyond it.

The position on 9/Leics front was "obscure".[88] A number of runners were sent forward with messages for the attacking companies, but none returned. Accordingly, at around 07.00, Lieutenant Walker was sent forward with fifty men and a Lewis Gun to work his way down Wood Trench. Twenty minutes later he had established telephonic communication with Battalion HQ and was able to report that the enemy were holding the sunken road in front of Fontaine Wood and the village [River Road] and that the men of the 9/Leics were in a line of shell holes fifty yards short of this road. Others were holding Rotten Row and a couple of strongpoints manned by Lewis Gun teams had been established. A message was also received at 08.45 to the effect that Captain H.E. Milburn, with one other officer and thirty Other Ranks, was holding a trench "with enemy on both flanks and in front",[89] but that he was unable to identify his position. It was later reported that an enemy strongpoint at U.1.b.85.15 (approximately just south of the point where York Trench meets Bush Trench) had held up the Leicesters' advance with fire from a single machine gun "with a very wide traverse in it",[90] and that enemy counter attacks down Fontaine Trench and up Wood Trench and Bush Trench had isolated a number of 110 Bde parties. The attack had "lost cohesion and disintegrated".[91] Many of the troops in forward positions were effectively cut off: indeed, Captain Milburn's party was not heard from again.[92]

The enemy advance up Bush Trench was met by a party of six men of 6/Leics, under Second-Lieutenant Bernays. This battalion was moving up in support of the two attacking battalions, with A and C Coys on the right, and B and D Coys on the left. Bernays and his small group were unable to push the Germans back, all the men becoming casualties. Another party of 6/

---

86   TNA PRO WO 95/2165: 8/Leics War Diary.
87   TNA PRO WO 95/2163:. 'Narrative of Operations' 110 Bde HQ War Diary.
88   TNA PRO WO 95/2165: 9/Leics War Diary.
89   Ibid.
90   TNA PRO WO 95/2163: 'Narrative of Operations', 110 Bde HQ War Diary.
91   Falls, *Military Operations France and Belgium 1917*, Vol. I, p.435.
92   Captain Milburn was later reported as having been taken prisoner. Richardson, *The Tigers*, p. 185.

Leics (under Captain McLay of C Coy) established themselves in what would appear to be part of York Trench,[93] but could do no more than hold that line. On the left, B Coy, ordered by Brigadier-General Hessey (OC 110 Bde) to attack Fontaine Wood to protect the left flank of the men who had already gone over the top, managed to push forward almost as far as Fontaine Trench, with D Coy 150 yards behind them. B Coy's commanding officer was killed and D Coy's wounded, and the diarist of 6/Leics regrets that it was "difficult to obtain a reliable narrative of events".[94]

At around 09.15, 18th Division had reported that they had cleared the village of Chérisy and were consolidating ground along the ridge in squares O.33. b & d. Accordingly, just over an hour later, 21st Division issued an order that the ground gained on the right was to be held, and the attack "pushed home"[95] on the left. The German counter attacks, as mentioned above, frustrated these preparations, and it was not until after three o'clock in the afternoon that it was decided that three companies of 7/Leics would carry out this new assault: a renewed artillery bombardment was to begin at 17.30 and the Leicesters would go in forty-five minutes later. Their objectives were, firstly, the consolidation of River Road, and secondly, to secure the southern edge of Fontaine Wood. A postponement of one hour followed, and – for reasons that remain unclear – 7/Leics' war diary makes no mention of the battalion's second objective.[96]

As the men moved forward at 19.15, the Germans brought down heavy artillery bombardment on the very area into which they were to advance. A Coy (Captain Vanner) was able to push on down Rotten Row as far as the centre of square U.1.b., and C Coy (Second-Lieutenant White) moved simultaneously down Wood Trench, but found it difficult to follow, the trench not being fully dug in places. Exposed above ground, they were subject to very heavy machine gun fire from the north-east and were eventually forced to seek the protection of the sunken section of Rotten Row. B Coy's job was to keep C Coy supplied with grenades, but found it impossible to make any ground through the artillery and machine gun fire.

The plan had already fallen apart, and to make matters worse, Vanner's men were forced to defend their newly-won outpost from a German counter attack emanating from River Road. Rifle and Lewis Gun fire eventually drove the attackers back. Once he had re-established a line running roughly from the eastern end of Pug Lane to a point near the junction of Wood Trench and Fontaine Trench, Vanner proceeded to reconnoitre his flanks. All he found were an NCO and four men of 6/Leics on his right, and an NCO and fourteen men of the same battalion on his left.

110 Bde HQ were informed at around 21.50 that the 18th Division troops on their left had been forced to retire from Chérisy and were for the most part back where they had started on the Brown Line. Accordingly, at 22.55, orders were issued to withdraw all battalions to positions behind the Brown Line, where re-organisation could take place. The men made their way back, some crawling from shell hole to shell hole, and it was not until well after two o'clock the following morning that the withdrawal was completed, one company of 7/Leics in Rotten Row and one of 6/Leics in Pug Lane having not received the original withdrawal order.

---

93   The name of the trench is not mentioned in the relevant war diary.
94   TNA PRO WO 95/2164: 6/Leics War Diary.
95   TNA PRO WO 95/2163: 'Narrative of Operations', 110 Bde HQ War Diary.
96   The omission is in any case academic. The attack did not reach Fontaine Wood, let alone its southern edge.

180 To Do the Work of Men

Casualties for this failed attack were heavy. Most of the officers of 8/Leics had become casualties: Captain Astle and Second-Lieutenant Pratley were known to have been killed; Major Warner and Second-Lieutenants Johnson, Harris, Bennett and Hill were wounded. Second-Lieutenants Clarke and Pitts were believed to be prisoners of war, as was Lieutenant Oliver. Frank Pitts of A Coy had been wounded and left behind when his company withdrew. Unfortunately, he died of his wounds soon after his capture and was buried by the Germans in Bouchain Military Cemetery.[97] Total battalion casualties were reported as 11 Officers and 291 Other Ranks. The 9/Leics lost two officers killed, with ten wounded and four missing. Other Ranks casualties amounted to thirty killed, 179 wounded and 92 missing.[98]

The war diaries of 6 and 7/Leics do not report casualties for this battle, but it can be estimated that the 6th Battalion lost twenty-four men killed and the 7th seventeen. Captain Vanner was awarded the Military Cross for his actions on 3 May, as was the 7/Leics Medical Officer, Captain Robert Bruce Wallace, who had gone out with stretcher bearers to bring wounded men back to safety.

The 21st Division was withdrawn once more from front line positions. Between 13 and 18 May they were in the vicinity of Adinfer Wood, undergoing training, particularly in musketry. By the start of June, they were back holding the new front-line positions in the old Hindenburg Line – in the very sector south of Fontaine-lez-Croisilles that 64 Bde had failed to capture on 3 May. The old German front line had been renamed Burg Trench, the support line now known as Tunnel Trench. This latter was still in German hands. It was the 110 Bde that was called upon one last time to try and push the front line forward, this time from these new positions. For this assault, the 12 and 13/NFus were attached to the brigade, and would form the main attacking force, with one company each from 6 and 8/Leics in support (See Map 23).

The 12/NFus moved up into their positions on the right of the Brigade front during the night of 15/16 June with little difficulty, relieving 7/Leics in Burg Trench and completing the process by 23.45. The experience of 13/NFus was very different: they were effectively pinned down in the communication trenches for two hours near the village of Croisilles as the German artillery pounded the area between ten and midnight. The battalion suffered heavy casualties and were forced to continue their move "in small parties and by various routes",[99] only arriving in their jumping off positions in Humber Trench between one and two o'clock in the morning. It was impossible to reorganise all of their units before Zero Hour – D Coy still had only half a platoon in place by 02.40 – and it was hastily arranged that C Coy of 8/Leics (and two Lewis Guns from 6/Leics) would be 'lent' to 13/NFus "to replace casualties caused on the way up"[100] and take part in the assault..

The objective of the two Northumberland Battalions was Tunnel Trench between its junction with Lump Lane and U.14. a. 40.45. (See map). The British artillery barrage commenced at Zero Hour, 03.10, just as the men went over the top, but did not provoke a serious response from the German artillery which continued to shell the area behind the British front line.

---

97   In 1924 he was reinterred in Cabaret Rouge Cemetery, grave reference XVI. G. 7. Captain Albert George Astle, age 22 and Second-Lieutenant Joseph Edward Pratley, age 37, are commemorated on the Arras Memorial. Pratley had previously served sixteen years with the 9th Lancers.
98   As reported in TNA PRO WO 95/2165: 9/Leics War Diary.
99   TNA PRO WO 95/2132: 21st Div HQ War Diary.
100 Ibid.

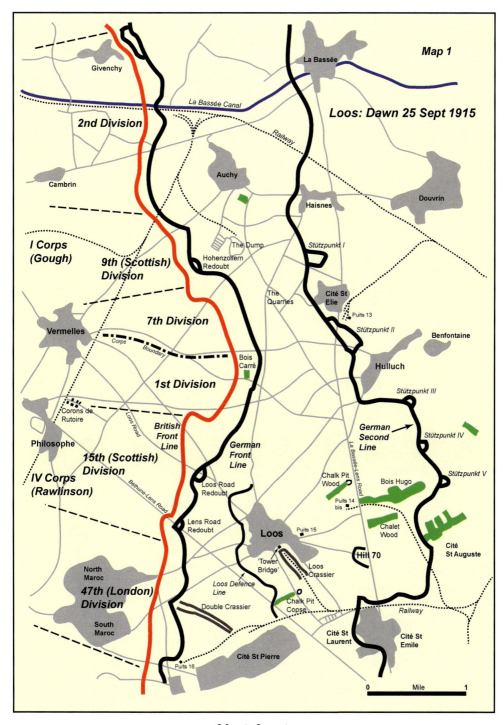

Map 1. Loos 1.

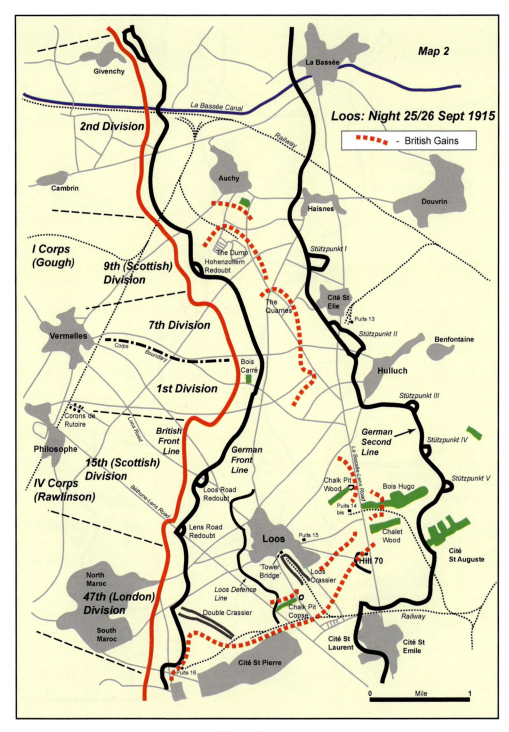

Map 2. Loos 1a.

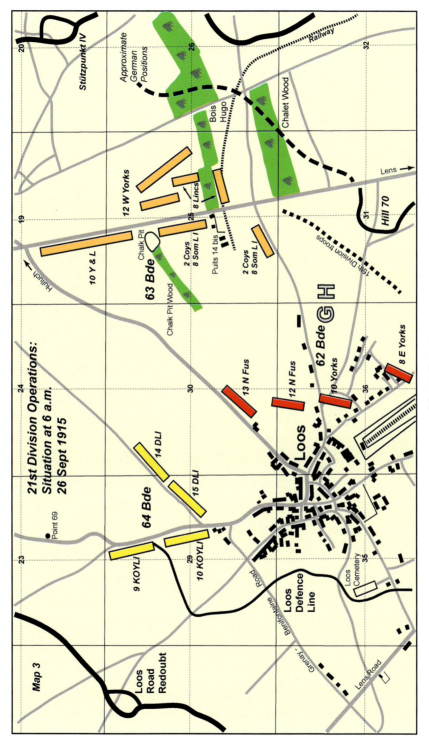

Map 3. Loos 2.

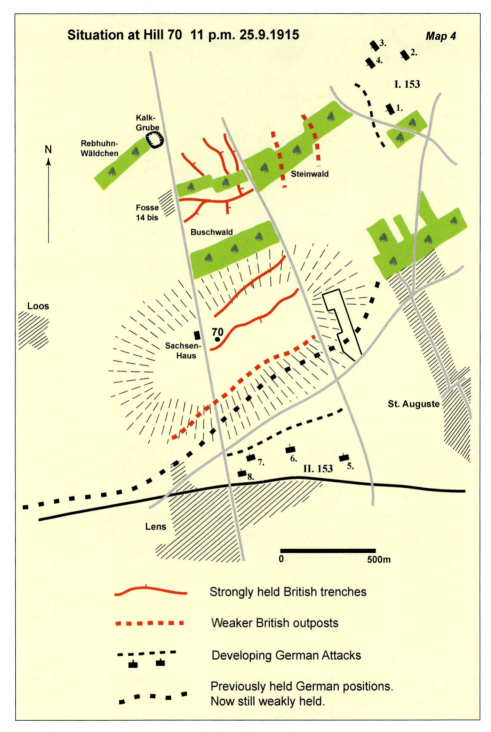

Map 4. Altenberger 1.

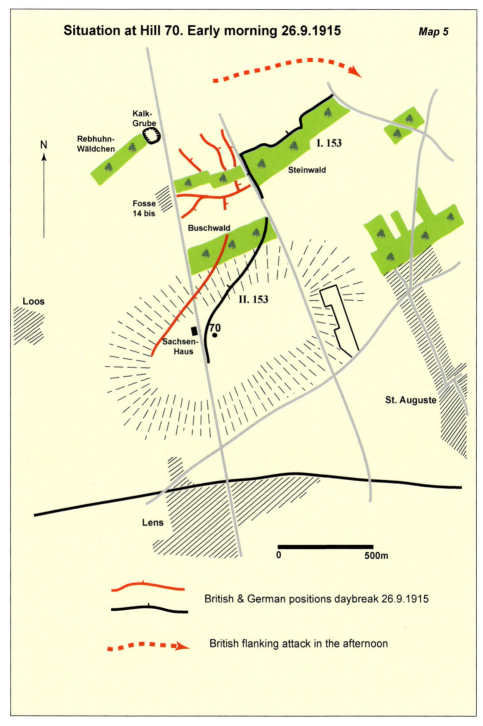

Map 5. Altenberger 2.

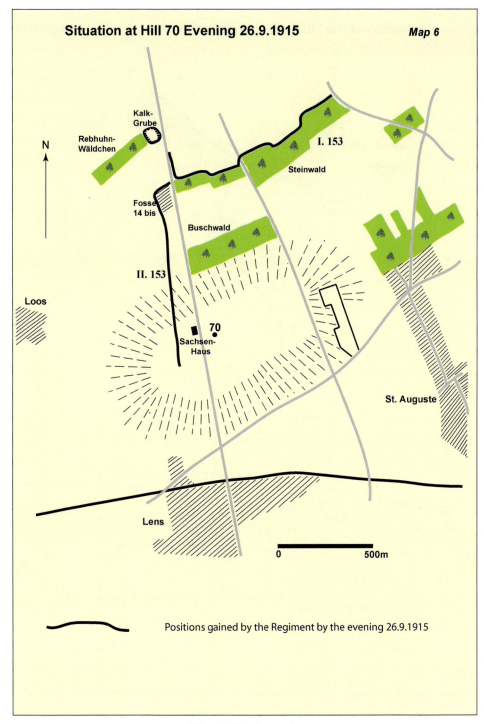

Map 6. Altenberger 3.

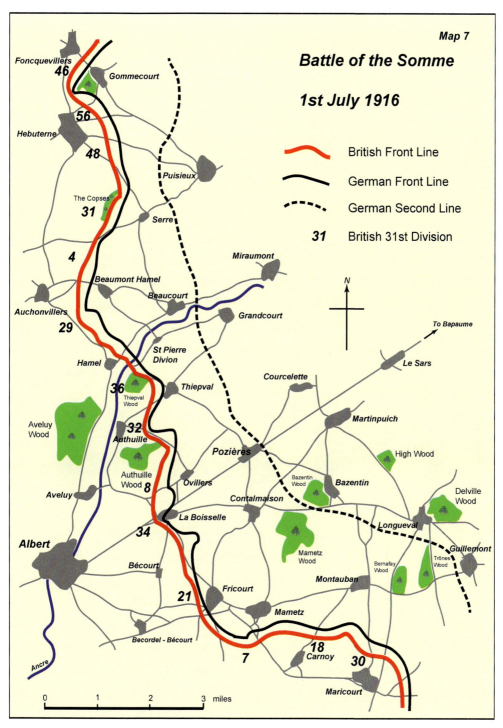

Map 7. Somme 1.

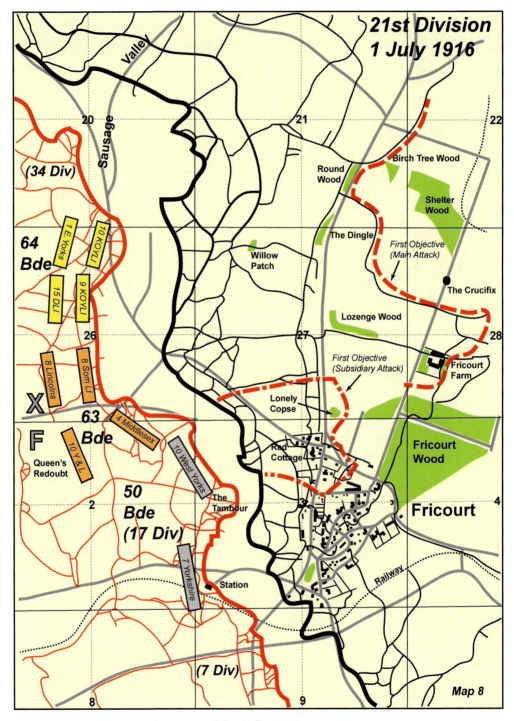

Map 8. Somme 2.

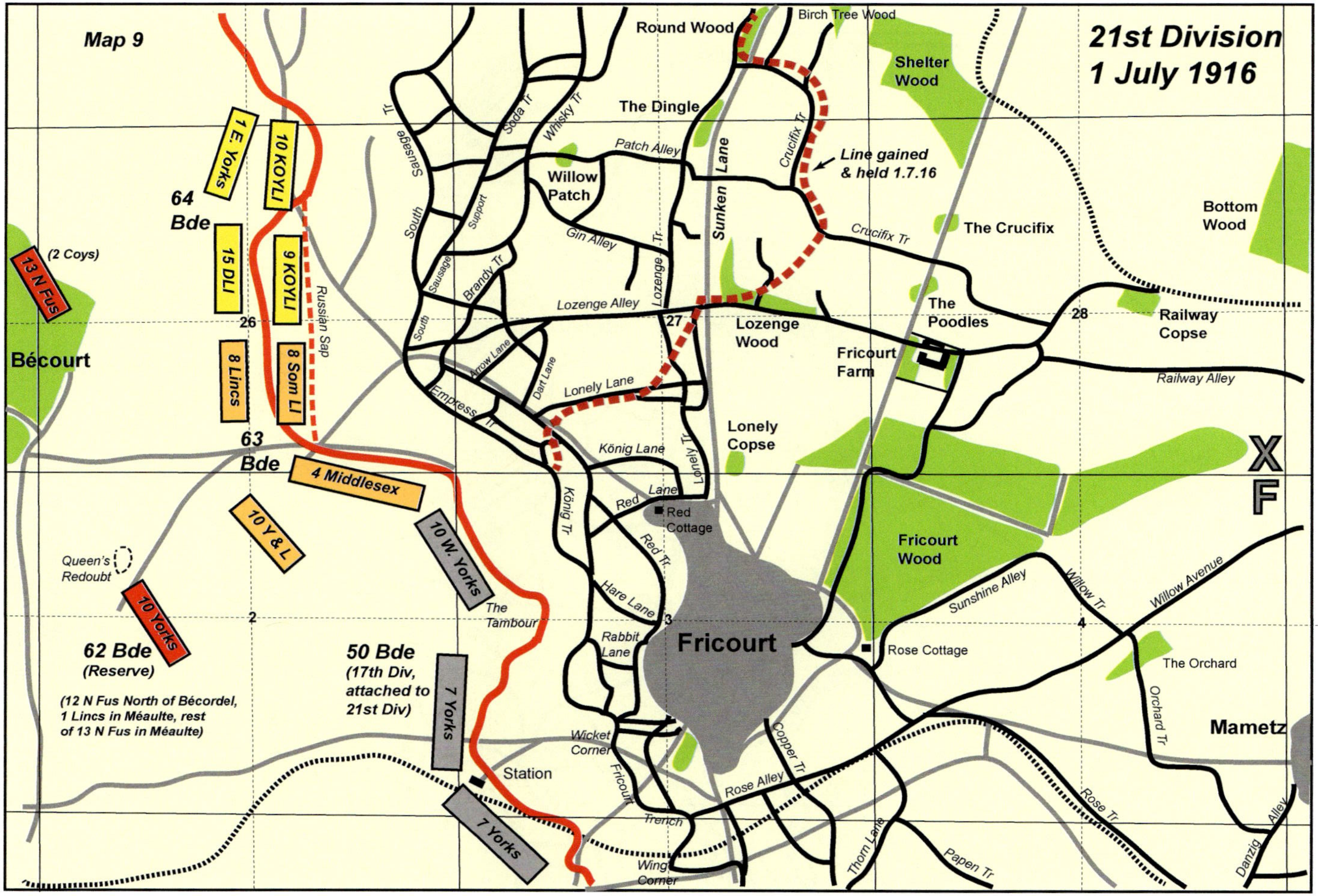
Map 9
21st Division
1 July 1916
Bécourt
(2 Coys)
13 N Fus
1 E. Yorks
10 KOYLI
64
Bde
15 DLI
9 KOYLI
8 Lincs
8 Som LI
Russian Sap
63
Bde
4 Middlesex
10 Y & L
10 W. Yorks
Queen's
Redoubt
10 Yorks
62 Bde
(Reserve)
(12 N Fus North of Bécordel,
1 Lincs in Méaulte, rest
of 13 N Fus in Méaulte)
50 Bde
(17th Div,
attached to
21st Div)
7 Yorks
7 Yorks
Station
The
Tambour
Wicket
Corner
Fricourt
Trench
Wing
Corner
Sausage
South
Support
Sausage
South
Soda Tr
Whisky Tr
Brandy Tr
Arrow Lane
Empress
Tr
Dart Lane
The Dingle
Willow
Patch
Patch Alley
Gin Alley
Lozenge
Tr
Lozenge Alley
Lonely Lane
König Lane
König Tr
Red
Lane
Red
Cottage
Red Tr
Hare Lane
Rabbit
Lane
Round Wood
Birch Tree Wood
Sunken Lane
Crucifix Tr
Line gained
& held 1.7.16
Crucifix Tr
Lonely Tr
27
Lozenge
Wood
Lonely
Copse
Fricourt
Shelter
Wood
The Crucifix
The
Poodles
Fricourt
Farm
Fricourt
Wood
Rose Cottage
Sunshine Alley
Copper Tr
Rose Alley
Thorn Lane
Papen Tr
28
Railway
Copse
Railway Alley
Bottom
Wood
X
F
Willow Tr
Willow Avenue
4
The Orchard
Orchard Tr
Mametz
Rose Tr
Danzig
Alley
2
3
26

Map 9. Somme 3.

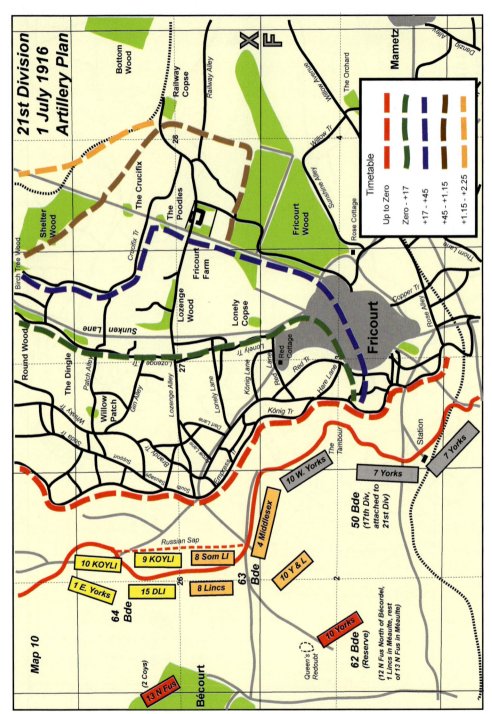

Map 10. Somme 4 Artilley Map.

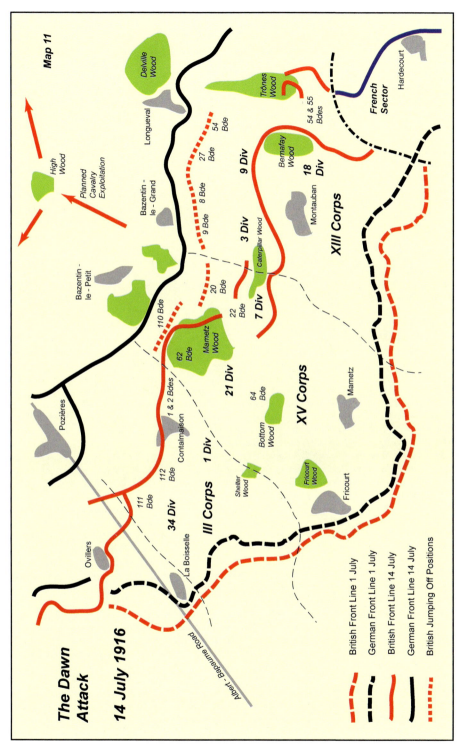

Map 11. Bazentin 1.

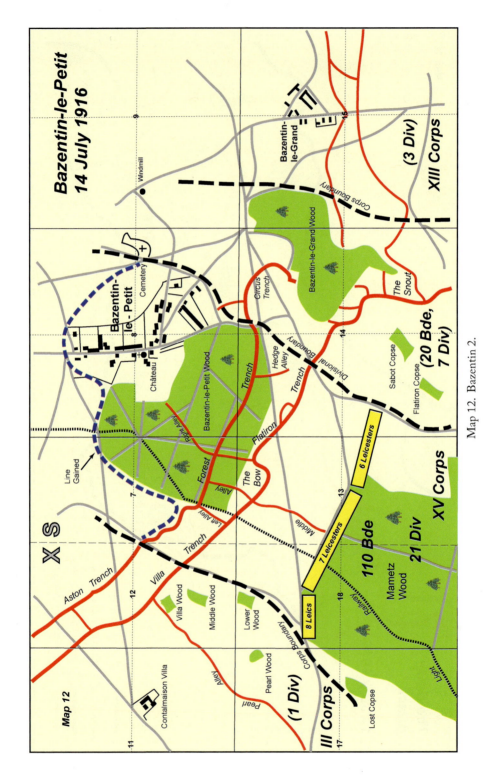

Map 12. Bazentin 2.

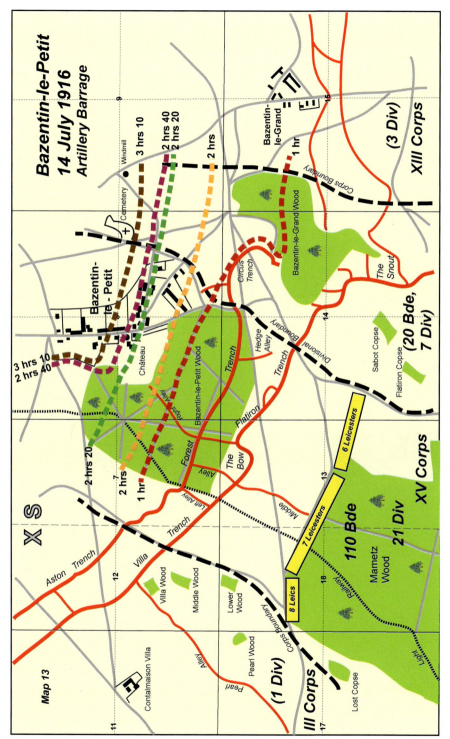

Map 13. Bazentin 3 (Artillery Barrage).

xiii

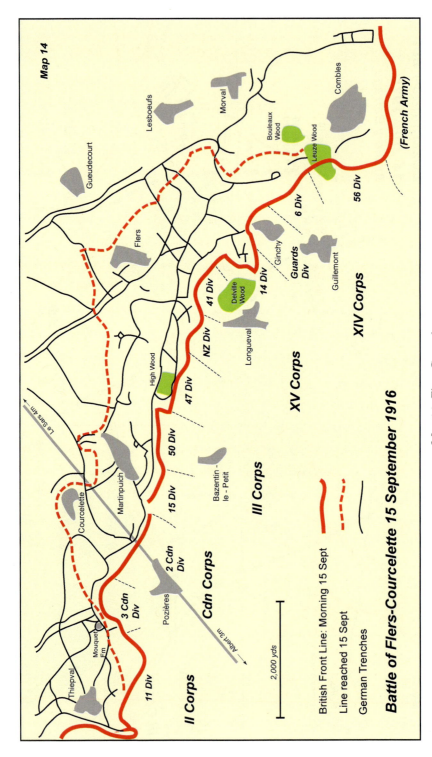

Map 14. Flers-Courcelette.

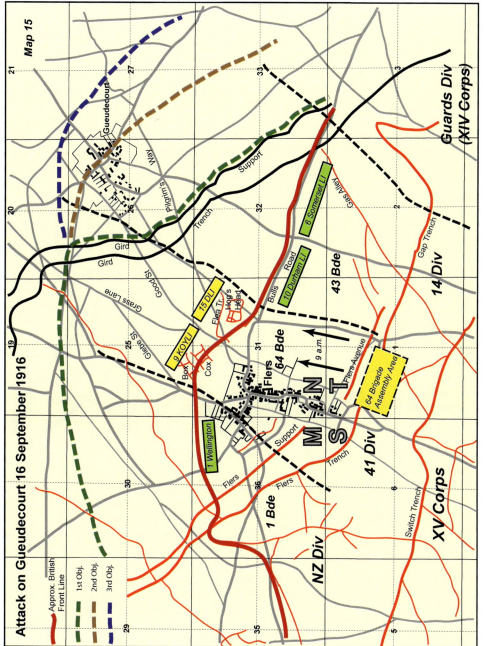

Map 15. Gueudecourt 1.

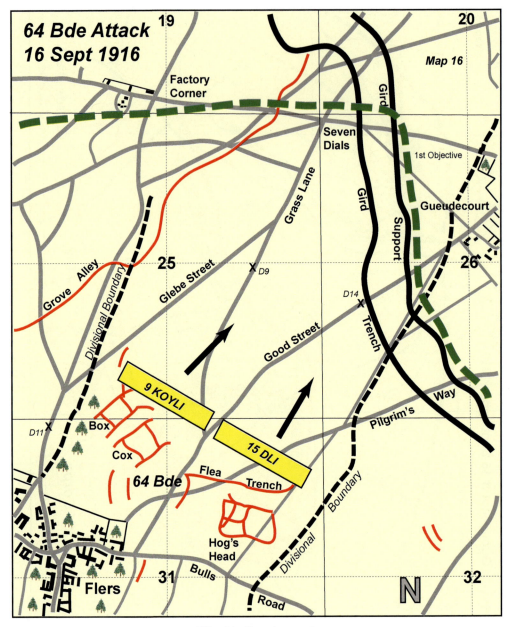

Map 16. Gueudecourt 2.

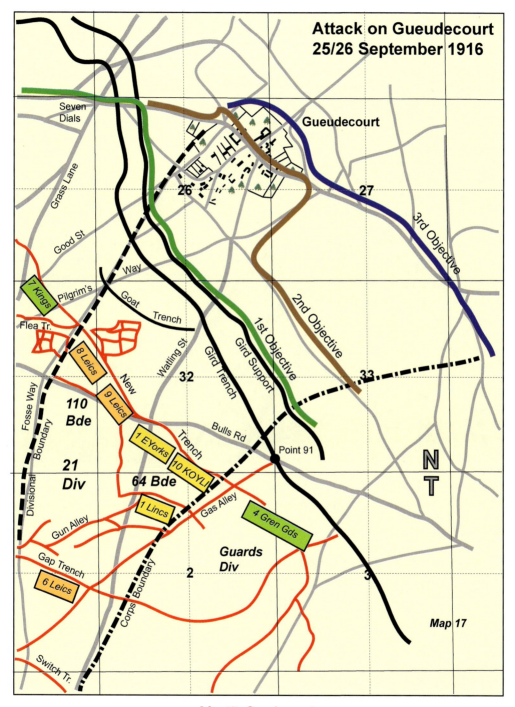

Map 17. Gueudecourt 3.

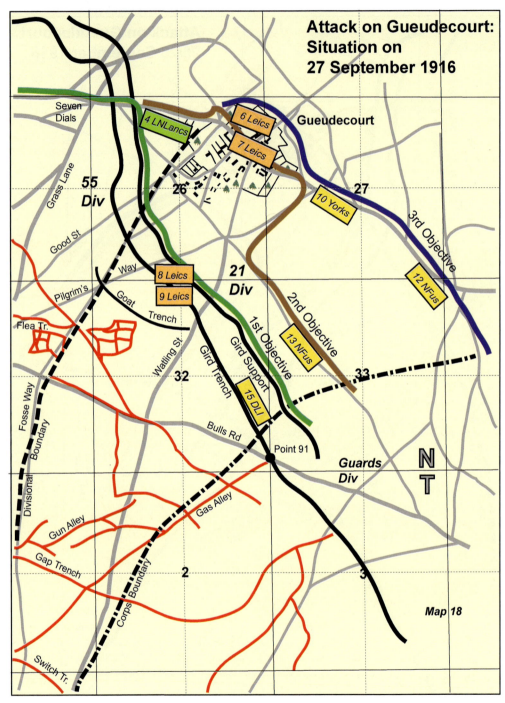

Map 18. Gueudecourt 4.

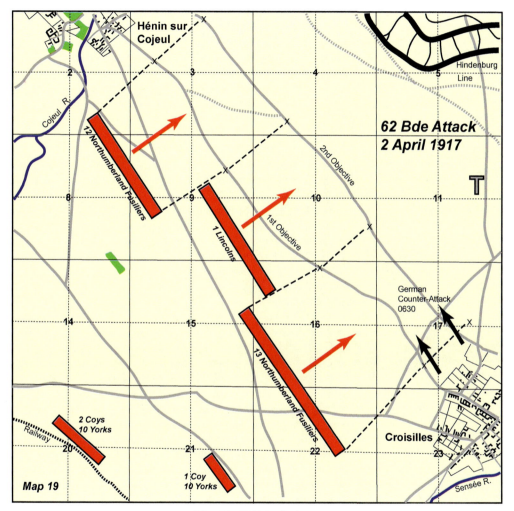

Map 19. 62 Brigade Arras.

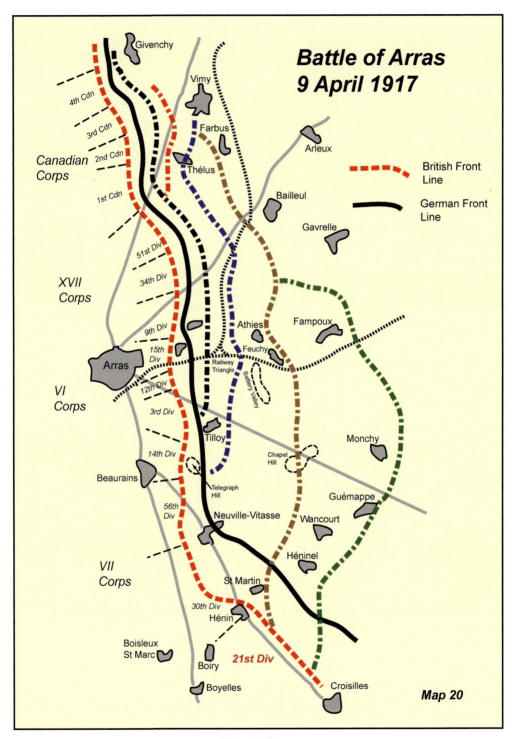

Map 20. Arras.

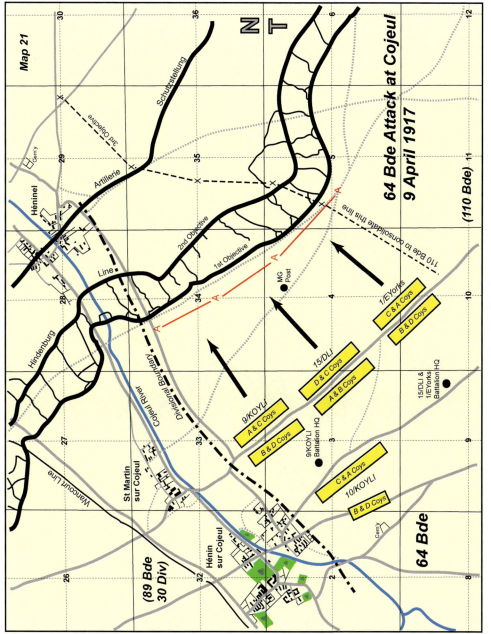

Map 21. Cojeul.

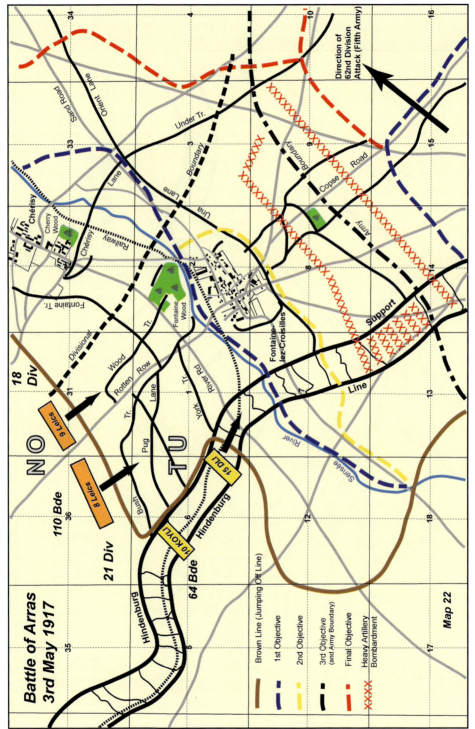

Map 22. Arras 3 May 1917.

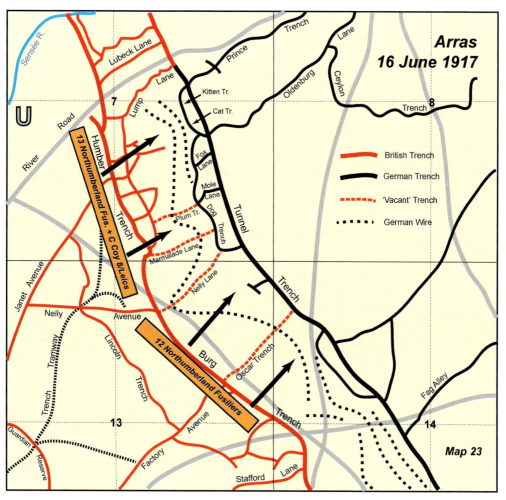

Map 23. Arras 16 June 1917.

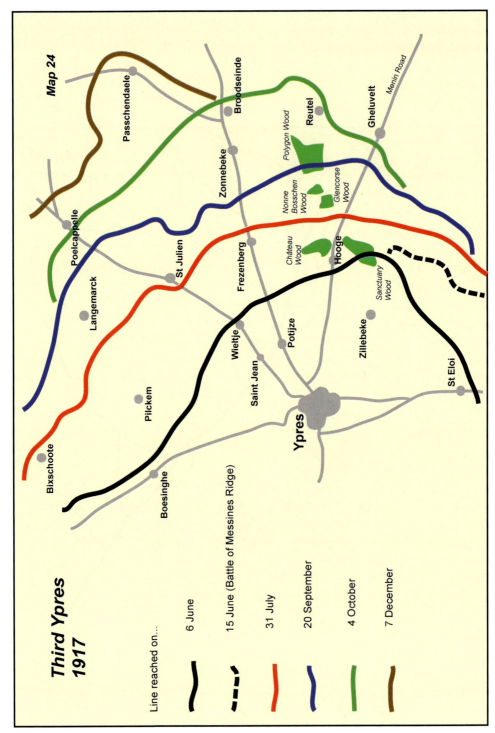

Map 24. Third Ypres 1.

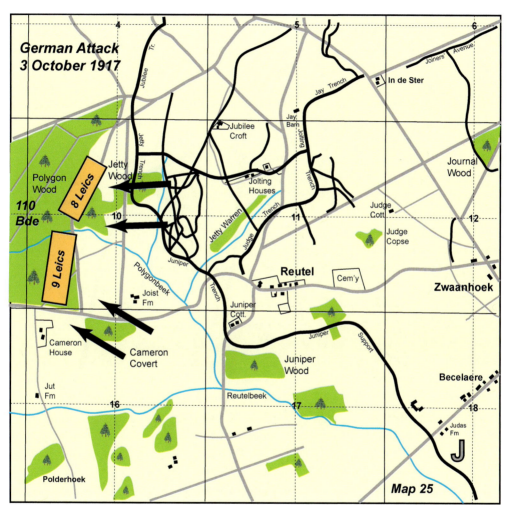

Map 25. Broodseinde 3.10.17.

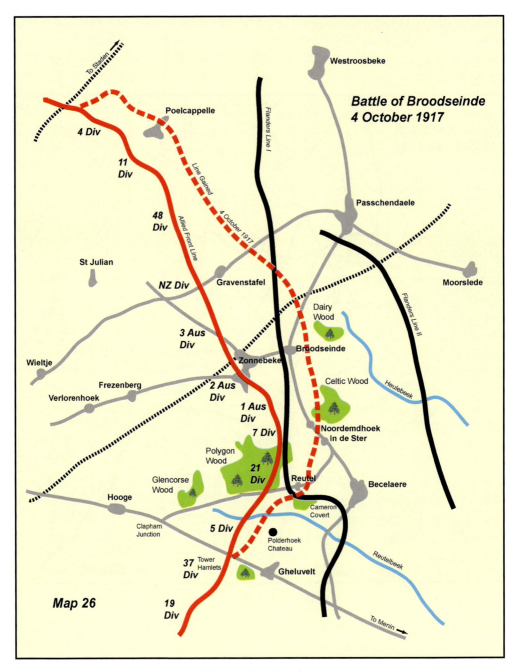

Map 26. Broodseinde 1.

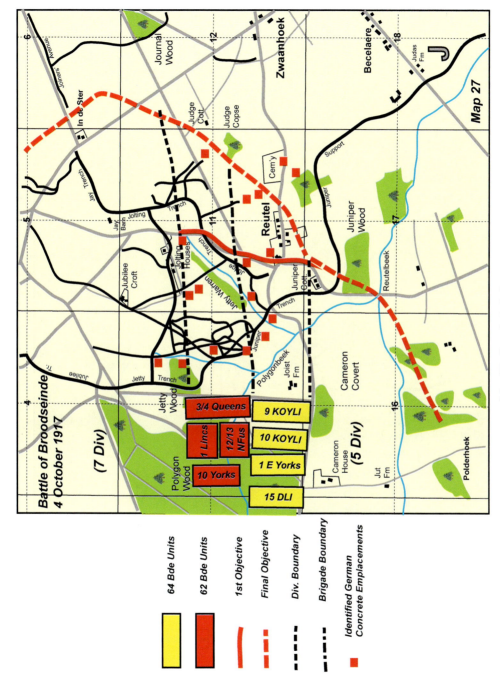

Map 27. Broodseinde 2a.

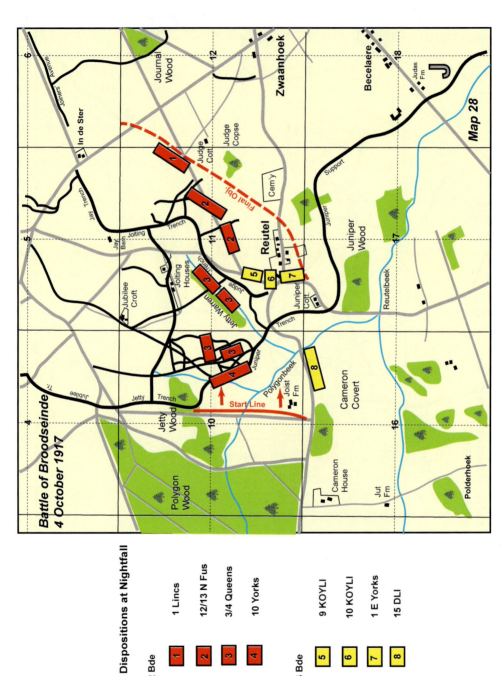

Map 28. Broodseinde 2b.

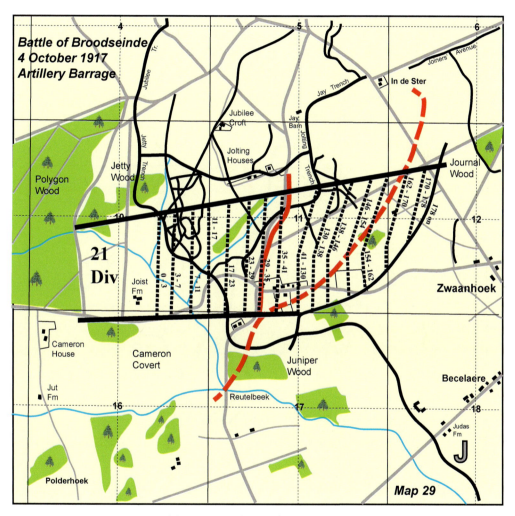

Map 29. Broodseinde Artillery Map.

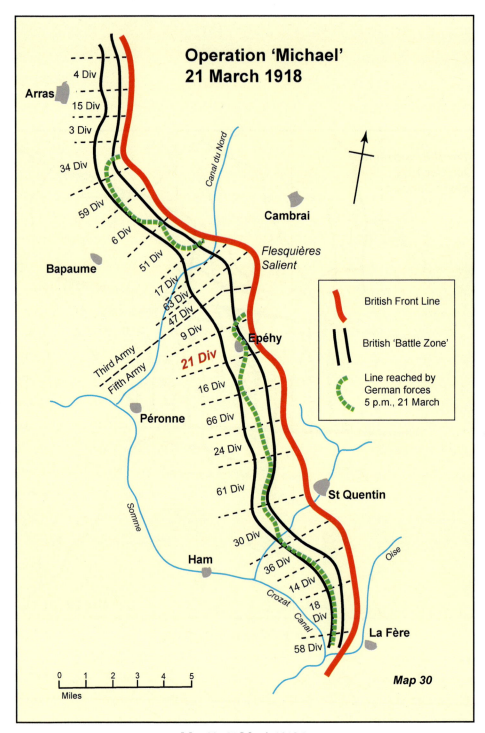

Map 30. 21 March 1918 1.

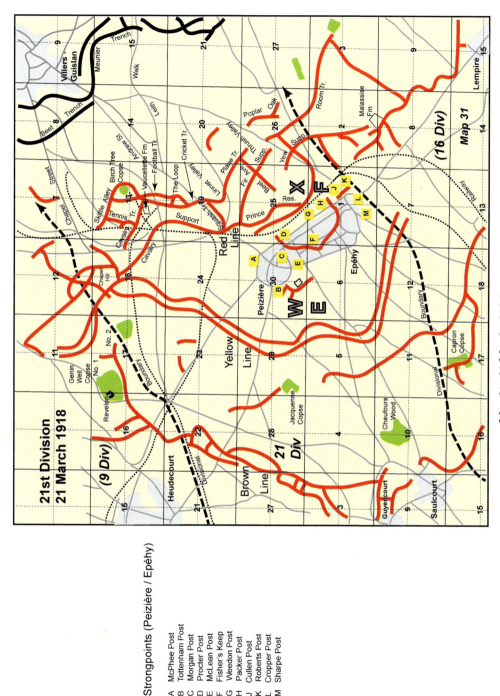

Map 31. 21 March 1918 2.

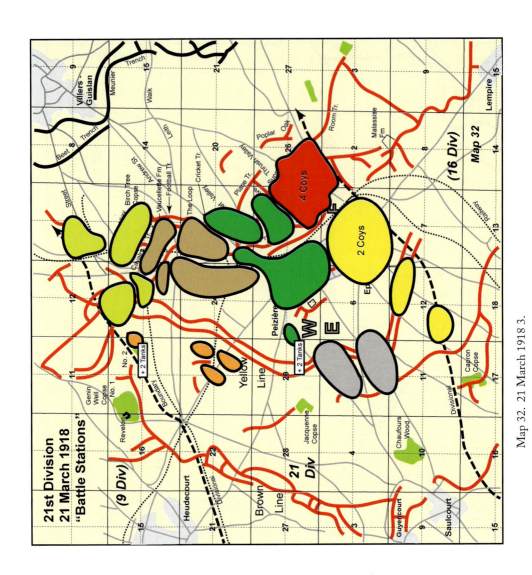

Map 32. 21 March 1918 3.

xxxii

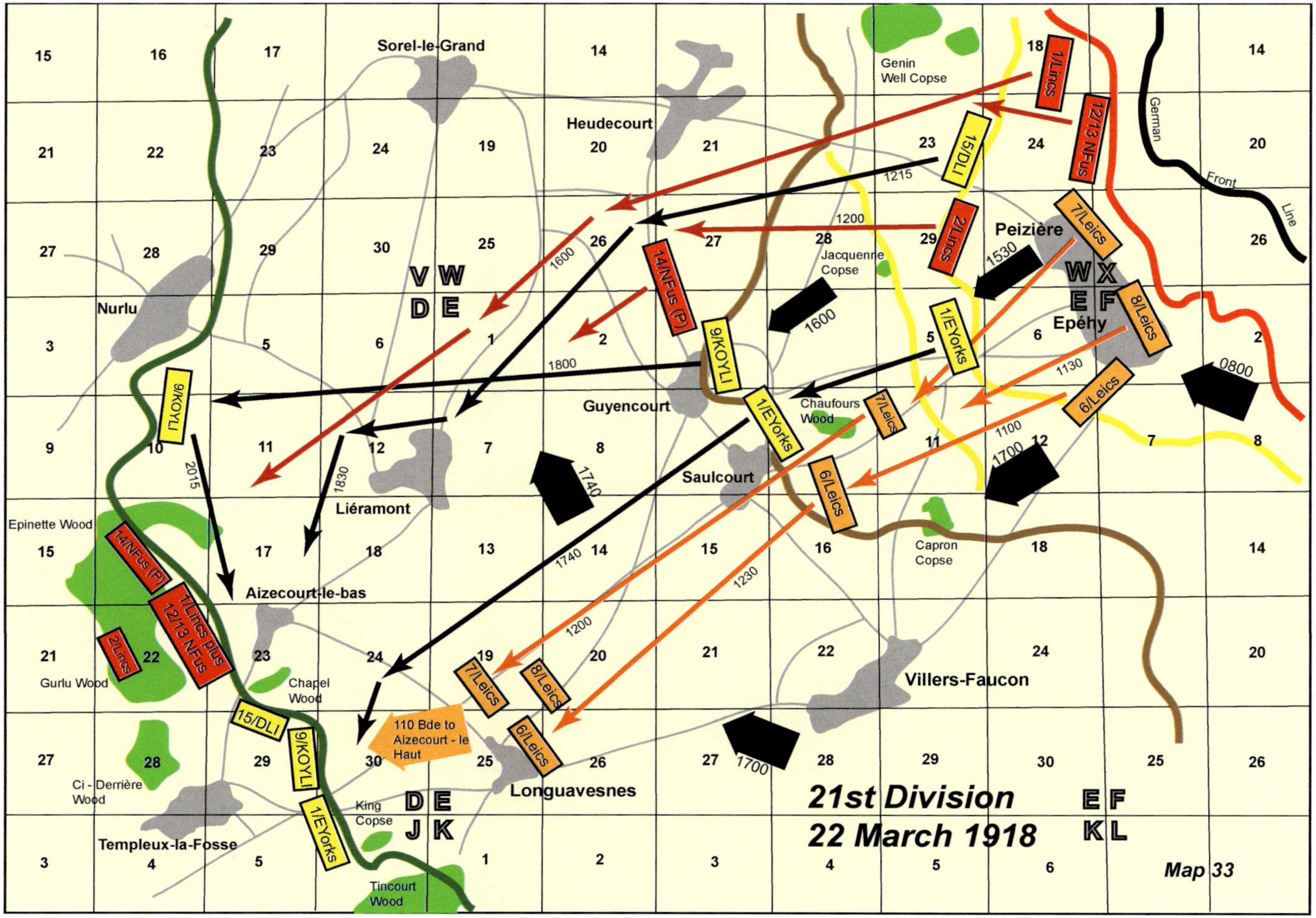

Map 33. 22 March 1918.

xxxiii

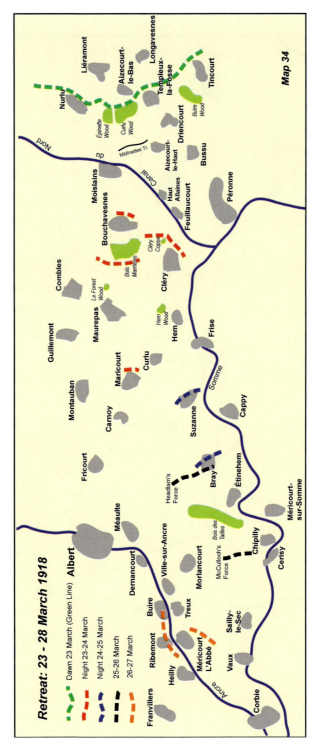

Map 34. Retreat March 1918.

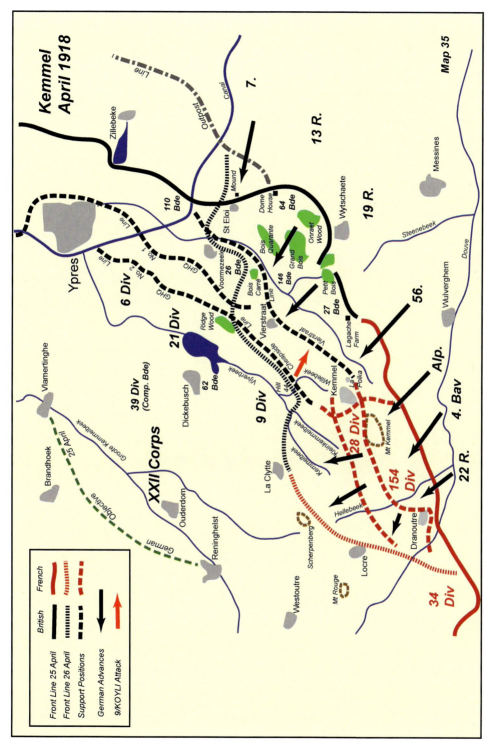

Map 35. Kemmel April 1918 1.

xxxv

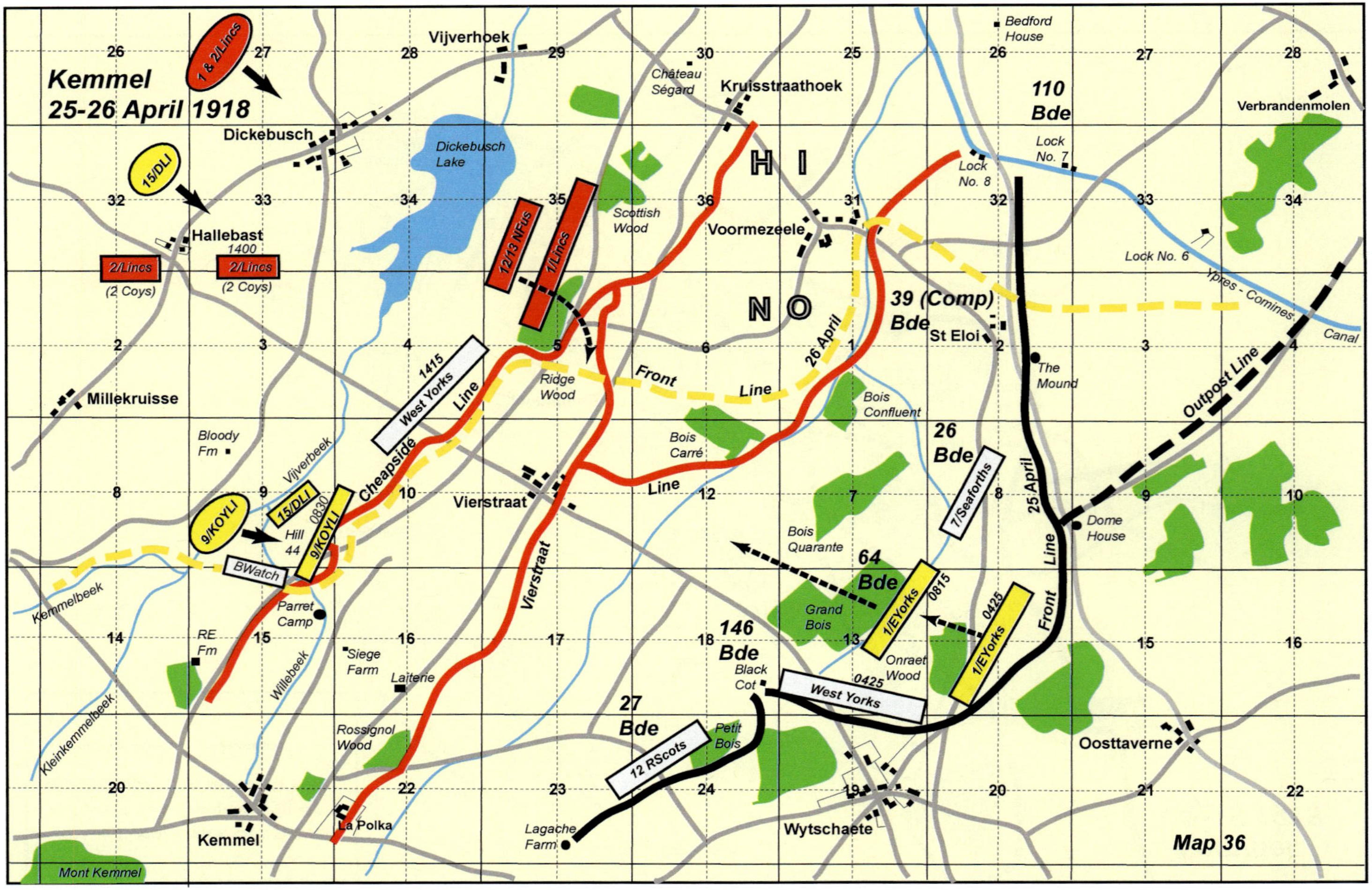

Map 36. Kemmel April 1918 2.

xxxvi

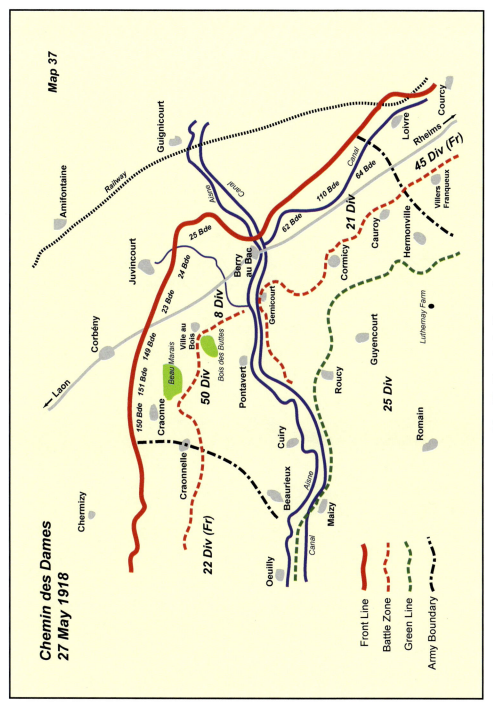

Map 37. Chemin des Dames 1.

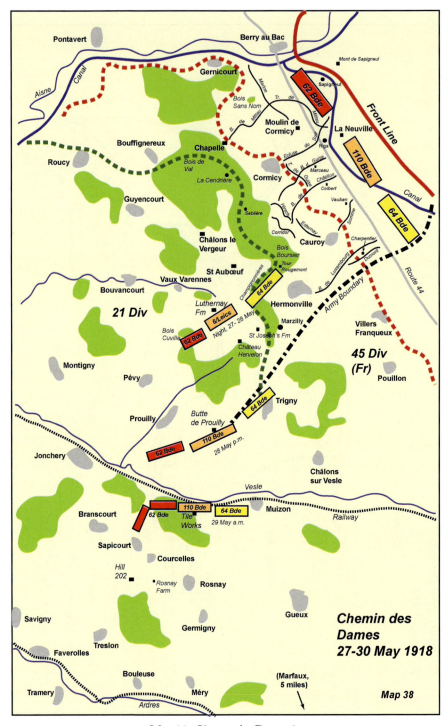

Map 38. Chemin des Dames 2.

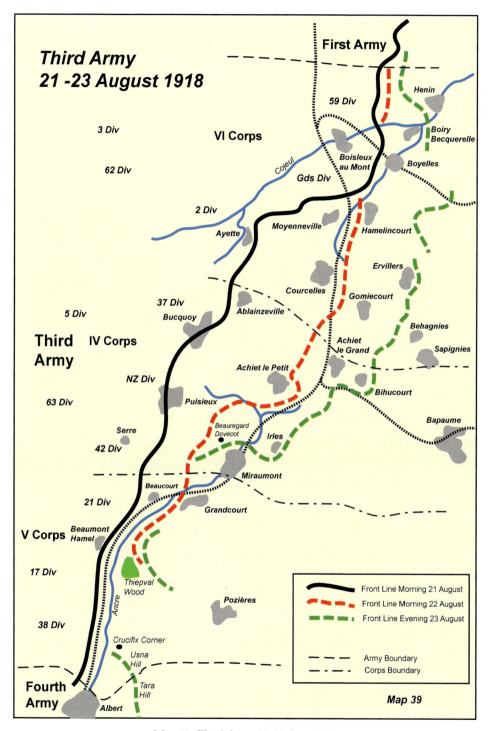

Map 39. Third Army 21-23 Aug 1918.

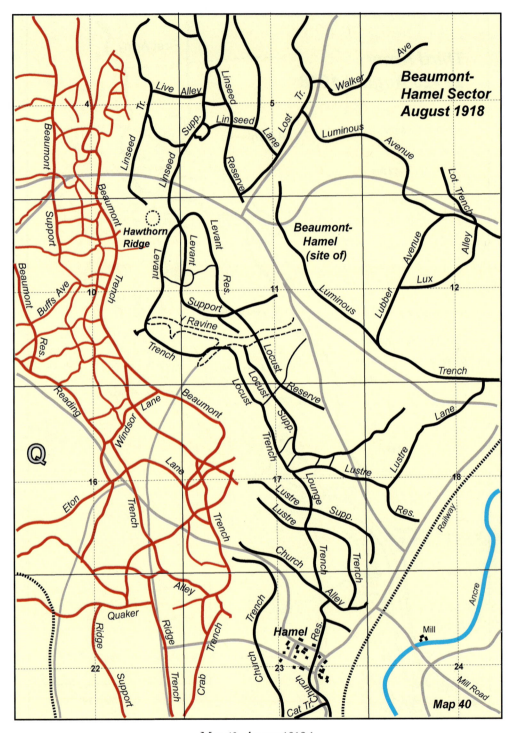

Map 40. August 1918 1.

xl

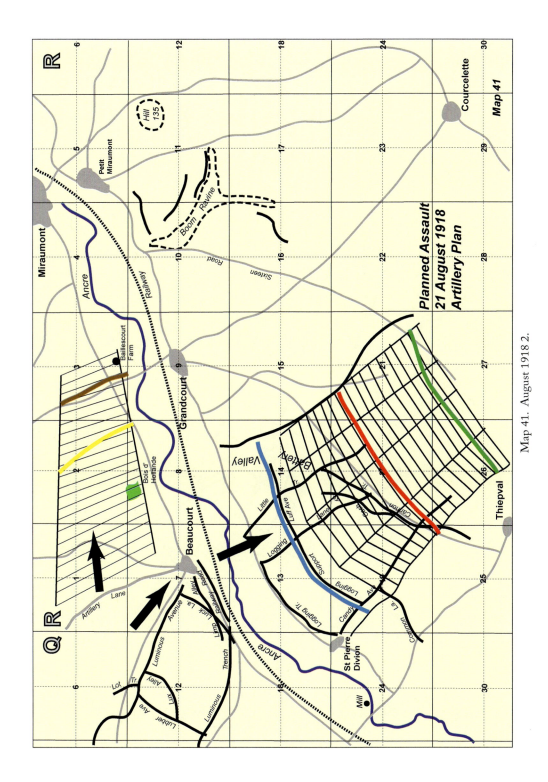

Map 41. August 1918 2.

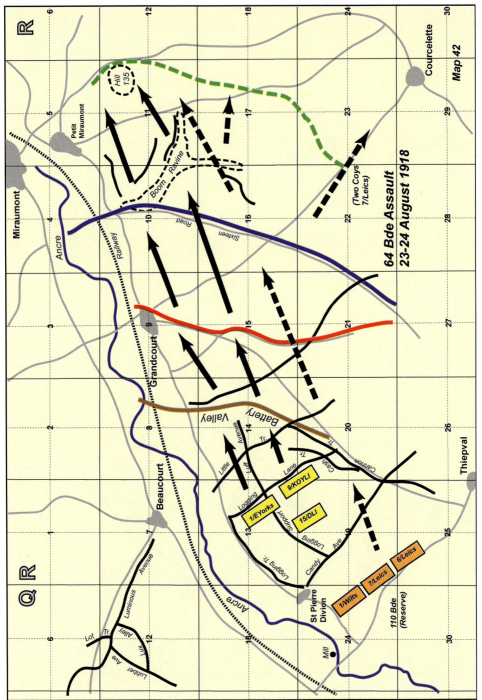

Map 42. 24 August 1918.

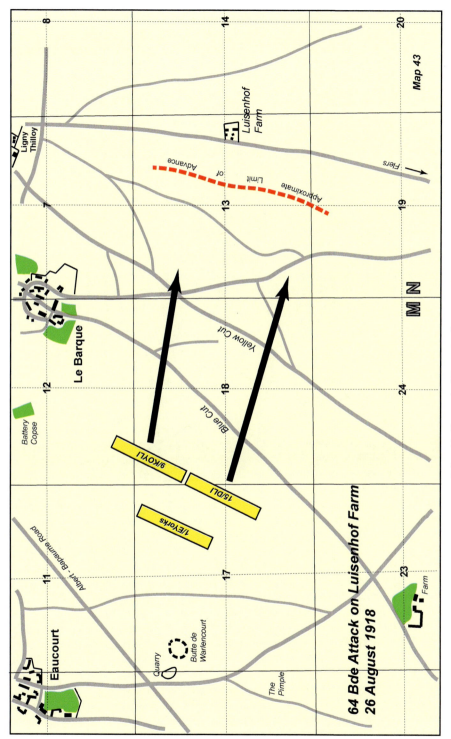

Map 43. Luisenhof Farm 26 August 1918.

xliii

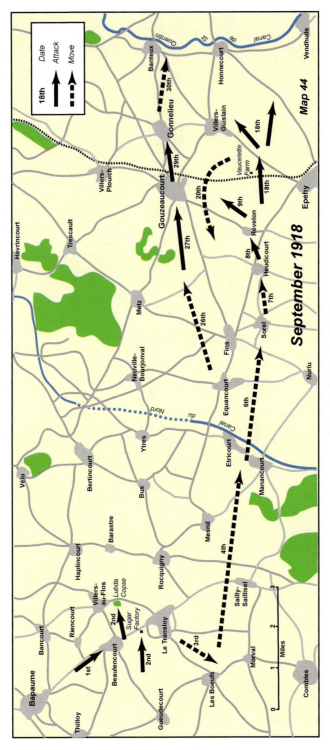

Map 44. September 1918.

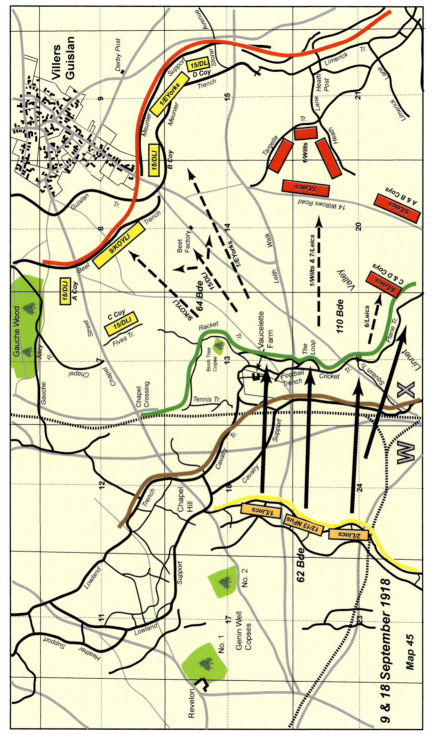

Map 45. 9 & 18 September 1918.

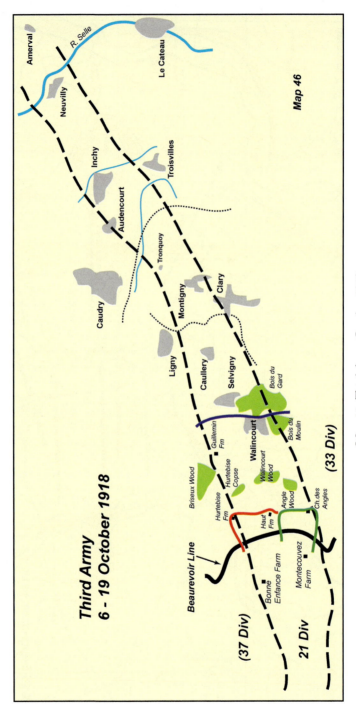

Map 46. Third Army October 1918.

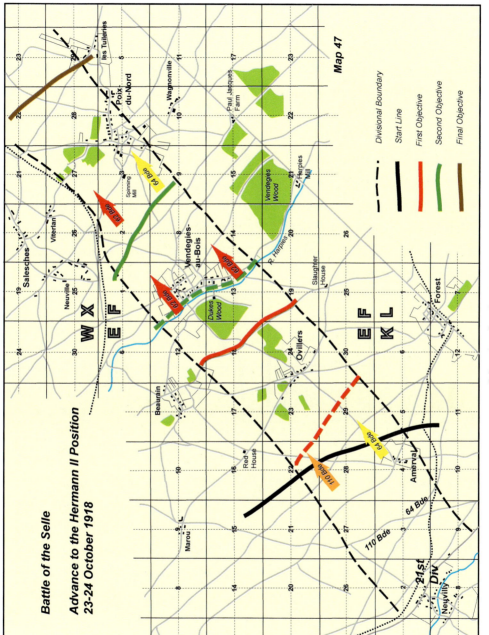

Map 47. October 1918.

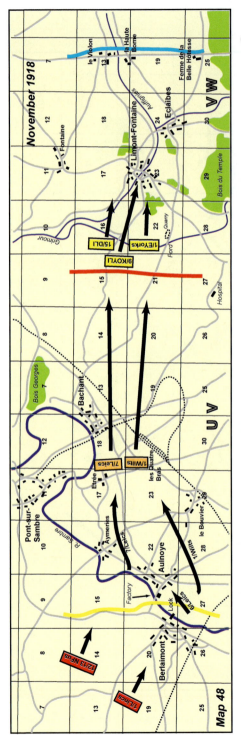

Map 48. November 1918.

On the left, the 13/NFus advanced on a four-company front, with A Coy on the right, then B and C Companies with C Coy of 8/Leics (Captain Matthews) on the extreme left. The rest of D Coy caught up just in time to go over in the second wave. The story of their attack is best left to the 13/NFus war diarist:

> The Germans were holding a trench in front of TUNNEL TRENCH in great numbers[101] and the trench was well wired with 3 rows of crinoline wire that was untouched by the Artillery barrage. The 1st waves got up to within 20 yds of our barrage and got through the 1st row of wire but were unable to penetrate the second. The enemy put a very heavy hand grenade barrage on his wire and kept up a very intense rifle and machine gun fire despite this however the men with wire cutters lay on their backs and cut the wire till they became casualties while the remainder threw all their bombs (4 bombs per man, bombers 7 bombs each) and the Lewis Gunners opened fire causing heavy casualties to the enemy. As it was impossible to penetrate the wire (a few men got through) and all bombs had been used the Battalion withdrew to HUMBER TRENCH.[102]

According to the 110 Bde war diarist, the whole sorry affair was over within the hour, around ninety men being reported as back in Humber Trench by four o'clock. The cost was crippling: the battalion had gone into the attack with 16 Officers and 380 Other Ranks; casualties were initially reported as 14 Officers and 214 men. Six of the Officers were killed, and Commonwealth War Graves Commission records indicate 66 Other Ranks fatalities.[103] The 8/Leics suffered ten fatalities.[104]

On the right flank of the assault, 12/NFus also attacked with all four companies in the front line. They had 300 yards to go to their objective, Tunnel Trench. As well as rifle and machine gun fire, the Fusiliers were met with "showers of stick grenades".[105] Nevertheless, a number of men from D Coy under Second-Lieutenant Queen and a handful of C Coy men led by CSM Byron managed to force their way into Tunnel Trench, whereupon a desperate hand-to-hand struggle began. Out of bombs and faced by superior numbers, all of these men became casualties. The rest of D Coy did not make it as far as the parapet of Tunnel Trench, having lost its commanding officer, Captain McLean, to a serious wound and Second-Lieutenant Field killed.[106] To their left, B Coy made it into a series of shell holes between 50 and 200 yards short of their objective, having also lost their commanding officer, Second-Lieutenant Findlay.[107] A

---

101 This would be the line of Kitten, Cat and Dog Trenches. See Map 23.
102 TNA PRO WO 95/2155: 13/Northumberland Fusiliers War Diary.
103 Captain Albert Ayland Evans (OC A Coy), Second-Lieutenants Samuel Walton White, age 20, Charles Hubert Quarrell, age 20, John George Dixon, age 19 and John Donald Parland Duncan, age 26, are all commemorated on the Arras Memorial. Second-Lieutenant K. Garry died of his wounds on 18 June and is buried in Grevillers British Cemetery, grave VI.A.4. All four Company Commanders were killed, wounded or reported missing that day.
104 These include platoon commander Lieutenant Frank Percy Haines, age 29, who is commemorated on the Arras Memorial, and their Medical Officer, Captain S. Pool MC, RAMC, who is buried in Croisilles British Cemetry, grave I.D.12.
105 TNA PRO WO 95/2155: 12/Northumberland Fusiliers War Diary.
106 Second-Lieutenant Gordon Stewart Field, age 27, is commemorated on the Arras Memorial.
107 Second-Lieutenant James Findlay, age 21, is commemorated on the Arras Memorial.

182   To Do the Work of Men

Coy, on the extreme left of the battalion frontage, could not reach Tunnel Trench, but were able to fight their way into the advanced German trenches and consolidate their gains. This party, under Lieutenant Byrne, consisting of six Lewis Gunners with one gun, four bombers and two riflemen, held out against strong bombing attacks from both flanks until it became dark enough on the evening of the 16th to allow them to make their way back to the safety of Burg Trench. The 12/NFus had gone into the attack with 10 Officers and 391 Other Ranks. Six Officers and 208 men became casualties, all, in the end, for no gain.

A disturbing report found its way to 21st Divisional HQ. It was submitted by Second-Lieutenant V.C. Cherryman, of 13/NFus, who had been sheltering in a shell hole during the 16 June attack, unable to move until dark:

> On the morning of the 16th of June, after the attack had been held up, I was in a shell hole about 10 yards from the German lines. One of my wounded men came crawling towards me, (he was shot badly in the leg) and could not be mistaken for an unwounded man, because he crawled on one side, and his trousers were soaked in blood. He had hardly moved towards me five yards when a Boche shot him in the back of the head from his parapet. The man tumbled into my shell hole dead.
>
> Then five or six Boches came out and stood up shooting at the others who were in and about the wire.
>
> I cannot be certain if all shots took effect, because I feigned death, and by doing so was left alone. But I am certain that they shot the man I mentioned above".[108]

This report had clearly been seen by Major-General Campbell, who commented on it in his congratulatory letter, dated 20 June1917. Its construction was predictable: congratulations on the men's gallantry, followed by an absolution from guilt for its failure, concluding with an exhortation to further efforts in the future.

> I wish to take this opportunity of expressing to the Officers, Non-commissioned Officers, and Men of the 12th & 13th Battalions Northumberland Fusiliers, and 'C' Company, 8th Battalion Leicestershire Regiment, my admiration for the gallant manner in which they fought on June 16th under the most adverse conditions.
>
> Circumstances over which they had no control robbed them of the fruits of their splendid efforts.
>
> I am convinced, by all evidence procurable, that on no previous occasion has any Battalion fought with greater gallantry than that displayed by the above Units on June 16th.
>
> The barbarities committed by the enemy on the wounded will not, I am sure, be forgotten when this Division next takes part in an attack.
> David G.M. Campbell
> Major-General
> Commanding 21st Division[109]

108 TNA PRO WO 95/2132: 21st Div HQ War Diary.
109 Ibid.

A report written by Lieutenant-General Thomas D'Oyly Snow,[110] commanding VII Corps, on 23 June 1917, gave three reasons for the failure of the 16 June attack:

The failure of the attack was due:

1. To the casualties and disorganisation caused by the enemy barrage on the way up to the trenches.
2. To the presence of uncut wire: the ground had been very carefully reconnoitred and observed from land and air previously and statements as to its condition go to shew that the wire had probably been put out earlier during the same night as the attack took place.
3. To alertness on the part of the enemy due to repeated attacks at a similar time of day.

The principle lessons to be learnt are:

1. Necessity for alternative routes to assembly trenches.
2. Necessity for preventing the enemy from wiring immediately prior to the attack.
3. That the German has learnt to expect an attack at dawn".[111]

But for some routine trench holding duties, the 21st Division had no further involvement in the Battle of Arras. The Official History lists its casualties during the battle as:

Officers			Other Ranks			Total
Killed	Wounded	Missing	Killed	Wounded	Missing	
13	71	5	295	1,173	292	1,849

The 21st Division entrained for Flanders in September 1917. The Third Battle of Ypres had been raging there since 31 July. 21st Division was about to play its part in the struggle.

110 Major-General Campbell had gone on leave to England on 20 June 1917.
111 Ibid. In the original document, point two under "lessons to be learnt" has been crudely crossed out.

4

Third Ypres

Field Marshal Sir Douglas Haig had for a long time nurtured plans to capture the high ground to the south and east of the ancient Belgian town known to his men as "Wipers". This ground had been lost in the costly and desperately-fought First and Second battles of Ypres in 1914 and 1915 respectively. In 1917 the BEF was clinging on to a salient, Ypres at its hub, overlooked from the German lines, stubbornly refusing to surrender what was left of the shell-ravaged town whose strategic importance was perhaps outweighed by its symbolic status. The re-capturing of these ridges would be only the first stage of Haig's objectives: the advance would sweep over the Passchendaele Ridge as far as Roulers and Thourout, the former town being a vital railway hub whose loss would almost inevitably force a German tactical withdrawal from the Belgian coast and its hinterland. Thereafter, the axis of the offensive would veer northwards and this, in conjunction with an amphibious assault – landing infantry and tanks from the sea – behind the German lines, would liberate the ports of Zeebrugge and Ostend, thus depriving Germany of two important submarine bases. Such a breakthrough would hand Haig his coveted strategic victory. It might even win the war outright.

Offensive planning had begun in earnest in November 1916: Sir Herbert Plumer, commanding Second Army, which had occupied the Ypres Salient since 1915, was asked to submit plans for an offensive that would take place the following spring. An initial requirement would be to drive the Germans off the Messines Ridge to the south of Ypres, thus depriving them of the high ground from which they could overlook and therefore severely disrupt the right flank of the main assault. Plumer's proposals required a series of 'phased' attacks, the tempo dependent upon the speed at which captured ground could be consolidated and artillery brought up to support the next stage. This found little favour with the C-in-C: such an approach would rob the offensive of any meaningful momentum and Plumer was instructed to review his plan accordingly. Haig also – presumably not convinced that Plumer would come up with the goods – asked General Sir Henry Rawlinson to submit his own ideas for the offensive. Plumer's revised plans, submitted at the end of January 1917, still reflected the General's natural caution. Rawlinson's ideas were not much better: his 'one trench line at a time' approach had been overruled on the Somme the previous summer and Haig was going to have no truck with it this time. The two men had, by the very nature of their recommendations, done themselves out of a job.

Haig needed a commander who could share his vision of the decisive breakthrough, someone with a more ambitious philosophy, someone who could be described – in the language of the period – as a "thruster". His gaze fell upon General Sir Hubert Gough, commander of Fifth

Army, a man with little knowledge of the Flanders area. Gough was given the responsibility of executing the main assault. Plumer would conduct the Messines Ridge operation and Rawlinson would busy himself with the details of the amphibious landing.

By 7 May, with the Nivelle Offensive closed down and operations pertaining to the Battle of Arras winding down, Haig was able to focus fully on his Northern Operation. It had become clear that the attack would, in the end, have to be split into two phases: the first would comprise the capture of Messines Ridge; the second, after a delay of a number of weeks to allow for artillery to be moved into position, would be the main advance eastwards from the salient.

The Messines Ridge assault went in during the early morning of 7 June, when, at 03.10, nineteen mines were detonated under the German positions. This, in conjunction with a stupendous artillery barrage and the availability of seventy-two Mark IV tanks, meant that the 80,000 assault troops in the leading divisions were able to overrun the ridge, gaining their first objectives within thirty-five minutes. The reverse slope was in British hands by 09.00.[1] This has been trumpeted as a remarkable achievement, "perhaps the finest example of a 'bite-and-hold' operation ever conducted – proving that, under the right conditions, the BEF could secure even the most heavily defended locations".[2]

A detailed analysis of the main Third Ypres assault is beyond the scope of this work, but a brief account will place the action of 21st Division in context.[3] The land around Ypres is generally low-lying. The ridges, whose captures were vital to the BEF's initial operations, were low and gentle, Gheluvelt Plateau, for example, only reaching sixty-four feet above sea-level at its highest point. Even this small differential gave the German defenders the huge benefit of being able to overlook British positions and, crucially, preparations.[4] The landscape of small valleys, woods and villages is crossed by numerous streams, many of them traversing the line of the intended British attack. The land between them, with its high water-table, is only kept relatively dry by a substantial system of drainage channels, dykes and sluices. Any artillery barrage could quickly destroy this system and even moderate rainfall thereafter could turn the salient into a quagmire. Digging deep trenches and dugouts under these conditions was impossible, and the German defensive system consisted largely of breastworks, concrete emplacements and pill-boxes.

The preliminary bombardment for the northern offensive threw four and a half million shells into the salient. At 03.50 on 31 July, troops of twelve British divisions advanced on a front of some eleven miles, into mist and rain, which, with impeccable timing, had begun to fall the

---

1   For a detailed account of the attack on Messines Ridge, see Ian Passingham, *Pillars of Fire: The Battle of Messines Ridge June 1917* (Stroud, Sutton Publishing, 1998), *passim*.
2   Nick Lloyd, *Passchendaele: A New History* (London, Penguin/Viking, 2017), pp.56-57.
3   For detailed accounts of Third Ypres, see, inter alia: Robin Prior & Trevor Wilson, *Passchendaele: The Untold story* (London: Yale University Press, 1996); Nick Lloyd, *Passchendaele: A New History* (London, Penguin/Viking, 2017); Peter Liddle (ed.), *Passchendaele in Perspective. The Third Battle of Ypres* (London: Leo Cooper, 1997); Jack Sheldon, *The German Army at Passchendaele* (Barnsley: Pen & Sword, 2007); Nigel Steel & Peter Hart, *Passchendaele: The Sacrificial Ground* (London: Cassell & Co., 2000). Lyn Macdonald, *They Called it Passchendaele* (London: Papermac, 1984). Sir James Edmonds, *Military Operations, France & Belgium 1917*, Vol. II (London: HMSO, 1948).
4   It is difficult to assess the nature of the terrain when looking east from the town of Ypres. If the visitor to the battlefield looks back towards the town from, say, Tyne Cot Cemetery, the advantage – in terms of observation – enjoyed by the German defenders becomes obvious.

186   To Do the Work of Men

previous evening. Progress on the first day could perhaps be described as promising: XIV Corps in the north was able to capture two German defensive lines; Pilckem Ridge had been taken and the line of the Steenbeek reached, an advance of 3,000 yards. Further south, 39th Division (XVIII Corps) captured the village of St Julien. On their right, XIX Corps advanced 4,000 yards, crossing three defensive lines, but fire enfilading the right-hand division (15th Div) from the south indicated that all had not gone well on the II Corps front on Gheluvelt Plateau. Difficult ground conditions resulting in the loss of the creeping barrage meant that the attack had stalled by 07.00 after an advance of only 1,000 yards. German counter attacks later in the day enjoyed some success in the centre where St Julien had to be relinquished.[5] That evening, the weather broke in spectacular fashion and it rained heavily almost non-stop for a week. Gough nevertheless renewed his efforts along the Gheluvelt Plateau, but ground conditions became so difficult that the troops' best efforts were mostly in vain.

It had been envisaged that Roulers would be reached by 7 or 8 August. It was not until the 16th that any meaningful attempt to improve the gains made on the first day could be made. The ensuing Battle of Langemarck ran for three days. The ruins of the village that gave the battle its name were eventually taken, but on the right, a heavy price was once more paid for very little gain. Further attacks on 22 and 24 August resulted in more heavy casualties – by this point Fifth Army had suffered 60,000 losses – and the Gheluvelt Plateau was still in German hands. Rain set in once again and the landscape began to resemble a swamp. General Gough at this point informed Haig that, under the prevailing conditions, he believed that the campaign should be abandoned. The lack of progress had forced Haig to postpone (and later abandon) the notion of an amphibious landing on the Belgian coast, and his patience with Gough had also reached its end. On 25 August Haig visited Second Army HQ and told General Plumer that he would be taking over responsibility for the continuation of the main attack along the Gheluvelt Plateau. "[Plumer] told Haig, clearly and firmly, that he would need three weeks to prepare [for the next attack]. Haig, whose options were narrowing by the day, had little choice but to accept".[6] Haig would also, willing or otherwise, have to accept Plumer's methodology.

Plumer planned to complete the capture of the Gheluvelt Plateau – an advance of about 4,000 yards – in four stages. This was text-book 'bite and hold': each advance would be made under the cover of a protective artillery barrage; the newly-gained positions would be consolidated against German counter attack; artillery would be brought forward and the process repeated. Ideally, a 1,000 – 1,500 yard advance would take place every six days or so. The keys to success were the limited extent of the advance – infantry would not be overstretched and would not be asked to go beyond the range of the creeping barrage – and the intensity and sheer weight of the artillery bombardment itself:

> When Zero Hour came, five creeping barrages – about 1,000 yards in depth – would cover the advancing troops, sweeping the ground in front of them with an invincible wall of shrapnel and high-explosive. Once their objectives had been secured, standing barrages would be fired on enemy counter-attacks or possible approach routes to ensure German

5   For an overview of ground gained at various stages of the campaign, see Map 24.
6   Lloyd, *Passchendaele*, p.156.

reserves were fully engaged. In order to achieve this, Second Army would need a prodigious amount of guns and ammunition. For the seven-day preliminary bombardment, and to ensure the attack was thoroughly supported, General Plumer requested (and then received) over 1,800 guns (principally 18-pounders, but also a significant number of heavier howitzers to take on German bunkers) and upwards of 3.5 million shells.[7]

The first of these steps was scheduled for 20 September. In what became known as the Battle of Menin Road, nine divisions of the BEF captured five square miles of territory, with ten German counter attacks successfully repulsed. It all went pretty much to plan and was announced in *The Times* of 21 September as a "Big British Success". Nevertheless, the cost must be regarded as high, with the BEF losing around 21,000 men, killed, wounded or missing. The salient drew breath and awaited the next phase of the assault.

For once, the weather appeared as if it might stay dry for some significant time, prompting Haig to push for the next attack to take place as soon as possible. On 21 September, he wrote: "In view of the fine weather which our weather experts think is likely to last for a week, it is most desirable to take full advantage of it, and of the superiority which we have now gained, for the time being, over the enemy's aeroplanes and artillery".[8] The battles of Third Ypres were not an unceasing litany of rain and mud. The artillery bombardment that fell on the German positions on the morning of 26 September – the beginning of the next phase, known as the Battle of Polygon Wood – raised a "dense wall of dust and smoke".[9] All did not go to plan. In the northern sector V Corps took most of its objectives but were held up by machine gun fire along the Zonnebeke stream. They finished the day 600 yards short of the final objective. On the right flank, on X Corps front, 33rd Division had already suffered heavy casualties on the day before the planned assault in their efforts to hold back a German attack. They had already been fighting for over twenty-four hours when they launched their own attack at Zero Hour. Not surprisingly, the advancing lines faltered, the barrage was lost, and the attack ground to a halt short of its objectives. Further to the right, south of the Menin Road, the 39th Division was not quite able to capture the whole of the 'Tower Hamlets' spur: the German defensive strongpoint known as the 'Quadrilateral' on its southern extremity remained in enemy hands.

The primary thrust of the assault was in the centre, and was entrusted to I ANZAC Corps. The 5th Australian Division followed their barrage as closely as they dared into Polygon Wood, with 4th Division advancing to the north, between the wood and the village of Zonnebeke. Resistance from strong points and pill-boxes was quickly overcome and by 09.00 final objectives just to the east of the wood had been reached. Nine German counter attacks along the assault frontage were checked, and by the end of the day, a victory of sorts could be claimed. The cost to the British and Australian divisons was a total of 15,375 casualties.[10]

Haig was in optimistic mood. He was not, as he had explained to his commanders at a conference on 2 September, about to "repeat the mistake made by the Germans on the 31st October 1914, when they failed to take advantage of the exhaustion of the British forces after their repeated attacks on this same battleground at 'First Ypres': he had decided to abandon projects

---

7   Lloyd, *Passchendaele*, p.158.
8   TNA PRO WO256/22: Haig Diary.
9   Edmonds, *Military Operations 1917*, Vol. II, p.284.
10   Ibid, p. 293, fn. 3.

188   To Do the Work of Men

for operations elsewhere […] and to employ all available strength for the Ypres operations so long as weather conditions permitted".[11] Indeed, he was eying the possibility of a breakthrough by the middle of October. The next stage of the campaign was, however, to be another 'bite and hold' operation, scheduled to go in on 6 October. Haig, fearing that the spell of fine weather might break, instructed Plumer to bring this forward by two days. Accordingly, the Battle of Broodseinde was set to begin on 4 October and would involve units of 21st Division.

The 21st Division had been transferred to X Corps by an order dated 13 September. The division moved, by rail, into the Second Army area between the 15th and 17th of the month. Orders regarding the proposed attack were issued by the 21st Division Staff on 29 September: in a similar vein to the division's attack on 9 April at Arras, they were placed on the right flank of the battle frontage, tasked to "form a defensive flank facing South, South East and East with a view to protecting the Southern flank of the attacking troops in the North, and obtaining observation of the REUTELBEEK Valley and the Spur running S.E. to BECELAERE".[12]

The attack was to be prosecuted by 62 and 64 Brigades and would be launched from a start line just to the east of Polygon Wood (See Map 26). On the night of 30 September / 1 October, troops of 110 Bde relieved the 8th Australian Brigade in the front-line positions in the right sector of 5th Australian Division. With 8 & 9/Leics on the left and right respectively, their job was to hold the 'line' until the assault troops could be brought forward to replace them. This 'line' consisted of "shell holes and isolated portions of trenches",[13] and the men dug "as well as possible, […] and with the aid of some old wood planks lying about, contrived to make a little shelter and firing position. At midnight, we lay down in the mud with the idea of sleeping, each one taking turn at sentry".[14] Behind them, in the wood, the 7 & 6/Leics were respectively in support and reserve positions, with Brigade HQ located in an old German concrete emplacement, or 'pill box'.

The relief had been completed without any casualties, and "the night was extremely quiet, the absence of hostile shelling [being] particularly noticeable",[15] but any hopes of a quiet, undisturbed stint of duty were to be very quickly dashed.

At around 05.15 on the morning of 1 October, the Germans opened up a very heavy artillery barrage along the whole of the divisional frontage. (And on the positions of the neighbouring divisions). Heavier guns began to pound the rear areas, from Polygon Wood all the way back to the outskirts of Ypres itself. The diarist of 9/Leics recorded a "smoke screen all along Battalion front",[16] and at 05.27 German infantry were seen advancing through the smoke. These were the first waves of two converging assaults: one from the south-east – from the direction of Cameron Covert – and a second from the north-east – launched from Jetty Trench, just north of Jetty Wood (See Map 25).

---

11   Ibid, p.297.
12   TNA PRO WO 95/2132: 'Divisional Order No. O.O. 132', 29 September 1917, 21st Div HQ War Diary.
13   TNA PRO WO 95/2165: 8/Leics War Diary.
14   Unpublished typescript account by Private D.A. Bacon, 9/Leics, Leicestershire Record Office. Cited in Richardson, *The Tigers*, p.197.
15   TNA PRO WO 95/2165: 8/Leics War Diary.
16   TNA PRO WO 95/2165: 9/Leics War Diary.

On the right brigade flank, the first wave of German attackers was driven back by concentrated rifle and Lewis Gun fire by the men of A Company, 9/Leics. They were unfortunate to lose Captain A.A.D. Lee MC, killed at this early stage of the encounter.[17] A second wave only three minutes later was also halted in front of the battalion's positions, but on the right flank, A Company was coming under severe pressure and was eventually driven back. It fell to D Company – in reserve positions behind A Coy – to attempt to stabilise the situation. Lieutenant-Colonel Bent led two platoons forward, in conjunction with a number of men from B Coy under Lieutenant Burn, in a counter-attack which successfully repelled the enemy incursion into the line. Bent was killed leading the charge, but he was awarded the Victoria Cross for his actions.[18]

By this time, both front-line Leicester battalions had sent up SOS rockets and the British artillery put down a "heavy barrage [...] in and in front of the enemy lines".[19] Nevertheless, a third German wave came forward and once again pushed back the right flank of the 9/Leics. Two platoons of C Coy

Captain Audley Andrew Dowell Lee, "A" Coy, 9/Leics, kia 1 Oct 1917. Age 22. (*Oundle School Roll of Honour*)

were thrown forward into the mix and the German advance ground to a halt once more. It was during this episode that Lieutenant Burn of B Coy was killed.[20]

At 06.00, Battalion HQ received the welcome news that the enemy assault seemed to have ground to a halt, but it had made significant progress against the 9/Green Howards (69 Bde, 23rd Division) on their right. Two more platoons of C Coy were rushed forward to reinforce the right flank and to get in touch with the Green Howards who were themselves counter-attacking. The Germans were pushed back by the two defending battalions, who "regained the lost ground, with the exception of a couple of pillboxes in Cameron Covert".[21] The 9/Leicesters had suffered heavily to repulse the enemy attacks and were forced to form a defensive line some 100 yards behind their original front line. There they remained, under continuing enemy shelling. At around 09.30, reinforcements from 7/Leicesters began to arrive.

---

17 Captain Audley Andrew Dowell Lee, age 22, is commemorated on the Tyne Cot Memorial.
18 For the full VC Citation and a brief biography, see Appendix IV. Lieutenant-Colonel Bent is commemorated on the Tyne Cot Memorial.
19 TNA PRO WO 95/2165: 8/Leics War Diary.
20 Lieutenant Cuthbert John Burn, age 22, son of the late Bishop Burn, is commemorated on the Tyne Cot Memorial.
21 Edmonds, *Military Operations*, 1917 Vol. II, p.302.

190   To Do the Work of Men

The 7/Leicesters had earlier dug in in reserve positions in what was left of Polygon Wood. They themselves were already suffering casualties under the German artillery bombardment when news of the precarious situation of 9/Leicesters reached them. They immediately sent a platoon of B Coy under Lieutenant V.C. Hales forward to form a right defensive flank. This they managed to do but Hales was wounded in the process. Subsequently, C and D Companies (Captain H.H. Hendricks and Captain A.A. Clarke), along with the remaining platoons of B Coy, were also sent forward. They had to advance through the enemy barrage, and the battalion war diarist estimates that they suffered fifty percent casualties before even reaching the front line positions. This included Captain Clarke, who was killed by shell fire.[22] The diarist of 9/ Leics welcomed the arrival of these reinforcements but put their numbers at seventy only. Some members of D Coy, including Second-Lieutenant R.T.W. Miles, had arrived in time to take part in one of the counter attacks. Miles, who had been sent forward merely to reconnoitre, was killed.[23]

The German shelling continued for the rest of the morning as the Leicesters dug in along the eastern edge of Polygon Wood. It was also reported that enemy aircraft were "very aggressive".[24] Remarkably, at around 10.30, Corporal Outhwaite of 9/Leics managed to shoot down a German aeroplane that was flying over the British trenches at an altitude of about 200 feet. It came down in No Man's Land and was subsequently destroyed by shell fire.[25]

There were no more German attacks for the rest of the morning and enemy stretcher bearers were observed removing their wounded comrades from the battlefield. It was around noon that Major Howitt, commanding 7/Leics, arrived at 9/Leics Battalion HQ. He assumed command of both battalions and ordered that consolidation and improvements to the new positions be carried out during the afternoon as a German prisoner had stated that another attack would be launched at dusk. Indeed, the enemy was seen massing in Cameron Covert at around 16.30, but they were quickly dispersed by British artillery and small arms fire. Another 'alarm' was similarly dealt with late in the evening.

The left sector of the brigade frontage was held by 8/Leics. Other than sheltering from the German artillery barrage, for the first hour of the action on 1 October, they were merely spectators to what was going on to their right. At around 06.30, however, it was noticed that small parties of Germans were seen in the open near Joist Farm. They were moving in short rushes towards the right flank of 8/Leics, but were quickly dissuaded from continuing down the slope towards the Leicesters' positions by rifle and Lewis Gun fire. For the next four hours, repeated, if less than energetic, attempts were made to attack the 8/Leics' right flank. All were dealt with in the same way as had been the first. Just after ten o'clock, it was decided that a more aggressive approach might be needed, and Captain J.B. Matthews was accordingly sent forward to assess the possibility of launching a counter attack against the enemy units occupying the high ground near Joist Farm. Unfortunately, he was "killed instantly by a sniper when making a personal reconnaissance, preparatory to the attack, and at 10:30 a.m., the hostile artillery put down a

---

22   Captain Arthur Aubrey Clarke MC is buried in Hooge Crater Cemetery, grave reference X.L.17
23   Second-Lieutenant Roger Thomas William Miles, age 34, is buried in Tyne Cot Cemetery, grave reference LXI.D.8. The Commonwealth War Graves Commission records his date of death as 2 October 1917.
24   TNA PRO WO 95/2165: 9/Leics War Diary.
25   Ibid.

Captain Arthur Aubrey Clarke MC, kia 1 Oct 1917, 7/Leics. Hooge Crater Cemetery, X.L.17. (Author)

192   To Do the Work of Men

heavy barrage on the E. Side of POLYGON WOOD. Consequently this counter-attack did not materialise".[26]

The diarist of 8/Leics plays down the intensity of the German artillery barrage and mentions only two real attempts by the enemy to attack from the direction of Jetty Warren. The first was beaten off by rifle fire, but it was noted that the commanding officer, Lieutenant-Colonel Utterson DSO, was wounded in the arm shortly after 14.00 hrs by machine gun fire. The second came just after three o'clock in the afternoon, when small parties made "a determined effort [...] to move down the slope from JOIST FARM towards Battalion Headquarters, but this attempt was stopped by rifle fire from the Battalion HQ Concrete Emplacement, the enemy retiring and leaving several dead behind them".[27] Later that evening, they were spectators once again as a German attack against the Royal Welch Fusilier battalion on their left was driven back by an SOS barrage. Nevertheless, casualty figures for the 8/Leics would indicate a very uncomfortable day indeed: it had cost them 11 Officers and 175 men.[28]

The 8/Leics and the rest of 110 Bde were relieved on the night of 2/3 October and moved back to Scottish Wood Camp. Casualty figures have proven difficult to finalise: the following table is taken from the 110 Bde War Diary and denotes total casualties for the entire month of October 1917. Since the brigade saw practically no action after their relief on 2/3 October, the figures can give a reasonably accurate picture of the 1 October battle.

	Officers			Other Ranks		
	K	**W**	**M**	**K**	**W**	**M**
6/Leics[29]	2	7	0	24	179	11
7/Leics	3	11	0	63	235	8
8/Leics	6	8	0	73	208	11
9/Leics	5	7	0	46	195	35
110 TM B'ty	0	1	0	1	4	2
110 MG Coy	0	2	0	7	20	1
Total	16	36	0	214	841	68
Overall Total						1,175

The 110 Bde was relieved by units of 62 and 64 Bdes as these latter moved into their jumping off positions for the 4 October attack. On the left, 62 Bde had 3/4 Queen's in the front line, with 1/Lincs and 12/13/NFus close behind them in support, left and right respectively. In reserve, a little further back, were 10/Yorks. On the right divisional front, 64 Bde formed up on a single battalion frontage, with 9/KOYLI in the front line, 10/KOYLI behind them, then 1/EYorks

26   TNA PRO WO 95/2165: 8/Leics War Diary. Captain John Bredel Matthews MC is commemorated on the Tyne Cot Memorial.

27   Ibid.

28   In addition to Captain Matthews, four other officer fatalities can be confirmed: Second-Lieutenants Victor Edward Ellingham, age 29, Albert Henry Hearn, William George Robinson, age 26, and Alfred Shaw, age 20, are all commemorated on the Tyne Cot Memorial. Other ranks fatalities can be confirmed at 47. (Commonwealth War Graves Commission records).

29   The 6/Leics did no more than hold their reserve positions in Polygon Wood on 1 October. The casualties were due entirely to enemy artillery fire.

in support and 15/DLI in reserve.[30] Original plans called for the 3/4 Queen's and 9/KOYLI to take the first objective, the second objective being entrusted to 12/13/NFus and 15/DLI. On the afternoon of 3 October, however, shelling of the rear areas by German heavy artillery caused severe casualties amongst the 15/DLI.

> [Consequently], Lieut Col J.Falvey-Beyts (Comdg 15th D.L.I.) felt compelled to send his Adjutant with a letter to Bde H.Q. in which he stated that, owing to the casualties sustained and the shaken state of his battalion due to the shelling, he felt that his men would be unable to undertake the attack on the second objective to which they had been allotted.[31]

As a result, Brigadier-General Headlam decided to shuffle his pack: 10/KOYLI would take the second objective, 1/EYorks would move up into support positions and 15/DLI would remain behind in reserve. This arrangement was only decided upon at 22.00 hrs on 3 October, and the message had to be delivered in person by Headlam's Brigade Major, Major Macdougall, as the battalions were already on the move from the back areas. This last-minute change, Headlam was sure, would not be a problem, as "all Battalions had been warned (and had arranged plans) to be prepared to take up any task".[32]

The jumping off positions had been marked out with tape and the battalions were all in place by 05.00, ready to move off at 06.00. At 05.20, a heavy German barrage fell on the British front line: the Germans – therefore seemingly unaware of British intentions – were about to launch an attack by three battalions of *212th Reserve Regiment* along a 2,000-yard front to recapture the terrain lost on 26 September. The German advance was to commence at 06.10, but when the British barrage pre-empted it, falling on the crowded German trenches at 06.00, the men of the *212th* suddenly found themselves forced onto the defensive.

A brief account of the general assault will serve to place the actions of 21st Division into context (See Map 26). The 4th Division, on the extreme left of the attack, attempted to cross terrain which had been turned into a swamp by the shelling. Raked by heavy machine gun fire, they lost the protective barrage and fell short of their objectives, losing 1,600 casualties in the process. To their right, 11th and 48th Divisions' main objective was the village of Poelcappelle: with the help of a dozen tanks, they were able to capture all but the very northern edge of it.

I and II Anzac Corps, in the centre of the attack frontage, fared well, despite having suffered significant casualties under the aforementioned German preparatory barrage. On the left, the 3rd Australian and New Zealand Divisions (II Anzac) went forward, the latter crossing the Hannebeek swamp and managing to capture strongpoints behind the village of Gravenstafel, the former successfully arriving on their final objective by 09.00. The 1st Australian Division (I Anzac) swept over the crest of Broodseinde Ridge and, deeming the planned one-hour halt at 07.15 unnecessary, reached the second objective by 08.10. The 2nd Australian Division captured the ruins of Zonnebeke and then pushed on to take the hamlet of Broodseinde. In the end, the exposed nature of these newly-won positions prompted commanders to decide to dig in along

---

30 See Map 27.
31 TNA PRO WO 95/2160: 64 Brigade War Diary.
32 Ibid.

194   To Do the Work of Men

an old British trench line, last occupied in the winter of 1914-15, about 200 yards short of the final objective. This assault had cost the Anzacs over 8,000 casualties.

On the left of the X Corps front, the 7th Division managed to keep pace with the Australians on their left, advancing their 20 and 9 Bdes as far as the plateau edge between Nordemdhoek and In de Ster. On the right of X Corps, 5th Division was able to occupy Cameron Covert and Polderhoek Chateau, though the latter had to be given up by nightfall. On the extreme right of the British front, the IX Corps could not get forward, leaving Gheluvelt Wood and the Tower Hamlets Spur in German hands.

The artillery barrage on 21st Division front commenced at Zero Hour, 06.00, coming down on a line 150 yards in front of the waiting infantry. This meant that Joist Farm (see Map 27) escaped the basic barrage, so instead it was to be shelled by 6" howitzers between 06.00 and 06.03, at which time the main barrage would begin its advance at a rate of 100 yards every four minutes for the first 200 yards, before continuing at a rate of 100 yards every six minutes to a line 200 yards beyond the first objective. Here it would pause between Zero plus 41 and Zero plus 130, providing a protective shield as the first objective was consolidated and the second wave troops prepared to advance. Thereafter, the barrage would creep onto, and then beyond the final objective at the slower rate of 100 yards every eight minutes. It will be seen from the Barrage Map [Map 29] that the artillery plan, though a 'proper' creeping barrage, was quite linear, with no real regard for geographical features, arriving at different parts of the objective lines at different times. Artillery provision was developing in complexity, but at this stage of the war could still be a rather blunt instrument.

The nature of the ground over which they were to advance weighed heavily on the minds of those who would lead the attack. Throughout the summer, rain had appeared with almost malevolent regularity: just as the British attacked, the weather would turn the ground into an almost impassable morass. As mentioned before, however, the days leading up to this attack had been dry. Harold Yeo wrote home on 1 October, stating that "Thousands of flies and tons of dust are the chief features of the situation".[33] A report from 21st Division reflects a certain level of optimism: "The ground represents no formidable natural obstacles. Going should be extremely good on the high ground, and though the low ground is rather wet in places, and the REUTELBEEK and the POLYGONBEEK are broken up by shell fire, it ought not to be difficult to make headway".[34] The infantry were soon to discover for themselves the true state of affairs.

The 3/4 Queen's (Lieutenant-Colonel K.A. Oswald) were about to go into action for the first time. They had served in England from October 1914 to May 1917 before landing at Le Havre on 1 June. After short spells with 9th and 12th Divisions, they joined 62 Bde, 21 Div, on 9 August 1917.[35] Their war diarist wrote a very detailed and evocative account of their exploits in October 1917, including an assessment of the ground and the enemy defences that stands in stark contrast to the 21st Division report:

33   IWM Colonel H.E. Yeo MBE MC 1915-1919 Papers, Doc 3132.
34   TNA PRO WO 95/2132: 'Report on Country and the Enemy's Defences Opposite Xth Corps Front, Ref. O.O.132', 21st Div HQ War Diary.
35   The battalion was disbanded on 11 February 1918.

The night was dark with occasional drizzle. The configuration of the ground and the natural obstacles gave every advantage to the defenders.

The place of assembly was thirty feet below the first objective and in full vision of the enemy. Three streams separated the opposing forces. Each stream ran through soft and boggy ground 50 yards in width. This ground had been churned by the continuous shelling to an almost impenetrable morass. Scrub covered the slopes of the small spurs and this was all heavily wired. About 50 yards to the east of the POLYGON BEEK and again to the East of JETTY WARREN powerful concrete blockhouses, some containing three compartments, and each provided with loopholes, and manned by garrisons of 20 or 30 with machine guns and trench mortars commanded all approaches.

4' to 5' deep trenches were sited on all the prominent positions. The beds of the streams were swept by machine gun fire from CAMERON COVERT and POLDERHOEK CHATEAU. As seen in daylight after the attack the position seemed impregnable.[36]

At Zero, the battalion was lined up with A, B and D Companies in the front line, left to right, each on a frontage of eighty-five yards, with C Coy in close support. C Coy was flanked by sections of 62nd Machine Gun Company and two guns of the 62nd Trench Mortar Battery followed in the rear. As soon as the artillery barrage opened, the assaulting units moved up as close to it as they dared. They found the 'going' rather heavy but were able to keep up with the barrage as it began to creep forwards at Zero plus 3. Almost immediately, the assaulting troops came up against a line of "concertina and barbed wire"[37] which ran across the whole of their front, and that earlier patrols had not been able to clear. To add to their problems, at this juncture they also came under enfilade machine gun fire from the right. The wire did not hold them up for long, but when they reached the Polygonbeek they found a stretch of swamp tens of yards wide. The leading companies only had four "mud mats" and a few trench boards and by the time they had struggled to the far bank they had lost the barrage and units were somewhat mixed up. Nevertheless, they lost no time in assaulting the first German defensive line, Juniper Trench. They caught the Germans emerging from their dugouts and, "owing to the darkness it was impossible to tell their intentions, and the majority were killed".[38] The only serious resistance encountered at this stage of the attack came from one of the concrete emplacements: a bombing party under Lieutenant A.B. Frost was able to storm it and then set in on fire with phosphorous grenades. The rest of this position fell to the Queen's with little difficulty.

The rapidity with which Juniper Trench fell meant that by the time the advance from there had reached Jetty Warren, the men were once more up with the barrage. The next defensive line, Judge Trench, had been largely obliterated by artillery fire and but for some brief, but stubborn resistance from an advanced machine gun post, the German garrison showed little fight, a number of them surrendering quite readily. The first objective, the Red Line, had been secured on time, and the Queen's wasted no time before beginning their consolidation of the position, digging six strongpoints and placing four Lewis gun posts to their front. Company runners and pigeons were sent back with messages confirming the capture of the objective: the first of these to arrive at 62 Bde HQ was one of the pigeons, timed at 07.45. With their support

---

36 TNA PRO WO 95/2156: 3/4 Queen's War Diary.
37 Ibid.
38 Ibid.

196   To Do the Work of Men

company digging in 200 yards behind the Red Line, the 3/4 Queen's work for the day was done. The diarist's account of the attack plays down the level of German resistance to some extent, but casualties were in fact quite significant: three officers were killed[39] and seventeen wounded, leaving some of the battalion's forward positions "not directly under the control of a commissioned rank".[40] Other Ranks had suffered equally badly, with 49 killed, 184 wounded and 19 missing.[41] The diary of 62 Bde HQ paints a more serious picture, but is fulsome in its praise of the brigade's new component battalion:

> Several unsuspected and well-hidden concrete emplacements on the eastern bank of the POLYGON BEEK, each manned by a garrison of 20 to 30 men and 3 machine guns, immediately the barrage had passed opened fire on the advancing troops, causing many casualties. The offensive spirit of 3/4th "Queens" in this, their first fight, was beyond all praise and their recent hard training enabled them to instinctively work round these 'Mebus'[42] and reduce them with skill and rapidity.
>
> The capture of those powerful concrete shelters, in all of which the enemy put up a determined resistance, were amongst the brightest features of the day and were only accomplished by previous good training, absolute determination to win, and a complete disregard of self".[43]

By this stage of the war, the re-organisation of the platoon to include Lewis Guns, rifle grenades, bombers and rifleman had made it into a self-contained, flexible and effective fighting unit. New tactics meant that machine gun nests and pillboxes no longer represented insurmountable obstacles – the return to a version of fire and movement allowed such strong points to be attacked and overcome with an increasing chance of success. Even so, it was still accepted – and to some extent inevitable – that casualties would nevertheless be high.

The capture of the second objective was originally down to the 12/13 NFus and the 10/Yorks. Mirroring the experience of 64 Bde, however, the 10/Yorks suffered such heavy casualties moving up to the front line, that their role was reduced to being in reserve. The 1/Lincolns took their place in support.

When the 3/4 Queens faltered and lost the barrage in front of Jetty Warren, the commanding officers of the support battalions (Lieutenant-Colonel Evans, 1/Lincs, and Lieutenant-Colonel Dix, 12/13 NFus) were quick to react and got their formations to close up quickly on the assault battalion positions: Evans then sent his two leading companies (C & D Coys) through the northern companies of the Queens. These managed to scramble across the swampy ground in Jetty Warren and rushed on as far as the first objective. The advance was not without incident, however: as they passed the Mebus at J.10.d.5.6 – the one set on fire earlier by men of 3/4 Queens

---

39   Commissioned officers killed were Lieutenant John Jocelyn Brooke, age 23, 2/6 Suffolks, attached 3/4 Queen's; Lieutenant Arthur Herbert Augustus Cooper; Lieutenant Alexander Egan Barrow, age 29. All three are commemorated on the Tyne Cot Memorial.
40   TNA PRO WO 95/2156: 3/4 Queen's War Diary.
41   As reported in the battalion war diary. Commonwealth War Graves Commission records confirm the Other Ranks fatalities on 4.10.17 at eighty.
42   Mebu was a slang derivative for the German *Mannschafts-Eisen-Beton-Unterstände* (Team Iron Concrete Dugouts) or ferro-concrete pillboxes.
43   TNA PRO WO 95/2152: 62 Bde HQ War Diary.

Third Ypres   197

– it was realised that the northern compartment had not been 'mopped up' by the support troops and one machine gun opened up on the advancing Lincolns. Lieutenant-Colonel Evans rushed up to the emplacement and silenced the machine gun by "firing his revolver through the loophole".[44] The Fusiliers, on the right, advanced with the Queens as far as Judge Trench, and then C Coy attacked a Mebus just behind it, at J.11.c.78, initially using rifle grenades, "large numbers of Germans being killed and few prisoners taken".[45] Lieutenant-Colonel Dix had himself led the charge to Judge Trench, but was killed in the process.[46] Captain Riddell, himself already wounded, took command. A Coy, under Second-Lieutenant Edmonds, was similarly employed as he and his men strayed briefly into 64 Bde territory before resuming their correct position in support of D Coy.

As the artillery barrage, now including smoke shells paused on the protective line 150 yards ahead of the first objective for an hour and forty minutes, the two support battalions reorganised and got themselves ready for the next stage of the attack. Unfortunately, they were still taking enfilade fire from the south from the German machine gunners still active in Cameron Covert and Polderhoek Chateau. (The 5th Division on the right had been held up). It was at this point that Captain Riddell of 12/13 NFus was severely wounded and command passed to the Lewis Gun Officer, Lieutenant McKinnon, all officers in the battalion senior to him having been either killed or wounded. By now, each of the four companies only had one officer left: A Coy was commanded by Second-Lieutenant Edmonds, B Coy by Lieutenant Jackson, C Coy by Second-Lieutenant Cherryman and D Coy was the responsibility of Second-Lieutenant Hutchinson. The 1/Lincolns were also short on officers by this time, only six, plus Lieutenant-Colonel Evans, were still at duty. It was estimated, by the 62 Bde diarist, that each of the three leading battalions "had now lost 40% of its effectives".[47] And the advance to the second objective was still to come.

At zero plus 100 minutes, at 07.40, the artillery barrage recommenced its forward movement, 1/Lincolns and 12/13 NFus close on its heels. On the left, the 1/Lincs "went smoothly through to the final objective",[48] the only real resistance coming from machine gunners near Judge Copse and from snipers "esconsed [sic] in shell holes".[49] The ridge had sheltered the Lincolns from the worst of the machine gun fire from the right flank, and they were able to begin consolidating along the line of their objective. The snipers remained a nuisance, however, one managing to wound Lieutenant-Colonel Evans, who eventually collapsed through loss of blood. For his single-handed assault on the German concrete emplacement and for his leadership during the rest of the attack, Evans was awarded the Victoria Cross.[50] The battalion was down to four officers and 160 Other Ranks.[51] The Germans did not launch any counter attacks, but around

---

44   TNA PRO WO 95/2154: 1/Lincs War Diary. The diarist then states that "Germans then came out with their hands up but were not taken back as prisoners. Men showed a decided preference to use the rifle rather than the bayonet."
45   Ibid.
46   Lieutenant-Colonel Stephen Hamilton Dix MC, Leinster Regt,, OC 12/13 Northumberland Fusiliers, age 39, is buried in Tyne Cot Cemetery, grave reference XLVI.B.1.
47   TNA PRO WO 95/2152: 62 Bde HQ War Diary.
48   TNA PRO WO 95/2154: 1/Lincs War Diary.
49   TNA PRO WO 95/2152: 62 Bde HQ War Diary.
50   For the full citation and a brief biography, see Appendix IV.
51   Commonwealth War Graves Commission records indicate 59 Other Ranks fatalities on 4 October 1917. The six officers killed were: Second-Lieutenant S.W. McClay, buried in Hooge Crater

Second-Lieutenant S.W. McClay, 1/Lincs, kia 4 Oct 1917. Hooge Crater Cemetery, XX.L.11. (Author)

midday, one company of German troops moved forward from Becelaere and began to dig in on a line running roughly from Judge Copse to Reutel Cemetery. Lewis Gun and rifle fire dissuaded them from advancing any nearer towards the Lincolns' positions.

With the 5th Division still held up, and 64 Bde also hung up on the first objective,[52] the 12/13 NFus advanced with their right flank in the air and still subject to heavy machine gun fire from the south. They got to within 250 yards of their objective before it was decided to dig in where they were, A Coy throwing back a defensive flank on the right in order to maintain touch with the 9/KOYLI. Spared the threat of counter attack, they began the process of consolidation. The war diary estimates casualties at 7 Officers and 44 Other Ranks killed, 12 Officers and 320 Other Ranks wounded.[53]

On the right frontage of the 21st Division assault, the men of 9/KOYLI had taken up their positions in the assembly trenches during the darkness of the early hours of 4 October. All was ready by 05.00. Two sources of annoyance were evident as they waited for the off: the German artillery had bombarded them twice, once at midnight and again at 05.30 – in preparation for their own counter attack. Probably equally galling was the fact that the rations and the rum were late.[54]

Directly across their line of advance lay the shallow valley of the Polygonbeek. The ground sloped gently down to this stream for some 500 yards or so. The far bank rose rather more steeply for a further 300 yards to a crest, over which, and therefore out of sight, lay the village of Reutel. The crossroads just before the village marked their objective. They lined up with C and D Companies in the front line, left and right respectively, with A and B Companies likewise behind them in support. Bayonets were fixed shortly before zero, as per brigade orders: "Care is to be taken that they are fixed quietly and do not glitter in the moonlight".[55]

The men moved off precisely at zero hour, each company on a one platoon front, each platoon going forward in "artillery" or "snake" formation, with a gap of about thirty yards between them. They were met almost immediately by heavy rifle and machine gun fire, and Joist Farm (it will be remembered that this location was not subject to the 18 pdr barrage – see artillery map) was still strongly held, its wire defences intact.

An account of the assault was written by Captains J.H. Frank and A.E. Day of 9/KOYLI six days after the action. Their words describe the beginning of the battle and the true state of the ground near the Polygonbeek:

> This sector was broken by the Polygonbeek [...] and the Reutelbeek, which drain this south-eastern corner of the plateau. Normally a few feet wide and a few inches deep, the

---

Cemetery, grave reference XX.L.11. Lieutenant Samuel Vergette, age 19 and Second-Lieutenants John Conway Adamson, age 19, Edward John Gayer, age 19, James Norman Losh, age 22, and John Robertson Lish are all commemorated on the Tyne Cot Memorial.

52 See below.

53 Commonwealth War Graves Commission records indicate 72 Other Ranks fatalities on 4 October 1917. The officers killed were: Lieutenant John Halifax Feggetter MC, age 22; Second-Lieutenants John Leslie Lowth, age 27, Walter Edmund Waistell, age 23, Ralph Lummis, age 26, Percy John Gregory, age 27 and William Henry Lethbridge, age 21. All are commemorated on the Tyne Cot Memorial.

54 The rum ration was issued "shortly before zero". TNA PRO WO 95/2160: 64 Bde HQ War Diary.

55 Ibid.

200   To Do the Work of Men

bed of these brooks, broken by shell craters, had become belts of oozing mud of uncertain depth; joining near the objective, they formed a muddy valley of well over half a mile wide between Reutel village and Polderhoek Spur to the south.[56]

The two captains continue the narrative. The grammar is their own:

> Just before six o'clock all was more or less quiet, at zero the barrage opened with a fearsome noise and we leapt from our shell holes and went forward in snake formation. It was the darkness that precedes the dawn and one could recognise nobody. We are thankful to say that we got away from our own assembly positions before the full force of the German barrage descended – but were immediately subjected to a withering machine-gun fire, men were falling right and left, but who cared?, our one care was to get forward. Joist Farm proved to be our first stumbling block and was a tough nut to crack.[57]

The capture of Joist Farm was to be a shared enterprise: some of the leading troops on the right of the brigade frontage had avoided the farm altogether. The machine gun fire emanating from it coupled with the difficulty in negotiating the flooded riverbed – some attempted to bridge it by using tree trunks – led many to veer to the south and cross the Polygonbeek by the road (10.d.8.1 – see Map 27). In the end, two sections of D Coy under Captain Sykes and one section of C Coy under Sergeant Pyott, 9/KOYLI, along with B Coy of 10/KOYLI under Second Lieutenant Rooke, advancing in close support, were able to storm the farm buildings once the tanks had broken through the barbed wire defences. The tanks were advancing behind the infantry, their job being to support the advance onto the second objective. The Joist Farm garrison, it turned out, comprised one officer, twelve men and four machine guns. Then, even before reaching the Polygonbeek valley, the right hand companies of both 9 & 10/KOYLIs were held up by single machine gun in a shell hole: once more, the arrival of a tank proved decisive: just as the strongpoint was about to be attacked with rifle grenades, the very sight of the tank – still at this point behind the front troops – prompted an immediate surrender. Our two 9/KOYLI captains take up the story once more:

> The swamp proved a veritable death trap we were up to our knees in slush and at the same time subjected to enfilade machine gun fire from the right. [Mostly from Juniper Wood]. A small strongpoint not concreted and immediately on the west bank of the swamp we took by surprise and the garrison surrendered without firing a shot. On the same bank were a considerable number of German bivouacs constructed of 'elephants' [curved panels of corrugated iron] and filled with Germans, most of these had been blown in by our bombardment. The remainder containing Germans were bombed by our men and the Germans shot as they ran out. On the east side the ground rose rapidly and contained a number of concreted strongpoints two of which were in our area. These fired at us until we were within 50 yards. The garrisons then surrendered, the majority of them being bombed

56   TNA PRO WO 95/2162: 9/KOYLI War Diary.
57   Ibid.

and shot. The left strongpoint turned out to be battalion HQ and was an elaborate concern. Each contained two machine guns.[58]

The delay at Joist Farm, the difficulty in crossing the Polygonbeek and the detour taken by some had all resulted in units of the first two attacking battalions becoming quite mixed up. Casualties were also beginning to mount, and it was a depleted force of both 9 & 10/KOYLI men that made for the next German line, Juniper Trench. This was strongly held, but the defenders seemed to prefer flight to fight, a number of them surrendering to Second-Lieutenant L.B. Spicer, 9/KOYLI, who had managed a quick manoeuvre to their rear. German resistance had temporarily melted away, and this mixed force was able to advance up the hill from the valley with little difficulty, arriving at the first objective more or less to time. They were quickly joined by "stray" groups from the Northumberland Fusiliers, Queens, and D.C.L.I., all of whom had lost direction, the latter quite drastically.[59] The right front company of 10/KOYLI (C Coy) did not arrive on the first objective until the barrage had started to move forward towards the second. Frantic efforts to re-organise while the barrage was static had restored some semblance of order, but it became clear that all the officers of C and D Coys, 10/KOYLI, had been either killed or wounded. The battalion only had two officers remaining. One of them realised the parlous nature of their position. He could see no sign of 5th Division troops on the right flank; some of the men were, indeed, at this time digging in as best they could in order to create a defensive flank position. With about only fifty rifles now available – including the men from the other battalions – the advance to the final objective was looking hopeless. It did not help that the men in this newly-captured position were under sporadic fire from a German strongpoint east of Reutel.[60] Nevertheless, an attempt was made. After working their way forward behind the barrage for about 200 yards, they realised the desperate nature of their position and called a halt. Lengthening their unprotected right flank any further could only make matters worse. The 9/KOYLI meanwhile dug in slightly in advance of the first objective, some 100 yards in front of the road running north-south on the western extremity of Reutel and managed to make contact with the refused right flank of A Coy of the Northumberland Fusiliers. 9/KOYLI fatal casualties for the period 3 to 6 October amount to eight Officers and 103 Other Ranks.[61]

The 1/EYorks (Lieutenant-Colonel R.H. Waithman) had left camp at Scottish Wood at 23.00 hrs on 3 October, still under the impression that they were to be the reserve battalion. New orders were received as they arrived at Brigade HQ, and accordingly formed up behind 10/KOYLI, eventually getting into position soon after 05.00, with the exception of D company (Captain W.C. Green), which had adopted "snake" formation to pass through the by now active German artillery barrage, had become bogged down in Polygonbeek and ended up losing direction. Two platoons had veered off to the right into 5th Division territory and finally went into

---

58 Ibid.
59 The 1/DCLI (Duke of Cornwall's Light Infantry) were part of 95 Bde, 5th Division.
60 This nuisance was soon knocked out, however, by one of the tanks, which made its way along the road through the village as far as the cemetery. There, it was hit by enemy fire and promptly retraced its route to the rear areas.
61 Officers not specifically mentioned elsewhere in this chapter are: Second-Lieutenant Robert Granville Bennett, Second-Lieutenant Norman Davis, Acting Captain Archibald Hardman, Second-Lieutenant Gilbert Arthur Hyde, Second-Lieutenant Frank Lionel de Marche Logsdon and Second-Lieutenant Percy Douglas Stanley. All are commemorated on the Tyne Cot Memorial.

the attack with the left flank of that formation. Captain Green and about a dozen of his men eventually reached the correct jumping off line just before zero.

B Coy (Lieutenant Oughtred) had been attached to 10/KOYLI, and as it advanced Oughtred noticed that some 9/KOYLI men "were held up owing to the presence of wire or some other obstacle".[62] B Coy went forward and helped to capture a part of Juniper Trench.[63]

The other two complete companies moved off at Zero plus 140, A Coy (Captain A.R. Case) on the right, C Coy (Lieutenant C.C. Rice) on the left, closing up as near as was practicable behind 10/KOYLI. They crossed the Polygonbeek and the first line of trenches before advancing up and over the crest, finally being re-organised by Captain Case,[64] and digging in along the right flank of the first objective line.

The advance through the German barrage and the attack had cost them four officers killed[65] in action, with a further five wounded. Other Ranks losses amount to 76 killed and over 170 wounded.

The diary of 15/DLI tells a short, yet sorry, tale. The 3 October entry simply states: "Battalion was heavily shelled and unable to attack".[66] On the 4th, the heavy casualty count forced the amalgamation of

Lieutenant Francis James Ellwood, 1/EYorks, kia 4 Oct 1917, age 19. (*Mill Hill School Book of Remembrance*)

---

62 TNA PRO WO 95/2161: 1/East Yorks War Diary.
63 In his after-action report, the 1/EYorks diarist mistakenly identifies Juniper Trench as the 'first objective'. He then mistakes the real first objective for the second. He also reports that the battalion moved off at Zero Hour, (06.00). In fact they did so as per the plans, at zero plus 140. The late change of orders and objectives has clearly led to confusion. The author has corrected this error in the narrative.
64 Lieutenant-Colonel Waithman had remained in Battalion HQ.
65 Lieutenant Francis James Ellwood, age 19, is buried in Bedford House Cemetery, Enclosure 4, grave VIII.H.40. Second-Lieutenant H.S. Mintoft in buried in Oosttaverne Wood Cemetery, grave reference V.F.1. The Commonwealth War Graves Commission records give his battalion as 3/EYorks. The original Graves Registration Form, however, has him correctly in the 1/EYorks. Second-Lieutenant Robert Ernest Howe, age 19, originally recorded as missing, is buried in Ypres Reservoir Cemetery, grave VII.C.7. Second-Lieutenant Reginald Hooper Crane, age 28, is commemorated on the Tyne Cot Memorial.
66 TNA PRO WO 95/2161: 15/DLI War Diary.

A & B, and C & D Companies into two composite units. With 5th Division struggling to advance on the right flank, the newly-designated AB Coy was sent forward at around midday form a defensive flank facing south along the Reutel road (See Map 28 for 21st Division units' final positions on 4 October). At 01.30 on 5 October, CD Coy was sent forward to join them.

The 10/Yorks played no real active part in the attack. They stood fast in Polygon Wood for the most of 4 October under an enemy artillery barrage that "continued unceasingly",[67] until they eventually moved up under the cover of darkness to occupy positions in the old German front line, Juniper Trench. Incredibly, they suffered 61 fatalities on that day, and a further 131 in the three days that followed.[68]

During the afternoon of 4 October, the Germans attempted a number of counter attacks. One at around 13.00 hrs was disrupted by British artillery fire when SOS rockets were sent up from front line positions. The main effort, timed at 14.15, was directed at Polderhoek Chateau and Cameron Covert:

> Heavy barrage fire was opened on our lines and the enemy could be seen forming up in large number in the vicinity of BECELAERE. The lowest estimate of the number to be seen forming up was 500, and it may have been double that number.[69] This attack was apparently directed against POLDERHOEK CHATEAU and the left of the 5th Divisional frontage. As there was at this time a gap of some 600 yards on the right of the troops which were south-east of REUTEL the attack looked somewhat dangerous. However, the S.O.S. barrage was […] called for and at the same long range (over 1,000 yards) machine gun and rifle fire was brought to bear on the enemy. The enemy could not only be seen forming up but was also seen to move off in small 'snake' formation, similar to our own. He must have suffered tremendous casualties from our S.O.S. barrage and from our rifle and machine gun fire, but he commenced to advance. How far he got it was impossible for anyone to see except for those who were actually in front of him".[70]

One of those units "in front of him" was the amalgamated 15/DLI company under Lieutenant J. Sedgwick. As some of the Germans reached Cameron Covert, Sedgwick's men "opened sustained fire on to these with seven Lewis guns and their rifles. The firing was at 500 yards range and the severest casualties were inflicted on the enemy who got no nearer and were broken up".[71]

The two 9/KOYLI captains also saw this attack developing, also noticing that some of the Germans were moving up from the south, in the vicinity of Gheluvelt. In response

> we sent out a party under 2nd-Lt [L.B.] Spicer with two Lewis Guns and one Vickers to flank the advancing enemy and get enfilade fire to bear on them, later in the day this party disappeared and that evening we searched the ground both to the right of us and in front of

---

67 TNA PRO WO 95/2156: 10/Yorks War Diary.
68 Only one officer was killed. This was Lieutenant Frank Pearce Cliff, age 22. He is commemorated on the Tyne Cot Memorial.
69 The 64 Bde diarist puts the number at 1,500.
70 TNA PRO WO 95/2162: 10/KOYLI War Diary.
71 TNA PRO WO 95/2160: 64 Bde HQ War Diary.

204   To Do the Work of Men

the village for signs of them or their bodies but found nothing. We can only conclude that they were cut off and probably taken prisoners".[72]

Another party with the strength of one platoon under Second-Lieutenant Burton was also dispatched similar orders. This party returned, but Spicer's group was never seen again. Leonard Baker Spicer's death at the age of 23 was later confirmed, but he has no known grave, being commemorated on the Tyne Cot Memorial.

Later that evening, another SOS call resulted in a retaliatory barrage of Polygon Wood by the German artillery. At 22.30, a German shell exploded at the entrance of the 9/KOYLI battalion headquarters. The signalling corporal was killed outright and both the signalling officer and intelligence officer wounded. The commanding officer, Lieutenant-Colonel Daniell, was hit by shrapnel in the stomach and right thigh. The wounds proved mortal. On the orders of the Brigadier, Lieutenant-Colonel Festing, CO 10/KOYLI, took command of both battalions.[73]

During the night of 4/5 October, the units facing the village of Reutel dug a single continuous trench line. Captain A.E. Day, now in command of the forward troops of both KOYLI battalions, had an estimated 150 rifles at his disposal. Soon, large numbers of German troops were seen in Reutel. Fearing a counter attack, the KOYLIs opened up with their Lewis Guns and forced the Germans to take cover. No counter attack developed, but KOYLI snipers were busy for the rest of an uneasy day.

The situation on the right flank was still not resolved: it was reported that the enemy were occupying blockhouses on the north-western edge of Cameron Covert. The commanding officer of 15/DLI, Lieutenant-Colonel J. Falvey-Beyts, organised and then led an attack on these blockhouses. The German garrison was forced to surrender and three machine guns were captured, but Falvey-Beyts was killed.[74] Lieutenant Sedgwick took over the command of the battalion.

The situation on the right improved that evening when units of 95 Bde, 5th Division, established themselves in Cameron Covert and took over the positions occupied by 15/DLI. The Durhams were thus able to withdraw to Zillebeke. Over the next four days, various reliefs took place, the Leicester battalions taking over the front-line positions, and by 10 October, the entire 21st Division was out of the line. The division's action was its only real involvement in the Third Battle of Ypres, being described in the Official History as a "success [that] gave possession of a dominant position overlooking the Reutel valley to the south-east, and so completed the security of the southern flank of the main Broodseinde battlefront. [...] The final objective was not gained, but the casualties show with what stubborn courage this important sector of the battlefield, at the eastern edge of Gheluvelt Plateau, was captured and held".[75]

---

72   TNA PRO WO 95/2162: 9/KOYLI War Diary.
73   Inexplicably, the body of Lieutenant-Colonel Neville Reay Daniell DSO, age 28, was lost and he is commemorated on the Tyne Cot Memorial on the panel dedicated to his original regiment, the Duke of Cornwall's Light Infantry.
74   Lieutenant-Colonel J.Falvey-Beyts DSO, age 29, is buried in New Irish Cemetery, grave reference XXXIII.B.27.
75   Edmonds, *Military Operations 1917*, Vol. II, p.313-314.

The casualties had indeed been heavy. The Official History records them as follows:

Officers			Other Ranks		
Killed	Wounded	Missing	Killed	Wounded	Missing
10	51	10	364	1,699	482
Total:	2,616				

Units of the division completed trench holding duties in and around the Ypres Salient before spending a short time in positions near Arras.[76] On 1 December, they moved by train to a Royal Flying Corps camp at Longavesnes, coming under orders of VII Corps, part of Third Army. On 8 December, having spent a few days in trenches east of the town of Epéhy, Lieutenant Ellenberger of 9/KOYLI wrote home describing the battalion's new surroundings: "There is a distinct resemblance to open warfare. The ground in front of me is full of dead cavalry horses and the Bosches are the best part of a mile away".[77] He added that the weather was bitterly cold and frosty, and that he had not seen his kit nor been able to take his clothes off for over a week. He wrote home again ten days later, saying: "We are pretty comfortable, and this is a 'cushy' section".[78]

They were to remain in this 'cushy' sector until March 1918, by that time coming under Fifth Army orders, though still being part of VII Corps.

21st Division Christmas Card 1917.

In February 1918, the division, like many others along the Western Front, underwent a drastic re-organisation. Following the 1917 battles, the BEF was quite simply short of men. In response to Field Marshal Haig's demands for appropriate reinforcements, the War Cabinet proposed a scheme that would indeed bring units up to strength but would not entail providing any extra men. The British infantry division had up to this point consisted of twelve battalions, four in each brigade. This number would now

---

76 Sadly, during this 'quiet' time, Brigadier-General Rawling, commanding 62 Bde, was killed by a shell in Hooge Crater. Cecil Godfrey Rawling, age 47, is buried in Huts Cemetery, grave reference XII.C.20.
77 IWM Brigadier G.F. Ellenberger Papers, Doc.4227, 8.12.17.
78 Ibid.

be reduced to nine, requiring each brigade to lose one battalion. The problem was, of course, that from then on, three battalions were expected to do exactly the same job as had previously been done by four. This reorganisation affected the 21st Division as follows: 62 Bde lost 3/4 Queens and 10/Yorks but gained 2/Lincs; 64 Bde lost 10/KOYLI; 110 Bde lost 9/Leics. The composition of the division was now:

62 Bde	64 Bde	110 Bde
12/13 NFus	9/KOYLI	6/Leics
1/Lincs	15/DLI	7/Leics
2/Lincs	1/EYorks	8/Leics

It was these units that would face the German Spring offensives of 1918.

5

Kaiserschlacht

The decisive events of 1918 were undoubtedly influenced by two major developments that had occurred the previous year: the entry of the United States into the war in April 1917 and the Bolshevik seizure of power in Russia in November which subsequently took Russia out of the conflict.[1]

The first of these developments meant that the Allies could eventually look forward to a manpower advantage on the Western Front as the United States began to send their troops across the Atlantic. The second, however, meant that Germany was able to transfer a number of divisions from the Eastern Front to France and Flanders: at the end of November 1917, Germany had 150 divisions on the Western Front. By February 1918 this had risen to 180, and by the middle of March had reached 192. The rate at which American troops were arriving was, however, to begin with, no more than a trickle: even by November 1917 there were only 78,000 in France. By March 1918 this had risen to no more than 220,000.[2] It was estimated that the manpower balance in the west would not begin to tip back into the Allies' favour until June 1918, by which time General Pershing[3] estimated that there would be 20 American divisions on the Western Front. The German High Command already knew that if they were going to win the war, they would have to gamble everything on a Spring Offensive in the west. The narrow window of opportunity offered by their temporary manpower superiority would be firmly closed by the summer.

On 3 December 1917, Sir Douglas Haig gathered his Army Commanders together and shared with them his thoughts on the Allied position. The situation on the Italian Front was little short of perilous – Haig had been forced to send five British divisions to Italy in order to help prop up the struggling Italian forces – and that in Russia was disastrous. He concluded that this,

---

1   The "October Revolution", as it was called, took place during late October 1917, according to the Julian Calendar still in use in Russia at the time. By the Gregorian Calendar, used by most other countries, this was early November.

2   David Stevenson, *With Our Backs to the Wall: Victory and Defeat in 1918* (London: Allen Lane, 2011), p.43.

3   General John Joseph 'Black Jack' Pershing (1860-1948), C-in-C American Expeditionary Force from May 1917 until the end of the war.

... combined with the paucity of reinforcements which we are likely to receive,[4] will in all probability necessitate our adopting a defensive attitude for the next few months. We must be prepared to meet a strong and sustained hostile offensive. It is therefore of first importance that Army commanders should give their immediate and personal attention to the organisation of the zones for defensive purposes and to the rest and training of their troops.[5]

Ludendorff[6] understood only too clearly that Germany had one more throw of the dice: he had met with his Chiefs of Staff in November 1917 in order to discuss the prospects for 1918. A major assault was the only option on the table: exactly where it should take place was still a matter for debate. An attack in Flanders would have one obvious advantage: the proximity to the front of the Channel ports vital to the BEF's continued participation in the war. The need to wait until at least April for the terrain to dry out sufficiently rendered this option unacceptable.

Another attack at Verdun was considered, but Ludendorff was of the opinion that the British would be unlikely to rush to the aid of their French counterparts and in his view, it was vital that the attack target the BEF. After a tour of the Western Front, Ludendorff decided upon an assault, codenamed 'Michael', which would take place near St Quentin, this being close to the junction of the British and French armies. The plan envisaged a breakthrough between the Scarpe and Oise rivers and would take his troops over the old Somme battlefield in the direction of Amiens. 'Mars' – an assault on Arras – would go in a few days later. Preparations for attacks elsewhere along the Western Front were to continue, just in case 'Michael' failed. If it succeeded, the German Army would follow up its breakthrough by turning northwards and rolling up the British line in flank and in rear.

Haig was not a happy man. He estimated in early 1918 that he would need 615,000 men to bring his divisions up to strength: the Cabinet Committee, forced to take into consideration the needs of the Navy, the Royal Flying Corps, shipbuilding, munitions and food production, deemed that Haig would have to make do with 100,000 Category 'A' men (i.e. fit for active front line duties) and a similar number of men in lower medical categories. This was barely enough to keep up with the normal daily casualties, or 'wastage' and sickness. If this were not enough, a recommendation by the newly-inaugurated Supreme War Council meant that Haig had to extend his front southwards, taking over twenty-eight miles of front-line trenches from the French. A further twelve miles were then added, meaning that General Gough's newly-created Fifth Army now had its right wing extended as far south as the town of Barisis, some five miles south of the Oise river. Haig's reaction was perhaps understandable: he remarked that "the whole position would be laughable but for the seriousness of it".[7] It must also be remembered at this point that the manpower crisis had forced the reduction in January and February of 1918 of every division in the BEF from twelve to nine battalions.

---

4   See Alison Hine, *Refilling Haig's Armies. The Replacement of British Infantry Casualties on the Western Front 1916-1918* (Solihull: Helion & Company, 2018) pp. 215-226.
5   J.E. Edmonds, *Military Operations France and Belgium 1918*, Vol. I (London HMSO, 1935) p.37.
6   Erich Ludendorff (1865-1937), together with Paul von Beneckendorff und von Hindenburg (1847-1934), was supreme commander German Forces in the West 1916-1918.
7   Gary Sheffield & John Bourne,(eds.), *Douglas Haig. War Diaries and Letters 1914-1918* (London: Weidenfeld & Nicolson, 2005) p. 372, 14 January 1918 entry.

The War Council had also recommended the creation of a 'Reserve Force' which could be held back to bolster any part of the front which found itself in peril. The proposal did not take into account the paucity of available troops, however. Haig refused to give up any men for this formation and Pétain took a similar stance. The two commanders were to rely on mutual support: troops from unopposed sectors could move to help any area encountering real difficulties, regardless of national considerations and Army boundaries. That was the theory, anyway.

The British line, as of March 1918, therefore extended from Ypres in the north to just beyond the Oise in the south. This meant that the entire front of the 'Michael' offensive would now be faced by British troops. In the north, Second Army manned a frontage of twenty-three miles with twelve divisions around Ypres. First Army, with fourteen divisions on a thirty-three-mile frontage extended almost as far south as Arras. From there, the next twenty-eight miles belonged to fourteen divisions of Third Army, including, on its right, the Flesquières Salient, a remnant of the gains made during the Battle of Cambrai the previous autumn. The Fifth Army then held the next forty-two miles, but only had twelve divisions with which to cover them. Taking divisions per mile of frontage into consideration, this put Fifth Army at a distinct disadvantage: each division was responsible for an average of three-and-a-half miles. The equivalent figure for Second Army was less than two miles.

To some extent, this was a sensible strategy on Haig's part. He had to keep his left wing strong: with less than fifty miles between the front line and the Channel ports he would have little room for manoeuvre should the German hammer fall here. He could not envisage the possibility of losing this vital lifeline to Britain and thus leaving his formations in an untenable position, cut off from their lines of supply. Likewise, a successful German breakthrough in the centre near Arras would effectively cut the BEF in half. On the right wing, however, Fifth Army would be able to give ground if necessary, and by doing so surrender nothing of vital strategic importance to the Germans. 'Elastic' defence was a possibility here.

The section of line taken over from the French by Fifth Army was in poor condition and would need a great deal of work to prepare it for effective defence against a concerted German offensive. The new defensive theory ran thus: the front-line system would be called the Forward Zone, code-named the Blue Line. This would consist of outposts only, where pockets of infantry and machine gun emplacements would inflict as many casualties as possible on an advancing enemy before giving ground. The main defensive area, or Battle Zone (Red Line), would be carefully sited 2,000 to 3,000 yards behind the front line and would be of similar width itself. A number of strong redoubts would be built into this system, giving the machine gunners potentially devastating and overlapping fields of fire. It was here that an attack would be held up and turned back. Behind it, the Brown Line or Corps Line would be from where reserve troops could be moved forward as required. Green and Yellow Lines even further back were planned. These latter were to be "constructed as opportunity offered".[8] The actual situation was far from ideal. Martin Middlebrook puts it succinctly:

> ...the entire front of the Fifth Army... never did achieve the status of a fully defended front. The British had come too late, the front was too long, there were not enough men. The front line was reasonably well protected by barbed wire but not a continuous trench.

8   J.H. Johnson, *1918: The Unexpected Victory* (London: Arms & Armour Press, 1997), p.24.

210   To Do the Work of Men

> The Battle Zone was not complete, especially in the extreme south, and the Corps Line in the rear was almost non-existent [...], scattered outposts [...] watched the front, hoping to cover the empty ground between the posts with machine gun fire. Scattered along the front line area [...] were a series of 'redoubts' or 'keeps'. These were all-round defensive positions sited on natural features dominating the surrounding ground. Like the smaller posts further forward, they covered the gaps to the neighbouring redoubts with machine gun fire, but the redoubts were too distant from each other to give much mutual support. What would happen if the enemy attacked in the dark or in a fog or smoke screen and infiltrated between the outposts and redoubts did not bear thinking about.[9]

The trenches further to the rear, as earlier mentioned, were either scratched out to a minimum depth in the grass awaiting completion or simply marked out by lines of tape. Sometimes they were nothing more than a line on a map. John Terraine describes them as "pious hopes rather than military realities".[10]

The British had not fought a major defensive action on the Western Front since the Second Battle of Ypres in April 1915. The BEF liked to fight from well-prepared positions; units preferred to have their flanks secure, and the voluntary surrender of ground was not usually to be contemplated. Just how were the men going to cope with a new, rapidly-imposed philosophy that went against most of their fighting instincts and traditions?

The 21st Division formed part of VII Corps under Lieutenant-General Sir W.N. Congreve.[11] This Corps was positioned on the extreme left flank of the Fifth Army front, just south of the Flesquières Salient (See Map 30). The 15,000-yard frontage was divided almost equally between its three divisions: the 16th (South Irish) on the right; the 21st in the centre; the 9th (Scottish) on the left. Each division had one brigade and its Pioneer battalion in reserve. The 16th Division had five battalions in the Forward Zone, the 21st and 9th each having four similarly positioned. This left only five battalions for the entire Corps Battle Zone, but

> this strong manning of the Forward Zone was judged necessary on account of the short field of view on the high ground, on which the front line had settled down after the Battle of Cambrai, and the ease with which the enemy could mass in the defile, through which the Schelde Canal ran close at hand, free from ground observation".[12]

The 21st Division front contained two natural defensive positions: Chapel Hill and the twin villages of Epéhy and Peizière. Between the two sat Vaucellette Farm, garrisoned, but not so advantageously placed as the other two. These three positions were technically in the Battle Zone, but geography dictated that they were not the requisite distance back from the front line: Vaucellette Farm, for example, was no more than 200 yards behind the Forward Zone.

---

9   Martin Middlebrook, *The Kaiser's Battle.21 March 1918: The First Day of the German Spring Offensive* (London: Penguin, 1983) p. 80.
10 John Terraine, *To Win A War. 1918: The Year of Victory* (London: Papermac, 1986), p.60.
11 Walter Norris Congreve (1862-1927), GOC XIII Corps, 1915-1917, VII Corps 1918. The only corps commander to be wounded during the war, losing his left hand at Arras in summer 1917.
12 Edmonds, *Military Operations France and Belgium 1918*, Vol.1, p.130.

Major-General Campbell was not going to allow his forward units to be overrun by any precipitate German attack, however. Once it was clear that an attack was imminent, the order to "Man Battle Stations" would be issued, whereupon the Forward Zone would be largely evacuated, leaving only observation parties behind, whose job it would be to "keep a look out for enemy movement and send up the SOS signal in case of attack".[13] The bulk of the troops would withdraw to positions in the Red Line: 62 Bde would be on the extreme left, with 1/Lincs occupying Chapel Hill and the adjacent areas;[14] the 12/13th NFus took up positions between the 1/Lincs and Epéhy–Peizière, including Vaucellette Farm; 2/Lincs were placed just behind the Yellow Line in support positions. (The most northerly Company near Genin Well Copse No.2 had two tanks attached.) The twin villages and the Red Line positions in front of them were occupied by 110 Bde: 7/Leics on the left, with 8/Leics and 6/Leics on the right, the former in front, the latter garrisoning the village.[15] Two companies of 1/EYorks were sent forward into the Yellow Line positions directly behind the villages, but the rest of 64 Bde were kept a couple of miles further back near the villages of Saulcourt and Guyencourt.

Campbell clearly intended that Epéhy-Peizière be held: Appendix 'C' of 21st Division's War Diary details the elaborate defensive system:

> EPEHY-PEZIERES (sic) is roughly 1,800 yards long and 500-600 yards broad – with its long side running parallel to the front. The RED LINE was 200-400 yards in front of the village and constituted its outer defence.
>
> The inner defences consisted of 12 strong works[16] and an elaborate system of wiring. 8 of these works were sited on the outskirts of the NE & S faces of the village, forming a perimeter defence. The intervals between the works were covered by cross fire in every case except between ROBERTS and CULLEN and between PROCTOR and MC.PHEE where the nature of the ground made it impossible. These areas were denied by means of additional wiring. The northern end of the village being the most vital was further defended by a second series of three works, MORGAN, MC.LEAN and TOTTENHAM – the two former being sited amongst ruined houses and commanding all the main streets – whilst TOTTENHAM was on high ground covering the exits from this part of the village. Finally a central Keep, "FISHER" was made. Each work was for a garrison of one platoon and was prepared for all round defences. The greatest care was taken to conceal the works and all trenches were completely covered.
>
> […] Each post was provided with a deep mined dug-out or strongly protected cellar – except WEEDON and PACKER where dug-outs were just about to be begun.
>
> Every work was wired all round and a continuous wire obstacle connected all the works. A strong wire obstacle was erected along the West side of the main road, and the road

---

13   TNA PRO WO 95/2133. War Diary 21st Division General Staff. "Summary of a Conference held at Div. HQ on 1st March".

14   See maps 31 and 32 for dispositions.

15   German shelling on the mornings of 15th, 16th and 17th March all prompted the "Man Battle Stations" order to be given and acted upon. The order was also given on the following three mornings, so it can perhaps be assumed that these false – and therefore 'practice' – alarms resulted in its efficient implementation on the 21st.

16   These can be seen on Map 31, marked A – M.

212   To Do the Work of Men

was swept by Lewis Guns from MORGAN Post and from the road junction just North of CROPPER Post, where a special concrete emplacement was under construction.

[...] Headquarters of the battalion holding the village were in deep dug-outs in FISHER'S KEEP, to which a buried cable was led.[17]

In November 1917, the 21st Division had been earmarked for transfer to the Italian Front. Fate intervened to prevent this move: when the Germans counter-attacked at the Battle of Cambrai, 21st Division – and in particular 110 Bde – were rushed down from the Ypres sector to help stem the flow. As it turned out, they arrived only after the front had stabilised once more, and, with the move to the Southern Alps cancelled, began, in early December, holding the line and improving the defences in the Epéhy sector.

As March 1918 dawned, it became apparent to the units rotating through stints in the front line that the routine of trench life was anything but normal. The diarist of 62 Bde noted that:

"The first 20 days of the month were marked by the passive attitude of the enemy, whose troops opposite the Bde. sector (personnel of the 227th R.I.R., 107th Div.) were very unenterprising. There was very little activity in all arms by the enemy".[18]

The battalions of 110 Bde manning the positions in and around Epéhy-Peizière also became aware of what appeared to be the eerie calm before a possible impending storm. The 7/Leics, in the front line at the beginning of March, observed that:

... after the first few days [...] raiding on the part of the enemy ceased and from then onwards to the commencement of the attack his guns were remarkably quiet, the hostile shelling being mainly confined to a few gas shells mixed with HE fired during the night. [...] In spite of considerable harassing fire from our artillery [...] the hostile artillery was almost completely silent.[19]

It was, of course, patently clear that the Germans were preparing an attack. What was not definitively known was the date:

The attitude of the enemy still remained very suspicious. His artillery made no reply to our continued heavy bombardments of his front line system and back areas, and it was evident that the enemy desired to conceal the positions of his guns. Prisoners still continued to give information of an impending attack.[20]

The prisoners mentioned above were captured during a series of trench raids: 'A' Company of the 12/13th NFus had raided Beet Trench at 23.00 hrs on 14 March; on the night of the 15/16th, a patrol under Second-Lieutenant Dickinson of 7/Leics ran into severe opposition – thirty Other Ranks were wounded and Dickinson captured; sixty Other Ranks and two officers of C Coy,

17   TNA PRO WO 95/2133: 21st Div HQ War Diary.
18   TNA PRO WO 95/2153: 62 Bde HQ War Diary.
19   TNA PRO WO 95/2164: 7/Leics War Diary.
20   TNA PRO WO 95/2165: 8/Leics War Diary.

2/Lincs, – Second-Lieutenant F.C. Harper in command – conducted another raid on Beet Trench, in particular a strongpoint at X.8 central (see Map 31) at 03.00 on 19 March. There was no retaliation by the enemy artillery or machine guns on this occasion, despite two green lights being sent up by the front-line German garrison. Five Other Ranks of *227th R.I.R.* were taken:

> One of the prisoners, a Pole, upon whose statements too much reliance should not be placed, said that his Regiment is to be relieved prior to the great attack, that is due to take place on the 20th, having been postponed from the 15th. He affirms that there is to be a heavy bombardment of our battery positions with a special kind of 'BLUE CROSS' gas shell.[21] As a safeguard against this each man of his Company was supplied on the 17th at MONTECOUVEZ FARM with a new and additional disc to be fitted at the bottom of the gas mask. He states that he saw men of the 95th I.R. (18th Div.) in VILLERS OUTREAUX on the 17th. His Coy. expected to be relieved at any time now by troops who were to take over the front for the attack.[22]

Operation 'Michael' was launched on 21 March 1918. The magnitude of this offensive was unprecedented: at 04.40 a single white rocket arced into the air over the town of St Quentin, signalling the commencement of the artillery barrage. Over 6,000 guns, supported by almost 3,500 trench mortars, poured 1,160,000 shells onto the positions of Fifth, Third (and as a feint, First) Armies. The bombardment was to be of relatively short duration – five hours. For the first two hours, fire was directed chiefly at British artillery positions, with a ratio of four gas shells to every one of high explosive. Thereafter, a gas and high explosive barrage (this time with a ratio of 1:1) was directed against the British defensive positions until 09.35, five minutes before Zero, at which point "all howitzers [were to] fire as near to the front line of the First Position as is possible, without endangering their own infantry".[23] As the infantry attacked, the barrage would advance in "deep bounds",[24] the first being 300 metres, thence 200 metres for the field artillery and 400 metres for the heavies. The rate of advance could be reduced in an emergency by the firing of green rockets by the infantry, but there was no signal for halting it.

The war diaries of the 21st Division units do not agree on the time of the commencement of the enemy artillery barrage – they range from 04.00 to 04.45, with most settling for 04.30. The one thing they do agree on was that the entire divisional front was wreathed in a thick fog: "When daylight came just after 6 a.m. it was quite impossible to see the wire in front of the trenches".[25] The order to 'Man Battle Stations' had been sent out by 21st Div HQ at 05.20. If divisional HQ knew the date of the offensive, they did not, it would seem, communicate it to lower units: their war diary entries of 19 March suggest ongoing uncertainty, stating that the attack might be expected on the 20th, 21st or 22nd. On the 21st, raids were therefore still

---

21 "Blue Cross" gas shells are incorrectly named. They contained Diphenylchloroarsine, a solid that was dispersed on detonation as a fine powder which could penetrate a respirator filter and cause irritation and pain to the upper respiratory tract. This would, it was hoped, make the victim remove his gas mask, thus making him susceptible to other forms of gas.

22 TNA PRO WO 95/2153: 62 Bde HQ War Diary.

23 Edmonds, *Military Operations France and Belgium 1918*, Vol.1, p.160.

24 Ibid, p.160.

25 TNA PRO WO 95/2165: 8/Leics War Diary.

being sent out to try and identify the German units facing them. One Officer and twenty Other Ranks of 8/Leics went out at 01.00 hrs: "This patrol met with no opposition whatsoever and on his return the Officer in charge was able to report that not a single German had been seen".[26]

It soon became clear, however, that this was the real thing. Any lingering doubts not assuaged by the intensity and duration of the enemy artillery barrage were finally dispelled at 09.40 when the shelling slackened and through the misted eye pieces of the gas masks that they had been forced to wear for several hours, the British infantry in the front lines saw German assault troops appearing through the thick mist.

Campbell's 'Battle Stations' order had worked just as he had hoped: the German artillery bombardment had fallen on largely empty front line trenches and had also concentrated on areas behind the Red Line positions. The diarist of the 8/Leics was able to report that the battalion had suffered "very few casualties" and that "all ranks were fully prepared for the appearance of the hostile infantry".[27] These men, on the right of the brigade frontage, poured rifle and machine gun fire into the advancing German ranks. Suffering heavy losses – and perhaps taken by surprise by the intensity of the defensive fire – they went to ground in the recently vacated British front line 'Poplar' and 'Oak' trenches (see Map 31, square X.26). The fog and smoke was still problematic: the F.O.O.s[28] were not able to call down artillery fire on the enemy's positions, but accurate rifle grenade and Lewis Gun fire forced them to keep their heads down and precluded any immediate resumption of the attack.

On the left brigade front, the German artillery barrage had effectively destroyed the British wire in front of the original front line and the infantry crossing No Man's Land were able to occupy Plane Trench (see Map 31, squares X.19 & 20). Second-Lieutenant Farey, 7/Leics, commanding the observation party in that section had just enough time to give the SOS signal before his position was overrun. The wire in front of Fir Support and the Red Line was still intact, however, and the 7/Leics were able to hold their lines against repeated enemy incursions.

To their left, the situation appeared a little more precarious: the 7/Leics diarist reported that at ten o'clock that morning, the enemy, around 200 strong, had "broken through the front lines of the Bn on our left [12/13th NFus] and at this hour small parties attacked the northern post (McPHEE) in PEIZIERE and got into the railway cutting behind the RED LINE".[29] Somewhat out on a limb, McPhee Post was captured, six men of 7/Leics being taken prisoner. Almost immediately, C Coy, standing in reserve in square W.30.c, along with two tanks, was ordered to counter attack. The tanks moved around the northern end of the village whilst C Coy attacked along the road leading north from McLean Post. The enemy, presumably in fear of being cut off, retired from the village and indeed beyond the railway cutting. The action was completed by 11.00 hrs and C Coy and the tanks were withdrawn to their original positions. One of the six men captured in the original attack on the Post was able to rejoin his comrades.

On 62 Bde and 16th Division fronts, respectively north and south of 110 Bde, the enemy had met with more success. At 07.30, the 12/13th NFus had reported that all was well except for a breakdown

---

26 Ibid.
27 Ibid..
28 Artillery officers in the front-line trenches designated as "Forward Observation Officers" (FOOs) whose job it was to call down artillery strikes on targets of opportunity, such as attacking forces, or when attacking, to adjust fall of shot as appropriate. Their efficacy depended on good observation.
29 TNA PRO WO 95/2164: 7/Leics War Diary.

in communication with their right company. Almost as soon as the German attack began, at around 09.30, this company was "overwhelmed",[30] and Battalion HQ soon fell to the enemy. It was reported that the following officers were either captured or killed: Major G. White MC, Captain E.H. Griffin DSO MC RAMC, Captain & Adjutant J.McKinnon MC and Second-Lieutenants Elliott and Comley.[31] From this point on, the battalion war diary is silent. A report from 12/13 NFus was received at divisional HQ at 10.25 to the effect that the enemy was attacking the Red Line "in force",[32] but there is no mention thereafter. The 62 Bde story must therefore be told from the points of view of the other formations. The breakthrough on the 12/13 NFus front meant that the enemy were able to outflank Vaucellette Farm to the south. The farm was heavily shelled throughout the morning and was reported to be still holding out at midday.[33] As the tactics of the day dictated, the Germans bypassed this centre of resistance and advanced westwards, threatening to encircle and isolate Chapel Hill, which was held by units of 1/Lincs, including C Coy and the Battalion HQ. The gap was a narrow one, however: D Coy 1/Lincs, in Skittle Alley and Tennis Trench, was able to hold those trenches throughout the day, despite having to form a defensive flank on their right to guard against any enemy advance from the direction of Vaucellette Farm. Meanwhile, A Coy, stubbornly holding Cavalry Trench and Cavalry Support, realised that they were in danger of being totally encircled and captured and attempted to break out to the west: those that succeeded were able to reach Chapel Hill, where B Coy had formed a defensive flank between the hill and Genin Well Copse.

The situation at around 13.00 hrs was reported as follows: Epéhy-Peizière was still firmly in British hands: the Germans had attempted several flank attacks from Squash Trench to the north of the village which threatened the Fir Support position:

> The defence of FIR SUPPORT was conducted by 2nd Lt Wright with about 20 men against numerous bombing attacks in one of which *flammenwerfer*[34] were used but these were stopped on our wire by rifle fire and the cylinders catching alight. The enemy were burnt with there (sic) own weapons. Good work was done by the whole of this platoon and particularly by Pte HICKIN who on 2 or 3 occasions walked along the parapet firing a Lewis Gun from his hip at the enemy concentrating in the trenches on the flanks. Pte HICKIN was eventually killed in making one of these attacks. This platoon held out until dark when with only 6 men left it was ordered to fall back on the RED LINE.[35]

Unconfirmed reports had told of the fall of Vaucellette Farm as the Germans outflanked it to the south and attacked the 12/13 NFus garrison from the rear. The 2/Lincs, in brigade support, were occupying trenches near the railway in square W.23.b. The 1/Lincs were in touch with 9th Division on the railway east of Chapel Hill. This hill was still being held by 1/Lincs, with a defensive flank on its southern slopes. Enemy troops were reported to be occupying the sunken road in W.18.d. from

---

30 TNA PRO WO 95/2155: 12/13 NFus War Diary.
31 Of that list, only one is confirmed killed. Second-Lieutenant John William Elliott, age 26, of County Durham, is commemorated on the Pozières Memorial, Panel 16.
32 TNA PRO WO 95/2133: 21st Div HQ War Diary.
33 Ibid.
34 Flamethrower.
35 TNA PRO WO 95/2164: 7/Leics War Diary. 25264 Private Thomas Hickin, 7/Leics, is commemorated on the Pozières Memorial. It would seem that he did not receive any gallantry award for his actions on 21 March.

216   To Do the Work of Men

where they attempted to advance against the left flank of 2/Lincs. This incursion was spotted as the Germans reached W.18.c. and they were engaged by Battalion HQ troops and a gun team from the Machine Gun Battalion. "A number were killed and the remainder (about 50) surrendered".[36]

Other than the limited and narrow incursion between Epéhy-Peizière and Vaucellette Farm, the 21st Division units were holding their positions in the Red Line, and in some cases in advance of it. On the left, 9th Division had not been seriously troubled, although the South African Brigade troops had eventually been forced to relinquish their hold on Gauche Wood. On the right, however, it was noticed, as the fog began to lift just after midday, that the 16th Division was in trouble. Unlike 21st Division, the men of 16th (Irish) Division had been concentrated largely in the Blue Line, or Forward Positions. These were quickly surrounded and overrun in the fog, the garrisons having suffered heavy casualties under the German preparatory artillery barrage. Malassise Farm (see Map 31, F.2.d.) fell at around 11.00 hrs and with enemy troops seen advancing through Lempire a couple of hours later, the right flank of 21st Division could soon be threatened. The defence of this flank, and of Epéhy village, was the responsibility of 6/Leics. As the orders to 'Man Battle Stations' were given that morning, A and D Coys were garrisoning the Posts in the village,[37] and B and C Coys were making their way forward from Saulcourt to take up positions in the Yellow Line, reaching these by 07.30. There they remained, under constant shell fire, for the rest of the morning. In the village itself, Company Commander, Lieutenant E.G. Lane-Roberts, was in his company HQ, a ruined cellar in Epéhy High Street. The men of his company, D Coy, upon receipt of the 'alarm', would move from their respective cellars to man Fisher's Keep, and Weedon, Packer and Cullen Posts. Lane-Roberts had decided that at that point, he would move his Company HQ into Cullen Post, just behind the town cemetery. In his memoir, he describes the events of the early morning:

> At 4:45 a.m. on the morning of the 21st March I was awakened by hearing a rough and loud rumbling going on outside & on getting to the top of the dugout I soon came to the conclusion that the long expected German Offensive had started. The enemy were putting a heavy barrage fire down on the village, including a large proportion of gas shells. Everyone was soon aroused & after seeing Officers on their way to their respective platoon dugouts to meet their men & guide them to their "Battle" positions. I went off to mine accompanied by my runner, servant & 2 signallers carrying a telephone. The gas being very thick & objectionable we had to don our gas-masks but after falling down a few times & colliding with walls etc we took them off again. We all reached our position safely – in fact every man was soon reported ready to "try our odds" with any Germans that choose to come our way.[38]

The Posts stood to arms for the rest of the day as the fight developed in front of them. Even though they were spared much of the intense fighting of that day, 6/Leics suffered twenty fatalities.[39]

---

36   TNA PRO WO 95/2154: 2/Lincs War Diary.
37   Posts marked F to M on the map.
38   Leicester Records Office, Doc P170. "How I was Captured": A record of the service of Lt E.G.L. Roberts with the 6th Leicestershire Regiment and as a Prisoner of War.
39   These included Captain Archibald McLay MC, age 31, who was in command of the Epéhy defences manned by A & D Coys. He is commemorated on the Pozières Memorial.

Large numbers of enemy troops, possibly three brigades, were seen massing in Thrush and Linnet valleys at about 15.00 hrs. The subsequent attack was repelled, but the right flank situation "was very critical".[40] Accordingly, units of 6/Leics, B and C Coys,[41] were ordered to form a defensive flank pivoting on the southern edge of Epéhy: three Vickers Machine Guns, two Field Companies R.E. and one company of 1/EYorks were attached during the evening. By doing so, they were able to gain touch with units of 16th Division in the Brown Line. In response to German troops collecting in the sunken road to the south of these positions, a counter attack involving one tank was sent out at around 16.45. Soon after, it was decided that the survivors of 8/Leics who were still manning the trenches ahead of the Red Line should withdraw to said line just to the east of Epéhy, in order to conform with 7/Leics on their left who had eventually been driven out of their original lines. Both battalions were now ensconced in Prince Reserve Trench (See Map 31, X.25). One other 'rearrangement' was made to tidy up the Epéhy-Peizière defences: two platoons of the counter attack company, C Coy of 7/Leics, were moved to form a defensive flank facing north between the railway cutting and McPhee Post. The remaining platoons concentrated on McLean Post and settled down to spend an uneasy night. Patrols were sent out between 21.00 hours and 06.30 the following morning, but there was no sign of the enemy.[42]

Lieutenant John Lambert Roberts MC, 6/Leics, kia 21 March 1918, age 19. (Rugby Roll of Honour)

The German incursion to the north of the villages had reached and occupied trenches in the Yellow Line system from W.24.2.0 northwards as far as the Heudecourt to Vaucellette road. At 18.10, the 15/DLI were ordered to retake it. Zero Hour would be 19.45. The 15/DLI had spent most of 21 March in positions in the Brown Line system to the east of Heudecourt. At Zero, they advanced with three companies in line: the attack, in the face of heavy machine gun fire, was completely successful. The Yellow Line was recaptured, and one Officer and sixty Other Ranks taken prisoner. Losses were fairly heavy: fatalities for the day can be confirmed at forty-two. Among the dead was the 15/DLI's commanding officer, Lieutenant-Colonel Festing.[43] Captain S.D. Thorpe MC assumed command.

---

40   TNA PRO WO 95/2163: 110 Bde HQ War Diary.
41   A Coy were already manning Roberts, Cropper and Sharpe Posts on the southern edge of the village.
42   TNA PRO WO 95/2164: 6/Leics War Diary.
43   Lieutenant-Colonel Hubert Wogan Festing, age 35, is commemorated on the Pozières Memorial. He was the fourth commanding officer of the 15/DLI to be killed in action during the war and had taken

218 To Do the Work of Men

As darkness fell on 21 March, activity along the 21st Division front decreased, and indeed a number of unit diaries recorded the fact that the Germans made no further attacks during the night. The 21st Division HQ diarist summed up the action of the day:

> The enemy attacked all along the Divisional front, but only succeeded in penetrating between PEIZIERE and VAUCELLETTE FARM. After having broken through, the enemy turned outwards and captured VAUCELLETTE FARM from the rear. In spite of having forced an entry into PEIZIERE on at least two occasions, the 7th Leicester Regt. with the aid of two tanks ejected the enemy each time by counter attacks and at the end of the day PEIZIERE WAS INTACT.[44]
>
> After the capture of VAUCELLETTE FARM and the YELLOW LINE (between the railway and CHAPEL HILL) the enemy made repeated efforts to capture CHAPEL HILL itself, but the hill was successfully defended by the 1st Lincolnshire Regt. throughout the day. The counter-attack made by the 15th Durham Light Infantry late in the evening succeeded in restoring the situation in the YELLOW LINE.
>
> On the right flank of the Division the 16th Division had been forced back to the BROWN LINE: this involved the formation of a defensive flank of 3,000 yards. The only Reserves available to hold this flank were elements of the 6th Leicestershire Regt. and two Field Coys R.E. The enemy were undoubtedly held off on this flank for a considerable period by the action of the batteries of the 94th Brigade R.F.A. who continued firing at the enemy at point blank range up till the last possible moment.[45]

Lieutenant-Colonel Hubert Wogan Festing, commanding 15/DLI, kia 21 March 1918, age 35. (*The Sphere*, 1 June 1918)

The full story of the events along the whole BEF front on 21 March 1918 is beyond the scope of this work. These events did, however, go some way to determining the fate of 21st Division on the days that followed: as can be seen from Map 30, the Germans had overrun the Front

---

over command less than a month before, on 24 February 1918.
44 These episodes are taken from the war diary of 7/Leics. The first incursion and counter attack is timed at 10.00 hrs, the second at 18.00 hrs. The wording is almost identical each time: was the event written up twice by mistake, or did history indeed repeat itself that day?
45 TNA PRO WO 95/2133: '21st Division Report on Operations from March 21st to March 30th, 1918', 21st Div HQ War Diary.

positions along the entire frontage of the attack, and in many places were into or through the Battle Zone. The situation was most critical in the south, and General Gough was already considering a fighting withdrawal behind the line of the Crozat Canal. As trench lines were lost, units on the flanks, left 'in the air' were inclined to conform, fearing encirclement, this resulting in a general retreat, whether precipitated by unit commanders on the spot or by orders from higher formations. The combination of fog, the speed of the advance and infiltration tactics had, in places, resulted in large numbers of prisoners falling into German hands. Where British units had been able to engage the enemy effectively, however, German casualties had been extremely high. The 'balance sheet' for the day makes interesting reading, bringing into question the often-touted assertion that the opening day of 'Michael' had been an overwhelming success for the German Army. That the British forces had suffered a considerable defeat cannot be denied, of course, but German commanders were less than jubilant: the hoped-for decisive victory had proved elusive. They expected the British artillery positions to be overrun on the first day: they were not. General von Kuhl, noted that "the hoped-for objectives were not reached".[46]

German and British Casualties, 21 March 1918

	Killed	Wounded	Prisoners	Total
Germany	10,581	28,778	300	39,929
Britain	7,512	10,000	21,000	38,512[47]

Sir Douglas Haig, ever the optimist, sums up the events of 21 March in his diary:

Having regard to the great strength of the attack (*over* 30 extra divisions having reinforced those holding the original German front line for the battle) and the determined manner in which the attack was everywhere pressed, I consider that the result of the day is highly creditable to the British troops: I therefore sent a message of congratulation to the Third and Fifth Armies for communication to all ranks".[48]

Reality was soon dawned on the Commander-in-Chief, however. The following day he authorised Gough's proposal to withdraw the right wing of Fifth Army to the line of the Somme.

The 21st Division, despite having held on valiantly through the first day of the battle, was soon to be swept up in the general retreat that followed.

The 22 March also dawned misty with poor visibility. At 02.35 that morning, orders had been received at 21st Division HQ from VII Corps that Epéhy was to be held and that the division's right flank should be extended back to "W.12.d.8.1".[49] This was an attempt to gain touch with the troops of 16th Division who had been driven back to the Brown Line the previous day. One company of 1/EYorks was detached and placed at 110 Bde's disposal for this purpose, along with one company 97th Field Coy RE. Also during the night, troops of 39th Division (Brigadier-General M.L.Hornby) had been rushed forward: they had dug a switch line from

---

46 Quoted in Edmonds, *Military Operations France and Belgium 1918*, Vol.1,. p.260.
47 Stevenson, *With Our Backs to the Wall*, p.55, quotes figures reproduced in Middlebrook, *The Kaiser's Battle*, p.322.
48 Sheffield & Bourne (ed.), *Douglas Haig, War Diaries and Letters 1914-1918*, p.390.
49 This reference is clearly wrong. It should read 'E.12.d.8.1'. See Map 33.

220   To Do the Work of Men

Saulcourt to Tincourt Wood in order to protect a very vulnerable right flank and to help cover any subsequent withdrawal (For unit dispositions and movements on 22 March 1918, see Map 33).

In the Peizière-Epéhy positions, the men of the Leicestershire battalions were getting ready to "Hold On", as per Captain McLay's original orders. At around 04.00[50] on the 22nd, the Germans began a fresh artillery bombardment of the villages: this was in preparation for an assault by *79th Reserve* and *183rd Divisions*. This attack began at around 08.00 and included an advance from the south in an attempt to outflank the 110 Bde positions.[51] By 09.00 this wing of the attack had pushed into the southern outskirts of Epéhy and had surrounded Roberts, Cropper and Sharpe posts, the enemy now able to rush them from the rear.[52] The situation was becoming critical as the Germans threatened to cut off the entire British garrison. Lieutenant Lane Roberts, 6/Leics, emerged from his dug out in Epéhy at about 09.00 and in attempting to reach his Company HQ was forced to dive into a trench as machine gun fire burst out "from the right rear of the village". His account of his eventual capture surely reflects the confusion that typified the fight to hold the village and deserves to be quoted extensively.

Having checked that everyone was still at his post in the trench, he realised that he had left his kit and his papers in his dug out and began to make his way back to the house underneath which the dugout was situated:

> As I came around the bend in the trench I saw two Germans entering the House. I fired & shot one of them & the other turned and jumped into the trench grasping me as he did so. His rifle fell & we started to struggle in the trench. He was heavily equipped & handicapped by being packed up ready for Paris. 4 times I managed to get my revolver into such a position as to shoot him but none of the bullets exploded. Finally at the 5th attempt my big, burly opponent dropped with a bullet through his heart. I afterwards examined the shots & found the striker had pierced the cap but that the cap had not exploded – Faulty Caps – Hearing shots my Sergeant Major came along & got up to see if anyone was in view. He was immediately shot down & fell in the trench.[53] A Sergeant further along met with the same fate. Some few minutes later I saw there were Germans in the cemetery in front of us, hiding behind gravestones. We cleared the Germans out of there & devoted our attention to those who had got behind us. We kept up a continual fire of bullets, bombs & rifle bombs. Every moment I was expecting the 8th Battalion in front to retire on us & hoped then to break through the Germans. As long as there were English troops in front it was impossible & out of the question to retire & and leave them out in front. At 1/30 o'clock I decided to make a dash for it, risk the 8th Bn having retired to the left & try & gain our Yellow Line some way in the rear of the village. I started off & expecting Germans to be in

50   Accounts vary as to the exact time. The latest time given is 06.30.
51   Again, different units report different times, but an SOS signal sent up from Epéhy and seen by 110 Bde HQ at 0815 would perhaps indicate that 0800 is correct.
52   TNA PRO WO 95/2165: 8/Leics War Diary.
53   Commonwealth War Graves Commission records indicate two Company Sergeant Majors of 6/Leics killed in action on 22 March 1918. It is not possible to determine which of the two is featured in Lane Robert's account. CSM Samuel Jackson MM is commemorated on the Pozières Memorial and CSM H C May, age 24, is buried in Unicorn Cemetery, Vendhuile, Grave reference III G 14.

the trench ahead bombed my way down. Lt Thirlby, who was with me, brought up the rear. The Germans were closing in on us now & we had not gone very far when they jumped in the trench in between us & completely surrounded us on top. Escape was hopeless now & we had to surrender – 13 out of about 35 who started.[54]

Lane Roberts asked his captors if he could go back to look for Lieutenant Thirlby, who, he suspected, was wounded. The request was refused.[55]

The 110 Bde was still in contact with 8/Leics, thanks to an intact buried phone cable. At around 09.30, as the German troops were advancing northwards through Epéhy, a message ordering a withdrawal to the Saulcourt – Epéhy road was sent. Lieutenant-Colonel Utterson, CO 8/Leics, was able to pass this on to the 6/Leics, but he himself and a considerable number of the Epéhy garrison were surrounded and captured before they could get away. The commanding officer of 6/Leics had been killed shortly before the withdrawal order: "Lieutenant-Colonel W.N. Stewart DSO was killed, being shot through the head by a sniper: death being instantaneous: Command of the battalion being taken over by Major J.C. Burdett".[56]

The 6/Leics war diarist abruptly recorded that at 09.30, the "Enemy worked round both flanks & we were surrounded".[57] A fighting retreat ensued "under very difficult circumstances, as the enemy were rapidly closing in from three sides".[58] Those men who could, attempted to move back along the communication trenches, but these only stretched so far and the Germans had machine guns trained on the exits. The new positions along the Saulcourt – Epéhy road were eventually reached at around eleven o'clock, but the withdrawal had proven much more costly than the previous day's defensive action. It had fallen to the 7/Leics to cover this withdrawal from their positions in Peizière, and every available man had been used to form a defensive flank facing south. The German advance was halted briefly: at 11.00 hrs, "it was seen that the enemy were entering EPEHY in force from the south [and] two tanks[59] were ordered forward to check his advance and if possible clear EPEHY. The enemy retired on seeing their approach and they report having inflicted heavy casualties. Unfortunately they were running short of petrol and as the engines required repairs they were unable to proceed further and attempting to withdraw to Saulcourt both were knocked out".[60] At noon the 7/Leics received orders to move back behind the Brown Line and wasted no time in implementing them: the withdrawal began at 12.15, and up to that point, Captain Vanner's company was still holding the Red Line and repelling enemy

54   Leicester Records Office: Doc: P170: "How I was Captured": A record of the service of Lt E.G.L. Roberts with the 6th Leicestershire Regiment and as a Prisoner of War.
55   Sadly, Second Lieutenant Stuart Longsdon Thirlby, age 24, from Littleover, Derbyshire, was dead. He is commemorated on the Pozières Memorial. Lane-Roberts was initially reported missing. It was not until 10 April that a telegram was sent confirming that he was a prisoner of war. He had been transported via Le Cateau and Rastatt to an officers' camp in West Prussia at Gradenz. He left there on 13 December 1918 and reached the UK six days later.
56   TNA PRO WO 95/2164: 6/Leics War Diary. The description of Stewart's death in such terms is only too familiar. Its veracity cannot be verified, and it must be treated with some scepticism. Lieutenant-Colonel William Norman Stewart DSO, age 44, North Somerset Yeomanry, attd 6/Leics, is commemorated on the Pozières Memorial.
57   Ibid.
58   TNA PRO WO 95/2165: 8/Leics War Diary.
59   Of 4th Tank Battalion.
60   TNA PRO WO 95/2164: 7/Leics War Diary.

222   To Do the Work of Men

attacks. Even as they withdrew, Vanner remained to supervise the successful demolition of the bridges over the railway cutting. He was eventually able to rejoin his men.

Enemy machine gun fire from both the north-east and south-east accompanied the 7/Leics' withdrawal and "of the two companies […] which covered the retirement, only one officer and fourteen other ranks escaped being hit, and they were captured".[61] The Leicestershire battalions had suffered over 1,200 casualties, killed, wounded and missing, over 800 of which fell into the latter category, many of them having been captured. The brigade, initially ordered to fall back on village of Saulcourt, was effectively finished as a fighting force. An order from 21st Division reached them just after noon: they were to fall back to Longavesnes and then withdraw to Aizecourt-le-Haut, a further four miles to the rear. By 18.00 hrs the remnants of the Leicestershires were in camp enjoying a meal. For the time being, they were well out of the firing line.

The left flank of the 21st Divison, 62 Brigade plus 15/DLI attached from 64 Bde, did not come under such severe attack as their compatriots on the right. The withdrawal of 110 Bde and the proposed evacuation of the Flesquières Salient to the north would of course render their positions untenable. Accordingly, the 1/Lincs on Chapel Hill were relieved by the South African Brigade of 9th Division and at 11.30, orders for the retirement of 62 Bde were issued. At first, they moved to Pioneer Camp on the Heudecourt – Liéramont road, but the enemy "tried to follow up closely, assisted by low-flying aeroplanes".[62] A and D Companies of 2/Lincs suffered particularly heavily as they tried to withdraw, and two companies of 15/DLI holding a strongpoint between Peizière and Chapel Hill had not received the retirement orders. This isolated post held out until around three that afternoon, when, with ammunition running short, a number of men managed to make their way back to the British lines.

By 17.00 hrs, the German advance was threatening the village of Heudecourt and it was decided that 62 Bde would fall back to the Green Line and take up positions between Epinette Wood and Chapel Wood to the north of Templeux-la-Fosse (See Map 33). The Germans harassed the retreating British all the way back, the contact not being broken off until nightfall. It was almost midnight by the time all units were in position. The Green Line was far from being completed: the diarist of 1/Lincs describes it as "not finished – in many places it was only 1 ft deep, the CTS [communication trenches] to the support line were not dug nor was the support line".[63] The 62 Bde lined up with the Pioneer Battalion, the 14/NFus on the left, 1/Lincs with the remnants of the 12/13 NFus on the right, with 2/Lincs in support in Gurlu Wood.

The 15/DLI had begun the day under shell fire, repulsing two German attacks on the Yellow Line with Lewis Gun fire. Just as the Germans appeared to be preparing for a further concerted attack on their positions at around noon, the orders to withdraw were received. The battalion reorganised once they had reached Pioneer Camp and set off to march to Liéramont. With that village coming under artillery fire as they arrived, they moved out onto the Nurlu road before further orders saw them take up positions in the Green Line to the north-east of Templeux-la-Fosse.

It fell to the remaining two battalions of 64 Bde, the 9/KOYLI, (Lieutenant-Colonel A.J. McCulloch) who had not yet been seriously engaged, and 1/EYorks, (Lieutenant-Colonel

---

61   Edmonds, *Military Operations France and Belgium 1918*, Vol.1,, p.294.
62   Ibid, p. 294.
63   TNA PRO WO 95/2154: 1/Lincs War Diary.

J.B.O.Trimble) to hold back the German advance long enough to enable the rest of the division to complete its retirement to, or in some cases, beyond, the Green Line.

The 1/EYorks, with their right flank very quickly exposed on the morning of 22 March owing to the withdrawal of 16th Division, pushed out patrols towards Capron Copse and Villers-Faucon. With the precariousness of their situation thereby confirmed, Trimble withdrew his right flank to join up with 39th Division units. Once A and B Coys had returned from their attachment to 110 Bde, the battalion was ordered to take up positions on the Brown Line, to the right of 9/KOYLI and in front of the village of Saulcourt. They were in position, with six extra machine guns having been sent up to bolster their line, by 14.30.

Until noon, the men of 9/KOYLI had been mere spectators to the action taking place ahead of their positions on the high ground to the north-east of the village of Guyencourt. C and B Coys, left and right respectively, were in front, with D Coy in support. A Coy was slightly isolated in positions to the south of the village. Desultory enemy artillery fire had been no more than a slight annoyance during the morning, but this had increased in intensity around noon as 8" shells began to fall amongst them. C Coy took the brunt of this, but "being spread out did not suffer greatly and only lost 30 O.R. killed and wounded".[64] From about 14.00 hrs, the KOYLI positions were the object of enemy low-level aircraft reconnaissance flights during which the pilots expended a great deal of ammunition in strafing the battalion's positions while they were about it. Their efforts were limited to the wounding of Second-Lieutenant Hargreaves and two Other Ranks of D Company.

It was not until an hour and a half later that the KOYLI units got their first view of German ground troops as they were observed advancing from Peizière along the road to Saulcourt and from the direction of Chapel Hill up to the ridge at Jacquenne Copse directly in front of the battalion's elevated positions. As the Germans crested this ridge, they were met with rifle and Lewis Gun fire from all three front-line companies, which halted them in their tracks. A German officer was seen to have been shot from his horse during this encounter. In response to the German advance from Peizière, McCulloch sent two Vickers Machine Guns to his right flank and notified an artillery battery to their right rear in square E.9.a. The combined fire "had the effect of stopping the German attack with great loss".[65] A number of small parties attempted to push forward from the ridge, but each effort was repulsed: the war diary estimates that they killed 250 Germans that afternoon in front of Guyencourt.

The situation on the right, however, seemed to be turning to the Germans' advantage. The 1/EYorks had observed the enemy massing for an attack on Villers-Faucon, as had units of 39th Division. The latter had sent up an SOS signal, but the response from the British artillery had fallen on 39th Div trenches, forcing some of the men to run back into 1/EYorks positions. Lieutenant Waite, commanding C Coy, pushed his reserve platoon forward to 'retake' the abandoned trenches. The German attack materialised at about 17.00 hrs and C and D Coys were driven back into Saulcourt. The Battalion HQ party under Second-Lieutenant Mansfield was ordered back from the hedge line it was defending and came under heavy machine gun fire as the southern part of the village was overrun. On the left flank, A and B Coys managed to "put up a very strong resistance and no Officer got away, only isolated parties of men working their

---

64   TNA PRO WO 95/2162: 9/KOYLI War Diary.
65   Ibid.

224   To Do the Work of Men

way back".[66] The village was lost, and Trimble attempted to get across to 9/KOYLI positions in order to inform McCulloch of the developing crisis, but "was cut off by advancing enemy and had to abandon the attempt".[67] All Trimble could do now was to reform his battalion at the quarry near Longavesnes and then occupy his allotted section of the Green Line behind that village.

From the 9/KOYLI positions, McCulloch was able to keep an eye on the deteriorating situation on his right flank. He sent parties out to find out what they could, and their reports did nothing to lighten his mood: the enemy were seen advancing in a northerly direction in large numbers across the ridges to the south-west of Villers-Faucon. The possibility of being cut off was now very real. McCulloch gave orders that his men were to be ready either to counter-attack or move to their rear at very short notice. At 17.40, Battalion Observers reported the 1/EYorks withdrawing from the Brown Line, and McCulloch was himself able to watch "a running fight taking place between the E.YORKS. R. and the GERMANS through SAULCOURT".[68] He immediately telephoned A Coy – the line was at that moment intact, though it had been broken and repaired eight or nine times that afternoon – and ordered their withdrawal. Most of the company got away in time, but the speed of the German advance meant that one platoon was surrounded before it could move back. "These gave a good account of themselves and killed more than their own number of Germans. Some Germans indicated by motions of holding up their hands that our men should surrender. The men did not take the hint but shot the enemy down. Capt. CHALK, A. Coy shot a German officer with his Pistol at 5 yards".[69] It is not recorded whether any members of the platoon were able to affect their escape. Captain Chalk survived the action.

Second-Lieutenant Gregg, on McCulloch's orders, ran across to B and C Coys to expedite their immediate withdrawal. This move was also accomplished just in time, as the German spearhead managed to get in amongst the right wing of B Coy but was crucially held up by some wire entanglements. Return fire from the KOYLI rear guard kept the enemy back just long enough for the withdrawal to be successfully implemented.

Forced to cross the open valley behind them under intense enemy artillery fire, the battalion inevitably suffered casualties. C Coy was the last to retire:

> the enemy were at E.13. central [*behind* Guyencourt] when C. Coy the last to withdraw was at E.3 central, and if the enemy had not been wonderfully unenterprising when advancing on LIERAMONT, he ought to have cut off at least half of the battalion. 2nd Lieut. GREENSHIELDS carried out the retirement of C. Coy with skill and coolness.[70]

It was shortly before eight o'clock in the evening that 9/KOYLI reached their positions on the Green Line between Epinette Wood and Nurlu (See Map 33). Reports from the four companies seemed to show that five officers and seventy men had been either killed or wounded during the withdrawal and that about a further 200 were still unaccounted for. Atop this new ridge

---

66   TNA PRO WO 95/2161: 1/EYorks War Diary.
67   Ibid.
68   TNA PRO WO 95/2162: 9/KOYLI War Diary.
69   Ibid.
70   Ibid.

stood only 16 Officers and 160 Other Ranks. They would not stay there long: orders from Bde HQ at 20.15 required them to march two miles or so to the south. Halting briefly to fill their water bottles in the village of Aizecourt-le-bas, the battalion was in position, again in the Green Line, in front of the small town of Templeux-la-Fosse, overlooking Longavesnes, and flanked by the 15/DLI to the left and 1/EYorks to the right. The move was completed by 22.30. Patrols found enemy units only 1,000 yards away, but the day's action was over. It had cost the battalion seventy-two fatalities, including three officers: Lieutenant Arthur Hetherington and Second-Lieutenants Stanley Makin and Clifford Moon.[71]

64 Bde had suffered 159 fatalities on 22 March: to the seventy-two KOYLIs must be added sixty-nine EYorks, including Lieutenant Thomas Stockham and Second-Lieutenants Percy Wadsworth and George Mansfield[72], along with eighteen Durhams.

Over two days of the battle, the 62 Bde had experienced a severe decrease in manpower numbers, including almost 200 fatalities. Necessity had seen the Pioneer battalion taking on front line duties, and as the brigade took up their positions in the Green Line on the evening of the 22nd, 21st Division HQ became aware of just how badly weakened they had become. Accordingly, the three Leicestershire battalions of 110 Bde were sent forward during the hours of darkness to reinforce the left sector of the divisional front, this allowing the 14/NFus to move back into a reserve position. "This step was essential in view of the fact that under orders from the Corps, the GREEN LINE had to be held at all costs".[73] This Corps-inspired imperative was to prove short-lived.

The night was spent improving the fortifications in the Green Line: this was necessary work, as the 'trench' was reported, in places, to be only one foot deep.[74] The only enemy activity reported was a German patrol that reached the wire in front of the 1/EYorks positions, but they were easily driven off. By daybreak on the 23rd the British lines were once more swathed in a thick mist.

At the headquarters of 62 Bde, orders had been received at 06.45 from 21st Division for a "gradual withdrawal",[75] beginning immediately, to a line running north-south from Bussu, through Aizecourt-le-Haut, to Moislains. Just after 07.00, Major-General Campbell delivered similar instructions in person to the 64 Bde staff, having "explained the situation".[76] The Leicestershire battalions had not been in the line more than four hours when the same message reached them. They had been under desultory enemy artillery fire – most of which fell behind them – since 06.40, and receipt of the orders at 08.00 was supposed to precipitate an immediate withdrawal. Written orders had not, however, reached any of the 21st Div. forward units before "the enemy made a sudden heavy attack and broke the sector held by the 7th Leicester R.".[77] At this point in the narrative, the accounts in the numerous war diaries of the units involved offer a confused and sometimes contradictory picture. The diary of 7/Leics

---

71 These officers are all commemorated on the Pozières Memorial.
72 The EYorks officers are also commemorated on the Pozières Memorial. Mansfield was seen earlier in the narrative defending a hedge line in the village of Saulcourt.
73 TNA PRO WO 95/2133: '21st Division Report on Operations from March 21st to March 30th, 1918', 21st Div War Diary. .
74 TNA PRO WO 95/2164: 7/Leics War Diary.
75 TNA PRO WO 95/2153: 62 Bde HQ War Diary.
76 TNA PRO WO 95/2160: 64 Bde HQ War Diary.
77 TNA PRO WO 95/2153: 62 Bde HQ War Diary.

226   To Do the Work of Men

confirms an enemy attack, but not until 09.00 hrs: this came from a south-easterly direction and managed to penetrate between Curlu and Épinette Woods. The battalion was, however, able to hold new positions slightly to the rear along the Nurlu – Péronne road for a further two hours before receiving orders to withdraw to the 'Midinettes' line. (See Map 34). By 13.00 hrs, however, the enemy were working around the battalion's right flank, and with enfilade machine gun fire raking their positions, they were forced to move back across the Canal du Nord, ready to make a stand on the high ground between Moislains and Haut Allaines.[78] Their sister battalion, the 6/Leics, merely conformed with the movement of their neighbours at around 10.00 hrs, this, it would seem, due to the fact that on their right, the 8/Leics had been under attack since 07.00, and were able to observe a German breakthrough to the south of Templeux-la-Fosse. It was clear that encirclement was a real possibility: Lieutenant-Colonel Fisher, commanding 1/Lincs, was given overall command of 62 and 110 Bde troops in the Green Line and was ordered to affect an immediate withdrawal. The 62 Bde sector was also under attack and 1/Lincs had withdrawn some 2,000 yards to the Midinettes Line. This was an old German trench stretching northwards from Aizecourt-le-Haut and the diarist noted that the wire was "behind instead of in front of us", although "the trench itself was a good one and the field of fire very fair".[79] The next rearward movement involved a risky retirement under heavy machine gun fire through the village of Haut Allaines. "The men were very tired & much scattered. About 40 men under Capt Neilson held a line in front of Bouchavesnes during the night".[80] The rest of the battalion were by nightfall much further back near the town of Maricourt.

The story of 2/Lincs is not dissimilar: they received orders to withdraw to Aizecourt-le-Haut at 09.30 – another risky manoeuvre under fire during which their CO, Lieutenant-Colonel Lloyd, was wounded. Major Baker took command. The German breakthrough on the right precipitated a further move, this time across the canal to positions immediately north-west of Haut Allaines. Even this was temporary: the six Officers and only forty Other Ranks that remained as a coherent unit were moved back to a position half way between Cléry and Bois Marrières. Fortunately, they were able to remain there for the night, as "enemy pressure by this time had slackened",[81] and some reorganisation was able to take place. It would seem, with no word to the contrary from the battalion war diarist, that the remnants of the 12/13 NFus were still mixed up with the Lincolns. By the end of the night, the Leicesters, having briefly held a line on the west bank of the Canal du Nord, had consolidated a line just to the west of Bois Marrières where they were able to establish touch with 9th Division on their left. Having had the canal between themselves and the advancing German troops, hopes had been raised briefly that they might have been relatively safe for a short time:

> All around stretched the old wilderness of shell holes, mostly overgrown with grass. At our feet lay the canal, on the further side of which the German vanguards were already in view but halted on coming under direct fire from two solitary field guns. South of us we could

78   For this and subsequent movements of 21st Div units up to and including 28 March, see Map 34.
79   TNA PRO WO 95/2154: 1/Lincs War Diary.
80   Ibid.
81   TNA PRO WO 95/2154: 2/Lincs War Diary.

see the towering hill of Mount St Quentin, the ownership of which was a matter of specu-
lation. Neither to the right nor the left of us were any British troops to be seen.[82]

This lull, as we shall see, would be temporary.

It is from the 64 Bde, on the right of the Green Line positions, that emerges the most detailed
account of the German attack that morning. The left sector was held by the 15/DLI, with 9/
KOYLI in the centre, and 1/EYorks on the right. Orders had been sent, as per Campbell's
instructions, for an immediate withdrawal, but events intervened. The 15/DLI were attacked
at around 08.15, but seeing the Lincolns withdrawing on their left, they moved back through
Ci-Derrière Wood to a trench line north-west of Aizecourt-le-Haut. A further attack at 12.30
and the perceived need to conform once again with the 2/Lincs on their left saw the battalion
move through Haut Allaines, cross the canal and take up positions north of Feuillaucourt. To the
south, just north of Péronne, it was observed that the Mont St Quentin position had been evacuated by 117 Bde, 39th Division: consequently, under "personal instructions from the G.O.C.
64th BRIGADE, the Battn withdrew to a position from CLERY COPSE to the RIVER
SOMME, EAST of CLERY".[83] Further German advances required a defensive flank to be
formed to the south-east of Cléry, this including some stragglers from 39th Division and a
number of machine guns of 21st MG Bn under Lieutenant-Colonel Settle.

On the right of the brigade sector, 1/EYorks came under attack at 08.30 on the morning of
23 March. Their rifle and machine gun fire were able to thwart any serious German advance,
but orders to withdraw reached them at about 09.30. Two factors imperilled the retreating
Yorkshiremen: the fog lifted, German machine gunners being able to sweep the open ground to
the south of Templeux-la-Fosse and a number of platoons did not receive the withdrawal order
and were only too quickly overrun. The 1/EYorks men retreated through Haut Allaines, where
they briefly took up positions on the left flank of the 15/DLI, but the remaining eight Officers
and ninety Other Ranks were soon ordered to the Bouchavesnes-Cléry Copse ridge line, where
they took station for the night, in touch with 2/Lincs on their left.

In the centre, the 9/KOYLI had repelled a German attack at 06.30:

> the attack got within 30 yards of our wire and was repulsed with slaughter. [...] A second
> attack was launched about 7:30 a.m. again under the cover of mist and advantage was taken
> by the enemy of the gutters and mud heaps along the LONGAVESNES-PERONNE
> ROAD. This time fire was with-held until really useful targets exposed themselves.
> Consequently there was a good number of German dead and wounded near our wire and
> in the above-mentioned road.[84]

Once the attack had died down, Major Greenwood MC, and 38787 Private H.Wright (9/
KOYLI) along with Lieutenant Stephenson and Lance Corporal Hardy of 1/EYorks rushed
out to where the wire abutted onto the road to try and bring in two abandoned German machine
guns, many of the brigade's Lewis Guns having been lost during the previous days' withdrawals.

---

82 D.V. Kelly, *39 Months with the Tigers* (Ernest Benn, 1930) p.92 quoted in Richardson, *The Tigers*,
    p.221. Mount St Quentin was in German hands by 1500 hrs on 23 March.
83 TNA PRO WO 95/2161: 15/DLI War Diary.
84 TNA PRO WO 95/2162 War Diary 9/KOYLI.

228   To Do the Work of Men

As Greenwood approached a heap of German dead, an Officer and two Other Ranks suddenly rose from the pile and held up their hands in surrender:

> The Officer noticing that MAJOR GREENWOOD was unarmed, was inclined to be unpleasant, and to retract his surrender, but the immediate arrival of the two men with rifles[85] reduced him to a more amenable frame of mind. The prisoners were brought [in]. They belonged to the 221st Machine Gun Coy. The officer, who was in civil life a Professor of Philosophy said that he hated the whole business. […] The action of Major GREENWOOD MC and the 2 O.R. was worthy of the highest praise and did much to cheer up the spirits of the troops, who were anxious to witness deeds of retaliation.[86]

The diarist, not without a certain level of indignation, continued the story:

> At about 9. a.m. orders were received to withdraw to a trench line at AIZECOURT le HAUT. This was a terrible blow, because having repulsed two attacks without loss, we hoped to stay in the GREEN LINE, and a withdrawal up a slope behind the GREEN LINE under fire of the German machine guns and rifles meant that anything from a quarter to half of the Battn. would be wiped out in the withdrawal. The withdrawal was carried out and no sooner had the movement begun than the quiet, which had preceded, was turned into a veritable 'hell' let loose. About 8 Officers were killed or wounded. Names as follows: Capt TEAZ MC and 2nd Lt. S.MAKIN – killed. Capt. DAY MC, 2nd Lt[s]. J.MAGIN, A.V. GREGORY, T.SLATER, V.R. GREGG, C.A. MOON wounded. And about 100 O.R. out of 16 Officers and 180 O.R.[87]

The reason for the withdrawal soon became apparent, however. The Germans were already in the village of Templeux-la-Fosse, *behind* the KOYLI positions and it fell to Second-Lieutenant James, commanding D Coy, to organise a flank defence of Lewis guns which would allow the rest of the battalion to skirt the southern edge of the village. Some men lost direction and it was "scattered remnants"[88] of the battalion that arrived at their new positions between Aizecourt-le-Haut and Bussu. Others of those 'scattered remnants' found themselves in the village of Feuillacourt: they were soon to be joined by their comrades, as Moislains had fallen to the Germans and this precipitated a further withdrawal. By the afternoon, the 9/KOYLI were also across the Canal du Nord in line with 1/EYorks on their left, extending some 2,000 yards along a spur to the east of Cléry. By this time, according to the 110 Bde diarist,

> the enemy were everywhere in possession of the East Bank of the Canal, somewhat earlier enemy artillery had caused considerable losses in material to conjested [sic] transport on

---

85   The 9/KOYLI war diary makes no mention of Lieutenant Stephenson. His presence is recorded only in the 1/EYorks war diary.
86   TNA PRO WO 95/2162 War Diary 9/KOYLI.
87   Captain Homer Nevin Teaz MC is buried in Péronne Community Extension Ste Radegonde Cemetery, grave reference III H 29.
88   TNA PRO WO 95/2162: 9/KOYLI War Diary.

the HAUT ALLAINES – CLERY RD, where the rough country of the old SOMME battlefield made cross-country traffic impossible".[89]

A further withdrawal to rather more commanding ground just to the east of Bouchavesnes turned out to be no more than temporary: with both flanks effectively in the air here, it was decided that 110 Bde should move back to the Bois Marrières ridge, thus coming more or less into line with the rest of the division.

The night, but for a less than energetic push by the Germans against 64 Bde positions at around 22.00 hrs, which was easily repulsed, passed quietly. It was against the 64 Bde that the main thrust of the German attack in that sector on 24 March was to fall. Yet again, the day dawned, after a bitterly cold night, with a heavy mist shrouding the countryside.

Orders were issued by 21st Division at 08.25 requiring the present line to be held: this was clearly more of a hope than an expectation, as the same orders gave details of two defensive lines, the latter level with the village of Curlu, onto which the division would withdraw should the original requirement prove impossible. The division's right wing was designated as the course of the River Somme and the left should remain in contact with 9th Division. These orders originated at GHQ and had been relayed to his divisions by Lieutenant-General Congreve (VII Corps): it was he who added the "withdrawal clause".

Captain Charles William Tone Barker, 15/DLI, kia 24 March 1918. (*The Sphere*, 25 May 1918)

The main thrust of the German attack that morning, commencing at around 0830, came from the south-east: the village of Cléry was taken "without much difficulty"[90] by ten o'clock, and the remnants of 9/KOYLI and 15/DLI were withdrawn to high ground north-east of Hem. The 1/EYorks joined them there once the Lincolns on their left had also been forced to withdraw, leaving the former's left flank in the air. The 2/Lincs diarist claims that the 1/EYorks were the first to withdraw, thus precipitating the general rearward movement: neither claim can be verified. The 2/Lincs were a spent force by this time, the diarist affirming that casualties had been "severe and only 4 Officers and 19 O.Ranks (including 5 stragglers from other units) remained".[91]

---

89 TNA PRO WO 95/2163: 110 Bde HQ War Diary.
90 TNA PRO WO 95/2160: 64 Bde HQ War Diary.
91 TNA PRO WO 95/2154: 2/Lincs War Diary.

230   To Do the Work of Men

To the north, the 9th Division was also being forced back and this meant that 62 and 110 Bde units were obliged to conform, reaching the high ground to the south of Maurepas just in time to regain touch with 64 Bde to the south.

It was around this time that units of 35th Division – rushed forward by train during the previous night and having marched seventeen miles from the railhead – began to arrive on the scene. Two battalions each of 105 and 106 Bde counter attacked and managed to throw the Germans back a little way astride the Hem–Cléry road.

The German attack continued to build, however, and appeared to be still directed across the divisional frontage in a north-westerly direction. This massing of troops was in full view of the 9/KOYLI men who were still clinging on to their elevated position. With the enemy seemingly unable to locate their exact whereabouts, the KOYLIs were able to frustrate German attempts to advance at 12.50, 14.00 and 14.30:

> After taking our position [...] and getting in touch with the LECESTERS on our left, a German attack was seen developing [...] across our front, about 12:50 p.m. Fire was withheld until it had arrived at B.16.c. when we commenced and drove the enemy back with a few losses. The enemy attack then proceed (sic) by crawling until about a Battalion were accumulated. [...] It appeared from the observation through glasses that the Officers of the Bn. were puzzled to know where the fire was coming from as they kept looking round to their left and left front, sending back messages and compelling their men to keep down. As a result a light machine gun barrage was sprinkled about the hill we occupied, but the enemy appeared to have difficulty in locating our position. At about 2 p.m. the Germans again started to advance, but bursts of fire again stopped them with a few losses. A third attempt was made to advance about 2:30 p.m. but again we put them to earth.[92]

The impasse could not endure, however: the Germans brought up some 5.9 guns and redoubled their efforts, this time with a line of machine gunners in front of their infantry and men lighting grass fires so as to improvise a smoke screen. The KOYLIs hung on until 16.00 hrs, and, in typical fashion, blaming troops on their flanks, were 'forced' to withdraw. A Brigade Staff Officer arrived on the scene at this juncture, met with Lieutenant-Colonel McCulloch and instructed him to move what was left of his battalion back to the village of Suzanne where they would spend the night in billets. They arrived at around 20.30 and were able to spend the night in the relative comfort and safety of barns. The noise of gunfire was still audible, emanating from the direction of Maurepas, but it is likely that this did not disturb the slumbers of the battalion's exhausted survivors for long.

The 9/KOYLI withdrawal was, of course, not an isolated incident: 62 Bde had been withdrawn through Suzanne to Bray, and 110 Bde followed a similar route, halting in Suzanne for the night before making for Bray early the next morning. With the KOYLIs also moving to Bray at 06.00 hrs on the morning of 25 March, the whole of 21st Division was gathered in one place, command of the sector from which they had withdrawn having passed to C.O. 35th Division, Major-General Franks. The countryside across which the troops were forced to withdraw was still scarred by the Battle of the Somme some two years earlier: nevertheless, some

92   TNA PRO WO 95/2162: 9/KOYLI War Diary.

of the French civilian population had returned to their partly ruined villages and were now caught up in the fighting for a second time. Quartermaster Sergeant Bacon of the Leicestershire Brigade witnessed their plight as they were once more forced out:

> Until reaching Suzanne, the area passed through had been that of the old Somme battle-field, but this village was behind the old trench lines of 1916, and therefore to within a few hours previous, had been populated. The scene was now one of utter desolation and presented a picture worse in some respects than the ruins of the villages further east: houses and buildings were quite intact, but there were signs everywhere of a hurried evacuation by the civil population. Such articles of value or necessity as were able to be got away on carts, trucks, peramulators (sic) or by hand, had been taken. For the rest, furniture, articles of Clothing, contents of shops, and the like, lay about in tangled confusion, having been roughly and hurriedly sorted over in the frenzied endeavour to be off. Under these conditions, billets presented no difficulty and the men secured a well-deserved and very much needed rest.[93]

Bacon, from the rear areas, also witnessed the frenzied rearward movement of troops, guns, transport, supplies and so on as they attempted to fall back in some semblance of order and avoid getting mixed up in the fighting, or worse still, falling into the hands of a rapidly advancing foe:

> The Transport of a single division is very considerable, far greater than generally imagined, and from the outset the roads became congested, and the scene extraordinary. In this part of the country, the roads going Westwards were few, and those few converged at many points and gradually but one or two main routes were available. Traffic on every road, all in the Westerly direction, was without interval for miles (2 or 3 divisions were compelled to use one road), consequently at a converging junction the wagons or guns had perforce to fit in like a cog-wheel (this was admirably controlled by Military Police), and the pace diminished throughout. The open country was studded with deep shell-holes and old trenches and tangled with barbed wire, therefore, that proved useless for the passage of Transports. As the enemy followed up our infantry, his guns and observation balloons were brought in daring proximity, and all villages and roads within 3 or 4 miles of the ever receding Line, were systematically shelled. This, in addition to enemy low-flying Bombing Planes, played havoc among the Transports and in several instances, […] the enemy advanced more quickly than the withdrawing Transport Convoys were able to, and much of the tail-end had to be abandoned.[94]

During the night, VII Corps had been transferred to Third Army. It is doubtful that any of the Other Ranks knew of this 'move' and even less likely that they would have cared anyway. They were far enough from the fighting to allow the establishment of bivouacs, followed by a rest and a substantial midday meal, before the inevitable re-organisation began.

93 Leicester Records Office: Doc. 22D63/146, Unpublished memoir of D.A. Bacon MM, late Quartermaster Sergeant, 110 Infantry Brigade. p. 103.
94 Ibid, p.102.

232   To Do the Work of Men

The 21st Division was badly depleted and it was decided that one Composite Brigade would be formed under the command of Brigadier-General Headlam (64 Bde). Each brigade was able to furnish one under-strength battalion as follows: 62 Bde, 650 men, all ranks; 64 Bde, 400 men; 110 Bde, 450 men. The total of 1,500 officers and men, along with a Machine Gun Company consisting of eight guns, were to be ready to move at fifteen minutes' notice. Small nucleus parties of each brigade were sent back to the transport lines north of Chipilly.

Headlam's Brigade consisted of one 'battalion' formed from each brigade in the division, made up of one 'company' from each battalion. They were commanded as follows:

64 Bde:	Major Coles (1/EYorks)
	15/DLI – Captain Herbert
	1/EYorks – Captain Stephenson
	9/KOYLI – Captain Shaw
62 Bde:	Lieutenant-Colonel Howlett (12/13 NFus)
	1/Lincs – Captain Newbury
	2/Lincs – Lieutenant Holliday
	12/13 NFus – ???
110 Bde:	Major Burdett (6/Leics)
	6/Leics – ???
	7/Leics – Lieutenant Carnley
	8/Leics – Captain Gregory

At 20.00 hrs on 25 March, a telegram (GX.720) from VII Corps was received at 35th Division Headquarters: due to events further north, the 35th Division was to withdraw during the night and take up new defensive positions along the Albert – Bray road. Orders to that effect were dispatched at 21.10, emphasising that the move was to take place immediately. The new dispositions included Headlam's Brigade, which would take its place on the right of this new line, its right flank in the village of Bray. In the centre of the line were 35th Division units, with 9th Division completing the line, its left on the River Ancre.

The move was carried out efficiently, successfully and for once, "without molestation from the enemy",[95] and on arrival the troops found supplies of bully beef, biscuits and tins of water which had been dumped along the Albert-Bray road at around 02.00 hrs on the 26th. It soon became apparent that this line was not to be held for long: VII Corps Order 248 was issued at 02.15 that morning, stating that:

> VII Corps will fight to-day on the line ALBERT-BRAY in order to delay the enemy as long as possible without being as involved as to make retirement impossible. Retirement when made will be to the North of the ANCRE which is to be held again as a rearguard position all bridges being destroyed after the crossing. [...]
>
> The retirement will be from the right, 21st Division via MERICOURT l'ABBE, 35th Division via VILLE, 9th Division pivoting on ALBERT.[96]

95   TNA PRO WO 95/2469: 35th Div HQ War Diary.
96   Ibid.

Once across the river, Headlam's Force would take up positions between Ribemont and Buire, with, as before, 35th and 9th Divisions filling in the line as far as Albert. These instructions were reinforced by a personal visit from Lieutenant-General Congreve (VII Corps) who spoke to each brigade commander in turn:

> impress[ing] strongly upon these Officers and upon all others with whom he spoke the fact that it was important to gain time for the removal of valuable stores and guns in rear, but that the value of them was not to be held so great as to entail the troops suffering heavy losses. It was clearly understood that the retirement should take place during the day, beginning on the right flank, which indicated a methodical withdrawal on a prearranged plan, as existed in the 35th Division Orders already issued".[97]

He also added that should the troops on the right flank find their way across the Ancre blocked, they should cross the Somme and join Fifth Army, although he was of the opinion that this would not be necessary. He told Headlam to "stay on as long as you can; you should be able to hold on until 10 a.m.".[98]

At 11.00 hrs, mounted German scouts appeared on the ridge to the east of the Albert-Bray road, soon to be followed by troops moving slowly forward, as if uncertain as to exact location of the British positions. They began to probe for weak spots in the British line, which was not continuous, in an effort to turn flanks: one bold attempt on 105 Bde front was foiled by the arrival of a section of tanks, but pressure continued to mount.

Accounts of how the eventual withdrawal began are contradictory. Most accounts do agree that the retirement was triggered at around 14.30. The 35th Division diary states simply that Headlam ordered the move at 14.00 hrs, his positions being under severe attack from the enemy, and that 104 Bde on his left followed suit as per orders at 14.45. The Official History's version is slightly different: British heavy artillery had begun to shell the village of Bray at around two that afternoon, and Headlam's troops still to the east of it were forced to move back. This caused 104 Bde troops to believe that the planned withdrawal had begun and thus conformed as per orders. Headlam, on seeing this, sent a message to 104 Bde saying that he did not intend to withdraw until after dark. The message did not arrive, however, and 104 Bde's retirement continued. Half an hour later, 105 Bde joined the rearward movement, passing through Morlancourt at around 16.00 hrs. Some men on Headlam's left flank nervously began to move back, but were successfully halted before the trickle became a flood: although now enfiladed from the north, they held on until ordered to move back at 16.00 hrs. Headlam sent a message back to 21st Div HQ, explaining his situation:

> I was finally forced to leave my line at 4:00 p.m. as the left and centre brigades were then in full retreat. The Bosches were bringing up guns very quickly and there were considerable numbers following on. It is quite possible that some of the extra foot weary men will get cut off but I hope not. The men will be very weary and really not fit to put up a show in defence of the river if Bosches push on hard. Necessity is food and hot drink. Can I have

---

97 Ibid.
98 Edmonds, *Military Operations France and Belgium 1918*, Vol.1,, p.511, fn. 2.

234   To Do the Work of Men

1,500 rations put at Sucrerie and also some cookers brought there for all battalions. Please give me orders re an entrenching Bn and the reinforcing Bn who were put under my orders. They are no use, in my opinion, and were the cause of several 'stampedes'. They might be a more useful reserve after a day's rest. They also want rations – no. about 800 each. I am trying to get these Bns assembled just east of Buire.[99]

Meantime, Third Army HQ had tried to change the rules: news of the withdrawal had reached them at around three o'clock. Orders were immediately dispatched stating that "no voluntary retirement from our present line is intended. Every effort is to be made to maintain our present line".[100] Congreve immediately called Major-General Franks (35th Div) on the telephone, instructing him to halt the withdrawal. Orders dispatched at 15.31 and 18.18, bluntly affirming that "The BRAY-ALBERT line is to be held at all costs"[101] came too late. The message never reached 104 Bde and Headlam did not receive it until 19.05, by which time he was in the village of Buire, already safely across the Ancre. Franks had motored through congested traffic to Morlancourt, just in time to meet the 105 Bde coming the other way. After consulting with his brigadiers, he decided that it was too late to stop the retirement.

Bray was by now in enemy hands. On the western side of the Bois des Tailles between Chipilly and Morlancourt, stood 'McCulloch's Force'. This detachment, consisting of 1,200 men, under the command of 9/KOYLI's CO, had been formed from the remnants of 21st Div – those pioneers and infantry left once Headlam's Brigade had departed – and had taken up station at 08.00 hrs but had not yet been threatened. As McCulloch saw troops on his left withdrawing through Morlancourt at around 17.30, he gave the order for his men to conform. Just as his men started to fall back, the brigade major of 106 Bde brought him a written message from Brigadier-General Pollard. This required him to maintain his position until nightfall. McCulloch managed to stop the last 500 or so of his men from joining in the withdrawal and got them into position just south of Morlancourt, thus prolonging the right flank of Pollard's 106 Bde. They were reinforced by a detachment of troopers from the 1st Cavalry Division under Brigadier-General Beale-Browne.

The Germans could now be observed across the valley north of the Bois des Tailles and by 18.30 they were attacking Morlancourt in force. The 106 Bde took the brunt of this assault and, half an hour later, judging that they had by now fulfilled their holding role, began to pull back westwards and across the Ancre. Beale-Browne's men withdrew to the Sailly-le-Sec – Ribemont line at about the same time, but McCulloch's Force held on for another fifteen minutes. With their communications threatened, they slipped away in the dark, but did not reach the Ancre at Ribemont until around 21.30. They were under fire for much of the way, but thankfully casualties were slight: one Officer and six Other Ranks were wounded, the only fatality was 'Sawdust', a riding horse of the 9/KOYLI, "an old battalion pet, whose loss was much deplored".[102]

Headlam had by now received the orders cancelling his original retreat. Accordingly, he and Brigadier-General Marindin (105 Bde) made arrangements to re-cross the Ancre and retake

99   TNA PRO WO 95/2133: 21st Division General HQ War Diary.
100 Edmonds, *Military Operations France and Belgium 1918*, Vol.1,, pp.513-514.
101 TNA PRO WO 95/2469: 35th Div HQ War Diary.
102 TNA PRO WO 95/2162: 9/KOYLI War Diary.

Morlancourt. Mercifully, with their much-depleted force exhausted and short of ammunition, a staff officer from VII Corps, Major Kelly, arrived just in time to countermand the move.

McCulloch's men were still south of the Ancre, now combined with 'Cumming's Force',[103] which was experiencing "an anxious time, especially for [Cumming], with a hastily organised and unknown force under his command, and with an attack of unknown strength imminent at any moment".[104] They were still there, unmolested, on the morning of 27 March. The Germans had taken Morlancourt but had not pushed on beyond the Bois des Tailles. Less than determined attempts by the Germans to cross the Ancre at Dernancourt against 9th Division positions on the 27th were repelled, mainly by artillery fire, and before long, the 4th Australian Division arrived to relieve the hard-pressed defenders, completing the task by dusk. On the right, the 3rd Australian Division took over the outpost line held by Cumming's Force during the afternoon and pushed their cavalry patrols forward in the direction of Morlancourt. McCulloch's and Cumming's men remained in support behind them for the time being. They were to be ready to attack in the direction of Sailly-le-Sec should the situation south of the Somme deteriorate to the extent that a German attack northward across the river might become a possibility. Such a situation never arose, and the 21st Div men were finally relieved on 28 March. The rest of the division – what was left of it – had already moved back to Allonville, a small village just to the north-east of Amiens, some fourteen miles to the rear of Albert, where McCulloch and Cumming rejoined them on the 30th.

The 21st Division's involvement in the 'Michael Offensive' was over. It had been a very costly enterprise. Casualty figures for the infantry and artillery between 21st and 31st March recorded in the 21st Division War Diary amount to 4,432 killed, wounded and missing. The following detailed breakdown is, of course, bound to be slightly inaccurate, compiled as it was before the figures "settled down", but the overall picture is nevertheless indicative of the difficulties entailed in a prolonged fighting retreat before a determined and skilful enemy. It is even more astonishing that the defence could be prosecuted at all during its latter stages when it is realised just how under-strength the battalions were by that time: none escaped with less than 300 casualties, most surpassing 400.

---

103 This third composite unit had been formed at Heilly that morning, consisting of 2,000 men from an Entrenching Battalion, numerous stragglers and a number of drafts and men returning from leave. It was ordered to occupy a line from Ribemont to Heilly, subsequent orders taking it forward to an old trench system running from Ribemont to Sailly-le-Sec. They were under command of 110 Bde CO, Brigadier-General Hanway R. Cumming.

104 Hanway R. Cumming, *A Brigadier in France* (London: Jonathan Cape, 1922) p. 122.

236   To Do the Work of Men

Summary of Casualties 21st to 31st March 1918

	Killed		Wounded		Missing		Total	
	Off	OR	Off	OR	Off	OR	Off	OR
62 Bde								
12/13 NFus	1	19	2	87	20	318	23	424
1/Lincs	2	39	8	131	3	272	13	442
2/Lincs	1	33	10	103	5	248	16	384
62 TM Bty	–	1	1	5	–	4	1	10
Bde Total:							53	1,260
64 Bde								
Bde HQ	–	–	–	7	–	3	–	10
1/EYorks	4	37	7	194	7	183	18	414
9/KOYLI	3	29	13	103	1	166	17	298
15/DLI	4	35	7	232	6	228	17	495
64 TM Bty	1	–	1	3	1	5	3	8
Bde Total:							55	1,225
110 Bde								
6/Leics	5	35	7	125	6	262	18	422
7/Leics	3	22	9	130	9	280	21	432
8/Leics	–	29	8	116	6	274	14	419
110 TM Bty	1	1	–	–	–	31	1	32
Bde HQ	–3	–7	–12		–	22		
Bde Total:							54	1,327
14 NFus (P)	1	18	7	109	3	67	11	194
21st MG Bn	2	18	9	93	15	181	26	292
Div. Artillery								
HQ	–	–	–	1	–	–	–	1
94 Bde RFA	1	6	7	30	–	2	8	38
95 Bde RFA	1	12	7	55	1	9	9	76
21st DAC	–	1	–	12	–	7	–	20
21st TM Bde	1	–	1	5	–	4	2	9
RA Total:							19	144
Total:	31	338	104	1,548	83	2,556	218	4,432[105]

Once Engineers, Signallers, Medical Staff and Transport Troops are added, then overall total rises to 238 Officers and 4,702 Other Ranks.

Operation 'Michael' failed. The Germans had overrun the British positions along a sector totalling fifty miles; 1,200 square miles of territory was occupied; 90,000 prisoners had been captured, along with 1,300 guns. However, they had not taken Amiens – and one final attempt

---

105 TNA PRO WO 95/2135: 21st Div HQ War Diary.

to capture Arras on 28 March ended in disaster – and they had not split the British from the French and rolled up the former's lines as planned. The initial tactical victory was not followed by strategic success: all they had acquired was "masses of strategically unimportant territory".[106] They had also suffered very heavy casualties: Allied casualties totalled around 212,000, but German figures are higher, reaching 239,000 dead and wounded. Ludendorff closed the operation down on 5 April, but he could not revert to the defensive: if the Germans were to win the war in 1918, the unpalatable fact was that it would still have to be done before the summer. On his map of the western front, his eyes had wandered northwards: even before 'Michael' had finally petered out, orders were given (on 3 April) to instigate "Georgette". This offensive became known to the British as the Battle of the Lys.

The 21st Division was transferred to Second Army on 1 April 1918 and a twelve-hour train journey saw them arrive in Belgium just after dark on the 2nd. They concentrated in an area near Kemmel, just to the south-west of Ypres, and the men, including a substantial draft of new arrivals, were able to rest during the following day while brigade and battalion staffs visited the section of front line that they were going to take over from the 1st Australian Division. On 4 April, they completed the relief, with 62 Bde taking over the right sector of the front line, with 64 Bde on the left, and 110 Bde in reserve. The following day "passed quietly, there being little activity on either side".[107] The welcome respite was not to last.

106 Stevenson, *With Our Backs to the Wall,* p. 67.
107 TNA PRO WO 95/2133: 21st Div HQ War Diary.

6

Kemmel

The entry in the 9/KOYLI War Diary for 5 April 1918 was short and simple but could not have suited the men better: "A quiet day on the front. Nothing to report".[1] Captain G.F. Ellenberger MC, now in command of C Company, put his thoughts about the new location in a letter home:

> The comparative safety of the front line, except in an actual attack contrasted strikingly with the increasing harassment of the areas behind. In reserve, by Dickebusch Lake, we spend nights and days moving up shell-beaten paths to dig fresh targets in ground merely to pass over which was fearsome, and on which the gunners stayed for weeks. Our rest was nightly disturbed by German aeroplanes – we had scarcely known them on the Somme: to watch their silvered wings shining like angels' toys in the crossed searchlight beams was entrancing enough; but tents afforded no sense of security either from enemy bombs or from our own avenging missiles. Up in the line, on the other hand, it was often strangely quiet; the enemy's guns found better targets behind us, and when his shells dropped short, the 'lengthen range' signal flared up from a German forward post: maybe we should have mopped up that isolated 'pill-box', but as it was it served us well.[2]

One of the most important tasks of early April was to bring the depleted battalions of 21st Division back up to full complement. During the first four days of the month, badly-needed reinforcements had arrived as follows: 1/Lincs, 1 Officer and 236 Other Ranks; 2/Lincs, 1 Off. and 176 O.R.; 12/13 NFus, 335 O.R; 1/EYorks, 1 Off. and 475 O.R.; 9/KOYLI, 1 Off. and 384 O.R.; 15/DLI, 1 Off. and 492 O.R.; 6/Leics, 1 Off. and 565 O.R.; 7/Leics, 519 O.R.; 8/Leics, 219 O.R.; 14/NFus, 250 O.R.; 21st MG Battn., 19 Off. and 84 O.R.; RAMC, 60 O.R.[3] This comes to a staggering total of 3,820 men, the equivalent of four battalions. By the end of the month, this figure had risen to over 6,000. Brigadier-General Cumming, 110 Bde, commented on the quality of these replacements:

> New drafts of men were quickly forthcoming to fill the vacancies but these were of course comparatively raw, and to a certain extent untrained, although good material if time could

---

1   TNA PRO WO 95/2162: 9/KOYLI War Diary.
2   IWM Brigadier G.F. Ellenberger MC papers, Doc. 4227, 3 April 1918.
3   TNA PRO WO 95/2135: 21st Division HQ War Diary.

238

be given to let them settle down and be properly organised and trained with their battalions. This respite was, however, from force of circumstances not procurable.[4]

On 8 April, a message was received at 21st Div HQ to the effect that the division was to transfer to XXII Corps (Lieutenant-General Sir A.J. Godley) as of 18.00 hrs that day. At 04.05 the following morning, heavy firing was heard to the south and reports came in announcing an extensive and heavy enemy attack going in between the La Bassée Canal and the town of Fleurbaix. The Battle of the Lys had begun.[5]

The Germans' code name for this attack was 'Georgette', it being a scaled down version of the original 'George I' and 'George II' plans. The key objectives were the railway junction at Hazebrouck, the main road running west from Ypres through Poperinghe, and the 'Flemish Hills, including Mount Kemmel, Mont des Cats and Scherpenberg. This would render the British positions on Messines Ridge untenable. With the southern half of the Ypres salient outflanked, and the Germans threatening a breakthrough to the coast – Dunkirk is less than 25 miles from Hazebrouck – the British would probably be forced to abandon Ypres entirely. The successful implementation of 'Georgette' could even see the British knocked out of the war.

The preliminary assault was delivered at 08.45 on the morning of 9 April by eight German divisions. Four of them, once more under cover of thick fog, were directed against the Portuguese Corps between Neuve Chapelle and Laventie. An hour later, a precipitous Portuguese retreat had become a rout. The 55th Division, on the Portuguese right, somehow managed to hold their ground. On the left, 40th Division was forced to withdraw. The result was a German advance of nearly three miles on a ten-mile-wide front, the forward troops having reached the River Lys at Estaires. On the next day, the focus of the attack moved north: Ploegsteert and Messines had been taken by noon, though the latter was recaptured later in the day. Armentières was outflanked and had to be abandoned.

As the attacks continued on 11 April and Messines Ridge finally fell, Haig's worst nightmare was in danger of becoming a reality. He sent a letter to Foch asking that he send at least four French divisions north to support the British and issued his now famous 'Order of the Day'. This uncharacteristic exhortation concluded:

> There is no other course open to us but to fight it out. Every position must be held to the last man: there must be no retirement. With our backs to the wall and believing in the justice of our cause each one of us must fight on to the end. The safety of our homes and the Freedom of mankind alike depend on the conduct of each one of us at this critical moment.[6]

Units of 21st Division had replaced the 1st Australian Division on the Wytschaete – Messines Ridge on 4 April, but they were relieved by 19th Division three days later and moved to new positions astride the Menin Road in the Polderhoek sector, ready to repel a German attack. On the night of 9 / 10 April, troops of 110 Bde were in the right sector of the front line, with

4   Cumming, *A Brigadier in France*, p. 129.
5   For a detailed account of this engagement, see Chris Baker, *The Battle for Flanders: German Defeat on the Lys 1918* (Barnsley: Pen & Sword Military, 2011), *passim*.
6   J.E .Edmonds, *Military Operations France and Belgium 1918, Vol. II* (London HMSO, 1937, Appendix 10, p.512.

240   To Do the Work of Men

6/Leics (Lieutenant-Colonel Chance) on Tower Hamlets spur, 8/Leics (Lieutenant-Colonel Irwin) in support at Zillebeke Lake and 7/Leics (Lieutenant-Colonel Sawyer) in reserve at Scottish Wood. To their left was 146 Bde (49th Division), to whom 9/KOYLI was temporarily attached. The rest of 64 Bde and 62 Bde were in reserve positions in and around Hooge. No attack ensued, and for the next few days units of 64 and 62 Bde were sent to and fro in the sector, attached to various formations, presumably in response to the ever-changing situation to the south. 110 Bde positions remained basically unchanged. Captain Harold Yeo, on 64 Bde Staff, summed up the situation rather neatly in a letter to his mother, dated 13 April 1918; "One can't analyse the situation at all, chiefly because one doesn't know much about it".[7]

By the evening of 10 April, 62 Bde HQ was at Bedford House (see Map 36, square I.26.a.), with its three battalions scattered around various camps in the vicinity. Almost as soon as they had arrived, orders were received that the brigade, (less 1/Lincs who were to come under orders of 64 Bde), was to move immediately to Parret Camp (Square N.15.b.) and come under command of 26 Bde: this was as a result of a heavy German attack that morning against 9th and 19th Divisions. A conference of Brigadiers (26, 57 & 62 Bdes) was held at the camp at 23.00 hrs and the 12/13NFus and 2/Lincs, who arrived there at around one o'clock the following morning, were given orders to retake the village of Wytschaete and "re-establish themselves on the Messines – Wytschate Road […] before dawn".[8]

Accordingly, the 12/13NFus (Lieutenant-Colonel Howlett) and 2/Lincs (Lieutenant-Colonel Bastard), right and left respectively, moved into the gap south of Onraet Wood. They advanced at 05.30, by which time the Germans were aware of their presence and had put down an artillery barrage on the road they were occupying. One hundred yards into Wytschate the 12/13NFus encountered a number of the enemy:

> … pushing their way up to the ridge with M.G. detachments and infantry; our advanced guards rushed these detachments and hand to hand fighting took place for about half an hour, the enemy putting down a heavy barrage after the first five minutes; eventually the enemy was forced to retire and we occupied the strong points EAST of WYTSCHAETE.[9]

Later that evening they were able to repel a German counter attack that came in just after dusk.

The 2/Lincs were able to match their compatriots' advance, despite the fact that "[t]he advance was carried out during a very dark night, at very short notice and over ground which was only known to a very few people in the battalion and was carried out without a hitch".[10]

The hard-pressed 62 Bde remained in the line until relieved on 16 April, having endured repeated shelling and several incursions by enemy patrols. A sequence of reliefs had taken place in the meantime, and on the morning of 16 April, the line was being held by 12/13NFus and 1/Lincs. At 04.30 a "terrific bombardment"[11] fell on the front line and the village. It lasted for an hour, and

7   IWM Colonel Harold Yeo Papers, Doc. Ref. 3132, 13 April 1918.
8   TNA PRO WO 95/2153: 62 Bde HQ War Diary.
9   Ibid. April 1918. Appendix IV.
10   Ibid.
11   Ibid.

under cover of a dense fog the enemy attacked on the flanks of [1/Lincs] and succeeded in breaking our line just North of the Stanyer Cabaret cross roads and at Peckham. Strong parties of the enemy then wheeled inwards and attacked both flanks of the battalion, the frontal attack does not appear to have been pressed.

Owing to the dense fog and bombardment it was impossible to get a clear idea of the situation, and the Companies did not know they were attacked until the enemy appeared at close quarters. Fighting under every disadvantage, as the fog denied them the full use of Lewis Guns and rifles and made it impossible to locate the enemy, the battalion stood firm, and fought it out to the last. No Officer, platoon post or individual surrendered, and the fighting was prolonged until 6:30 a.m. Ample evidence of this is provided by the Commanding Officer and Battn. H.Q., who made a last stand at the Cross Roads, and did not leave there until 7 a.m. They, a mere handful of men, withdrew slowly, fighting all the way through WYTSCHAETE WOOD.

The withdrawal was covered by the Adjutant, Captain MCKELLAR, with revolver and bombs, firing into the enemy at close quarters. This enabled the Commanding Officer, Major GUSH, to get away his wounded and the Commanding Officer of the 12/13th Northumberland Fusiliers, who was also wounded.[12]

The account of this defensive action in the diary of 12/13NFus is brief, recounting that a defensive flank was formed on the high ground from Black Cot to Onraet Wood, five machine guns having been gathered together. It does mention the arrival of 1/EYorks on the scene at 11.30. The 'fog of war' is evident in the 1/EYorks account, which recounts the "disappearance of 62nd Bde".[13] The establishing of a defensive flank is attributed to D Coy of 1/EYorks who, after losing all the men in the right hand platoon, including Second-Lieutenant Foster, "held fast all day although the enemy three times penetrated into their trenches".[14] B Coy and two platoons of A Coy arrived to bolster this position and they were soon joined by a company of 15/DLI.[15]

The situation was stabilised later on 16 April by a counter attack by units of 9th Division, which went in at 19.30. This also involved units of 62 & 64 Bde, which had been under 9th Division command since 10 April.[16] They captured their first objective, but were unable to move on to their second, as the planned attack by the French on their right failed to materialise. Between 16 and 18 April, all battalions of 62 Bde were relieved and withdrew to Siege Farm, (Square N.16.c.), leaving the village of Wytschaete in German hands.

Casualties for this engagement were heavy. The war diary of 1/Lincs puts their strength at only five Officers and 103 Other Ranks on 17 April. The 12/13NFus reported casualty figures of eleven Officers and 320 Other Ranks. The 1/EYorks enumerate one officer (Second-Lieutenant Johnston-Stuart) and 37 Other Ranks killed[17], two Officers and 61 Other Ranks missing, with two Officers and 113 Other Ranks wounded. This is an overall total of 216.

12   Ibid. By 22 April, Major Gush is being referred to as "Lt-Colonel Gush" in the battalion war diary. See TNA PRO WO 95/2154: 1/Lincs War Diary.

13   TNA PRO WO 95/2161: 1/EYorks War Diary.

14   Ibid.

15   The 15/DLI diarist confirms their involvement in this action, but incorrectly dates it as 17 April.

16   The 2/Lincs were certainly involved, as were 1/EYorks at dawn the following morning. Due to the mix up of dates in the 15/DLI account, it is unclear as to whether this battalion was involved. The 9/KOYLI were at this time engaged in work on the GHQ Trench Line in the vicinity of Vierstraat.

17   Lieutenant (?) Cyril George Johnston-Stuart, age 24, is commemorated on the Tyne Cot Memorial.

242   To Do the Work of Men

64 Bde units do not all record their casualties for these few days[18], but overall numbers for 62 Bde can also be estimated through the 21st Division Quartermaster's returns, as reported to him by 9th Division:

	Officers	Other Ranks
12/13NFus	12	300
1/Lincs	6	300
2/Lincs	4	150

Fatalities for the engagement (12-19 April) can be ascertained from Commonwealth War Graves Commission records:

64 Bde	9/KOYLI	1/EYorks	15/DLI
	5	44	38
62 Bde	1/Lincs	2/Lincs	12/13NFus
	61	47	60

The 64 Bde remained under orders of 9th Division: the 1/EYorks and 15/DLI were still holding trench lines in Onraet Wood. The former was relieved by 9/KOYLI on19 April. The diary described this relief as "intricate" – there were many gaps in the line and no communication trenches, but the relief was completed by 03.00 hrs on the 20th. The new positions were very close to Wytschaete (see Map 35), which was, as we have seen, now in German hands. British artillery, in an attempt to shell enemy positions there, managed to land a disturbing number of rounds on B Coy trenches at around two o'clock that afternoon. To add to the insult, more shells also fell short in reply to an SOS flare sent up at nine o'clock that night: in spite of messages sent back to the artillery, one gun continued to fire short until the early hours of the 21st, resulting in the deaths of ten 9/KOYLI soldiers, including Second-Lieutenant Stanley Cundall.[19] A similar number were wounded. The war diarist gave vent to his anger as he recorded the day's events: "The strongest protest was made against this discreditable performance and it is to be hoped that the officer of the artillery concerned will be tried at Court Martial for this carelessness".[20] If any disciplinary action was ever taken, it was not recorded in the 9/KOYLI diary.

One of the Other Ranks killed by shell fire was 24554 Private Sid Waldron. It is impossible to be certain whether he was killed by friend or foe, but that would have been of no importance to his mother in Bulwell, Nottinghamshire, as she read the War Office telegram. She wrote to one of Sid's friends, Willie Simpson, enquiring after further details of what had happened to her son. Willie posted his reply on 10 May, by which time he was in hospital suffering from the effects of gas:

18   64 Bde casualties will be for the period 16-30 April 1918 are listed below.
19   Second-Lieutenant Cundall is buried in Klein-Vierstraat British Cemetery, Grave Ref. V. A. 8, along with 34708 Private Joseph Ward, Grave Ref. IV.D.2. The other eight are commemorated on the Tyne Cot Memorial.
20   TNA PRO WO 95/2162: 9/KOYLI War Diary.

Dear Mrs Waldron,

Just a few lines answering your most welcome letter which I received today. I was very pleased to hear from you, and I know how you will feel about Sid. I can hardly realize it yet because we were chums. I cannot tell you much more about him because I was only up the line at the time and had to come down again with the CO. He was in a dugout at the time, and a shell hit it, but none of the shell hit him, it must have been a beam or something that hit him or shock because he was not marked anywhere, it is hard luck. I was only telling him a week or two ago we would have a good time when we got home, I should like to get home to tell you but I don't think their [sic] is much luck this time. I am getting better, but gas is an awful thing. I don't want any more of that, I only got a slight wound besides I will give you a call if I get to Blighty. I expect I shall be in hospital a little while yet. I must conclude now. Hoping you are getting over your great loss, which I know will be hard,

I remain your Sincere Friend, Willie Simpson.

P.S. Write back and let me know if you get this".[21]

On 10 April 110 Bde received orders that they were to take part in the "general withdrawal from the Ypres Salient to a line immediately East of Ypres".[22] The line to which they were to withdraw ran along what was the old GHQ line (See Map 35). This "had been dug in 1917 and had now partially fallen in and required digging out".[23] The withdrawal did not take place until the night of 15/16 April, when the two front line battalions (7 & 8/Leics) vacated their positions after dark, retiring through two companies of 6/Leics under Major Burdett MC who were left in position in what became known as the 'Outpost Line' as a rearguard until the new line was ready. The digging was completed two nights later and the system was occupied by 7 & 8/Leics. The other two companies of 6/Leics joined their comrades in the Outpost Line during the night of 20/21 April before being able finally to vacate it on the 23rd when 7/Leics relieved them. The position was finally vacated on 26 April. The 110 Bde diary gives little detail about what happened in the Outpost Line, stating that it was "very little molested and enemy attitude was cautious and unaggressive".[24] Brigadier Cumming's memoirs give us a little more detail:

> The holding of this isolated position was a very trying and arduous duty, entailing incessant watchfulness and care on the part of all concerned. It was only a skeleton force, scattered over a wide extent of front in small posts with practically no support. It was really a colossal piece of bluff to cover, in the first instance, the construction of a new line; but it was continued for some time longer as it prevented the enemy from gaining a commanding bit of ground from which observation of the whole area was possible. It proved a most successful device, as the enemy advanced very slowly and cautiously towards it, and it was not until the 17th that he pushed forward and established a general line in front of it.[25]

---

21 Liddle Collection. Item No. 55. 24554 Private Sid Waldron is commemorated on the Tyne Cot Memorial.
22 TNA PRO WO 95/2163: 110 Bde HQ War Diary. This enforced withdrawal gave up much of the territory that had been hard-won the previous summer and autumn during the Battle of Third Ypres.
23 Cumming, *A Brigadier in France*, p.140.
24 TNA PRO WO 95/2163: 110 Bde HQ War Diary.
25 Cumming, *A Brigadier in France*, pp.141-142.

244   To Do the Work of Men

The 6/Leics' war diary also shows that the position was far from being a comfortable one. They endured snow during the day on 19 April and at 21.00 hrs on the evening of the following day, an SOS was received from the post on the far right flank: Captain Scott was sent out to investigate and was soon requesting stretcher bearers. Lieutenant Vernall's platoon was repelling a sizeable German trench raid. The fight lasted for half an hour before the Germans were finally repulsed, but it had cost the Leicesters three dead and a number of wounded.[26]

On 23 April the 9/KOYLI were relieved in Onraet Wood by 1/EYorks and withdrew to a hutted camp on the banks of the Vijverbeek (within square N.9.c. – see Map 36) "with a view of being rested and 'fattened up' for 2 nights, preparatory to taking part in an attack on Wytschaete on the morning of the 26th".[27]

9th Division, to whom 9/KOYLI was still attached, issued D.O. 218 on 24 April. This detailed an attack on a wide front, involving 9/KOYLI and 9/Black Watch (27 Bde) retaking Wytschaete and the French 28th Division on their right launching an assault astride Spanbroekmolen. The CO of 9/KOYLI (Lieutenant-Colonel A.J. McCulloch) reconnoitred the ground over which the attack was to take place with his opposite number in 9/Black Watch on 24 April. This turned out to be a fruitless exercise: the following morning the Germans launched a huge offensive between Bailleul and Ypres, the main initial objective being the capture of Mount Kemmel. 21st Division was thrown onto the defensive once again.

The Official History describes this sector of the Allied line as "an international front".[28] The right was held by the 34th, 154th and 28th French divisions, the left consisting of the British XXII Corps (Lieutenant-General Sir A. Godley) – 9th and 21st divisions (with the 39th Composite Brigade under command of the latter) – and II Corps (Lieutenant-General Sir C. Jacob) – 6th, 41st and 36th divisions.

Occupying the front line trenches were six French regiments, each of three battalions, on a 9,000 yard front, and five "very weak"[29] British brigades, similarly of three battalions each, on a frontage of 7,000 yards. The trench system consisted of three lines of defence: the front line, the Vierstraat Line and the Cheapside Line (See Map 35).

The XXII Corps was in the process of modifying the front line system: it had been decided that between Lagache Farm and Dome House, the main line of resistance would be the front line, and with this in mind, the curve in the line forming the salient around Onraet Wood would be straightened by digging a new trench across its base from Petit Bois to The Mound. When the German artillery bombardment began at 02.30 on 25 April, this undertaking was far from complete. For two hours, the rear areas were drenched with gas and high explosive shells. At 05.00, after a thirty-minute pause, the barrage resumed, this time targeting mainly the front line trenches. The bombardment had proven particularly effective against the allied artillery positions: by 08.30, hardly one gun per battery was still in action in the French sector. The British artillery had suffered slightly less, their guns having been more spread out than those of

---

26   Privates 31629 William Freestone, age 36, and 235444 Albert Holmes, age 35, are buried in The Huts Cemetery, grave references XI.A.8 and XI.A.11 respectively. 235421 Private Henry Smith, age 28, is buried in Hooge Crater Cemetery, grave reference VI.G.5. The Commonwealth War Graves Commission records their date of death as 21 April 1918.
27   TNA PRO WO 95/2162: 9/KOYLI War Diary.
28   .Edmonds, *Military Operations France and Belgium 1918*, Vol. II, p.409.
29   Ibid, p.410.

their French counterparts, but the high percentage of gas shells used ensured that the gunners were forced to keep their gas masks on until 11.00 hrs and they also "incurred heavier losses per battery than on any other day in the war".[30]

The main thrust of the German assault, which went in at 06.00, was against the French held sector in front of Mount Kemmel and was prosecuted by three and a half divisions. The *22nd Reserve, 4th Bavarian*, The *Alpine Corps* and part of the *56th Division* pushed forward in a north-westerly direction and had overrun the French front line so promptly that many of the French support troops were still in their dugouts when the Germans overwhelmed their positions. By 07.10, the *Leib Regiment* of the *Alpine Corps*, advancing with fire support from low-flying aircraft, had reached the summit of Mount Kemmel and 800 French soldiers had become prisoners. To their right, the *56th Division* captured the town of Kemmel, taking 1,600 prisoners in the process. An almost immediate but ill-judged counter-attack by a company of the 19/ Lancashire Fusiliers was met by withering machine gun fire resulting in their near annihilation.

The German forces pushed on down the northern slopes of Mount Kemmel, crossed the Kleinkemmelbeek and halted around 11.00 hrs just short of the village of La Clytte. On the left wing, a defensive flank had been formed facing Locre to the west (See Map 35). Luckily for the hard-pressed French, who had only managed to bring up two battalions of the 99th Regiment from reserve, and whose men were hopelessly spread out over nearly three miles from Locre to La Clytte, the German timetable required a pause at this juncture so that artillery could be brought up to support the next stage of the assault. The attack was not to be resumed that day, however: the artillery was slow to move forward, patrols sent forward further north met with solid resistance, and as more allied troops moved forward to strengthen the line, General von Lossberg (Chief of Staff of *Fourth Army*), was fearful of counter attack.

It had been hoped that this incursion into the French line would force the British to abandon the Ypres Salient and German attacks against the British sector to the south of the town threatened to outflank the whole position. These attacks did not have the intensity, nor it seems, the determination, to match that of the assault on Kemmel, however, and a fighting withdrawal involving the formation of a new south-facing defensive flank, coupled with stubborn resistance at a number of key points saw the German attacks falter and come to a halt in front of the British second and third lines, the Vierstraat and Cheapside Lines. (See Map 36).

The British sector of the line, manned, right to left, by 27, 146, 64 and 26 brigades, with some units of 39 Composite Brigade on the left flank, faced attacks by the right wing of the German *56th Division*, and by the *13th Reserve Division* and *7th Division*.

The right of the line, as it abutted the French sector near Lagache Farm, was held by three companies of the 12/Royal Scots (27 Bde). In the salient east of Black Cot were the 1/5 and 1/6 West Yorks (146 Bde), with the 1/E Yorks – the only 21st Division presence at this time – in the vicinity of Onraet Wood. Two companies of the 7/Seaforth Highlanders were in close support behind the left flank. Each brigadier held one battalion in the front line with other units further back in the Vierstraat and Cheapside lines or beyond.

It was the 64 Bde that bore the brunt of 21st Division's involvement on 25 April: the actions of the other two brigades can be briefly outlined. The 110 Bde was still in positions to the north of the Ypres-Comines Canal and came under nothing more than diversionary artillery fire and

---

30   Ibid, p.413.

246   To Do the Work of Men

limited infantry incursion. The 6/Leics were not attacked but were forced to suffer an initial artillery bombardment. This had subsided by 05.00 hrs, but one gas shell had landed in the HQ Runners' dugout – "all runners & signallers inside were gassed"[31] – and at 10.00 hrs a high explosive shell scored a direct hit on the battalion kitchen. Casualties amounted to thirteen wounded and four gassed.

The war diary entry for the 7/Leics on 25 April is brevity personified: "Battalion in the line. 1 O.R. wounded".[32] The 8/Leics' response to a small German force probing the defences was to withdraw its men from the outpost on Torr Top. Other than that, the day passed without incident.

The units of 62 Bde started the day in reserve positions to the west of Dickebusch Lake. By 09.00 hrs the 1 & 2/Lincs were in square 27.a (see Map 36), ready to move forward if needed. It was not until 2 o'clock in the afternoon that two companies of 2/Lincs were moved to positions between Hallebast and Dickebusch Lake. Battalion HQ and the two other companies echeloned back on their right to the west of the crossroads.

The 1/Lincs were 'stood to' at 04.25 and told to be ready to move at five minutes' notice. The previous day, with their numbers still down after the action of the previous week, the battalion had been reorganised into two companies, each of four platoons. A and B Coys were formed as No.1 Company under Captain T.G. Newbury MC, C and D Coys becoming No.2 Company, commanded by Captain S.S. Edinborough MC.

These companies moved to positions on the Ouderdoom – Vlamertinghe Road at around nine o'clock that morning, and remained there until 18.30, when they were ordered to take up new positions in the Cheapside Line (also known as GHQ Line No.2), spread thinly between the south-west corner of Ridge Wood and the northern edge of Scottish Wood. This move was completed by 23.20.

The 12/13 NFus, also having been 'stood to' since 04.45, were finally issued orders at 19.00 hrs. They moved off two hours later and took up support positions behind the 1/Lincs. Reliable information regarding the action of 1/EYorks in Onraet Wood and Grand Bois in the early morning of 25 April is scarce: the after action account in the war diary of 64 Bde makes only one reference to the battalion during its narrative, stating that at 08.30, "1st E.York. R. were apparently holding GRAND BOIS".[33] At the end of the narrative, its author, the Brigade Major, Captain L.D. Spicer, formerly of 9/KOYLI, also observed:

> After the attack on the 25th April, of the 1st. E. Yorks who were holding the line, only 3 Officers (including the M.O.) and 34 other ranks managed to escape. Of the rest very little is known and until the names of prisoners come to hand, the majority must be classed as missing.[34]

31   TNA PRO WO 95/2164: 6/Leics War Diary.
32   TNA PRO WO 95/2164: 7/Leics War Diary.
33   TNA PRO WO 95/2160: 'Appendix I. Account of part taken by 64th. Infantry Brigade in the Operations of April 25th to 28th 1918', 64 Bde HQ War Diary.
34   The Commonwealth War Graves Commission records 66 fatalities for the 1/EYorks in this engagement.

Furthermore:

> There would seem to be no doubt that the battalion put up a very fine show. The Germans attacked about 6.a.m. They were in great force but only reached ONRAET WOOD a little after 8.a.m. and GRAND BOIS at 9.a.m. The distance from WYTSCHAETE to GRAND BOIS can be walked in about 15 minutes, so the East Yorks and [1/]5th. West Yorks on their right stopped the German advance for several hours.[35]

The Official History account is similarly brief:

> [...] in the mist, the Germans, using flame throwers and trench mortars, had broken through the front of the 1/East Yorkshire and 1/6th West Yorkshire at two places and by working outwards were getting in the rear of these units. The two battalions fell back fighting a rearguard action and making prolonged stands in the various woods: a particularly effective resistance was offered by the 1/East Yorkshire in Onraet Wood.[36]

The battalion war diary entry for 25 April was clearly written some days after the event and can only tell the story from the point of view of Battalion HQ. Nevertheless, it fills in many vital details and should be quoted in full:

> About 2:30 a.m. the enemy opened a heavy bombardment with gas shells which continued for about 1 1/2 hours. Intermittent shelling continued until about 5 a.m. and then a very heavy barrage was put down on all the valleys and possible assembly positions in rear of the front line defences. The enemy then attacked under a smoke barrage and was greatly assisted by the fog. After 2.30 a.m. all communication with BHQ from coys ceased, telephone lines broke down and repeated attempts to get runners thro' failed, although touch was maintained with the front line coys of the left & right battalions for two hours after. No news whatsoever came from the front coys but about 7 a.m. small parties of Germans wandered over the BLACK COT RIDGE and into the E. Side of GRAND BOIS. BHQ was then organised into two parties, each about 12 strong, and a stand was made around BHQ for nearly two hours and the enemy sniped as he appeared over the ridge. By 8.30 a.m. the enemy had established machine gun posts on the ridge and was advancing in strength (in snake formation) down the ravine from PETIT BOIS & BOIS de WYTSCHAETE. The party around BHQ was by this time obliged to withdraw and during the withdrawal under heavy machine gun fire the C.O. – Major J.H. COLES was killed.[37] Only three officers and 30 OR succeeded in getting through the withdrawal. (No definite news reached the battalion headquarters but from information gathered from one or two men who succeeded in getting away from the front line coys, the enemy succeeded in enveloping the front line

---

35 Ibid.
36 Edmonds, *Military Operations France and Belgium 1918*, Vol. II, p.419.
37 Lieutenant-Colonel (?) Coles is commemorated on the Tyne Cot Memorial. The Commonwealth War Graves Commission record his date of death as 24 April. The 64 Bde account, written by Captain Spicer, gives his date of death as 29 April. The author is of the opinion that the battalion War Diary account, giving his date of death as 25 April, is correct.

coys under the cover of his smoke barrage). 2/Lt B.W. HOWARD, A/Adjt. 2/Lt A.D. ROBINSON, O.C. D Coy and the M.O. Capt R.T. RAINE got safely thro' the barrage. The two former reported @ nucleus camp DEVONSHIRE CAMP, OUDERDOOM during the afternoon.[38]

The remnants of 1/EYorks, back in camp at Ouderdoom, played no further part in the action.

The actions of neighbouring units help to fill out the overall picture. As the Germans reached the British wire, concentrated machine gun fire nullified their attempts at a swift breakthrough. By 07.00 hrs, however, with the French in full retreat to their right rear, the 12/Royal Scots, on the right flank of the British sector, were already outflanked. Even the King's Own Scottish Borderers behind them were in danger of encirclement. These two battalions therefore fought their way back to the Vierstraat Line, only to find it partly in German hands, forcing them to continue their withdrawal to the Cheapside positions. The cost had been appalling: the Royal Scots arrived with only three officers and forty men. (These numbers doubled as stragglers came in during the night, but the losses remain very heavy.)

Further up the line, the 1/5th West Yorks managed to hold back the grey onslaught for two and a half hours, but to their left, the 1/6th West Yorks and 1/EYorks had been broken. Both West Yorks battalions fell back, fighting rearguard actions as they went. Again, losses were heavy: the 1/6th West Yorks were reduced to forty-six officers and men by the time they reached the Cheapside Line. Their sister battalion fell back to the Vierstraat Line, reaching it at around 11.00 hrs, where they joined the 1/7th West Yorks (146 Bde reserve) and the 9/Scottish Rifles. Here they attempted to form a defensive flank. Soon after midday, the village of Vierstraat fell into German hands, but there the advance stalled briefly. Just to the west, on Hill 44, McCulloch's 9/KOYLI awaited developments.

In the early hours of 25 April, as the German artillery barrage commenced, 9/KOYLI were about a mile NE of Beaver Camp (within square N.9.c. – see Map 36). At 02.45 they received orders to be ready to move at short notice and to send an Officer patrol in the direction of Grand Bois in order to ascertain what was going on. Lieutenant-Colonel McCulloch led the patrol himself and three hours later arrived at Brigade HQ to report that he had got as far as Grand Bois and that no infantry attack had developed. The heavy shelling of the front line positions suggested, however, that such an attack was probably imminent. By the time McCulloch returned to camp, his battalion had been sitting around in gas masks for the best part of two hours. Fortunately, by around 06.15, the breeze had dispersed any lingering gas and the CO ordered that breakfasts be served. Fifteen minutes later, more gas shells arrived and the men were forced to move to higher ground, to Hill 44, in the Cheapside system, where trenches had been dug. Breakfast was "carried up along with the troops".[39]

---

38   TNA PRO WO 95/2161: 1/EYorks War Diary. Captain Raine MO arrived back at Devonshire Camp the following day. The diarist then lists as missing the following officers: Captains Robinson, Ball and Sleath. Lieutenant Bolton and Second Lieutenants Coverdale, Wisbey, Witley, Tatlow, Stephens, Mayhew, Wallis, Yates, Farmer, Hardy and Toogood. Of those listed, only Second-Lieutenant Richard Yates, age 30, is recorded as killed in action. He is commemorated on the Tyne Cot Memorial and his date of death is recorded erroneously as 24 April 1918.

39   TNA PRO WO 95/2160: Brigadier-General McCulloch's Diary, "Account of events on 25th April 1918", 64 Bde HQ War Diary.

From this higher ground, French troops could be seen retreating on the battalion's right from Kemmel in the direction of Millekruisse "in a more or less demoralised conditions (sic)".[40] Officers who spoke to them could get no coherent picture of the situation: many of those approached simply replied with the single word: "gaz". Mount Kemmel, it was also noted, was "hidden in a cloud of smoke and [...] a fleet of about 30 German Aeroplanes were reconnoitring it".[41] With the Germans reportedly only 1,000 yards from the Cheapside Line, Brigadier-General Headlam (64 Bde) sent orders to the 9/KOYLI at 08.30 to the effect that they were to hold Hill 44 and stop any German advance. He added reassuringly that a detachment from the Tank Corps – no tanks but ten Lewis Gun teams – was on its way forward to protect the flanks and that he hoped to send some of the 15/DLI forward in support. Accordingly, orders were sent to 15/DLI at 09.50 to report immediately to Brigade HQ.[42]

The 9/KOYLI had been under intermittent shelling on Hill 44, a number of 5.9s falling amongst their positions, but a breathing space finally allowed breakfast to be served. Before long, however, at around midday, the Germans could be seen advancing once more from the main Vierstraat – Kemmel road. "The troops were put in a position of readiness with Lewis Guns ready to shoot at once and before long we were closely engaged with the Germans".[43] Accurate small arms fire brought the German advance to a halt and they were forced back "in a certain amount of disorder".[44]

"This unexpected resistance took the Germans by surprise: they were thrown into considerable disorder and suffered many casualties".[45] Thus ran the *Official History's* account. The Battalion War Diary makes the same point in rather more effusive terms: "[The battalion] got into position and dealt out death with such success that the German attack came to a standstill and nothing could be seen except for a few furtive skirmishers and some more stout-hearted machine gunners who kept up a desultory fire on our front".[46]

The situation was helped by the fact that "we had one field gun with us and a couple of sporting artillery officers. They swung the gun round and fired direct at some Bosches advancing 1,200 yards away in our right rear: at the same time we opened up on him and he fled".[47]

This attempt by the Germans to outflank the KOYLI position, via Laiterie, Siege Farm and RE Farm (see Map 36, squares N.15 & 16) got no further than the line of the Kemmelbeek. Concentrated fire from Hill 44 drove them back into the woods near RE Farm. The Germans then adopted a new tactic: they would attempt to shell the KOYLIs off the hill. It was a severe bombardment, but it fell largely behind the firing line as the German artillery could not risk

40 Ibid.
41 TNA PRO WO 95/2160: 'Appendix I. Account of part taken by 64th. Infantry Brigade in the Operations of April 25th to 28th 1918', 64 Bde, HQ War Diary.
42 According to the 15/DLI War Diary, the battalion moved forward "immediately" to support the KOYLIs. The 64 Bde account, however, records that the order to report to HQ was sent to the 15/DLI again at 11.30 and again at 12.55. They finally reported at 13.50 and by 14.30 three companies, some 240 men and four machine guns, were on their way forward.
43 TNA PRO WO 95/2160: Brigadier-General McCulloch's Diary, "Account of events on 25th April 1918', 64 Bde HQ War Diary.
44 Ibid.
45 Edmonds, *Military Operations France and Belgium 1918*, Vol. II, p.422.
46 TNA PRO WO 95/2162: 9/KOYLI War Diary.
47 IWM Brigadier G.F. Ellenberger Papers, Doc Ref. 4227, 2 May 1918.

250   To Do the Work of Men

hitting their own forward troops. By now, the Lewis Gun teams from 13th Tank Battalion had turned up and a company of Black Watch was in position protecting the right flank. Once the 15/DLI contingent arrived, the firepower arraigned on Hill 44 proved more than adequate, "checking any attempts of the enemy to advance against or past them".[48]

Later in the evening, units of 49th Division came up to occupy positions to the north and south of Hill 44, thus forming a continuous line, linking with the French on the right. By 22.00 hrs, it was clear that the Germans had decided to call it a day: they were seen digging in just to the west of Kemmel village and in front of the KOYLI positions. The action that day had cost 9/KOYLI twenty-four fatalities. At some point, McCulloch had been wounded in the face by a sniper, but he was able to stay at duty. The Durham's had lost eight men killed, with one officer, Captain M.R. Pease, wounded.

The overall position of the British line at nightfall was as follows: from the junction with the French just south of La Clytte, it ran east and then south-east to join the Cheapside Line at Hill 44. It followed the Cheapside Line for two miles as far as Ridge Wood, where it cut across eastwards and then veered northwards to join the Vierstraat Line just to the east of Voormezeele. From there, it ran just to the north of St Eloi before reaching the original outpost line on the Ypres-Comines Canal. [This is shown by the yellow dotted line on Map 36]. The Germans had created a large bulge in the allied lines but had not achieved the hoped for breakthrough.

At 23.30, the 9/KOYLI and 15/DLI received fresh orders. They were to participate in an attack the following morning in conjunction with the 39th French and 25th British Divisions. These two divisions would attack in a southerly direction and recapture Kemmel. The 9/KOYLI would advance to the south-east and retake a section of the Vierstraat Line. The 15/DLI would then take over the line vacated by the KOYLIs. The finer details of the attack were delivered in person to 9/KOYLI HQ at one o'clock in the morning of 26 April by the Brigade Major, Captain Spicer. Zero hour would be 04.25. A creeping barrage would advance in front of them at a rate of 100 yards every four minutes, halting on a line 250 yards beyond the Vierstraat – La Polka trench line. The 147 and 148 Bdes, left and right of 9/KOYLI respectively, were to conform with their advance. This hastily conceived plan would soon fall apart. McCulloch described it simply as "a good example of a very badly organised counter-attack".[49]

The 9/KOYLI lined up for the attack with A, C and B companies in the front line, left to right, with D Coy behind them in close support. They were to go forward in two waves of two lines each. Each company had two platoons in the front line and the remaining two forty yards in the rear. D Coy was 150 yards behind the first wave.

The promised artillery barrage failed to materialise: it was "of the most feeble description".[50] A few eighteen pounders firing at a rate of one round per minute was all that was forthcoming, but nevertheless the men advanced at the appointed time. As soon as the assault got under way, it became clear that the 9/KOYLI were on their own.

The main attack on the Kemmel position by the French 39th and British 25th Divisions had gone in at 03.00 after a miserable night of heavy rain. As the rain eased in the small hours, a fog descended over the battlefield. Floundering across the muddy ground, and coping with poor

48   Edmonds, *Military Operations France and Belgium 1918*, Vol. II, p. 423.
49   TNA PRO WO 95/2160: Brigadier-General McCulloch's Diary, 'Account of events on 25th April 1918', 64 Bde HQ War Diary.
50   Ibid.

visibility and a flooded Kemmelbeek, the 39th Div troops – who had arrived late at the jumping off positions – made only slow progress in the face of machine gun fire from the Alpine Corps units securely dug in atop Mount Kemmel and were forced to halt short of their objectives. The 25th Division did make it as far as the village of Kemmel, but – and this was to prove critical – lost touch with 147 Bde on their left. By 08.00 the 25th realised that their position – they were already suffering from machine gun fire from their right rear where the French should have been – would soon become untenable, especially as the mist was starting to dissipate, so at 09.00 both brigades withdrew to the north bank of the Kemmelbeek and dug in the best they could. The right battalion of 147 Bde, the 1/4th Duke of Wellington's, with orders only to conform to the movement of the units on their right, advanced no further than the Cheapside Line and then formed a defensive flank.

As the KOYLIs moved out across No Man's Land, Second-Lieutenant Marsden, commanding B Coy on the right front of the attack, soon became aware that the battalion on their right had not left their trenches. Marsden reorganised his company and formed a defensive flank facing south before going across and remonstrating with them, but they informed him that they had received no orders for the attack and refused to budge. A similar situation had occurred on the left also – the West Yorks were later to complain that their attack had been stalled almost as it had begun by heavy machine gun fire. A Coy on the left of the KOYLI attack was therefore also forced to throw back a defensive flank. Both of these companies were suffering heavily from machine gun fire once the Germans realised that only one battalion was on the move, A Coy particularly being in serious trouble. Second-Lieutenant Dore MC, commanding D Coy, saw this from his rearward position and steered his men across and moved through A Coy in an attempt to bolster this exposed left flank.

In the centre, C Coy under Captain Ellenberger MC had managed to work forward some 1,200 yards. They had suffered casualties from German small arms fire, but luckily German SOS flares had failed to bring down very much on them in the way of shelling. A report was received back at 64 Bde HQ around 06.30 from Ellenberger, who, aware of his exposed position, had decided to withdraw his men to a line approximately 400 yards ahead of the jumping off point. This he managed to do without incurring any casualties under the cover of the heavy morning mist that still lingered. Somehow, by this stage, the battalion had managed to capture seventy prisoners. Between 04.30 and 05.15, only twenty-three had passed through Battalion HQ. The war diary asserts that "apparently the escorts had taken summary action with the remainder".[51]

McCulloch was quickly aware that the attack had faltered and that any attempt to reinvigorate it would be pointless. At 07.00 he ordered that all companies should conform to C Coy's withdrawal. "There being plenty of trenches hereabouts, the taking up of the line was not very difficult".[52] By 10.45, however, all companies were reported to 64 Bde HQ as being back in their original jumping off line, this move having taken place on the initiative of the company commanders on the spot before McCulloch's message had been received. The counter-attack had failed.

---

51   TNA PRO WO 95/2162: 9/KOYLI War Diary.
52   Ibid.

The troops concerned felt it had failed on account of bad staff arrangements, poor artillery support, and the lack of drive exhibited by the French infantry. There had been a useless waste of life; one battalion commander even sent in a very strongly worded protest against what he called 'this discreditable affair'.[53]

The fighting had more or less subsided. Small gains had been made by the Germans on their right wing, gaining ground along the Ypres-Comines canal and thereby forcing 110 Bde units back once and for all from their 'outpost' positions. This attack cost the 6/Leics six fatalities. The two 62 Bde battalions still in line between Ridge Wood and Scottish Wood came under prolonged and heavy artillery fire during the day, but no German attack materialised. Nevertheless, casualties were quite heavy, 83 for the 12/13 NFus and 74 reported by 1/Lincs. The village of St Eloi also fell.

202351 Private Arthur Burkhill, 9/KOYLI, kia 26 April 1918, age 37. (*Yorkshire Rugby Union Roll of Honour*)

This pause in the conflict allowed two members of 9/KOYLI to put their thoughts on the recent attack down on paper. In a letter home Captain Ellenberger wrote:

> Rather sudden and a bit of a rush, but we did it and got on pretty well, only the people on either flank who were supposed to come with us never left their trenches, so we killed some Bosches, took some prisoners, and had to come back again. A complete muddle on the part of the Staff from beginning to end. All they can do is send us complimentary chits – they don't come up and see the situation themselves: they rest content to call the situation 'obscure'; it's safer for them that way. Well there's not much more about it that I can put in here. Except, as I told you, that I've been put in for a bar to my MC – rather amusing, but very silly: just a reward for not being killed!!.[54]

Lieutenant-Colonel McCulloch wrote a letter of complaint to 64 Bde:

> […] I wish to complain about the artillery barrage, which was put down, which was of the most futile description, in fact, unless one had been told, one would not have known it was intended for a barrage at all. I cannot see how more than four guns could have been

---

53 .Edmonds, *Military Operations France and Belgium 1918, Vol. II*, p.434.
54 IWM Brigadier G.F. Ellenberger Papers, Doc Ref. 4227, 2 May 1918.

235421 Private Henry Lincoln Smith, 6/Leics, kia 21 April 1918, age 28. Hooge Crater Cemetery VI.G.5. (Author)

254   To Do the Work of Men

firing over my front, and it had absolutely no effect on the German machine gunners, who remained at their posts and worked their guns with their accustomed skill.[55]

On 27 April, the 64 Bde diarist estimated that the 9/KOYLI and 15/DLI had a strength of approximately 160 rifles each. The entire brigade could barely muster 400.[56] McCulloch's face wound was now becoming painful and he was also suffering from the effects of gas: accordingly he relinquished command of 9/KOYLI, temporarily, to Major Harry Greenwood MC. Relief finally came during the night of 27 / 28 April in the form of 148 Bde, completed by 04.15. By the end of the morning the brigade was in camp near Ouderdoom. The 62 Bde units were by this time also out of the line in bivouacs near Lederzeele, but the three Leicester battalions manned their defences for a day or so longer before being relieved by 58 Bde (19 Div) on the 30th.

Adjutants began counting the cost of 'Georgette' and were able to estimate casualties for the month of April. With the usual caveats regarding their accuracy, they were recorded as follows:

110 Bde	Officers	O.R.	
6/Leics	9	198	
7/Leics	1	75	
8/Leics	2	95	
110 TMB	–	2	
110 Bde HQ	–	4	
Total:	**12**	**374**	
62 Bde			
12/13 NFus	13		
1/Lincs	9		
2/Lincs	7		
Other Ranks total:	**1,259**	**Overall total:**	**1,288**
64 Bde			
1/EYorks	21	677	
9/KOYLI	17	425	
15/DLI	9	290	
64 TMB	–	11	
Total:	**47**	**1,403**	

These figures amount to a divisional total of 3,124.

Chris Baker, author of *The Battle for Flanders. German Defeat on the Lys 1918,* sums up the battle in his final chapter:

> There is no doubt that the Allies inflicted a serious defeat on the German army in Flanders in April 1918. [...]

55   TNA PRO WO 95/2162: 9/KOYLI War Diary. The 64 Bde response has not been preserved.
56   TNA PRO WO 95/2160: 64 Bde HQ War Diary.

The defeat was of a strategic nature; time, men and resources that the Germans could ill afford to lose had been squandered. No strategic goal had been achieved. The territorial gain had served only to extend the line being held and to place the German army in a tactically difficult salient. It is true that the British had suffered severe losses and several divisions were completely or temporarily disabled, but Allied resources had not yet been so badly injured that their defensive ability had been crippled. Of itself, failure on the Lys and in the Flemish hills was not sufficiently damaging to cause Germany to give up, but in combination with ultimate defeats on the Somme, Marne and Metz it contributed significantly to a collapse of morale and fighting capability. [...]

Operationally and strategically, the German high command made a significant contribution to its own defeat. The force assembled was not as strong as that for 'Michael' and was not given time to make sufficient preparations. Divisions were kept in line, hammering away for too long, day after day, without respite. The attack frontage became narrower from 12 April onwards, and operations were broken off increasingly quickly when there were many instances where one more determined push might have brought results. Most crucially, the initial north-west thrust towards Hazebrouck was abandoned and attention moved to Ypres, just at the time when the brilliant strategic prize of Hazebrouck was within reach. This decision cost Germany the battle. [...]

Foch's influence on the battle was a key factor in the defeat of the enemy. His firm and oft-repeated doctrines brought a nervelessness, a steel, to high command, where all too often Haig and Wilson were looking at withdrawal and a demand for more and more men. In such a situation someone had to draw a line – and Foch did so.

But neither German shortcomings nor Foch represent the central reason why the Battles of the Lys were won. Countless were the occasions where positions were held, or delay and loss inflicted on the enemy, simply through personal bravery and a bloody-minded will not to be beaten. [...] The battle was won by the many thousands of junior leaders, NCOs and men, a proportion of whom were just 18 years old and in action for the first time, coping with improvised circumstances and doing their bit".[57]

If there was one thing that the men of 21st Division were beginning to learn how to do rather well in the late spring of 1918, it was how to conduct a successful fighting withdrawal. Such undertakings, successful or otherwise, tend to be costly, however, and by the end of April the division was badly in need – for the second time that year – of replacement drafts, and of sufficient time in which to train them and integrate them into their new units. A scheme was devised to make this possible. For a short time, it appeared that the conflict was on hold, and Foch saw the opportunity to create a sizeable General Reserve force, this to be positioned behind the Franco-British front in the north, where both he and Haig feared a renewal of the German offensive. In order to be able to add fresh French divisions to this reserve, Foch and Haig had agreed to a system of *roulement*: the French formations would be withdrawn from a quiet sector of the line and their place taken by tired British divisions. Four of the five divisions thus chosen were placed under the command of the staff of IX Corps (Lieutenant-General Sir A.H. Gordon) and sent to the French Sixth Army sector on the Aisne River, west of Reims. The four were the 8th, 21st, 25th and 50th Divisions. None was yet back up to full strength. Some

---

57   Baker, *The Battle for Flanders*, pp.185-188.

256　To Do the Work of Men

anxiety was expressed by the British General Staff as to the suitability of the sector chosen for this 'rest and recuperation', but they were assured by the French that the region was "suitable and quiet".[58] The British formations arrived there over a period of fifteen days, between 27 April and 11 May.[59] Sixteen days after they were all in place, the Germans launched their third, massive offensive, codenamed 'Blücher-Yorck', across the Chemin des Dames Ridge. The left wing of this attack came up against the four newly-arrived British divisions.

58　J.E. Edmonds, *Military Operations France and Belgium 1918,* Vol. III (London: HMSO, 1939) p.31.
59　The 19th Division was also dispatched to this sector, arriving on 18 and 19 May. It was placed in reserve, some seven miles south-east of Châlons.

7

Chemin des Dames

The Chemin des Dames assault (*Operation Blücher*), the third major German offensive of spring of 1918, had been under preparation for some time, initial orders for an attack in this sector having been issued as early as 17 April. First thoughts had been of a renewed assault in Flanders, even while the *Georgette* offensive was still underway there, but Ludendorff's gaze had, for the time being, drifted to the south. A week later, Major-General von Unruh, Chief of Staff of *4th Reserve Corps*, was instructed to undertake a detailed reconnaissance of the Allied positions and address the feasibility of the proposed offensive. His report was favourable, and preparations went ahead. The Chemin des Dames attack would "compel the French to bring their reserves to it from Flanders",[1] thus paving the way for the original proposal of a further attack at Ypres to follow. This latter offensive was postponed until July in order to allow for "maximum preparedness".[2]

The original objective of the attack was the line of the River Aisne. This would require the capture of just the Chemin des Dames ridge. Ambition blossomed, however, and by the time it was launched, the objective line had been extended "some kilometres beyond the [River] Vesle".[3]

On 26 May, the eve of the battle, thirty German divisions and 1,150 artillery batteries were in place. Fifteen of these divisions were completely fresh, and none of the others had taken part in the Lys Offensive: "all had enjoyed at least seven weeks rest"[4] since their exertions in March. Facing these along the attack frontage were, left to right, the French 61st, 21st and 22nd Divisions, covering nearly twenty miles between Leuilly and Craonelle. Then came the British 50th, 8th and 21st Divisions (with 25th Division in reserve), stretching eastwards and then south-eastwards for a further fourteen miles, where the right flank of 64 Bde abutted the French 45th Division near Loivre (See Map 37).

The principles of defence had been lain down by Foch on 19 April, these reflecting old-established practices championed by Pétain in his directive dated December 1917. Unlike in certain sectors further north where ever yard of ground had to be vigorously contested, here, "it was

---

1   Edmonds, *Military Operations France and Flanders 1918*, Vol. III., p.27.
2   Stevenson, *With Our Backs to the Wall*, p. 79. This offensive in Flanders, codenamed "Hagen", would once more target the Flanders Hills and Hazebrouck. It never took place: pre-empted by the French attack on the Marne, it was eventually shelved.
3   Edmonds, *Military Operations France and Belgium 1918*, Vol. III, p. 28.
4   Ibid, p.29.

257

258   To Do the Work of Men

possible, without serious inconvenience, to abandon a certain amount of ground in the face of a violent enemy onslaught".[5] In short, defence in depth. The Front Zone, or 'First Position' as it was known to the French, should be lightly held and could only be expected to delay and disrupt any serious attack. The enemy should be properly engaged and stopped only as they reach the Battle Zone, or 'Second Position'. General Duchêne,[6] commanding the French Sixth Army, did not embrace this doctrine, however. He was of the opinion that in a sector so close to Paris, and on a ridge that had been won at such devastating cost the previous year, no ground should be voluntarily surrendered to the enemy. Accordingly, he placed the majority of his troops – including those in the British IX Corps under his command – in the First Position trenches. Foch, faced with this reality, had a choice: remove Duchêne from command, or give way to his subordinate. He chose the latter course.

The French Sixth Army thus lined up with twenty-six battalions in the First Position, five in the Second, and a further seven behind them. The position on the British front was similar, and when Lieutenant-General Gordon, along with his three divisional commanders, went personally to protest, suggesting that he was courting disaster, they were met by Duchêne's curt reply: 'J'ai dit', (I have spoken). On 27 May, the disaster duly arrived.

When the men of 21st Division arrived in the Champagne region, it must have appeared to them a stark contrast to the areas of war-ravaged France and Belgium to which they had become accustomed: Sidney Rogerson, author of *The Last of the Ebb*, is quoted by John Terraine:

> To battered, battle-weary troops, whose only knowledge of France was based upon their experience of the Northern front, the Champagne country in the full glory of spring was a revelation. Gone the depressing monotony of Flanders, drab and weeping, with its muds, its mists, its pollards and its pavé; gone the battle-wrecked landscapes of Picardy and the Somme, with their shattered villages and blasted woods. Here all was peace. The countryside basked in the blazing sunshine. Trim villages nestled in quiet hollows beside lazy streams, and tired eyes were refreshed by the sight of rolling hills, clad with great woods golden with laburnum blossom; by the soft greenery of lush meadowland, shrubby vineyards and fields of growing corn.[7]

Harold Yeo, 64 Bde Staff, writing home soon after his arrival in that sector, puts it more succinctly, yet his phonetic spelling conveys all that he and the men of 21st Division must have felt about their new surroundings: "We have at last [...] settled down in a bee-autiful spot". Later, in the same letter, he goes on to describe the almost idyllic scene from the point of view of Staff HQ, idyllic in the sense that neither side seemed at that point in time all that keen on inflicting any damage on their adversaries:

5   Ibid, p.39.
6   General Denis Auguste Duchêne (1862-1950). GOC Sixth Army since December 1917, he was dismissed on 9 June 1918.
7   John Terraine, *To Win A War. 1918, the Year of Victory.* (London: Papermac, 1986) p. 70.; Sidney Rogerson, *The Last of the Ebb* (London: Arthur Barker 1937)). Rogerson served in the 2/West Yorkshires, 8th Division.

... a few miles away we can see where the Hun Brigade headquarters sits on a similar hill. Every morning at eleven o'clock the Hun shoots five shells at our hill and we shoot five at his – but of course care is taken to shoot where nobody lives, and at a nice convenient time too when everyone is usually out.[8]

The first few days in the sector were taken up with training, including some time on the rifle range, though this was limited to the earlier hours of the morning owing to the very hot weather.[9] By the middle of the month, the British units began taking over sections of the line from their French counterparts. The 62 Bde were on the left of the divisional front, just south the town of Berry au Bac. The brigade diary sums up their first fortnight in the trenches as follows: "... the enemy displayed very little activity in any arm".[10] The diaries of the individual battalions in the brigade paint a similar picture, although the 1/Lincs dispersed an enemy raiding party of between 20 and 30 men with Lewis Gun fire on the night of 19 / 20 May and the German artillery did launch a number of shells onto the Moulin de Cormicy (See Map 37).[11]

110 Bde was in the centre of the divisional front, geography dictating that most of its units were in positions to the east of the canal. This was to prove extremely problematic. With their sector equally dormant, it was decided to poke the hornets' nest by organising a raid on the German front line positions. The honour fell to two Officers and seventy Other Ranks of 7/Leics: the raid was to take place at 01.00 hrs on 26 May. The battalion war diary relates the episode:

> "Raiding party consisting of 2Lt. Bone & 2Lt Hughes & 70 ORs from the Bn & 12 Sappers under Lt Warmesby left TENAILLE DE GUISE at about 10 p.m. to get into position. The RE were responsible for placing Bangalore Torpedoes in position prior to Zero Hour.
> 1 a.m. – Zero hour for raid. 2 Torpedoes successfully blown & Artillery opened on MT. SPIN & MT SAPIGNOL (sic). Raiding party advanced through enemy's wire with no difficulty but found enemy's front line trench and ground behind thick with wire which was impossible to cut a way through. The left party under 2Lt. HUGHES got into the trench but were soon held up by wire. None of the enemy were met with. The raiding party were all back in our trenches by 2 a.m. Casualties nil. Retaliation by enemy very slight".[12]

The raid had been carried out at no cost to the Leicesters, but it is hard to imagine what intelligence, if any, had been gleaned.

64 Bde occupied the right sector of the divisional front. Their most advanced positions were also to the north-east of the canal, but the main defensive line consisted of a series of bastions to the south-west of the waterway. It was the job of the advanced parties, in the event of a large-scale attack, to withdraw across the canal, blowing up the bridges as they went.

In the days prior to the German attack, various company and battalion reliefs had taken place, but on the evening of 26 May, the division was deployed thus (See Map 38): On the

8   IWM Private Papers of Harold Yeo, Doc.Ref. 3132, 18 May 1918.
9   TNA PRO WO 95 /2161: 1/EYorks War Diary.
10   TNA PRO WO 95/2153: 62 Bde HQ War Diary.
11   TNA PRO WO 95/2154: 1/Lincs War Diary.
12   TNA PRO WO 95/2164: 7/Leics War Diary.

left, 62 Bde (Brigadier-General G.H. Gater), with 12/13 NFus and 2/Lincs in the front line, left and right respectively. 1/Lincs were in reserve near Châlons le Vergeur. In the centre, 110 Bde (Brigadier-General H.W. Cumming) had 7/Leics on the left front, with 8/Leics on their right, 6/Leics being placed in support between the villages of Cauroy and Cormicy. The 64 Bde (Brigadier-General H.R. Headlam) on the right divisional flank had 9/KOYLI in their left sector and 1/EYorks on the right. 15/DLI were initially in and around Châlons le Vergeur, but the gas bombardment forced them to move forward almost immediately to Cauroy. Crucially, as previously mentioned, too many units were to the east of the canal: two companies of 12/13 NFus, three of 2/Lincs, two companies each of 7 & 8/Leics, and one company each of 9/ KOYLI and 1/EYorks.[13] It was becoming perfectly clear to everyone that a German assault was imminent. Two sources indicated the 27 May, one of them also predicting the exact hour of the start of the artillery bombardment.

At 21.30 on 26 May, Second-Lieutenant F.A. Marsden, commanding C Coy on the right of the 9/KOYLI sector, sent a message to Battalion HQ saying that he had been warned by the French Zouaves Regiment on the right that there were signs of an impending attack apparent in the German lines:

> This had been suspected for the past two or three days, for new dumps had appeared, wire had been cleared and the movements of troops on the roads in the rear of the German trenches had been detected. Listening sets had confirmed the existence of unusual telephone activity, and that Germans were speaking 'in clear' of barrages, trenches, and troops.[14]

Apparent confirmation of the date, plus an indication that Zero Hour would be one o'clock in the morning, was given by a German prisoner captured by the French on the 26th. The information was taken seriously, and by 22.00 hrs all the units of the division had been made aware of the situation.

It is unnecessary to include here a detailed narrative of the events across the whole Allied front, but a brief account will help place the fate of 21st Division in context. At 01.00 hrs, as predicted by the German prisoner, a tremendous barrage from over 4,000 guns opened on the Allied positions. "Every battery position, village, farm, and railway station, every bridge and road junction was systematically shelled",[15] as far back as the River Vesle, that is to a depth of around twelve miles, with high explosive and gas. In the British sector, the bombardment covered the Forward and Battle zones to a depth of over 3,000 yards: battalion and brigade headquarters came under fire and before long, all communication with forward units had been severed:

> The Front Zone had nearly everywhere been rendered untenable; the strongpoints obliterated. Casualties in the infantry had been very heavy, and most of the machine guns and artillery were out of action. [...] So thorough had been the preliminary destruction that all

---

13 Edmonds, *Military Operations France and Belgium 1918,* Vol. III, p. 61.
14 R.C. Bond, *The King's Own Yorkshire Light Infantry in the Great War 1914-1918* (London: Percy Lund, Humphries & Co. Ltd., 1929), p. 958.
15 Edmonds, *Military Operations France and Belgium 1918,* Vol. III.,p. 47.

resistance was crushed and the [German] infantry had only to advance to take possession of the front position.[16]

At 03.40, twenty minutes before it began to get light, the creeping barrage began to edge forwards.[17] This was the signal for the German infantry to leave their jumping off trenches and advance through the mist and smoke towards what was left of the Allied front line. The Allies were outnumbered by seventeen divisions to six (the Germans held six more in reserve, the Allies four). The German forces were not evenly distributed across the whole attack frontage, however: the French 21st and 22nd divisions bore the brunt, facing three and five German divisions respectively along the main Chemin des Dames ridge. The French 61st and 21st Divisions on the extreme left were forced out of their forward positions very quickly and by 11.00 hrs the villages of Charonne and Vailly on the northern bank of the Aisne – and some four and a half miles behind the original front line – had fallen.

The 22nd Division fared little better: they had been forced off the ridge by 05.30; the Germans were pushing on near the Aisne by 09.00, and the bridge over the river at Oeuilly was in enemy hands an hour later. Two more bridges were lost intact by midday, and the German storm troopers were soon swarming across the river between Oeuilly and Maizy (See Map 37).

Moving eastwards, the next sector was the responsibility of the British 50th Division. Their left sector, including the Californie Plateau to the north of Craonne, was manned by troops of 150 Bde. Only small, isolated groups managed to escape the initial onslaught: the plateau was completely overrun by 06.00. "By 8.00 a.m., therefore, the 150th Brigade, except the usual detachments left in billets for administrative duties, had ceased to exist".[18]

The 151 Bde was next on the right, with 6 & 8/DLI and a pioneer company of 7/DLI in the front line. 150 Bde's withdrawal allowed the Germans to attack the Durhams from the front and from the left rear: they managed to hold out for three quarters of an hour, but each position was successively outflanked and surrounded, resulting in the almost complete destruction of these DLI units. The remnants of the brigade managed to hold out at Cuiry, on the north bank of the Aisne, until around 11.00 hrs, but they were once more outflanked and overrun from the west and south.

Brigadier-General Riddell's 149 Bde had only one battalion in the front line: the 4/NFus. Four German tanks (probably captured British ones) helped their infantry break through the line and the survivors of the 4th, along with their sister battalion, the 6/NFus, clung on as best they could near the village of Ville au Bois. The tanks managed to turn the flank, however, and the fate of the by now surrounded defenders was sealed.

Further along the line, the nine under-strength and battle-weary battalions of 8th Division faced twenty-one fresh, full-strength German battalions. Of the 23 Bde, on the left, only three companies of 2/West Yorks were in the front lines: their resistance was predictably brief. The enemy advance into the Battle Zone was rapid, and the three companies of 2/Middlesex holding a line of redoubts in front of it were soon overwhelmed. There remained D Coy of 2/Middlesex

16 Ibid, p.49.
17 For a detailed description of the German artillery bombardment, see Edmonds, *Military Operations France and Belgium 1918*, Vol. III, pp. 48-49.
18 Ibid, p.53. The CO of 150 Bde, Brigadier-General Rees, was captured sometime later whilst trying to cross the Aisne.

262   To Do the Work of Men

and the 2/Devonshires in the Bois des Buttes, a wood covering a conical hill just to the south-west of Ville au Bois. They came under fire at around 05.15 but were able to hold out for nearly three hours. By 08.00 hrs, the Devonshires had all but ceased to exist and their CO, Lieutenant-Colonel Anderson-Morshead, decided to try and fight a rearguard action back to the River Aisne. For its gallant stand against overwhelming odds at the Bois des Buttes, the battalion was later awarded the Croix de Guerre.

The 24 Bde troops were quickly forced to withdraw to the Battle Zone, where 2/Northants and 1/Worcs held on until 05.00 hrs, when their flank was turned by a German advance down the Miette valley: it was all over by 06.00 hrs. The 25 Bde sat in what was in effect a mini-salient. They were attacked from both the north and south-east and were forced back. Brigade HQ, to the north of Berry au Bac, was surrounded almost before the Staff were aware of the situation, and they were forced to fight their way back to the village of Gernicourt. Brigadier-General Husey was badly wounded and captured, however. He succumbed to his wounds three days later.[19]

Gernicourt enjoyed an elevated position overlooking the canal and river from the south. It was garrisoned by the 22/DLI and the French II/23rd Territorial Regiment: between them they had twenty-four machine guns. Early in the morning they were reinforced by two companies of 2/East Lancs and a number of engineers from 2nd and 490th Field Companies RE. On their left, in the woods, the 1/Sherwood Foresters were able to watch as all but one bridge over the canal was blown up. Such was the intensity of machine gun fire concentrated on the one remaining bridge that the German advance was held up for several hours. Eventually, the inevitable happened and the village was outflanked on both sides: at 13.00 hrs the survivors, their position now untenable, made their way back to the Green Line. "Less than ten companies had held up twelve enemy battalions for over six hours".[20]

The 21st Division front was spread across nearly five miles of flat ground, through which ran the Aisne-Marne Canal. This waterway was about twenty yards wide, not quite full of water, but unfordable nevertheless, with swampy ground on both sides. It could – and perhaps should – have been turned into a formidable defensive barrier, but with so many units deployed to the east of it, it soon became an acute hindrance to communication and a serious obstacle to any organised withdrawal. Brigadier-General Cumming, 110 Bde, described the position as

> tactically unsound: it was dominated by the enemy positions and it had a very serious obstacle in the rear. The ground East of the Canal could have no sentimental value, being composed of marsh and a medley of shell holes and trenches of no use to anyone. The only reason that could be adduced for retaining it was that it had been won and therefore must be held at all costs. In war such reasons are folly, and worse than folly – they are almost criminal. In this particular case the advantages gained if this ground had been given up

---

19   Brigadier-General Ralph Hamer Husey DSO and Bar, MC, age 36, was wounded and captured as he defended the northern end of the bridge at Gernicourt. He died of his wounds in a German Field Hospital and was buried in the German Cemetery in the village of Le Thour. After the armistice, his body was exhumed and reinterred in Vendresse British Cemetery, grave reference II.G.1. He had served on the Western Front since November 1914 and had previously been wounded four times. The inscription on his gravestone reads Cor Immobyle – "A Steadfast Heart".

20   Edmonds, *Military Operations France and Belgium 1918*, Vol. III., p. 55.

would have been immense. A strong line existed to the West of and commanding the Canal and this would have possessed the obstacle of the Canal and marsh in front of it, well within range – an ideal combination.[21]

The "folly" of such deployments was soon to become apparent. In addition, the position of 21st Division and the speed and depth of the German penetration across the Aisne and Vesle rivers meant that for the next three days, the constant threat was one of being outflanked on the left: in order to counter this threat, it became necessary over and over again not only to withdraw, but to pivot the line in an anti-clockwise direction. On 27 May, the 21st Division faced roughly north-east. By the evening of 29 May, the remaining units were facing almost due west (See Map 38).

The diarist of 12/13 NFus, on the extreme left flank of the divisional frontage, recorded the commencement of the German artillery barrage at one o'clock in the morning on the 27th, remarking on the "many gas shells"[22] that accompanied it. 62 Bde reported to division that the shelling appeared much heavier on their left, to the north of the Aisne, and that their front positions were "practically immune from shelling, the bulk of which was concentrated on back areas including the vicinity of Brigade H.Qrs".[23] The picture all along the attack frontage was a similar one: the Germans were making every effort to disrupt and cause "irremediable confusion"[24] in the rear areas, firing at all targets within reach – battalion, brigade and divisional headquarters, artillery batteries, bridges, roads, telephone exchanges and camps, forcing the allied soldiers to wear gas masks for an uncomfortably long period of time. Between 02.15 and 03.40 the emphasis was on counter-battery work, again using a high proportion of gas shells. Disruption, rather than destruction, was the aim. Communications were severely disrupted: 110 Bde records that "all telephonic communication forward of Brigade Headquarters ceased within a few minutes [of the start of the barrage] and could never be restored".[25] 64 Bde HQ reported simply that by 01.30, "all communications with Battalions was cut".[26] Only on 62 Bde front were the telephone wires still intact. Once battalion headquarters had been overrun, however, the system did fail.

At 03.40, the German guns concentrated their fire on the Allied front lines prior to commencing a creeping barrage. The mist and the heavy gas clouds meant that observation from the rear was impossible, and this, allied with the communication problems, and the fact that few, if any of the men in the front lines made it back to the Battle Zone, meant that although some units held out for a number of hours, the details of their travails remain obscure. Indeed, the 110 Bde HQ diarist bemoans that "owing to the virtual annihilation of the Companies East of the Canal, it is impossible to state the exact time of the enemy attack; the indications are that it was launched between 3 and 4 a.m."

21 Cumming, *A Brigadier in France 1917-1918*, pp. 193-194.
22 TNA PRO WO 95/2155: 12/13 NFus War Diary.
23 TNA PRO WO 95/2153: 62 Bde HQ War Diary.
24 Edmonds, *Military Operations France and Belgium 1918*, Vol.III, p. 48.
25 TNA PRO WO 95/2163: 110 Bde HQ War Diary.
26 TNA PRO WO 95/2133: 64 Bde HQ War Diary.

264   To Do the Work of Men

The other war diaries of the units of 21st Division cannot agree on the time of the attack either,[27] but the *Official History* states that the German infantry assault was launched at 03.40.[28]

On the extreme left of the 21st Division front, the first news of the 12/13 NFus did not arrive at 62 Bde HQ until 07.10: it was apparent that the forward positions had been overrun in the fog and Battalion HQ had also been captured. HQ Company and the reserve companies (C & D Coys) were holding the Boyau de la Marine, but "the enemy were gradually approaching on both flanks".[29] This meant that the enemy had crossed the canal and Route 44 by this time. It was also suspected that the Moulin de Cormicy, to their right, was in German hands (See Map 38).[30]

In the right sector of 62 Bde front, the 2/Lincs had also had a hard time of it. The account in the battalion diary is once again brief but relates that the enemy had broken through on the right where the company in the front trenches "seem to have been almost immediately surrounded". Only two Officers and around thirty Other Ranks had managed to extract themselves from the fight.[31]

The reserve battalion, 1/Lincs, had received orders at 05.12 to move forward from their positions near Châlons le Vergeur and by 06.20 were in the Green Line, with A & B Coys (Captain Samuelson & Lieutenant Carr) north of the Châlons le Vergeur to Cormicy road "covering La Chapelle", C & D Coys (Lieutenant Swaby and Lieutenant Tapsell) to the south of it "covering Cormicy".[32]

Before ten o'clock, the remnants of the 12/13 NFus were beginning a fighting withdrawal from their positions in the Boyau de la Marine down the Boyau de Mittau and were able to join forces with the two companies of 1/Lincs. Captain Samuelson managed to form a defensive flank on the left just in time to prevent the Germans gaining a foothold in the woods. The rest of A & B Coys meanwhile were able to hold up a determined enemy attack to the north of Cormicy, repulsing them "with heavy loss".[33] The situation remained acute, however, and once more it became apparent that the enemy "had broken through on our left and had completely worked round the left flank".[34]

By this time, parties of the 3rd French Territorial Regiment and some units of 75 Bde (25th Div) had been moved up from their reserve positions and were holding a line somewhere near Bouffignereux and orders were soon received from division (at around 12.30) telling 62 Bde to swing back its left flank from La Chapelle to the Bois de Val Spur and form a defensive flank between Cormicy and La Cendrière. The withdrawal of C & D Coys, 1/Lincs, executed

---

27   According to 64 Bde HQ, the attack started at 03.45; 1/EYorks record 03.00, as do 9/KOYLI. 7/Leics record the start-time as 03.15, 2/Lincs 04.00 and 12/13 NFus see the division *on their left* attacked at 03.30.
28   Edmonds, *Military Operations 1918 France and Belgium,* Vol.III. p. 49. It appears that this simply equates to the German artillery plan.
29   TNA PRO WO 95/2153: 62 Bde HQ War Diary.
30   This is contradicted by the 21st Div HQ diary, which "believed" the Moulin de Cormicy was still "in our possession" at 08.25. TNA PRO WO 95/2133: 21 Div HQ War Diary.
31   TNA PRO WO 95/2154: 2/Lincs War Diary.
32   TNA PRO WO 95/2154: 1/Lincs War Diary.
33   Ibid.
34   Ibid.

reluctantly "after smashing three successive attacks"[35] meant that by 13.00 hrs, the Germans had occupied Cormicy.

The forward units of 110 Bde, the 7 & 8/Leics, in the centre of the divisional front, were seemingly able to hold off the frontal German attacks for some short while, but once the Germans had taken La Neuville and had crossed the canal to their north, the enemy was able to move along the captured third line[36] trench to the *west* of the waterway and effectively cut off the four companies still in position to the east of it. All they could do was establish trench blocks as best they could and "f[i]ght their positions to the end".[37] A report to this effect arrived, courtesy of a runner, at 8/Leics Battalion HQ at around 05.30 and half an hour later small parties of German soldiers were seen advancing to the west of the canal. A & B Coys were effectively cut off and no further reports from them were received.

The four remaining companies of the two Leicestershire battalions were now all that stood between the Germans and the main line of resistance. One company of 6/Leics

Private J.H. Hutton, 12/13NFus. Wounded 27 May 1918, died Bar-le-Duc Hospital 6 June 1918. Buried in Bar-le-Duc French National Cemetery, grave reference 2790. (*Yorkshire Rugby Union Roll of Honour*)

was sent forward at 08.00 to reinforce the Esternay trench on the right of the brigade front, and two platoons from the nucleus party of 8/Leics had also been sent up and joined two from 7/Leics, forming a 'Nucleus Coy' under Major H.C. Tyler MC, 7/Leics. At 09.50, a message timed at 08.40 from 7/Leics arrived at 110 Bde HQ. It stated that the main line of resistance to the west of the canal was still holding out against frontal attack, but that the enemy was in the Boyau de Ecluse du Sud and that the Riga defence works, though surrounded, "was still fighting".[38] By 10.00 hrs, it was finally confirmed that the Moulin de Cormicy had been lost.

Also at this time, the 110 Bde HQ diarist gives us a situation report: the 8/Leics were in touch with 64 Bde in the Boyau de la Somme and held the line Somme – Vauban – Colbert. The 7/Leics, with one company of 6/Leics in Esternay trench, continued the line northwards

---

35   Ibid.
36   The first two 'defence' lines ran to the east of the canal. The third and fourth lines were just to the west of it, along the western edge of Route 44. The fifth line was about 700 yards west of the canal and the sixth just east of the Cauroy – Cormicy road. See TNA PRO WO 95/2165: 8/Leics War Diary.
37   TNA PRO WO 95/2164: 7/Leics War Diary.
38   TNA PRO WO 95/2163: 110 Bde HQ War Diary.

266   To Do the Work of Men

through Marceau. "All strong points between ROUTE 44 and the canal had been cut off, though not all had been overcome".[39]

Four hours later, the determined resistance of 110 Bde was only just beginning to crack: Colbert had been lost, but Vauban held out still. Another company of 6/Leics had been sent forward to occupy Hirsch trench and the southern sector of Boyau de Guise. To the north, the line had been broken at Marceau, but despite repeated bombardments and enemy attacks, the Tenaille de Guise was still firmly in British hands. At 16.15, the line had been adjusted again:

the remnants of 8/Leics were in 'Corridor' trench; the 7/Leics were to their left near Sablière, though not in touch, and 6/Leics were still in occupation of 'Hirsch' and 'Esternay'.[40]

On the left of 64 Bde front, D Coy of 9/KOYLI (the one company of that battalion in positions to the east of the canal) sent out a patrol under the initial German bombardment and were able to report at 02.15 that no attempt had been made up to that point by the enemy to cross No Man's Land and cut their wire. The men sat, waited and watched as best they could in the darkness and the fog for any signs of a German advance, forced to wear their box respirators the whole time. "The result was that our men were fatigued, sore about the face and without breakfast to commence a long day's battle". The diarist adds ruefully: "The Germans probably had breakfast in comfort".[41] Back at Brigade HQ, the staff officers were also suffering under a gas attack and "sucked [their] gas helmets and cursed the Hun".[42]

The German attack materialised through the mist sometime after three o'clock that morning. Rifle fire, grenades, but most importantly, Lewis Gun fire from the KOYLI trenches held up the Germans as they initially struggled to get through the British wire. The assault developed into a grenade fight, and although D Coy held out stubbornly for over an hour, their posts were eventually surrounded and overrun. Almost all were either killed, wounded or captured. Two officers, Lieutenant Shaw and Second-Lieutenant Holmes were among those captured. They managed to evade their captors, however, and were able to bring back a report of the engagement to Brigade HQ at around five o'clock. Only those two officers and around five or six men made it back across the canal. The CO of D Coy, Lieutenant Kenneth James, was killed.[43] Instructions had been given to blow up the bridges over the canal, but – and under the circumstances it is not surprising – at least one remained intact and the Germans were able to cross without too much difficulty.

To the west of the canal, 9/KOYLI units were concentrated in five redoubts, or 'bastions' as follows: on the left flank, Redoute des Chasseurs and Redoute de Wattignies were held by C Coy; in the centre of the sector was Jemmapes Bastion, garrisoned by A Coy. To the right and slightly to the rear were Redoute des Grenadiers and Redoute des Mousequetaires, manned by B Coy.

'Chasseurs' was the first of these redoubts to come under attack, somewhere between 03.30 and 04.30. The three platoons of C Coy managed to repel the initial assault, but the Germans were happy to pause and pour rifle fire and grenades into the KOYLI positions from the east,

---

39   Ibid.
40   Leicester Records Office, Doc 22D63/146, Unpublished memoir of D.A. Bacon MM, late Quartermaster Sergeant 110 Inf. Bde. p. 116.
41   TNA PRO WO 95/2162: 9/KOYLI.
42   IWM Harold Yeo Papers, Doc. Ref. 3132, 5 June 1918.
43   Lieutenant Robert Kenneth James, age 21 from Leeds, is commemorated on the Soissons Memorial.

north and west. Meanwhile, 'Wattignies' also came under attack, but managed to hold out for three hours, aided by a counter attack just after seven o'clock, during which a prisoner was taken from the *74th Regiment*. It was only a matter of time until the inevitable happened, however, and at 08.45 Bde HQ received a message carried by pigeon, stating that the Germans were across the canal in force and that 'Chasseurs' had fallen. Captain G.F. Ellenberger, commanding C Coy, was wounded and captured here. He was able to recall his experiences some days later in a letter home from captivity:

> My Company, 'C' Coy, was relieved in the front line, or outpost line as it really was, only that evening [26 May] by 'D' Coy and I did not get back to Chasseurs Redoubt (my new post west of the canal) until about 10.30 p.m. I had three platoons and my headquarters together in Chasseurs and the remaining platoon in Wattignies – though it was really absurd to talk of having platoons, as the total strength of the company was only about eighty men. About midnight came a message to the effect that prisoners stated the bombardment would commence at 1.00 a.m., and the attack at 2.00 a.m. We did not really, even then, believe that an attack was actually coming on such a quiet sector. I went down with Shaw, my Second in Command, to see the French 'listening set' operators, who had their instruments in Chasseurs, to ask if they had any information. We took a tin of Gold Flake cigarettes with us to promote the 'entente' feeling – how I wish I had that tin here now!
>
> The Frenchmen were quite certain nothing serious was taking place: but even while they were saying it was only to be a 'coup de main', the bombardment started. Shaw and I went at once to see how things were.[44]

These two officers were making their way to Wattignies Redoubt when a gas shell landed nearby. Ellenberger, it seems, was suffering slightly from the effects of the gas, but Shaw managed to get him back to his dug out in Chasseurs. Ellenberger continues the narrative, initially with uncertainty, but his recollections become more detailed and assured as the morning progresses:

> … the rest of the night seemed like a dream. I remember going on with Shaw in a sort of nightmare. I think he was trying to get me back to the dugout. We passed my servant, Miller – I think he said he was gassed. I saw him no more, but hope he got away. In the dugout I remember Shaw told me Sgt. Tilbrook was badly and probably fatally hit, but he was taken down alive.[45]
>
> Shaw gave Sgt. Watson Tilbrook's respirator as Watson had lost his in hospital two days before. My next recollection is of finding myself with Shaw standing in the trench two or three hours later in the early morning. The Germans suddenly appeared and seemed to be all around us in no time. No 'SOS' went up from the front line.
>
> We fired at figures advancing through the mist: one Lewis Gun, I remember, was completely driven from its position by a machine gun firing from somewhere close at hand. We were bombed from both sides, and found the French bombs, which were all we had, absolutely ineffective and outclassed.

---

44 IWM Brigadier G.F. Ellenberger Papers, Doc. Ref. 3132, 4 June 1918.
45 It would appear that Sergeant Tilbrook survived.

268   To Do the Work of Men

The trenches, too, made the confusion worse as the French make their trenches very deep with insurmountable sides – you cannot see out of them and it is very hard to get up anywhere to have a look. It was soon all over, and we found ourselves prisoners. Shaw, I lost, he was wounded I believe, but I hear he was brought back safely by the Germans. I was wounded in both legs […] but could hobble along. […] After crossing the canal we met Taylor, another of my officers, untouched. We were passed back through our old trenches and taken over no man's land and along the old German line to a dressing station at Mont Spin. We were decently treated all the way. One German gave me a stick to help myself on with, but another, less polite, took it from between my knees while we were sitting outside the dressing station".[46]

Ellenberger's family must have been very surprised and even more relieved to receive this letter, as an Official Telegram had by this time reached them, informing them that he had been killed in action. Indeed, on 6 June, Lieutenant-Colonel McCulloch wrote a letter to the family:

Your son's company was holding the post close to the Aisne-Marne Canal about five miles SE of Berry-au-Bac. On Mon. morning 27th May the Germans attacked. Your son and his men offered most gallant resistance. Eventually your son's company was surrounded and he died in a hand to hand encounter with the enemy.
McCulloch
Lt-Col. CO 9th KOYLI".[47]

Some days later McCulloch wrote another letter to Ellenberger's family giving a more detailed – and somewhat different – version of events: "… killed instantly at close quarters whilst making a counter-attack on Germans who had entered his trench. This is the account I got from Lt. J. Shaw who was with him".[48]

After the fall of Wattignies and Chasseurs redoubts, the full force of the German attack fell on A Coy in the Jemmapes Bastion. Lieutenant Greenshields was seriously wounded by a shell and was evacuated. The garrison held out for two hours, and even drove the enemy back with two counter attacks. Each time, the Germans withdrew a short distance and bombarded the company again. A final attack at 09.30 proved successful. Thirty-eight men under Second-Lieutenant Hurley were all that managed to get out. They moved to the south-east and encountered units of the 1/EYorks. At this point in his narrative the 9/KOYLI diarist backs up Captain Ellenberger's opinion of the French hand grenade:

It was found during grenade conflicts that the French grenade with the tin cover inflicted few injuries on the enemy. Good up to a point for intimidation purposes, but of little use compared to the Mills grenade when it came to killing and mutilating Germans. Our men were not as proficient in grenade fighting as men of the battalion a year ago as it had been relegated to a secondary position in training of the last six months. Still, 'A' and 'B' Coys'

46   IWM Brigadier G.F. Ellenberger Papers, Doc. Ref. 3132, 4 June 1918.
47   Ibid.
48   Ibid. Lieutenant Shaw was obviously mistaken. Ellenberger spent the remainder of the conflict as a prisoner of war. It was whilst he was in captivity that the Bar to his Military Cross was confirmed.

hand grenade fights ('B' Coy under 2nd-Lt Scott) were carried out in a courageous and determined manner against superior forces.[49]

Second-Lieutenant Scott and his B Coy men in the Mousequetaires and Grenadiers redoubts were in a similar position to those in Jemmapes. At 10.30, both redoubts were holding out, but both were also surrounded. With the Germans in secure possession of the main road running behind the redoubts, and with Battalion HQ forced, as a result, to move back to the Battle Zone line at Cauroy, no more reports from B Coy ever made it back. By 14.00 hrs, with the sounds of rifle fire and grenades having ceased from that direction, it was assumed that the two redoubts had been overwhelmed.

On the extreme right of the division frontage, 1/EYorks, (Lieutenant-Colonel N.S. Alexander DSO) had D Coy, under Lieutenant Greenwood, to the east of the canal. Like their counterparts in 9/KOYLI, they were also occupying a string of redoubts to the west of it. North to south, they were Fleurus, Arcole and Marengo. The next redoubt, Iena, on their right, was occupied by the French. Behind them, on Route 44, was the Luxembourg redoubt.

The fate of D Coy is easily and predictably summarised: It came under attack at around 03.00 hrs and was "enveloped".[50] Their exact fate remains obscure, as they are not mentioned again in any of the unit diaries. With the Germans doing their best to advance in a southerly direction along the western bank of the canal, they did not immediately see the need to launch frontal assaults on the 1/EYorks' garrisons in the redoubts: indeed, a message sent from battalion headquarters to Bde HQ at 06.10 stated that "at that time our main line of resistance was intact and that they had not had many casualties. There had been no enemy rifle fire against the BASTIONS FLEURUS and MARENGO and little against the BOYAU de LUXEMBOURG".[51]

This state of affairs was not to last long, however: just over an hour later 1/EYorks reported that the enemy had crossed the canal in front of them and were advancing up the communication trench that led directly to the Fleurus redoubt. Lieutenant-Colonel Alexander immediately sent two platoons of B Coy forward to reinforce the line. By 09.00 hrs, they were in place, one in Fleurus and the other in Arcole, the former facing north in order to be able to defend against a flank attack. Before long, C Coy in Bastion Arcole were reporting that the French had been forced to evacuate 'Iena' after a period of continuous heavy shelling.

At 11.25 a message was sent to Brigade announcing that the 1/EYorks was forming a defensive flank facing north and was about to fall back "gradually"[52] on Hermonville. This move was prompted, according to the battalion diarist, by the withdrawal of 9/KOYLI on their left. Accordingly, B Coy moved back down the Boyau de Luxembourg. A Coy followed and occupied the Charpentier Redoubt, whilst C Coy were able to dribble back along the Boyau Dumont. Battalion HQ was quickly established at a road junction to the south-east of Hermonville.

The support battalion of 64 Bde, the 15/DLI, (Lieutenant-Colonel Holroyd-Smyth), in camp near Châlons le Vergeur as the German artillery bombardment commenced at one o'clock that

---

49 TNA PRO WO 95/2162: 9/KOYLI War Diary.
50 TNA PRO WO 95/2161: 1/EYorks War Diary.
51 TNA PRO WO 95/2160: Bde HQ War Diary. The fate of D Coy was presumably at this time unknown.
52 TNA PRO WO 95/2161: 1/EYorks War Diary.

morning, was ordered to move off almost immediately and made their way forward "through dense clouds of gas"[53] to take up positions near the village of Cauroy. From there, C Coy went forward at ten o'clock with instructions to reinforce the 9/KOYLI. They arrived only in time to see the 9/KOYLI forced back as the Germans swarmed across Route 44 and took up defensive positions in the Avancée de Cauroy (a trench just to the east of that village) where they were able to gain touch with the 14/NFus (21st Division's pioneer battalion). D Coy occupied trenches to the north-west of Cauroy, whilst B Coy meanwhile headed for the Boyau de la Somme. The advancing grey tide soon pushed them back to C Coy's trenches, however, and hastily arranged bombing raids, meant to drive the enemy back, made no impact. Both sides then paused for breath. At 19.30, a determined German attack finally pushed the defenders back to positions west and south of Cauroy, although, just as darkness set in, stern resistance on the right managed to halt the advance and even push the Germans back a short distance.

In the rear areas, which had been under enemy artillery fire since the start of the bombardment, it very quickly became clear that a huge amount of supplies, stores and ammunition would have to be moved back to prevent them from falling into German hands:

> [...] when it became evident that the attack assumed large proportions and was likely to lead to big developments all surplus baggage, stores, Office equipment etc., in the Line Head Qrs., was as far as possible moved back to the transport Lines; and this was carried out under dangerous and difficult conditions. The opening barrage of the enemy was deep and intense, extending to Chalons-le-Vergeur and beyond, and enveloping Divisional Head Qrs., and the Brigade Transport Park in its depredations. Several casualties were inflicted among the Transport personnel, and men, horses and wagons had to scatter to avoid grouping which provided a good target. After loading all the stores, etc., at the transport Lines and cutting out that portion of the column used for conveyance of Ammuntion (sic), very little was available for the Line, and such as could be spared were required to make several journeys, each time over the now deadly St. Auboeuf Ridge. All stores with the forward Brigade Head Qrs., were loaded and got away safely, which was perhaps short of a miracle as during the loading and conveyance, shells fell like hail, while the road over the hill was torn with gaping holes, covered with fallen trees, reeking with Gas and Powder, and under direct observation by the enemy. The majority of the Battalion stores and such documents as were in the forward Zone, had to be destroyed.[54]

It soon became clear to 21st Division that the disjointed line occupied on the late afternoon of 27 May was in danger of being completely outflanked on the left and ultimately individual units would be surrounded, cut off and destroyed. The German troops in the centre of their attack had, in places, pushed the French 21st and 22nd Divisions back, in places, across the Vesle river:

> In the course of a summer day the enemy crossed two, and in places three, rivers; he had driven a salient twenty-five miles wide at the base and extending nearly twelve miles into the Allied line; he had destroyed four of the Divisions originally in the line, and nearly

---

53   TNA PRO WO 95/2161: 15/DLI War Diary.
54   Leicester Records Office, Doc 22D63/146, Unpublished memoir of D.A. Bacon MM, late Quartermaster Sergeant 110 Inf. Bde, p. 116.

destroyed two more (the British 21st and French 61st), besides two others (British 25th and French 157th) sent up from the reserve.[55]

With the alarming news coming in around eight o'clock that evening that the Germans had occupied Châlons le Vergeur, and, two hours later, that Bouvancourt had also fallen, it was imperative that the remnants of 21st Division withdraw even further. Original orders sent out at 20.15 were soon rendered obsolete – it was no longer possible to hold an east-west orientated line through St Auboeuf and Vaux Varennes as proposed – and with the enemy now suspected to be pushing patrols *eastwards* between Vaux Varennes and Pévy, further instructions were hurriedly compiled. The division would take up positions as follows:

The 64 Bde would occupy a line south-westwards from the Tour Rougemont (NW of Hermonville. The 6/Leics were to act as rearguard at Luthernay Farm while the rest of 110 Bde were moved back to Pévy. In the end, due to the dispatch rider being wounded, the order to finally withdraw never reached the 6/Leics and they spent the next day fighting alongside 64 Bde. 62 Bde took up positions in the Bois Cuville. In the early morning, at around 02.15, this garrison was reinforced when Lieutenant-Colonel Stevenson of 12/13 NFus arrived with 160 men, followed half an hour later by Lieutenant-Colonel Gush with 50 men of 1/Lincs.

The situation of the three Leicestershire battalions of 110 Bde was, to say the least, obscure: by ten o'clock on the evening of the 27th, the whereabouts of the two forward companies of the 7 & 8/Leics – and of one company of 6/Leics – were completely unknown. Accordingly, the remnants of the brigade were organised into one composite battalion, this under the command of Lieutenant-Colonel Chance (6/Leics). Runners failed to find either troops of 25th Division to their right or of 8th Division on their left, so with both flanks in the air and the threat of encirclement a rapidly approaching probability, the new order to move back to the village of Pévy came just in time. It was decided to move along a cross-country track running to the south-west of Hermonville. Brigade Headquarters was set up in the chateau at Pévy before midnight, by which time they were able to report thankfully that enemy shell fire had practically ceased. Just before the composite battalion assembled to move out, a strange occurrence unfolded: "shortly after midnight a few of the enemy were found among our Positions (fully armed and equipped) and these were quite surprised on being captured, having evidently advanced through one of the many gaps in our lines, and thus had got cut off from the main body of the enemy advance guards".[56] It was 03.30 by the time the Leicesters moved off and, having left the rearguard at Luthernay Farm as they passed through it, continued unmolested until, as it was now beginning to get light, a number of enemy aircraft spotted the column and began bombing them. "Though falling within a few yards, no direct hits were obtained, and as a matter of fact, owing to the cheeky nature of the low flying, the 'planes were thought to be our own until the first bomb was dropped".[57]

Just like 6/Leics, the 9/KOYLI had also not received any orders to withdraw. About thirty Other Ranks and half a dozen men of 1/EYorks, under the command of Lieutenant Holmes, had been placed in a shallow trench in front of a farm about a mile north-east of Hermonville,

---

55 Edmonds, *Military Operations France and Belgium 1918*, Vol. III, p. 84.
56 Leicester Records Office, Doc 22D63/146., Unpublished memoir of D.A. Bacon MM, late Quartermaster Sergeant 110 Inf. Bde, p. 117.
57 Ibid, p.117.

from where they had a reasonable field of fire. They were joined here by sixteen stragglers of 15/DLI under Captain Clarke, who extended the line southwards and gained touch with the 3rd Zouaves on the right. During the night, the Germans were seen to advance to within thirty or forty yards of the KOYLI trench, but they made no attempt to attack. The Yorkshiremen sat and awaited developments.

Dawn found them still in these positions, completely alone and exposed. A German advance from the direction of Cauroy developed at 05.30 on the 28th but was held up by this small detachment of fifty or so men. Probably more surprised than anything to find British troops still there, the Germans went to ground and were, for the moment, content to pour rifle and machine gun fire into the KOYLI trench. Lieutenant-Colonel McCulloch was hit in the side by a bullet at around six o'clock and was forced to go off to hospital. On his way back, he found time to report the situation to the HQ of 3/Zouaves in Hermonville and to 64 Bde HQ at Luthernay Farm. Lieutenant Walby assumed command.

The Germans pushed forward once again and reached as far as the trench block that the men had constructed during the night, and it was at about this time that the KOYLIs became aware of their perilous position: an NCO was sent out to find out more about the situation from the 15/DLI but came back with the news that they had gone. Hardly surprising was the dawning realisation that with a remaining strength of barely one platoon, a hasty withdrawal was probably the best course of action.

The new 21st Division line was coming under increasing pressure once again. The 15/DLI were bombed out of their positions on the Montigny ridge near Luthernay Farm, where they had been sent to counter a German force advancing south from Vaux Varennes, driven back some 500 yards and forced to defend against an enemy once more determined to turn their left flank. It was during this engagement that their CO, Lieutenant-Colonel C.E.R. Holroyd-Smyth was wounded. Command passed to Major S.D. Thorpe MC. The 1/E Yorks, who had by this time been "reduced to about forty men,"[58] were also being gradually forced back southwards but were able to make a brief stand – with the help of a "French Mitrailleuse Coy"[59] – at St Joseph's Farm, just to the west of Marzilly. The 9/KOYLI, still out of touch with the other units of 64 Bde, began an independent withdrawal through Marzilly towards Trigny.

The 62 Bde positions were also under threat. The 1/Lincs report that although no attack was directed squarely at their position, hostile patrols had been seen approaching from the north-west, and before long, "both flanks became completely exposed and another withdrawal became necessary to conform with the general line".[60] Orders sent by Brigade HQ at 06.10 that morning to hold the current line became redundant as "the enemy attacked in great numbers with many machine guns, and a further rear-guard action was unavoidable, the Left Flank West of PEVY having been turned to such an extent that it was impossible to hold the ridge any longer".[61]

It remains unclear in all the 21st Division formation and unit diaries whether specific messages were sent ordering the withdrawal to the next line of defensive positions running between Trigny, across the Butte de Prouilly and continuing south-west to a point half a mile south of Prouilly village itself. The 21st Division HQ diary is clear that orders were issued at

---

58   Edmonds, *Military Operations France and Belgium 1918*, Vol. III, p. 108.
59   TNA PRO WO 95/2161: 1/E Yorks War Diary. *Mitrailleuse* is French for machine gun.
60   TNA PRO WO 95/2154: 1/Lincs War Diary.
61   TNA PRO WO 95/2153: 62 Bde HQ War Diary.

05.25 to hold the previous 'Montigny Ridge' line, but states simply thereafter that at 08.00, "the line held by the Division was withdrawn".[62] The diary of 62 Bde HQ merely records the establishment of this new line at around midday, and the 64 Bde after-action account recounts how the Brigadier, (Headlam), whilst riding across to reconnoitre his right flank and having his horse shot from under him, on his way back to Brigade HQ "found that an organised line already existed along the ridge running from Trigny to Hill 220 and that a certain number of French troops were already in position there. A certain number of 14th N.F (Pioneers) were found close to here and were put into this trench with orders that any stragglers of the Brigade were to be collected here".[63] Brigadier Cumming, in his narrative of the events, sums up the command situation:

> About this time it became apparent that the enemy was advancing so rapidly, and the situation changing in consequence so often, that it was impossible for the Division to keep pace with it and issue and deliver orders in time for them to be acted upon. It therefore devolved upon Brigadiers to make decisions and order movements on their own initiative, endeavouring as far as possible to carry out the general scheme without orders and with no information – a by no means easy task, as the point of view of a Brigadier is necessarily somewhat limited. This was especially the case during this day's operations (28th), when the enemy moved so fast around the left flank that it became merely a question of delaying his advance as long as was compatible with withdrawing the troops before they were actually surrounded and cut off.[64]

Brigadier Headlam (64 Bde) went round this new line at midday and found the situation thus:

> The line was held by a somewhat mixed party of troops. On the right, there was a French battalion, then came mixtures of the 64th Bde with a fair percentage of Officers, and then a French Battalion. The French Commander had a liaison officer of the 62nd Inf. Brigade with him and the 62nd Inf. Bde were on his left. The situation on the left was somewhat obscure, as the enemy were known to be in Prouilly and Jonchery. […] The line was situated just on the forward slope and was about 2'6" deep and had good wire, but thick woods in front of most of it obscured the view […] Men of course were tired and naturally somewhat disorganised. The remainder of the 15th Dur. L.I. were only just then arriving at this line. They must have put up a very good show on the Luthernay Farm – Montigny Ridge.[65]

Headlam reported this situation to Division and at 15.15, (message sent at 13.10). Division came back with a rather self-contradictory order. There was to be no withdrawal from this line, unless such a move became imperative.

What remained of 110 Bde was still working its way back to Pévy, but after a short halt for breakfast, it became clear that the heights above the village were held by the enemy. The appearance of the Leicesters provoked a veritable hail of machine gun bullets: the Leicesters, in reply,

---

62 TNA PRO WO 95/2133: 21st Div HQ War Diary.
63 TNA PRO WO 95/2133: 64 Bde HQ War Diary.
64 Cumming, *A Brigadier in France 1917-1918*, pp. 177-178.
65 TNA PRO WO 95/2133: 64 Bde HQ War Diary.

274   To Do the Work of Men

turned south and made for the Prouilly ridge on the other side of the valley. Brigadier Cumming takes up the story:

> This move entailed crossing a swamp in the centre of the valley and a stiff climb up to the ridge on the opposite side, followed the whole way by heavy but fortunately inaccurate fire, from the Boche machine guns on the hill. No one was hit and the movement was carried out without mishap; but it was not pleasant, especially for those men with bicycles, who had to carry them across the marsh and haul them [up] the opposite side. The Headquarters mess waiter, Meadows, was in charge of the few utensils that were being used and the rations, all of which were in a sack. This he insisted on carrying; nothing would induce him to leave it, and he finally bore it in triumph to safety on top of the ridge – a fine feat of doggedness and muscle on a hot day.[66]

On the crest, the Leicesters found parties of various units, including some men of 14/NFus, some elements of the 8th and 25th Divisions, and one company from 12/13/NFus. Cumming set about reorganising the line and settled in with every intention of defending the ridge.

It was around 15.30 hrs that the next determined effort by the Germans saw them gain a foothold on parts of the Prouilly ridge. The British line was shelled very heavily and with the machine gun fire being particularly accurate this time, casualties began to mount. From the heights, it was possible to see that 21st Division was once more being outflanked, and as German troops "were now swarming by the hundred"[67] up the forward slopes of the ridge, it was time to invoke the second clause of the 21st Div order and get away to new positions across the Vesle river. Almost inevitably, the orders did not reach all of the units on the ridge: the 1/Lincs, acting as rearguard for their brigade, did not retire until after nine o'clock – and only then once they were sure that the French battalion on their right had themselves received orders to comply with the rearward move. Brigadier Headlam did not find out about the withdrawal of the troops on his left until 23.30 and it was not until around 02.00 hrs on the 29th that his 64 Bde units began to fall back across the Vesle. The 1/E Yorks and 15/DLI diarists give the time of the order to withdraw as 01.30, but it would seem that the message once more failed to reach the 9/KOYLI: an officer doing his rounds at 03.00 hrs "discovered that the troops on our left and right had disappeared, and that the Germans were coming through the wire in front of the trench in twos and threes".[68] A recce by the Adjutant revealed that the village of Trigny and the defensive line along the Trigny heights "had been evacuated".[69] Realising that their position was now "rather impossible",[70] the remnants of the battalion made their way south, crossing the Vesle at Muizon where they found the rest of the brigade. Fortunately, it was not until after the KOYLIs' arrival that the bridges over the river were destroyed.

It was also fortunate that the main thrust of the German advance on 28 May had been further to the west: the town of Soissons had fallen and the Forward troops were across the Vesle

---

66   Cumming, *A Brigadier in France 1917-1918*, p. 179.
67   Leicester Records Office, Doc 22D63/146, Unpublished memoir of D.A. Bacon MM, late Quartermaster Sergeant 110 Inf. Bde, p. 118.
68   TNA PRO WO 95/2162: 9/KOYLI War Diary.
69   Ibid.
70   Ibid.

everywhere to the west of Jonchery. By German admission, their follow-up attacks against the British sector of the line had been less than energetic:

> The infantry of the *7th Reserve Division* [facing 21st Div] was greatly lacking in attack ardour on this day [and] stopped in the face of weak resistance, […] went forward very slowly with hour-long pauses, without their being a question of any real fighting. […] The *86th Division* went forward even more slowly than the *7th Reserve* and, going no further than Thil-Trigny, lost all touch with the Allies.[71]

As the exhausted and badly depleted battalions of 21st Division settled into their new positions south of the river, they would probably not have agreed with the above-propounded idea that they had had a relatively easy day of it.

As dawn broke on 29 May, the division was deployed thus (See Map 38): With the railway line designated as the first line of defence, 64 Bde were on the right, with their right flank on Les Vautes (800 yards south-west of Muizon). 1/E Yorks and 15/DLI were, right and left respectively, in the forward positions, with the 9/KOYLI party attached to the former, placed behind them with a Lewis Gun team from the Nucleus Party. They were in touch with the French 45th Division on the right. The line was continued westwards near the Tile Works by 110 Bde, which had been reduced to a single composite battalion under the command of Lieutenant-Colonel Sawyer. On the left flank of the divisional front, and with their left battalion (12/13/NFus) echeloned back slightly towards Sapicourt, was 62 Bde.

By 08.00 hrs, the intentions of the German formations were becoming clear: they were launching an attack to the south and south-east of Jonchery, their aim to outflank the 21st Division once again by capturing Branscourt, Savigny, Faverolles and eventually Treslon. To support the French, who were holding a line to the south of Sapicourt, a detachment of fifty men of 110 Bde were sent to bolster this position. The right flank of 21st Division was not, it seemed, about to be troubled other than by artillery fire, so the 1/Lincs and 12/13 NFus were sent across to strengthen the Hill 202 – Sapicourt line during the afternoon.

This artillery fire was to some extent provoked by the fact that all four brigades (this includes 7 Bde of 25th Division) had established their headquarters in a large house on the top of a hill on the south side of Rosnay, a location that was clearly in full view of the enemy, who could observe "the number of Mounted Orderlies which came riding up to it every minute".[72] At around 15.00 hrs, just after a number of enemy aircraft had circled low over the building, a salvo of 5.9s landed just to the south of it. The Germans could not have known just how valuable a target this building was, with four Brigadier-Generals in residence, but they persisted with their bombardment, landing a second salvo just short. Brigadier-General Cumming immediately ordered everyone to clear the house as quickly as possible. The majority were able to make it outside, whilst some headed, just in time, for the cellars: the third salvo demolished the house completely.

At 18.45, Lieutenant-Colonel Sawyer (7/Leics) reported to Brigade HQ that all was quiet along the Muizon front, but that he could see around 400 of the enemy advancing on Sapicourt.

---

71 Edmonds, *Military Operations France and Belgium 1918*, Vol .III, p. 119.
72 TNA PRO WO 95/2162: 9/KOYLI War Diary.

In fact, that sector of the front had been under attack for some time. The 1/Lincs were caught up in the first German attack on Hill 202 at around 14.00 hrs and had managed to repel it. Two hours later the Germans had worked around the left flank and had positioned machine guns which could now sweep the reverse slope of the hill. Equally worrying was the fact that the village of Treslon had fallen to the enemy at around 17.00 hrs.

Hill 202 was defended by a mixture of 62 Bde, 110 Bde and French troops. Nominally in charge was Lieutenant-Colonel Chance, 6/Leics. He had taken his already depleted force from Rosnay and occupied positions on the wooded summit on the morning of the 29th. The 6/Leics diarist continues the story:

Captain, Brevet Major, acting Lieutenant-Colonel Edward Seton Chance, 2/Dragoon Guards, attached and commanding 6/Leics, kia 29 May 1918, age 36. (*The War Illustrated*, Vol. 10)

> A patrol was pushed forward to get in touch with the situation at Branscourt and a reconnaissance was carried out by Lt Col Chance of situation W. of Hill 202. The enemy shelled Hill 202 heavily during the morning. About 40 OR were placed in position on the forward slope of Hill 202 where they were able to bring considerable fire to bear on enemy advancing over the Branscourt Valley.
>
> The general tendency of all enemy movements after 11 a.m. was across our front to SW along the Branscourt – Savigny road when infantry, horsed vehicles and guns were frequently seen. Fire was kept up on this road but the range was too long for rifle fire to be effective. At 1 p.m. on the left towards Treslon troops were observed withdrawing. Col Gush of the Lincolns and the CO SW Borderers of 25th Division reported to Col Chance and after reconnaissance brought their battalions into action on the left of Hill 202 to check the enemy advance on the left. About this time 3 Coys of French Colonials took up a position with our troops in front of Hill 202 and a battalion of French Territorials took up a position on the S. of the Rosnay – Treslon Rd. 4 p.m. enemy attacked in strength from Branscourt southwards. Excellent results were obtained by rifle & MG fire and attack brought to a standstill opposite our front.[73]

At 19.45, the enemy began a heavy bombardment of the wood on Hill 202 "with field guns at point blank range and heavy minenwerfer. Lt Col Chance whose personal bravery and skillful (sic) handling of troops had enabled Bn to maintain its position throughout the day, was killed".[74]

---

73 TNA PRO WO 95/2164: 6/Leics War Diary.
74 Ibid. Captain (Brevet Major) acting Lieutenant-Colonel Edward Seton Chance, 2nd Dragoon Guards (Queen's Bays) attached as Commanding Officer, 6/Leics, age 36, is commemorated on the

By this time, the Germans had reached the crest of Hill 202 and the French troops on the left, completely outflanked as they were, began to withdraw. The 1/Lincs, numbering no more than 70 Other Ranks, had already withdrawn to new positions between Germigny and Bouleuse and the rest of the 110 Bde vacated the hill and were holding a line just to the west of Rosnay Farm, commanded now by Captain Tooth of 6/Leics.

21st Division's involvement in this battle was coming to an end: the French 45th Division were tasked with taking over the sector, and orders were issued to the effect that once British unit commanders were satisfied that their part of the line was secure in French hands, they could withdraw their men. By the evening of 29 May, most 110 Bde units were being reorganised on high ground just to the south of Rosnay. They received verbal orders from Division at 21.00 hrs authorising their immediate withdrawal: they eventually moved off between one and two o'clock the following morning and gathered in the Epernay Forest. They were in billets in Etrechy on 31 May and were being reorganised into a Composite Battalion of 350 men under Lieutenant-Colonel Irwin DSO MC, 8/Leics.

The 1/Lincs were pulled out of the line at eight-thirty and they trudged back as far as Méry Premecy where they found the rest of 62 Bde. They continued their march back through Marfaux and by 31 May had also found billets, this time in Soulières. The total strength of the three infantry battalions was 68 Officers and 1,154 Other Ranks.

Finally gathered more or less in the same place, 64 Bde received notification of their impending relief at 21.30 hrs, 29 May. "GOC (Major-General Campbell) however wished Brigadiers to satisfy themselves that French troops were in position and that the withdrawal of the British troops would not have any material effect".[75] The Brigade Major was then sent to each unit in turn in order that they could be sure that this criterion had been met, whereupon written orders would be issued to bring the troops back to Marfaux. It was three o'clock the following morning by the time he returned, his mission only partly successful: the 14/NFus (Pioneers) were apparently already on their way back and he was unable to find the 1/EYorks. It turned out that Lieutenant-Colonel Alexander had "received the orders from a different source"[76] and was also already heading back. By seven o'clock the following morning, the whole of 64 Bde was bivouacked at Marfaux. Their stay was a short one, and after a night in a forest clearing at Epernay, a four-hour march saw them arrive at Chaltrait on the last day of May. Here they were able, finally, to rest and clean up. With some stragglers still turning up at this juncture, battalion strengths were somewhere around 250. Harold Yeo, 64 Bde staff, summed up his experiences in a letter posted home on 6 June:

> Since we got up on the morning of the 26th, in the ordinary way I hadn't got any sleep until that night of the 30th (i.e. five days and four nights) except on three occasions when I got about two hours' sleep each time, at the very most. That's the worst part of these shows, the lack of sleep. It seems not to affect some people as much as others; for instance, the General[77] doesn't sleep the whole time and yet never seems to yawn even.

Soissons Memorial.
75   TNA PRO WO 95/2133: 64 Bde HQ War Diary.
76   Ibid.
77   Presumably Brigadier-General Headlam.

278 To Do the Work of Men

Since then we've been trekking about the place and are now in quite a good village and have got pretty decent billets. Thus ends the third battle we've had since the Bosches started their pushes: so far as we are concerned, it is ended, at any rate, pro tem.[78]

The 21st Division was temporarily reorganised into a composite brigade under Brigadier-General G.H. Gater DSO, re-christened the 21st Independent Brigade, and sent to undertake trench holding duties, still in the French sector, on the Marne. An uneventful fortnight later, relief on the night of 16/17 June meant that they were able to return to the British sector, arriving in the Abbeville area by train to find an immediate draft of 2,500 men waiting to join the Division.

Casualties for the Chemin des Dames offensive are, as ever, difficult to finalise. The best estimate comes from the 21st Division A & Q diary and is partly reproduced here:

	Killed		Wounded		Missing		Total	
	Off	OR	Off	OR	Off	OR	Off	OR
62 Bde								
12/13 NFus	2	12	5	39	11	454	18	505
1/Lincs	3	26	8	127	3	95	14	248
2/Lincs	–	7	2	55	17	340	19	402
62 TM Btty	–	5	–	6	1	18	1	29
Bde Total	**5**	**50**	**15**	**227**	**32**	**907**	**52**	**1,184**
64 Bde								
1/EYorks	1	6	7	55	8	314	16	375
9/KOYLI	2[79]	4	6	28	6	319	14	351
15/DLI	–	21	7	17	8	414	15	452
64 TM Btty	–	–	1	2	–	3	1	5
Bde Total	**3**	**31**	**21**	**102**	**22**	**1,050**	**46**	**1,183**
110 Bde								
6/Leics	1	21	6	95	5	158	12	274
7/Leics	2	15	5	57	12	431	19	507
8/Leics	1	5	3	15	15	559	19	579
110 TM Btty	–	–	–	–	–	8	–	8
Bde Total	**4**	**41**	**14**	**167**	**32**	**1,156**	**50**	**1,364**
14/NFus (P)	4	18	3	140	9	206	16	354
21 Bn MGC	1	16	4	57	3	103	8	176
Div. Artillery	2	7	6	52	1	40	9	99
Royal Eng.	–	14	5	50	4	46	9	110
RAMC[80]	–	3	–	5	4	47	4	55
Div. Total	**19**	**180**	**68**	**800**	**107**	**3,355**	**194**	**4,335**
Overall Total							**45**	**29**

78 Private Papers of Harold Yeo, IWM. Letter dated 6 June 1918. Doc.Ref. 3132.
79 This includes Captain G.F. Ellenberger, who, it was subsequently discovered, was a prisoner of war.
80 A Casualty Clearing Station in the village of Jonchery was overrun before the personnel and the wounded could be withdrawn.

What is extraordinary about these figures is that over 76 percent of the divisional total are classified as 'missing'. Commonwealth War Graves Commission figures for those killed would suggest that the vast majority of the 'missing', though perhaps wounded, of course, were taken prisoner. This can be partly blamed on geography – the fact that the main German thrust was southwards and therefore behind the 21st Division's front line positions – and on the rapidity of the enemy advance. War diaries, however, bemoan the almost immediate loss of those units placed forward of the canal on the morning of 27 May, and the responsibility for that lies squarely with the French Commander, GOC Sixth Army, General Duchêne.

The 21st Division played no further part in the Chemin des Dames offensive. By 3 June, the Germans had crossed the Marne, but the fall of the town of Château Thierry, some sixty miles from Paris, was to prove the high-water mark of their advance. The Germans had created a salient forty miles wide at its base and extending to a depth of thirty miles. Its defence had cost the Allies dear: the British had suffered almost 29,000 casualties, the French over three times that number. As with the two previous German offensives, however, the advance had simply run out of steam, and the badly-extended forces were susceptible to counter attacks on both flanks. Ludendorff knew that he would have to try and widen the salient: an attempt to reach Compiègne to the west of the Chemin des Dames ridge was to end in failure, despite an initial advance on 9 June of six miles. Thereafter the pace slowed dramatically and on the 11th, the French, under General Mangin,[81] who had replaced the disgraced Duchêne, launched a counter attack using 144 tanks and aircraft support. The battle ended, in effect on 13 June, and although other small, local actions were fought, the tide of the war had begun to turn. Mangin, prior to the counter attack, had exhorted his men by assuring them that there were to be no more defensive battles, promising a renewal of Allied offensives. Just how much faith he had in his own pronouncements can only be surmised, but he was to be proved right.

The number of casualties suffered by 21st Division was such that it was decided to reduce the 9/KOYLI and 8/Leics to 'Training Cadre' status – in effect this meant disbanding the unit, leaving only a handful of Officers and fewer than 200 men in each battalion. The 9/ KOYLI received the order for their disbandment on 24 June, and arrangements were made for the transfer of the bulk of the men to other units. On the same day, Brigadier-General Headlam inspected them for the last time and gave what amounted to a farewell speech. However, at 23.30 on 27 June, the message came down from Brigade that the reduction of 9/KOYLI had been 'reconsidered'. The battalion was, after all, to live on. The 2/South Lancs, who had arrived on 25 June to replace 9/KOYLI, were unceremoniously shunted off with immediate effect to the 30th Division.

Sadly, no such reprieve arrived for 8/Leics, and the cadre set off to return to England on 29 June. The vast majority of the men 'left behind' were moved to their sister battalion, the 7/Leics, one exception being Lieutenant-Colonel Irwin, who went to 1/Lincs. Their place in 110 Bde was taken by 1st Battalion Wiltshire Regiment.

---

81 Charles Marie Emmanuel Mangin (1866- 1925) commanded 5th Division in its recapture of Forts Vaux and Douaumont at Verdun in 1916. He was subsequently promoted to command Sixth Army in the failed Nivelle Offensive of May 1917. His career was resurrected in 1918 by the June 1918 counter attack on the Marne. He commented during the battle of Verdun that 'whatever you do, you lose a lot of men'. His aggression and willingness to sacrifice his own men in the pursuit of victory earned him the sinister nickname of 'The Butcher'.

280   To Do the Work of Men

It was a period of uncertainty for 21st Division. On 24 June they received orders to be ready for a move to Second Army. The very next day the order was confirmed and it was decided that they should join XXII Corps in Belgium, leaving on the 26th. The move was subsequently cancelled, however, and by early July they were back on the Somme as part of V Corps, (Lieutenant-General Shute), Third Army (General Byng). July turned out to be a "month of waiting",[82] a month of re-organisation, training and trench-holding. The 21st Division's next action would be part of the "Advance to Victory". The defensive battles were over.

82   Cumming, *A Brigadier in France 1917-1918*, p. 200.

8

Somme Redux

Major-General David Campbell was fortunate to have under him at this point in the war three "truly outstanding brigade commanders", who were "well equipped to meet the demands of decentralised command in the semi-open warfare of the 'Hundred Days' ".[1]

The GOC 62 Bde was George Gater, who had had no military experience before the war other than a brief time in the Winchester Officer Training Corps. After obtaining a history degree and a Diploma in Education at Oxford, he was, in 1914, Assistant Director of Education for Nottinghamshire. He was soon commissioned into the 9/Sherwood Foresters and was in temporary command of the battalion when it was evacuated from the Gallipoli peninsula in December 1915. Eight months later he was given command of 6/Lincolnshires and just over a year later was promoted to command 62 Bde at the age of thirty. His rise from civilian to brigade commander had taken just over three years. Campbell portrayed Gater as a brigadier "of the very highest class", a "very good disciplinarian" and one who had "the absolute confidence of all serving under him".[2]

Andrew McCulloch, CO 9/KOYLI since October 1917, was promoted to command 64 Bde on 28 July 1918. He was 42 years old. Son of a Scottish judge, and originally planning a career as a barrister, he joined the City Imperial Volunteers and fought in the South

Brigadier-General George Gater.

---

1 Peter Simkins, *From the Somme to Victory: The British Army's Experience on the Western Front 1916-1918* (Barnsley: Pen & Sword, 2014), pp. 166 & 167.
2 Ibid, p.166.

African War, being awarded a DCM before receiving a commission in the Highland Light Infantry. He graduated from Staff College in 1910 and in 1914 was a Captain in the Dragoon Guards before transferring to 14/Hussars. His next command was the 9/KOYLI.

Brigadier-General Hanway Cumming, 50 years old, was GOC 110 Bde. He was commissioned into the Durham Light Infantry in 1889 and attended Staff College between 1901 and 1902. In August 1916 he was given command of 2/DLI and only three months later he was promoted to command 91 Bde. His penchant for questioning orders that he found ill-advised got him into trouble at Bullecourt in May 1917 and he was sent back to England where he commanded the Machine Gun Training School at Grantham until February 1918. It became apparent that he was too good an officer to leave back in 'Blighty' and he was brought back to the Western Front and given command of 110 Bde just three days before it faced the onslaught of the German March Offensive. Campbell soon learnt to value his advice and described him as "a magnificent leader of men" and "a soldier of the very highest class".[3]

The beginning of August 1918 saw the 21st Division, now part of General Shute's V Corps (Third Army), back on what for some must have been familiar territory: when not on front-line duty, units were billeted in the area around the villages of Auchonvillers, Mailly-Maillet and Englebelmer.

In March 1918, the scope of the German advance meant that they had been able once more to establish themselves on the west bank of the Ancre between Albert and Beaumont Hamel. The month of August was, however, a good one for the Allies: there were to be no

Brigadier-General Andrew McCulloch, pictured after the War. (Peter Simkins)

Brigadier-General Hanway Cumming.

---

3 Cumming, *A Brigadier in France 1917-1918*, Introduction by David Campbell.

more German offensives and the Allies were gathering themselves after the setbacks of the Spring. The Americans were arriving in larger numbers and the Germans were soon to be forced onto the back foot, never to regain any significant forward movement. On 8 August, the Allies launched a massive and decisive attack eastward from the city of Amiens.[4] One hundred thousand troops of Fourth Army – Canadian, Australian and British – along with the French First Army on their right, went into the assault at 04.20, backed by 2,000 guns, over 400 tanks and ground-attack aircraft, achieving an advance of up to eight miles that day. The Germans lost an estimated 27,000 men, 18,000 of them being taken prisoner. The battle continued for another three days, the advance finally running out of steam by the 11th, whereupon Haig – against Foch's wishes – closed the battle down. It had been a severe blow to the German forces, in territorial, material and manpower terms, not to mention the crushing morale effect of a very impressive and overwhelming all-arms attack that had taken the defenders by surprise. It is no wonder that Ludendorff described the 8 August as a "black day" for the German Army.

It was necessary to keep the pressure on the German Army, however, and only two days after Haig shut down the Amiens battle, he gave orders for General Byng, Third Army, to prepare for an attack on the Somme in the direction of Bapaume and Péronne. This was part of a larger scheme whereby this northern pincer, combined with an attack by the French Tenth Army east of the Oise, between Soissons and St Quentin, would effectively outflank the German defensive system on the Somme and force the enemy into a deeper retirement.

In the meantime, the opposing forces facing each other on the western bank of the Ancre between Hamel and the eastern slopes of the Redan Ridge were engaged in a deadly cat-and-mouse game of patrol and counter-patrol: "the Germans rarely occupied the same position two nights running, and were hard to locate, sometimes holding one series of posts, sometimes another. More than one British officer described the Ancre valley as a happy hunting ground for night patrols. […] [R]aids, patrols and skirmishes were frequent".[5]

It was into and out of this labyrinth of trenches atop the Hawthorn Ridge[6] that the units of 21st Division were rotated. A detailed account of each relief, re-positioning and withdrawal would produce a tangled, impenetrable and frankly unproductive narrative: a representative sample of unit engagements will suffice to give the reader a flavour of the action taking place in early August that year.

Reports were reaching 21st Division that the Germans were in the process of withdrawing from positions on the western bank of the Ancre. Conformation would only come from aggressive patrolling. On the night of 6 / 7 August, 64 Bde sent out "fighting patrols"[7] to ascertain the situation on their front. The report came back that both Lustre Trench and Lustre Support in square Q.17.d were indeed unoccupied, but that the patrol "was sniped"[8] from Lustre Reserve. Further to the south, Church Trench in Q.23.a was also found to be empty.

The following night, D Coy of 2/Lincs under Captain C.W. McConnan was tasked with carrying out a raid on Levant Trench. (Square Q.10. b & d. See Map). They had spent the day

4   For a detailed examination of the Battle of Amiens, see James McWilliams & R. James Steel, *Amiens 1918: The Last Great Battle* (Stroud: Tempus Publishing, 2007), *passim.*
5   Simkins, *From the Somme to Victory.* p. 158.
6   See Map 40.
7   TNA PRO WO 95/2160: 64 Bde HQ War Diary.
8   Ibid.

284   To Do the Work of Men

in Acheux and were moved from there to Mailly Maillet by motor lorry at eight o'clock in the evening, prior to marching up to their assembly positions. The company was divided into four parties, each one platoon strong: the right, or southern, party would enter Levant Trench just south of the sap at Q.10.d.5.6 and work southwards along it towards Locust Trench. One of the centre parties would occupy the sap; the other would then pass through and move on into Y Ravine. The left party's objective was to take the section of Levant Trench just north of the sap, which would then allow some of their number to push on into Levant Support. While all of this was happening, two Lewis Gun sections, one on either flank, would be stationed in No Man's Land as flank guards.

As they formed up at 23.00 hrs on a line fifty yards east of Beaumont Trench, the artillery put down a box barrage isolating the salient formed by the German front line system.[9] A creeping barrage then came down on Levant Trench itself before advancing at a rate of 100 yards every four minutes. Trench Mortars and machine guns added to the mayhem. The raiding parties started forward as soon as the barrage commenced and were able to enter the German trench as it lifted from there.

Such levels of sound and fury proved to be unnecessary: all parties reached their objectives without encountering any of the enemy directly and were back in their own trenches by 00.20 hrs. Retaliation was limited to a rather weak artillery shoot, and rifle and machine gun fire from the Locust trench system. Nevertheless, there were casualties: three Other Ranks killed and five wounded.[10] Brigade and Battalion War Diaries both add a positive spin to the experience: the 2/Lincs diarist, only too well aware of the large number of new recruits reaching the front line battalions at this stage of the war, states:

> Although the raid did not produce any prisoners, the lessons learnt were most useful. The majority of the men had never before advanced under a barrage and the ease with which they were able to follow it gave them confidence for future operations.[11]

The 62 Bde diary focuses on the lack of 'action', concluding that "the men, who were very keen, were very disappointed that they had been deprived of a fight".[12]

On 12 August, it was the sister battalion, 1/Lincs, that began practising for the next raid, which was scheduled to go in "not earlier than the 17th/18th".[13] Events were to render their practices redundant. On the 14th, 62 Bde was receiving more reports that the Germans were

---

9   This 'box' barrage, owing to the shape of the salient formed by Levant Trench, constituted two sides of a triangle, running from Q.10.b.8.2 to Q.11.a.6.1 and then back to Q.11.c.6.0. It prevented any German reinforcements moving either forward or sideways to help defend the incursion, and isolated the German front line garrison.

10   Commonwealth War Graves Commission records show five deaths for the 2/Lincs between 7 and 9 August 1918 inclusive: 38542 Private George William Westmoreland (29), buried in Mailly Wood Cemetery, II.P.13; 52069 Private E. Blewett (19) is buried in the same row, in grave II.P.5. 1947 Private Arthur Dean (22), 238139 Sergeant S. Morrey (26) and 1245 Private H.D. Williamson are all buried together in Gézaincourt Communal Cemetery Extension, graves II.O.21, II.O.20 and II.O.22 respectively.

11   TNA PRO WO 95/2154: 2/Lincs War Diary.

12   TNA PRO WO 95/2153: 62 Bde HQ War Diary.

13   Ibid.

"carrying out a gradual withdrawal from this front".[14] Observers both on the ground and in the air could see no movement in the forward areas back as far as square Q.6: the roads and tracks, it seems, were devoid of transport and personnel. That afternoon, a party of New Zealanders from 42nd Division on the left had found the enemy's front trench system evacuated. Accordingly, patrols were sent forward immediately by the 12/13 NFus: three parties moved off at 15.00 hrs and two of them were able to establish posts in Linseed Reserve. (Squares Q.5.a & b.). The other passed through the deserted ruins of Beaumont Hamel, only gaining contact with enemy outposts 1,000 yards further east. By the evening, these groups had pressed on as far as the ridge in square Q.6 and only when they approached the high ground in squares R.2 a & c (see Map 41), did they find the enemy in any strength. By nightfall, "platoon posts were established in WALKER AVENUE and LUMINOUS AVENUE, Q.6.a & c, with Platoons in Support in WAGGON ROAD and LINSEED RESERVE".[15]

That night, these units were relieved by battalions of 64 Bde who had earlier also found Levant and Locust Reserve Trenches empty. Parties of 9/KOYLI were able to push even further forward, ending the day with men in Lubber Avenue and Lux Alley (Q.12), with plans to continue the advance the next morning. At 08.00 hrs on 15 August, however, it became clear that the Germans had finally decided to put up something of a fight: an enemy artillery barrage fell on the KOYLI positions, all four companies suffering casualties as a result. In front of them one machine gun post was also proving particularly troublesome. With the help of some Stokes Mortar fire, A Coy was able to rush this post and deal with the machine gunners. This temporary belligerence overcome, it was possible to push forward as far as Artillery Lane, a trench line running northwards from the village of Beaucourt. B, C and D Coys occupied this line, with A Coy now in support in Luminous Avenue. They got no further that day: machine gun and artillery fire increased once more and checked any further thoughts of advance. They were relieved by units of 15/DLI that night. The action had cost the KOYLIs eleven fatal casualties, including Second-Lieutenant Grafton, who had joined the battalion only eight weeks before.[16]

Meantime, the 110 Bde had not been idle. The village of Hamel had been vacated by the German garrison and a number of patrols were sent forward to try and establish a bridgehead over the River Ancre. One such formed of units of 7/Leics, commanded by Second-Lieutenant Boss, succeeded in pushing across the river a little to the south of the Mill. They quickly encountered the enemy dug in on either side of Mill Road, however, and were forced to fight a rearguard action as they were pushed back across the waterway. "Formation of ground afforded good view of fight from our old line, and patrol was very favourably commented on" writes the battalion diarist.[17] By 20 August the brigade had settled into positions in Hamel itself (C Coy) with A Coy in the old front line and B and D Coys in Church Alley, these latter two ready to move forward across the river once more as part of the large-scale attack planned for the 21st.

Sir Julian Byng's Third Army, in mid-August, was made up of three corps: from north to south these were VI, IV and V Corps. These, in turn, were made up of thirteen infantry divisions. Opposite them were eight German divisions (with two more in reserve). Although by this

14 Ibid.
15 Ibid.
16 Second-Lieutenant William Salter Grafton, age 29, is buried in Mesnil Communal Cemetery Extension, grave reference II. C. 3A.
17 TNA PRO WO 95/2164: 7/Leics War Diary.

286   To Do the Work of Men

time in the war British divisions were numerically superior to their German counterparts, Byng was still inclined to caution: 50 percent of his infantry "were said to be 'boys', who would do well if the first action in which they took part was a success".[18] These eighteen and nineteen year-olds had had little, if any, training for open warfare, but "their discipline [...] was good [and] they were keen and physically fit".[19]

The official historian, sums up the conditions in August 1918 as "closely resembl[ing] open warfare, continuing thus:

> As the operations progressed, although the ground was seamed with old trenches, the Germans did not occupy continuous lines, and thus there was room for manoeuvre. Their system of defence was to hold the ground by fire, in depth, artillery and machine guns furnishing not only the framework but also the resistance. In these circumstances, the British artillery, except in the attack of localities, could not support the infantry either as closely or as quickly as in trench warfare: information could not be passed back to the guns with telephone rapidity, and the machine gun is a very small target which takes much time and ammunition to hit. [...] In attacks ordered at short notice, as most of them were, it was not always practicable to employ the carefully calculated trench-warfare type of creeping barrage.[20]

Orders for the 21 August offensive were circulated on the 18th. On the left, or northern, wing of the attack frontage, the right wing of Haldane's VI Corps and the left wing of Harper's IV were to make a limited advance of a mile or two in order to capture the villages of Bucquoy and Ablainzeville. Should this preliminary move prove successful, both corps would exploit the success and push on to (and if possible, beyond) the north-south running section of the Albert – Arras railway line. IV Corps would also capture the Serre – Miraumont ridge. V Corps had only a subsidiary role in the assault. It boiled down to two tasks[21]: north of the Ancre, units would advance eastwards in the direction of Miraumont, thus extending IV Corps' right wing. Others would capture the village of Beaucourt, cross the Ancre and push on in a south-easterly direction towards the Pozières Ridge, thus threatening to outflank the German positions on the Thiepval heights. Third Army was about to join Foch's *bataille générale*.

The terrain in the V Corps sector was not ideal country across which to launch an attack. Peter Simkins describes it as follows:

> "The Ancre had been canalised at a higher level than the swampy approaches to the river and, because shelling had damaged the banks, much of the valley was flooded to a width of 300 yards. The main stream was now indistinguishable and the Ancre valley had become a stretch of marsh and water which was covered, in places, by a tangle of fallen trees and branches, reeds, barbed wire and mangled railway track.[...] Bridges and causeways had been largely destroyed by artillery fire while German artillery and machine guns were ranged on the existing crossing-places. Indeed, the Ancre valley resembled a moat

18   Edmonds, *Military Operations France and Belgium 1918 Vol. IV* (London: HMSO, 1947), p.181.
19   Ibid, p.184.
20   Ibid, p.184.
21   See Map 39.

defending the Thiepval heights which loomed above the men of V Corps 'like a great, black hump', scarred with old trench lines".[22]

Tellingly, 21st Division Order No. 205 included the following paragraph:

> Should Battle Patrols meet with serious resistance either on the line of the ANCRE or in their subsequent advance, it is NOT the Divisional Commander's intention to deliver a costly attack on the THIEPVAL RIDGE.[23]

The order divided the operation into three distinct phases (see Map 41): the first, with Zero Hour set at 05.45, was the capture of the village of Beaucourt. This would be the responsibility of 62 Bde. The second was the advance eastwards along the north bank of the Ancre: this too fell to 62 Bde. Thereafter, the third phase would require "Battle Patrols of the 110th Inf. Bde. on the right and the 62nd Inf. Bde. on the left, [to] cross the ANCRE and advance to the BLUE LINE".[24] At this point, units of 114 Bde (38th Division), having crossed the Ancre at the Mill Bridge, (Q24.a.7.4 – see map) would "endeavour to get touch with the right of the 110 Bde"[25] and join in with any subsequent move. After consolidation, at Zero plus 3 hours, the advance would continue to the Red Line. After a further pause of two hours, the creeping barrage would lead the men onto the Green Line and the prospect of pushing patrols "out in the direction of Pozières"[26] might just beckon. The launch of each phase of the attack depended upon the success of the previous one.

The village of Beaucourt would be assaulted by 2/Lincs (62 Bde). On the evening of 20 August, the two 'outpost' companies, B and C, were in positions in squares Q.6.d and Q12.b respectively. A and D Companies were in support. Just 300 yards in front of the Lincolns' positions, the Germans held a series of strong posts, and one particular troublesome machine gun nest in Luminous Avenue (Q.12.b.9.4) was only 150 yards away. At around 21.00 hrs, the Germans launched a "determined but unsuccessful"[27] raid against B Company's left flank: rifle fire and a 'counter patrol' party sent out under Second-Lieutenant Fairmann drove the enemy back. Just after midnight:

> the enemy opened an intensive gas bombardment of the area occupied by the 2 support companies. [...] and considerably interfered with these two companies while they were preparing to move forward. Several severe gas casualties were sustained, but the remainder of the men, although all were suffering from the effects of the gas shelling, remained at duty".[28]

---

22 Simkins, *From the Somme to Victory,* p.167.
23 TNA PRO WO 95/2133: 'Order No. 205', paragraph 8, 21 Div HQ War Diary. Interestingly, this paragraph was repeated verbatim in 110 Bde Order 165, issued 20 August 1918. It did not appear, however, in 62 Bde Order 102, issued the same day, even though the advance south of the Ancre would include two companies of 1/Lincs and two companies of 12/13 NFus.
24 TNA PRO WO 95/2163: 'Order No. 165', 110 Bde War Diary.
25 Ibid.
26 Ibid.
27 TNA PRO WO 95/2154: 2/Lincs War Diary.
28 Ibid. Approximately 100 men were put out of action by the mustard gas bombardment. See Simkins, *From the Somme to Victory,* p.168.

288   To Do the Work of Men

At 02.00 hrs on 21 August the two support companies moved through their comrades' outposts into jumping off positions, ready to spearhead the attack. A Coy "formed up on a line running north-east from LUMINOUS AVENUE with their right on Q.12.b.8.6."[29] D Coy continued this line to the south of the trench. The attack frontage was quite narrow – 100 yards per company with two platoons in the leading wave, and two more in a second wave. Each platoon had a Lewis Gun section on its flank. Between the two companies, in Luminous Avenue, was a bombing party from C Coy.

All were in position by 05.35: a smoke barrage arranged to hide the troop movements was in the end cancelled, as a thick mist hung over the countryside. The forward German machine gun post was however alerted by the sound of the men forming up and opened fire blindly through the fog. A few rounds from a Trench Mortar Battery soon silenced them. Ten minutes later, at Zero Hour, twelve Stokes Guns began to pound the unfortunate German machine gunners, who were forced back into their dug outs. Simultaneously, a hurricane bombardment from 18 pdrs was put down for eight minutes on the ruins of Beaucourt village. As the bombardment began, the Lincolns launched their assault: the C Coy bombing party under Second-Lieutenant Sharpe rushed the German machine gun post, capturing both the gun and eight prisoners, and this allowed A and D Coys to begin their advance unopposed. "So eager were the men that they were able to keep close up to the fast-moving barrage".[30]

Subsequent events might suggest that the German resistance in and around Beaucourt was perhaps less than determined. A Coy was able to move quickly towards Railway Road, hindered only by a single machine gun firing at them from the left flank. A Lewis Gun section despatched in their direction expedited the crew's precipitous withdrawal and A Coy reached the railway where they began to dig in. D Coy's leading platoons made a similarly rapid advance, a party of Germans in Railway Road on the right flank surrendering after being fired upon by the Lincolns' Lewis Gun. The two supporting platoons coming on behind came across a number of Germans emerging from their dug outs. "These were bombed and many taken prisoner".[31] The left leading platoon of D Coy slightly lost direction and ended up at the crossroads in Beaucourt at Q.7.d.3.8, but was able, as it turned out, to form an effective defensive flank there. The fight for the village did not last long: the 62 Bde War Diary reports Beaucourt as having been captured by 06.15, despite a "short delay"[32] whilst dug outs in the village were cleared.[33] The assault cost the battalion only thirty casualties[34] and the Lincolns captured 93 prisoners, three of them officers, of the *68th R.I.R., 16th Div*. By 10 o'clock that morning the mist had lifted and the 2/Lincs men in their new positions along the railway line came under machine gun fire from Logging Support Trench on the slopes south of the river, and during the afternoon had to endure a bout of heavy shelling.

To the north of the Ancre, the 1/Lincs launched the attack in the direction of Baillescourt Farm. They had been in their preliminary assembly positions in Waggon Road since 03.00 hrs that morning and moved to their jumping off positions at Zero minus 50 minutes. At 05.45 the

29   Ibid.
30   Ibid.
31   Ibid.
32   Ibid.
33   The Official History states that Beaucourt was captured by 06.38.
34   The Commonwealth War Graves Commission records confirm seven fatalities on 21 August 1918.

leading companies, B and D, advanced under the creeping barrage. Assembly in the thick mist had not gone entirely to plan and the attack was in the end made on a narrow 200 yard frontage, their left flank on the northern boundary of the bombardment. They reached the sunken road in R.1.b & d without opposition, surprising the few Germans who were there and taking them prisoner. Any further advance was suddenly hampered by German machine gun fire from the high ground straight ahead in square R.2. One of the support companies, C Coy, was sent south along the sunken road, from where it could then attack in a north-easterly direction along the valley spur and then up through the Bois d'Hollande, thus gaining touch with D Coy, who had reached the Yellow Line. Just afterwards, A Coy was sent by the same route to support their comrades, whilst B Coy were withdrawn and placed behind D Coy, on the left flank of the attack. D Coy had managed to gain and keep touch with 42nd Division on their left, but the advance had come to a halt once more as it encountered more heavy German machine gun fire from directly ahead. It was decided that they should call a temporary halt and consolidate their current line. (N – S through R.2 central. See map).

Orders were subsequently received just after midday that two companies of 2/Lincs would be attached to the battalion, and these would pass through and capture the road in R.4.a, an advance of a little over a mile. B and C Coys 2/Lincs turned up as promised and at 14.00 hrs went forward, but only got as far as the sunken road in R.3.c, some 1,000 yards short of their ultimate objective[35]. As they attempted to consolidate their gains, the position was enfiladed "by direct machine gun, rifle and trench mortar fire from GRANDCOURT".[36] Enemy parties also tried to work round the left flank of B Coy, and during the subsequent skirmishes, Lieutenant Walton was killed.[37] The position only stabilised when D Coy of 12/13 NFus came up at around eight o'clock that evening and took up positions on the left flank.

The enemy were, it seemed, determined to recapture the approaches to Miraumont, and counter attacks were launched at 19.30 on 22 August and at 07.30 on the 23rd, but the 62 Bde men stood firm: "A few got within 30 yards of our position in the sunk road and those not killed were dispersed. Over fifty dead were counted next day on the front".[38]

We return now to the action on the banks of the Ancre to the south of Beaucourt. The advance south of the river, with ambitions reaching as far as the Pozières Ridge, was the responsibility of the remaining companies of 12/13 NFus: D Coy was employed forming a defensive flank on the left of the 2/Lincs positions after taking part in the earlier attack alongside 1/Lincs; A Coy relieved two companies of 2/Lincs and took over the defence of Beaucourt; this left B and C Coys earmarked for the crossing of the Ancre.

B and C Coys had advanced via Waggon Lane and Luminous Avenue in the early hours of 21 August and had moved forward to the railway embankment south of Beaucourt once the village had been cleared. Any thoughts of a rapid advance were dispelled as they suffered a number of casualties under very heavy fire from across the river in Logging Support and from the Thiepval Ridge. It was not until 15.30 that the first patrols (B Coy) managed to cross the waterway, struggling through the swampy wastes and pushed forward to within fifty yards of the Blue

---

35   The 1/Lincs War Diary states that the men thought they had reached their final objective.
36   TNA PRO WO 95/2154: 2/Lincs War Diary.
37   Lieutenant George Pears Walton, age 29, 4/NFus, attached 2/Lincs, is buried in Queen's Cemetery, Bucquoy, grave reference IV.B.10.
38   TNA PRO WO 95/2154: 2/Lincs War Diary.

Line. C Coy, on the right flank, also threw men across the marshes, but they were forced back to the railway embankment. A second attempt some hours later managed to reach a trench 100 yards short of the Blue Line. A patrol was subsequently able to work up Little Trench and, out on a limb, established a post in Luff Avenue. Two further platoons were sent forward and a section of Luff Avenue was occupied. They were able to get in touch with B Coy on the left, but their right flank remained in the air. They managed to hold on to their newly-won positions but attempts during the night by other units of 62 Bde "to get liaison"[39] with them came to nothing.

Further downstream, units of 6 and 7/Leics were under orders to cross the Ancre at dawn on 21 August and "establish themselves in COMMON LANE & LOGGING SUPPORT".[40] B and D Coys of 7/Leics crossed the bridge on Mill Road, as they had done six days earlier, covered by a thick ground mist. As before, they were held up by very heavy machine gun fire, and having lost Lieutenant Hackett,[41] were forced to retrace their steps, harried by German artillery fire. Units of 6/Leics fared no better on the 21st, and it was not until the following day that a second foray saw them reach, and maintain, positions in Common Lane, having advanced some 80 yards east of the river.

To the south of 21st Division, the 38th Division initially met with the same problems as they tried to push across the Ancre. It was not until the night of 22/23 August that six sections of the 14/Welch (115 Bde) managed to occupy a trench in Thiepval Wood.

The continuingly cautious Byng, "anxious not to overtax inexperienced troops and wishing to move his guns forward",[42] called a temporary halt to operations for Third Army on 22 August. His plans for a "trifle over-cautious"[43] advance the following day incurred Haig's displeasure, however, and he was forced to revise his ideas and began preparing for a more vigorous attack.

Haig had already arranged for an attack by III Corps, aimed at recapturing the town of Albert and the ridge of high ground to its east between the Somme and the Ancre. At 04.45 on 22 August, the 18th Division made its assault on the town: within five hours, Albert was once more in British hands. To the south, 47th, 12th and 3rd Australian Divisions also made ground, although 47th Div troops were pushed back out of 'Happy Valley' later that evening.

It was late that same evening, the 22 August, that Haig sent a telegram to the commanders of all the British Armies exhorting a redoubling of efforts and announcing a bolder attacking doctrine. It is worth quoting extensively:

> I request that Army Commanders will, without delay, bring to the notice of all subordinate leaders the changed conditions under which operations are now being carried on [...]
>
> The methods which we have followed hitherto, in our battles with limited objectives when the enemy was strong, are no longer suited to his present condition.
>
> The enemy has not the means to deliver counter-attacks on an extended scale, nor has he the numbers to hold a position against the very extended advance which is now being directed upon him.

---

39   TNA PRO WO 95/2153: 62 Bde HQ War Diary.
40   TNA PRO WO 95/2164: 7/Leics War Diary.
41   Lieutenant David Frederick Mackness Hackett MM, age 35, is buried in Mill Road Cemetery, Thiepval, grave reference XI.A.3.
42   Simkins, *From the Somme to Victory*, p. 169.
43   Ibid, p.169.

To turn the present situation to account the most resolute offensive is everywhere desirable. Risks which a month ago would have been criminal to incur, ought now to be incurred as a duty.

It is no longer necessary to advance in regular lines and step by step. On the contrary, each division should be given a distant objective which must be reached independently of its neighbour, and even if one's flank is thereby exposed for the time being.

Reinforcements must be directed against the sectors where our troops are gaining ground, not where they are checked [...]

The situation is most favourable; let each one of us act energetically, and without hesitation push forward to our objective".[44]

This approach may have been desirable, and it could indeed at times be feasible in the situation developing on the Western Front in the autumn of 1918, but it was no universally-applicable panacea: throughout the 'Hundred Days', there were times when a pause, followed by a set-piece assault would prove necessary, even if Haig's new methodology was evident on a small scale – tactical and occasionally operational – within these battles. The hope that positional warfare was a thing of the past remained just that. And as Harris and Barr state:

> Though the Germans did not always withdraw in a completely orderly fashion, they normally managed to cover their retreats with rearguards composed of the most reliable and determined troops. Enfilading machine gun fire delivered by such people was as dangerous as ever. In order to bring the Germans to breaking point without crippling losses to themselves, British forces would have to apply pressure with somewhat greater caution than Haig's message of 22 August suggested.[45]

Machine guns would prove to be an enduring and serious obstacle during the final offensives: despite the ongoing and increasingly serious manpower deficiencies evident in German divisions, which saw rifle strength almost halved in some units, "machine gun firepower declined by less than a quarter".[46]

Byng's plans for 23 August had, as requested, been beefed-up: VI Corps would start the ball rolling by capturing the town of Gomiecourt during the night of 22/23rd, before pushing on to Ervillers and Sapignies. IV Corps would then attack the German positions between Achiet le Grand and Irles. Converging attacks by V Corps and III Corps (Fourth Army) would aim at pinching out the Thiepval Heights, even though Rawlinson was of the opinion that only 18th Division was fit for action on that day.

The outcomes can be briefly described (See Map 39). Preliminary attacks by IV Corps – going in at 02.30 – took Beauregard Dovecot and the ridge north-east of it. Gomiecourt had fallen by 05.00 hrs. VI Corps' main attack was then able to commence at 04.55: the ridge beyond the villages of Boiry Becquerelle, Boyelles and Hamelincourt was captured by 08.00 hrs. Further

---

44 TNA PRO WO 158/241: Haig to the Armies, OAD 911, 22 August 1918.
45 J.P. Harris with Niall Barr, *Amiens to the Armistice. The BEF in the Hundred Days' Campaign, 8 August – 11 November 1918* (London: Brassey's 1998), pp. 146-147.
46 Jonathan Boff, *Winning and Losing on the Western Front: The British Third Army and the Defeat of Germany in 1918* (Cambridge: Cambridge University Press, 2012), pp. 48-49.

advances by 2 Div at 11.00 hrs met with mixed fortune: Ervillers was in British hands by 13.00 hrs, but the twin targets of Behagnies and Sapignies remained out of reach. On IV Corps front, the main assault went in at 11.00 hrs: 37 Div targeted Achiet le Grand and Bihucourt, whilst 5 Div aimed for Irles. All three were captured before nightfall.

On the Third and Fourth Army boundary near Albert, 113 Bde of 38 Div, V Corps, attacked and took Usna Hill, before capturing Crucifix Corner and pushing patrols into Thiepval Wood. On the southern side of the Albert – Bapaume road, Tara Hill fell to 53 Bde, 18 Div. The action was all over by 06.00 hrs. Third Army's total haul on 23 August was 5,000 prisoners.

The grand plan was developing. The next stage demanded a two-prong assault. In the north, 21st and 38th Divisions, with 50 Bde from 17th Division, would attack in a south-easterly direction, taking Thiepval in the flank. Once the high ground and the village of Grandcourt had been secured, they would join up with the southern pincer – 38 and 18 Divs driving north-east – half a mile north-north-east of Ovillers. If successful, the ultimate goal was a line from Contalmaison, through Pozières to a point 1,000 yards south-east of Miraumont.

Miraumont was still in German hands, however. It was therefore deemed vital that the high ground to the south-east of the town, Hill 135, "should be taken as rapidly as possible, in order to forestall any attempt by the garrison of Miraumont to destroy the bridges over the Ancre prior to the attack".[47] This unenviable task was allotted to Campbell's 21st Division.

Time pressure meant that this attack would have to take place that night. The initial orders,[48] issued at 15.15 on 23 August, proposed a two-stage attack (See Map 42). The first stage, designated "A" Attack, would be prosecuted by 64 Bde. Having taken up positions south of the Ancre between Little Trench and Logging Lane, the three battalions would advance under a creeping artillery barrage with their left flank on the river, their first and second objectives being respectively the Brown and Red Lines. The latter position was to be reached by Zero plus 90 minutes. Both positions were to be consolidated – twelve machine guns would accompany 64 Bde to aid in this matter – and patrols pushed out ahead of the Red Line "to cover consolidation".[49] These patrols would be withdrawn by 05.00 to allow a second barrage to be put down 300 yards east of the Red Line, this heralding the start of "B" Attack. This second stage was the responsibility of 110 Bde, which had been relieved in its positions south of the river by 50 Bde, 17 Div, the previous night. They would capture the Blue Line and then "exploit the success towards LE SARS and PYS, with the special object of capturing the high ground (marked GREEN DOTTED on Map 42)".[50]

Progress would be marked by the foremost troops by the use of red flares – for the contact aeroplane of 15 Squadron RAF – and green Very Lights for ground observers. Each officer would carry a map with the objectives marked.

Plans, it is said, rarely survive first contact with the enemy. These didn't survive the afternoon. Reports of German withdrawals prompted Third Army to instigate last-minute changes. At 17.30, Brigadier-General McCulloch, 64 Bde, received a telephone call from his divisional

47   Simkins, *From the Somme to Victory*, p.176.
48   TNA PRO WO 95/2133: 21st Divisional Order No. 210, 23 August 1918, 21 Div HQ War Diary.
49   Ibid.
50   Ibid.

commander: Campbell asked him to report immediately to Divisional HQ in Mailly-Maillet for amended orders.[51]

On arrival McCulloch learned that the entire advance as far as Hill 135 would now be down to 64 Bde, and that they were to attack as soon as possible. 110 Bde were to do no more than advance echeloned to the rear right of McCulloch's men and link up with their right flank and 17th Division's left flank on the Green Dotted Line. McCulloch was less than impressed. In his after-action report he takes up the story:

> I explained that I should prefer to carry out the well-arranged plan for the 1 a.m. attack rather than a hurried and impromptu performance which owing to scattered positions of my units could not commence before 10.30 p.m. at the earliest. I also knew from my own patrols that the Germans were still holding their old Miraumont – Grandcourt – Thiepval Line.
>
> However it was decided that the early attack was to take place, and that I was to advance without troops on my right or left. I did not care much for this idea but I quite realised that others knew the situation in rear of the German outposts better than I did. […] At the first blush it appeared somewhat ambitious".[52]

The Brigadier-General did not relish a three-mile, unsupported advance at night, but his protests were in vain and zero hour was fixed for 23.30 hrs.

Back at Brigade HQ, McCulloch held an impromptu conference with his battalion commanders, impressing upon them "that the situation demanded boldness".[53] It was dark and raining by this time and "conditions did not admit of elaborate written orders".[54] A verbal briefing would have to suffice.

The first objective was now the Red Line, running along the Grandcourt – Courcelette road. A halt would be made there to reorganise and the order for any further advance would be given in person by McCulloch. Dispositions were as follows: 9/KOYLI (Lieutenant-Colonel H. Greenwood DSO MC) – less one company- would be on the right of the attack, with 1/EYorks (Lieutenant-Colonel F.L. du Moulin MC) – also less one company – on the left. The two 'detached' companies, plus one more from 15/DLI and eight Vickers Guns would constitute the reserve, under Major Constantine of 9/KOYLI.[55]

In order to try and maintain some sort of cohesion in the dark, an unusual attack formation was adopted: each battalion would have two companies in front and one behind; each company would form a square with a platoon at each corner, twenty yards between each platoon in both directions. Ten yards in front of the centre of the brigade formation, (ten yards to the left of 9/KOYLI's left front platoon and ten yards to the right of 1/EYorks right front platoon), out on his

---

51 McCulloch's Bde HQ was by this time at the junction of Lot Trench and Luminous Avenue. Captain Spicer, Brigade Major 64 Bde was unimpressed by this location, noting in the brigade diary that it "could hardly be called a commodious dwelling. It consisted of an old deep Bosche Dug-out, which was by no means clean and smelt somewhat foul". TNA PRO WO 95/2160: 64 Bde HQ War Diary.
52 TNA PRO WO 95/2160: 'Report on Night Attack by Brigadier-General Andrew McCulloch', 64 Bde HQ War Diary.
53 Ibid.
54 Ibid.
55 Constantine had joined the battalion on 9 August.

294   To Do the Work of Men

own, was Captain Ennals of 9/KOYLI who, compass in hand, would act as guide. The reserves would advance 100 yards in the rear. Each battalion was to have a party on its exposed flank "ready to rush out and capture any hostile party or Machine gun attacking our flank".[56] Any firing from a substantial distance was, however, to be ignored. Communication with the rear was to be by runner, signal lamp or pigeon.

The ground over which the attack was to take place (see Map 42) sloped down from right to left into the valley of the Ancre. The terrain could best be described as gently 'rolling'. Four shallow valleys ran more or less directly across the line of advance. 'Battery Valley' was the nearest, less than 800 yards on average from the jumping-off lines. A similar distance further on lay the next 'valley'. This was in effect no more than a sunken road, the last half-mile or so of the Thiepval to Grandcourt road. The also slightly sunken Grandcourt to Courcelette road formed the next obvious transverse feature a few hundred yards further on still. The fourth valley, arguably the only one to merit the name, was known to the British as Boom Ravine, and lay approximately a mile and a half from the start line. Reaching the final objective, Hill 135,[57] required a total advance of just over 4,000 yards.

The 64 Bde passed through the line held by 62 Bde troops and assembled just to the rear of Logging Lane. By 22.30, they were formed up, ready for the attack. The artillery barrage commenced at 23.15 and the men set off into the darkness over ground "pitted with craters, gulleys (sic) and small ravines. The advance was in the face of the enemy, but no signs of his presence were obvious at first".[58] Indeed, the first problem encountered was one of friendly fire: as the men approached Battery Valley, some of the heavy artillery failed to lift at 23.45 and five bursts fell on the forward companies of 9/KOYLI. One shell knocked Lieutenant-Colonel Greenwood "violently off his feet",[59] throwing him against a post. He apparently suffered some internal bruising but was able to continue leading his men forward. Thirty men had been injured by this friendly fire: McCulloch later described the mistake as "inexcusable".[60]

One or two machine guns were encountered, but these were quickly dealt with and Battery Valley was reached with a final rush, urged on by McCulloch who gave the word for the charge as they neared this first objective: "Charge, charge! The shout was quickly taken up by everyone, and the battalions vied with each other in the vigour of their shouting, and their rush into Battery Valley".[61] Luckily, the German defenders did not open fire until the 64 Bde men were within fifteen yards of their positions. Once in the valley, the men cleared several dug outs and strong points, capturing one machine gun, a 4.2 gun and thirty prisoners in the process. One unidentified platoon, leaderless by this time, started to fall back, however. McCulloch, in his personal account, describes how they were dealt with:

---

56   TNA PRO WO 95/2160: 'Report on Night Attack by Brigadier-General Andrew McCulloch', 64 Bde HQ War Diary.
57   This is just to the north of the site of Adanac Cemetery.
58   *The Snapper*, Article by Lieutenant Howard: "Story of the 1st Battalion [East Yorks] in the War", Part VII. (KOYLI Association, Pontefract Barracks). p. 59. Lieutenant Howard's sketch of the terrain is reasonably accurate 'topographically', but the slopes of the hills and ravines are far too pronounced.
59   TNA PRO WO 95/2162: 9/KOYLI War Diary.
60   TNA PRO WO 95/2160: 'Report on Night Attack by Brigadier-General Andrew McCulloch' 64 Bde HQ War Diary.
61   *The Snapper*, p. 59.

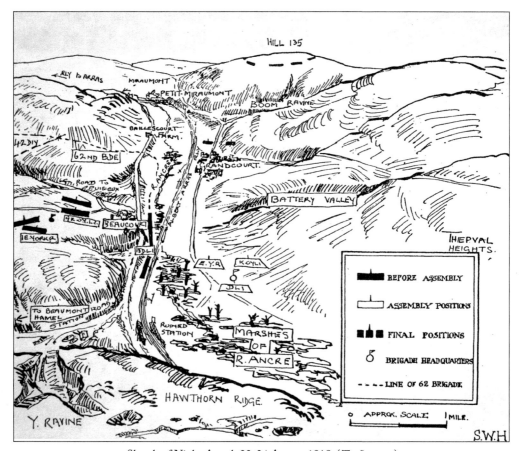

Sketch of Night Attack 23-24 August 1918. (*The Snapper*)

One platoon only, when leaders had been killed or wounded, came back. They were brought to me and reported that they had lost touch and were trying to find the rest of their company. They were somewhat shame-faced when I cursed them for heading away from the enemy and went forward again willingly and rejoined. I do not think that these men were panic-stricken. They simply had faced a blow – had their directing hand removed and were in a sort of invertebrate state with no will to guide them. I mention this because it is in this that the danger of night fighting lies. Directly these men met me and found someone who meant business they responded willingly and went on with their task.[62]

The advance continued, the men "full of confidence",[63] and a number of small strong points were rushed and captured before they arrived at the Red Line at about one o'clock in the morning.

62   TNA PRO WO 95/2160: Report on Night Attack by Brigadier-General Andrew McCulloch, 64 Bde HQ War Diary.
63   Ibid.

The 9/KOYLI dug in about 400 yards ahead of the Red Line and McCulloch ordered a pause to allow for reorganisation. The 1/EYorks, having lost six Other Ranks and one Officer[64] killed by this stage, pushed on into the village of Grandcourt and "mopped up",[65] capturing 100 prisoners and twenty machine guns.

With the brigade's right flank in the air, it was inevitable that hostile fire would come from that direction, and signs of German troops encroaching from the south provoked McCulloch into sending some of the reserve and a number of Vickers guns in their direction with orders to shoot at the muzzle flashes. "This was most successful and silenced the enemy who was evidently puzzled as to what we were doing. I consider these Germans were very poor troops. They evinced no desire to close in with us. […] The prisoners we caught were frightened".[66] Taking into consideration their isolated position and the fact that the 15/DLI were slow coming up – their three companies eventually appeared on the 9/KOYLI's right flank at 02.15 – McCulloch decided to postpone any further advance until 03.15 and sent a report back to divisional HQ to that effect. He did not dare make it any later, as he "wanted to have at least half an hour before daylight on our final objective so as to get defence arranged and digging done in case it was necessary".[67]

The advance resumed at the appointed hour and Boom Ravine was reached in quick time. Although there was some initial resistance, many of the German garrison fled, discarding their weapons as they scrambled out of the steep-sided valley. The men pressed on, and despite encountering machine gun fire from the flanks and from dead ahead, reached Hill 135 at 04.30 hrs. They now had around fifteen minutes of darkness left in which to reorganise and occupy a line of shell holes before they became clear targets for the nearby German defenders. The 15/DLI, having had to fight off a German attack on their right flank as they crossed Boom Ravine, arrived forty-five minutes later and established a short defensive flank to the right of the 9/KOYLI. The 1/EYorks had not managed to reach the line gained by the 9/KOYLI and settled into positions from where they would try to guard the left flank, albeit a thousand yards to the rear.

McCulloch had reached Hill 135 with his men but had then gone a few hundred yards south to see if he could find the 15/DLI. Just as he found them, he was hit in the thigh by a machine gun. His report completes his story:

> As I was bleeding a lot and unable to walk I considered that if I stayed I would be more of a hindrance than a help. I therefore told the Bde. Major that in view of the Germans being aggressive and of the isolated position we were in that a defensive position must be taken up and communication opened with the Division who were to be told that no troops were coming up on our right and left as was promised. The next Senior Officer was to take command.

---

64 Second-Lieutenant Cecil Ullyott, age 27, is buried in Connaught Cemetery, Thiepval, grave reference VIII.F.1.

65 TNA PRO WO 95/2161: 1/EYorks War Diary.

66 TNA PRO WO 95/2160: Report on Night Attack by Brigadier-General Andrew McCulloch, 64 Bde HQ War Diary.

67 Ibid.

I told Lt. Perrott (Gas Officer) to find Lt. Col. de Moulin and tell him to go up to Bde. H.Q. and take command. It then appeared that Lt. Col. de Moulin had been lost with his battalion [1/EYorks] and had stayed on the ridge at Grandcourt.

On my way back (carried by Germans whom I had captured) I met Capt. Somerville 15/D.L.I. who commanded one of the Companies of the reserve. He was unable to say what had held up the reserve. I told him to pass on the order that the reserve was to move up to Bde. H.Q. (in rear of Hill in R.11.b).

I also saw Major Muirhead, D.S.O., Commanding 1st Wilts and told him the situation and that the 64th Bde. wanted support. He agreed to push on and do what he could. I then went and saw the Divl. Commander at Mailly Maillet and explained the situation to him".[68]

In the end, command of the brigade passed to Lieutenant-Colonel Holroyd-Smyth of the Durhams.

In a letter home dated 6 September 1918, Captain L.D. Spicer, Brigade Major, 64 Bde HQ, gave his own slant on McCulloch's wounding:

General McCulloch was wounded by *our* men, I regret to say. It was during a night operation and he would go gallivanting ahead catching Boche prisoners himself, until finally he with Brigade HQ consisting of about 10 men was ahead of everyone. Then when he turned to come back he was (not unnaturally) shot by our own men. Fortunately it is not a serious wound, tho' I am afraid it is rather painful. We now have as our Brigadier one General Edwards, a nice old fellow, whom I think I shall like better as I get to know him. At present tho' I quite like him; his exterior rather frightens me".[69]

Despite its "outstanding success",[70] the brigade's position was precarious. The Germans were gradually working their way around both flanks of the Hill 135 position and were able to pour rifle and machine gun fire onto the isolated garrison. Signallers had tried to set up a lamp station on the hill, but the equipment was immediately smashed by enemy rifle fire. As the position became more critical, a more traditional means of communication came into its own: a pigeon message timed at 07.28 (received at 09.20) reported that they were surrounded. The Germans had filtered back into Battery Valley and Boom Ravine, and casualties were mounting. German counter attacks were repulsed, but there was no immediate respite: from strong positions a "few yards" in front of the 64 Bde line, the Germans "subjected us to very deadly sniping Machine Gun Fire and Bombing. […] [E]very inch of ground was held".[71]

From their adjacent positions, the Germans called upon the 64 Bde men to surrender. It is doubtful that the answer given was polite: suffice it to say that it was definitely in the negative. Captain Spicer, Brigade-Major of 64 Bde, had managed to break out of the Hill 135 positions and had made his way back to Divisional HQ in Mailly Maillet to present his report in person. Aerial reconnaissance had confirmed his report and aeroplanes had dropped messages onto the

68 Ibid.
69 Spicer, *Letters From France 1915-1918*, pp.119-120.
70 Simkins, *From the Somme to Victory*, p.179.
71 TNA PRO WO 95/2162: 9/KOYLI War Diary.

298   To Do the Work of Men

hill promising that help was on its way. Ammunition was also sent by aeroplane, along with a congratulatory message, but neither reached their destination.[72]

By noon, the sun had burnt off the mists in the river valley and the day had turned out hot. British troops could be seen advancing along the heights to the north of the Ancre in the direction of Miraumont. Suddenly, enemy fire ceased. Influenced by the sights to the north and no doubt by the general Allied advance now underway, the Germans (*16th Reserve Division*) retired. Lieutenant Howard of 1/EYorks had been separated from his battalion earlier in the day and had found himself amongst members of 15/DLI on Hill 135. He stood up from his shell hole and saw Lieutenant-Colonel Greenwood walking about. Others began to do the same, and before long the collection and evacuation of the wounded was being organised. In front of their positions, the 64 Bde men counted 130 German dead.

Units of 110 Bde arrived on 64 Bde's right flank at around 14.30. They had originally concentrated in Battery Valley just after midnight, ready to follow up 64 Bde's advance, with 6/Leics on the right, 7/Leics in the centre and 1/Wilts on the left. As 6/Leics approached Battery Valley, they realised that the southern end of it was still occupied by the enemy. Lieutenant-Colonel Martyn (6/Leics) led his men in an assault on these positions and cleared the valley, but the reorganisation required afterwards necessitated a change in brigade formation: 6/Leics would now follow the other two battalions in support. They began their move from Battery Valley at around 05.00 hrs but there was no sign of 17th Division on their right flank. With that flank in the air, machine gun fire from the south bedevilled the whole advance and it stalled just west of Boom Ravine. Brigadier-General Cumming ordered the 1/Wilts to push on, with 7/Leics slightly echeloned on the right with one company sent to the south to protect that flank. In the end, two companies (under Captains H.R. Horne and J.C. Vanner) veered to the right and approached the village of Courcelette. (This was in 17th Division's sector). They entered the village and captured a number of prisoners, including a battalion commander, after overrunning four machine gun posts. Captain Horne received a bar to his Military Cross for his part in this action.

As 110 Bde extended 64 Bde's line to the south along the Green Dotted Line, the 12/13 NFus (62 Bde) were moving forward to do the same to the north. The two Lincoln battalions pushed through the 64 Bde positions later in the afternoon in the direction of Pys and were able to gain touch with 42nd Division to the north. Despite initial delays, 17th and 38th Divisions to the south had also made good their objectives. Thiepval Ridge had fallen. V Corps had also captured La Boisselle, Ovillers and Pozières. Villages fought over for months during the summer of 1916 had all fallen to the British in the space of twenty-four hours.

At 19.00 hrs on 24 August, the 64 Bde was withdrawn into Divisional Reserve positions. The men spent a chilly night in Boom Ravine. Lieutenant Howard's article in *The Snapper* ends thus:

> The 64th Brigade had some cause for self-congratulation, having fought its own bridgehead positions, crossed the Ancre, and on a pitch dark night advanced from 2.5 – 3 miles to their allotted objective over craters and shell hole country and holding that objective in face of determined outflanking enemy until relieved some fifteen hours afterwards".[73]

---

72   TNA PRO WO 95/2160: 'Account of the part taken by the 64th Infantry Brigade in the Operations of August 19th to 27th 1918', 64 Bde HQ War Diary.

73   *The Snapper*, Part VII, p. 61.

McCulloch, by now safe and well to the rear, was still concerned for his men's welfare: "From Hospital in Le Tréport I wired to know how the fight ended and to ask that the ground between St Pierre Divion and Miraumont be searched for my wounded".[74]

Casualties for this audacious attack could be regarded as relatively slight. It is impossible to finalise exact figures, as unit war diaries give numbers for differing periods of time: overall divisional figures were assembled later in the campaign. (See end of chapter). Fatalities for 23/24 August, as given in the Commonwealth War Graves Commission records, are as follows:

64 Bde
9/KOYLI: 23[75]   1/EYorks: 26[76]   15/DLI: 51

110 Bde
6/Leics: 6   7/Leics: 1   1/Wilts: 2

With no fatalities in 62 Bde, this gives a total of 109.

Plans were already in place for 25 August. The Germans were to be given no time to reorganise and settle into new defensive positions. Commencing at 06.00 hrs, the 62 Bde was to pass through the line held by 110 Bde and capture both the village of Sars on the main Albert – Bapaume road and the Butte de Warlencourt just beyond it.

Orders for the advance were received by the three battalions at 03.00 hrs. The ultimate objective was the sunken road running south from the village of Le Barque and known to the British as "Yellow Cut" (See Map 43). The brigade advanced with 1/Lincs on the left, 12/13NFus on the right, 2/Lincs in support, under cover of a heavy mist that did not begin to lift until nearly seven o'clock. The two leading battalions were then held up by heavy machine gun fire short of the summit of the ridge running north-south to the west of Le Sars. Artillery support was accordingly called for and a thirty-minute barrage was arranged, starting at 10.30. By ten o'clock, however, B Coy of 2/Lincs had managed to work around the northern flank of the German positions on the ridge and two Stokes Mortars had directed fire on "the most active M.G.",[77] silencing it. These twin challenges forced the enemy to retire from the ridge, but it was too late to cancel the artillery barrage and the brigade was forced to delay its advance, using the pause to reorganise. German resistance began to evaporate, and at 11.00 hrs the Lincolns and the Northumberland Fusiliers moved forward again, "through Le Sars and advanced without further opposition to their final objective".[78] The 12/13 NFus' Diary records the battalion arriving on the objective at 12.30, having captured one Officer and forty Other Ranks on the Butte de Warlencourt. On arrival at "Yellow Cut", they found the northern section of it already

---

74 TNA PRO WO 95/2160: 64 Bde HQ War Diary.
75 This includes one officer fatality: Second-Lieutenant Frederick Gillard is commemorated on the Vis-en-Artois Memorial.
76 Three officer fatalities, Captain Frederick Cecil Longden, age 30, Lieutenant Hugo Burr Craig Watt MC, age 25, and Second-Lieutenant Charles Walter Bodman, age 28, are all commemorated on the Vis-en-Artois Memorial.
77 TNA PRO WO 95/2154: 1/Lincs War Diary.
78 TNA PRO WO 95/2153: 62 Bde HQ War Diary.

occupied by troops of 63rd Division and so B Coy settled into "Blue Cut", around 500 yards to the rear, whilst C Coy extended 63rd Division's line to the south in "Yellow Cut". The 62 Bde diarist's assertion that the advance had been unopposed is not confirmed by the 12/13 NFus account: they note one Officer killed, with four wounded, and Other Ranks casualties amounting to fifty-five.[79] Likewise, the 2/Lincs, on arriving at "Blue Cut", were obliged to send B Coy up into Le Barque to repel a German counter-attack. Throughout the rest of the day, they "were continually engaged with the enemy in LE BARQUE, but were able to maintain their position",[80] suffering only two fatalities in the process. On the right of the brigade front, 1/Lincs were first into "Yellow Cut" at around 12.30,[81] only to find that 17th Division on their right had been held up, forcing A Coy to form an echeloned defensive flank. So, as evening approached, the 62 Bde units began to consolidate their positions, 1/Lincs on the right, 12/13 NFus in the centre, and one company of 2/Lincs on the left. Plans for 110 Bde to leapfrog and continue the advance had been cancelled: a German counter attack in the direction of Eaucourt l'Abbaye during the afternoon had seen the two Leicestershire battalions rushed forward to support 62 Bde and fill a 1,000 yard wide gap in the line that had opened up opposite that village. They managed to repel the counter attack and they were kept in the line well into the night, as enemy machine gun and artillery fire persisted through the hours of darkness. The action had cost the 7/Leics only three fatalities, their sister battalion the 6/Leics suffering rather more with twelve.[82] The commanding officer of the 6/Leics, Lieutenant-Colonel M.C. Martyn, was taken prisoner sometime during this encounter, but the incident is oddly not mentioned at all in the battalion war diary: Martyn is recorded only as 'missing' at the end of the month,[83] and the details of his capture must remain obscure.

It was important that the momentum of the British attacks of the last few days was not lost. With that in mind, and with Lieutenant-Colonel G.H. Sawyer DSO, 7/Leics, taking temporary command of 64 Bde on the afternoon of 25 August, planning for the next phase of the advance was able to go ahead: the troops of 64 Bde had been able to spend the day resting in the vicinity of Hill 135, but by tea time, orders for their next attack were ready to be issued.

Orders for 26 August involved the First, Third and Fourth armies: the general advance was to continue against a retreating German Army which was preparing to halt and hold the old Hindenburg Line. The overall picture need not be detailed here: suffice it to say, V Corps was to push on eastwards. Narrowing the field of vision even further, 21st Division was to advance towards and occupy the road running north – south between Ligny-Thilloy and Factory Corner (just north of Flers). The road was sunken for most of its length, except at its highest point,

---

79 The Officer killed was Lieutenant John Murphy, age 27. He is buried in Adanac Cemetery, grave reference VI.C.8. Twelve Other Ranks are confirmed killed on 25 August 1918 by Commonwealth War Graves Commission records.

80 TNA PRO WO 95/2154: 2/Lincs War Diary.

81 This timing, and the claim to being first there, is according to the battalion war diarist. The 12/13 NFus diarist gives a similar time of arrival, however, for that battalion.

82 These fatalities included Second-Lieutenant Robert Miles Jalland, age 24, of 6/Leics and Lieutenant George William Crutwell Burrows, age 22, Duke of Cornwall's Light Infantry, attchd 7/Leics. They are buried side by side in Warlencourt British Cemetery, grave references respectively VIII.K.29 and VIII.K.30.

83 Command of the 6/Leics fell to Major J.C. 'Jimmy' Burdett, who remained in post for the rest of the war.

halfway between the two villages and directly in the line of advance, where the terrain was dominated by the German-held strongpoint of Luisenhof Farm (See Map 43).

On the left flank of 21st Division, 38th Division was to clear the Bazentin Woods and advance on Longueval and High Wood. On the right, 17th Division would have the village of Flers as its objective.

No definite Zero Hour had been fixed at Army level, but "it was well understood that an early start should be made".[84] Orders were delayed, however, not being issued at divisional level until between one and two o'clock in the morning. A violent thunderstorm also hampered their delivery to brigades and it was therefore not possible to begin the assault before daylight. The German machine gunners would have clearly visible targets from the outset.

Zero hour was set for 05.30 hrs. The 64 Bde assembled for the attack, its HQ in a dug out in a quarry behind the Butte de Warlencourt, on a front of approximately 1,000 yards, the 15/DLI on the left, 9/KOYLI on the right and 1/EYorks in support 300 yards in rear. The two front battalions were in the 'dead' ground to the west of 'Blue Cut', just under a mile from their objective. With only weak artillery support,[85] which was "not sufficient to keep all the M.G. and rifle fire quiet",[86] the advance did not go well. Both flanking divisions were held up and the 64 Bde, unable to keep up with the creeping barrage, was soon taking machine gun fire not only from the front but from both flanks. "Advancing over the Blue Cut the increasing hail of machine-gun bullets from the enemy broke up the advance, and it soon became a shell hole scramble".[87] The 9/KOYLI managed to cross Yellow Cut, harassed by machine gun fire from low-flying German aircraft, but by 10.00 hrs the advance had faltered. Patrols were sent out along trenches on the flanks and a number of German machine gun posts were located. By this time, the men of 1/EYorks, moving up from support, had "become involved in the front-line fighting",[88] and a few of their number managed to push on to within 100 yards of the objective. They got no further and were rewarded for their efforts by intense enemy machine gun fire from the high ground beyond the farm and from both flanks. On their left, the right-hand company of 9/KOYLI under Major Walsh got to within 300 yards of the sunken road and was able to hold the position for several hours: they too, however, could get no further. On the right flank of the attack, 15/DLI met with a similar fate. Heavy machine gun fire held them up short of their target, and an attempt to push a patrol forward towards the farm and establish a post at M.13.d.00.25 (see map) at around 15.00 hrs signalled the foremost extent of their advance.

By mid-afternoon, it was obvious that the attack had failed, and all three battalions withdrew a short distance and attempted to hold on as best they could. A German counter attack around 16.00 hrs developed and the enemy attempted to establish a post about 500 yards in advance of Luisenhof Farm. Two Stokes Mortars replied and the 1/EYorks managed to overrun the new German position, capturing two machine guns and killing four of the garrison, the rest escaping back in the direction of the farm.

---

84   Edmonds, *Military Operations France and Belgium 1918*, Vol. IV, p.299.

85   Such was the weakness of the artillery support, the 1/EYorks diarist insisted that the attack was made "without barrage" See TNA PRO WO 95/2161: 1/EYorks War Diary.

86   TNA PRO WO 95/2160: 64 Bde HQ War Diary.

87   *The Snapper*, p.61.

88   TNA PRO WO 95/2161: 1/EYorks War Diary.

302   To Do the Work of Men

As far as HQ was concerned, the position was rather hazy: no runners had managed to get back over the open ground and observers on the Butte de Warlencourt had reported a lull in the fighting. Discretion won the day, and it was decided that a withdrawal was required, but that this could not take place until nightfall. Orders finally reached the front line at around nine o'clock that evening: the 1/EYorks moved back into trenches just to the south-east of the Butte and the two other battalions took up positions in or near to the Yellow Cut. Heavy losses meant that the 9/KOYLI had to be reorganised into one composite company, but even so a line of posts was established 300 yards in front of Yellow Cut. Owing to a wound and sickness, Lieutenant-Colonel Greenwood made his way back to the nearest Dressing Station, having handed over command of his battalion to Major Walsh. An uncomfortable night was spent under intermittent enemy fire. Lieutenant Howard later wrote that:

> The only tangible result of our day's operations was to prove that the German resistance was thickening, and that it was getting increasingly necessary to have artillery preparation and assistance for further advances of any distance or importance.[89]

Despite the 9/KOYLI later managing to get a patrol forward into the sunken road objective, it was decided that as the village of Ligny-Thilloy had not fallen to the 63rd Division, any further attempts to get forward should be put on hold. A planned "leapfrogging" by 110 Bde onto the high ground east of Luisenhof Farm was therefore wisely abandoned. By the evening of 27 August, relief was on its way: 64 Bde was able to move back through 62 Bde – by then established in Yellow Cut – into Divisional Reserve. On the 28th, 62 Bde also moved back, leaving 110 Bde in Yellow Cut.

On 29 August, 110 Bde, thanks in part to a successful attack by 38th Division the previous evening in the direction of Ginchy, which had triggered an enemy withdrawal, was able to advance on Luisenhof Farm unopposed, and then beyond it to positions just to the west of Beaulencourt. Patrols sent forward by 7/Leics quickly established that this village was strongly held: it was shelled heavily by British artillery for lengthy periods during the next two days and nights, but further patrols were still "unable to approach nearer than 300 yds of the village".[90] At 10 o'clock in the morning of 31 August, orders were received from 21st Division HQ that 110 Bde should "be prepared to attack Beaulencourt at short notice".[91] It was deemed important that the tempo of the British attacks be maintained, giving the Germans little time to rest, recuperate or reorganise: keeping the enemy off-balance was essential. Beaulencourt would be no push over, however.

Casualty figures for this period demonstrate that the successful advances of the Hundred Days' offensives were bought at consistently heavy cost for the British Army. The A & Q section of 21st Division HQ compiled a complete list for August 1918:

89   *The Snapper*, p. 63.
90   TNA PRO WO 95/2163: 110 Bde HQ War Diary.
91   Ibid.

The figures for the component infantry brigades are as follows:

Unit	Killed		Wounded		Missing		Total	
	Off	OR	Off	OR	Off	OR	Off	OR
62 Bde								
12/13 NFus	2	44	15	278	–	21	17	343
1/Lincs	3	39	10	208	–	17	13	264
2/Lincs	1	31	5	133	–	7	6	171
62 TM Batt.	–	1	–	17	–	–	–	18
Total:	**6**	**115**	**30**	**636**	**–**	**45**	**36**	**796**
64 Bde								
1/EYorks	7	54	12	193	4	205	23	452
9/KOYLI	6	42	18	270	–	39	24	351
15/DLI	9	74	15	344	1	112	25	530
64 TM Batt.	–	–	1	2	–	–	1	2
Total:	**22**	**170**	**47**	**809**	**5**	**356**	**73**	**1,335**
110 Bde								
6/Leics	2	21	5	170	1	9	8	200
7/Leics	2	16	12	218	1	32	15	266
1/Wilts	2	17	10	154	–	6	12	177
110 TM Batt.	2	3	–	11	–	–	2	14
Total:	**8**	**57**	**27**	**553**	**2**	**47**	**37**	**657**
Overall Total:	**41**	**342**	**104**	**1,998**	**7**	**448**	**146**	**2,788**

When the Artillery, Engineers, R.A.M.C., ASC, AVC[92], Army Chaplains and 64 Bde HQ casualties are added, the total climbs to 167 Officers and 2,992 Other Ranks.

92 33rd Mobile Veterinary Section.

9

Playing Leapfrog

Things were beginning to move rather quickly. Although the fighting on the Western Front in the autumn of 1918 never quite matched the 'war of movement' seen during the initial German attacks of 1914, and the chimera of breakthrough remained only in the imagination of High Command, the Allied operations of this period can be characterised by the increased tempo of attacks all across the front, this designed to give the German Army no respite as it was pushed back relentlessly across the terrain that it had won at such heavy cost during the preceding spring. Efficient BEF staff work meant that attacks could be organised and executed within days or even hours of their inception, and a loosening of the reins allowed for decision-making and improvisation by commanders 'on the spot'. Not all of these attacks succeeded, of course. Allied over-confidence – attacking without adequate artillery support, for example – and grim defiance by German units could combine to give the British an occasional bloody nose, and when geography gifted the Germans a strong defensive position, such as along the waterways that traversed the line of advance, it became necessary for the Allies to pause and then revert to the tactic of the 'set-piece attack'.

Both sides were fighting the final encounters of the war with dwindling numbers of infantry, but this style of "mobile attrition"[1] inevitably cost the Allies dear. German rifle strength may have been approaching fifty percent by the end of the conflict, but as mentioned in the previous chapter, German machine guns remained a potent weapon. British unit war diaries testify regularly to both the efficacy and the abundance of German machine guns. Platoon tactics had, however, developed: the re-organisation of the structure of the platoon to include rifle grenade and Lewis Gun sections produced an integrated combined-arms unit capable of fire and manoeuvre tactics supported by its own increased fire-power capabilities. The cards were no longer heavily stacked in favour of the defender.

The series of assaults undertaken by 21st Division during September 1918 reflect perfectly the situation outlined above: small unit assaults, quickly organised and launched, met with varying degrees of success or failure; two larger 'set-piece' attacks did likewise. Nevertheless, the overall picture was one of relentless eastward advances: a decisive victory in 1918 was perhaps possible.

The German defenders of Beaulencourt had, during the last few days of August, endured heavy allied artillery fire and successfully thwarted attempts by infantry patrols to penetrate

---

1   Boff, *Winning and Losing on the Western Front*, p. 37.

the outskirts of the village. Final orders for its capture were issued to 110 Bde at 21.00 on 31 August.[2] The attack was to go in at 02.30 the following morning, only five and a half hours later. The idea of a daylight frontal attack had been considered, but perhaps wisely shelved: Brigadier-General Cumming outlines the reasons:

> A daylight operation would have necessitated a frontal attack, but a night attack which allowed a certain amount of manoeuvring could take the position from the flank. The approaches to Beaulencourt from the front presented a glacis-like slope with no cover, which would have made a frontal attack very risky and costly. A night attack from the North however presented less difficulties and would introduce the element of surprise. Moreover the necessary movements could be made under cover of darkness".[3]

Tactical methods had changed significantly from those employed earlier in the war. The 110 Brigade Intelligence Officer sums up the thinking:

> … it was a small masterpiece achieved with one tenth the casualties it would assuredly have cost us in 1916. The long, western front of the village, which appeared the main line of approach, was defended by numerous well-concealed pits for riflemen and machine guns, and had we been attacking in the 1916 method the course of events would probably have been as follows. A tremendous artillery bombardment, perhaps for two days, would have annihilated the village and churned up the ground, and at zero hour our troops would have advanced in waves across the belt of land commanded by the various posts, who, as our barrage passed on behind them, would have opened a murderous direct fire on them and taken an enormous toll in casualties. Very possibly we should never have reached the village but consolidated a line of shell holes a few hundred yards beyond the starting point, from which a fresh attack would have been delivered perhaps several days later.[4]

Whilst 7/Leics held the trenches to the west of the village, 1/Wilts and 6/Leics would perform the flanking attack from the north. The 6/Leics would be on the left, with their left flank on the Bapaume Road and 1/Wilts on the right. The jumping off line was some 1,600 yards north – north – west of the crossroads in the village.[5] Their advance would be preceded by an artillery and machine gun barrage. At seven o'clock in the evening on 31 August, 110 Bde also received a telephone call from Division ordering a supplementary attack on the Sugar Factory to the north of Le Transloy: this task fell to one company of 7/Leics which would go in at 05.30 in support of an assault on the village itself by 17th Division. At the time, the village of Riencourt, to the north, was held by 42nd Division, but Beaulencourt, Le Transloy and the road linking them were still strongly held by the enemy.

---

2   The original orders to prepare for the scheme were sent from Division at ten o'clock that morning.
3   Cumming *A Brigadier in France 1917-1918*, p. 225.
4   Quoted in Jonathan Boff *Winning and Losing on the Western Front*, p.123.
5   See Map 44. This map provides an overview of movements and attacks during the month of September 1918.

306   To Do the Work of Men

The Beaulencourt assault is described only in the briefest of terms by the 6/Leics diarist,[6] so the following account relies largely on an after-action report from 1/Wilts.At 02.00 hrs, with both battalions already in place, a standing barrage was put down on an east-west line to the north of Beaulencourt, where it remained for twenty minutes. Meanwhile, heavy artillery pounded the village itself and the high ground to the east of it. At 02.30, both the infantry and the creeping barrage set off for the village.

The *208th Reserve Infantry Regiment (RIR)* had relieved units of *205th RIR* in and around Beaulencourt during the night of 31 August – 1 September and had taken up positions mainly to the west of the village.[7] Three companies were in a forward outpost line 500 yards west of Beaulencourt: the strongest company, numbering around 80 men,[8] was holding a line of about 400 yards in length. The main line of resistance was between Beaulencourt and Villers-au-Flos, but this was not a proper trench line – the men were in the open. Another outpost line was in place to the south of the village and one company was defending the Sugar Factory further to the south. It became clear from prisoners' statements that "the direction of [the] attack was a surprise".[9]

The 1/Wilts advanced with two companies in the first line (A & B), with the other two following in support. The main resistance encountered came from enemy machine gun fire: the Germans were later reported to have had around thirty in the village. They pressed on regardless and, making good use of Lewis guns and Trench Mortars,[10] were able to push on through the village: by 05.30 it was all over, Beaulencourt was in British hands. A Coy consolidated a trench line 200 yards to the south of the village, and D Coy moved up into support positions on the right, B Coy performing the same task on the left. C Coy 'mopped up' the village. The right flank was also protected by a section of Vickers Machine Guns from 21st Machine Gun Battalion. The Germans attempted a counter attack under a smoke barrage at around 06.30, but it was a weak affair and quickly and easily repulsed. Three German Officers, (all company commanders),[11] and 130 Other Ranks were captured, along with two 77mm guns,[12] two *Minenwerfer*, 30 machine guns and five anti-tank rifles. Also taken intact was a Field Hospital with 101 beds, 500 blankets and 176 stretchers.[13] According to the three German company commanders, their orders had been to hold the position to the end, there being no question of withdrawal. Weak in numbers they may have been, but morale remained reasonably solid:

> The examination of some 30 prisoners, including 3 Coy Commanders, left the impression that whilst a certain depression existed, there was a strong element not only trusting in

---

6   "Attack successful". See TNA PRO WO 95/2164: 6/Leics War Diary.
7   Details of German dispositions are taken from a report on the examination of prisoners captured at Beaulencourt on the morning of 1 September 1918. TNA PRO WO 95/2134: 21st Div HQ War Diary.
8   The weakest company was said to have only 13 men.
9   TNA PRO WO 95/2134: 21st Div HQ War Diary
10   Cumming, *A Brigadier in France 1917- 1918*, p. 226.
11   Commanders of the 4th, 9th and 11th coys, *208th RIR*.
12   Both damaged in the British artillery barrage.
13   TNA PRO WO 95/2163: 110 Bde HQ War Diary. This account puts the number of anti-tank guns captured at nine, and of *Minenwerfer* at four. It can be assumed that the extra numbers were captured by the 6/Leics.

their Higher Command, but holding also a belief in the possibility of final victory for the German Army or at worst a satisfactory Peace by Agreement.[14]

The attack on the Sugar Factory, due to commence at 05.30, never materialised. Initial reports to 21st Division HQ said that the attack had been held back by machine gun fire, but the reality was that the units of 7/Leics, with little or no time to reconnoitre the position, failed to reach the forming up line in time.[15]

Casualties suffered in the capture of Beaulencourt could be assessed as slight: the 6/Leics do not record any figures in the war diary, and only one fatality occurred: 235499 Private Percy Thorpe, age 27, is commemorated on the Vis-en-Artois Memorial; 1/Wilts reported eighteen fatalities, including one officer,[16] and forty-two wounded.

Pausing for breath at this point was not an option. Whilst the captors of Beaulencourt remained in place, other units moved through them to continue the advance. At 20.15, 110 Bde received the order for 7/Leics to make a second attempt at capturing the Sugar Factory, this time using three companies. Zero hour was set for 02.00 hrs, 2 September. Meanwhile, 64 Bde was tasked with the capture of Lubda Copse near the Villers-au-Flos to Le Transloy road. This attack would commence at 05.15 hrs and would be executed by 1/EYorks, with 9/KOYLI in reserve just in case. On the left flank of 21st Division, 42nd Division would be attacking the village of Villers-au-Fos, and on the right, 17th Division were to make another attempt to capture Le Transloy, this time using an encircling attack from both north and south.

The men of 7/Leics were on their forming up line in good time this time: again, to catch the defenders off guard, the assault would be made from the north, astride the Bapaume to Le Transloy road. A & D Coys lead the assault, and by 05.30 the Sugar Factory was in British hands. The Germans were determined not to surrender the position that easily, however, and after heavily shelling the factory, they launched a determined counter-attack. By 10.00 hrs, it was back in German hands and the Leicesters had been forced back to the line of their original assembly positions. An hour and a half later, the Leicesters attacked again and re-captured the factory. This time, with 17th Division troops now moving through to the south, there was no chance of a second German counter attack: the Leicester men pushed on towards the high ground near Lubda Copse. They had taken around forty prisoners and captured three machine guns. This see-saw battle had cost the 7/Leics just six fatalities. Second-Lieutenant George Waite Beesley was awarded the Military Cross for his actions:

> For conspicuous gallantry and devotion to duty. During an attack on a sugar factory he skilfully organised and controlled mopping-up parties. When he saw some of the enemy making for some trench mortars, which were out in front of the line, he dashed out and drove them back single-handed. He showed marked ability and leadership.[17]

14 TNA PRO WO 95/2134: 'Report on Examination of Prisoners', 21 Div HQ War Diary.
15 The 17th Division (52 Bde) attack on Le Transloy faltered in the face of machine gun fire from the unmolested Sugar Factory. Further attacks were postponed until the following day.
16 Second-Lieutenant Arthur Wilfred Healey, age 19, is buried in Beaulencourt British Cemetery, Ligny–Thilloy, grave reference IV.G.10.
17 *London Gazette*, 11 January 1919, Ref: LG:31119.

308   To Do the Work of Men

North of the sugar factory, the 1/EYorks set off towards Lubda Copse at about 05.00 hrs. Almost immediately, they were subjected to heavy enfilade machine gun fire from the direction of the factory, which was still in German hands, and the right-hand company was unable to get forward. Lieutenant-Colonel du Moulin went across to assess the situation himself, and by the time he arrived, the enfilade fire had ceased. Erring on the side of caution, he formed the right-hand company into a defensive flank position, facing south-east, and the rest of the battalion pushed on. The objective was reached at around 11.30, the copse cleared, and fifty prisoners, including two officers, taken. This small wooded area had been a costly prize, however: the 1/EYorks had suffered eighty casualties, eleven killed, thirty-one wounded and thirty-eight missing.[18]

The attacks to the north and south of 21st Division had also been successful. Units of 42nd Division had captured Villers-au-Flos and then pushed on some 700 yards beyond it. Le Transloy had fallen to 17th Division after the Germans abandoned it around midday. Troops of 52 Bde were soon on the ridge about a mile to the south-east of the town and at 17.00 hrs, 50 Bde leapfrogged their compatriots and by 22.00 hrs were in possession of the village of Rocquigny, their men ensconced in a trench line just beyond it. On 3 September, Barastre fell and with the advances of the 42nd and 17th Divisions, the narrowing of the front effectively squeezed out the 21st Division. By the evening of 3 September, all three brigades were in Corps Reserve: Divisional HQ had moved back to Le Sars, 62 Bde was in Les Boeufs, 64 Bde in Le Barque and 110 Bde in Beaulencourt. The 7/Leics diarist was able to boast of a "piano captured & in use".[19] Brigadier Cumming welcomed the badly needed rest:

> It was wonderful what these short periods of rest did for the men. After constant fighting, moving with little rest or sleep and with periods during which the tactical situation did not admit of proper food being taken, the men at times were strained to the limit of human endurance. Fatigue became almost a pain: yet one day's complete rest with good hot food and a comprehensive wash, worked wonders. Of course the moral effect of advancing and hammering the Boche was a great asset in keeping the men going and added to their ardour. Their tails were right over their heads; fatigue and hardship no longer counted.[20]

Farther north, the Germans had been dealt a severe hammer blow. The Canadian Corps had broken through the Drocourt-Quéant Line, sending shock-waves back to OHL.[21]

> The breaking of the D-Q Position had immediate effect: O.H.L. recognized defeat. About midday they issued orders for retirement behind the Sensée [River] and the Canal du Nord and, further south, to the Hindenburg Position, beginning that very night. [...] In the retirement, the *Seventeenth Army* on the right, holding from near Combles (Fourth Army area) to the D-Q Position, was to move first on the night of the 2nd/3rd September, and the *Second* south of it, on the night of 3rd/4th. The *Eighteenth* and the *Ninth*, farther south

---

18   This is according to the battalion war diary. Commonwealth War Graves Commission records confirm thirteen fatalities that day.
19   TNA PRO WO 95/2164: 7/Leics War Diary.
20   Cumming, *A Brigadier in France 1917- 1918*, pp. 228-229..
21   *Oberste Heeresleitung*: German High Command.

again, were to follow in succession. [...] The whole great salient won in March 1918 was to be abandoned".[22]

Sir Douglas Haig once more succumbed to optimism:

Advance is continuing to the Canal du Nord. I expect that the results of our success in yesterday's great battle should be very far reaching".[23]

The period of bathing, refitting, training and musketry practice was not to endure for too long. From 5 September, a series of reliefs saw the 21st Division units move forward:[24] 62 Bde were in the line near Etricourt and Manancourt by the evening, and the following day 64 Bde crossed the Canal du Nord to take up positions on its eastern bank. With no sign of the retreating Germans, 62 Bde was able to leapfrog onto a line running through the villages of Sorel and Fins by nightfall. Only on the next day, the 7th, did they bump into the German rearguards: the 2/Lincs, advancing on Heudecourt, were held up by machine gun fire from positions south of the village. The next objective would have to be taken by force.

The next move, on the morning of 8 September could probably be best described as tentative: the extent of the advance depended upon the success or otherwise of units of 58th Division which were attacking Peizière-Epéhy to the south. The task fell to 62 Bde : in their left sector, 1/Lincs would capture Revelon Farm, the Genin Well Copses and Lowland Support; on the right, 2/Lincs with two companies of 12/13 NFus attached, would look to take the "Yellow Line", the double trench system running south from Chapel Hill (see Map 45), but only if no more than slight opposition was met on the Spur in square W.23. No attempt to push on to the Vaucelette Farm – Peizerat ridge was to be contemplated until Chapel Hill had been secured.

A & B Coys of 12/13 NFus had occupied their jumping off trenches by 05.00 hrs, and A & B Coys 2/Lincs were directly behind them in support.[25] They moved off at 07.30 as the artillery barrage commenced and in spite of machine gun fire from the direction of Chapel Hill, and some from directly ahead, the two companies quickly reached their objectives: A Coy occupied the trenches south of the railway in square W.24.c, B Coy doing likewise to the north. As troops of 2/Lincs began to consolidate the captured positions, – two Lewis Gun teams had been sent forward to establish posts in the Yellow Line system – A Coy 12/13 NFus pushed patrols out eastwards along the railway in an attempt to gain touch with 58th Division troops on the right, but this endeavour failed and the men were forced back by enfilade machine gun fire from the south.

To the north, 1/Lincs met with some success and were able to capture Revelon Farm and the adjoining Genin Well Copse No.1 and pushed patrols on into Lowland Support. By noon, the patrols had retired and the men began to consolidate their positions in the farm and the copse.

To the south, 58th Division "could not get within a thousand yards of Epéhy".[26]

---

22 Edmonds, *Military Operations France and Belgium 1918*, Vol. IV, p.413.
23 Sheffield & Bourne (eds.), *Douglas Haig*, pp. 455-456.
24 See Map 44.
25 C and D Coys 12/13 NFus had moved into support positions further to the north behind 1/Lincs.
26 Edmonds, *Military Operations France and Belgium 1918*, Vol. IV, p.453.

310   To Do the Work of Men

The 21st Division casualties had not been heavy: 1/Lincs had suffered no fatalities; their sister battalion lost five men killed; the 12/13 NFus had taken the brunt, losing twenty-two men, including one officer.[27]

The Germans were clearly intending to make a determined stand on the Gouzeaucourt – Chapel Hill – Vaucelette Farm – Peizière Ridge: strong patrols and piecemeal attacks would not be enough to dislodge them, but before a full assault could be undertaken, the Lowland Trench system, from where German defenders could easily enfilade any attack on the ridge, needed to be taken.[28] Orders for its capture[29] were issued to 64 Bde units on 8 September. Zero Hour was 04.00 hrs the following morning.

Two battalions would launch the attack: on the left, 9/KOYLI would take Lowland Ridge; on the right, 15/DLI was to assault Chapel Hill. The former's jumping off line was just to the east of Genin Well Copse No.1. The latter's depended upon whether Copse No.2 was in German hands or not. Ideally,

Captain William Stanhope Hutchinson MC & Bar, "B" Coy, 12/13NFus, kia 8 Sept 1918, age 22. Served in Gallipoli in 6/Leics. (*The Sphere*, 19 October 1918)

15/DLI would form up along the eastern edge of the copse, but Brigade HQ was ignorant of the true situation: the Germans were still occupying Genin Well Copse No.2.

Creeping artillery barrages would fall at Zero along the northern half of Cavalry Support (Barrage A) and along Lowland Support (Barrage B). At Zero plus fifteen minutes, they would begin to creep forward at a rate of 100 yards every four minutes until Barrage A reached Cavalry Trench and Barrage B reached an east-west line through W.11.c central. Sixteen machine guns would target Vaucelette Farm and the southern section of Cavalry Support.

9/KOYLI moved forward from Equancourt at around midnight and marched to their assembly positions via Fins and Heudecourt. With B and D Coys in the front line and C Coy in support, they awaited the start of the artillery barrage. On their left, 52 Bde (17th Div.) and 3 New Zealand Rifle Bde (NZ Div.) were ready to attack Gouzeaucourt Wood.

The attack went in on time, but "some gas shelling, which affected the eyes, made it difficult to keep direction in the darkness; but in the early stages, this darkness prevented the enemy's machine gun fire from being very effective, and good progress was achieved".[30]

27   Captain William Stanhope Hutchinson MC & Bar, age 22, is buried in Varennes Military Cemetery, grave reference IV.A.70.
28   This trench system can be seen on Map 45, in squares W.11, 12, 17, 18.
29   TNA PRO WO 95/2160: 'Operation Order No. 206', 8 September 1918, 64 Bde HQ War Diary.
30   Edmonds, *Military Operations France and Belgium 1918*, Vol. IV, p.454.

Lowland Support Trench was quickly occupied and the battalion paused to reorganise before pressing on to its second objective. This time, opposition was much more determined, and the men met with heavy machine gun fire, trench mortars and grenades. Lowland Trench was reached, however, and after some vicious hand-to-hand fighting, taken and held.

The 15/DLI had begun their move forward at 00.30 hrs.

> The battalion moved up to assembly position. Eastern edge of GENIN WELL COPSE No. 2 had been selected for the assembly position as the copse had been reported clear of the enemy, but as the leading Coys arrived immediately West of the Copse they came under heavy M.G. fire from the Western edge. Orders were then issued for Coys to assemble West of the Copse.[31]

These machine guns were quickly overrun as the attack began and the Durhams, with C & D Coys leading and A Coy in support, were soon approaching their first objective. Heavy machine gun fire from Cavalry Support did not delay its capture, however, but fire from Cavalry Trench prevented any immediate continuation of the advance.

In the meantime, the 9/KOYLI CO,[32] with both flanks in the air and facing the very real threat of enveloping counter attacks, decided that it would be wise to withdraw to the first objective, Lowland Support. Consolidation of this position went ahead, although outposts were pushed out into the communication trenches in the direction of the recently abandoned line.

Orders for the renewal of the attacks were sent out, and both battalions went forward once more at 17.00 hrs. The KOYLIs were able to reach their final objective for the second time that day, but at heavy cost: the Germans had managed to work around the Yorkshiremen's left flank and with the threat of isolation once more evident, Walsh again chose discretion over valour and ordered a second and frustrating withdrawal to Lowland Support. Indeed, the situation was deemed precarious enough for a company (C Coy) of 1/EYorks to be moved up in support just in case.[33]

The 15/DLI diarist recorded the second advance as going in at 17.30 hrs and Cavalry Trench captured soon after. An immediate German counter attack from the direction of Chapel Crossing was repelled, but a second pushed the Durhams back again and by 19.00 hrs they were back in Cavalry Support and early the following morning were successfully seeing off a third counter attack as around thirty of the enemy made one more attempt to enter their positions.

The remainder of 1/EYorks had been idle up to this point, but it was decided that one more push might prove successful. Three companies were accordingly sent forward to positions in Lowland Support and Cavalry Support – D Coy on the left, C Coy in the centre and B Coy on the right – ready to attack at 04.00 hrs. Heavy rain during the night made it difficult for these units to reach their assembly positions in time, however, and zero hour was altered to 05.15.

Hastily organised attacks and late alterations to timings combined with difficult weather conditions rarely augur well, and this occasion was no exception. The men arrived late, wet,

---

31 TNA PRO WO 95/2161: 15/DLI War Diary.
32 This was Major Walsh. Lieutenant-Colonel Greenwood was in hospital recovering from his recent wounds.
33 B Coy was later sent up to support 15/DLI.

312   To Do the Work of Men

miserable, and took up positions too far to the left. They set off in a northerly direction instead of moving to the north-east as planned and soon lost the barrage.

> The enemy had apparently anticipated a further attack on his position and was fully prepared to meet it. The right coy met with very heavy M.G. fire from its right flank and as they had lost the barrage had to withdraw. From further verbal reports it appears that the left coy went too much to its left and the enemy counter attacked and apparently captured abt 20 of them.[34]

The three assault companies were soon back in the assembly trenches, interspersed between units of the KOYLI and Durham battalions. By midday, arrangements had been made for the withdrawal of the 1/EYorks men. This shambles of an attack had cost them dear: the war diary reports one Officer and five Other Ranks killed, two Officers and thirty-six Other Ranks wounded, but tellingly four Officers and 138 Other Ranks missing. Later records confirm fifty-one fatalities for that day.[35]

The 9/KOYLI had suffered twenty-five fatalities, including three Officers.[36] Over the two days, the 15/DLI lost forty-four men killed, including two Officers[37]. The war diary also lists 221 wounded and missing. The remnants of 64 Bde were relieved by 110 Bde units during the night of 10/11 September "without incident",[38] and the three battalions were able to begin a spell of rest, reorganisation and training in the trench systems around the village of Equancourt. 62 Bde was also taken out of the line and was occupied in like manner in and around Manancourt and Etricourt.

It was the turn of 110 Bde to take up the baton and continue, at least initially, the small-scale attacks across terrain that they had defended so stubbornly only six months before. Commanders were determined to maintain the tempo of the attacks: this, on the one hand, gave the German defenders no respite, but on the other meant that there was no time for careful and considered preparation, and the fluidity of the situation meant that attacks were often cancelled at short notice. Equally, German counter attacks were numerous, if often not particularly strongly executed. A confused and obscure picture when viewed from brigade or even divisional level can be understood, however, if the wider perspective is appreciated. GHQ had the strategic overview in mind: the Allied forces were approaching the formidable defensive system of the Hindenburg Line. It was vital that advantageous jumping off positions were reached and that a pause for rest, the introduction of new drafts into the badly depleted infantry formations, for the moving up of supplies and artillery, and for repairs to road and rail supply routes was incorporated into the strategic thinking. Orders were therefore issued stating that "no deliberate operation on a large scale will be undertaken at present, […] with a view to the resumption of

---

34   TNA PRO WO 95/2161: 1/EYorks War Diary.
35   The officer was Captain Charles Edward Wright Spragg, age 25, BA and Senior Scholar of Trinity College, Cambridge. He is buried in Gouzeaucourt New British Cemetery, grave reference III.D.5.
36   Second-Lieutenants Henry Cooil, age 29, Percy Green, 24, and John Giles Overman, 21, are all buried in Gouzeaucourt New British Cemetery, grave references respectively I.H.11, I.A.10 & I.H.8.
37   Second-Lieutenant Edwin John Brinkworth, age 27, is buried in Rocquigny-Equancourt Road British Cemetery, Manancourt, grave reference XIII.C.13. Second-Lieutenant George Seatter is commemorated on the Vis-en-Artois Memorial.
38   TNA PRO WO 95/2160: 64 Bde HQ War Diary.

a vigorous offensive in the near future in conjunction with an operation to be carried out on a large scale by our allies".[39] "An operational pause followed", states Jonathan Boff.[40] The necessary jumping off positions had not yet been secured, however, and for some formations there was to be no let up just yet.

It was important for the British to be in full control of the "Yellow Line" trench system running southwards from Chapel Hill if they were going to be able to launch a planned substantial attack on 18 September in support of a wider assault on the approaches to the Hindenburg Line. With this in mind, 7/Leics were ordered to attack these trenches early on the morning of 11 September. The 1/Wilts had meanwhile taken over Lowland Support to the north. The Leicesters' attack was on a relatively wide frontage, from Chapel Hill to a point almost a mile to the south (W.23.d.8.0 – junction with 58th Division, see Map 45). It was completely successful, with 50 prisoners and 6 machine guns captured, although a stubborn pocket of German troops on the slopes of Chapel Hill prevented touch from being gained with the 1/Wilts. This enterprise had cost the battalion sixteen fatalities, including four NCOs and one Officer.[41] A further thirty-five men were wounded. Touch was eventually gained with the 1/Wilts when 6/Leics relieved their sister battalion the following day.

At around 09.20 on 13 September, a German deserter arrived at 110 Bde HQ. He announced that a *Flammenwerfer* attack was to be launched on Chapel Hill from Cavalry Support at 10 o'clock that morning. Messages were rapidly despatched to appropriate units and artillery retaliation was requested. The deserter had told only half the story. A German artillery barrage came down on 1/Wilts positions at 09.45 and attacks from both south *and north* ensued. The battalion war diarist takes up the tale:

> Enemy opened a heavy barrage on and behind our line and attacked under cover of flame projectors. The attacked (sic) consisted of two strong parties, the Northern Party worked down reserve switch and attacked 'D' Company at the junction between 'D' Company and the Division on our left.[42] The Southern Party worked along Cavalry Support and attacked 'C' Company at the junction between 'C' Company and Battalion on our right. The two left posts of 'D' Company were forced to withdraw, but a counter attack was at once organised and original line restored. The Southern Party was driven off without difficulty.[43]

The Wiltshires captured ten prisoners and one machine gun at the cost of three Other Ranks killed[44] and twenty-four men wounded. One man was reported missing.

Two days later, the 110 Bde units were relieved and moved back to the rear areas west of Manancourt. That same day, Brigade HQ was bombed:

---

39 TNA:PRO WO158/227: 'Third Army Operations OAD 915', 3 September 1918.
40 Boff, *Winning and Losing on the Western Front*, p.29.
41 Second-Lieutenant John Aubrey Hawkes, age 24, is buried in Fins New British Cemetery, Sorel-le-Grand, grave reference VIII.B.10.
42 Trench junction at W.11.c.8.6.
43 TNA PRO WO 95/2165: 1/Wilts War Diary.
44 The three men, 30041 Pte H.F.Abbott, 39954 Pte Herbert Edward Cadle & 29764 Pte George Rees Chilcott MM, are buried side by side in Gouzeaucourt New British Cemetery, grave references respectively I.F.19, I.F.18 & I.F.17.

314   To Do the Work of Men

The night of the 16th was a most unpleasant one for Brigade Headquarters, which were under canvas in the vicinity of a sunken road immediately West of Manancourt. Dinner had just been finished about 6 p.m. and all were very busy with orders and preparations for the coming attack, when without warning an enemy aeroplane dropped 6 bombs into the small camp. A direct hit was obtained on the office tent; Sergeant Winney, the chief "G" clerk, was killed instantaneously and Private Osie, assistant clerk, so badly wounded that he died shortly afterwards. Typewriter, stationery, files and correspondence were of course blown to atoms. The Brigade despatch rider was also killed. Altogether, out of a total of 30 officers and men, the casualties amounted to 6 killed and 10 wounded. There were some extraordinary escapes. The Officers' Mess tent was riddled with splinters but none of the officers were touched although all were blown off their feet by the force of the explosion.[45]

As if that were not enough, a violent thunderstorm at two o'clock the following morning washed away what was remained of the camp.

Following a conference at 62 Bde HQ at 09.30 on 16 September, orders for the 18 September attack arrived at Brigade Headquarters at around noon. The scheme, part of a much wider assault, involved only the right Corps of Third Army, namely V Corps, who would protect the left flank of Fourth Army as it tried to "establish [itself] within striking distance of the enemy's main defences on the general line St Quentin–Cambrai".[46]

Immediately to the south of 21st Division, 58th and 12th Divisions would respectively take Peizière and Epéhy before, if possible, pushing on. The 21st Division scheme involved the successive capture of the Brown, Green and Red Lines (See Map 45). The Brown and Green Lines would be the responsibility of 62 Bde. Their capture would require the crossing of the railway, the taking of Vaucelette Farm and the double trench system extending southwards from there towards Peizière. "The enemy", states 62nd Brigade Order No. 18, "is holding the general line CHAPEL HILL, VAUCELETTE FARM, PEIZIERE, EPEHY, in considerable strength but, it is believed, in little depth".[47]

After this, 110 Bde and 64 Bde, right and left respectively, would leapfrog and make for the Red Line, widening the front and capturing the trench system that ran west and south of Villers Guislain.

The attacking units of 62 Bde moved off at around midnight to the assembly position, which was a white tape running along the Yellow Support trench line (W.24.a.3.0 – W.18.c.5.0 – W.18.a.6.0), 1/Lincs on the left, 12/13 NFus in the centre, 2/Lincs on the right. The successful completion of this deployment was to be notified to Brigade HQ by the code word "SOUP". Zero Hour was 05.20.

---

45   Cumming, *A Brigadier in France 1917-1918*, p. 233. Brigadier Cumming recalled the two named casualties phonetically but spelt their names wrongly in his memoirs. 25062 Sergeant Walter Gordon Whinney, age 24, is buried in Fins New British Cemetery, Sorel-le-Grand, grave reference VIII.C.19. 27940 Private F. Osey is buried in Five Points Cemetery, Lechelle, grave reference C.3.

46   Edmonds, *Military Operations France and Belgium 1918*, Vol. IV, p.474. The wider details of the 'Battle of Epéhy' need not be included in this work. The curious reader should see pp. 474-496 of the Official History.

47   TNA PRO WO 95/2153: 62 Bde HQ War Diary.

A hurricane artillery bombardment fell 200 yards or so ahead of the infantry jumping off positions, comprising trench mortars and a creeping barrage of 18 pdrs. Two other barrages of 4.5-inch howitzers and 6-inch howitzers moved ahead of these, the latter up to 800 yards beyond the rearmost line of shells. For the first half hour, a smoke screen was laid down across the whole Corps front, this switching to masking the southern divisional boundary and the village of Villers Guislain thereafter. For the men waiting to advance, it must have been an awe-inspiring spectacle. As Private R.H. Kiernan of the Leicesters (still some distance back from the front-line trenches at this stage) recollected:

> We have come up and are 'lying out' to 'go over'. The air is alive and shaking with fire. It is hardly dawn yet, just grey and black. Along the railway line our barrage is down, a great wall of grey smoke covered with yellow flashes. It is the first time I have seen a barrage from behind. It is raining and very cold. Everything is banging and roaring, and there is the steely shriek of hundreds of shells, and that great wind overhead. There's the big whistle and 'shee-ing' and hammering of the machine guns, firing over us from the railway embankment.[48]

The machine gun barrage was delivered by D Coy 21st MG Bn and A and C Coys 33rd MG Bn and supported the troops up to the Brown Line. Once this line had been taken, D Coy was to move forward into positions on Peizière Ridge (X.19.a & c) and continue firing over the heads of the advancing infantry as far as the Red Line. A further eight guns (C Coy, 21st MG Bn) were to set up on Vaucelette Farm spur, once it was in British hands, and assist this final assault. Appendix C of the Bde Attack Order added that "All forward guns will be used with the utmost boldness, and every opportunity taken of ground from which direct overhead fire can support the attack".[49]

On the left of 62 Bde frontage, the 1/Lincs (Lieutenant-Colonel N.M.S. Irwin) were formed up in two lines, A and D Coys in front, B and C directly behind. Their third objective, the Green Line, just to the east of Vaucelette Farm, was the old British front line of 21 March 1918. All accounts of their attack are brief: it was completely successful and the Green Line was reached at the cost of one Officer and 60 Other Ranks.[50] They had taken six Officers and 150 Other Ranks prisoner. The taking of Vaucelette Farm must have been particularly sweet; they had held the same position bravely and successfully on 21 March 1918 as the massive German Spring Offensive had got under way.

In the centre of the brigade sector, 12/13 NFus (Lieutenant-Colonel R. Howlett) advanced "midst a downpour of rain",[51] capturing all their objectives by 07.10. The diarist makes light of

---

48 R.H. Kiernan, *Little Brother Goes Soldiering* (Edinburgh: Constable & Co, 1930) p. 135.
49 TNA PRO WO 95/2153: 'Order No. 18, Appendix C 'Machine Gun Arrangements', 62 Bde War Diary. In 1918 each machine gun battalion was composed of four companies and had a total of 64 Vickers Medium Machine Guns.
50 Commonwealth War Graves Commission records records eight fatalities, including Second-Lieutenant Walter George Clough, age 29. He is buried in Gouzeaucourt New British Cemetery, grave reference V.H.7.
51 TNA PRO WO 95/2155: 12/13 NFus War Diary.

316   To Do the Work of Men

German opposition, but this attack had cost the Fusiliers eighty-seven casualties, eight of them ultimately fatal.

On the right, the 2/Lincs (Lieutenant-Colonel E.P. Lloyd) set off at 05.20, following the barrage which was moving forward at a rate of 100 yards every four minutes, as closely as they dared, A, C and D Companies in front, B Coy close behind. They were greeted by heavy machine gun fire from the railway embankment but "these […] posts were successfully dealt with and did not materially check the advance".[52] Luckily, the German artillery retaliation was very weak. The first objective was taken in a gallant rush, overwhelming an otherwise stubborn garrison, and touch was established with the 12/13 NFus who had seemingly matched their rate of advance. It had taken just over forty minutes, and the artillery barrage obligingly remained stationary for another eighteen minutes as the men caught their breath and reorganised, ready for the next leap forward. At Zero plus one hour, the three companies continued their advance. A Coy, (Captain E.T. Welsh), met with little opposition and were quickly into positions in the sunken road that paralleled Squash Trench. D Coy, (Captain C.W. McConnan), on the right, also reached Squash Trench, but had had to eliminate a number of machine gun nests on the way. C Coy (Lieutenant J. McVey) left two platoons in the first objective, the other two advancing to the junction of Squash Trench and Cavalry Support. B Coy (Captain J. Dawson MC) then moved through D Coy and made it as far as Plane Trench, just as two platoons of A Coy moved across into a section of Cricket Trench.[53] Captain Dawson then led two of his platoons beyond their final objective, and they soon encountered a battery of German 77mm guns. Dawson's men went to ground and began firing at the German gunners who were doing their best to keep their guns in action.

With all objectives taken, the stage was set for 110 and 64 Bdes to continue the advance. The 64 Bde units, on the left of the divisional sector, and which had arrived on their assembly lines only at 05.00, moved up immediately at 05.20 into the trenches just vacated by 62 Bde. Then at 06.10 they moved forward once more and "formed up for the assault"[54] on the railway line running north-south through squares X13 & 19. The 9/KOYLI (Major Walsh) was on the left, 1/EYorks (Lieutenant-Colonel du Moulin) on the right, and 15/DLI (Lieutenant-Colonel Holroyd Smyth) in support. The way in which this second stage of the attack developed is indicative of the state of the German defences at this stage of the war: positions could not be held in any great depth and real resistance could only be offered from prepared defence lines. Between the two main trench systems in this sector, other than an odd isolated machine gun post or artillery battery, there was nothing to slow down any determined advance.

The 9/KOYLI leapfrogged the 62 Bde positions at 09.47 "and advanced with very little opposition"[55] until they neared Beet Trench, their final objective. "Here sharp fighting took place but the enemy were cleared and the trench occupied".[56] The positions were consolidated and the companies were disposed as follows: D Coy on the left, B Coy in the centre and C Coy on the right. A Coy was in close support. Battalion HQ had moved forward and been established at the road junction at X.7.d.9.5. The 9/KOYLI's travails were not over, however.

---

52   TNA PRO WO 95/2154: 2/Lincs War Diary.
53   These movements are depicted on Map 45.
54   TNA PRO WO 95/2160: 64 Bde HQ War Diary.
55   TNA PRO WO 95/2162: 9/KOYLI War Diary.
56   Ibid.

The situation on their left, according to the war diary, was "somewhat obscure", and before long heavy machine gun and rifle fire was enfilading the KOYLI positions from the eastern edge of Gauche Wood. An enemy counter attack from that location at 12.30 drove the troops on 9/KOYLI's left[57] back several hundred yards, leaving D Coy's flank in the air. The situation was in danger of becoming critical, but a platoon of A Coy and a number of men from Battalion HQ under the personal command of Major Walsh were rushed forward to fill the developing gap. "The retiring troops seeing reinforcements arriving, turned, and the whole charged the enemy and the line was regained and many casualties inflicted on the enemy".[58] Unfortunately, Major Walsh was wounded during this action and command of the battalion fell to Captain A.F. Ennals. Two platoons of A Coy were brought up from reserve to reinforce the extreme left flank, and at this point, the situation settled down. Captain Ennals was also given one company of the15/DLI later that evening, who remained at his disposal for the rest of the night.

The 1/EYorks, on the KOYLI's right, enjoyed a similarly unopposed advance across the stretch of countryside between the trench systems, before capturing and occupying Meunier Trench. The war diary claimed 400 prisoners and "numerous" machine guns.[59] They also overran the artillery battery that had earlier been pinned down by fire from Captain Dawson's B Coy of 2/Lincs, listing one 7.7, two 5.9s, two 4.2 howitzers, limbers and accompanying ammunition wagons along with the entire battery personnel as "captured". The commander of *3rd Battalion, 403rd Regiment, 201st Division* and his adjutant were reported as killed.[60]

Mirroring the experience of 9/KOYLI to the north, 1/EYorks came under attack from their open right flank.[61] Enemy troops bombed the newly-won positions from Storar Avenue and the 1/EYorks were pushed back along Meunier Trench, but with the arrival of two companies of the 15/DLI, the situation stabilised and the trench was held as far south as X.15.b.2.8.

The 15/DLI had moved up in rear of their two sister battalions in 64 Bde, dropping off C Coy along the way, this unit occupying Birch Tree Copse. The rest of the battalion continued the advance, but during this time, Lieutenant-Colonel Holroyd Smyth was severely wounded.[62] Captain C.P. Grant MC, the battalion adjutant, took over command.

A Coy advanced "with and on the left of"[63] 1/EYorks and captured and held the Beet Factory on the Peizière – Villers Guislan Road (X.14.a.9.6). Its presence was later deemed superfluous and the men were withdrawn into trenches some 1,000 yards to the rear.

B Coy ended up in Meunier Trench between 9/KOYLI and 1/EYorks. Patrols were sent forward at about midday to ascertain the situation regarding the village of Villers Guislain: they returned having found it firmly still in German hands. It was D Coy that finished the day on the right of 1/EYorks in Meunier Trench, where Lieutenant Stephenson, commanding, personally led the counter-bombing that halted the enemy counter attack from Storar Avenue. By the end

---

57   Likely troops of 17th Division.
58   TNA PRO WO 95/2162: 9/KOYLI War Diary.
59   TNA PRO WO 95/2161: 1/EYorks War Diary.
60   The *201st Division* was disbanded in October 1918.
61   The 110 Bde had been unable to reach their objective. See below.
62   Lieutenant-Colonel Charles Edward Ridley Holroyd Smyth DSO MC, age 36, 3rd Dragoon Guards (Prince of Wales' Own), commanding 15/DLI, died of his wounds on 23 September 1918. He is buried in Landsdown Burial Ground, Somerset, grave reference 4.O.5A.
63   TNA PRO WO 95/2161: 15/DLI War Diary.

318   To Do the Work of Men

of the day, as the situation stabilised, A and C Coys found themselves manning a reserve line between Fives Trench and the Beet Factory.

As has already been hinted, the advance of 110 Bde on the right divisional front did not go to plan. This was due to some extent to the fact that 38th Division on their right were only able to reach the trenches immediately to the east of Peizière and 12th Division further south were unable to capture of Epéhy which allowed German units to harass 110 Bde's right flank. They assembled as planned, 1/Wilts (Lieutenant-Colonel Ward) on the left, 6/Leics (Lieutenant-Colonel Burdett) on the right, with 7/Leics (Lieutenant-Colonel Sawyer) in support.

The 1/Wilts had been delayed on their move up to their assembly positions but were able to move off on time and followed the 62 Bde units "closely"[64] as far as the railway. At the appropriate time they set off towards their objectives, namely Limerick Trench from its junction with Limerick Lane in X.21.d. northwards as far as its junction with Storar Avenue. The plan was for A and C Coys to capture Heath Post in the centre of the objective line, and for bombing parties to then work their way "outwards and establish touch with troops on both flanks".[65] B Coy was given the task of mopping up Linnet Valley and D Coy was to take up support positions. To begin with, all went to plan: Heath Post was taken and parties began to extend north and south. No contact was made with friendly units on either flank, however, and the bombing parties were driven back. The Germans also counter attacked and recaptured Heath Post, forcing the 1/Wilts to withdraw initially to positions in Heath Lane. As B and D Coys arrived on the scene, B Coy having supposedly completed its earlier task, Battalion HQ was established in 14 Willows Road and the battalion consolidated positions along the ridge line in Targelle Trench and Heath Lane, forming their own small salient with echeloned defensive flanks.

The 6/Leics, advancing on the right, were confronted almost immediately by a German counter attack up Linnet Valley. They managed to repel this attack, but with German troops still in the 'Green Line' trenches to the south, and therefore with their right flank in the air and under threat of enfilade fire, they were forced to leave C and D Coys in Plane Trench. A and B Coys made it as far as 14 Willows Road, but no further.

The support battalion, the 7/Leics, reached the railway triangle north of Epéhy at around 09.30 and then pushed on across Cricket Trench, coming under machine gun fire from the south as they did so. They reached the northern sector of 14 Willows Road an hour later. B and C Coys began to dig in where they were whilst D Coy set off to try and establish contact with 64 Bde on their left. A Coy was sent forward to reinforce the 1/Wilts on the ridge, from where they repelled a rather half-hearted German attack during the afternoon.

Orders were sent out for another attack on Heath Post, but these were cancelled as the situation on the right flank had not improved. An attack the following morning was also suggested, but this was only to go ahead if 58th Division had captured Poplar Trench.[66] They had not, and relief was organised for the night of the 19th – 20th.

Brigadier Cumming, in his memoir, described the day as "very successful",[67] but even with a haul of 20 officers, 400 men and eight field guns captured, this assessment seems a little rosy. The brigade had been operating across ground rather familiar to them and "many evidences

---

64   TNA PRO WO 95/2165: 1/Wilts War Diary.
65   Ibid.
66   This was just off Map 45, to the south of Plane Trench.
67   Cumming, *A Brigadier in France 1917- 1918*, p. 236.

of [their] former occupation were found,[68] including old trench signs. Remarkably, Cumming himself found an old dugout that had been the headquarters of the 12/13 NFus in March 1918, and there discovered on a shelf under six months' worth of dust, an old regimental cheque book "in which the last cheque drawn was dated March 19".[69]

The focus of the narrative must now briefly return to the northern brigade sector. The situation along the front had more or less stabilised, but just ahead of the 15/DLI's positions on the right of the 1/EYorks in Meunier Support, a German strongpoint at Derby Post "was causing considerable trouble".[70] A raiding party from D Coy was sent out to capture it, but the endeavour failed, costing two killed and seven wounded.[71] The war diary entry for that day also details one particularly noteworthy episode:

> During the morning L/C [Lance-Corporal] Mitchell (Stretcher Bearer) whilst looking for wounded in No Man's Land came across an enemy M.G. post in front of 110th Bde. With great gallantry he collected some bombs lying about & single-handed rushed the M.G. post, killed the team of 6 men & brought the Machine Gun back to our lines. He received several bullet wounds in the legs in doing so.[72]

By the night of 20 September, all units of 21st Division had been relieved and were in the rear areas: 110 Bde was in the vicinity of Etricourt and Manancourt; 64 Bde was bivouacked to the east of Etricourt, and 62 Bde was a little further back at Mesnil. During this respite, Major H.H. Tyler MC took over command of 9/KOYLI, and Lieutenant-Colonel H.H. Neeves DSO, MC arrived to command 15/DLI.

The respite, largely taken up by training, was a brief one: at 21.00 hrs on 24 September, a conference of commanding officers took place at 64 Bde Headquarters, so that a proposed attack on the towns of Gouzeaucourt and Gonnelieu could be discussed.[73]

On the night of 25/26 September, the 62 Bde and 110 Bde moved forward to relieve 17th Division in the front line west of Gouzeaucourt. The proposed attack on the two villages – due to take place on the 26th – was dependent on success achieved first by other formations to the north: success eluded them, however, and orders were cancelled. The 26 September passed relatively quietly.

African Trench, extending roughly north-south and situated to the west of Gouzeaucourt, was attacked by three companies of the 12/13 NFus at 07.50 on 27 September. The right-hand

68 Ibid, p.232.
69 Ibid, p.232.
70 TNA PRO WO 95/2161: 15/DLI War Diary.
71 Commonwealth War Graves Commission records confirm nine fatalities on 19 September 1918 for the 15/DLI.
72 TNA PRO WO 95/2161: 15/DLI War Diary. 19263 Lance-Corporal Robert Mitchell was awarded the Distinguished Conduct Medal for this action. His award of the DCM was gazetted on 16 January 1919 and the citation reads: "For conspicuous gallantry and devotion to duty on 19th September, 1918, near Villers Guislain. Locating an enemy machine-gun which was inflicting casualties, he collected some bombs and rushed it single-handed in broad daylight, killing six men and capturing the gun. He received several wounds in this daring action but showed utter indifference to danger". He had been with the 15/DLI since September 1915.
73 See Map 44.

320   To Do the Work of Men

company reached its objective and occupied its sector of the trench, a message to that effect reaching Brigade HQ at 09.13. The other two companies joined them soon after. The success was to be short-lived, however: at 19.00 hrs, a strong German counter attack under a very heavy artillery and trench mortar barrage drove the Northumberlands out of African Trench. Such were the 12/13 NFus casualties that the battalion was forced to reorganise into three companies. War diaries do not give casualty numbers, but forty-two fatalities can be confirmed, including two officers.[74] Sadly, it seems that a twenty-four hour delay would have saved these lives: at 10.30 on 28 September, reports were received that aerial reconnaissance had discovered that the Germans had "vacated his trenches in the vicinity of Gouzeaucourt".[75] Patrols were sent out to confirm the situation on the ground, and it was revealed that the whole village had been abandoned. New positions were secured without opposition just beyond the railway line to the east of the village.[76] An attack on Gonnelieu was ordered for the next morning.

History was about to repeat itself. An artillery barrage came down at 03.30 on the morning of 29 September. The 1 and 2/Lincs were to lead the assault, on the right and left respectively, but owing to orders arriving very late, it was impossible for all companies of 2/Lincs to reach their assembly positions in time and the resulting advance was chaotic: the start-line of the artillery barrage was some 1,500 yards east of the jumping off line, so 1/Lincs had decided to set off at 03.00 hrs in order to try and catch it up. At this point, 2/Lincs were still trying to make their way through Gouzeaucourt under an enemy gas barrage. They pushed on as best they could over "difficult and unknown country in the dark",[77] but inevitably the cohesion of the attack was lost. The two tanks designated to support the advance were given orders to go forward on the left of 1/Lincs "in place of the 2nd Lincolns".[78] It did not help that one of the tanks broke down before it had made any ground at all. The other, "Kintore", reached the enemy's front line, but was knocked out.

The 1/Lincs came under heavy machine gun fire almost immediately in the intermittent bright moonlight, and despite reaching the German defence line, it was unable to press home its attack. With both flanks in the air, it was forced to withdraw. The 2/Lincs also met machine gun fire and the advance stalled some 500 yards west of Gonnelieu. The attack had failed at the cost of thirty-six fatalities, and proof, if proof were needed, was demonstrated that two unsupported tanks cannot fulfil the role of an infantry battalion.

Patrols dispatched at 04.00 hrs on 30 September found the enemy still in situ, but five hours later "there was every indication that the enemy had withdrawn from Gonnelieu".[79] This was quickly confirmed and the 2/Lincs were able to push through the village and establish themselves in positions to the east without encountering any opposition. They had found several of their own men in dug outs in Gonnelieu who had been wounded and taken prisoner the previous day. They were leapfrogged by 1/Lincs who were able to push on as far as the canal at

---

74   Captain J.C. Coy is buried in Gouzeaucourt New British Cemetery, grave reference II.A.15. Second-Lieutenant James Arthur Mitchell, age 21, lies in Fins New British Cemetery, Sorel le Grand, grave V.E.6.
75   TNA PRO WO 95/2153: 62 Bde HQ War Diary.
76   See Map 44.
77   TNA PRO WO 95/2154: 2/Lincs War Diary.
78   TNA PRO WO 95/2154: 1/Lincs War Diary.
79   TNA PRO WO 95/2154: 2/Lincs War Diary.

Banteux. On their right, 110 Bde was also pushing patrols forward: the 7/Leics encountered no enemy troops to the west of the canal but came under intermittent light machine gun fire as they approached Honnecourt. They found all the bridges over the canal destroyed, one of them blowing up just as the patrol reached it.

Remarkable events had been taking place farther south, where, on 29 September, units of Fourth Army had smashed through the German defences along the St Quentin Canal and had broken through the Hindenburg Line to a depth of 5-6,000 yards on a front of 10,000 yards. The units of 21st Division were content to consolidate their positions on the western bank.

Casualties for September 1918 were not insignificant. The frequency of attacks undertaken meant that numbers mounted steadily and unceasingly. Figures in brigade war diaries may not be totally accurate, but they give a sense of the cost of victory.

62 Bde: 32 Officers and 988 Other Ranks
110 Bde: 22 Officers and 621 Other Ranks
64 Bde: 37 Officers and 864 Other Ranks
Total: 91 Officers and 2,473 Other Ranks

The various war diarists are not too often given to overt expressions of unit pride. The advances in the summer and autumn of 1918 are also not too often trumpeted, but the adjutant of 2/Lincs included two passages in the battalion war diary that seem to reflect a growing pride in the achievements of his men, and an increasing confidence that the tide of war had turned irrevocably in their favour:

Since August 21st, 21st Division have driven enemy back a total distance of about 31 kilometres, from BEAUMONT HAMEL to PEIZIERES (sic). During this period Battn has taken part in hard fighting during the first 10 days and last 3 days. From the night 5th/6th, Battn was fighting over and regaining the identical ground, over which it withdrew during the enemy's offensive in March, 1918, including the villages SOREL LE GRAND and HEUDICOURT. Fighting on afternoon of Sept. 8th actually took place in the same trenches which were held with great gallantry on March 22nd 1918. [...] The knowledge that the Battn was fighting over ground which had been given up in face of superior numbers and after hard fighting in March was the means of being a great incentive to the men, whose dash and eagerness regained in the face of considerable opposition a depth of 8000 yards in 27 hours [...]

The attack on the morning of the 18th was carried out in a heavy storm of rain. In reaching its final objective, the Battn had recaptured the line held by the Brigade on March 21st, 1918.

Once again the dash, determination and enthusiasm of all ranks ensured the brilliantly successful results obtained by the Battn, which, since the opening of the offensive on August 21st has considerably added to its record, the retaking of our old front line coming at the climax".[80]

80 TNA PRO WO 95/2154: 2/Lincs War Diary

322   To Do the Work of Men

As the Hindenburg Line fell to the Allies on 29 September, a conference was being held at the Hotel Britannique in Spa, Belgium. Generals Hindenburg and Ludendorff met with the Kaiser and advised him to seek armistice terms. The request was subsequently made by the German Government to President Wilson on 4 October. It was to take a further thirty-eight days of fighting for the request to become a reality, and 21st Division would have its part to play.

10

The End is Nigh

On 2 October 1918, in a message received at 21st Division HQ at around 15.30, V Corps policy was communicated to the lower formations. With the situation on the Canal de l'Escaut – and the state of the German defences on or near it – obscure, Lieutenant-General Shute's dictates included rest, re-organisation and reconnaissance. Offensive action was not proscribed, however: patrolling would continue and the German positions would be 'sniped' by machine gun fire. No frontal attacks were to be attempted if opposition appeared strong: the enemy was to be "manoeuvred out of his position".[1] Attempts to cross the canal in the first days of the month had been met by German snipers and machine gunners in positions on the eastern bank of the waterway. Early on the 2nd, a bridge had been "swung across the Canal",[2] but the two men of 1/Lincs, 62 Bde,[3] advancing from their trenches south-west of Banteux, who had succeeded in crossing it, were promptly forced back.

The following day, the divisional front was taken over by 110 Bde. The 4 October passed without serious incident, but on the 5th it was discovered that the Germans had begun to retire on the whole V Corps front: troops of 33rd Division were the first to get across the canal at Honnecourt that morning, but by midday all three battalions of 62 Bde, comprising "large patrols in artillery formation"[4] were across and the "Hindenburg Line and Hindenburg Support Line [were] occupied without resistance".[5] A number of German stragglers were taken prisoner during this advance and interrogated the following day. The information gleaned sheds valuable light on the state of both the German defensive positions and the morale of those manning them. One soldier of the *9th Coy, 105th IR, 30th Division*, tells an interesting tale. It is illuminating, even when taken with the advisory pinch of salt:

> According to the statement of the prisoner, the 9th Coy, then strictly the outpost Company, as soon as they discovered that they had been left behind in the lurch, threw all their rifles

---

1 TNA PRO WO 95/2162: 9/KOYLI War Diary.
2 TNA PRO WO 95/2134 : 21st Div HQ War Diary.
3 TNA PRO WO 95/2153. The 62 Bde War Diary indicates two bridges being thrown across the canal but confirms the same outcome. The diary of 1/Lincs speaks of *one* bridge being subsequently destroyed by the enemy.
4 TNA PRO WO 95/2163: 110 Bde HQ War Diary.
5 TNA PRO WO 95/2134: 21st Division HQ Diary.

324   To Do the Work of Men

and Machine Guns into a heap in disgust, and walked back, their Officer acquiescing and laughing. After a time they fell out on the side of a track for a rest and one man got wounded by a bullet. The man examined put him in a dug out and bandaged him up, subsequently being found by one of our patrols. The men of this regiment are chiefly Saxons and are of very poor moral and fighting quality. The 9th Coy is said to be about 50 strong.[6]

Another prisoner, belonging to *2nd Coy, 99th IR*, believed that preparations for a general retirement of at least 20 kilometres were underway in the rear areas, where a new defensive line was being dug.

Of more immediate concern to 21st Division was the trench system known as the Beaurevoir Line (see Map 46), this being approximately 1,000 yards from the newly-captured and occupied Bonne Enfance and Montecouvez Farms. These, and the road running between them had been taken by 15/DLI and 1/EYorks of 64 Bde on the morning of the 6th, having moved through the 110 Bde positions. Although the farms had been abandoned, the approaches were machine gunned from strong points in the Beaurevoir Line and the farms themselves shelled for the rest of the day. The 1/EYorks reported three Officers wounded and Other Ranks casualties amounting to fifty.[7]

The Beaurevoir Line was to be assaulted on 8 October. The veracity of the prisoners' statements made two days earlier was about to be tested. The report concluded as follows:

The Beaurevoir Line was held on the morning of the 6th instant by troops composing the screen and support troops of the previous day. The line is only said to be held in Sectors with both light and heavy machine guns with the Infantry Companies. The trenches are at the most only waist deep, several prisoners saying that they were only knee deep. The wire is very strong but that at the time the gaps where tracks and roads passed through were not believed to have been blocked.[8]

The 21st Division attack was part of a much wider assault involving the formations and units of three Armies (First,[9] Third and Fourth), totalling six Corps (IX, XIII, V, IV, VI and XVII). A conference of brigadiers was held at 110 Bde HQ at ten o'clock on the morning of 7 October, followed by a second involving Battalion Commanders at two that afternoon. Written orders from Division were issued at half past seven the same evening.

---

6   Ibid. Report dated 6 October 1918.
7   Commonwealth War Graves Commission records indicate that the 1/EYorks suffered five fatalities that day. The diary of 15/DLI casually reports that "the Battalion came under very heavy Trench Mortar and Machine Gun fire". See TNA PRO WO 95/2161: '15/DLI fatalities for 6 October 1918 number twenty-three', but this merits no mention, 15/DLI War Diary.
8   TNA PRO WO 95/2134: 21st Div HQ War Diary.
9   First Army involvement was limited to the Canadian Corps, which, on the right wing of First Army to the west and north of Cambrai, was to co-operate on the 8th by means of artillery fire and active patrolling, before advancing to secure crossings over the Schelde Canal at Ramillies, two miles north of Cambrai.

Zero Hour was set at 01.00 hrs, 8 October[10] and the 21st Div units were allocated three objectives: the first, the Green Line, 1,000 metres beyond the Beaurevoir Line, and extending across the right-hand sector of the divisional front only (see Map 46) would be assaulted by 64 Bde on the right and 110 Bde on the left. The second, the Red Line, running more or less due south from Hurtebise Farm, would also be the responsibility of 110 Bde, which would now attack initially in a northern direction before veering to the right. The third, the Blue Line, just to the east of the village of Walincourt, was entrusted to 62 Bde.

Phase one of the attack would commence at Zero Hour, 01.00 hrs. The second would begin at 05.15 and the third at 08.00 hrs. Once the final objective had been reached, patrols would be sent out beyond the Bois du Gard and into the village of Selvigny. This last phase would be the responsibility of 62 Bde's Cyclist Squadron who, if the above locations were found to be unoccupied, was to push reconnoitring patrols on towards Caullery.

Six Mark V tanks of 11th Tank Battalion were allocated to assist: four would support the second phase of the attack onto the Red Line and two were to be available to 64 Bde once it had got light – if needed – to help clear up the area around the Château des Angles. All six would then support 62 Bde's attack on the Blue Line and would be used "for clearing up 'pockets' of the enemy during the advance".[11]

On the right of the attack frontage, 64 Bde troops, with 9/KOYLI and 15/DLI leading the attack, had formed up in their assembly positions on the road running south-east from Montecouvez Farm by 00.30 hrs. The artillery barrage fell on the Beaurevoir Line positions exactly on time at 01.00 hrs, the KOYLIs and the Durhams, left and right respectively, moving forward, in order to be as close to the barrage as possible when it lifted at Zero plus eight minutes.

The Beaurevoir system was "carried with a rush",[12] the only real opposition coming from one stubborn German machine gun post on the Durham's right flank. This was "eventually rushed and captured",[13] allowing the front companies to push on towards the Green Line. A German counter barrage did come down, but it fell behind the advancing troops and did little damage, although one or two shells landed perilously close to 9/KOYLI Battalion HQ. All the objectives were reached by 02.30, including the Château des Angles, which had been surrounded and then taken after "a very stiff fight",[14] by the Durhams. The assault party was down to 2 Officers and 30 men by this point, however, and a German counter attack retook the château, forcing the Durhams back about 200 yards into a sunken road. Reinforcements arrived and at 06.00, a second attack captured the château once more. It would seem that the Germans had booby-trapped the château, however, as "at this moment mines commenced to explode all round the building, and the force once again withdrew to the Sunken Road".[15] Once any remaining mines had been rendered harmless, the château was finally, and this time definitively, occupied.

10 This first stage was in effect a 'preliminary' operation, undertaken by V Corps who would seize the Beaurevoir Line in order that the right wing of Third Army could then move forward in conjunction with the left wing of Fourth Army, whose forward troops were already across the Beaurevoir Line.

11 TNA PRO WO 95/2134: 'GHQ Order No. 246, issued 7 October 1918 at 19.30 hrs', 21 Div War Diary.

12 TNA PRO WO 95/2162: 9/KOYLI War Diary.

13 TNA PRO WO 95/2161: 15/DLI War Diary.

14 Ibid.

15 Ibid.

The 9/KOYLIs, on the left of the attack, also reached their objectives "at very little cost",[16] and were then withdrawn to join the 1/EYorks in positions in the Beaurevoir Line itself, their active part in the day's business over. The action had cost the KOYLIs six fatalities, including one officer.[17]

This left the 15/DLI to consolidate the captured Green Line positions from the Château des Angles to Haut Farm. The Durhams had taken the brunt of the German retaliation and had suffered five Officers wounded, 24 Other Ranks killed, with 146 wounded and 49 missing.[18]

On the left of the preliminary attack, the 1/Wilts, 110 Bde, had begun their assault from positions east of Montecouvez Farm, with two companies, C and D, in front, the others close behind in support. They came up against uncut wire, A Coy (in support on the right) in particular being held up and suffering casualties from German shell fire, but the other companies found gaps and were able to force their way through. The Germans had a number of machine guns "clearly sighted in the open"[19] on the slope in front of their trench lines, but the Wiltshires carried the Beaurevoir Line, despite enfilade machine gun fire also coming from the direction of the Château des Angles and were able to consolidate their gains at moderate cost. One officer had been killed, along with fourteen Other Ranks, with the wounded totalling eighty-one.[20]

This permitted the two Leicester battalions to form up behind them, ready to launch the second phase of the attack: they took up positions in a shallow communication trench, facing northwards. This communication trench was only one foot deep in places and had proven very difficult to find during what was an exceptionally dark night. Again, German artillery retaliation fell well behind the front-line troops, Montecouvez Farm being particularly badly hit, as Captain David Kelly of 6/Leics later recalled:

> The German batteries […] were now very active, and as I entered Montecouvez Farm – in reality a small village – falling shells and a shower of bombs from a low-flying aeroplane combined to produce a terrifying uproar. Houses were crashing and bricks flying in every direction, always a specially (sic) unpleasant sound in the darkness, and I ran hard through the village and along a road which brought me to the positions just taken by the Wiltshires.[21]

The British artillery were perfectly capable, by this stage of the war, of putting down a creeping barrage at 90 degrees to the general direction of the attack, and behind this one, moving south to north, the 6 and 7/Leics, right and left respectively, moved off at 05.15. All contemporary narratives of this attack are brief, pointing to the fact that it was regarded as a 'routine' assault: casualties were "fairly light"[22], the prisoner haul was extensive – 430 men captured along with

---

16 TNA PRO WO 95/2162: 9/KOYLI War Diary.
17 Second-Lieutenant Charles Woodley, age 26, is buried in Prospect Hill Cemetery, Gouy, grave reference V.A.20.
18 Commonwealth War Graves Commission records show 19 fatalities for 15/DLI on 8 October 1918.
19 TNA PRO WO 95/2165: 'Operations 7th to 8th October', 1/Wilts War Diary.
20 The officer was Second-Lieutenant Reginald Hall, age 21. He is buried in Prospect Hill Cemetery, Gouy, grave reference III.F.14.
21 D.V. Kelly, *39 Months with the Tigers*, (Ernest Benn, 1930) pp.146-147.
22 TNA PRO WO 95/2164: 7/Leics War Diary. Commonwealth War Graves Commission records show 18 fatalities for 6/Leics on 8 October 1918, with 26 for 7/Leics.

The End is Nigh   327

67 machine guns – and the objective was taken to time. Other narratives[23] suggest that the Germans were taken somewhat by surprise: the attack went in *behind* the Beaurevoir system, and parallel to it, thus avoiding much of the wire and possibly accounting for the large number of machine guns captured, many of which would have been assaulted from the rear. One German battalion, the *2nd Battalion, 105th Regt, 30th Division*, was "cut off and completely destroyed".[24] The attacking battalions consolidated their gains and began to re-organise, with 1/EYorks, 64 Bde, sent forward to occupy the Haut Farm position.

The third phase of the attack was due to go in at 08.00 hrs: the 62 Bde was to capture the village of Walincourt and the high ground to the north of it near Guillemin Farm. All three battalions would be in the front line, 1/Lincs on the left, 12/13 NFus in the centre, and 2/Lincs on the right.

The 1/Lincs, moving up to their assembly positions a little too early, came under machine gun fire as they crested the ridge to the west of the Beaurevoir Line, 110 Bde not yet having completed their mopping up of the northern sector of that system. Two officers, Lieutenants Richardson and Wright, were thus wounded before any attack commenced. They finally made it to their jumping off positions with only ten minutes to spare. Four tanks were supposed to co-operate with the 1/Lincs in this attack, but only one made it to the start line and it broke down soon after.

As the attack commenced at eight o'clock, the 1/Lincs men were met by machine gun fire from Hurtebise Farm and the copse to the east of it. A captured enemy field gun and a section of 18 pdrs were fortunately able to fire directly at these positions and the German garrison surrendered. The men pushed on, encountering little opposition until they approached Guillemin Farm, where machine gun fire once more halted the advance. On the left, there was no sign of 37th Division and enemy machine guns in Briseux Wood were able to enfilade the 1/Lincs as they sheltered in the valley.

In the centre, the details of the 12/13 NFus attack must remain obscure: the battalion war diary devotes only two lines to the day's events, and even within those wrongly claims that they had taken the village of Walincourt. The truth was that at 12.15, the men had got as far as the eastern outskirts of Angle and Walincourt Woods and were in touch with 2/Lincs on their right. Two Officers[25] and twenty-six Other Ranks had been killed. Over one hundred were recorded as wounded or missing.

On the right, 2/Lincs were immediately subjected to enfilade machine gun fire from their right, where 33rd Division had been slow to get moving. A and D Coys pushed on, however, and were able to reach the western edge of Angle Wood before momentum was once more lost. As B Coy began to dig in on the ridge to the east of the Château des Angles, C Coy came up on the left in support of the two leading companies. A great deal of enemy fire was coming from the right, from two quarries just within the 33rd Division sector. Two tanks were dispatched and were able to force the enemy out of these positions, but enemy field guns hidden in the numerous copses and woods were proving difficult to dislodge.

---

23   For example, see Cumming, *A Brigadier in France 1917-1918*, pp.242-243.
24   J.E. Edmonds, *Military Operations, France and Belgium 1918*, Vol. V (London: HMSO, 1947, p.202.
25   Second-Lieutenants Gibbon and France were killed. Frederic Gibbon, age 27, is commemorated on the Vis-en-Artois Memorial. William France, age 28, is buried in Bois-des-Angles British Cemetery, Crevecoeur-sur-l'Escaut, grave reference I.A.49.

328   To Do the Work of Men

At two o'clock in the afternoon, patrols from B and D Coys were sent forward to try to establish what was happening ahead of them: meeting no opposition, the battalion was able to push A and D Coys on as far as the sunken road running north-south just two or three hundred yards short of the western environs of Walincourt.

With the advanced stalled across the entire attack frontage, even though 62 Bde HQ was receiving reports of a possible general German withdrawal, orders were given for a resumption of the attack at 18.00 hrs under a renewed artillery barrage.

Even with the added strength of the 1/EYorks and 1/Wilts who were moved up to support this effort, the attack failed to reach the Blue Line. Indeed, very little ground was gained at all. Walincourt, the high ground to the north of it and Guillemin Farm all remained in German hands.

The two Lincolnshire battalion war diarists enumerate the day's losses: 1/Lincs record two Officers killed,[26] with four wounded. Other Ranks casualties amount to eleven killed, fifty-four wounded and thirteen missing. 2/Lincs suffered three Officers wounded, with fourteen Other Ranks killed, seventy wounded and nine missing.[27]

On the evening of 8 October, General Ludendorff, realising that the town of Cambrai was no longer tenable, issued orders for a general withdrawal of all German troops to the 'Hermann Position I', a line of defences that ran, opposite the V Corps sector, along the River Selle, almost ten miles north-east of Walincourt. When 17th Division relieved 21st Division at 05.20 on the morning of 9 October, they were able to advance through Walincourt unopposed. By 18.00 hrs, after being held up for four hours in front of Montigny, they had pushed on to Tronquoy (see Map 46), completing an advance of five and a half miles.

The units of 21st Division were able to move forward and find billets in Caullery, which "contained almost a full complement of civilians".[28] Quartermaster – Sergeant Bacon, 110 Bde, explains in his memoir that this was not a straightforward operation:

> Prior to his retreat, the enemy had mined all the crossroads, and large buildings – the huge craters at the crossings greatly impeding the passage of Transports and Guns; as a result of his propensity, all houses and buildings in the village were examined by Tunnelling Companies, R.E., before occupation as billets, and in some instances as much as 1000 lbs of dynamite were found in cellars, with fuzes set. Long after our arrival, many houses, cross-roads and portions of the railway, blew up. The food distribution and administration of the civilians was entrusted to the French gendarmerie (several of whom had followed closely our advance) in conjunction with the British Military Authorities. Nothing whatever of value had been left by the enemy, and the civilians, in many cases, were in sad plight. Everything possible here was done to make the billets as comfortable as conditions afforded, and while considerable assistance was given to the civil population, they in turn gave us a warm welcome and out of their meagre resources, were extremely hospitable.[29]

26 Lieutenant John Edward Tillett, age 22, is buried in Prospect Hill Cemetery, Gouy, grave reference V.B.7. Second-Lieutenant John Jacob Wipf is buried in Naves Communal Cemetery Extension, grave reference III.E.17.
27 2/Lincs Other Ranks fatalities eventually numbered eighteen for 8 October 1918.
28 Leicester Records Office, Doc. 22D63/146, Unpublished memoir of D.A. Bacon MM, late Quartermaster Sergeant, 110 Infantry Brigade, p. 136.
29 Ibid, p. 136.

On 10 October, with 21st Division now officially in "Corps Reserve", 62 and 64 Bde troops moved into billets in Walincourt, which had suffered very little damage from shelling. The 64 Bde diarist rejoiced in the fact that "many of the houses were furnished".[30] The 9/KOYLI Medical Officer, Captain Guy de H. Dawson had been able to treat some of the civilians that had stayed behind in the neighbourhood, and at five o'clock that afternoon, the battalion band gave a concert from the village bandstand, playing selections "highly appreciated"[31] by both civilian and military inhabitants alike. Two days later, Brigadier-General Edwards, 64 Bde, ordered the battalion to parade and an address from the Divisional Commander was read out to the men:

> The Army and Corps Commanders have requested me to convey to all ranks under my command, their high appreciation of the magnificent success gained by the 21st Division during the past few days.
>
> I personally have nothing to add to what I have already told you, namely that I was confident you would live up to the tremendously high standard you had already set yourselves. That you intend to do so is already proved by your success in the recent fighting, especially as your success has been gained in the face of the greatest difficulties. I would ask all ranks to note the ruthless havoc wrought by the enemy on the person and property of defenceless women and old men. You are fighting a vicious beast and you must treat him as such.
>
> The enemy is rapidly reaching the end of his tether and it is up to you to see that his final defeat is as complete as possible.
>
> What you suffered in the early days of the year, the enemy is suffering now with, moreover, the prospect of an overwhelming defeat staring him in the face.
>
> Good luck,
> (Signed) David G.M. Campbell
> Major-General, Commanding 21st Division

The following twelve days out of the line were taken up largely by training. The 62 Bde diarist summed up the programme:

> The units of the Bde carried out the programme of intensive training, paying special attention to the training of subordinate commanders, for example section and platoon commanders. Tactical schemes for Companies and Battalions were also carried out. The conditions for training during the period were excellent, the ground W. of Walincourt being particularly suitable for both field and range work, and the weather, on the whole, being good.[32]

Other unit diaries mention instruction in the use of the Lewis Gun, various practice attacks at both battalion and brigade level, and musketry training. All also mention numerous drafts of both Officers and Other Ranks who arrived to bring battalions up to somewhere near full strength. Total reinforcements for the division for the month of October 1918 amounted to 119

---

30 TNA PRO WO 95/2160: 64 Bde HQ War Diary.
31 TNA PRO WO 95/2162: 9/KOYLI War Diary.
32 TNA PRO WO 95/2153: 62 Bde HQ War Diary.

330 To Do the Work of Men

Officers and 3,150 Other Ranks.[33] It was not all work, however: on 12 October, 64 Bde organised an inter-company football competition. A full record of the results has sadly not survived, the only match subsequently mentioned being one played between C Coy 9/KOYLI and D Coy 15/DLI. Even then, the actual score is not revealed: "The latter [...] were the superior team and won rather easily".[34]

In the two weeks during which 21st Division was out of the line; the Allied advance had continued. Pushing on from their positions in Tronquoy, 17th Division found that fighting intensified as the village of Neuvilly was approached, and the struggle to establish bridgeheads across the River Selle became a costly and vicious encounter: Neuvilly was not finally cleared until 20 October and with the railway to the north-east of the village also secured on that day (see Map 47), the village of Amerval fell at the second attempt in the early hours of the following morning.

This first stage of the Battle of the Selle had cost V Corps almost 6,000 casualties. The offensive was initially supposed to continue almost immediately, but "on account of the slow arrival of the ammunition trains in the Third Army area",[35] two postponements meant that the next attack would take place on 23 October. The Germans did not waste the breathing space offered them: their trench systems were relatively poor, but strong points and machine gun nests in villages, orchards and enclosed fields were strengthened and strongly wired. An outpost line was also established, and carefully-sited machine guns covered the approaches to every village and wood.

This second phase of the Battle of the Selle was to involve Fourth, Third and First Armies. The plan was to swing the left wing of the Allied front forwards so that the line would run north to south,[36] and face the Hermann II position, which ran along the Sambre-Oise Canal in the south and thence northwards through a line of fortified villages to the west of the Forest of Mormal.

V Corps was allocated a succession of five objectives spread over 9,500 yards, which involved the capture of three villages, Ovillers, Vendegies-au-Bois and Poix-du-Nord (See Map 47). "The ground in front presented no special difficulties: it consisted of a series of long, low ridges with the valleys of small streams between them descending to the Scheldt; it was closely cultivated, and dotted with small villages, nearly all in the valleys, surrounded as usual by orchards".[37] This was well suited for the use of tanks, but the numbers available across the BEF as the autumn set in was dwindling, and V Corps was given only six tanks from 11th Tank Battalion for this attack.

Zero Hour was set at 02.00 hrs on 23 October. This was forty minutes later than that of Fourth Army on the right, as Third Army's right wing was already approximately 1,000 yards

33 TNA PRO WO 95/2135 : 21st Div Adjutant and Quartermaster General War Diary.
34 TNA PRO WO 95/2162: 9/KOYLI. War Diary. The diarist was presumably too embarrassed to enumerate the scale of the defeat.
35 Edmonds, *Military Operations France and Belgium 1918*, Vol. V, p. 351. By this point in the 100 Days Offensive, the Allied supply lines were becoming stretched and a constant supply of ammunition, shells and food could not be maintained. The tempo of the Allied attacks therefore inevitably slowed at certain times.
36 The general axis of attack had been up to this point in a north-easterly direction.
37 Edmonds, *Military Operations France and Belgium 1918*, Vol. V, p. 361.

ahead of Fourth Army's left wing. This meant that some early German artillery retaliation fell on 21st Division units as they waited in their assembly positions.

The British artillery barrage was to advance at a rate of 100 yards every four minutes – fairly standard for this stage of the war – as far as the Green Dotted Line. It consisted of four Field Artillery Brigades: two thirds of the 18 pdrs would fire shrapnel with 10 percent smoke, the rest firing high explosive one hundred yards ahead of the shrapnel. The heavy guns would also fire ahead of the creeping barrage, concentrating their fire on sunken roads and the outskirts of villages. The villages themselves were not to be bombarded as it was believed that a large number of French civilians were still in residence. One and a half Machine Gun Companies would also provide overhead covering fire. The barrage would not extend beyond this line. The troops' rate of advance was strictly timetabled: the Red Dotted Line was to be reached at 03.40. Forty minutes later the men would move off from there and arrive at the Red Line at 06.00 hrs. The rest of the schedule was as follows:

Leave Red Line	08.00
Arrive Green Dotted Line	08.40
Leave Green Dotted Line	09.20
Arrive Green Line	10.50
Leave Green Line	12.50
Arrive Brown Line	15.20

The 64 Bde, on the right, and 110 Bde on the left, would launch the attack and prosecute it as far as the Green Dotted Line, whereupon the 62 Bde would leapfrog and continue as far as the Brown Line. Three tanks were available to help clear the village of Ovillers; they were to work around the edges of the village, one to the north and two to the south, and "be ready to assist the Infantry to 'Mop up' when required".[38] Exploitation beyond the Brown Line was included in the Divisional Orders, but this was probably added more in hope than in expectation. Indeed, needless to say, once the advance started, the timetable very quickly became a work of fiction.

The final paragraph of 110 Bde's orders for this attack reflects a growing confidence that German resistance was beginning to falter. The last sentence might, however, give the local commander, on the spot, pause for thought:

> It has been proved in the operations of the last few days that the counter-attacks delivered by the enemy are not determined and that they break if resolutely countered. If, therefore, Counter-attacks develop, Officers in charge of local Reserves will be instructed to Charge at once with the Bayonet.[39]

The 64 Bde moved up for the attack on the evening of 22 October, halting for four hours just east of Inchy for tea, before assembling at the railway embankment just to the north-east of Neuvilly. The 15/DLI went ahead and occupied the front line, relieving the 9/Duke of Wellington's, (52

---

38   TNA PRO WO 95/2163: 'Brigade Order No. 174. Paragraph 11', 110 Bde War Diary.
39   Ibid. Paragraph 15.

332   To Do the Work of Men

Bde, 17th Div) and at 23.30 the 9/KOYLI and 1/EYorks moved into their jumping off positions, right and left respectively, the latter having already been peppered by enemy gas shells.

On 110 Bde front, on the left of the divisional sector, similar dispositions were in place. The 6/Leics had occupied the front line and the 1/Wilts, on the right, and 7/Leics, on the left, were poised to move through them and into the attack. The 1/Wilts diarist noted that a thick mist was by this time obscuring all the ground level features, but that the stars were still visible. The battalion had advanced to their forming up line "guided by the stars".[40] Luckily, they emerged from the mist some 300 yards short of the jumping off line and were able to watch as the forming up tape was being laid out in front of them. It was also at this point that enemy shells began to fall amongst them. Casualties were incurred, but the front-line companies, A and C, were still able to move off on time.

The British artillery bombardment came down exactly on time at 02.00 hrs, and the four attacking battalions moved through their line-holding comrades and set off towards their first objective. The Red Dotted Line was reached and occupied to time, the report of this success reaching Bde HQ at around 04.30. The next objective proved more of a challenge: on the left, the 7/Leics were subject to enfilade fire from the direction of Red House, which was still in enemy hands due to the slow advance of 5th Div, and 1/Wilts were taking casualties before reaching the outskirts of Ovillers from machine gun fire coming from the right flank. The 6/Leics were by now moving up ready to leapfrog onto the next objective and it was only with their help that the village of Ovillers was finally taken.

On the right, the 1/EYorks and 9/KOYLI had also run into difficulties: the 9/KOYLI on the right flank was held up by fire from a machine gun post bypassed by units of 33rd Div. This machine gun was located on a ridge overlooking the approaches to Ovillers and from this elevated position they had a clear view of the British troops as they struggled forward. Lieutenant-Colonel Greenwood (9/KOYLI) realised that this machine gun had to be eliminated – and quickly – if the attack was to succeed. Single-handedly, he rushed up the ridge and, seemingly taking the German crew by surprise, killed all four of them. He, along with two battalion runners, was forced to repeat this act of gallantry very soon afterwards as his battalion was held up by another machine gun located at the "eastern entrance"[41] to Ovillers village. The crew suffered the same fate as their unfortunate aforementioned comrades.

The village was eventually cleared with the help of two of the tanks which had destroyed a number of machine gun posts,[42] the 7/Leics having outflanked Ovillers to the north and taken up positions in the sunken Ovillers – Beaurain road. They began taking fire from Beaurain but were able to push on and secure the Red Line. C and A Coys of 1/Wilts also made it forward this far, but the other two companies had lost direction in the dark and took some time to re-orientate themselves. The attack on the left-hand sector of the Green Dotted Line was down to 6/Leics: they crossed the Red Line at 07.10 and immediately came under heavy enemy fire from the edge of Duke's Wood. With the rest of the battalion pinned down, one company

---

40   TNA PRO WO 95/2165.: 'Operations 22/23rd Oct. 1918', 1/Wilts War Diary.
41   Derek Hunt, *Valour Beyond All Praise: Harry Greenwood VC.* (London: The Chameleon Press, 2003), p. 74.
42   Afterwards, one of these tanks fell into a gravel pit and the other broke a track. The third had lost direction and ended up in the 33rd Division area. See Edmonds, *Military Operations France and Belgium 1918*, Vol. V, p. 364.

worked around the southern flank of the wood and managed to reach the château (reference F.13.a.8.8). Once outflanked, the Germans in the wood were forced to retire and the Green Dotted Line was reached at about 10.00 hrs

On the right, the 9/KOYLI, having left one company to form a defensive flank on the right, were down to around 250 rifles. Nevertheless, they advanced faster than the 1/EYorks and found themselves in the open to the south of Dukes Wood with both flanks in the air. A German counter-attack from the right managed to get within forty yards of the Yorkshiremen before it was finally repulsed and Greenwood was able to lead a charge across the open, capturing 150 prisoners, eight machine guns and one field gun on their way to the Green Dotted Line.[43]

The Green Dotted Line was in British hands by 08.05 and the 64 and 110 Bde units had completed their work for the day. The 15/DLI had moved forward and taken over the Green Dotted Line positions, thus allowing the 9/KOYLI and 1/EYorks to form a substantial defensive flank facing south-east. The 1/Wilts took up positions in the Red Line, with 7/Leics on their right. Patrols had also been sent through the village of Vendegies-au-Bois, which was found to be full of French civilians.

The advance to the Green Line was down to 62 Bde. The three battalions had assembled on the original start line, having stopped just north of Neuvilly at 04.30 for breakfast, ready to move off at Zero plus 300 (07.00 hrs). With 1/Lincs on the left, and 2/Lincs on the right, (12/13 NFus) were in reserve), it was nearer 07.30 when the leading companies set off, the plan being to reach the Green Dotted Line by 08.40. The 2/Lincs squeezed past the southern outskirts of Ovillers before re-organising into a two-company front, coming under enemy shell fire as they did so. They were also advancing through a ground mist, and D Coy, on the right, lost direction and ended up wandering into 33rd Div territory. They were able to rectify this situation when the mist lifted at about ten o'clock and half an hour later, the Harpies river had been crossed and Vendegies-au-Bois finally cleared of all German defenders. With the 1/Lincs on the left, they pushed on to the Green Line, but German machine gunners on the high ground to the west of Poix du Nord, with the help of some quite heavy retaliatory shelling from the German field gunners, were able to halt the advance on the high ground adjacent to the road running north-west to south-east just short of the Green Line. By two that afternoon, the men had edged forward onto the Green Line and orders were issued for the support companies to leapfrog their comrades and continue the advance onto the Brown Line. These were soon countermanded, however, when enemy shelling intensified and the Germans attempted a counter attack on the right flank. At 17.00 hrs, the 2/Lincs on the right flank were ordered to withdraw to the road and dig in there. The Northumberland Fusiliers had moved up in support as far as Vendegies. Divisional HQ decided that no further attempts to advance would be made that day: orders for the resumption of the attack at 04.00 hrs the next morning were issued at 20.30. The 62 Bde staff settled down in Vendegies château for the night.

The advance to the Brown Line – and if possible, beyond – would be prosecuted initially by 62 and 64 Bdes. Exploitation was to be entrusted to 110 Bde. A second objective was set about a mile beyond the Brown Line,[44] and an ambitious third line running along the Jolimetz to Le Quesnoy road represented the limit of 21st Division's hopes.

---

43   Bond, *The King's Own Yorkshire Light Infantry in the Great War*, Vol. II., pp. 1012-1013.

44   This line ran through Grand Gay Farm and is located just beyond the top right-hand corner of Map 47.

334   To Do the Work of Men

On the left flank of the divisional frontage, the first stage of the attack was executed by the 1/Lincs, who moved off behind an artillery barrage at 04.00 hrs. It was all over very quickly: with C Coy on the left and A Coy on the right, the Brown Line was reached and captured by 06.00. Over 100 prisoners had been taken at a cost of three Other Ranks killed, with 32 wounded and 12 missing. As they halted to consolidate their newly-won position, the 12/13 NFus leapfrogged and continued the attack. German resistance appeared to stiffen at this point, and with 64 Bde on the right also finding the going difficult, the advance stalled, and it was not until 16.00 hrs that the Fusiliers were able to push on to their objective. The cost was not inconsequential this time: three officers had been killed, with a further three wounded.[45] Other Ranks casualties amounted to 13 killed, 100 wounded and 30 missing.[46]

On the right divisional front, 2/Lincs stood fast in the road just short of the Green Line, allowing 15/DLI and 9/KOYLI to pass through them and head for the village of Poix-du-Nord. Almost straight away, machine gun fire from the shallow ridge immediately ahead of them held up the advance. This line was also heavily wired, and 9/KOYLI were stuck there for almost two hours, losing the barrage as a consequence. A frustrated Lieutenant-Colonel Greenwood decided to take a look for himself and crept out towards the German line. There was a weak spot: he found that one sector of the ridge was held by a solitary machine gun post that was out of sight of the others, so he crawled to within twenty yards of the gun before standing up and rushing the position single-handed, taking the crew by surprise and killing all of them with his pistol. He was now able to direct his men through this gap in the defences, and with the other machine guns now outflanked, the battalion was able to push on towards Poix-du-Nord. The village was "taken with very little resistance",[47] and the KOYLIs continued the advance and occupied the Salesches – Englefontaine road, just short of the Brown Line. As it turned out, they had arrived on this line before their compatriots and found both of their flanks in the air. The Germans saw this as a perfect opportunity to launch a counter attack, which they did under a fierce artillery bombardment. British casualties started to mount, but with Greenwood walking calmly up and down in front of his advanced posts to encourage his men, the attack was repulsed. By 10.00 hrs two companies of the 1/EYorks had moved up from their initial support positions and joined the KOYLIs on their objective, extending their right flank. Two hours later, the 15/DLI were able to do the same on the left, having lost their commanding officer, Lieutenant-Colonel H.H. Neeves, wounded, in the advance. Captain J.Sedgwick took command.[48] It was a further two hours before touch was gained with 33rd Division on the right.

At 14.40, 21st Division issued orders for the continuation of the attack. Accordingly, at 16.00 hrs, the 12/13 NFus on the left and 15/DLI and 1/EYorks on the right pushed on against a now somewhat demoralised enemy and were able to reach their objective – the road running south-east from Grand Gay Farm in square X.24 – by 18.00 hrs. They spent the night digging in,

---

45   Second-Lieutenants Benjamin Alexander Watson, age 26, Oliver Tunnell, age 33 and John Greenwell, age 24, are all commemorated on the Vis-en-Artois Memorial.

46   TNA PRO WO 95/2155: 12/13 NFus War Diary.

47   TNA PRO WO 95/2162: 9/KOYLI War Diary. Over 2,500 French civilians were found to be still living there.

48   Lieutenant-Colonel A.C. Barnes arrived to take command of 15/DLI on 29 October.

preparing to repel any German counter incursion, with 9/KOYLI forming an echeloned defensive flank on the right. During the two days' fighting, 15/DLI had suffered substantial casualties: two Officers had been killed on the 23rd,[49] and Other Ranks casualties numbered 32 killed, 156 wounded and 57 missing. The 9/KOYLI diarist does not mention casualties, but records show 47 fatalities, including Lieutenant John Philip Webster, who had joined the battalion only seven days before. Second-Lieutenants Walter Lowe Percival and William Byron Smith died of wounds on the 24th and 25th respectively, their stays with the battalion also being brief, both having joined in mid-October.[50]

Original plans had allowed for 110 Bde to push on even further to the east, but by mid-afternoon on the 24th, it was realised that the attack had been checked, "presumably for the day",[51] and its three battalions were content to take up positions between Vendegies and the Green Line and await developments on the morrow. Patrols were sent out by 62 Bde at 06.30 on the morning of 25 October, "to ensure that the enemy still maintained the position to which he had retired the night before on the Western outskirts of LOUVIGNIES".[52] He did: the patrols met very heavy fire from a line of machine guns in the orchards and withdrew immediately. Advanced posts were established, but no further attempts at infiltration were attempted that day. All battalions were then placed on alert in case of German counter attack, but none materialised. Both sets of front-line troops seemed happy to pause and catch their breath, but German artillery continued to bombard the village of Poix-du-Nord:

> No sooner had billets been obtained however, than the enemy, with accustomed viciousness, commenced to shell violently the most congested portions of the village – and this wanton and despairing effort continued all the morning. To complete the discomfort of civilians and troops alike, at 11-0 a.m. he increased the terror with an avalanche of aerial bombs, inflicting many casualties and destroying much property. In striking contrast to such perfidy, was the fact that our Artillery had fired on no village East of the Beaurevoir System.[53]

During the night of 25/26 October, 110 Bde relieved 62 and 64 Bde units in the front line. This was in itself a temporary measure, as 17th Division took over the line the following night. 62 Bde had moved back to billets in Neuvilly, 64 Bde units were further back in Inchy, and 110 Bde were soon "at rest" [54] in and around Ovillers. The Division would not be called into action again for just over a week, so casualties could be calculated and new drafts welcomed and integrated.

49 Lieutenant John Hyman Marks, age 21, is buried in Ovillers New Communal Cemetery, grave reference A.47. Second-Lieutenant Peter Hodkinson is commemorated on the Vis-en-Artois Memorial.
50 Webster and Smith are buried in Awoingt British Cemetery, grave references I.B.15. and I.E.11 respectively. Percival is buried in Poix-du-Nord Communal Cemetery Extension, grave reference II.B.17.
51 TNA PRO WO 95/2163: 110 Bde HQ War Diary.
52 TNA PRO WO 95/2153: 62 Bde HQ War Diary.
53 Bacon: unpublished memoir, p. 138.
54 TNA PRO WO 95/2163: 110 Bde HQ War Diary.

336   To Do the Work of Men

21st Division casualties for the month of October 1918 were recorded as follows:

	Killed		Wounded		Missing		Total	
	Off	OR	Off	OR	Off	OR	Off	OR
62 Bde								
12/13 NFus	6	39	6	199	–	51	12	289
1/Lincs	2	28	7	130	–	42	9	200
2/Lincs	1	43	7	188	–	39	8	270
Total:	*9*	*110*	*20*	*517*	*–*	*132*	*29*	*759*
64 Bde								
1/EYorks	–	22	7	272	–	74	7	368
9/KOYLI	1	27	13	165	–	59	14	251
15/DLI	2	60	15	305	1	107	18	472
Total:	*3*	*109*	*35*	*742*	*1*	*240*	*39*	*1,097*
110 Bde								
6/Leics	3	39	8	120	–	31	11	190
7/Leics	1	35	8	155	–	30	9	220
1/Wilts	3	38	7	192	–	11	10	241
Total:	*7*	*112*	*23*	*467*	*–*	*72*	*30*	*651*
Overall:	**19**	**331**	**78**	**1,726**	**1**	**444**	**98**	**2,507**[55]

Drafts had just about kept up with the losses:[56]

	Officers	Other Ranks
62 Bde	41	1,160
64 Bde	42	1,025
110 Bde	19	541
Total:	**102**	**2,726**

For his gallant actions on 23 and 24 October 1918, Lieutenant-Colonel Harry Greenwood, 9/KOYLI, was awarded the Victoria Cross.[57] His thoughts at the time are not recorded, but in early 1919 he wrote a letter to his friend Captain Ellenberger, who had been repatriated after his capture and incarceration in May 1918:

My Dear Ellenberger,
Many thanks for your letter which turned up last evening and for the nice things you say therein about myself. I'm afraid I don't deserve them all, however, as I did really nothing save drive on, kill a few Huns and cheer our fellows on a bit when they flagged. It was topping fighting really and I would not have missed it for anything. Lots of Bosche to kill

55   TNA PRO WO 95/2135: 21st Division Adjutant & Quartermaster General War Diary.
56   Ibid.
57   The full VC Citation and a brief biography can be found in Appendix IV.

and plenty of time to kill them in, in fact one could almost choose one's bird. Our fellows were splendid and with any kind of leadership would have gone anywhere. It is a great shame of course that you were not there to get a little of your own back".[58]

The next major offensive was to be an attack on the German defensive line running north-south through the villages to the west of the Forêt de Mormal and along the banks of the Sambre-Oise Canal. The Battle of the Sambre, the last large-scale set-piece attack of the war, was, in scale, similar to that of the first day of the Battle of the Somme.[59] The German Army was determined to hold their defensive line, hoping to buy time for a strategic withdrawal to as yet incomplete defensive positions between Antwerp and the River Meuse and thereby negotiate a compromise peace in the Spring of 1919. As before the 23 October attack, logistics dictated a pause while ammunition, guns and other materiel were moved up the stretched Allied supply lines.

Lieutenant-Colonel Harry Greenwood VC, commanding 9/KOYLI. (Michael Greenwood)

The assault would go in on 4 November. The 21st and 17th Divisions had been leapfrogging each other on a regular basis throughout the autumn offensives, and on this occasion 17th Division would be in the front line for the attack, with 21st Division held in reserve. The V Corps attack (with 17th Div on the left and 38th Div on the right) would take the men deep into the central section of the Forêt de Mormal and included the capture of the rather isolated village of Locquignol. The scale of any involvement of 21st Division would depend on the level of success – or otherwise – of the initial assault.

On 4 November the 17th Division struggled a little fighting its way through the Forêt de Mormal: it came up short of its final objective, but a general German withdrawal that night prompted by British success elsewhere along the line meant that units were able to push on towards the eastern edge of the forest more or less unopposed in the early hours of the following morning.

---

58 IWM Brigadier G.F. Ellenberger. Doc: 4227, 5 January 1919.
59 For a detailed account of the Battle of the Sambre, see Derek Clayton, *Decisive Victory. The Battle of the Sambre 4 November 1918* (Solihull: Helion & Company Ltd, 2018), *passim*.

338 To Do the Work of Men

21st Divisional Order No. 258, issued at 23.10 on 4 November, delineated a series of objective lines, Green, Black and Yellow,[60] which were allocated respectively to 62, 110 and 64 Bdes. Zero Hour for 62 Bde was 05.30 the next morning.

They moved off, not quite knowing what to expect, with 12/13 NFus on the left and 1/Lincs on the right. It was raining hard. Little opposition was encountered and so the two battalions were ordered to continue the advance as far as the Yellow Line. The 1/Lincs diarist notes that opposition "in strength" was first encountered "from spurs and orchards N of Berlaimont. The town itself was clear of enemy".[61] The battalion was then disposed as follows: A Coy was in the orchards just to the north-east of the Berlaimont – La Grande Carrière road (running diagonally through Square U.20 on map). D Coy extended the line down to the canal and C Coy took up positions in reserve to the west of the village. Meanwhile, B Coy was ordered to advance along the railway line towards the canal. Once there, they found that all the bridges had been destroyed, and so were content for the time being to take up positions astride the railway and to await developments. The decision not to place men in Berlaimont village itself turned out to be a wise one, as the Germans shelled it heavily during the afternoon and on into the night.

On the left, the 12/13 NFus had been held up briefly by machine gun fire from the high ground to the north of Berlaimont, but the Germans were executing a fighting retreat and did not resist for long. The Fusiliers were able to take up positions in the sunken road in Square U.15 and then proceeded to push patrols out towards the canal. The advance had cost them two fatalities.[62]

At 17.00 hrs, the 1/Lincs began to investigate the possibility of bridging the canal: it seemed possible that a crossing might be viable at the Lock (see map square U.21.c.), and by using the debris of the lock gates, temporary bridges were extemporised and a platoon of D Coy was ordered to establish a bridgehead on the eastern side of the waterway. Unfortunately, the canal splits into three channels at this point, and the platoon discovered that the third had not been bridged. It was not until a further reconnaissance was made by Royal Engineers (from 126 Field Coy) that an intact bridge was found: it had been prepared for demolition, but the Engineers were able to remove the explosive charges and at around three o'clock on the morning of the 6th, two companies of 1/Lincs (B & C Coys) – albeit under machine gun fire – were able to cross and pushed on in the direction of the village of Aulnoye. C Coy managed to take about twenty prisoners as they established a bridgehead. By five o'clock, they had cleared the area to the south-west of the village, but opposition was stiffening and no advance into the village was attempted. At 12.00 hrs, the 1/Lincs received orders to move back into billets in Berlaimont and the rest of the day, apart from a "heavy burst of shelling"[63] between three and four o'clock, was quiet. During the last two days, the battalion had advanced 9,000 yards and had captured two villages and about thirty prisoners. Five Other Ranks had been killed, with one Officer – Second-Lieutenant F. Hotson – and twenty-seven Other Ranks wounded.

---

60   The Yellow Line is marked on Map 48. It runs roughly north-south just to the east of Berlaimont.
61   TNA PRO WO 95/2154: 1/Lincs War Diary.
62   83404 Private Thomas Carr, age 19, and 19813 Private J. Logan are buried in St Sever Communal Cemetery Extension, grave references II.Y.10 and II.Y.25 respectively.
63   TNA PRO WO 95/2154: 1/Lincs War Diary.

The 62 Bde had unknowingly taken part in its last action of the war. Just after 05.15, units of 110 Bde were to leapfrog through their positions to carry on the advance. The men of 62 Bde were soon in billets in Berlaimont; their role in the Great War was over.

The 110 Bde commenced their long move forward at midday on the 5 November:

> Their march had been much delayed by the congestion on the road caused by the large and deep craters which had been blown by the Boche in the road, at Locquignol and West of Tête Noire. It was pouring with rain too, which made the roads through the forest very muddy and difficult.[64]

They had been ordered to billet in Tête Noire for the night and the following morning, two entire battalions of 110 Bde, the 6/Leics and 1/Wilts, had crossed the canal by means of a bridge at the site of the old lock at Berlaimont:

> This bridge merely consisted of single planks, about two feet wide, laid zigzag across the dilapidated masonry, with no handrail or supports on either side. It was a most rickety structure over which to cross troops on a pitch dark and rainy night, the more so as the river below was swift running.[65]

As this had taken the best part of an hour, they were not ready to make any kind of move forward until nearer 08.30. The crossing had been done under heavy fire from machine guns in Aulnoye, and with 6/Leics on the left, all that had been immediately viable was for D Coy of that battalion to work its way northwards along the eastern canal bank as far as the factory at U.21.d.0.7.

It was decided that a frontal assault on the village might prove costly. Accordingly, 7/Leics were brought forward from support positions: they crossed the canal by means of a pontoon bridge and by noon were ready to continue the advance. They succeeded in outflanking Aulnoye to the north and by mid-afternoon were digging in on the high ground in Square U.23, well to the east of the village. In the meantime, the 1/Wilts had completed a similar manoeuvre to the south of Aulnoye and had gained touch with the 7/Leics. Most of the German garrison, fearful of encirclement, had beaten a hasty retreat: A and B Coys of 6/Leics were then able to advance through the village, leaving B Coy behind to mop up any stragglers. By 18.00 hrs, the day's final objective had been reached: the road northwards from les Quatre Bras and running through Etrée (See Map 48). Some desultory machine gun fire was still coming from the direction of les Quatre Bras, but touch had been gained on the right with 33rd Division. The division's left flank was, however, still in the air, 5th Division having not kept up with the rate of advance. This was not as serious as it might appear: the risk of German counter attack at this point was negligible. The important thing now was to keep the enemy on the back foot and give him no time to regroup or establish any kind of prepared defensive line. At 22.20 hrs, orders were issued by 21st Division HQ for a resumption of the advance at dawn on 7 November.

---

64 Cumming, *A Brigadier in France 1917-1918*, p.256.
65 Ibid, p.257.

340   To Do the Work of Men

Once more it was the turn of 110 Bde to lead the way. Initial plans included two new objective lines: the Red Line was drawn seemingly fairly arbitrarily from north to south along the ridge of high ground to the west of the village of Limont-Fontaine, through the centre of squares V.15 and V.21; the second objective, the Blue Line, was in effect the line of the Maubeuge – Avesnes road, again running north-south, some 2,000 yards east of Limont-Fontaine. Once 110 Bde had secured the Red Line, 64 Bde would move through onto the second objective. If all went well, patrols would be sent out beyond the road to "exploit the village of Beaufort",[66] another thousand yards or so to the east.

Zero Hour was 05.45 on 7 November, and the 7/Leics and 1/Wilts, left and right respectively, moved off to time under a creeping artillery barrage. It quickly became clear that the Germans had withdrawn quite some distance during the night: at 08.45, 110 Bde HQ received a report from 7/Leics saying that the village of Bachant was "clear of the enemy" and that the leading companies had crossed the railway in V.13.b & c by 06.30; by 07.10 they had crossed the sunken road in V.14.c. "Little opposition was met with".[67] The 1/Wilts diarist paints a similar picture, remarking that "little opposition was met with until the Battalion reached the high ground in V.20 [1,000 yards short of the Red Line] where they came under heavy machine gun and artillery fire".[68] Both battalions reached the Red Line and began to dig in. Once more, the 33rd Division on the right had kept pace, but 5th Division on the left had not crossed the railway in V.8 and 7/Leics were obliged to throw a defensive flank back facing north along the high ground in V.14.[69] Brigadier Cumming (GOC 110 Bde) had advanced his initial HQ to a brewery in Aulnoye at approximately 07.30, and thence ninety minutes later to Etrée, "being received everywhere with open arms by the inhabitants who were crazy with joy at being free once more. Flowers and everything they had – mostly coffee – were pressed on the troops, and flags sprang out everywhere like mushrooms in a night".[70]

As 64 Bde units passed through them at around 09.00 hrs, 110 Bde could begin to breathe a little more easily. It was obviously not known to them at the time, but they too had completed their last action of the war. It had cost the 7/Leics ten fatalities, the 1/Wilts losing just one man.[71]

Units of 64 Bde had moved off in column, crossing the Sambre at Berlaimont at 05.30 and then marching on through Aulnoye and Bachant. The 15/DLI and 1/EYorks, left and right, deployed into attack formation before passing through the Red Line positions at around 08.30,

66   TNA PRO WO 95/2160: 64 Bde HQ War Diary.
67   TNA PRO WO 95/2163: 110 Bde HQ.War Diary
68   TNA PRO WO 95/2165: 1/Wilts War Diary. By this stage of the war, which was in effect a 'pursuit', German defences consisted mainly of machine gun posts and small groupings of artillery pieces. On occasion, single guns came into action.
69   There is some confusion here: the 7/Leics diarist places 1/Wilts on the left flank of the attack. Brigadier Cumming's memoir states, however, that 7/Leics threw back the defensive flank on the left. The 110 Bde HQ diary does not mention dispositions. Taking into consideration the line of the 7/Leics' attack, and the fact that the 1/Wilts diary has them digging in in square V.20, (although in reality it was probably V.21), the author favours the Brigadier's version.
70   Cumming, *A Brigadier in France 1917-1918*, pp.259-260.
71   28070 Private E. Mears is buried in Berlaimont Communal Cemetery Extension, grave reference B.4. Three graves away from him lies 39926 Corporal Walter Waring, age 19, who died from wounds the day after the attack.

with 9/KOYLI in support. They walked straight into an enemy artillery barrage and very heavy machine gun fire. The 15/DLI were also taking enfilade fire from the left flank. Brigade HQ was obliged to send a detachment of cyclists and a machine gun section out to cover this flank, and only then could the Durhams continue their advance. They were now some distance behind the front companies of 1/EYorks: their D Coy had crossed the Grimour stream and had taken up positions in the quarry just beyond the ford, and C Coy, on the left, had also managed to cross the stream, but in trying to establish contact with the Durhams, had formed a defensive flank facing north. At around 13.15, their commanding officer, Lieutenant-Colonel F.L. du Moulin, was killed.[72]

Although the 15/DLI had also belatedly managed to cross the Grimour stream, it was clear to division that the attack had stalled, and orders were sent out to hold on and consolidate the positions already captured. The attack on Limont-Fontaine and Eclaibes would resume under a re-arranged artillery barrage at 17.00 hrs, but not before patrols had been sent out by 9/KOYLI to try and locate some of the machine gun posts and artillery batteries.

Captain Reginald Claud Moline Gee MC, 15/DLI, kia 7 Nov 1918, age 22. (*The War Record of Old Dunelmians 1914-1919*)

The artillery barrage opened at 16.45 and with 9/KOYLI leading, the attack went in five minutes later. The only detailed account of this assault is to be found in the KOYLI War Diary, and even this is short on detail, if not on hyperbole:

> ... the 9/KOYLI, covered by supporting fire, advanced. From now onwards this battalion, ably led, made excellent progress, and literally carried everything before it by sheer determination and will to win. A strong stand was made by the enemy, but all to no purpose. In the fierce fighting that took place in front, and in the streets of the villages, men of the 9th. K.O.Yorks.L.I. refused to be denied victory which they had set out to gain. Once again the enemy were entirely outmanoeuvred and outfought. By 21.30 hrs. so great had been the force of the assault that the villages of LIMONT FONTAINE and ECLAIBES – thoroughly cleared of the enemy, were added to the ever growing list of Allied gains.[73]

---

72 Lieutenant-Colonel Francis Louis du Moulin MC, age 29, Royal Sussex Regiment, commanding 1/East Yorks, is buried in the south-western part of Berlaimont Communal Cemetery.
73 TNA PRO WO 95/2162: 9/KOYLI War Diary.

The capture of these villages had cost the KOYLIs sixteen fatalities, including Second-Lieutenant A. Hunter, who had only joined the battalion three weeks before.[74] The attack had also resulted in the death of a Victoria Cross recipient: Captain A.M. Lascelles of 15/DLI was killed during the capture of Limont-Fontaine. He had won his VC on 3 December 1917 when serving with 14/DLI, 18 Bde, 6th Division.[75] The line now ran through squares V.18 and V.24 – and it fell to 17th Division units to continue the advance to the Maubeuge – Avesnes road the following day.

The 64 Bde units were relieved by 51 Bde during the night of 7/8 November, and by dawn, all three battalions were having a tea break in Bachant before moving into billets in Berlaimont. Here, they were able to re-organise, bathe, clean up generally and count the cost of the recent action. The 21st Division A & Q diary finalises the casualties for November 1918 as follows:

Captain Arthur Moore Lascelles VC MC, 15/DLI, kia 7 Nov 1918, age 38. The inscription on his gravestone reads: "Utterly regardless of fear, he died for God, King and Country" (www.findagrave.com)

	Killed		Wounded		Missing		Total	
	Off	OR	Off	OR	Off	OR	Off	OR
62 Bde								
12/13 NFus	–	2	1	9	–	1	1	12
1/Lincs	–	5	1	26	–	2	1	33
2/Lincs	–	1	1	14	–	–	1	15
64 Bde								
1/EYorks	1	9	2	44	–	4	3	57

74 Second-Lieutenant Archibald Hunter, age 19, is buried in Dourlers Communal Cemetery, grave reference II.C.22., along with ten Other Ranks of the battalion.
75 Captain Arthur Moore Lascelles VC MC, age 38, is buried in Dourlers Communal Cemetery Extension, grave reference II.C.24. For a description of the action during which Lascelles won his Victoria Cross, see: Peter Hodgkinson, *A Complete Orchestra of War: A History of 6th Division on the Western Front 1914-1919* (Solihull: Helion & Company Ltd, 2019), pp.273-275.

9/KOYLI	1	11	2	49	–	6	3	66
15/DLI	2	13	1	90	–	11	3	114
110 Bde								
6/Leics	–	4	–	29	–	–	–	33
7/Leics	–	4	2	19	–	3	2	26
1/Wilts	–	4	–	32	–	2	–	38
Total:	**4**	**53**	**10**	**312**	–	**29**	**14**	**394**

These figures do not match exactly the records of the Commonwealth War Graves Commission, but they suffice to give an overall impression of the level of losses sustained during the last days of the war.

On the 9 and 10 November, the 21st Division was "resting and re-organising",[76] with all three battalions of 64 Bde in or around the town of Berlaimont. The 1/EYorks paraded at 07.00 hrs on the 9th for the funeral of their commanding officer, with D Coy providing the firing party. The next day, a draft of two Officers and 200 Other Ranks joined the battalion. The 15/DLI also received three Officers and 140 Other Ranks that day.

The 10 November signalled the resumption of training, and the following morning, battalions marched off to new billets in Limont– Fontaine and Eclaibes. On the way, news of the signing of the Armistice reached the columns. Only the 9/KOYLI diarist records the reaction of the men to the news: "…while inward satisfaction was undoubtedly felt, no outward demonstration was made".[77]

Once the news had had time to sink in, and the constraints of march discipline had been removed, celebrations that evening were perhaps a little more effusive. Captain Harold Yeo, 64 Bde Staff, wrote home that evening:

> Everyone smiling and sounds of cheers ringing out in all the villages. What a strange feeling! These great events never are quite so great when they actually come about. I think one's senses have been rather numbed by all the shocks they have received during the last four and a half years […] and now to go to bed to dream of a blue suit and a bowler hat.[78]

On 12 November, the War Diary of 9/KOYLI declared that "No parades were engaged in, it being considered that for this day at least, training was subservient to rest".[79] At 64 Bde HQ, however, a conference of commanding officers was taking place in order to discuss training and a general programme of work and recreation for the next month. It was important to keep the men occupied. In 110 Bde, it would be a question of "Company Drill & Field Training in the mornings, one Ceremonial Parade and one Route March a week, while Recreational Training [that is, Sports] was carried on during the afternoons".[80]

76 TNA PRO WO 95/2134: 21st Div HQ War Diary.
77 TNA PRO WO 95/2162: 9/KOYLI War Diary.
78 IWM Colonel H.E. Yeo. Papers, Doc. 3132., 11 November 1918.
79 TNA PRO WO 95/2162: 9/KOYLI War Diary.
80 TNA PRO WO 95/2164: 110 Bde HQ War Diary.

344   To Do the Work of Men

On 18 November, a Memorial Service was held in the village church at Limont-Fontaine in memory of those who had fallen in its liberation. Men of 9/KOYLI were invited to take part, and a wreath, made by the villagers, was presented to the battalion. The local 'curé', Abbé J.Hégo, gave a stirring speech, praising the British Army for its valiant efforts since 1914. He spoke in emotive terms of the battle that had resulted in the liberation of his village:

> But our hearts, those of the inhabitants of Limont-Fontaine, share a common and acutely felt pain when we reflect upon the cost paid by the English Army for the retaking of our tiny village. [...] Blood flowed, many brave men fell: officers, as well as their men, were offered up as sacrificial tributes to Death, and it seems that he chose those amongst you of whom you were most proud.
>
> So, it is to recognise the qualities of all the brave men that the English Army has lost in the course of this war: it is to celebrate the memory of the Officers, NCOs and men who have fallen in our homeland; it is to beseech the Almighty to have mercy upon their souls. It is for these reasons that the young people of this commune wanted this ceremony. In the name of all my parishioners, I thank you, General, you the Officers, for being able to enhance it by your presence, and for allowing your men to take part".[81]

He went on to apologise for the conditions under which the ceremony had to be held: the Germans had burned his church in 1914 and shelled it in 1918: "Quelle triste église pour vous recevoir, Messieurs".[82]

It would have been unusual had messages of congratulations not been sent to battalions of 21st Division by formation commanders. Two such have been preserved in the War Diary of 1/Wilts. On 11 November, Major-General Campbell issued his "21st Division Special Order":

> The work which the Division has done, whilst helping to win the great series of victories which have forced GERMANY to sue for peace, has been surpassed by no Division and equalled by few, if any, in the whole of the Allied Armies.
>
> The record of the Division during the past eight months is absolutely unique.
>
> Every Officer, N.C.O., and Man who has ever belonged to the 21st Division may well be proud of the fact, and especially those who fought so doggedly through the dark days of the Spring, and early Summer, and then returned to the attack with a spirit which no troops in this world could have surpassed.
>
> Proud indeed you may be, and proud indeed am I to have the honour of commanding such a glorious Division during the greatest epoch making period in the history of the whole world.
>
> Peace is not yet ensured, and, until it is, I confidently rely on every Officer, N.C.O. and Man so training himself that, whatever the result of the peace negotiations may be, you will be prepared to live up to the magnificent reputation which you have so rightfully and worthily earned and which will cause the name of the 21st DIVISION to be remembered and honoured as long as our Empire exists.

81   Extract from a copy of the 'Programme of the Ceremony' held by the KOYLI Association, Pontefract. Translated from the French by the author.
82   Ibid.

David G.M. Campbell
Major-General,
Commanding 21st Division.[83]

The following day, 12 November, Brigadier-General Cumming issued his "110th Infantry Brigade Special Order of the Day":

Now that active operations have ceased, and everything points to an eventual Victorious Peace, the Brigadier wishes to place on record his appreciation of the work done by Officers, N.C.O.'s and Men while he has had the honour to command the 110th Infantry Brigade.

Since March 21st the Brigade has practically been continuously in action, till the announcement of the present Armistice. Never has the Brigade failed to hold positions in defence, when it was humanly possible to do so, or to obtain its objective in attack.

The defence of EPEHY will remain in history as one of the finest feats of arms performed during the war.

At YPRES the Brigade fell back onto its final position with veteran precision and steadiness, and although greatly reduced in numbers it repelled in no uncertain manner the German attacks on the 27th, 28th and 29th April.

Its reputation for dogged and determined resistance was never more clearly shown than during the retreat in CHAMPAGNE, where although reduced to a skeleton it kept its line intact during the four strenuous days, until finally relieved by the French on the line of the VESLE and came out of action again attenuated in numbers but with its cohesion and morale still intact.

During the recent operations from 14th August onwards it has more than kept up its former record. It has never failed to obtain and hold its objective, and at BEAULENCOURT, the MASNIERES – BEAUREVOIR Line, and finally the crossing of the SAMBRE at BERLAIMONT, it carried out difficult operations with a dash and gallantry which is beyond all praise.

It is a fine record and one that every Officer, N.C.O. and Man may well be proud of in the days to come.

The Brigadier congratulates all ranks on this short epitome of their record during the past eight months, and at the same time wishes to thank them for their gallantry, their cheery acceptance of hardships and privations, and their loyalty and bravery in carrying out his orders at all times.

H.Cumming
Brigadier-General,
Commdg. 110th Infantry Brigade[84]

As 1918 drew to a close, the men of 21st Division settled into a routine of route marches, church parades, salvage working parties, sporting distractions, concert parties and educational classes. The Education scheme allowed men to enrol on various courses, including Advanced English,

83   TNA PRO WO 95/2165 1/Wilts War Diary and WO 95/2160: 64 Bde HQ War Diary.
84   Ibid. During the Irish War of Independence, Brigadier-General Cumming was shot and killed by IRA gunmen in what became known as the Clonbanin Ambush, on 5 March 1921.

346   To Do the Work of Men

Mathematics, Languages, and technical subjects such as the Theory of Engines, Electricity and Magnetism. Brigadier-General McCulloch also offered lectures on history.

The danger of death by enemy action may have receded, but other factors were still at play: on 2 December, the 1/EYorks diarist sadly notes the death of Second-Lieutenant G. Manley from influenza two days earlier at 19 Casualty Clearing Station.[85]

The most popular sport by far was Association Football. Inter-company, battalion and brigade competitions were held: Brigadier-General Edwards provided a silver cup for the 64 Bde Competition; the final was played on the afternoon of 28 November between A Coy 1/EYorks and B Coy 9/KOYLI. After extra-time, the KOYLI team emerged triumphant by a score of two goals to one. Through December, battalion teams contested the 'General Headlam Football Cup', this being played for on a league basis. The 1/EYorks diarist details the situation after each team had played three matches: the 15/DLI led the table with six points, but 64 Bde HQ & TMB propped up the rest having lost all of their games. Sadly, none of the diaries record the final standings. It was not until 28 February that the Divisional Championship was decided, when 21 Div RASC MT Coy[86] beat 1/EYorks in the Final Tie by two goals to one.

Boxing also proved popular; the divisional heavyweight competition being won in January 1919 by Private Long of 12/13 NFus. Hockey and rugby matches were also recorded, and by April, cricket was also on the agenda.

One event that merited comment in almost all the unit diaries took place on 3 December. King George V visited the village of Pont-sur-Sambre and all battalions of 21st Division were assembled on the town square just after 10 o'clock that morning and "gave the Royal party a most hearty reception".[87]

Whilst all this was happening, the process of demobilisation began. The first men to return to England were those needed to bolster a struggling economy: 258 miners left 15/DLI on 6 December. The miners in 1/Lincs had been sent back a week earlier. Other priorities were married men, men who had "release slips" – guaranteeing immediate re-employment from pre-war employers – and men with over three years' service. The overall process proved too slow for some, however, and in an address to 9/KOYLI and 1/EYorks on 6 January in the hangars at Bovelles aerodrome, General Campbell deemed it necessary to explain the delay before General Demobilisation took place and asked the men to show patience. The system, perhaps slightly cumbersome and over-complicated, was as follows:

> Corps Concentration Camps were formed at the chief Railhead in each Corps Area (that of the 5th. Corps was at Saveuse, near Amiens), and here all men for demobilisation in the Corps were collected and despatched in parties by train daily to the Base Port (Calais, Boulogne, Havre or Dunkirk, as the case might be). Usually a night or two was spent at the Corps Camp. Every man was despatched from his unit in a good serviceable uniform and boots, and fully equipped with the exception of Arms and Ammunition. All were warned that this was very important as any deficiencies on arrival in England would have to be made good. On arrival at the Base Port, the men were marched to a Camp for the night.

85   Second-Lieutenant G. S. Manley is buried in Caudry Cemetery, grave reference II.D.5. The inscription on his headstone reads: 'He went with Gladness when Duty called'.
86   Royal Army Service Corps Motor Transport Company.
87   TNA PRO WO 95/2154: 2/Lincs War Diary.

The End is Nigh   347

[...] As a general rule the boats left the Base Ports fairly early in the morning, between 7-0 a.m. and 10-0 a.m., and on arrival in England (Folkestone or Dover) each man would proceed to his Dispersal Area Station for demobilisation. Special trains were provided to London, from whence the journey was continued by ordinary train if necessary. The whole of the British Isles had been divided into Dispersal Areas, [...] and the men were dealt with at the Station nearest their home. [...] But a very short time was required at the Dispersal Station before the Soldier was a civilian – a tour of the Station being made, the man handing in equipment on the way round, and signing, receiving and giving up, various documents. On leaving the Dispersal Station, each man was given [...] a free Railway Warrant to his destination and £2 in notes. His gratuity, any money he might be in credit, full pay and ration allowance for one month, and a civilian suit or 52/6 in lieu,[88] were forwarded later from the Record Office concerned".[89]

There was a gradual acceleration in demobilisation and by March / April of 1919 all battalions were preparing for the last of their numbers to embark for England. On 30 April, for example, 1/Wilts recorded a strength of 10 Officers and 92 Other Ranks. A month later, the last 3 Officers and 60 men embarked for home. The 12/13 NFus had already completed their disbandment: on 26 April, "one Officer and 15 OR [were] loading transport on S.S. HUNSCLYDE. The Cadre embarked on S.S. NOPATIN at 17.30 for Southampton prior to proceeding to destination Catterick".[90]

On 19 May 1919 the 21st Division ceased to exist. Major-General Campbell had left on 9 February to take command of 33rd Division, leaving Brigadier-General Cumming in charge. Its duty to the nation was complete and the list of Battle Honours reflects the magnitude of the part it played in the struggle:

Battle of Loos
Battle of Albert (first phase of the Battle of the Somme 1916)
The Battle of Bazentin (second phase of the Battle of the Somme 1916)
Battle of Flers-Courcelette (sixth phase of the Battle of the Somme 1916)
Battle of Morval (seventh phase of the Battle of the Somme 1916)
Battle of Le Transloy (eighth phase of the Battle of the Somme 1916)
German Retreat to the Hindenburg Line
First Battle of the Scarpe (first phase of the Arras Offensive)
Third Battle of the Scarpe (fourth phase of the Arras Offensive)
Battle of the Polygon Wood (fourth phase of the Third Battle of Ypres)
Battle of Broodseinde (fifth phase of the Third Battle of Ypres)
Battle of St Quentin (first phase of the First Battles of the Somme 1918)
First Battle of Bapaume (second phase of the First Battles of the Somme 1918)
Battle of Messines, 1918 (second phase of the Battles of the Lys) (62nd Brigade)
Second Battle of Kemmel (seventh phase of the Battles of the Lys)

88   Fifty-two shillings and sixpence: in modern currency, £2.62½p. (This is equivalent to around £100 today).
89   D.A. Bacon unpublished Memoir, p.144.
90   TNA PRO WO 95/2155: 12/13 NFus War Diary. This is the last entry in the War Diary.

348   To Do the Work of Men

Battle of the Aisne 1918
Battle of Albert (first phase of the Second Battles of the Somme 1918)
Battle of Bapaume (second phase of the Second Battles of the Somme 1918)
Battle of Epéhy (second phase of the Battles of the Hindenburg Line)
Battle of the St Quentin Canal (fourth phase of the Battles of the Hindenburg Line)
Battle of Cambrai 1918 (sixth phase of the Battles of the Hindenburg Line)
Battle of the Selle
Battle of the Sambre

The deeds of 21st Division have long since passed from the realm of first-hand human memory. During the conflict, the division lost a total of 55,581 men killed, wounded and missing.[91] It is to their memory that this history is dedicated.

Their Name Liveth For Evermore

---

91   This is the highest figure for any 'New Army' division in the Great War. The approximate average casualty figure per month on active service is 1,490. Figures taken from Martin Middlebrook, *Your Country Needs You: Expansion of the British Army Infantry Divisions 1914-1918* (Barnsley: Pen & Sword, 2000) p.94.

Appendix I

21st Division 1915-18

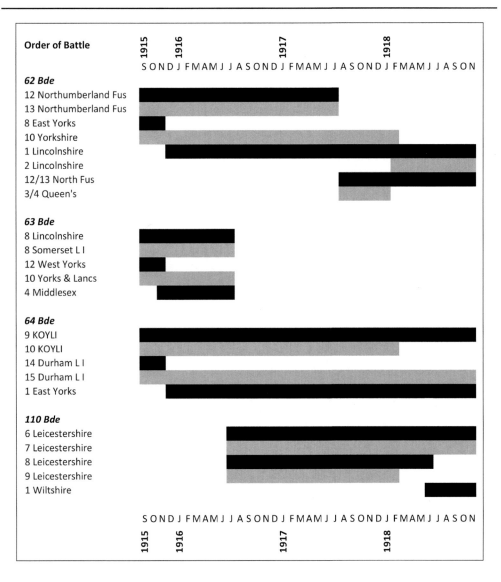

Appendix II

Divisional and Staff Commands

G.O.C. (General Officer Commanding)

16.9.14	Lt-Gen Sir E.T.H. Hutton
11.4.15	Maj-Gen G.T. Forestier-Walker
18.11.15	Maj-Gen C.W. Jacob (wounded 4.3.16)
4.3.16	Br-Gen G.M. Gloster (acting)
1.4.16	Maj-Gen C.W. Jacob
22.5.16	Maj-Gen D.G.M. Campbell

G.S.O. 1. (General Staff Officer.1)

19.9.14	Capt. L.W.G. Butler (acting)
29.3.15	Lt-Col F Cunliffe-Owen
18.6.15	Lt-Col T.F. Fremantle (temp)
21.6.15	Lt-Col F Cunliffe-Owen
5.7.15	Maj. D. Forster (acting)
16.8.15	Lt-Col F.E.Ll. Daniell (kia 4.3.16)
4.3.16	Maj. D. Forster (acting)
7.3.16	Lt-Col A.T. Paley
17.10.17	Lt-Col H.E. Franklyn

A.A. and Q.M.G. (Assistant Adjutant and Quartermaster-General)

18.9.14	Maj. H.W.W. Wood (acting)
13.10.14	Col. R.H.D. Thring
12.10.15	Lt-Col F.H. Dansey
21.11.15	Maj. H.J. Pack-Beresford (acting)
28.11.15	Lt-Col G.J. Acland-Troyte

B.G.R.A. (Brigadier-General Royal Artillery)

9.11.14	Br-Gen C.H. Alexander
6.10.15	Br-Gen R.A.C. Wellesley
12.5.17	Br-Gen F. Potts (temp)
13.5.17	Br-Gen H.W. Newcome
30.10.18	Lt-Col H.A. Boyd
10.11.18	Br-Gen W.B. Browell

C.R.E. (Commander Royal Engineers)

13.10.14	Col. H.F. Chesney (sick 1.6.15)
1.6.15	Maj. C. Coffin (acting)
9.6.15	Lt-Col C Coffin
9.1.17	Maj. H.J. Couchman (acting)
16.1.17	Lt-Col G.H. Addison
19.7.18	Lt-Col G. Master

Appendix III

21st Division Brigade and Battalion Commanders

Only those in command during their brigades'/ battalions' time in 21st Division are shown.

Brigade Commanders

62 Brigade
Brigadier-General T.G.L.H. Armstrong	18/9/1914
Brigadier-General E.B. Wilkinson	4/9/1915
Lieutenant-Colonel H.B. Warwick (acting)	11.6.1916
Brigadier-General C.G. Rawling	13.6.1916 (kia 28/10/1917)
Captain G.M. Sharpe (acting)	28.10.1917
Brigadier-General G.H. Gater	1/11/1917

63 Brigade
Brigadier-General G.J. Fitz M. Soady	18/9/1914
Colonel A.L. Lindesay (acting)	26/6/1915
Brigadier-General N.T. Nickalls	31/8/1915 (kia 26/9/1915)
Lieutenant-Colonel E.R. Hill (temp)	27/9/1915
Brigadier-General E.R. Hill	7/10/1915
(Brigade transferred to 37th Division on 8/7/1916)	

64 Brigade
Brigadier-General H.S. Fitzgerald	18/9/1914
Lieutenant-Colonel R.A. Smith (acting)	30/7/1915
Brigadier-General G.M. Gloster	18/8/1915
Lieutenant-Colonel J.L.J. Clarke (acting)	5/3/1916
Lieutenant-Colonel C. Coffin (acting)	18/3/1916
Brigadier-General G.M. Gloster	31/3/1916
Brigadier-General H.R. Headlam	13/6/1916
Brigadier-General A.J. McCulloch	28/7/1918 (wounded 24/8/1918)
Lieutenant-Colonel C.E.R. Holroyd-Smith (acting)	24/8/1918
Brigadier-General C.V. Edwards	28/8/1918

Appendix III   353

110 Brigade
(Brigade joined from 37th Division on 8/7/1916)
Brigadier-General W.F. Hessey   9/6/1916
Lieutenant-Colonel W.N. Stewart (acting)   20/6/1917
Brigadier-General Lord Loch   22/7/1917
Lieutenant-Colonel W.N. Stewart (acting)   4/1/1918
Brigadier-General D.E. Cayley   4/1/1918
Brigadier-General H.R. Cumming   16/3/1918

Battalion Commanders

62 Brigade
Northumberland Fusiliers
12th (Service) Battalion
Lieutenant-Colonel Willoughby Brooking Mullins 01/10/1914 to 09/08/1915
Lieutenant-Colonel Henry Branston Warwick 09/08/1915 to 07/09/1916
Lieutenant-Colonel Francis Joseph Frederick Edlmann 07/09/1916 to 10/12/1916
Lieutenant-Colonel Percival Henry Stevenson 10/12/1916 to 14/11/1917
Lieutenant-Colonel Francis Joseph Frederick Edlmann 15/11/1917 to 21/12/1917
Lieutenant-Colonel Edward Seton Chance 21/12/1917 to 10/02/1918
Lieutenant-Colonel Reginald Howlett 10/02/1918 to 11/11/1918

13th (Service) Battalion
Colonel William Prior 01/10/1914 to 23/06/1915
Lieutenant-Colonel Arthur Edward Lowther Crofton 23/06/1915 to 10/06/1916
Lieutenant-Colonel Harry Allardice 11/06/1916 to 01/07/1916 Killed in action.
Lieutenant-Colonel Henry George Grist 03/07/1916 to 26/10/1916
Lieutenant-Colonel Theobald Alfred Walsh 26/10/1916 to 25/06/1917
Lieutenant-Colonel Stephen Hamilton Dix 25/06/1917 to 10/08/1917 Killed in action
The 12th and 13th Battalions were amalgamated in August 1917 and became the 12/13th Bn.
    Its commanding officers are listed under 12th Bn above.

East Yorkshire Regiment
8th (Service) Battalion
Lieutenant-Colonel Leslie Charles Fryer 01/10/1914 to 14/08/1915
Lieutenant-Colonel Benjamin Irby Way 14/08/1915 to 26/09/1915 Wounded
Lieutenant-Colonel Francis Bertie Brewis 27/09/1915 to 15/03/1916

Yorkshire Regiment
10th (Service) Battalion
Colonel Arthur De Salis Hadow 12/10/1914 to 27/09/1915 Killed in action.
Lieutenant-Colonel William Black Eddowes 27/09/1915 to 10/07/1916
Lieutenant-Colonel Valentine Fowler 10/07/1916 to 18/11/1916
Lieutenant-Colonel Thomas Gilbert Mathias 18/11/1916 to 20/10/1917 Wounded

354   To Do the Work of Men

Lieutenant-Colonel Reginald Howlett 26/10/1917 to 09/02/1918

Lincolnshire Regiment
1st Battalion
Lieutenant-Colonel Dudley Harcourt Fleming Grant 16/06/1915 to 03/07/1916 Wounded
Captain Thomas Grindall Newbury 03/07/1916 to 04/07/1916
Lieutenant-Colonel Richard Henry George Wilson 04/07/1916 to 18/09/1916
Lieutenant-Colonel Henry Montague Cave Orr 18/09/1916 to 13/12/1916
Lieutenant-Colonel Edmund George Francis Langdon Gould 13/12/1916 to 01/03/1917
Lieutenant-Colonel Lewis Pugh Evans 01/03/1917 to 04/10/1917 Wounded
Captain Thomas Grindall Newbury 04/10/1917 to 06/10/1917
Captain William H Littleton 06/10/1917 to 08/11/1917
Lieutenant-Colonel Edmond William Wales 09/11/1917 to 24/01/1918
Lieutenant-Colonel Bertie Drew Fisher 24/01/1918 to 10/04/1918
Lieutenant-Colonel Henry Wood Gush 10/04/1918 to 30/06/1918
Lieutenant-Colonel Noel Mackintosh Stuart Irwin 30/06/1918 to 11/11/1918

2nd Battalion
Lieutenant-Colonel Noel Mackintosh Stuart Irwin 19/08/1917 to 01/02/1918
Lieutenant-Colonel Edward Prince Lloyd 01/02/1918 to 22/03/1918 Wounded
Major Euston Edward Francis Baker 22/03/1918 to 09/04/1918
Lieutenant-Colonel Reginald Bastard 09/04/1918 to 27/05/1918 Wounded
Major Euston Edward Francis Baker 27/05/1918 to 05/06/1918
Lieutenant-Colonel Edward Prince Lloyd 05/06/1918 to 11/11/1918

Royal West Surrey Regiment (Queen's)
3/4th Battalion
Lieutenant-Colonel Kenneth Allan Oswald 21/06/1917 to 05/10/1917 Wounded
Lieutenant-Colonel Herbert Cooper Cannon 05/10/1917 to 21/11/1917
Lieutenant-Colonel Guy Henry Sawyer 21/11/1917 to 11/02/1918

64 Brigade
King's Own Yorkshire Light Infantry
9th (Service) Battalion
Lieutenant-Colonel Guy Lushington Holland 01/10/1914 to 21/06/1915
Lieutenant-Colonel Colmer William Donald Lynch 22/06/1915 to 01/07/1916 Killed in action
Lieutenant L.D. Spicer 01/07/1916 to 04/07/1916
Lieutenant G.L. Gordon 04/07/1916 to 09/07/1916
Lieutenant-Colonel Arthur George McClintock 09/07/1916 to 11/09/1916
Lieutenant-Colonel Charles Edensor Heathcote 11/09/1916 to 25/09/1916
Captain R.J. McMullin 25/09/1916 to 04/10/1916
Lieutenant-Colonel Clement Arthur Milward 04/10/1916 to 18/03/1917
Lieutenant-Colonel Neville Reay Daniell 18/03/1917 to 04/10/1917 Killed in action
Lieutenant-Colonel Harry Greenwood 04/10/1917 to 20/10/1917
Lieutenant-Colonel Andrew Jameson McCulloch 20/10/1917 to 27/07/1918

Lieutenant-Colonel Harry Greenwood 27/07/1918 to 28/08/1918 Wounded
Major Herbert William Henry Tyler 21/09/1918 to 15/10/1918
Lieutenant-Colonel Harry Greenwood 15/10/1918 to 11/11/1918

10th (Service) Battalion
Lieutenant-Colonel Arthur William Alsager Pollock 01/10/1914 to 01/11/1915
Lieutenant-Colonel William B Stewart 02/11/1915 to 06/04/1916
Lieutenant-Colonel Harry John King 07/04/1916 to 01/07/1916 Wounded
Major Francis Seward Laskey 01/07/1916 to 11/07/1916
Lieutenant-Colonel William Basil Charles Bridge 11/07/1916 to 02/12/1916
Lieutenant-Colonel Francis John Marshall Postlethwaite 02/12/1916 to 22/08/1917
Lieutenant-Colonel Hubert Wogan Festing 22/08/1917 to 06/02/1918

Durham Light Infantry
14th (Service) Battalion
Colonel Robert Eccles 01/10/1914 to 18/06/1915
Lieutenant-Colonel Archibald Samuel Hamilton 22/06/1915 to 13/10/1915 Died of Wounds
Lieutenant-Colonel George Feilden Menzies 14/10/1915 to 10/10/1916
Lieutenant-Colonel John Brenchley Rosher 10/10/1916 to 01/02/1918

15th (Service) Battalion
Lieutenant-Colonel Robert Astley Smith 21/09/1914 to 24/08/1915
Lieutenant-Colonel Edward Townshend Logan 24/08/1915 to 26/09/1915 Killed in action
Captain Albert Edward Babbage 26/09/1915 to 29/09/1915
Lieutenant-Colonel Alfred Edward Fitzgerald 29/09/1915 to 01/07/1916 Killed in action
Major Raymond Bazeley Johnson 01/07/1916 to 01/08/1916
Lieutenant-Colonel Stanhope Humphrey Pedley 06/08/1916 to 09/02/1917
Lieutenant-Colonel Neville Reay Daniell 10/02/1917 to 13/03/1917
Lieutenant-Colonel Julian Falvey Beyts 13/03/1917 to 05/10/1917 Killed in action
Lieutenant John Sedgwick 05/10/1917 to 04/12/1917
Lieutenant-Colonel Frank Alexander Wilson 05/12/1917 to 24/02/1918
Lieutenant-Colonel Hubert Wogan Festing 24/02/1918 to 21/03/1918 Killed in action
Captain Sydney Douglas Thorpe 21/03/1918 to 30/03/1918
Lieutenant-Colonel Charles Edward Ridley Holroyd-Smyth 30/03/1918 to 28/05/1918 Wounded
Major Sydney Douglas Thorpe 28/05/1918 to 28/06/1918
Lieutenant-Colonel Charles Edward Ridley Holroyd-Smyth 29/06/1918 to 18/09/1918 Killed in action
Captain Charles Percy Grant 18/09/1918 to 21/09/1918
Lieutenant-Colonel Horace Hunter Neeves 21/09/1918 to 24/10/1918 Wounded
Captain John Sedgewick 24/10/1918 to 26/10/1918
Lieutenant-Colonel Anthony Charles Barnes 26/10/1918 to 11/11/1918

356   To Do the Work of Men

East Yorkshire Regiment
1st Battalion
Lieutenant-Colonel John Louis Justice Clarke 20/11/1914 to 17/03/1916
Lieutenant-Colonel Montague Bruce Stow 17/03/1916 to 01/07/1916
Lieutenant-Colonel Harold Cecil Rich Saunders 02/07/1916 to 02/11/1916
Major Pipe 02/11/1916 to 08/11/1916
Lieutenant-Colonel Roland Henry Waithman 08/11/1916 to 28/11/1917
Lieutenant-Colonel John Brereton Owst Trimble 28/11/1917 to 08/04/1918
Lieutenant-Colonel James Hugh Coles 08/04/1918 to 25/04/1918 Killed in action
Lieutenant-Colonel William Nathaniel Stuart Alexander 02/05/1918 to 31/07/1918
Lieutenant-Colonel Francis Louis Du Moulin 31/07/1918 to 07/11/1918 Killed in action
Major Thomas William Baron 07/11/1918 to 11/11/1918

63 Bde
Lincolnshire Regiment
8th (Service) Battalion
Lieutenant-Colonel Ernest Berdoe Wilkinson 01/10/1914 to 04/09/1915
Lieutenant-Colonel Harold Ernest Walter 09/09/1915 to 26/09/1915 Killed in action
Major Henry Pattinson 29/09/1915 to 10/10/1915
Lieutenant-Colonel Richard Henry George Wilson 10/10/1915 to 18/11/1915 Wounded
Lieutenant-Colonel Robert Hector Johnston 18/11/1915 to 09/12/1916

Somerset Light Infantry
8th (Service) Battalion
Colonel Henry Cuthbert Denny 12/10/1914 to 11/10/1915
Lieutenant-Colonel Lewis Charles Howard 11/10/1915 to 23/12/1915 Killed in action
Captain Albert W Phillips 23/12/1915 to 21/01/1916
Lieutenant-Colonel John Willoughby Scott 21/01/1916 to 01/07/1916 Wounded
Lieutenant-Colonel Neil Alister Henry Campbell 10/07/1916 to 08/10/1916

West Yorkshire Regiment
12th (Service) Battalion
Colonel Francis Richard Loveband 16/10/1914 to 07/07/1915
Lieutenant-Colonel Robert Anthony Cleghorn Linington Leggett 07/07/1915 to 26/09/1915
    Wounded
Major Joseph Hodgson Jaques 26/09/1915 to 27/09/1915 Killed in action
Major Charles Cyrus Bullock 27/09/1915 to 03/11/1915
Lieutenant-Colonel Claude Henry Campbell 03/11/1915 to 12/02/1916

York & Lancaster Regiment
10th (Service) Battalion
Colonel James Corbet Yale 01/10/1914 to 21/03/1915
Colonel Alexander Lumsdaine Lindesay 21/03/1915 to 27/02/1916
Lieutenant-Colonel Cecil Hugh Taylor 28/02/1916 to 18/06/1916
Lieutenant-Colonel John Herbert Ridgway 18/06/1916 to 23/04/1917 Killed in Action

Appendix III   357

Middlesex Regiment
4th Battalion
Lieutenant-Colonel George Augustus Bridgman 26/02/1915 to 13/10/1915
Lieutenant-Colonel Francis John Duncan 13/10/1915 to 22/10/1915
Lieutenant-Colonel Henry Percy Frank Bicknell 27/10/1915 to 12/03/1917

110 Brigade
Leicestershire Regiment
6th (Service) Battalion
Lieutenant-Colonel Edward Lacy Challenor 19/08/1914 to 16/03/1917
Lieutenant-Colonel Robert Burrell Unwin 16/03/1917 to 06/06/1917
Lieutenant-Colonel William Norman Stewart 07/06/1917 to 22/03/1918 Killed in action
Lieutenant-Colonel Edward Seton Chance 23/03/1918 to 29/05/1918 Killed in action
Lieutenant-Colonel Michael Cleeve Martyn 30/05/1918 to 25/08/1918 Prisoner of war
Lieutenant-Colonel James Charles Burdett 25/08/1918 to 11/11/1918

7th (Service) Battalion
Lieutenant-Colonel William Drysdale 01/10/1915 to 13/07/1916 Wounded
Lieutenant-Colonel Robert Burrell Unwin 26/07/1916 to 01/09/1916
Lieutenant-Colonel William Drysdale 01/09/1916 to 29/09/1916 Killed in action
Lieutenant-Colonel Robert Burrell Unwin 29/09/1916 to 30/09/1916 Wounded
Lieutenant-Colonel Albert Arthur Aldworth 30/09/1916 to 03/12/1916
Major Thomas Cecil Howitt 03/12/1916 to 05/01/1917
Lieutenant-Colonel Charles Edensor Heathcote 05/01/1917 to 18/05/1917
Lieutenant-Colonel Albert Arthur Aldworth 18/05/1917 to 15/07/1917
Major Thomas Cecil Howitt 15/07/1917 to 15/08/1917
Lieutenant-Colonel Albert Arthur Aldworth 15/08/1917 to 15/02/1918
Lieutenant-Colonel Thomas Cecil Howitt 15/02/1918 to 20/02/1918 Wounded
Lieutenant-Colonel Guy Henry Sawyer 20/02/1918 to 15/06/1918
Lieutenant-Colonel Thomas Cecil Howitt 15/06/1918 to 15/07/1918
Lieutenant-Colonel Guy Henry Sawyer 15/07/1918 to 11/11/1918

8th (Service) Battalion
Lieutenant-Colonel Jephson George Mignon 28/07/1915 to 14/07/1916 Killed in action
Major Herbert Luis Beardsley 14/07/1916 to 16/07/1916
Lieutenant-Colonel Gerald Charles Irwin Hervey 16/07/1916 to 25/10/1916
Lieutenant-Colonel Herbert Luis Beardsley 26/10/1916 to 17/04/1917
Lieutenant-Colonel Gerald Charles Irwin Hervey 17/04/1917 to 28/06/1917
Lieutenant-Colonel Archibald Tito Le Marchant Utterson 29/06/1917 to 01/10/1917 Wounded
Lieutenant-Colonel Robert Rennie Yalland 04/10/1917 to 01/11/1917
Major Thomas Cecil Howitt 01/11/1917 to 15/11/1917
Lieutenant-Colonel Archibald Tito Le Marchant Utterson 15/11/1917 to 21/03/1918 Prisoner
    of war
Lieutenant-Colonel Noel Mackintosh Stuart Irwin 21/03/1918 to 28/06/1918

9th (Service) Battalion
Lieutenant-Colonel Claude Henry Haig 01/10/1915 to 26/10/1916 Wounded
Lieutenant-Colonel Philip Eric Bent 26/10/1916 to 23/03/1917
Lieutenant-Colonel William Arnold Eaton 23/03/1917 to 11/05/1917
Lieutenant-Colonel Philip Eric Bent 11/05/1917 to 01/10/1917 Killed in action
Lieutenant-Colonel Thomas Cecil Howitt 15/11/1917 to 20/02/1918

Wiltshire Regiment
1st Battalion
Major Herbert Cooper Cannon 27/04/1918 to 19/06/1918
Lieutenant-Colonel John Victor Bridges 19/06/1918 to 07/07/1918 Wounded
Lieutenant-Colonel Guy Bernard Campbell Ward 07/07/1918 to 11/11/1918

Appendix IV

21st Division Victoria Cross Winners

Major Stewart Walker Loudoun-Shand, 10th Battalion Yorkshire Regiment

Date of VC Action: 1 July 1916

For most conspicuous bravery. When his company attempted to climb over the parapet to attack the enemy's trenches, they were met by very fierce machine gun fire, which temporarily stopped their progress. Maj. Loudoun-Shand immediately leapt onto the parapet, helped the men over it and encouraged them in every way he could until he fell mortally wounded.

Even then he insisted on being propped up in the trench and went on encouraging the non-commissioned officers and men until he died.

Stewart Walter Loudoun-Shand was born in Ceylon on 8 October 1879, where his father was a tea planter and Chairman of the Planters' Association of Ceylon. Stewart had ten siblings.

He was educated in England at Dulwich College from 1891 to 1897 and excelled at sport, especially cricket. On leaving school he was employed by William Deacon's Bank. He enlisted in the London Scottish Rifle Volunteers on the outbreak of the Boer War, but only served for five months because he was debarred from service overseas due to his age. He transferred to the Pembroke Yeomanry on 26 January 1900 and served in South Africa as a Lance Corporal with 30th Company, 9th Battalion, Imperial Yeomanry until July 1901.

On discharge, he remained in South Africa and took up a mercantile appointment at Port Elizabeth. Three years later his father arranged for him to return to Ceylon as a tea merchant, a post that he held until the outbreak of the First World War.

Having passed his medical examination in Ceylon, he returned to Britain and was commissioned as a Lieutenant in the 10th Battalion The Yorkshire Regiment on 28 November 1914. He was promoted Captain in June 1915 and went to France on 9 September that year. He was promoted Major on 28 December 1915 and was wounded on 2 March 1916. He returned to duty eight days later.

He was commanding B Company, 10th Yorkshire Regt on 1 July 1916 when he earned his Victoria Cross. He is buried in Norfolk Cemetery, near Bécourt, France.

His VC was presented to his father by King George V at Buckingham Palace on 31 March 1917. He is commemorated on the Dulwich College War Memorial and on the Loudoun-Shand memorial in West Norwood Cemetery.

30144 Private Horace Waller, 10th Battalion King's Own Yorkshire Light Infantry

Date of VC Action: 10 April 1917

For most conspicuous bravery when with a bombing section forming a block in the enemy line. A very violent counter-attack was made by the enemy on this post, and although five of the garrison were killed, Pte. Waller continued for more than an hour to throw bombs, and finally repulsed the attack. In the evening the enemy again counter-attacked the post and all the garrison became casualties, except Pte. Waller, who, although wounded later, continued to throw bombs for another half an hour until he was killed. Throughout these attacks he showed the utmost valour, and it was due to his determination that the attacks on this important post were repulsed.

Horace Waller was born on 23 September 1896 at 11, Woodhill Terrace, Batley, Yorkshire. His father, John Edward Waller was a plumber. His mother, Esther, died when Horace was two years old and he and his father moved in with his maternal grandmother. His father remarried in October 1903.

Horace was educated at Purlwell Primary School in Batley and won a free scholarship to Batley Grammar School, beginning his studies there in the autumn of 1909. He left school at seventeen and was apprenticed into the family plumbing business, all the while continuing his education at Batley Technical College.

Horace joined the army on 30 May 1916. This was his third attempt to enlist, having been classed as medically unfit on the first two occasions. His date of arrival in France is unknown, but on 9 April 1917 he was with the 10th King's Own Yorkshire Light Infantry, ready to advance in an attack on the German Hindenburg Line, south of the town of Arras. On the second day of the battle, he won his Victoria Cross defending his position against a German counter attack.

He is buried in Cojeul British Cemetery, near where he fell. His parents received his VC from King George V at Buckingham Palace on 21 July 1917. In 1992, a road was named after him in his home town: 'Horace Waller VC Parade' was officially opened by the Mayor of Batley.

4/9720 Private Michael Wilson Heaviside, 15th Battalion Durham Light Infantry

Date of VC Action: 6 May 1917

For most conspicuous bravery and devotion to duty. When the Battalion was holding a block in the line a wounded man was observed about 2 p.m. in a shell hole some sixty yards in advance of our block and about forty yards from the enemy line. He was making signals of distress and holding up an empty water bottle. Owing to snipers and machine gun fire it was impossible, during daylight, to send out a stretcher party. But Pte. Heaviside at once volunteered to carry water and food to the wounded man, despite the enemy fire. This he succeeded in doing, and found the man to be badly wounded and nearly demented with thirst. He had lain out for four days and three nights, and the arrival of the water undoubtedly saved his life. Pte. Heaviside, who is a stretcher bearer, succeeded the same evening, with the assistance of two comrades, in rescuing the wounded man.

Michael Heaviside was born in Station Lane, St Giles, Durham on 28 October 1880. He was educated at Kimblesworth Colliery School and was then employed as a miner at Burnhope Colliery. He enlisted in the Royal Army Medical Corps and served as a stretcher bearer in the Boer War. He was returned to England after a bout of enteric fever.

He returned to mining and in 1913 moved to the Oswald Pit. He married Elizabeth Draper on 30 December. They went on to have fifteen children. (One of the sons, Victor, was killed in action during the Second World War).

Michael enlisted in the 10th Durham Light Infantry on 7 September 1914 and was posted to France in June 1915. Soon after, he transferred to the 15th Battalion DLI.

Shortly after his VC action, on 12 July 1917, he returned home to a hero's welcome. He received his VC from King George V at Buckingham Palace on 21 July 1917. He was discharged from the army on 8 June 1919.

Michael returned to England and continued working as a miner. The effects of gas poisoning during the war, coal dust and heavy smoking resulted in his death at his home in Craghead on 26 April 1939. His family could not afford a headstone and he was buried in an unmarked grave in St Thomas' Churchyard, Craghead. Burial records were later lost in a fire, but his grave was eventually located and a headstone, paid for by the family and the Durham Light Infantry Association, was dedicated on 1 November 1999.

A four-minute film of Michael Heaviside VC arriving at Shield Row Station and being paraded through the streets in a motor car to Stanley Town Hall can be viewed at <www.iwm.org.uk/collections/item/object/1060000167>

Lieutenant-Colonel Philip Eric Bent, 9th Battalion Leicestershire Regiment

Date of VC Action: 1 October 1917

On 1st October 1917, east of Polygon Wood, Zonnebeke, Belgium, during a heavy hostile attack, the right of his own command and the battalion on his right were forced back. The situation was critical owing to the confusion caused by the attack and the intense artillery fire. Lt. Col. Bent personally collected a platoon that was in reserve, and together with men from other companies and various regimental details, he organised and led them forward to the counter-attack, after issuing orders to other officers as to the further defence of the line. The counter-attack was successful and the enemy were checked. The coolness and magnificent example shown to all ranks by Lt.-Col. Bent resulted in the securing of a portion of the line which was of essential importance for subsequent operations. This very gallant officer was killed whilst leading a charge which he inspired with the call of "Come on the Tigers."

Philip Eric Bent was born in Halifax, Novia Scotia on 3 January 1891. He was educated in England, at Ashby de la Zouch Grammar School between 1904 and 1907, where he was Head Boy, and at the Royal High School, Edinburgh. He joined HMS Conway, the Merchant Navy training ship, in 1909 and became a senior cadet captain. He became an apprentice on the barque "Vimeria" in December 1910 and qualified as a 2nd Mate early in 1914.

Being ashore when war broke out, he enlisted 'for a bit of fun' as a private in the 15th Battalion Royal Scots on 2 October 1914. He was commissioned in the Leicestershire Regiment on 30 November and joined the 7th Battalion at Aldershot in April 1915. He was promoted to Lieutenant on 1 June and transferred to 9th Battalion just over a month later. He went to France on 31 August 1915 and was Grenade Officer when he applied for a regular commission in March 1916. He was appointed temporary Captain on 21 April and joined the Bedfordshire Regiment in May.

After being mentioned in dispatches, he transferred back to the Leicestershire Regiment on 5 July 1916, joining the 9th Battalion as Major and Second in Command. He was wounded in September and October and in February 1917 he was promoted to temporary Lieutenant-Colonel. On 4 June 1917 he was awarded the DSO.

He was commanding the battalion on 1 October 1917 in positions in Polygon Wood, near Zonnebeke, Belgium, when he won his Victoria Cross.

His body was not recovered after the action and he is commemorated on the Tyne Cot Memorial. His mother presented his medals to Ashby Boys' Grammar School in 1923. In 2015, a new road in Ashby de la Zouch was named 'Philip Bent Road'. Bent's sword is on display in All Saints Church in his hometown of Halifax, Nova Scotia.

Lieutenant-Colonel Lewis Pugh Evans, 1st Battalion Lincolnshire Regiment

Date of VC Action: 4 October 1917

For most conspicuous bravery and leadership (Zonnebeke, Belgium) Lt.-Col. Evans took his battalion in perfect order through a terrific enemy barrage, personally formed up all units, and led them to the assault.

While a strong machine gun emplacement was causing casualties, and the troops were working round the flank, Lt.-Col. Evans rushed at it himself and by firing his revolver through the loop-hole forced the garrison to capitulate.

After capturing the first objective he was severely wounded in the shoulder, but refused to be bandaged, and re-formed the troops, pointed out all future objectives, and again led his battalion forward. Again badly wounded, he nevertheless continued to command until the second objective was won, and, after consolidation, collapsed from loss of blood. As there were numerous casualties, he refused assistance, and by his own efforts ultimately reached the Dressing Station.

His example of cool bravery stimulated in all ranks the highest valour and determination to win.

Lewis Pugh Evans was born at Abermadd, Wales, on 3 January 1881. He was educated at Eton and entered the army after training at the Royal Military College, Sandhurst with a commission in the Black Watch as Second-Lieutenant on 23 December 1899, and served with the 2nd Battalion in the Second Boer War in South Africa. At the end of the war he served in India. On his return to England, he went to Staff College in 1913, qualified as a Royal Flying Corps pilot with an aviator's certificate the same year, and on passing out of Staff College he was appointed GSO3 at the War Office. He was subsequently sent to France with the Royal Flying Corps No 3 Squadron, serving as a pilot/observer on the Aisne, mapping the German lines. He later returned to the Black Watch as a company commander.

In March 1917 Evans was appointed to command the 1st Battalion, Lincolnshire Regiment. It was in this role that he won his Victoria Cross on 4 October 1917, during the Battle of Third Ypres.

Following recovery from his wounds, Evans re-joined the Lincolnshire Regiment in January 1918, only to be given command of 1/Black Watch a fortnight later. He was made Brigadier-General on 10 June 1918 and took command of 14 Bde, a position that he held until the end of the war.

Lewis Evans married Dorothea Margaret Seagrove Vaughan-Pryse-Rice on 10 October 1918 and they had one son Griffith Eric Carbery Vaughan Evans who predeceased his father. Dorothea died on 5 December 1921.

In 1938 he retired from the army but returned to service in the Second World War as a Military Liaison Officer at the Headquarters of the Wales Region. He worked with the Special Operations Executive in India and between October 1947 and January 1951 he was Honorary Colonel of the 16th Battalion, the Parachute Regiment.

He was a Churchwarden at Llanbadarn Fawr, a Justice of the Peace, Deputy Lieutenant for Cardiganshire and a Freeman of the Borough of Aberystwyth.

Evans suffered a fatal heart attack on Paddington Station on 30 November 1962. He was buried in the family plot at Llanbadarn Church.

His medals are in the Ashcroft Collection at the Imperial War Museum.

Lieutenant-Colonel Harry Greenwood, 9th Battalion King's Own Yorkshire Light Infantry

Date of VC Action: 23-24 October 1918

For most conspicuous bravery and devotion to duty and fine leadership. When the advance of his battalion on the 23rd October was checked, and many casualties caused by an enemy machine-gun post, Lieutenant Colonel Greenwood single-handed rushed the post and killed the crew.

At the entrance to the village of Ovillers, accompanied by two battalion runners, he again rushed a machine-gun post and killed the occupants. On reaching the objective west of Duke's Wood his command was almost surrounded by hostile machine-gun posts, and the enemy at once attacked his isolated force. The attack was repulsed and, led by Lieutenant Colonel Greenwood, his troops swept forward and captured the last objective, with 150 prisoners, eight machine-guns and one field gun.

During the attack on the Green Line south of Poix Du Nord, on 24th October, he again displayed the greatest gallantry in rushing a machine-gun post, and he showed conspicuously good leadership in the handling of his command in the face of heavy fire. He inspired his men in the highest degree, with the result that the objective was captured, and, in spite of heavy casualties, the line was held.

During the further advance on Grand Gay Farm Road, on the afternoon of 24th October, the skilful and bold handling of his battalion was productive of most important results, not only on securing the flank of his brigade, but also in safeguarding the flank of the division. His valour and leading during two days of fighting were beyond all praise.

Henry 'Harry' Greenwood was born on 25 November 1881 in Victoria Barracks, Windsor, where his father was serving with the Grenadier Guards. He was the eldest of nine children.

Harry was keen to follow his father into the army and on 21 July 1897, aged fifteen, he joined the 1st Cadet Battalion, King's Royal Rifle Corps. Two years later, he had reached the rank of Sergeant.

He volunteered for service in the Boer War, enlisting in the City of London Imperial Volunteers (CIV). He fought at Diamond Hill in June 1900. As volunteers, once they had served their allotted time, they were sent home. Arriving back in England in October 1900, Harry immediately arranged a transfer to the South African Light Horse, and served with them back in South Africa until June 1901. He then joined the South African Constabulary, but was invalided home in October that year after a fall from his horse.

After the Boer War, he re-enlisted in his old King's Royal Rifle Corps unit and served with them as Colour Sergeant until 1909. He remained on the Reserve List until 1914.

Harry married Helena Anderson – a nurse who had tended to him when was hospitalised with appendicitis – on 9 January 1909. They went on to have four children, three daughters and a son. Unfortunately, the son, also called Harry, died when he was four days old.

Before the First World War, Greenwood was working as private secretary to a diamond merchant, but as soon as war broke out, he volunteered for active service and was appointed Captain in the 9th KOYLI.

Captain Greenwood was awarded the Military Cross for his actions on 26 September 1915 at the Battle of Loos and in July 1918, he was awarded the DSO for action during the retreat from Epéhy four months earlier. He had been promoted Major in October 1915 and by the time of his Victoria Cross action he was commanding the 9th KOYLI as Lieutenant-Colonel.

He received his VC, and a Bar to his DSO, from King George V at Buckingham Palace on 8 May 1919. He retired from the army, but in 1920 was part of the VC Guard at the internment of the Unknown Warrior at Westminster Abbey.

Harry returned to Africa where he worked for a number of companies based in Angola until returning to England for good in 1935, settling with his family in Wimbledon.

During the Second World War he served in the Pioneer Corps and was awarded an OBE in 1944.

Harry died of cancer at his home on 5 May 1948, and was buried in Putney Vale Cemetery. His medals are on display at the KOYLI Museum in Doncaster.

Appendix V

Death Sentences Passed by 21st Division Military Courts

Twenty-seven men were sentenced to death whilst serving in the infantry battalions of the 21st Division. Only two of these sentences were carried out, both in 1916, the rest being commuted to lesser punishments. Two of these punishments cannot be confirmed (N/C), one man was given hard labour (HL), the rest penal servitude of varying lengths (PS). Some of the lesser sentences may have been suspended, allowing the man to return to serve with his unit:

Date	Name	Unit	Offence	Sentence
5.1.16	Anderson W. Pte.	10/KOYLI	Sleeping	5yrs PS.
8.3.16	Bladen C.F.H. Pte.	10/York & Lancs	Desertion	Shot 23.3.16
8.5.16	Burgess W. Pte	1/Lincs	Desertion	10 yrs PS.
31.7.16	Randall C. Pte	9/Leics	Desertion	10 yrs PS
15.8.16	Giles P. Pte	14/NFus	Desertion	Shot 24.8.16
1/11/16	Thompson G. Pte	12/NFus	Desertion	5 yrs PS
16.5.17	Atwell G. Pte	12/NFus	Desertion	2 yrs HL
16.5.17	Marston E. Pte	12/NFus	Desertion	N/C
16.5.17	Metcalfe W.E. Cpl	12/NFus	Desertion	10 yrs PS
16.5.17	Pringle J.W. Pte	12/NFus	Desertion	10 yrs PS
24.6.17	Williams W.W. Pte	10/KOYLI	Quitting	10 yrs PS
5.7.17	Hackett J. Pte	7/Leics	Desertion	5 yrs PS
8.8.17	Waring H. Pte	7/Leics	Cowardice	5 yrs PS
14.9.17	Dawson E. Pte	9/KOYLI	Desertion	10 yrs PS
14.9.17	Grozier A.E. Cpl	1/EYorks	Desertion	10 yrs PS
17.10.17	Rossington J. Pte	1/EYorks	Desertion	10 yrs PS
19.10.17	Dring T. Pte	1/EYorks	Desertion	10 yrs PS
19.10.17	Gibbon L. Pte	1/EYorks	Desertion	10 yrs PS
19.10.17	Sizer B. Pte	1/EYorks	Desertion	10 yrs PS
23.11.17	Hackett J. Pte	7/Leics	Disobedience	N/C
30.11.17	Duce J. Pte	9/KOYLI	Desertion	5 yrs PS
20.2.18	Paish G. Pte	12/13 NFus	Desertion	5 yrs PS
14.10.18	Bennett H. Pte	7/Leics	Mutiny	15 yrs PS
14.10.18	Knight F. Pte	7/Leics	Mutiny	15 yrs PS

11.11.18	Bentley W. Pte	15/DLI	Desertion x2	5 yrs PS
21.11.18	McEwan J.A. Pte	1/Lincs	Desertion	5 yrs PS
19.2.19	Emm A. Pte	13/NFus	Desertion	10yrs PS

Twenty-six-year-old Private Charles Bladen deserted from his battalion, the 10/York & Lancs, on 20 December 1915. He managed to get back to England, but was arrested by the police in Hornsey, London, on 19 January 1916. He told the police that he had simply failed to return on time from home leave. In reality, of course, no leave had been granted. Bladen tried to escape three times before he was finally returned to Armentières. He was executed on the morning of 23 March 1916 by a firing squad made up of men from his own battalion and which included his platoon commander, Lieutenant A. Lamond. 14357 Pte Charles Bladen is buried in Cité Bonjean Military Cemetery, Armentières, grave reference IX.G.94.

10018 Private Peter Giles, age 24, 14/NFus (Pioneers), was executed on 24 August 1916 in a back area near Arras. A week earlier, he had spent a night away from his unit and failed to return before roll call the following morning, at which point the Pioneers moved up to the front without him. Sources give different reasons as to where he was that night and why he failed to return to his unit on time. A letter from his sister, discovered in 1999 by Giles' great-niece, states that he had spent the night with his French girlfriend and had then overslept. (Reported on the BBC News Online web site, 23 March 1999). The ChronicleLive web site (23 August 2006) claims that the same letter described a night out with his friends, after which Giles caught up with his unit, remaining with them for three days before being called back for trial. Putkowski and Sykes[1] report Giles being absent for the best part of a week before his arrest. At his court martial, Giles simply claimed that he had been ill. He is buried in Louez Military Cemetery, Duisans, grave reference II.F.6.

---

1   Julian Putkowski & Julian Sykes, *Shot at Dawn* (Barnsley: Pen & Sword Books Ltd. 1993) p.103.

Appendix VI

Map References for Original Trench Maps and How to Interpret Them

The method of using map references is explained below, allowing the reader to find locations on the maps referred to in the text by First World War-style coordinates.

The areas shown on the maps are divided into large rectangles, each identified by a capital letter of the alphabet. These are, in turn, divided into smaller squares (1000 yards by 1000 yards on the ground) identified by a number.

Each numbered square is divided into four quarters, referred to as a, b, c & d, though only rarely marked as such on the maps. Each side of these 500 yard x 500 yard 'sub-squares' are considered to be divided into ten.

See below for example map references:

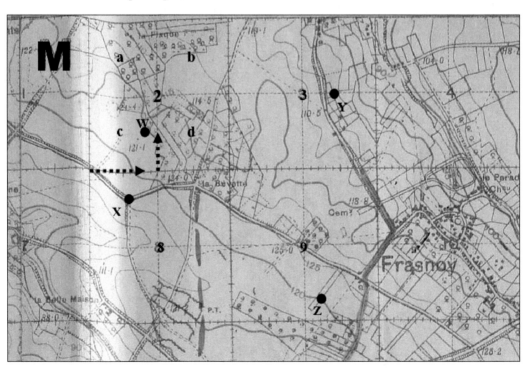

Appendix VI   369

The dot marked 'W' is in square M.2. It is in sub-square c, therefore M.2 c.

Count from left to right along the southern horizontal boundary of that sub-square – the dot is above the eighth division. Count upwards along the eastern vertical boundary and the dot is adjacent to the fifth division.

Therefore, this point can be described as being at **M.2 c 8.5**. Similarly, the dot marked 'X' is at **M.8 a 6.7**. The dot marked 'Y' is at **M.3 b 4.0** and the dot marked 'Z' is at **M.9 d 2.3**.

Any point on the map can therefore thus be identified to within 50 yards on the ground. On larger scale maps, each side of a sub-square is divided not into ten, but one hundred, therefore M.2 c 82.51 locates the centre of 'W' to an accuracy of five yards. (This notation is not often used in the text of this work).

Bibliography

Primary Sources

National Archives (Kew)
   TNA PRO 30/57/50: Kitchener Papers
   TNA PRO CAB 45/116: Official History Correspondence
   TNA PRO CAB 45/120: Official History Correspondence
   TNA PRO CAB 45/121: Official History Correspondence
   TNA PRO CAB 45/134: Official History Correspondence
   TNA PRO CAB 45/135: Official History Correspondence
   TNA PRO WO 95/110 War Diary 4 Brigade Tank Corps.
   TNA PRO WO 95/158: First Army War Diary
   TNA PRO WO 95/1223: 4/Grenadier Guards War Diary
   TNA PRO WO 95/1424: 8/East Yorks War Diary
   TNA PRO WO 95/1432: 12/West Yorks War Diary
   TNA PRO WO 95/1617: 14/Durham Light Infantry War Diary
   TNA PRO WO 95/1998: 50 Brigade HQ War Diary
   TNA PRO WO 95/2004: 7/Yorkshire War Diary
   TNA PRO WO 95/2128: 21st Division HQ War Diary
   TNA PRO WO 95/2130: 21st Division HQ War Diary
   TNA PRO WO 95/2131: 21st Division HQ War Diary
   TNA PRO WO 95/2132: 21st Division HQ War Diary
   TNA PRO WO 95/2133: 21st Division HQ War Diary
   TNA PRO WO 95/2134: 21st Division HQ War Diary
   TNA PRO WO 95/2135: 21st Division, Adjutant and Quartermaster General War Diary
   TNA PRO WO 95/2136: 21st Division Commander Royal Artillery War Diary
   TNA PRO WO 95/2151: 62 Brigade HQ War Diary
   TNA PRO WO 95/2152: 62 Brigade HQ War Diary
   TNA PRO WO 95/2153: 62 Brigade HQ War Diary
   TNA PRO WO 95/2154: 1/Lincolns War Diary
   TNA PRO WO 95/2154: 2/Lincs War Diary
   TNA PRO WO 95/2155: 12/ Northumberland Fusiliers War Diary
   TNA PRO WO 95/2155: 13/ Northumberland Fusiliers War Diary
   TNA PRO WO 95/2155: 12/13 Northumberland Fusiliers War Diary
   TNA PRO WO 95/2156: 3/4 Queen's (Royal West Surreys) War Diary
   TNA PRO WO 95/2158: 63 Brigade HQ War Diary

TNA PRO WO 95/2158: 10/Yorks & Lancs War Diary
TNA PRO WO 95/2158: 8/Somerset Light Infantry War Diary
TNA PRO WO 95/2158: 8/Lincolns War Diary
TNA PRO WO 95/2159: 64 Brigade HQ War Diary
TNA PRO WO 95/2160: 64 Brigade HQ War Diary
TNA PRO WO 95/2162: 9/KOYLI War Diary
TNA PRO WO 95/2161: 15/Durham Light Infantry War Diary
TNA PRO WO 95/2161: 1/East Yorks War Diary
TNA PRO WO 95/2162: 10/KOYLI War Diary
TNA PRO WO 95/2163: 110 Brigade HQ War Diary
TNA PRO WO 95/2164: 6/Leicesters War Diary
TNA PRO WO 95/2164: 7/Leicesters War Diary
TNA PRO WO 95/2165: 8/Leicesters War Diary
TNA PRO WO 95/2165: 9/Leicesters War Diary
TNA PRO WO 95/2165: 1/Wilts War Diary
TNA PRO WO 95/2469: 35th Division HQ War Diary
TNA PRO WO 95/2638: 11/Royal West Surreys War Diary
TNA PRO WO158/227: Third Army Operations File
TNA PRO WO 158/235: Fourth Army War Diary
TNA PRO WO 256/22: Haig Diary

Imperial War Museum (London)
Field Marshal Sir John French Papers
Colonel A. de S. Hadow Papers
Lieutenant J.H. Alcock Papers
Lieutenant-Colonel K. Henderson DSO Papers
Colonel H.E. Yeo MBE MC Papers
Brigadier G.F. Ellenberger MC Papers

Miscellaneous Archives
KOYLI Association, Pontefract Barracks: *The Bugle* journal
KOYLI Association, Pontefract Barracks: *The Snapper,* Article by Lieutenant Howard: "Story of
     the 1st Battalion [East Yorks] in the War", Part VII
Leicester Records Office, DE8145/38. Lieutenant A. C. N. March Phillips De Lisle, 'The Story
     of a Leicestershire Company in the Great Push' by 'One who was there'. An account of the
     actions of 'D' Company, 9th Battalion, on the Somme, July 1916.
Leicester Records Office, 22D63/146. D.A. Bacon MM, '110th Leicestershire Brigade, 21st
     Div. A Personal Account'.
Leicester Records Office, Doc. P170: How I was Captured: A record of the service of Lt E.G.L.
     Roberts with the 6th Leicestershire Regiment and as a Prisoner of War.
Liddle Collection, Item No. 55.

372   To Do the Work of Men

Secondary Sources

Published Sources

Anon., *Dennis Ely: Captain, Durham Light Infantry* (Oxford: Frederick Hall, 1916).

Atter, Nigel, *In the Shadow of Bois Hugo: The 8th Lincolns at the Battle of Loos* (Solihull: Helion & Company Ltd, 2017).

Baker, Chris, *The Battle for Flanders: German Defeat on the Lys 1918* (Barnsley: Pen & Sword Military, 2011).

Boff, Jonathan, *Winning and Losing on the Western Front: The British Third Army and the Defeat of Germany in 1918* (Cambridge: Cambridge University Press, 2012).

Bond, R.C., *The King's Own Yorkshire Light Infantry in the Great War 1914-1918* (London: Percy Lund, Humphries & Co. Ltd., 1929).

Clayton, Derek, *From Pontefract To Picardy: The 9th King's Own Light Infantry in the First World War* (Stroud: Tempus Publishing, 2004).

—— *Decisive Victory: The Battle of the Sambre 4 November 1918* (Solihull: Helion & Company Ltd, 2018).

Corrigan, Gordon, *Loos 1915: The Unwanted Battle* (Stroud: Spellmount, 2006).

Cumming, Hanway R., *A Brigadier in France 1916-1917* (London: Jonathan Cape, 1922).

Dugmore, A.R., *When the Somme Ran Red: The Experiences of an Officer of the King's Own Yorkshire Light Infantry During the First World War* (Barnsley: Pen & Sword 2011 reprint of 1918 edition).

Edmonds, J.E., *Military Operations France & Belgium 1915*, Vol. II (London: HMSO, 1928).

—— *Military Operations France and Belgium 1916*, Vol. I (London: Macmillan, 1932).

—— *Military Operations France and Belgium 1917*, Vol. II (London: HMSO, 1948).

—— *Military Operations France and Belgium 1918*, Vol. I (London HMSO, 1935).

—— *Military Operations France and Belgium 1918*, Vol. II (London HMSO, 1937).

—— *Military Operations France and Belgium 1918*, Vol. III (London, HMSO 1939).

—— *Military Operations France and Belgium 1918*, Vol. IV (London: HMSO, 1947).

—— *Military Operations France and Belgium 1918*, Vol. V (London: HMSO, 1947).

Falls, C., *Military Operations France and Belgium 1917*, Vol. II (London: HMSO 1940).

Harris, J.P. with Niall Barr, *Amiens to the Armistice: The BEF in the Hundred Days' Campaign, 8 August – 11 November 1918* (London: Brassey's 1998).

Hart, Peter, *The Somme* (London: Weidenfeld & Nicolson, 2005).

Hine, Alison, *Refilling Haig's Armies: The Replacement of British Infantry Casualties on the Western Front 1916-1918* (Solihull: Helion & Company, 2018).

Hunt, Derek, *Valour Beyond All Praise. Harry Greenwood VC* (London: Chameleon Press, 2003)

Johnson, J.H., *1918: The Unexpected Victory* (London: Arms & Armour Press, 1997)

Kelly, D.V., *39 Months with the Tigers* (London: Ernest Benn, 1930).

Kiernan, R.H., *Little Brother Goes Soldiering* (Edinburgh: Constable & Co., 1930).

Liddell Hart, B.H. *Memoirs* (London: Cassell, 1965).

Liddle, Peter, (ed.), *Passchendaele in Perspective: The Third Battle of Ypres* (London: Leo Cooper, 1997).

Linge, Pam & Linge, Ken, *Missing But Not Forgotten* (Barnsley: Pen & Sword, 2015).

Lloyd, Nick, *Loos 1915* (Stroud: Tempus, 2006).

—— *Passchendaele. A New History* (London, Penguin/Viking, 2017).

Macdonald, Lyn, *Somme* (London: Papermac, 1983).

Middlebrook, Martin, *The First Day on the Somme, 1st July 1916* (London: Allen Lane, 1971).

—— *The Kaiser's Battle: 21 March 1918: The First Day of the German Spring Offensive* (London: Penguin, 1983).

—— *Your Country Needs You: Expansion of the British Army Infantry Divisions 1914-1918* (Barnsley: Pen & Sword, 2000)

Miles, W., *Military Operations France & Belgium 1916*, Vol. II (London: Macmillan, 1938).

Neillands, Robin, *The Great War Generals on the Western Front 1914-18* (London: Robinson Publishing, 1999).

Nicholls, Jonathan, *Cheerful Sacrifice: The Battle of Arras 1917* (London: Leo Cooper, 1993).

Oram, Gerard, *Death Sentences Passed by Military Courts of the British Army 1914-1924* (London: Francis Boutle Publishers, 1998).

Philpott, William, *Bloody Victory* (London: Little Brown, 2009).

Pidgeon, Trevor, *The Tanks at Flers* (Cobham: Fairmile Books, 1995).

Prior, Robin & Wilson, Trevor, *Command on the Western Front* (Oxford: Blackwell, 1992).

—— *Passchendaele: The Untold Story* (London: Yale University Press, 1996).

Putkowski, Julian & Sykes, Julian, *Shot at Dawn* (Barnsley: Pen & Sword, 1993).

Richardson, Matthew, *The Tigers, 6th, 7th, 8th & 9th (Service) Battalions of the Leicestershire Regiment* (Barnsley: Pen & Sword, 2000).

Schmidt-Osswald, Ernst, *Das Altenburger Regiment (8.Thüringisches Infanterie-Regiment Nr. 153) im Weltkriege* (Oldenburg: Stalling, 1927).

Sheffield, Gary, *The Somme,* (London: Cassell, 2003).

—— *The Chief. Douglas Haig and the British Army* (London: Aurum Press, 2011).

—— & Bourne, John (eds.), *Douglas Haig: War Diaries and Letters 1914-1918,* (London: Weidenfeld & Nicolson, 2005).

Simkins, Peter, *From the Somme to Victory: The British Army's Experience on the Western Front 1916-1918* (Barnsley: Pen & Sword, 2014).

—— *Kitchener's Army: The Raising of the New Armies 1914-1916* (Manchester: Manchester University Press, 1988)

Spicer, Lancelot Dykes, *Letters from France 1915-1918* (London: Robert York, 1979).

Stevenson, David, *With Our Backs to the Wall: Victory and Defeat in 1918* (London: Allen Lane, 2011).

Strong, Paul & Marble, Sanders, *Artillery in the Great War* (Barnsley: Pen & Sword, 2011).

Terraine, John, *To Win A War. 1918: The Year of Victory* (London: Papermac, 1986).

Wheeler, Philip L., Stuart M. Archer, Peter Wrigley & Ian B. Fallows, *Batley Lads: The Story of the Men on the Roll of Honour at Batley Grammar School Who Died in the Great War.* (Privately published, n.d.).

Wylly, H.C., *The Green Howards in the Great War* (Uckfield: Naval & Military Press, 2007).

Unpublished Sources

Snowden, K.L., 'British 21st Division on the Western Front 1914-18: A Case Study in Tactical Evolution' (Unpublished MPhil Thesis, University of Birmingham, 2001).

Index

PEOPLE

The rank given is the one held when the character appears in the text for the first time. Any subsequent promotions are not indicated.
The same principle applies to the unit / formation given.
Page numbers in italics denote a photograph.

Abbott, D.W.S., Capt. 10/Y&L. 55
Abbott, H.F., Pte. 1/Wilts. 313 fn.
Abbott, L.P. Lt. 7/Leics. *119*
Ackerman, Lt. 8/SomLI. 93
Adamson, J.C., 2/Lt. 1/Lincs. 199 fn.
Addison, G.H., Lt-Col. 21 Div CRE. 163 fn.
Alcock, J.H., 2/Lt. 8/Lincs. 52, 57, 60
Aldworth, A.A., Capt. 7/Leics. 117
Alexander, J., 2/Lt. 8/Leics. 121
Alexander, N.L., 2/Lt. 9/KOYLI. 88.
Alexander, N.S., Lt-Col. 1/EYorks. 269, 277
Allberry, C.C., Capt. 9/Leics. 144
Allenby, E.H.H., Gen. 155, 158, 175
Anderson, Capt. 1/EYorks. 90
Anderson-Morshead, Lt-Col. 2/Devons. 262
Armstrong, Lt. 13/NFus. 158
Asquith, Herbert. xvii
Astle, A.G., Capt. 8/Leics. 178, 180

Babbage, A.E., Capt. 15/DLI. 66
Bacon, D.A., QMS. 110 Bde. 123, 231, 270, 328, 335, 346-347
Baildon, C.N., 2/Lt. 10/KOYLI. 176 fn.
Baker, Maj. 2/Lincs. 226
Ball, Capt. 1/EYorks. 248 fn.
Barker, C.W.T., Lt. 15/DLI. 66, *229*
Barnes, A.C., Lt-Col. 15/DLI. 334 fn.
Barnett, 2/Lt. 4/M'sex. 110
Barrow, A.E., Lt. 3/4 Queen's. 196 fn.
Bartram, H.L., Capt. 7/Yorks. 102
Basker, R.H., 2/Lt. 8/SomLI. 61

Bastard, R., Lt-Col. 2/Lincs. 240
Beale-Browne, Brig-Gen. 1/Cav Div. 234
Beesley, G.W., 2/Lt. 7/Leics. 307
Bennett, 2/Lt. 8/Leics. 180
Bennett, A.S. Lt. 9/Leics. *122*
Bennett, R.G., 2/Lt. 9/KOYLI. 202 fn.
Benson, 2/Lt. 1/EYorks. 109
Bent, P.E., Lt-Col. 9/Leics. 189, *362*
Bernays, 2/Lt. 6/Leics. 178
Besant, Capt. 1/EYorks. 90
Bevan, Capt. M.G.C. 105
Bicknell, H.F.P., Lt-Col. 4/M'sex. 93, 95
Blewett, E., Pte. 2/Lincs. 284 fn.
Bodman, C.W., 2/Lt. 1/EYorks. 299 fn.
Bolton, Lt. 1/EYorks. 248 fn.
Boncker, B.R. 2/Lt. 1/EYorks. *91*
Bone, 2/Lt. 7/Leics. 259
Bosanquet, G.B., Maj. 64 Bde. 104-105
Boss, 2/Lt. 7/Leics. 285
Bosworth, A.W., 2/Lt. 8/Lincs. 60 fn., *61*
Bosworth,C.W., Lt. 8/Lincs. 60 fn., *61*
Box, R.H., 2/Lt. 9/KOYLI. 167
Bracecamp, 2/Lt. RFA. 157
Branch, H.G.S., Capt. 12/WYorks. 57, 63
Brewis, Maj. 10/KOYLI. 169 fn.
Bridge, W.B.C., Lt-Col. 10/KOYLI. 125, 150
Brierley, 2/Lt. 9/KOYLI. 174
Briggs, Pte. 8/Leics. 148
Brinkworth, E.J., 2/Lt. 15/DLI. 312 fn.
Brooke, J.J., Lt. 3/4 Queen's. 196 fn.
Brown, D.W. Capt. 6/Leics. *122*

Buckley, Maj. 64 Bde. 74
Burdett, J.C., Maj. 6/Leics. 221, 232, 243, 300 fn, 318
Burkhill, A. Pte. 9/KOYLI. *252*
Burn, C.J., 2/Lt. 9/Leics. 189
Burrows, G.W.C., Lt. att. 7/Leics. 300 fn.
Burton, 2/Lt. 9/KOYLI. 204
Bush, L/Cpl. 7/Leics.121
Byng, Sir J., Gen. Third Army. 280, 283, 285, 291
Byrne, Lt. 12/NFus. 182
Byron, CSM. 12/NFus. 181

Cadle, H.E., Pte. 1/Wilts. 313 fn.
Campbell, Lt-Col. 3/Coldstream Gds. 130
Campbell, D.G.M., Maj-Gen. 21 Div. 78-79, *79,* 105, 140-141, 150, 162, 169, 182, 211, 214, 225, 227, 277, 281, 292, 293, 329, 344, 346, 347
Campbell, C.H., Lt-Col. 21 Div. 67-68, *69,* 71
Carnley, Lt. 7/Leics. 232
Carr, Lt. 1/Lincs. 264
Carr, T., Pte. 12/13 NFus. 338 fn.
Cartman, F.J., 2/Lt. 15/DLI. 106, 165-166
Case, A.R., Capt. 1/EYorks. 202
Chalk, Capt. 9/KOYLI. 224
Chance, E.S., Lt-Col. 6/Leics. 240, 271, 276, *276*
Charlesworth, C. Sgt. 10/KOYLI. *70*
Charteris, T. Capt. 10/Yorks. 32, 48 & fn., *50*
Cherryman, V.C., Lt. 13/NFus. 182, 197
Chesterton, Sgt. 8/Leics. 148-149
Chilcott, G.R., Pte. 1/Wilts. 313 fn.
Clarke, Capt. 15/DLI. 272
Clarke, 2/Lt. 8/Leics. 180
Clarke, A.A., Capt. 7/Leics. 120, 121, 190, *191*
Clemson, Br-Gen. 124 Bde. 130
Cliff, F.P., Lt. 10/Yorks. 203 fn.
Clough, W.G., 2/Lt. 1/Lincs. 315 fn.
Coater, Capt. 10/Yorks. 126
Coles, J.H., Maj. 1/EYorks. 232, 247
Comley, 2/Lt. 12/13 NFus. 215
Congreve, Sir W.N., Lt-Gen. XIII Corps. 115, 210, 229, 233, 234
Constantine, Maj. 9/KOYLI. 293
Cookson, B., 2/Lt. 1/EYorks. 168
Cooil, H., 2/Lt. 9/KOYLI. 312 fn.
Cooper, A.H.A., Lt. 3/4 Queen's. 196 fn.
Cooper, L., Pte. 9/KOYLI. 90

Cooper, S., L/Cpl. 9/KOYLI. 90
Corbett, J.W., 2/Lt. 8/Leics. 178
Court, G.F., Lt. Tank Corps. 133
Coverdale, 2/Lt. 1/EYorks. 248 fn.
Cox, F.P., Capt. 9/Leics.177, *177*
Coy, J.C., Capt. 12/13 NFus. 320 fn.
Cragg, J.H., 2/Lt. 8/Lincs. 95 fn.
Crane, R.H., 2/Lt. 1/EYorks. 202 fn.
Crick, W.E. 2/Lt. 9/KOYLI. *165*
Croft, R.W.S., Capt. 7/Yorks. 102
Crofton, Lord. Lt-Col. 13/NFus. 39
Crone, Capt. 10/Yorks. 126
Crossland, RSM. 9/KOYLI. 108
Cumming, H.R., Br-Gen. 110 Bde. 235, 238-239, 243, 260, 262-263, 273, 274, 275, 282, *282,* 298, 305, 308, 318, 340, 345, 347
Cundall, J.E., 2/Lt. 10/KOYLI. 176 & fn.
Cundall, S., 2/Lt. 9/KOYLI. 242

Daniell, N.R., Lt-Col. 9/KOYLI. 167, 204
David, Lt. 7/Yorks. 102
Davis, N., 2/Lt. 9/KOYLI. 202 fn.
Dawson, G. de H., Capt. MO. 9/KOYLI. 329
Dawson, J., Capt. 2/Lincs. 316, 317
Day, A.E., 2/Lt. 9/KOYLI. 104, 106, 174, 199-201, 204, 228
Dean, A., Pte. 2/Lincs. 284 fn.
De Lisle, A.C.N.M.P., Lt. 9/Leics. 123
Denning, J.E.N.P., Capt. 1/Lincs. 150
Denny, H.C., Lt-Col. 8/SomLI. 66
Dent, W., Maj. 10/Yorks. 38, 48 & fn., *49*
Dickinson, 2/Lt. 7/Leics. 212
Dickson, A., Lt-Col. 10/WYorks. 98, 99, *100*
Dix, S.H., Lt-Col. 13/NFus. 156, 157, 172, 197
Dixie-Smith, J.W., Lt. 8/Leics. 148 fn.
Dixon, H.J. Cpl. 8/Som LI. *62*
Dixon, J.G., 2/Lt. 13/NFus. 181 fn.
Dodds, C.B., 2/Lt. 12/NFus, *50*
Dodds, R.W.L., Lt. 13/NFus, *44*
Dore, 2/Lt. 9/KOYLI. 251
Drysdale, W., Lt-Col. 7/Leics. 117, 152
Duchêne, D.A., Gen. French Sixth Army. 258, 279
Dugmore, A.R. Capt. 10/KOYLI. *128*
Duncan, J.D.P., 2/Lt. 13/NFus. 181 fn.

Eames, 2/Lt. 1/EYorks. 109
Eddowes, W.B., Lt-Col. 10/Yorks. 93

376   To Do the Work of Men

Edes, J. Capt. 1/Lincs. 150
Edinborough, S.S., Capt. 1/Lincs. 246
Edlmann, F.J.F., Capt. 12/NFus.50, 156
Edmonds, 2/Lt. 12/13 NFus. 197
Edwards, C.V., Br-Gen. 64 Bde. 297, 329, 346
Ellenberger, G.F., 2/Lt. 9/KOYLI. 77, 89, 90,
    92, 106, 108, 133, 136, 139, 205, 238, 251,
    252, 267-269, 336
EllinghamV.E., 2/Lt. 8/Leics. 192 fn.
Elliott, J.W., 2/Lt. 12/13 NFus. 215
Ellwood, F.J., Lt. 1/EYorks. 202 fn., *202*
Ely, D.H.J., Capt. 15/DLI. 106-107, *107*
Emmerson, H.H., Maj. 6/Leics. 149
Emmet, F.H., Capt. 9/Leics. 124, *124*
Ennals, A.F., Capt. 9/KOYLI. 294, 317
Escritt, George 9/KOYLI xvii
Evans, 2/Lt. 7/Leics. 120, 122
Evans, A.A., Capt. 13/NFus. 181fn.
Evans, L.P., Lt-Col. 1/Lincs. 156, 197, *363*
Ewens, T.W., 2/Lt. 13/NFus. 158 fn.

Fairmann, 2/Lt. 2/Lincs 287
Falvey-Beyts, J., Maj. 15/DLI. 167, 169, 176,
    193, 204
Farey, 2/Lt. 7/Leics. 214
Farmer, 2/Lt. 1/EYorks. 248 fn.
Featherstone, G.H., 2/Lt. 9/KOYLI. 90
Fegetter, J.H., Lt. 12/13 NFus. 199 fn.
Fellows, H., L/Cpl 12/NFus xvii
Festing, H.W., Lt-Col. 10/KOYLI. 119 fn.,
    204, 217, *218*
Field, G.S., 2/Lt. 12/NFus. 181
Fife, R.D'A. Lt-Col.7/Yorks. 98, 101, 102, 104
Findlay, J. 2/Lt. 12/NFus. 181
Fisher, B.D., Lt-Col. 1/Lincs. 226
Fitzgerald, A.E., Lt-Col. 15/DLI. 90, 92, 104,
    105, 107, *108*
Fitzmaurice, Lt. 8/SomLI. 61
Fletcher, A. Maj. 28
Foch, Ferdinand, Gen. 26, 114, 239, 255, 257,
    283, 286
Forestier-Walker, G.T., Maj-Gen. xx, *xxi*, xxii,
    26, 43, 71, 74, 76
Forster, Maj. GSO2, 21 Div. 33
Foster, Capt. 21 Div Staff. 56
Foster, 2/Lt. 1/EYorks. 241
Foulkes, C.H., Lt-Col. 28, 29
France, W., 2/Lt. 12/13 NFus. 327 fn.
Frank, J.H., Capt. 9/KOYLI. 199-201

Franks, Maj-Gen. 35 Div. 230, 234
Frazer, R.F., 2/Lt. 9/KOYLI. 106
Freestone, W., Pte. 6/Leics. 244 fn.
French, Sir J., Gen. 23-24, 26, 27, 31, 33, 34,
    73
Frost, A.B., Lt. 3/4 Queen's. 195

Gardner, T. L/Cpl. 8/Leics. *147*
Garforth, T.H. Pte. 1/EYorks. *134*
Garry, K., 2/Lt. 13/NFus. 181 fn.
Gater, G.H., Br-Gen. 62 Bde. 260, 278, 281,
    281
Gayer, E.J., 2/Lt. 1/Lincs. 199 fn.
Geary, CSM. 7/Leics. 120
Gee, R.C.M. Capt. 15/DLI. *341*
George V. 346
Gibbon, F., 2/Lt. 12/13 NFus. 327 fn.
Gilbart, W.S., 2/Lt. 9/Leics. 144, *146*
Gill, CSM. 10/KOYLI. 163
Gillard, F., 2/Lt. 9/KOYLI. 299 fn.
Glasgow, W.J.T., Br-Gen. 50 Bde. 81
Gloster, G.M., Br-Gen. 64 Bde. 56, 67, 68
Godley, Sir A.J., Lt-Gen. XXII Corps. 239, 244
Golding, F.A., 2/Lt. 9/KOYLI. 90
Goodman, J. Pte. A Coy, 8/Lincs. *59*
Gordon, Sir A.H., Lt-Gen. IX Corps. 255, 258
Gordon, B.L., Lt. 9/KOYLI. 83, 89, 91-92,
    104, 106, 108
Gough, Sir H. Gen. Fifth Army. 175, 184-185,
    186, 208, 219
Grafton, W.S., 2/Lt. 9/KOYLI. 285
Graham, Capt. 13/NFus. 171
Graham-Pole, D., Maj. 12/NFus. 50
Grant, C.P., Capt. 15/DLI. 317
Grant, D.H.F., Lt-Col. 1/Lincs. 110
Gray, E.J.W. 2/Lt. 14/DLI. *64*
Green, P., 2/Lt. 9/KOYLI. 312 fn.
Green, W.C., Capt. 1/EYorks. 201-202
Greenshields, 2/Lt. 9/KOYLI. 224, 268
Greenwell, J., 2/Lt. 12/13 NFus. 334 fn.
Greenwood, Lt. 1/EYorks. 269
Greenwood, H. Maj. 9/KOYLI. 227-228,
    254, 293, 294, 298, 302, 251 fn., 332, 334,
    336-337, *337, 364*
Gregg, V.R., 2/Lt. 9/KOYLI. 224, 228
Gregory, Capt. 8/Leics. 232
Gregory, A.V., 2/Lt. 9/KOYLI. 228
Gregory, P.J., 2/Lt. 12/13 NFus. 199 fn.
Griffin, E.H., Capt. (RAMC) 12/13 NFus.

215
Griffin, G.E., Capt. 9/KOYLI. 83, 85
Gush, H.W., Maj. 1/Lincs. 241, 271, 276
Gwyther, Capt. 7/Leics. 122

Hackett, D.F.M., Lt. 7/Leics. 290
Hadow, A. de S., Lt-Col. 10/Yorks. 32, 38, 45, *46, 47,* 46-48
Haig, C.H., Lt-Col. 9/Leics. 122, 148
Haig, Sir D. Gen. 24-25, 27, 28, 32, 33, 73, 77, 79-80, 114, 115, 129, 130, 155, 160, 174-175, 184-185, 186, 188, 205, 207-208, 209, 219, 239, 255, 283, 290-291, 308
Haines, Capt. 13/NFus. 157
Haines, F.P., Lt. 8/Leics. 181 fn.
Haking, R.C.B., Lt-Gen. 26, 34, 44, 73-74, 76
Hales, V.C., Lt. 7/Leics. 190
Hall, Lt. 15/DLI. 165
Hall, M.A., Lt. 8/Lincs. 60
Hall, Lt. 8/SomLI. 93
Hall, R., 2/Lt. 1/Wilts. 326 fn.
Hamilton, A.S., Lt-Col. 14/DLI. 64, *64,* 68
Hammond, Cpl. 10/KOYLI. 163
Hanning, J.H.R., 2/Lt 8/Lincs, *59*
Hardman, A., A/Capt. 9/KOYLI. 202 fn.
Hardy, 2/Lt. 1/EYorks. 248 fn.
Hardy, L/Cpl. 1/EYorks. 227
Hare, L.G., Capt. 7/Yorks. 102
Hargreaves, 2/Lt. 9/KOYLI. 223
Harper, Capt. MO. 7/Yorks. 104
Harper, F.C., 2/Lt. 2/Lincs. 213
Harris, 2/Lt. 8/Leics. 180
Hart, B.H.L., Lt. 9/KOYLI. 108, 127
Hastie, Lt. Tank Corps. 130
Haswell, G., Capt. 9/KOYLI. 85-86, *86*
Hawkes, J.A., 2/Lt. 7/Leics. 313 fn.
Hawkesworth, Capt. 1/EYorks.90, 109
Haynes, C.S., 2/Lt. 15/DLI. 90
Head, L.D., Capt. 9/KOYLI.88, *88*
Headlam, H.R., Br-Gen. 64 Bde. 81, *82,* 104-105, 125, 130, 131-132, 136, 139, 140-141, 150, 161-162, 164, 167, 168, 169, 193, 232, 233-234, 249, 260, 273, 274, 279
Healey, A.W., 2/Lt. 1/Wilts. 307 fn.
Hearn, A.H., 2/Lt. 8/Leics. 192 fn.
Heathcote, C. E., Lt-Col. 9/KOYLI. 141
Heaviside, M., Pte. 15/DLI. 176, *361*
Hégo, J., Abbé. 344
Henderson, K. Lt-Col. 64 Bde. 67-71, 72

Hendricks, H.H., Capt. 7/Leics. 190
Herbert, Capt. 15/DLI. 232
Hessey, W.F.,Br-Gen. 110 Bde. 125, 179
Hetherington, A., Lt. 9/KOYLI. 225
Hickin, T. Pte. 7/Leics. 215
Hill, 2/Lt. 8/Leics. 180
Hill, R.M., 2/Lt. 12/NFus. 39
Hill, E.R., Br-Gen. 63 Bde. 81
Von Hindenburg, Paul. 322
Hine, 2/Lt. 1/Lincs. 171
Hinings, F.W.C. Capt. 1/EYorks. *148*
Hobbs, A.W., 2/Lt. 10/KOYLI. 163 & fn.
Hodkinson, P., 2/Lt. 15/DLI. 335 fn.
Holdstock, Capt. 10/KOYLI. 167
Holliday, Lt. 2/Lincs. 232
Holmes, Lt. 1/EYorks. 271
Holmes, 2/Lt. 9/KOYLI. 266
Holmes, A., Pte. 6/Leics. 244 fn.
Holroyd-Smyth, E.R., Lt-Col. 15/DLI. 269, 272, 297, 316, 317
Hopkins, L., Lt. 8/SomLI. 61
Hornby, M. L., Br-Gen. 39 Div. 219
Horne, H.R., Capt. 7/Leics. 298
Horne, H.S., Lt-Gen. XV Corps. 115, 131, 150
Hotson, F., 2/Lt. 1/Lincs. 338
Howard, L.C. Maj. 8/SomLI. 56, 61, *62*
Howard, B.W., 2/Lt. 1/EYorks. 248, 298, 302
Howe, P., Lt. 10/WYorks. 98-99
Howe, R.E., 2/Lt. 1/EYorks. 202 fn.
Howlett, R., Lt-Col. 12/13 NFus. 232, 240, 315
Howitt, Maj. 7/Leics. 190
Hubback, Lt-Col. 1/20 Londons. 37
Huffam, V., 2/Lt. Tank Corps. 133
Hughes, 2/Lt. 7/Leics. 259
Hunter, A., 2/Lt. 9/KOYLI. 342
Huntriss, Capt. 1/EYorks. 90
Hurley, 2/Lt. 9/KOYLI. 268
Husey, R.H., Br-Gen. 25 Bde. 262
Hutchinson, W.S., 2/Lt. 12/13 NFus. 197, *310,* 311 fn.
Hutton, E.T.H.,Lt-Gen. xviii, *xix,* xx
Hutton, J.H. Pte. 12/13NFus. *265*
Hyde,G.A., 2/Lt. 9/KOYLI. 202 fn.

Ibbotson, Lt. 64 Bde. 167
Ingles, R.J., Maj. 8/EYorks. 38, 45, 50-51
Irwin, N.M.S., Lt-Col. 8/Leics. 240, 277, 279, 315

378 To Do the Work of Men

Jackson, Lt. 12/13 NFus. 197
Jackson, S. CSM. 6/Leics. 220 fn.
Jacob, Sir C.W., Maj-Gen. 21 Div. 76, *77*, 244
Jacobs, G., Capt. MO. 1/Lincs. 171
Jalland, R.M., 2/Lt. 6/Leics. 300 fn.
James, 2/Lt. 9/KOYLI. 228
James, R.K., Lt. 9/KOYLI. 266
James, S., Cpl. 9/KOYLI. 173
Jaques, A., Capt. 12/WYorks. 63, *63*
Jaques, J.H., Maj. 12/WYorks. 63, *63*
Joffre, J.J.C., Gen. 26, 79, 114, 155
Johnson, 2/Lt. 8/Leics. 180
Johnson, R.B., Maj. 15/DLI. 65, 66, 108
Johnston, R.H., Lt-Col. 8/Lincs. 93, 94
Johnston-Stewart, C.G., 2/Lt. 1/EYorks. 241
Jolley, J., Pte. 15/DLI. 106

Kearford, J., Pte. 9/KOYLI. 95
Keay, W.F., 2/Lt. 9/KOYLI. 108
Kellett, Lt. 8/SomLI. 93
Kelly, D., Capt. 6/Leics. 326
Kelly, Maj. VII Corps Staff. 235
Kemp-Welch, M., 2/Lt. 10/Yorks. 170 fn.
Kent, R.E.D., Maj. 7/Yorks. 102
Kiernan, R.H., Pte. Leics. 315
King, H.F., 2/Lt. 9/Leics. 114
King, H.J., Lt-Col. 10/KOYLI. 82, 87, 88
Kingston, H.F., 2/Lt. 9/KOYLI. 108
Kitchener, Herbert Horatio, Earl. xvi, xxii, 26
Knott, J. Maj. 10/WYorks. 99

Lane-Roberts, E.G., Lt. 6/Leics. 216, 220-221
Lascelles, A.M., Capt. 15/DLI. 342, *342*
Laskie, F.B., Maj. 10/KOYLI. 109
Lawford, Maj-Gen. 41 Div. 130, 131, 141
Lee, A.A.D., Capt. 9/Leics. 189, *189*
Leggett, R.A.C.L., Lt-Col. 12/WYorks. 40, 63, 74
Lethbridge, Q.H., 2/Lt. 12/13 NFus. 199 fn.
Levinge, T.V., Maj. 13/NFus. 39
Lillie, F. 2/Lt. 9/KOYLI. *153*
Lish, J.R., 2/Lt. 1/Lincs. 199 fn.
Lloyd, E.P., Lt-Col. 2/Lincs. 226, 316
Lloyd George, D. 155
Lockie, Capt. 12/NFus. 171
Logan, E.T., Lt-Col. 15/DLI. 65, 66, 68
Logan, J., Pte. 12/13 NFus. 338 fn.
Logsdon, F.L. de M., 2/Lt. 9/KOYLI. 202 fn.
Long, Pte. 12/13 NFus. 346

Longden, F.C., Capt. 1/EYorks. 299 fn.
Losh, J.N., 2/Lt. 1/Lincs. 199 fn.
von Lossberg, Gen. *Fourth Army Chief of Staff.* 245
Loudoun-Shand, S.W., Maj. 10/Yorks. 96, *97, 359*
Lowth, J.L., 2/Lt. 12/13 NFus. 199 fn.
Ludendorff, E., Gen. *OHL.* 208, 237, 257, 279, 283, 322, 328
Lummis, R., 2/Lt. 12/13 NFus. 199 fn.
Lynch, C.W.D., Lt-Col. 9/KOYLI. 68-69, 83-84, *85*, 86-87, 89
Lynch, J., Capt. 10/Yorks. 48 & fn.

Macdougall, Maj. 64 Bde. 193
Maconachie, A.D. 2/Lt. 9/KOYLI. *90*
Magin, J., 2/Lt. 9/KOYLI. 228
Makin, S., 2/Lt. 9/KOYLI. 225, 228
Mangin, C.M.E., Gen. French Sixth Army. 279
Manley, G.S., 2/Lt. 1/EYorks. 346
Mansfield, 2/Lt. 1/EYorks. 223, 225
Marindin, Brig-Gen. 105 Bde. 234
Marks, J.H., Lt. 15/DLI. 335 fn.
Marlin, H.J., 2/Lt. 1/Lincs. 170 fn.
Marsden, F.A., 2/Lt. 9/KOYLI. 251, 260
Marsh, Capt. 10/KOYLI. 167
Marsh, Lt. 8/SomLI. 56
Marshall, Lt. 1/EYorks. 109
Martin, Sgt. 12/NFus. 156
Martyn, M.C., Lt-Col. 6/Leics. 298, 300
Matthews, J.B., Capt. 8/Leics. 181, 190
Matthias, T.G., Lt-Col. 10/Yorks. 156
May, H.C. CSM. 6/Leics. 220 fn.
Mayhew, 2/Lt. 1/EYorks. 248 fn.
McClay, S.W., 2/Lt. 1/Lincs. 197 fn, 198
McConnan, C.W., Capt. 2/Lincs. 283, 316
McCulloch, A.J., Lt-Col. 9/KOYLI. 222, 223, 224, 230, 234-235, 244, 248, 250, 251-254, 268, 272, 281, *282*, 292-293, 294-297, 299, 346
McPherson, G. Sgt. 15/DLI. *135*
McKellar, Capt. 1/Lincs. 241
McKinnon, J., Lt. 12/13 NFus. 197, 215
McLay, A., Capt. 6/Leics. 179, 220
McLean, Capt. 12/NFus. 181
McNaught-Davis, Capt. 8/Lincs. 60
McVey, J., Lt. 2/Lincs. 316
Meadows, Mess Waiter. 110 Bde HQ. 274
Mears, E., Pte. 1/Wilts. 340 fn.

Index 379

Mignon, J.G., Lt-Col. 8/Leics. 121
Milburn, H.E., Capt. 9/Leics. 178
Miles, R.T.W., 2/Lt. 7/Leics. 190
Millwood, Sgt. 8/Lincs. 95
Millwood, Sgt. 4/M'sex. 110
Milward, C.A., Maj. 64 Bde. 150
Mintoft, H.S., 2/Lt. 1/EYorks. 202 fn.
Mitchell, J.A., 2/Lt. 12/13 NFus. 320 fn.
Mitchell, R., L/Cpl. 15/DLI. 319 & fn.
Montgomery, A.A., Maj-Gen. 27
Moon, C., 2/Lt. 9/KOYLI. 225, 228
Morley, A.S., 2/Lt. 15/DLI. 106
Morrey, S. Sgt. 2/Lincs. 284 fn.
Morris, F.G., 2/Lt. 9/KOYLI. 71
du Moulin, F.L., Lt-Col. 1/EYorks. 293, 297,
    307, 316, 341
Muirhead, Maj. 1/Wilts. 297
Murphy, J., Lt. 12/13 NFus. 300 fn.

Neeves, H.H., Lt-Col. 15/DLI. 319, 334
Neilson, Capt. 1/Lincs. 226
Newbury, T.G., Capt. 1/Lincs. 232, 246
Nichols, W.H., Capt. 8/SomLI. 42 fn., *62*
Nickalls, N.T. Br-Gen. 63 Bde. 39, 40, 41, 42,
    51-52, *52*, 55, 56, 63, 64
Nivelle, R., Gen. 155, 160, 174
Noble, Lt. 12/NFus. 156
Nolan, W.H., Lt. 9/Leics. 123
Noyes, R., Maj. 10/Yorks. 48 & fn.

Oldershaw, J.J.F., 2/Lt. 9/KOYLI. 88, *88*
Oliver, R., 2/Lt. 12/NFus. 39
Oliver, F.R., Lt. 8/Leics. 178, 180
Otter, Maj. 11/RWSurrey. 141-142
Osey, F., Pte. 110 Bde HQ. 314 & fn.
Oswald, K.A., Lt-Col. 3/4 Queen's. 194
Oughtred, Lt. att.10/KOYLI. 202
Outhwaite, Cpl. 9/Leics. 190
Overman, J.G., 2/Lt. 9/KOYLI. 312 fn.

Pearsall, H., 2/Lt. Tank Corps. 133
Pease, M.R., Capt. 15/DLI. 250
Pedley, S.H., Lt-Col. 15/DLI. 139, 141
Percival, W.L., 2/Lt. 9/KOYLI. 335
Perrott, Lt. 64 Bde. 297
Pershing, J.J., Gen. AEF. 207
Pétain, H-P.B.O.J., Gen. 174, 209, 257-258
Peter, A.E., 2/Lt. 9/Leics. 144
Phillips, Capt. 12/NFus. 38

Pitts, F., 2/Lt. 8/Leics. 180
Piza, D., A/Capt. 64 TMB. 165 fn.
Plumer, Sir H., Gen. Second Army.184,
    186-188
Pohl, Oberstleutnant, *IR153.* 52
Pollard, Brig-Gen., 2 Bde. 40
Pollard, Maj-Gen. 106 Bde. 234
Pollock, A.W.A., Lt-Col. 10/KOYLI. 68-69
Pool, S., Capt. RAMC, 8/Leics. 181 fn.
Postlethwaite, F.J.M., Lt-Col. 10/KOYLI.
    167-169
Potter, Rev. 7/Yorks. 104
Potterton, G., CSM. 9/Leics. 144, *145*
Pratley, 2/Lt. 8/Leics. 180
Pratt, J.S., Lt. 10/Yorks. 170 fn.
Preston, 2/Lt. 8/Lincs. 94
Prosser, Sgt. 4/M'sex. 110
Pulteney, Lt-Gen. III Corps. 129
Pyott, Sgt. 9/KOYLI. 200

Quarrell, C.H., 2/Lt. 13/NFus. 181 fn.
Quayle, Capt. 6/Leics. 149
Queen, 2/Lt. 12/NFus. 181

Raine, R.T., Capt. MO. 1/EYorks. 248 & fn.
Rawling, G.C., Br-Gen. 62 Bde. 81, 205 fn.
Rawlinson, Sir H.S., Gen. 44, 80-81, 114, 115,
    116, 129, 130, 184, 291
Read, Sgt. 8/Leics. 148
Reed, 2/Lt. 7/Leics. 120
Rees, Brig-Gen. 150 Bde. 261 fn.
Rennie, C.T., 2/Lt. 9/Leics. 144
Renwick, C.R. Pte. 15/DLI. *166*
Rhodes, W.H., CSM. 9/Leics. 144
Rice, C.C., Lt. 1/EYorks. 202
Richards, S.G., 2/Lt. 9/KOYLI. 174
Richardson, Lt. 1/Lincs. 327
Riddell, Brig-Gen. 149 Bde. 261
Riddell, Capt. 12/13 NFus. 197
Ridgway, J.H., Lt-Col. 10/Y&L. 93, 98
Roberts, J.L.R. Lt. 6/Leics. *217*
Robertson, Sir W.R., CIGS. 26, 155
Robinson, Capt. 1/EYorks. 248 fn.
Robinson, A.D., 2/Lt. 1/EYorks. 248
Robinson, W.G., 2/Lt. 8/Leics. 192 fn.
Rooke, 2/Lt. 10/KOYLI. 200
Rose, P.V. Capt. 21 Div Staff. 56, *56*

Samuelson, Capt. 1/Lincs. 264

Sanders, Lt. 15/DLI. 165
Santar, Capt. 10/KOYLI. 108
Sargeant, A.P., 2/Lt. 9/Leics. 126
Saunders, Lt. 15/DLI. 165, 166-167
Saunders, Maj. 1/EYorks. 109
Sawyer, G.H., Lt-Col. 7/Leics. 240, 275, 300, 318
Schafer, T.S., 2/Lt. 13/NFus, *44*
Schofield, J.H.C. Lt. 15/DLI. *151*
Scott, Capt. 6/Leics. 244
Scott, 2/Lt. 9/KOYLI. 269
Scott, J.W., Lt-Col. 8/SomLI. 93
Seatter, G., 2/Lt. 15/DLI. 312 fn.
Sedgwick, J., Lt. 15/DLI. 203, 204, 334
Settle, Lt-Col. 21/MGBn. 227
Shann, J.W., Lt. 10/WYorks. 99
Sharpe, 2/Lt. 2/Lincs. 288
Shaw, Capt. 9/KOYLI. 232
Shaw, A. 2/Lt. 8/Leics. 192 fn.
Shaw, J. Lt. 9/KOYLI. 266, 268
Shepherd, W.W., 2/Lt. 9/KOYLI. 108
Sherlock, L/Sgt. 7/Leics. 121
Shute, C.D., Lt-Gen. V Corps. 280, 282, 323
Simpson, W., Pte. 9/KOYLI. 242-243
Slater, T., 2/Lt. 9/KOYLI. 228
Sleath, Capt. 1/EYorks. 248 fn.
Smith, Capt. 8/EYorks. 45
Smith, Lt. 9/Leics. 123
Smith, H.L., Pte. 6/Leics. 244 fn., *253*
Smith, W.B., 2/Lt. 9/KOYLI. 335
Smith-Dorrien, H. Gen. xx
Snow, T. d'O., Lt-Gen. VII Corps. 156, 159, 172, 183
Somerville, Capt. 15/DLI. 297
Spicer, L.B., Lt. 9/KOYLI. 201, 203-204
Spicer, L.D., Lt. 9/KOYLI. 77, 83, 85, 108, 246-247, 250, 297
Spragg, C.E.W., Capt. 1/EYorks. 312 fn.
Stamper, F.P., Capt. 15/DLI. 90
Stanley, the Hon. F.C., Br-Gen. 89 Bde. 161
Stanley, P.D., 2/Lt. 9/KOYLI. 202 fn.
von Stein, Freiherr, Hauptmann. *IR153.* 54
Stephens, 2/Lt. 1/EYorks. 248 fn.
Stephenson, Capt. 1/EYorks. 232
Stephenson, Lt. 15/DLI. 317
Stephenson, Lt. 1/EYorks. 227
Stephenson, A., Capt. 9/KOYLI. 83, 85
Stevenson, P.H., Lt-Col. 12/13 NFus 271
Stewart, C.G., Br-Gen. 24 Div. 34, 75
Stewart, W.N., Lt-Col. 6/Leics. 221

Stockham, 2/Lt. 1/EYorks. 109, 225
Storer, J.Y., Maj. 8/Lincs. 52, 57, *57*
Storey, Lt. 10/Yorks. 158
Storey, C.E., 2/Lt. Tank Corps. 151
Stow, M.B., Lt-Col. 1/EYorks. 90, 91, 109
Summers, F., Maj. Tank Corps. 133
Swaby, Lt. 1/Lincs. 264
Swallow, H.L.St J., 2/Lt. 10/Yorks & Lancs *41*
Swift, W., 2/Lt. 8/Lincs. 95 fn.
Sykes, Capt. 9/KOYLI. 200

Tapsell, Lt. 1/Lincs. 264
Tatlow, 2/Lt. 1/EYorks. 248 fn.
Taylor, A.B., 2/Lt. 9/Leics. 114
Teaz, H.N., 2/Lt. 9/KOYLI. 174, 228
Tempest, W.N. Major. 9/KOYLI. *149*
Tenney, Lt. 7/Yorks. 102
Thirlby, S.L., Lt. 6/Leics. 220-221
Thompson, W.T. Pte. 8/Lincs. *60*
Thorpe, P. Pte. 6/Leics. 307
Thorpe, S.D., Capt. 15/DLI. 165, 167, 169, 176, 217, 272
Tilbrook, Sgt. 9/KOYLI. 267
Tillett, J.E., Lt. 1/Lincs. 328 fn.
Toogood, 2/Lt. 1/EYorks. 248 fn.
Tooth, G.E.G., Lt. 9/Leics. 148, 277
Topham, J. Capt. 8/Lincs. *59*
Trimble, J.B.O., Lt. 1/EYorks. 223, 224
Trotter, A.W.L., Maj. 9/Leics. 114
Tunnell, O., 2/Lt. 12/13 NFus. 344 fn.
Twentyman, D.C.T. Capt. 10/Yorks & Lancs. *98*
Tyler, H.C., Maj. 7/Leics. 265
Tyler, H.H., Maj. 9/KOYLI. 319
Tyler, H.W.H., Capt. 7/Leics. 151

Ullyott, C., 2/Lt. 1/EYorks. 296 fn.
von Unruh, Maj-Gen. *Chief of Staff, 4th Reserve Corps.* 257
Utterson, A.T. Le M., Lt-Col. 8/Leics. 192, 221

Vann, A.H.A., Capt. 12/WYorks. 63
Vanner, J.C., Capt. 7/Leics. 179, 180, 221-222, 298
Vergette, S., Lt. 1/Lincs. 199 fn.
Vernall, Lt. 6/Leics. 244
von Viereck, Rittmeister, *IR153.* 54

Wadsworth, P., 2/Lt. 1/EYorks. 225
Waistell, W.E., 2/|Lt. 12/13 NFus. 199 fn.

Index 381

Wait, C.F.W. Lt. 10/KOYLI. *126*
Waite, Lt. 1/EYorks. 223
Waithman, R.H., Lt-Col. 1/EYorks. 168, 201
Wakeford, Lt. 7/Leics. 121
Walby, Lt. 9/KOYLI. 272
Waldron, S., Pte. 9/KOYLI. 242-243
Wales, Maj. 1/Lincs. 171
Walker, Lt. 9/Leics. 178
Walker, A., L/Sgt. 1/Lincs. 170
Walker, Sgt. 7/Leics.121
Walker, W., Capt. 9/KOYLI. 88, 89
Wallace, R.B., Capt. MO. 7/Leics. 180
Waller, H., Pte. 10/KOYLI. 168, 173, *360*
Wallerston, Br-Gen. 45 Bde.45
Wallis, 2/Lt. 1/EYorks. 248 fn.
Walsh, T A. Maj. 9/KOYLI. 301, 302, 311 & fn., 316, 317
Walsh, H.J., 2/Lt. 7/Leics. 151
Walter, H.E., Lt-Col. 8/Lincs. 57, *58*
Walton, G.P., Lt. 2/Lincs. 289
Ward, Capt. 8/Leics. 118
Ward, G.B.C., Lt-Col. 1/Wilts. 318
Ward, J., Pte. 9/KOYLI. 242 fn.
Waring, W., Cpl. 1/Wilts. 340 fn.
Warmesby, Lt. RE. 259
Warner, T.L., Maj. 8/Leics. 178, 180
Warren, CSM. 9/KOYLI.108
Warwick, H.B., Lt-Col. 12/NFus. 39, 46, 50
Watson, Sgt. 9/KOYLI. 267
Watson, B.A., 2/Lt. 12/13 NFus. 334 fn.
Watt, H.B.C., Lt. 1/EYorks. 299fn.

Way, B.I., Lt-Col. 8/EYorks. 38, 45, 50, 51
Webb, Capt. 9/Leics. 144
Webster, J.P., Lt. 9/KOYLI. 335
Welch, J.E.H. 2/Lt. 8/Lincs. *59*
Welsh, E.T., Capt. 2/Lincs. 316
Wesselhoeft, G.H. 2/Lt. 15/DLI. *138*
Westmorland, G.W., Pte. 2/Lincs. 284 fn.
Wethered, J.H., Col. 62 Bde. 34, 37
Whinney, W.G., Sgt. 110 Bde HQ. 314 & fn.
White, 2/Lt. 7/Leics. 179
White, G., Maj. 12/13 NFus. 215
White, S.W., 2/|Lt. 13/NFus. 181 fn.
Wigham, R.D., Lt-Gen. GHQ. 75
Wilkinson, E.B., Br-Gen. 62 Bde. 35, 38, 39, 45
Williams, 2/Lt. 15/DLI.166
Williamson, H.D., Pte. 2/Lincs. 284 fn.
Willis, Capt. 1/EYorks. 91, 105, 109
Wilson, Woodrow. 322
Wipf, J.J., 2/Lt. 1/Lincs. 328 fn.
Wisbey, 2/Lt. 1/EYorks. 248 fn.
Witley, 2/Lt. 1/EYorks. 248 fn.
Woodley, C., 2/Lt. 9/KOYLI. 326 fn.
Wright, Lt. 1/Lincs. 327
Wright, 2/Lt. 7/Leics.215
Wright, H., Pte. 9/KOYLI. 227

Yates, 2/Lt. 1/EYorks. 248 fn.
Yeo, H.E., Lt. 9/KOYLI. 69, 76, 104, 127, 132, 139, 240, 184, 258-259, 277-278, 343
Young, A. Pte. 10/KOYLI. *137*
Zacharias-Jessel, V.A.V., Lt. 15/DLI. 163 fn.

PLACES

Abbeville 278
Acheux 284
Adinfer Wood 180
Ailly-sur-Somme 114
Aizecourt-le-bas 225
Aizecourt-le-Haut 222, 225, 226, 227, 228
Albert 112, 232, 233, 282, 290
Allonville 235
Amerval 330
Amiens 208, 236, 283
Angle Wood 327
Annay 35, 39
Armentières 32, 76, 83, 239
Auchonvillers 282
Aulnoye 338, 339, 340

Aylesbury xx

Bachant 340, 342
Baillescourt Farm 288
Bailleulment 114
Banteux 321, 323
Bapaume 88, 283
Barastre 308
Battery Valley 294, 297, 298
Bazentin le Grand 115
Bazentin le Grand Wood 120, 124
Bazentin le Petit 114, 124, 125, 126
Bazentin le Petit Wood 116, 120-121, 124, 125, 126
Beaucourt 286, 287, 288, 289

Beaufort 340
Beaulencourt 302, 304-307, 308
Beaumont Hamel 282, 285, 321
Beaurain 332
Beaurevoir Line 323-326
Beaver Camp 248
Becelaere 150
Bedford House 240
Bénifontaine 56
Berlaimont 338, 339, 342, 343.
Berles-au-Bois 114
Bernafay Wood 152
Berry-au-Bac 259, 262, 268
Béthune 153
Beuvry 27
Birch Tree Copse 317
Black Cot 241, 189.Boiry St Rictude 169
Bois Cuville 271
Bois Hugo 41, 43, 52, 54, 56, 57, 60, 64, 65, 69, 75
Bois des Buttes 262
Bois des Tailles 234, 235
Bois du Gard 325
Bois Marrières 226, 229
Bonne Enfance 324
Boom Ravine 294, 296, 297, 298
Bouchavesnes 226, 229
Bouffignereux 264
Bouleuse 277
Boulogne xvi, 23, 26, 113
Bouvancourt 271
Branscourt 275, 276
Bray 230, 234
Briseux Wood 327
Broodseinde 188, 193
Buire 233, 234
Bullecourt 175
Bussu 225, 228
Butte de Prouilly 272
Butte de Warlencourt 299, 301, 302

Calais 106
Cambrai 159, 174, 209, 212, 328
Cameron Covert 188, 189, 190, 194, 195, 197, 203, 204
Canal de l'Escaut 323
Canal du Nord 226, 228, 309
Capron Copse 223
Caullery 325, 328

Cauroy 260, 269, 270, 272
Chalet Wood 41, 54, 69
Chalk Pit 31, 40, 41, 51, 55, 60, 61, 64
Chalk Pit Copse 31, 37, 38
Chalk Pit Wood 40, 55, 56, 67
Châlons le Vergeur 260, 264, 269, 271
Chaltrait 277
Chantilly 79, 155
Chapel Crossing 311
Chapel Hill 210, 211, 215, 218, 222, 223, 309, 310, 313, 314
Chapel Wood 222
Château des Angles 325, 326, 327
Chemin des Dames 174, 256, 257, 261, 278
Chérisy 179
Cherry Wood 178
Chipilly 234
Cité St Auguste 30, 35, 50, 54
Cité St Laurent 31
Cité St Pierre 37
Cléry 226, 227, 228, 229
Contalmaison 114, 292
Corbie 127
Cormicy 264, 265
Courcelette 115, 129, 298
Craonne 261
Croisilles 156, 157, 158, 180
Cuiry 261
Curlu 226, 229
Curlu Wood 226

Delville Wood 128, 152
Dernancourt 111, 235
Dickebusch Lake 238, 246
Dome House 244
Doullens 114
Dukes Wood 332, 333

Eaucourt l'Abbaye 300
Eclaibes 341, 343
Englebelmer 282
Epéhy (-Peizière) 210, 211, 215-216, 217, 219, 220, 221, 309, 314, 318, 345
Epernay 277
Epernay Forest 277
Epinette Wood 222, 224, 226
Equancourt 310, 312
Etrechy 277
Etrée 339, 340

Etricourt 309, 312, 319

Faverolles 275
Feuillacourt 227, 228
Fins 309, 310
Flers 115, 129, 131, 136, 142, 151
Flesquières Salient 209, 210, 222
Fontaine-lez-Croisilles 175, 177, 180
Fontaine Wood 177, 178, 179
Forêt de Mormal 330, 337
Fosse No. 7 35, 44, 45
Fricourt 80, 82, 95, 99, 110, 111, 114, 130
Fricourt Spur 82, 90, 96, 98, 104
Fricourt Wood 96

Gauche Wood 216, 317
Genin Well Copses 211, 215, 309, 311
Germigny 277
Gernicourt 262
Gommecourt 113
Gonnelieu 319, 320
Gouzeaucourt 310, 319-320
Gouzeaucourt Wood 310
Grand Bois 246, 247, 248
Grandcourt 289, 292, 294, 296, 297
Grenay Ridge 30
Gueudecourt 130, 131, 133, 143-144, 150, 151, 152
Guillemin Farm 327, 328
Guillemont 115
Gurlu Wood 222
Guyencourt 211, 223, 224

Hallebast 246
Halton Park xix, xx, xxi
Hamel 283, 285-286
Harnes 35, 52, 55
Haut Allaines 226, 227
Haut Farm 326, 327
Hawthorn Ridge 283
Hazebrouck 239, 255
Heilly 91, 136, 235 fn.
Hellebroucq 32
Hem 229
Hénin sur Cojeul 156, 157, 163
Héninel 159, 161
Hermonville 269, 271, 272
Heudecourt 217, 222, 309, 310, 321
High Wood 115, 125, 128

High Wycombe xx
Hill 44 - 248, 249, 250
Hill 70 - 30, 31, 35, 37, 39, 43, 44, 45, 50, 52, 54, 64, 65, 66, 67, 68, 69, 75
Hill 135 –294, 296, 297, 298, 300
Hill 202 – 275-277
Hill 220 – 273
Hohenzollern Redoubt 28, 29
Honnecourt 321, 323
Hooge 240
Hulluch 30, 35, 47
Hurtebise Farm 325, 327

Inchy 331, 335

Jacquenne Copse 223
Jetty Warren 192, 195, 195, 196
Joist Farm 190, 192, 200, 201
Jonchery 273, 275
Judge Copse 197, 199

Kemmel 113, 245, 249, 250

La Cendrière 264
La Chapelle 264
La Clytte 245, 250
Lagache Farm 244, 245
Laiterie 249
Langemarck 186
La Neuville (Champagne) 265
La Neuville (Somme) 77
Le Barque 299, 300, 308
Lederzeele 254
Le Havre xvi, 23
Leighton Buzzard xx
Lens 50, 52
Le Sars 115, 292, 299, 308
Le Transloy 305, 307, 308
Les Boeufs 115, 130, 308
Les Vautes 275
Liéramont 224
Ligny-Thilloy 300, 302
Limont-Fontaine 340, 341, 342, 343, 344
Locquignol 337, 339
Locre 245
Loivre 257
Longueval 114, 115, 125, 132
Longavesnes 205, 222, 225
Loos 30, 35, 37, 40, 42, 50, 67, 71, 72

384 To Do the Work of Men

Lozenge Wood 94, 105, 109, 110
Lubda Copse 307, 308
Luisenhof Farm 301-302
Luthernay Farm 271, 272, 273

Maidenhead xx
Mailly Maillet 282, 284, 293, 297
Maizy 261
Malassise Farm 216
Mametz 82, 111
Mametz Wood 114, 115, 116-117, 118, 125
Manancourt 309, 312, 313, 319
Marfaux 277
Maricourt 226
Maroc 45
Martinpuich 115, 129
Marzilly 272
Maurepas 230
Mazingarbe 34, 45
Méaulte 112, 114, 127
Méricourt 114
Méricourt-l'Abbé 232
Méry Premecy 277
Mesnil 319
Messines Ridge 185, 239
Millekruisse 249
Miraumont 88, 286, 289, 292, 298
Moislans 225, 226, 228
Monchy-au-Bois 113
Monchy-le-Preux 160
Mondicourt 113
Montauban 81, 131
Montecouvez Farm 213, 324, 325, 326
Montigny 328
Montigny Ridge 272, 273
Morlancourt 233, 234, 235
Morval 115
Moulin de Cormicy 259, 264, 265
Mt Kemmel 239, 244, 245, 251
Mt de Sapigneul 259
Mt Spin 259, 268
Muizon 274, 275

Neuville-Vitasse 161
Neuvilly 330, 331, 333, 335
Nieppe 32
Noeux les Mines 27, 33, 34, 72, 153
Noyelles-les-Vermelles 50, 72
Noyon 23

Nurlu 224, 226

Oeuilly 261
Onraet Wood 240-248
Ouderdoum 248, 254
Ovillers 330, 332, 333, 335

Peizière 214, 218, 222, 223, 310, 314, 318, 321
Perham Down Camp 113
Péronne 227, 283
Pévy 271, 272, 273
Philosophe 35, 42, 50
Pilckem Ridge 185
Place à Bruay 33
Ploegsteert Wood 76
Poix-du-Nord 330, 333, 334, 335
Polderhoek Chateau 194, 195, 197, 203
Polygon Wood 187, 188, 190, 192, 203
Pont à Vendin 33, 35
Pont de la Deule 52
Pontefract xvii
Pont-sur-Sambre 346
Pozières 115, 287, 292
Pozières Ridge 286, 289
Prouilly 272, 273
Pys 292, 298

Quatre Bras 339

Redan Ridge 283
RE Farm 249
Reims 255
Reutel 199, 201, 203, 204
Revelon Farm 309
Ribemont 127, 233, 234
Ridge Wood 246, 250, 252
River Aisne 255, 257, 261, 262, 263
River Ancre 77, 232, 234, 235, 282, 285, 286,
    289, 290, 292, 294, 298
River Cojeul 159, 162, 171
River Marne 278, 279
River Oise 283
River Sambre 337
River Selle 328, 330
River Sensée 176
River Somme 77, 79, 155, 229, 233
River Vesle 257, 260, 270, 274
Rocquigny 308
Rosnay 275, 276, 277

Rosnay Farm 277
Rouen xvi
Roulers 184, 186
Round Wood 105, 107, 109, 110

Sailly la Bourse 72
Sailly-le-Sec 234, 235
Sambre-Oise Canal 330, 337
Sapicourt 275
Saulcourt 211, 216, 220, 221, 222, 223, 224
Savigny 275, 276
Scottish Wood 192, 201, 246, 252
Selvigny 325
Serre 81
Siege Farm 241, 249
Soissons 155, 274, 283
Sorel 309, 321
Soulières 277
Spanbroekmolen 244
St Auboeuf 271
St Eloi 250, 252
St Julien 186
St Martin sur Cojeul 159., 161, 162
St Quentin 208, 213, 283
Suzanne 230

Templeux-la-Fosse 222, 225, 226, 227, 228
Tête Noire 339
Thiepval 114, 286-287, 289, 292, 298
Thourout 184
Tilloy 160
Tincourt Wood 220
Tower Hamlets 187, 194, 240
Treslon 275, 276

Trigny 272, 273, 274
Tring xix, xx
Trônes Wood 114, 115, 125
Tronquoy 328, 330

Vaucelette Farm 210, 211, 215-216, 218, 309,
310, 314, 315
Vaux Varennes 271, 272
Vendegies-au-Bois 330, 333, 335
Verdun 79, 208
Vermelles 42, 57
Vierstraat 241 fn., 248
Ville au Bois 262
Ville-sur-Ancre 112
Villers-au-Flos 307, 308
Villers-Faucon 223, 224
Villers Guislan 314-315, 317
Vimy Ridge 156, 158, 160
Voormezeele 250

Walincourt 325, 327, 328, 329
Wancourt 161
Wendover xix
Westoutre 32
Wisques 32
Witley Camp, Surrey xxi
Wytschaete 239, 240, 241, 242, 244, 247
Wytschaete Wood 241, 247

Ypres 184-185, 209, 243, 244, 255, 257, 345
Y Ravine 284

Zillebeke (Lake) 240
Zonnebeke 187, 193

UNITS & FORMATIONS

British Army

Armies:
First Army 24, 27, 156, 158, 175, 213, 324
Second Army 184, 188, 237, 280
Third Army 156, 158, 175, 213, 231, 234, 280,
283, 285, 292, 324, 330
Fourth Army 114, 129, 131, 291, 292, 308, 324,
330
Fifth Army 175, 184, 205, 210, 213, 219, 233

Corps:
I Corps 25, 27, 35
II Corps 244
III Corps 129, 291
IV Corps 27, 35, 40, 44, 64, 285, 286, 291, 292,
324
V Corps 187, 280, 285, 286, 291, 292, 298,
300, 323, 324, 330, 337
VI Corps 158, 285, 286, 291, 324
VII Corps 156, 158, 159, 161, 205, 210, 219,
229, 231, 232, 233, 235

386   To Do the Work of Men

IX Corps 194, 255, 258, 324
X Corps 187, 188, 194
XI Corps 26, 27, 32, 33, 35, 40, 44, 73, 75
XIII Corps 115, 324
XIV Corps 186
XV Corps 115, 131, 142
XVII Corps 158, 324
XVIII Corps 186
XIX Corps 186
XXII Corps 239, 244, 280

Divisions:
Guards Div. 26, 72
1st Div. 25, 29, 31, 43
2nd Div. 25, 29, 292
3rd Div. 115, 158, 160
4th Div. 160, 193
5th Div. 194, 197, 199, 203, 204, 292, 332, 340
6th Div. 76, 244, 342
7th Div. 29, 81, 82, 111, 115, 120, 124, 125, 156, 157, 158, 194
8th Div. 255, 257, 261, 271, 274
9th Div. 29, 115, 158, 160, 194, 210, 216, 222, 226, 229, 230, 232, 233, 235, 240, 241, 244
11th Div. 193
12th Div. 158, 160, 194, 290, 314, 318
14th Div. 158, 159, 161
15th Div. 29, 30, 31, 42, 43, 55, 75, 112, 158, 160, 186
16th Div. 112, 210, 214, 216, 217, 218, 219, 223, 342
17th Div. 81, 292, 293, 298, 301, 305, 307, 308, 310, 319, 328, 330, 332, 337
18th Div. 111, 177, 179, 290, 292
19th Div. 239, 240, 254
23rd Div. 112, 115, 189
24th Div. 23, 26, 27, 32, 33, 34, 40, 43, 65, 66, 72, 73, 75
25th Div. 250-251, 255, 257, 264, 271, 274, 275, 276
30th Div. 111, 156, 158, 159, 161, 162, 279
33rd Div. 125, 173, 187, 323, 327, 333, 334, 340, 347
34th Div. 105, 106, 109, 158, 160
35th Div. 230, 232, 233
36th Div. 244
37th Div. 113, 160, 292, 327
38th Div. 115, 287, 290, 292, 298, 301, 302, 318, 337

39th Div. 187, 219-220, 223, 227
40th Div. 239
41st Div. 129, 131, 132, 140-142, 244
42nd Div. 285, 298, 305, 307, 308
44th Div. 113
46th Div. 114
47th Div. 29, 31, 37, 129, 290
48th Div. 193
49th Div. 240
50th Div. 129, 173, 255, 257, 261
51st Div. 158, 160
55th Div. 239
56th Div. 158, 161
58th Div. 309, 314, 318
63rd Div. 300, 302

Brigades:
1 Bde 30
2 Bde 29, 30, 40
7 Bde 275
9 Bde 194
18 Bde 342
19 Bde 173
20 Bde 194
21 Bde 171
23 Bde 261
24 Bde 262
25 Bde 262
26 Bde 29, 240, 245
27 Bde 29, 244, 245
28 Bde 29
44 Bde 30, 40
45 Bde 30, 35, 38, 39, 45, 50
39 Composite Bde 244, 245
46 Bde 30, 39
50 Bde 81, 95-96, 109, 292, 308
51 Bde 111
52 Bde 308, 310, 332
53 Bde 292
54 Bde 177
57 Bde 240
58 Bde 254
69 Bde 189
75 Bde 264
89 Bde 159, 161, 162, 163
91 Bde 282
95 Bde 204
98 Bde 127
104 Bde 233, 234

Index 387

105 Bde 230, 233, 234
106 Bde 230, 234
113 Bde 292
114 Bde 287
115 Bde 290
117 Bde 227
124 Bde 130, 142
140 Bde 31
141 Bde 31
146 Bde 240, 245, 248
147 Bde 250, 251
148 Bde 250, 254
149 Bde 261
150 Bde 261
151 Bde 261
165 Bde 140
169 Bde 171

Battalions (served in 21st Div)

62 Bde:
12/Northumberland Fusiliers: xvii, xviii, 35, 38-39, 45-46, 50, 109, 110-111, 156-157, 169, 171, 180-182
13/ Northumberland Fusiliers: xvii, 35, 38-39, 45, 110-111, 143, 156, 157-158, 169-170, 171-172, 180-182
12/13 Northumberland Fusiliers: 192, 193, 196-197, 206, 211, 212, 214-215, 222, 226, 232, 238, 240-241, 246, 252, 260, 263-264, 271, 274, 275, 285, 289, 298, 299-300, 309-310, 314, 315-316, 319-320, 327, 333, 334, 338, 346, 347
8/ East Yorks: xvii, 34, 37-38, 45, 50-51, 76
10/Yorks: xvii, 32, 34, 35, *36*, 37-38, 45-48, 50, 51, 96, 106, 109, 110, 111, 126, 156, 157, 169-170, 192, 196, 203, 206
1/Lincolns: 76, 106, 109, 110, 111, 126, 143, 150, 156, 157, 169-171, 192, 196-199, 206, 211, 215-216, 222, 226, 232, 238, 240-241, 246, 252, 259, 260, 264-265, 271, 272, 275, 276, 277, 279, 284, 288-289, 299, 309-310, 314-315, 320-321, 323, 327-328, 333, 334, 338
2/Lincolns: 206, 211, 213, 215-216, 222, 226, 229, 232, 238, 240, 246, 260, 283-284, 287-288, 289-290, 299-300, 309, 314, 316, 320, 321, 327-328, 333, 334
3/4 Queen's: 192, 193, 194-197, 206

63 Bde:
8/Lincolns: xviii, 39-40, 41-42, 52, 57-60, 73, 93, 94-95, 98, 109
8/Somerset Light Infantry: xviii, 39-40, 41, 55, 56, 60, 61, 93, 96, 98, 109, 110
12/West Yorks: xviii, 40, 41, 57, 63, 73, 74, 76
10/York & Lancs: xviii, 40, 41, 55, 56, 60, 64, 93, 98, 109, 110
4/Middlesex: 76, 93, 95, 96, 98, 109, 110

64 Bde:
9/KOYLI: xviii, xix, xx, 42, 43, 67-71, 76, 77, 83, *84,* 85-87, 88-90, 91-92, 104, 106, 108, 109, 127, 131, 132, 133-136, 139, 140, 141, 150, 153, 160, 163-167, 173, 174, 192, 193, 199-201, 202, 203-204, 205, 206, 222-225, 227-229, 230, 232, 234, 238, 240, 242-243, 244, 248-252, 254, 260, 266-268, 269, 270, 271-272, 274, 275, 279, 281, 285, 293-296, 301-302, 307, 310-311, 312, 316-317, 319, 325-326, 329, 330, 332-333, 334-335, 336, 341-342, 343, 344, 346
10/KOYLI: xviii, 42, 43, 67-69, 82, 83, 85, 87-88, 91, 108, 109, 125, 126, 131, 139, 140, 143-144, 149-150, 153, 160, 163, 167-169, 172, 175-176, 192, 193, 200-201, 202, 204, 206
14/Durham Light Infantry: xviii, 42, 43, 56, 62-64, 68, 73, 76, 342
15/Durham Light Infantry: xviii, 42, 43, 64-66, 68, 76, 83, 87, 90-91, 104, 106-107, 108, 109, 126, 131, 132-133, 139, 140, 141, 151, 153, 160, 162, 163-169, 174, 175-176, 193, 193, 202-203, 204, 206, 217, 218, 222, 225, 227, 229, 232, 238, 241, 242, 249-250, 254, 260, 269-270, 272, 273, 274, 275, 285, 293, 296, 298, 301, 310-311, 312, 316-317, 319, 324, 325-326, 330, 331, 333, 334-335, 340-342, 343, 346
1/East Yorks: 76, 83, 87, 90-91, 105, 109, 116, 125, 126, 128, 131, 136, 139, 140, 142, 143-144, 149, 153, 160, 163-164, 166-168, 174, 175, 192, 193, 201-202, 206, 211, 217, 219, 222-225, 227-229, 232, 238, 241, 242, 244, 245, 246-248, 260, 268-269, 271-272, 274, 275, 277, 293, 296, 297-298, 301-302, 307, 308, 311-312, 316-318, 319, 324, 326, 327, 328, 332-333, 340-341, 343, 346

388   To Do the Work of Men

110 Bde:
6/Leicesters: 112, 116, 117-118, 120-121,
124-125, 128, 149, 152, 172, 178-179, 188,
189, 206, 211, 216, 217, 218, 220-221, 226,
232, 238, 240, 243-244, 246, 252, 260, 265,
271, 276, 277, 290, 298, 300, 305-306, 307,
313, 318, 326, 332-333, 339
7/Leicesters: 112, 114, 116, 117-118, 120-122,
125, 128, 151-152, 179, 180, 188, 190, 206,
211, 212, 214, 218, 221-222, 225-226, 232,
238, 240, 243, 246, 259, 260, 265-266, 271,
275, 285, 290, 298, 300, 305, 307, 308, 313,
318, 321, 326, 332-333, 339-340
8/Leicesters: 112, 116-117, 118, 120-122, 125,
128, 143-148, 152, 176-180, 181, 188, 190, 192,
206, 211, 214, 217, 220, 221, 226, 232, 238,
240, 243, 246, 260, 265-266, 271, 277, 279
9/Leicesters: 112, *113,* 114, 116-117, 120,
122-124, 125, 126, 128, 143-148, 152,
176-180, 188-189-190, 206
1/Wiltshires: 279, 297, 298, 305-307, 313, 318,
326, 328, 332, 333, 339-340, 344, 347
14/Northumberland Fusiliers (Pioneers):
xviii, 173, 222, 225, 238, 270, 273, 274, 277

Battalions (not in 21st Div)
11/Argyll & Sutherland Highlanders: 45
2/Bedfords: 161
7/Bedfords: 177
9/BlackWatch: 39, 244
7/Border Regt: 111
8/Buffs (Royal East Kents): 62
1/Cameron Highlanders: 29, 174
6/Cameron Highlanders: 31
7/Cameron Highlanders: 31
3/Coldstream Guards: 130
2/Devonshires: 262
8/Devonshires: 29
6/Dorsets: 104, 109
1/4 Duke of Wellington's: 251
9/Duke of Wellington's: 331
2/Durham Light Infantry: 282
6/Durham Light Infantry: 261
7/Durham Light Infantry: 261
8/Durham Light Infantry: 261
22/Durham Light Infantry: 262
2/East Lancs: 262
7/East Yorks: 109.
1/Gloucesters: 31

10/Gordon Highlanders: 31, 39
4/Grenadier Guards: 143, 152
7/Highland Light Infantry: 39
19/King's Liverpool Regt: 161
20/King's Liverpool Regt: 161
19/Lancashire Fusiliers: 245
6/Lincolns: 281
17/Londons: 37
1/18 Londons: 31
1/19 Londons: 31, 38
1/20 Londons: 37, 38, 51
21/Mancchesters: 111
1/Middlesex: 127
2/Middlesex: 261-262
1/Northants: 31
2/Northants: 262
4/Northumberland Fusiliers: 261
6/Northumberland Fusiliers: 261
2/Queen's: 157
8/Royal Berkshires: 29
7/Royal Scots Fusiliers: 45
12/Royal Scots: 245, 248
13/Royal Scots: 45
9/Scottish Rifles 248
7/Seaforth Highlanders: 245
1/Sherwood Foresters: 262
9/Sherwood Foresters: 281
2/South Lancs: 279
1/4 Suffolks: 127
14/Welch: 290
1/5 West Yorks: 245, 248
1/6 West Yorks: 245, 247, 248
1/7 West Yorks: 248
2/West Yorks: 261
10/West Yorks: 81, 87, 98-99, 102, 109
1/Worcesters: 262
2/Yorks: 157
7/Yorks: 81, 99-104, 109
9/Yorks (Green Howards): 189

Miscellaneous Units / Formations:

Cavalry
1/Cavalry Division: 115, 234
3/Cavalry Division: 34
Deccan Horse: 125
3/Dragoon Guards: 51
7/Dragoon Guards: 125
14/Hussars: 282

2/Indian Cavalry: 115
19/Lancers: 152
South Irish Horse: 152

ANZAC
I ANZAC Corps: 187, 193
II ANZAC Corps: 193
1/Australian Div: 193, 237, 239
2/Australian Div: 193
3/Australian Division: 235, 290
4/Australian Div: 187, 235
5/Australian Div: 187, 188
8/Australian Bde: 188
3/New Zealand Div: 193
3/New Zealand Rifle Bde: 310

Canadian
2nd Canadian Div: 129
3rd Canadian Div: 129

Others
2/Field Coy Royal Engineers: 262
97/Field Coy Royal Engineers 219
126/Field Coy Royal Engineers 338
490/Field Coy Royal Engineers: 262
21/Machine Gun Bn: 227, 238, 315
33/Machine Gun Bn: 315
62/Machine Gun Coy: 110, 195
64/ Machine Gun Coy: 140
62/Trench Mortar Battery: 158, 195
110 Machine Gun Coy: 128
110/Trench Mortar Battery: 128
178th Tunnelling Coy RE: 87
11/Tank Bn: 325, 330

French Units / Formations
First Army: 283
Second Army: 23
Third Army: 23
Fourth Army: 23
Sixth Army: 258
Tenth Army: 7, 283
XX Corps: 115
21st Div: 257, 261, 270
22nd Div: 257, 261, 270
28th Div: 244

34th Div: 244
39th Div: 250-251
45th Div: 257, 275, 277
61st Div: 257, 261, 271
154th Div: 244
157th Div: 271
II/23rd Territorial Regt: 262
3/Territorial Regt: 264
3/Zouaves: 260, 272
99/Regiment 245

German Units / Formations
Alpine Corps (Leib Regt): 245, 251
4th Reserve Corps: 257
4th Bavarian Div: 245
7th Div: 245
7th Reserve Div: 275
13th Reserve Div: 245
15th Div: 189
18th Div: 213
22nd Reserve Div: 245
30th Div: 323, 327
56th Div: 245
79th Reserve Div: 220
86th Div: 275
107th Div: 212
183rd Div: 220
201st Div. 317
IR 74: 267
IR 95: 213
IR 99: 324
IR 105: 323-324, 327
IR 106: 54
IR 153: 52, *53,* 54-55, 67
IR 178: 54
111th Reserve Regt: 81
212th Reserve Regt: 193
403rd Regt. 317
99 RIR: 157
201 RIR: 317
205 RIR: 306
207 RIR: 156
208 RIR: 306
227 RIR: 212, 213
221/Machine Gun Coy 228

Wolverhampton Military Studies

www.helion.co.uk/wolverhamptonmilitarystudies

Editorial board

Professor Stephen Badsey
  Wolverhampton University

Professor Michael Bechthold
  Wilfred Laurier University

Professor John Buckley
  Wolverhampton University

Major General (Retired) John Drewienkiewicz

Ashley Ekins
  Australian War Memorial

Dr Howard Fuller
  Wolverhampton University

Dr Spencer Jones
  Wolverhampton University

Nigel de Lee
  Norwegian War Academy

Major General (Retired) Mungo Melvin
  President of the British Commission for Military
  History

Dr Michael Neiberg
  US Army War College

Dr Eamonn O'Kane
  Wolverhampton University

Professor Fransjohan Pretorius
  University of Pretoria

Dr Simon Robbins
  Imperial War Museum

Professor Gary Sheffield
  Wolverhampton University

Commander Steve Tatham PhD
  Royal Navy
  The Influence Advisory Panel

Professor Malcolm Wanklyn
  Wolverhampton University

Professor Andrew Wiest
  University of Southern Mississippi

Submissions

The publishers would be pleased to receive submissions for this series. Please contact us via email (info@helion.co.uk), or in writing to Helion & Company Limited, Unit 8 Amherst Business Centre, Budbrooke Road, Warwick, CV34 5WE, England.

Titles

1   *Stemming the Tide. Officers and Leadership in the British Expeditionary Force 1914* Edited by Spencer Jones (ISBN 978-1-909384-45-3)

2   *'Theirs Not To Reason Why': Horsing the British Army 1875–1925* Graham Winton (ISBN 978-1-909384-48-4)

3   *A Military Transformed? Adaptation and Innovation in the British Military, 1792– 1945* Edited by Michael LoCicero, Ross Mahoney and Stuart Mitchell (ISBN 978-1-909384-46-0)

4   *Get Tough Stay Tough. Shaping the Canadian Corps, 1914–1918* Kenneth Radley (ISBN 978-1-909982-86-4)

5   *A Moonlight Massacre: The Night Operation on the Passchendaele Ridge, 2 December 1917. The Forgotten Last Act of the Third Battle of Ypres* Michael LoCicero (ISBN 978-1-909982-92-5)

6   *Shellshocked Prophets. Former Anglican Army Chaplains in Interwar Britain* Linda Parker (ISBN 978-1-909982-25-3)

7   *Flight Plan Africa: Portuguese Airpower in Counterinsurgency, 1961–1974* John P. Cann (ISBN 978-1-909982-06-2)

8   *Mud, Blood and Determination. The History of the 46th (North Midland) Division in the Great War* Simon Peaple (ISBN 978 1 910294 66 6)

9   *Commanding Far Eastern Skies. A Critical Analysis of the Royal Air Force Superiority Campaign in India, Burma and Malaya 1941–1945* Peter Preston-Hough (ISBN 978 1 910294 44 4)